Ex Libris

KHAFRE

Kingship and the Gods

*A Study of Ancient Near Eastern Religion
as the Integration of Society & Nature*

HENRI FRANKFORT

With a new Preface by Samuel Noah Kramer

THE UNIVERSITY OF CHICAGO PRESS
CHICAGO & LONDON

To J

THE UNIVERSITY OF CHICAGO PRESS, CHICAGO 60637
The University of Chicago Press, Ltd., London

© 1948, 1978 *by The University of Chicago*
All rights reserved. Published 1948. Phoenix Edition 1978
Printed in the United States of America

82 81 80 79 78   54321

International Standard Book Number: 0-226-26011-9
Library of Congress Catalog Card Number: 48-5158

PREFACE TO THE
PHOENIX EDITION

THE problems relating to the rise and growth, the nature and character, of the two oldest civilizations known to man, the Egyptian and the Mesopotamian, have held and inspired the imaginations of archeologists, scholars, and humanists for over a century and a half. How, when, and why did the prehistoric Egyptians and Mesopotamians become city- and nation-oriented, develop a coherent cosmology, theology, and mythology, construct monumental temples, institute cathartic rites and propitiatory rituals, invent and develop an effective system of writing, and create a significant written literature? How did they influence the ancient Hebrews and Greeks? What traces, if any, remain of their civilization in our own modern society? In the ongoing efforts to discover and recover, to interpret and illuminate, the material remains and spiritual heritage of these two long-buried and forgotten civilizations, quite a number of oriental departments and archeological institutes have blossomed and flourished in the universities and museums of Europe and America. One of the most creative and productive of these is the Oriental Institute of the University of Chicago, where Henri Frankfort, the author of *Kingship and the Gods*, spent the most fruitful years of his scholarly career.

Frankfort was primarily an archeologist and art historian. He excavated in both Egypt and Mesopotamia and published extensively on the results of his archeological activities, with special emphasis on their significance for the history of art. For the preparation of *Kingship and the Gods*, however, expert knowledge of ancient texts was crucial, and Frankfort was no trained linguist. Fortunately, he had at his side in the Oriental Institute, two distinguished colleagues, the Egyptologist John Wilson and the cuneiformist Thorkild Jacobsen, each a leading scholar in his field. The three of them had been collaborating for some time on a series of lectures on the nature of speculative thought in the ancient Near East. These lectures were published in 1946 under the title *The Intellectual Adventure of Ancient Man*, a work that foreshadowed some of the psychological and philosophical under-

v

pinnings of *Kingship and the Gods*. The latter is therefore the distilled product of the most expert scholarship in archeology, art history, epigraphy, and philology.

Frankfort's central thesis in *Kingship and the Gods* is that the Egyptian and Mesopotamian civilizations differed fundamentally and profoundly in spite of their superficial resemblances, and that kingship, an institution which the ancients themselves regarded as the very foundation of all civilized life, was conceived of quite differently in the two lands. In Egypt the king was a god descended among men, whose coronation was a divine epiphany. In Mesopotamia, on the other hand, the king was a mortal—a "great man," to translate literally the Sumerian word for king, *lugal*—whose coronation was regarded at times as an apotheosis, a *consecratio*, but which did not make him a god incarnate. Frankfort's view ran counter to that held by many scholars, and he therefore concentrated all his expertise and erudition on a detailed, step-by-step demonstration of this crucial difference between the two civilizations.

Kingship and the Gods is divided into two books and seven parts: Book I, in four parts, is devoted to Egypt and Book II, in three parts, is devoted to Mesopotamia. Preceding Book I is a brief Introduction that focuses on the contrasting views of kingship in the two societies as expressed in their art. In Egypt the king is depicted as an integral component of the world of the gods and as the symbolic representative of the entire community. The Mesopotamian king, on the other hand, is rendered as a heroic man, a leader of his people, who is not essentially different from his fellow men.

Having demonstrated the significance and validity of his thesis as revealed directly and immediately in art, the author turns his attention to the Egyptian civilization, for which he seems to have a special affinity, and begins Part I with an examination of the historical and theoretical foundations of its kingship. Frankfort's treatment of this theme reveals and illustrates the perceptive penetration that characterizes the book as a whole. Thus the successful introduction of kingship by King Menes, the first king of the First Dynasty, was due not to utilitarian considerations, as most scholars assume, but rather to his psychological insight, conscious or unconscious, that in establishing himself as the sole ruler of the dual kingdom of Upper and Lower Egypt, he would perform an act in harmony with the Egyptian tendency to understand the world in dualistic terms, "as a series of pairs of contrasts balanced in unchanging equilibrium." As for the theoretical foundations of kingship, Frankfort's keen and detailed explication of the important "Memphite Theology" demonstrates not only that the king was conceived of as a god, but also that kingship entailed a mystic communion between two generations, between the living son, as Horus, and his dead predecessor, as Osiris.

As a god, the king of Egypt had absolute power over the land and its people, yet he could not act arbitrarily and capriciously but only in accordance with *maat*, "right order." The functioning of kingship is the concern of Part II, in which the author examines the nature of the king's potency as expressed by the elusive and allusive word *ka*, the ritual renewal and rejuvenation of the king's potency during the Sed festival, and the significance of the role played by the royal ancestral spirits sometimes designated as "Followers of Horus."

The king's death was a critical event in the life of all Egyptians, since it indicated that the powers of chaos and evil had the upper hand in the land, at least till the accession and coronation of the new king. This is the subject of Part III, in which the author reconstructs in a masterly fashion the main features of the coronation from temple reliefs, Pyramid texts, and the Mystery Play of Succession that is based on the script of a play performed at the accession of King Senusert.

Having discussed the Pharaoh's divinity and his place in the world of the gods as depicted in texts, rites, and pictorial representations, the author comes to the vast labyrinthine structure of Egyptian religion, the subject of Part IV, in which he examines, analyzes, unravels, and clarifies the main spheres of divine manifestation in Egyptian religious thought and practice. These are the power in the sun connoting creation, the power in cattle connoting procreation, and the power in the earth connoting resurrection.

Book II deals with Mesopotamian kingship, an institution whose origin and character cannot be followed as coherently as they can for Egyptian kingship, since several different peoples—the Sumerians, Akkadians, Babylonians, and Assyrians—are involved. Part V (the first part of Book II) therefore begins with a well-reasoned justification for the thesis that the concept of kingship in Mesopotamia was not significantly affected by ethnic changes and political developments. It continues with an analysis of the theological concepts of kingship in Mesopotamia which demonstrates that it lacked the more impressive aspects of its Egyptian counterpart, for though the king was considered divinely elected for his office, he had to grope his way through rites, dreams, and omens in order to learn how to perform his royal duties.

The functions of the king, explicated in Part VI, were threefold: the administration of the realm, the prayerful representation of the people before the gods in order to assure their prosperity and well-being; and the service of the gods by building and rebuilding their temples and officiating at state festivals.

Mesopotamian society was pervaded by a feeling of uncertainty and anxiety, and its religion, unlike that of the Egyptian society, was not dominated by such reassuring concepts as creation, procreation, and resurrection, but rather by the myth of a suffering god and a mourning mother goddess. This is the introductory theme of the last part of the book, which includes a detailed treatment of the problematical concept of the deification of the king, and of the profoundly religious character of the New Year Festival, as well as a remarkable excursus that refutes the universality of the "dying god" motif as conceived by Frazer in his *Golden Bough*.

Following a very brief epilogue concerned with the nature of kingship among the Hebrews, which differs fundamentally from that of both the Egyptians and Mesopotamians, the book concludes with more than sixty pages of clarifying notes directed primarily to the oriental specialist.

Kingship and the Gods, as should be evident from the preceding overview of its contents, is an innovative, stimulating, fundamental contribution to the study of the history of civilization. Not all scholars will agree with all its formulations, interpretations, and conclusions—I, myself, would take issue wth several relating to Mesopotamia. But by and large these disagreements and divergences are relatively trivial and in no way detract from the immense value of the book for the knowledge and understanding of man and his ancient past. It is my conviction that in due time *Kingship and the Gods* will be recognized as a classic in the field of oriental studies.

SAMUEL NOAH KRAMER

PREFACE

ἦλθον καὶ ἐθαύμασα

THE creations of the primitive mind are elusive. Its concepts seem ill defined, or, rather, they defy limitations. Every relationship becomes a sharing of essentials. The part partakes of the whole, the name of the person, the shadow and effigy of the original. This "mystic participation" reduces the significance of distinctions while increasing that of every resemblance. It offends all our habits of thought. Consequently, the instrument of our thought, our language, is not well suited to describe primitive conceptions.

We want to isolate a single notion. But, whenever we make the attempt, we find ourselves holding one mesh of a widely flung net; and we seem condemned either to trace its ramifications into the remotest corners of ancient life or to cut the skein and pretend that the concept thus forcibly isolated corresponds with primitive thought.

If, then, we propose to study the institution of kingship, which forms the very heart of the oldest civilized societies, we must be well aware of the difference in mentality which we have just indicated. Tracing the political and economic functions of kingship in the ancient Near East, we find irrational factors exercising influence at every turn. If, on the other hand, we take into account the religious implications of kingship and follow the line of theological reasoning, we find that it would only have us start with an account of creation in order to equate that First Day with every sunrise, with every New Year, with the accession of every king, nay, with his every appearance on throne or battlefield.

Nor can we follow chronology and, starting with the earliest known forms of the institution, describe its successive changes. In so doing, we should find ourselves dealing with insignificant modifications of a basic conception which would still be enigmatical. If, on the other hand, we should follow the fashion, trace a "pattern" of kingship supposed to be generally valid, and arrange our material to suit it, we should ignore peculiarities which are of the essence of the institution as it was known to the ancients.

Our treatment, then, will be unhistorical; but it will be so only because it disregards, not because it violates, historical truths. It will be phenomenological in that it will be a "systematic discussion of what appears." But it will not follow one single line of argument; rather it will

converge upon the central problem from different directions. This procedure is not without disadvantages. We shall find that the coherence of
the thought of the ancients will make itself disturbingly felt; at each
approach we are bound to touch upon phenomena which require another
avenue to be fully understood and which therefore try the reader's patience for the time being. Yet we believe that this method alone allows
us to do justice to the many-sidedness of ancient conceptions, a feature
too often misinterpreted as the fruit of "confusion" or "syncretism."

At the basis of our alienation from the ancients lie the achievements
of Greece and the teachings of the Old and New Testaments. It is,
therefore, logical to envisage the ancient Near East as a whole. But it is
fortunate that Egypt and Mesopotamia differ profoundly in spirit. For
if, across the chasm which separates us, we focus on now one and then
the other of these two great centers of civilization, we shall find that
the interplay of contrasts and similarities sharpens our sight not a
little. Both, moreover, are thrown in stronger relief by a comparison
with the Hebrews, who were familiar with the cultures of Egypt and
Mesopotamia and fanatically rejected the highest values recognized by
both.

We have stated our theme succinctly—and therefore, of necessity,
in a dogmatic form—in the Introduction, which is intended to be no
more than a provisional orientation of the reader, enabling him to survey the whole of the field before concrete details, proofs, and arguments require his attention. The Introduction also demonstrates the
difference between the Egyptian and the Mesopotamian views of kingship by means of the expression which these found in art. This evidence
is self-contained and unequivocal and can be grasped directly, irrespective of the conceptual differences between the ancient artists and the
modern spectator.*

In discussing the literary material, we have attempted to describe
texts, rites, and festivals as the outcome of politico-religious experiences. We have, moreover, presented the traditions in as concrete a manner as possible. This meant putting a good deal of detail before the reader. But abstractions and formulas like "divine king," "local god,"
"high god," etc., easily became obstacles to our understanding by inter-
posing their sham precision between us and the conceptions of the
ancients. No generalizations, however apt, can replace the actual forms
in which spiritual life has found expression. Images are not adjuncts or

* The Introduction is based on a paper read at the American Academy of Arts and Sciences in Boston on April 9, 1942, during the centennial celebration of the American Oriental
Society.

ornaments of ancient thought, which reaches its conclusions in a fashion
that is intuitive and imaginative as much as intellectual. Hence something essential is lost when we strip it of its imagery.

We should hope to share with the reader a mood best expressed in the
graffiti which visiting Greeks scribbled on the Pharaonic monuments:
I came and marveled. For though we have started this Preface by characterizing primitive mentality and have sometimes approached the ancients by way of modern savages, our work is borne by the conviction
that the structures of thought in which pre-Greek man apprehended his
world are as unprecedented an achievement as his more tangible monuments.

The literature bearing on our subject is voluminous. It fills twenty-
three pages of bibliography in a recent work, and we are content here
to refer to that list.* We have quoted when we felt that acknowledgment
was due or that a useful purpose would be served by explicitly refuting
an opinion; such discussions are relegated to the notes. In other
cases disagreement could be implied by silence and this book spared the
burden of controversy.

As regards the primary sources, those in cuneiform are closed to me,
while my knowledge of Egyptian is not sufficient to warrant independent judgment of moot points of grammar. My friends Professors Thorkild Jacobsen and John A. Wilson have been most generous in assisting
me in my dealings with the texts, though neither should be held responsible for any translation not explicitly marked as his own. Some of these
translations were made when we collaborated on a series of public lectures on "Speculative Thought in the Ancient Near East" (published
under the title *The Intellectual Adventure of Ancient Man* [Chicago,
1946]). For this reason, and because the processes of mythopoeic
thought are fully discussed there, it seemed desirable to publish our co-
operative effort first, although the present work was completed in essentials when the lectures were delivered.

Publications which appeared in Europe during the war could be used
only to a very limited extent before the manuscript went to press.

I am indebted to Drs. Harold H. Nelson, Keith C. Seele, S. I. Feigin,
Richard A. Parker, and Miriam Lichtheim for valuable suggestions and
to Miss Caroline Nestmann for an intelligent and conscientious revision
of the manuscript and for preparing the analytical Index.

CHICAGO AND NEW DENVER, B.C.
      1942–45

* Ivan Engnell, *Studies in Divine Kingship in the Ancient Near East* (Uppsala, 1943), pp.
223–46.

ACKNOWLEDGMENTS

T HE author wishes to thank the following persons for permission to reproduce figures from their publications or from original photographs which were kindly put at his disposal:

The Director of the Oriental Institute, the University of Chicago, for Figures 2, 3, 5, 9, 10, 12, 14, 42, 47, and 49.

Mr. Sidney Smith and the Trustees of the British Museum for Figures 8, 11, 36, 37, and 39.

The Curator of the Egyptian Collection, the Metropolitan Museum of Art, New York, for Figures 31, 32, and 34.

The Director of the University Museum, Philadelphia, for Figure 13.

Messrs. Martinus Nijhoff, Publishers, The Hague, for Figures 40 and 41.

Mr. Walter Hauser, New York, for Figure 4.

CONTENTS

INTRODUCTION

BOOK I. EGYPT

PART I. THE FOUNDING OF KINGSHIP

PART II. THE FUNCTIONING OF KINGSHIP

PART III. THE PASSING OF KINGSHIP

PART IV. KINGSHIP AND THE DIVINE POWERS IN NATURE

BOOK II. MESOPOTAMIA

PART V. THE FOUNDATIONS OF KINGSHIP

PART VI. THE FUNCTIONS OF THE KING

PART VII. KINGSHIP AND THE DIVINE
POWERS IN NATURE

EPILOGUE

LIST OF ILLUSTRATIONS

LIST OF ABBREVIATIONS

AJSL	*American Journal of Semitic Languages and Literatures.* Chicago, 1894–1941.
AO	*Der alte Orient.* "Gemeinverständliche Darstellungen herausgegeben von der Vorderasiatischen Gesellschaft." Leipzig, 1903——.
ASAE	*Annales du Service des Antiquités de l'Egypte.* Cairo. 1900 ——.
Borchardt, *Neuserre*	LUDWIG BORCHARDT. *Das Grabdenkmal des Königs Ne-user-re^c.* "Wissenschaftliche Veröffentlichung der Deutschen Orient-Gesellschaft," No. 7. Leipzig, 1907.
Borchardt, *Sahure*	LUDWIG BORCHARDT. *Das Grabdenkmal des Königs Śaȝḥu-re^c,* Vols. I and II. "Wissenschaftliche Veröffentlichung der Deutschen Orient-Gesellschaft," Nos. 14 and 26. Leipzig, 1910 and 1913.
Code	R. F. HARPER. *The Code of Hammurabi.* Chicago, 1904.
De Buck, *Oerheuvel*	ADRIAAN DE BUCK. *De egyptische Voorstellingen betreffende den Oerheuvel.* Leiden, 1922.
Erman, *Religion*	ADOLF ERMAN. *Die Religion der Ägypter.* Berlin, 1934.
Erman-Blackman, *Literature*	ADOLF ERMAN. *The Literature of the Ancient Egyptians.* Translated into English by AYLWARD M. BLACKMAN. London, 1927.
Gressmann, *AOTB*	*Altorientalische Texte und Bilder zum Alten Testament.* 2d ed. Herausgegeben von HUGO GRESSMANN. Berlin, 1926.
JAOS	*Journal of the American Oriental Society.* Boston, Baltimore, etc., 1849——.
JEA	*Journal of Egyptian Archaeology.* London, 1914——.
Jéquier, *Pepi II*	GUSTAVE JÉQUIER. *Le monument funéraire de Pepi II,* Vol. II: *Le temple.* Le Caire: Service des Antiquités, Fouilles à Saqqarah, 1938.
JNES	*Journal of Near Eastern Studies.* Chicago, 1942——.
JRAS	*Journal of the Royal Asiatic Society of Great Britain and Ireland.* London, 1834——.
Junker, *Giza*	HERMANN JUNKER. *Giza,* Vols. I and II. "Akademie der Wissenschaften in Wien, Phil.-hist. Klasse, Denkschriften." Wien, 1929 and 1934.
Kees, *Götterglaube*	HERMANN KEES. *Der Götterglaube im alten Ägypten. Mitteilungen der Vorderasiatisch-ägyptischen Gesellschaft,* Vol. XLV. Leipzig, 1941.
Kees, *Kulturgeschichte*	HERMANN KEES. *Ägypten,* in "Kulturgeschichte des alten Orients," Vol. I: "Handbuch der Altertumswissenschaft." Begründet von Iwan MÜLLER, herausgegeben von WALTER OTTO. München, 1933.

Kees, *Lesebuch*

Religionsgeschichtliches Lesebuch. 2d ed. Herausgegeben von ALFRED BERTHOLET. No. 10, "Ägypten," von HERMANN KEES. Tübingen, 1928.

Kees, *Opfertanz*

HERMANN KEES. *Der Opfertanz des ägyptischen Königs.* Leipzig, 1912.

Kees, *Totenglauben*

HERMANN KEES, *Totenglauben und Jenseitsvorstellungen der alten Ägypter.* Leipzig, 1926.

Labat, *Royauté*

RENÉ LABAT. *Le caractère religieux de la royauté assyrobabylonienne.* Paris, 1939.

MDOG

Mitteilungen der Deutschen Orient-Gesellschaft. Berlin, 1899——.

Moret, *Royauté*

ALEXANDRE MORET. *Du caractère religieux de la royauté pharaonique.* Paris, 1902.

OECT

"Oxford Editions of Cuneiform Texts." Edited under the direction of S. H. LANGDON.

"OIC"

"Oriental Institute Communications." Chicago, 1922——.

"OIP"

"Oriental Institute Publications." Chicago, 1924——.

OLZ

Orientalistische Literaturzeitung. Berlin, 1898–1908; Leipzig, 1909——.

Palermo Stone

HEINRICH SCHÄFER. *Ein Bruchstück altägyptischer Annalen.* *Abhandlungen der Preussischen Akademie der Wissenschaften, Phil.-hist. Klasse.* Berlin, 1902.

Pauly-Wissowa

Paulys Real-Encyclopädie der classischen Altertumswissenschaft. Neue Bearbeitung begonnen von GEORG WISSOWA. Stuttgart, 1894——.

PSBA

Proceedings of the Society of Biblical Archaeology. London, 1879–1918.

Pyr.

KURT SETHE. *Die altägyptischen Pyrimadentexte.* Leipzig, 1908–22.

RA

Revue d'assyriologie et d'archéologie orientale. Paris, 1884——.

Sethe, *Amun*

KURT SETHE. *Amun und die acht Urgötter von Hermopolis.* *Abhandlungen der Preussischen Akademie der Wissenschaften, Phil.-hist. Klasse.* No. 4. Berlin, 1929.

Sethe, *Dramatische Texte*

KURT SETHE. *Dramatische Texte zu altägyptischen Mysterienspielen.* "Untersuchungen zur Geschichte und Altertumskunde Ägyptens," Vol. X. Leipzig, 1928.

Sethe, *Sonnenauge*

KURT SETHE. *Zur altägyptischen Sage vom Sonnenauge das in der Fremde war.* Leipzig, 1912.

Sethe, *Urk.*

Urkunden des ägyptischen Altertums. Herausgegeben von GEORG STEINDORFF. Vol. I: *Urkunden des alten Reichs;* Vol. IV: *Urkunden der 18 Dynastie.* Bearbeitet von KURT SETHE. Leipzig. Vol. I, 2d ed., 1932–33; Vol. IV, 2d ed. 1927–30.

Speculative Thought

H. and H. A. FRANKFORT, JOHN A. WILSON, THORKILD JACOBSEN, and WILLIAM A. IRWIN. *The Intellectual Adventure of Ancient Man: An Essay on Speculative Thought in the Ancient Near East.* Chicago, 1946.

Thureau-Dangin, *ISA* — FRANÇOIS THUREAU-DANGIN. *Les inscriptions de Sumer et d'Akkad*. Paris, 1905.

Von Bissing–Kees, *Re-Heiligtum* — *Das Re-Heiligtum des Königs Ne-Woser-re*. Herausgegeben von F. W. VON BISSING. Vols. I, II, and III. Berlin, 1905, 1923, and 1928.

Von Bissing–Kees, *Untersuchungen* — F. W. VON BISSING and HERMANN KEES. "Untersuchungen zu den Reliefs aus dem Re-Heiligtum des Rathures." *Abhandlungen der Bayerischen Akademie der Wissenschaften, Phil.-hist. Klasse*, Vol. XXXII. München, 1922.

ZA — *Zeitschrift für Assyriologie und verwandte Gebiete*. Leipzig, 1886——.

ZÄS — *Zeitschrift für ägyptische Sprache und Altertumskunde*. Leipzig, 1863——.

CHRONOLOGICAL TABLE OF KINGS NAMED IN THIS BOOK

(Dates based on the work of Sidney Smith, Thorkild Jacobsen, and Richard A. Parker)

DATE (B.C.)	EGYPT		MESOPOTAMIA	
3100 / 2900	DYNASTY I	Narmer-Menes Aha Djer Djet Wedimu	EARLY DYNASTIC PERIOD	
2700	DYNASTY II			
	DYNASTY III	Djoser		
2600	DYNASTY IV	Snefru Khufu . . . . Khafre Menkaure		
2500		. . . .		Ur-Nanshe of Lagash Akurgal
	DYNASTY V	Sahure . . . . Neuserre . . . . Unas	PROTO-IMPERIAL	Eannatum . . . . Entemena . . . . Urukagina Lugalzaggesi
2340				
	DYNASTY VI	Teti . . . . Meryre Pepi I . . . . Neferkare Pepi II	FIRST IMPERIAL	Sargon of Akkad . . . . Naram-Sin . . . .
2180				
2130	FIRST INTER-MEDIATE		GUTIUM	
	DYNASTY XI	Kings called Intef and Mentuhotep	SECOND IMPERIAL (III DYNASTY OF UR)	Utu-hegal Ur-Nammu of Ur Shulgi Bur-Sin Shu-Sin Ibi-Sin
2000				

DATE (B.C.)	EGYPT			MESOPOTAMIA		
1900	DYNASTY XII		Amenemhet I Senusert I Amenemhet II Senusert II Senusert III Amenemhet III	POST-IMPERIAL *or* ISIN-LARSA (2025–1763)		Ishbi-irra of Isin Idin-Dagan Ishme-Dagan Lipit-Ishtar
1800 1785			Amenemhet IV	I DYNASTY OF BABYLON		Shamshi-Adad I of Assur Hammurabi (1792–50)
1580	SECOND INTERMEDIATE		Neferhotep Hyksos Kings			
1500 1400	DYNASTY XVIII		Ahmose Amenhotep I Tuthmosis I Tuthmosis II Hatshepsut Tuthmosis III Amenhotep II Tuthmosis IV Amenhotep III Akhenaten Tutankhamon	KASSITES	MIDDLE ASSYRIAN	Eriba-Adad of Assur Assur-Uballit I
1300	DYNASTY XIX		Haremhab Ramses I Seti I Ramses II			Tukulti-Ninurta I
900	DYNASTIES XX–XXI		Ramses III			
750 700 650	LATE PERIOD		Piankhi	LATE ASSYRIAN		Assurnasirpal . . . . Sargon II Sennacherib Esarhaddon Assurbanipal

INTRODUCTION

INTRODUCTION

CONCEPTS OF KINGSHIP IN THE
ANCIENT NEAR EAST

THE ancient Near East considered kingship the very basis of civilization. Only savages could live without a king. Security, peace, and justice could not prevail without a ruler to champion them. If ever a political institution functioned with the assent of the governed, it was the monarchy which built the pyramids with forced labor and drained the Assyrian peasantry by ceaseless wars.

But if we refer to kingship as a political institution, we assume a point of view which would have been incomprehensible to the ancients. We imply that the human polity can be considered by itself. The ancients, however, experienced human life as part of a widely spreading network of connections which reached beyond the local and the national communities into the hidden depths of nature and the powers that rule nature. The purely secular—in so far as it could be granted to exist at all—was the purely trivial. Whatever was significant was imbedded in the life of the cosmos, and it was precisely the king's function to maintain the harmony of that integration.

This doctrine is valid for the whole of the ancient Near East and for many other regions. But, as soon as we want to be more specific, we find that a contrast exists between the two centers of ancient civilization. Egypt and Mesopotamia held very different views as to the nature of their king and the temper of the universe in which he functioned.

Mesopotamian society was entirely adapted to the cyclic succession of the seasons. While each winter resolved its harshness in the spring and the plague of summer was succeeded by the autumn rains, human society moved in harmony with nature through a recurring sequence of religious festivals. These, again, meant more to the ancients than we are apt to realize. In celebrating them, the human community participated actively in the cosmic crises which the seasonal changes represented. For we must remember that, as Wensinck has it, "in that stage of development the idea of nature and natural laws has not arisen, and their place is taken by a dramatic conception which sees everywhere a strife between divine and demoniac, cosmic and chaotic powers."[1] No man could foresee the outcome of this conflict. But for this very reason the community could not remain passive, for it was involved to the extent of its very life. It had, somehow, to participate; and in the highly emotional atmosphere of the religious festivals the people passed from the deep uncertainty of the opening phases, through anxiety, to the ultimate elation of victory.

The most important seasonal celebrations in Mesopotamia centered around a deity who was worshiped under a great variety of names but whom we know best as Tammuz. The bewailing of his death in the scorching heat of summer was perhaps the most popular celebration of the year; but the outstanding state function was the New Year's festival, when the resurrection of the god, his victory over the powers of evil, and his sacred marriage to the mother-goddess were celebrated.

Egypt, too, reflected the natural rhythm of the seasons in the course of the official year. There were annual festivals connected with the rise of the Nile and the end of the inundation; with the resurrection of Osiris; and with the completion of the harvest. But these celebrations, which articulated the progression of the community through the year, differ profoundly in spirit from their Mesopotamian counterparts. In the Plain of the Two Rivers the festivals were never free from anxiety, and those which we know best show a change from deep gloom to exultation as the aim and the result of the solemnities. In Egypt, on the other hand, the festivals provided occasion to reaffirm that all was well. For Egypt viewed the universe as essentially static. It held that a cosmic order was once and for all established at the time of creation. This order might occasionally be disturbed, for the forces of chaos were merely subdued and not annihilated. Nevertheless, revolts against the established order were bound to remain mere ripples upon the surface. The feeling of insecurity, of human frailty, which pervades every manifestation of Mesopotamian culture, is absent in Egypt. This contrast in outlook is curiously in keeping with the physiographical differences between the two countries. The rich Nile Valley lies isolated and protected between the almost empty deserts on either side, while Mesopotamia lacks clear boundaries and was periodically robbed and disrupted by the mountaineers on its east or the nomads on its west. Egypt derived its prosperity from the annual inundation of the Nile, which never fails to rise, even if the floods differ greatly in effectiveness. But Mesopotamia is, for much of its grazing, dependent on an uncertain rainfall and possesses in the Tigris an unaccountable, turbulent, and most dangerous river.

In both Mesopotamia and Egypt religion centered round the problem of maintaining life. But in Mesopotamia it was not the immortality of the individual which caused concern. "For when the gods created man, they let death be his share, and life withheld in their own hands." This verse from the Epic of Gilgamesh voices the resignation with which the inevitability of death was accepted. But it was life on earth, the life of the family and of the crops and herds upon which it depends, which religion sought to maintain by harmonizing the life of the community with that of nature through the festivals. In this wider context, too, inescapable death was accepted; but it was counterbalanced by the recurring miracle of resurrection.

Egypt, in accordance with its static interpretation of the cosmos, considered life to be everlasting and paradoxically denied the reality of death. The body ceased to function, but man survived. As a bird he lived in the tomb but could visit the Nile Valley at will. Or he became one of the circumpolar stars which never set. He compelled certain spirits to form a ladder so that he could reach heaven. He became one of the eyes of the god of heaven—sun or moon. He joined the sun-god in his boat, which journeys through the sky by day and under the earth by night. Or the coffin—with a symbolism well known to psychoanalysis—became the mother-goddess Nut, who gives birth each morning to the sun, each night to the stars.

We remain here entirely within the sphere of paradox. For, notwithstanding these beliefs, a "soul" could not be abstracted from the body, or, rather, man's personality required both at all times; and, to gain eternal life, man's surviving part should not be entirely dissociated from the seat of his identity, his body. Hence the rich development of Egyptian sculpture; hence mummification; hence, also, the equipment of the tomb with the necessities of daily life.

But the ultimate paradox of all these beliefs is the fact that we meet them first of all in the pyramid texts applied to the king. And Pharaoh was not mortal but a god. This was the fundamental concept of Egyptian kingship, that Pharaoh was of divine essence, a god incarnate; and this view can be traced back as far as texts and symbols take us. It is wrong to speak of a deification of Pharaoh. His divinity was not proclaimed at a certain moment, in a manner comparable to the *consecratio* of the dead emperor by the Roman senate. His coronation was not an apotheosis but an epiphany.

In this respect also there is a complete contrast between Egypt and Mesopotamia. The earliest Mesopotamian term for king expresses a viewpoint which remains characteristic until the end of the Assyrian empire: Sumerian *lugal* means "great man." The Mesopotamian king was, like Pharaoh, charged with maintaining harmonious relations between human society and the supernatural powers; yet he was emphatically not one of these but a member of the community. In Egypt, on the other hand, one of the gods had descended among men.

The significance of this divergence is clear. In Egypt the community had freed itself from fear and uncertainty by considering its ruler a god. It sacrificed all liberty for the sake of a never changing integration of society and nature. In Mesopotamia the community retained considerable independence, since its ruler was but a man. It accepted as correlate the never ending anxiety that the will of the gods might be misunderstood and catastrophe disturb the labile harmony between the human and divine spheres.

The Hebrew prophets rejected both the Egyptian and the Babylonian views. They insisted on the uniqueness and transcendence of God. For them all values were ultimately attributes of God; man and nature were devaluated, and every attempt to establish a harmony with nature was a futile dissipation of effort.

It is obviously the Egyptian view of kingship which is least familiar to us. Pharaoh was divine—it is very difficult for us to attach any precise meaning to that phrase. And yet, if we are to understand the ancients, it is essential that we grasp so fundamental a concept.

There are two ways to penetrate behind the words of our texts. In the first place, there are alive today in Africa groups of people who are true survivors of that great East African substratum out of which Egyptian culture arose. Among other things we can study there how deeply the divine nature of the kings affects both the ruler and his subjects. Yet this evidence requires correction, for we are dealing here with savages who, either by tenacity or by inertia, have preserved through several thousand years the remnants of a primeval world of thought, while Pharaonic culture was the most highly developed and most progressive of its age. The other road to a more direct and vivid understanding of ancient thought approaches it, not in its conceptual, but in its pictorial or plastic, expression. Art is expression in form, a direct expression directly grasped by the spectator. As an introduction to our study we shall, therefore, consider how the varying concepts of kingship were expressed in ancient Near Eastern art.

In Egypt, in the predynastic period, no kings or chieftains were depicted. On the Gebel el Arak knife handle (Fig. 1) we see a battle between two parties which are clearly distinguished by their hairdress and by the ships that brought them to the scene of action. Their conflict is depicted as a mêlée of equivalent figures. The contemporary Hunters' Palette shows two groups of men in the same manner. But, with the unification of Egypt under the first Pharaoh, this method of representation changed abruptly. The king appeared now as representative of the community.

On one side of the votive slate palette of Narmer (who has the best claims to be the legendary Menes, first king of unified Egypt) we see the king inspecting beheaded enemies (Fig. 2). By a process which is common in primitive art there is a gradation of scale according to the importance of the persons. The king is the dominating figure. This "hierarchic scaling"[2] has nothing to do with the peculiar nonperspective method of representation of pre-Greek art. It derives from an emotional attitude toward the king. We also find it in drawings which use perspective. Figure 4 shows the modernized Persian army of the middle of last century. It is the setting for the dominating figure of the shah. The crown prince and the commander-in-chief are drawn on a smaller scale, the army yet smaller. The correspondence with the Narmer palette is complete, and the comparison underlines the difference between these and such predynastic monuments as Figure 1. With the first king of the First Dynasty, kingship—implying both the function of the ruler and the attitude of the subjects so well expressed by Narmer's artist—was born.

The other side of Narmer's palette (Fig. 3) shows the representative nature of the king even more clearly. It is quite likely that this scene shows one of the decisive victories, preceding the unification of the country, by which Menes and his men from Upper Egypt subjected one or more Delta states, for the vanquished enemy is identified as a Lower Egyptian. What matters for us at present is the remarkable fact that the whole conflict is represented as one between the king and the leader of the enemy. A glance at Figure 1 will show that this represents a complete break with predynastic usage. And the change is never undone. From this moment onward the community is never again rendered by a conglomerate of figures: Egyptian art steadfastly proclaims that, not the people's, but Pharaoh's, acts are efficacious. It is revealing that the representation of the community by the single symbolical figure of its ruler is consistently applied to Egypt only. The enemy is often rendered by a plurality. Even on the Narmer palette two dead opponents at the bottom of Figure 3 complete the picture of the defeat. The most common formula of the New Kingdom is an elaboration of the design on the Narmer palette. In Figure 5 Tuthmosis III is shown holding a mass of helpless captives. They serve as foil to the superhuman figure of the king, and, as we shall see, their confusion and their ineffectual opposition to Pharaoh possess a definite significance.

If we now consider a Mesopotamian monument of an early period, we are confronted with a very different concept of the king's nature. The ruler, Eannatum, marches in front of his phalanx or rides in his chariot at the head of his infantry (Fig. 6). On the other side of the stela (Fig. 7) a large symbolical figure has caught the enemy in a net. This figure represents the god Ningirsu, who is thus, most significantly, equivalent to the figure of Pharaoh in the Egyptian design of Figure 5. The Mesopotamian king leads his people, but he is not rendered as differing in essentials from his subjects; it is the god who belongs to a different order of being. This view of the ruler remains characteristic for Mesopotamian art of all periods. In Figure 8 we see Assurnasirpal in battle, standing in his chariot together with the charioteer and an archer; and, though some of the enemy submit, others do not hesitate to draw the bow against him. The god Assur supports the king.

The Egyptians represented a similar event in quite a different manner (Fig. 9). The whole scene is dominated by Pharaoh. Alone in his chariot, he has fastened the reins round his waist to have both hands free for the fight; and he is so absorbed in watching the effect of his last shot that his right hand remains beside his face where the bowstring had been released. Notwithstanding this charmingly "realistic" detail, the design is pure invention; it is impossible to fight single-handed from such a chariot. But no rendering of actuality could serve as an adequate rendering of Pharaoh. The rest of the design is similarly determined by the view which the Egyptian held as regards his ruler. The gods are represented by the vulture of Mut hovering above the king and recalling Assur in Figure 8. But Pharaoh stands less in need of assistance than the Assyrian. No enemy dares threaten him. Furthermore, no troops are conspicuous in battle. On the right the Egyptian army forms a decorative border behind the king, and only when we look carefully do we notice that Egyptian soldiers have penetrated the fortresses and are massacring the Syrians. The acts of the king alone count; he is invincible, nay, inassailable—intangible. For this reason the Egyptian texts always refer to the enemy in derogatory terms such as "the wretched Asiatics." No man can hope to resist the divine ruler and survive. Egyptian art sometimes waxes lyrical when rendering this theme. In Figure 10, another elaboration of the motif of the Narmer palette, Pharaoh appears in a hand-to-hand fight. Observe the magnificent contrast between the vigorous, agile figure of Ramses II and the utter collapse of the Libyan chief. Note, also, that the effect is again heightened by opposing two antagonists to the single figure of the king. The same contrast dominates Figure 5. But we may now be prepared to probe the full meaning of that scene; it is no mere assertion that so many are powerless a .1st the single figure of Pharaoh. The enemies in the design represent an element of chaos; the same applies to the enemies in Figure 8 and even to the two figures at the bottom of Figure 3. Victory is not merely assertion of power; it is the reduction of chaos to order. In Figure 5 the king is balanced by the gods whom he confronts; a divine order is vindicated.

This aspect of kingship we shall meet throughout the Egyptian texts which we shall presently discuss. It differentiates the Egyptian monarchy from mere despotism. Pharaoh does not act arbitrarily. He maintains an established order (of which justice is an essential element) against the onslaught of the powers of chaos. This function is independent of the accidents of history. It is an eternal truth and therefore the main subject of the artists at all times. The historical incidents in which the truth has become manifest may also be indicated, but in a subsidiary position, such as the large panels of text and the enumeration of the names of captured towns.[3] For the same reason many texts which we consider historical inscriptions exasperate us by the prevalence of generalities and clichés and the scarceness of factual information. But the latter had little significance for the Egyptian in comparison with the satisfaction which he felt because the static order, championed by Pharaoh, was once more firmly established.

We have hitherto used only battle scenes to illustrate the difference between Mesopotamian and Egyptian concepts of kingship. But it is evident that so thorough a contrast must appear in whatever context the king is shown. Figure 11 shows Assurnasirpal, while hunting, surprised by a wounded lion attacking from the rear. Soldiers come running to assist the king, who turns round with his bow held ready for more distant game. The charioteer attends to the horses. It is relevant to note that the lion is rendered as a magnificent, most powerful beast. Assurbanipal is pictured even more realistically in the same emergency.[4] The head of the maddened lion is forced aside by the spear of the king, who is assisted by another spearman, an archer, and, of course, the charioteer.

At Medinet Habu, Ramses III had himself depicted in exactly the same situation.[5] Of the lion only one claw is preserved, but this suffices; the difference between this and the Mesopotamian version could not be more striking. The king, with the reins tied round his waist, stands alone in the chariot. While he disposes of the beast attacking from behind, another lion is in headlong flight before his horses. It is rendered as a puny, frightened animal, just as, in another relief (Fig. 12), a tame lion of Ramses II is shown trotting beside his span like a not-very-large dog. These scenes do not mean that the Egyptians were under any misconception as to the potentialities of the lion; in fact, we have proof that at least one Pharaoh was very proud of his achievement in hunting these dangerous beasts. Amenhotep III issued in his tenth year a series of large commemorative scarabs on which we read: "Statement of the lions which His Majesty took by his own shooting from Year 1 to Year 10 (to wit) 102 fierce lions."[6] But ancient art is not bound to render merely what the eye can see. In both Egypt and Mesopotamia lion hunts were depicted to proclaim the valor of the king in a dangerous sport. But in Mesopotamia he appears in those scenes as a heroic man, in Egypt, as a god who destroys his victims in the perfection of his power, as in play. To us this rendering seems to overshoot the mark, since we deny virtue to a victory when the combatants are so unequal. But our reaction merely gives the measure of our distance from Egyptian mentality. Let us realize that the hunting scenes reflect the same view of the king as the battle pictures. The Egyptian designs show Pharaoh, in the manner of the gods in the *Iliad*, deciding the outcome of the battle, yet not endangered by the fray. In Mesopotamia the king appears at the head of his troops, risking his life as they do.

In one context only does Pharaoh appear on an equal footing with other figures, namely, in the company of the gods. And it is precisely in this context that the Mesopotamian king is shown, not as leader, but as subject. The stela of Ur-Nammu is characteristic for the Mesopotamian viewpoint at all times. The king stands in an attitude of worship and humility before the throne of his god (Fig. 13). In Assyrian times the relationship is not essentially different but has become less direct. The king is usually shown before a statue of the god.

A corresponding relationship is also known in Egypt, though the king is shown there, not merely worshiping, but carrying out in person all the acts of the daily ritual for all the gods throughout the land. But, in addition, there are scenes for which no parallel can be found in Asia. So we see Ramses II (Fig. 14), between the gods Horus and Khnum, netting birds in the marshes. The testimonial of this design, together with that of the battle scenes and hunting scenes, is quite eloquent: Pharaoh belongs not to the order of mankind but to that of the gods. Consequently, we need not be astonished to find him assuming that curious mixture of animal and human features which distinguishes the gods of Egypt. On the inside of the war chariot of Tuthmosis IV (Fig. 15), the only purely human forms are the agonizing enemies. The king is shown as the winged lion of the war-god Monthu, who himself appears falcon-headed. This rendering of the king is already known in the Old Kingdom.[7] Note in the design of the chariot how by purely formal means the figure of the king is assimilated to the divine figures around him. There are several areas, covered with close lines, which are significant in this connection: the wings of the king and those of the god; the royal fan behind the winged lion and the winged sun beetle; the vertically hatched wings of the latter, which harmonize with the feathered crowns of the god on the left and the king on the right. In this way, by purely aesthetic means, the king is made to appear as an integral part of the world of the gods, destroying the misguided mortals who move against it.

Upon this background we must consider a type of monument which is familiar to us and which, for that very reason, we are quite unable to appreciate. The sphinx, which for the Greeks remained an embodiment of mystery, has been vulgarized by the applied arts so that we consider it merely an odd freak of oriental fancy. It is, of course, no such thing. It represents the king, not only as a being of superhuman physical power, but of a quality of power which is, in Egypt, characteristic of the gods. In some works the realization is successful enough to impress even us (Fig. 16).

There remains one point which needs to be emphasized. In commenting upon works of art as the embodiment of two different concepts of kingship, we may have created the impression that we view them as products of deliberate thought. This is naturally not the case; and, confronted with the originals, one will recognize unhesitatingly the outcome not of intellectual calculations but of artistic inspiration. In other words, there was not, in the mind of the ancient artist, the question: "How can

I render the king as god or as hero?" In his mind was merely: "Now I must picture His Majesty," and according to his being an Egyptian or an Assyrian the result was as we have seen. The approach by means of art has this great advantage that, over and above our intellectual analysis, we can grasp directly the expressions-in-form in which the ancients expressed what they experienced to be the truth about their king. Their experience, however, was in the first place emotional; and this is comprehensible enough. For the truth about their king affected their lives in every, even the most personal, aspect, since, through the king, the harmony between human existence and supernatural order was maintained.

Fig. 3.—The Narmer Palette (*reverse*)

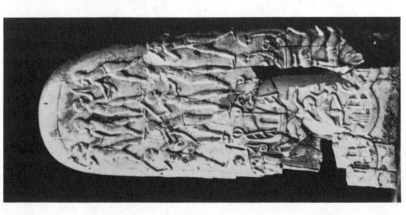

Fig. 2.—The Narmer Palette (*obverse*)

Fig. 1.—The Gebel el Arak
Knife Handle (Louvre)

FIG. 4.—PERSIAN WATER COLOR

Fig. 5.—Tuthmosis III Destroying Enemies (Karnak)

Fig. 6.—The Stela of the Vultures: Eannatum at the
Head of His Troops (Louvre)

FIG. 7.—THE STELA OF THE VULTURES: NINGIRSU
DESTROYING EANNATUM'S ENEMIES

FIG. 8.—ASSURNASIRPAL AT WAR (BRITISH MUSEUM)

Fig. 9.—Ramses III Attacking Hittite Cities (Medinet Habu)

Fig. 10.—Ramses II Destroying Libyans (Abu Simbel)

Fig. 11.—Assurnasirpal Hunting Lions (British Museum)

Fig. 12.—Ramses II in His War Chariot (Abu Simbel)

Fig. 13.—Ur-Nammu Making an Offering and Going To Build a Temple

Fig. 14.—Ramses II Netting Birds with the Gods Horus and Khnum (Karnak)

FIG. 15.—SIDE OF WAR CHARIOT OF TUTHMOSIS IV (CAIRO)

FIG. 16.—KING AMENEMHET III AS SPHINX (CAIRO)

BOOK I. EGYPT

PART I. THE FOUNDING OF KINGSHIP

CHAPTER 1

THE HISTORICAL FOUNDATION: THE
ACHIEVEMENT OF MENES

Egyptian kingship emerged at the end of the predynastic period. Of this the Egyptians were well aware; they recognized a first king of a first dynasty, Menes. Tradition named as his predecessors the "semidivine spirits" who had succeeded rule by the gods. These in their turn had been preceded by the Creator, Re. Monarchical rule, then, was coeval with the universe; the Creator had assumed kingship over his creation from the first. But the characteristic Egyptian form of kingship was remembered as one of those innovations which marked the beginning of history and a clear break with prehistoric times.

Modern scholars have almost unanimously rejected this view of the ancients without improving upon it. For, if we study the numerous predynastic and protodynastic monuments, we must admit that the emergence of Pharaonic rule coincides with an entirely unprecedented series of phenomena. The traditions regarding Menes can only mean that he unified the whole of Egypt. But this achievement appears, in the light of contemporary monuments, as the political aspect of one of those creative crises which mark the spasmodic growth of human culture. The rise of the First Dynasty is accompanied by the momentous introduction of writing, by the technological advance of a large-scale use of metal tools, by the new modes of expression of monumental art—in short, by the thoroughgoing change from a peasant culture, comparable to those found throughout prehistoric Europe and Asia, to the highest civilization which the world had yet known.

In this astonishing transformation the political unification of the country represents a more complex element than is usually recognized. It was not merely a practical solution of a problem of organization. The form given to this solution, Menes' dual monarchy, the kingdom of Upper and Lower Egypt, was as significant an invention and as fruitful in its consequences as any made in that formative phase of culture. Expressing a peculiarly Egyptian point of view, the dual monarchy was

capable of sustaining a symbolical significance which explains its permanence, its power as a cultural force, and also its valuation by the
ancients as a total break with the past. We must therefore describe
with some care the conditions under which it arose.

The roots of Egyptian unity reach back into the most distant past.
The population of the Nile Valley was as homogeneous, both physically
and culturally, as such a large group can ever be. The evidence of the
fauna and of flint tools suggests that the inhabitants descended in early
neolithic times from the surrounding desert plateaus. The change of climate which turned these wide pasture lands into deserts at the same time
made the marshes of the Nile Valley fit for human habitation. We know
that the physique of the inhabitants of this valley from the Delta deep
down into Nubia remained much the same from predynastic to late historic times.[1] They also shared a common material culture in predynastic
times. There are indications that this culture, the Amratian,[2] extended
well into Libya and reached the Red Sea in the East.[3] And somatic and
ethnological resemblances, and certain features of their language, connect the ancient Egyptians firmly with the Hamitic-speaking people of
East Africa.[4] It seems that Pharaonic civilization arose upon this Northeast African Hamitic substratum. In any case, the prehistoric inhabitants of the Nile Valley must have possessed a common spiritual culture
as a correlate to the homogeneous physical and archeological remains.

We may recognize parts of this common inheritance in certain ideas
which were at all times prevalent throughout the country, even though
their outward forms may have differed from place to place. One of these
basic beliefs held that divine power could become manifest in certain
animals and birds, especially bulls, cows, rams, and falcons. Another
made the visible world come forth from a primeval ocean and regarded
the Creator as the god manifest in the power of the sun. The basic unity
of all Egyptians must have been a contributing factor to the sudden
efflorescence of culture under the First Dynasty. The potentialities of
concerted action which such a unity implies could then, for the first
time, be realized and find adequate scope.

The differences which might have hampered unification did not descend very deeply into the fabric of Egyptian culture. They are such as
can be explained by the change from a roaming existence as hunters and
herdsmen on the highlands to the settled life of farmers in the valley.
Settlement strengthens particularism. Slight differences of old standing
would become more pronounced; special conditions, the peculiarities of
local chiefs or priests, religious and other experiences affecting some but

not all of the communities—all these and similar factors would give rise to those local cults and customs which have in recent years formed the main subject of study of Egyptologists, who, under the spell of these diversifications, have often lost sight of the underlying community of beliefs.[5] They have also accepted a brilliant but, in essence, mechanical conversion of religious contrasts into quasi-historical conflicts.[6] If we free ourselves from these hypotheses and consider the actual remains of predynastic and protodynastic times, a simpler picture emerges; and its correctness finds refreshing corroboration in observations made in modern Africa in regions where similar conditions still prevail:

> The social organization is essentially that of a number of villages united into a single community under a common chief. . . . . But throughout this form of political grouping it is generally possible to discover a unifying influence arising from a sense of kinship and therefore the possession of a common religious cult intensified by pressure from without.[7]

How well this description fits predynastic Egypt becomes clear when we view the modesty of the remains of predynastic villages; the homogeneity of the contents of thousands of predynastic graves; the division of Egypt, in later times, into nomes or provinces which go back, in the main, to the communities formed in early times; the ease with which these provinces became independent under their own local chiefs whenever the central power weakened; their representation by standards or emblems connected with a local cult; and the varying groups of these same standards—indicating an unstable and changing political conformation—which appear on predynastic monuments restraining enemies or demolishing cities (Figs. 27 and 28). There can be no doubt that our quotation from a description of modern conditions applies fully to those prevailing before the rise of Menes.

Within such a conglomerate of small communities, larger political units may originate: "It is in some such loose organization . . . . that in this part of Africa paramount chiefs may arise, when a strong man or war leader begins to extend his power beyond his own group, thus originating loose confederacies, which in the face of a hostile attack are welded into something approaching a small nation."[8] This is obviously the process reflected in the votive slate palettes which, by the varying groups of standards, prove the existence of "loose confederacies" (Figs. 27 and 28); these palettes are a little older than King Menes.[9] And since he was preceded (to judge by the style of the monuments) by an Upper Egyptian king, "Scorpion," who showed himself as conqueror and dedicated votive gifts to the Horus temple of Nekhen-Hierakonpolis as

Menes did,[10] it is quite clear that the final unification of the country under Menes followed a period of disturbance and that he was the "strong man" to whom our quotation refers. It is also clear from the monuments of Scorpion that Menes completed a task in which one or more of his predecessors had already been engaged. And yet his achievement differed radically from theirs; it was never undone.

Obviously, kingship was not created in a void, and the unification of the country can be viewed as a short process extending over a few generations. Scorpion is known as a conqueror. There must have been prehistoric chieftains of the type of the African rainmaker-king. But Egyptian tradition, in attaching the decisive change to the name of Menes, proclaimed that the rise of the First Dynasty marked a turning-point in the nation's existence; all we know confirms the correctness of that point of view. For this reason we retain the name of Menes for the founder of the united monarchy, even though some of his acts may have been performed by Scorpion, some by Narmer, and some by Aha. In this sense it can be said that kingship, as the peculiar concept which remained a living force throughout the country's history (or at least until the end of the second millennium B.C.), did not exist before Menes, for its premises are Menes' own achievements.

The lasting significance of Menes' conquests has a twofold root. In the first place, their completeness was of the essence. The king of the entire land was not the most successful of a number of chieftains but a ruler without peers. The conquest completed, it became possible to view the unification of Egypt, not as an ephemeral outcome of conflicting ambitions, but as the revelation of a predestined order. And thus kingship was, in fact, regarded throughout Egyptian history. Whenever in later times the central power collapsed and local centers assumed autonomy, this return to predynastic conditions was viewed not as a departure from a political norm but as a fall from grace. This is the characteristic mood of such writings as "The Admonitions of an Egyptian Sage,"[11] which describes the anarchy of the First Intermediate Period after the dissolution of the Old Kingdom. The description aims deliberately at the rendering of a situation which is not merely chaotic but in which social and moral norms are reversed—a world turned upside down. The Twelfth Dynasty, which overcame this anarchy; the Eighteenth Dynasty, which expelled the Asiatic Hyksos; the Ethiopians of the Twenty-fifth, who crushed the numerous kinglets who had usurped power—all these restorers of single rule proclaimed their achievement as the vindication of a divinely ordered state of affairs. Thus they took

Menes' achievement for granted; the united country under a single monarch was no longer considered an alternative to more decentralized forms of government but the only form admissible.

We may well ask how an institution introduced at the beginning of history could acquire this transcendent significance for the Egyptians. If it is suggested that unity was evidently most desirable from the point of view of efficient administration, one must answer that no merely utilitarian considerations could have given to single rulership the compelling character, the peculiar prestige, which it demonstrably possessed. Menes, in making himself a ruler without peers, had fulfilled one prerequisite for that sanction which power must obtain to rise above the sphere of historical vicissitude. He fulfilled the second prerequisite for a sublimation of his rulership when he imparted to it a form harmonizing so perfectly with Egyptian mentality as to appear both inevitable and perennial. That form was the dual monarchy, the kingship of Upper and the kingship of Lower Egypt united in the single person of the ruler. This extraordinary conception expressed in political form the deeply rooted Egyptian tendency to understand the world in dualistic terms as a series of pairs of contrasts balanced in unchanging equilibrium.[12] The universe as a whole was referred to as "heaven and earth." Within this concept "earth" was again conceived dualistically, as "north and south," the "portions of Horus and the portions of Seth," "the two lands," or "the two (Nile) banks." The last of these synonyms demonstrates their nonpolitical character most clearly. Each of them is equivalent to the second member of the more comprehensive pair, "heaven and earth"; they belong to cosmology, not to history or politics. Yet each of them was suitable to describe the king's domain, for the whole of mankind and all the lands of the earth were subject to Pharaoh. His realm was often described as "that which the sun encircles," the earth; and the Greeks, who, like ourselves, found literal translations of Egyptian phrases misleading, rendered "the Two Lands" by ἡ οἰκουμένη, "the whole inhabited earth." When Pharaoh assumed dualistic titles or called himself "Lord of the Two Lands," he emphasized not the divided origin but the universality of his power.[13] The dualistic forms of Egyptian kingship did not result from historical incidents. They embody the peculiarly Egyptian thought that a totality comprises opposites. Menes gave political expression to a basic Egyptian mode of thought when he styled his rule over the conquered and unified Nile lands a "kingship over Upper and Lower Egypt." The perfect consonance between the new political and the established cosmological con-

ceptions gave to his creation a compelling authority. A state dualistically conceived must have appeared to the Egyptians the manifestation of
the order of creation in human society, not the product of a temporary
constellation of power. It was in this respect that Menes' victory differed from any conquest which earlier kings, like Scorpion, had made.

It is important to realize that the dual monarchy had no historical
foundation; it was not as if an Upper Egyptian king had been confronted
with a united but antagonistic Delta over which he assumed sovereignty
in addition to his rule of Upper Egypt. The political structure of predynastic Egypt had been amorphous to a degree, as we have seen; if the
geographical configuration suggested a division of the country into
Delta and Nile Valley, there is no reason to believe that these were any
more thought of as political entities than the equally obvious divisions
of desert and arable soil, the "Red Land" and the "Black Land."

It is true that on the Palermo Stone—annals dating from the Old Kingdom—we find a series of pre-Menite kings wearing the Red Crown of
Lower Egypt.* But we must remember that this crown belonged originally, not to Lower Egypt as a whole, but to several Delta states, one
with its capital in Pe-Buto and another centered round Sais. Even in the
eastern Delta the Red Crown was worn by a local goddess.[14] It is due
to Menes' new conception of the rulership of Egypt that the Red Crown
, as well as the cobra-goddess Wadjet and certain usages and
institutions prevailing at Pe, became symbolical of Lower Egypt. They
were made to balance the White Crown , the vulture-goddess Nekhbet , and other features pertaining originally to the Upper Egyptian
principality from which the House of Menes derived and which included Nekhen-Hierakonpolis, This, and Abydos. The wider significance accorded to the symbols of Menes' homeland, on the one hand,
and of Pe, on the other, are part of the stylization of Egypt as a dual
monarchy, an artificial but meaningful symmetry which holds in its
spell even those modern authors who view his unification, not as a piece-
meal conquest in the manner of Piankhi the Ethiopian, but as the victory
of an established Upper Egyptian state over an equally developed Lower
Egyptian kingdom.[15]

The Egyptians themselves acknowledged throughout their history the
validity of Menes' conception, and they went to great lengths in its realization. Many departments of government, including the treasury,
were duplicated in an Upper and a Lower Egyptian office. The coronation ritual and the elaborate ceremonies of the Sed festival were, as

* See below, n. 15.

we shall see, repeated with different insignia, the king appearing once as the king of Upper and once as the king of Lower Egypt. There were dual shrines for the ancestral spirits of the royal house. The king's titulary included, besides the double title, "King of Upper and King of Lower Egypt," an epithet, "The Two Ladies," which proclaimed him the manifestation of the two goddesses whom we have mentioned and who represented the two halves of the realm.

Another epithet of the king, "The Two Lords," would seem to suggest a similar meaning; but here we touch upon more profound religious symbolism. "The Two Lords" were the perennial antagonists, Horus and Seth. The king was identified with both of these gods but not in the sense that he was considered the incarnation of the one and also the incarnation of the other. He embodied them as a pair, as opposites in equilibrium. Hence the ancient title of the queen of Egypt: "She who sees Horus-and-Seth."[16] In the pyramid texts a ruler appeals to the Creator Atum with the following reference to himself: "Look upon the two-dwellers-in-the-palace, that is Horus-and-Seth" (Pyr. 141d).[17] Another pyramid text explains the king's rebirth to eternal life as follows:

> Thou art born because of Horus (in thee)
> Thou art conceived because of Seth (in thee).[18]

This embodiment of the two gods in the person of Pharaoh is another instance of the peculiar dualism that expresses a totality as an equilibrium of opposites. In later times, when the titulary of the king had become standardized, it is no longer found; but the gods Horus and Seth are then used in art to express a similar idea. In symbolical designs connected with the king they appear as representatives of Lower and Upper Egypt when "the Union of the Two Lands" is represented, for instance, or in abbreviated renderings of the Sed festival (Fig. 25). They are always co-operating, and their antithetical gestures signify that the land in its totality honors or serves the king. Horus and Seth are therefore called rh.wy, "the partners"; and their use in art tallies well with the ancient texts in which they are said to be harmoniously combined in the single person of Pharaoh.

But this solidarity of the gods contrasts strangely with their mythological relationship. In the religious texts Horus and Seth form a pair, too, but the bond between them consists of an imperishable hostility. It is usual to translate the antagonism between the two gods from the sphere of cosmology, where it belongs, to that of politics, by postulating an ancient conflict between Upper Egypt (Seth) and Lower Egypt (Horus). Since we know that the unity of Egypt was achieved by the conquest of an Upper Egyptian king, Menes, the theory requires that the opposite movement, in which Horus (Lower Egypt) was victorious, have taken place in prehistoric times. This chimera comes into being by the unjustifiable projection into prehistory of symbols which derive their meaning from the dual monarchy as created by Menes and which therefore cannot be torn from that context.[19] The theory, moreover, bars the way to an understanding of an important aspect of royalty which was actually expressed when the king was viewed as Horus-and-Seth.

Horus and Seth were the antagonists per se—the mythological symbols for all conflict.* Strife is an element in the universe which cannot be ignored; Seth is perennially subdued by Horus but never destroyed. Both Horus and Seth are wounded in the struggle, but in the end there is a reconciliation: the static equilibrium of the cosmos is established. Reconciliation, an unchanging order in which conflicting forces play their allotted part—that is the Egyptian's view of the world and also his conception of the state. If the king is called (and that in early texts) Horus-and-Seth, this formula expresses more than "The Two Ladies." It indicates not merely that the king rules the dual monarchy but that he has crushed opposition, reconciled conflicting forces—that he represents an unchanging order.

In practice this aspect of kingship found expression in the numerous rites and festivals which we shall discuss and which combined references to Upper and Lower Egypt. Moreover, northerners were not at a disadvantage in the united kingdom though a southern dynasty reigned. Prominent officials and the courtiers buried in squares of graves round the tombs of kings of the First Dynasty[20] include men whose names show their devotion to Lower Egyptian gods. Two of the queens of the First Dynasty bear names compounded with that of the goddess Neith of Sais in the Delta. It is a mistake to see in these phenomena—as is commonly done—proof of practical wisdom only. The king's epithet "Horus-and-Seth" carries religious implications. The structure and practices of the new state show a distinct integration of religious zeal and expediency.

Menes' creation of a new capital for united Egypt must be viewed in the same light.[21] Just south of the apex of the Delta, near modern Cairo, land on the west of the Nile was reclaimed, and a fortress, "The White Walls" (later named "Memphis"), was constructed. The character of

* See below, p. 183.

the structure bore an obvious relationship to the recent date of the country's pacification. The name proclaimed it as the stronghold of a king who came from the South. In historical times the color of the North was red, that of the South, white.[22] On the southern side of the fortress a new temple was founded and dedicated to the god Ptah. It may be significant that one of this god's epithets was in later times "The (Upper Egyptian) King of the Two Lands."[23] The name of the new sanctuary is, in any case, full of meaning: "Balance of the Two Lands, in which the Upper Egyptian Land and the Lower Egyptian Land have been weighed." The name of the temple in the new capital explicitly proclaims the established equilibrium.

We have now gauged the full spiritual significance of Menes' achievement. The Egyptians always recognized it. Yet in their mode of thinking a historical innovation of such importance could be only the unfolding of a preordained order, the manifestation of what had always been potentially present.[24] Moreover, they retained as much as possible of the ceremonies and usages which Menes had introduced. Thus, for over three thousand years, the coronation of Pharaoh took place at Memphis and culminated in a double ceremony which in all likelihood goes back to the days when Menes had completed his new capital, since it is called "Union of the Two Lands; Circuit of the White Walls." We should be wrong if we estimated this tradition to be commemorative of Menes' deeds. Ritual is concerned with the present in which it is performed. Through the retention of these ancient ceremonies in the coronation of each successive king, his succession became to some extent a re-enactment of the original event, participating in its virtue and reaffirming its purpose.

CHAPTER 2

THE THEORETICAL FOUNDATION: THE MEMPHITE THEOLOGY

BY RARE good fortune we possess a text which, to all appearances, originated in an early phase of the Egyptian monarchy and which embodies, by implication, a theory of kingship. It seems indicated that we should present the document at this point. But that procedure entails peculiar difficulties. For this text, the "Memphite Theology,"[1] presents both the views and the mythological figures by which kingship was interpreted by the Egyptians throughout their long history and which our Book I is, in its entirety, intended to explain. We shall, then, be obliged to anticipate subsequent chapters and to present here somewhat apodictically conclusions which will be substantiated later.

The Memphite Theology presents the religious teaching for Menes' new capital. It combines views which we can recognize as new, since they concern the new foundation; others which we suspect to be new because they run counter to common Egyptian beliefs and could hardly have gained acceptance if they had not been part of the great movement at the dawn of history. Other doctrines again seem to be rooted in Egyptian, or even African, traditions of the greatest antiquity.

The text is a cosmology: it describes the order of creation and makes the land of Egypt, as organized by Menes, an indissoluble part of that order. Ptah, the *genius loci*, to whom a temple south of the wall of Memphis had been dedicated, is proclaimed the Creator of All; and in an argument of astonishing boldness and profundity the intellectual advantages of monotheism are combined with the variety of recognized Egyptian gods. But these remarkable speculations (for which the text is famous) form only its middle part, our Section V, set in a treatise upon the place of society in nature. It is characteristic of the Egyptian view of kingship that it should be clarified within such a context.

The document, in its present damaged state, suggests a division into six parts; there may have been more, or sections which now seem separate may originally have been joined together. It is exceptionally difficult to judge in this matter, since the text is not formally subdivided. The transition from our Section V to Section VI, for instance, shows that the literary construction is of the flimsiest; the text consists simply of a succession of statements (or, in the case of the related Mystery Play of the Succession [chap. 11], of scenes) which, from a formal point of view, are all equivalent and in no way subordinated to one another.[2] As literary forms, these early texts are most primitive.

Section I is badly damaged, but the main themes are recognizable. On the one hand, the land of Egypt is proclaimed to have its being in the creator-god Ptah-Ta-Tjenen, Ptah "the Risen Land." On the other hand, reference is made to the appearance of a united country under one king. What is left of this section reads:

> . . . . Ptah, that is, this [land] named with the Great Name of
> Ta Tjenen. . . . .
> He who unified this [land] has appeared as King of Upper Egypt
> and as King of Lower Egypt.[3]

The succeeding sentence states that Atum, the sun-god-creator of common Egyptian beliefs, acknowledged that Ptah had created him and all the other gods. The significance of this phrase will become clear as we proceed.

The various references to "the land" have to be understood with some appreciation of that polyphony of meaning which the Egyptians loved. It means the country, Egypt, with all that it contains. But it also means the fertile soil, and as such it is one with the creator Ptah-Ta-Tjenen. The "Risen Land" possesses, again, a multiple significance. It alludes to the universal Egyptian belief that creation started with the emergence of a mound, the Primeval Hill, above the waters of chaos.* Ptah, the fruitful earth, is one with this hill—the starting-point of all that is, even of life itself. But the epithet alludes, at the same time, to the land which Menes had reclaimed from the marsh waters to build Memphis and the temple of Ptah; and it furthermore alludes to the "Great Land," the name of the province of This, which, as we shall see, possessed some significance for the new theology.

Section II deals with the end of conflict which precedes the establishment of order both in the universe and in the state. The gods Horus and Seth, contending for the rulership of Egypt, are separated; and Geb, the earth-god, acts as arbiter. He first divides the country between the two, but he regrets this decision and rescinds it, giving the whole land to Horus. The two crowns of Upper and of Lower Egypt are now said to

* See below, chap. 13.

"grow" from the head of Horus; and Horus appears in the role of Menes (a role assumed by each king at his coronation) "uniting the lands" in his single rule. The Ennead, or nine gods, who assist, represent, as we shall see,* a formula which expresses the relation between king and gods. The text is damaged at the beginning of this section:

. . . . the Ennead gathered to him (Geb) and he separated Horus and Seth. . . . . He prevented them from quarreling and installed Seth as Upper Egyptian king, in Upper Egypt, at the place where he was born, in *Su* (near Herakleopolis). And Geb put Horus as Lower Egyptian king in Lower Egypt, at the place where his father was drowned, at the "Half of the Two Lands" (probably near Memphis). And so Horus was in his place, and Seth was in his place; and they agreed with each other as regards the Two Lands in Ajan (opposite Cairo), which is the frontier (or separation) of the Two Lands. . . . .

It suited Geb's heart ill that the portion of Horus was like that of Seth, and so Geb gave his heritage (entirely) to Horus, that is, the son of his son, his eldest (literally, "his opener-of-the-body").

Geb calls Horus an "opener-of-the-body" with a reference to the fact that he was a firstborn son. Horus is then identified with the wolf-god, Upwaut, whose name means "Opener-of-the-Ways," and whose ensign is closely associated with Pharaoh at all great ceremonies, as we shall see.[4]

The treatment of Horus in this text is remarkable. At the first division of the land, Seth goes to the place where he was born, but Horus to the place where his father was drowned. Horus, in contrast to Seth, seems to appear not as king in his own right but as the legitimate successor to his father Osiris. And, again, when Geb changes his mind and assigns the whole country to Horus, he justifies his act by acclaiming Horus as the eldest son of his predecessor. Horus assumes kingship over the Two Lands, not as conqueror, but as rightful heir. If we remember that this text was probably composed in the reign of Menes, a Horus king who had just conquered Egypt, we can gauge the relative importance, to the Egyptian mind, of historical and theological facts.†

It is interesting that Geb acts as arbiter. He was doubly entitled to do so, as father of Osiris and as earth-god.‡ In the first function he could act as head of the family with primitive, but universally acknowledged, authority. As god of the earth he was obviously concerned in a division of the land of Egypt. His successive decisions clearly represent the mythological form in which the whole complex of ideas involved in Menes' dual monarchy could be expressed: the fundamental view of a world in static equilibrium between conflicting forces (Horus and Seth); the kingship of Upper and Lower Egypt as the corresponding

* See below, chap. 15.   † See above, p. 9.   ‡ See below, chap. 15.

political form; and withal a rulership vested in the person of a single king.

The text, continuing, reasserts the relation between the land and Ptah—a relationship which was the subject of Section I also.[5]

Horus stood (as king) over the land. And so became united this country named with its Great Name, Ta-Tjenen-who-is-to-the-south-of-his-wall, the Lord of Eternity.

The two "Great in Magic" (the crowns) grew out of his head. Thus it was that Horus appeared as King of Upper Egypt and as King of Lower Egypt who united the Two Lands in the province of The (White) Wall, at the place where the Two Lands are united.

Now follows a ritual act signifying the acquiescence of the two parts of Egypt in the union. The heraldic plants—sedge 𐦢 for Upper, papyrus 𐦣 for Lower, Egypt—are placed at the entrance of the temple of Ptah:

It happened that sedge and papyrus were put at the two outer gates of the temple of Ptah. That means: Horus and Seth, who bore with each other and united in fraternizing so that their quarrel is ended wherever they may be. They are united in the temple of Ptah, the "Balance of the Two Lands in which Upper Egypt and Lower Egypt have been weighed."

Section III is very much damaged. It seems that the text, after having established the succession of Horus as rightful heir, now turns to his predecessor, Osiris, and explains the relation of this god to Ptah and to the new capital. Too much is lost for us to judge this relationship. Memphis is said to derive its significance as the "granary" of Egypt from the fact that Osiris was buried there. This statement is repeated in Section VI, where it is better preserved.

Section IV deals with the construction of the royal castle at Memphis, mentioned just before as the place where Osiris was buried and important also as the seat of authority over the whole of Egypt established by Menes. But the text is too damaged to allow further comment.

Section V is the famous exposé of the sole creatorship of Ptah, a closely reasoned theological argument which reduces the gods of Egypt to aspects or manifestations of Ptah. We shall be better able to appreciate its meaning when our study has progressed further,* but we may summarize it here. It is argued that everything that exists found its origin in the conceptions of Ptah's mind ("heart"), which were objectified by being pronounced by his "tongue." In this process of creation, one god after the other came into being; and through them Ptah evolved the visible and invisible universe and all living creatures, as well as justice, the arts, etc. This account imparts, at the same time, the character of an established order, valid for all time, to the phenomenal world. The cities

* See below, chaps. 13 and 15.

and sanctuaries of Egypt are part of this order. And the final phrase of the section closes the circle: while it had started by stating that the gods came forth from Ptah, objectified conceptions of his mind, it ends by making those gods "enter into their bodies" (statues) of all kinds of material—stone, metal, or wood—which had grown out of the earth, that is, out of Ptah.

The text starts with a series of eight equations in which the polytheism of Egypt is taken into account, but superimposed upon it is the novel thought of the ultimate oneness of the divine. The gods are declared to be manifestations of Ptah. The number eight is chosen in deference to a widely held view of creation which acknowledged the sun-god as creator* but maintained at the same time that the sun had been brought forth from the waters of chaos by eight strange gods, who were no more than a conceptualizing of chaos, as their names (Darkness, Primeval Ocean, etc.) testify.† Here, then, was a point where the Memphite Theology could build up a claim for Ptah as Creator; here were divinities older than the sun. Our text maintains that even these— in other words, chaos—were of the substance of Ptah, uncreated manifestations of his being.⁶ Thus the second of the eight equations runs: "Ptah—Nun the father who begat Atum." Nun is the primeval ocean from which Atum, the creator-sun, came forth. But Ptah is manifest in every god, hence in Atum: "Ptah—the Great One who is heart and tongue of the Ennead." The Great One stands for Atum, who created the Ennead of Heliopolis and who is called its heart and tongue because these are the organs of creation, according to the Memphite Theology. The epithet is no doubt given here because it throws the unique power of Ptah in bold relief: even Atum, generally worshiped as the creator of gods and cosmos, is but an emanation of Ptah.

The eight equations appear under a heading which reads: "The gods who came forth from Ptah";⁷ they present the whole theology of the text as a formula. But the theory is then stated once more in the form of a narrative of creation. And there we can watch how the ancient Egyptian language—which, as an instrument of expression for a mentality tending toward the concrete, is ill equipped to frame abstract thoughts— is made the vehicle of some truly astonishing abstractions. The author expresses no less than the conviction that the basis of existence is spiritual: ideas conceived by the Creator and objectified by his utterances. The text expresses this by describing the "heart" and the "tongue" as the organs of creation. These terms are concrete enough. But we should

* See below, chap. 13 and p. 232.   † See below, pp. 154–55.

misread our document completely if we took them at their face value. We know from numerous other texts that "heart" stands for "intellect," "mind," and even "spirit." The "tongue" is realizing thought; it translates concepts into actuality by means of "Hu"—authoritative utterance.* We must, then, read these passages as the true Egyptian equivalent of John's "In the beginning was the Word, and the Word was with God, and the Word was God." The Egyptian mode of expression strikes us as clumsy because we assume involuntarily that a more abstract mode was available; but, of course, it was not.

(There) originated in the heart and on the tongue (of Ptah) (something) in the image of Atum.

Great and exalted is Ptah who bequeathed his power to all the gods and their Ka's[8] through his heart and on his tongue. . . . .

It happened that heart and tongue prevailed over (all other) members, considering[9] that he (Ptah) is (as heart) in every body, (as tongue) in every mouth, of all gods, people, beasts, crawling creatures, and whatever else lives, while he thinks (as heart) and commands (as tongue) everything that he wishes. . . . .

Every divine word came into being through that which was thought by the heart and commanded by the tongue.

And thus the Ka's were made and the Hemsut[10] were created—they that make all sustenance and all food—by this speech (that was thought by the heart and was spoken by the tongue).

(And so justice is done to him) who does what is liked, (and evil is done to him) who does what is hated.

And so life is given to the peaceful, death to the criminal.

And so are done all labor and all arts, the action of the arms, the going of legs, the movement of all members according to this command which was thought by the heart and issued from the tongue and which constitutes the significance of all things.

Here we find, then, expressed in a most refractory medium, a statement proclaiming the unity of the divine, its spiritual character, and its immanence in living nature.[11]

We have omitted a theological argument which once again establishes that the thought and utterance of Ptah underlies Atum's work of creation, and a similar assertion follows the lines we have quoted. After that we read: "And so Ptah rested (or was satisfied) after he had made all things and all divine words." It has been argued[12] that these "divine words" really stood for a "divine order" in which "all things" found their appropriate places. The expression would rather seem once more to emphasize Ptah's peculiar process of creation through utterance of thought. For such "creative speech" turns each divine word into the *causa materialis*, *causa formalis*, and *causa movens* of an element of creation —all in one.[13]

* See below, pp. 51 and 61.

It is true, however, that the text describes how Ptah established a certain order. Our quotation explained that gods and other living beings, nay, their very life and the mechanics of their life, derived from Ptah's action as a demiurge. And the text continues by ascribing to him the establishment of the religious order of the land, namely, the local cults and all their peculiarities down to the very shapes in which the gods were worshiped; for their statues were made by Ptah and that from material "grown" upon him as earth-god.

He created the (local) gods, he made the cities, he founded the provincial divisions; he put the gods in their places of worship, he fixed their offerings, he founded their chapels. He made their bodies resemble that which pleased their hearts (i.e., the forms in which they wished to be manifest). And so the gods entered into their bodies of every kind of wood, of every kind of stone, of every kind of clay, of every kind of thing which grows upon him, in which they have taken form. Thus all the gods and their Ka's are at one with him, content and united with the Lord of the Two Lands.[14]

The diversified cults of all Egypt appear here as sanctioned by, or even due to, the initiative of the god of the united country. Our text thus imparts unity of a sort even to them.

Section VI continues to elaborate the close connection between the god and the land of Egypt by speaking about Memphis, the site of the temple of Ptah and the new capital of the country. Memphis is said to have a special significance for the "sustenance" of Egypt, and this fact is explained by the presence on its soil of the interred body of Osiris. The text acknowledges that Osiris had not always been connected with Memphis. He reached the city in the water of the Nile. Like the later myth, it speaks of Osiris' drowning, after which his body was drawn ashore by Isis and Nephthys. But the word "drowning" has connotations in connection with this god to which the straightforward translation cannot do justice.[15] The paradox of Osiris (with which we shall deal later in chap. 15) consists precisely in this—that in death the god becomes a center of vitalizing force. Hence the Nile, and especially the Nile in flood, counts as a manifestation of him. Osiris' connection with the river is not, therefore, rendered adequately by the statement that he was destroyed by the water—that he was drowned. The god was in the waters, and we have translated the verb here "to float." The notion that the god is the active force in, the beneficial influence of, the inundation can be expressed with the concreteness requisite in myth only by describing the anthropomorphic figure of Osiris as floating or submerged, "drowned," in the river;* the "finding" of Osiris, which our

* See below, pp. 191–92.

text describes as the recovery of his body by Isis and Nephthys, is represented in the ritual by the lifting-up of a jar of fresh Nile water. The statement that Osiris was buried at the new capital proclaimed it the center from which the vitalizing forces radiated. Hence Memphis could be said to be the "granary . . . . where the sustenance of the Two Lands is taken care of."

Since the text acknowledges explicitly that Osiris was not at home at Memphis, one may ask whence he "reached" that city. We are inclined to think of Abydos, contrary to current opinion. We shall consider the claims of Abydos in detail below,[16] but we may ask here why the god should be related to the capital founded by Menes at the apex of the Delta. It would seem, as we shall see, that Osiris was the dead ancestor of the kings of Menes' line, and the significance of dead kings— in ancient Egypt as in modern Africa—was so great that no blessing could rest upon the transference of the royal residence from the Thinite nome, in which Abydos is situated, unless the ancestral figure of Osiris was brought into a definite relationship with the new site. The Nile, in which Osiris was manifest and which streamed past Memphis as past Abydos, offered a means of creating a relationship that was expressed mythologically in the story of the rescue of Osiris' body from the waters.

The Memphite Theology, like the myth, ascribes the actual rescue to Isis and Nephthys; but the Theology, in contrast with the myth, insists that the goddesses acted on the orders of Horus. It agrees in this with the pyramid texts where Horus, the living king, appears as the instigator of all acts benefiting Osiris, his late predecessor.*

The text continues by describing the fate of Osiris after burial. His is a twofold destiny: he joins the sun-god in his daily circuit, but he also joins "the Court of Ptah-Ta-Tjenen," who must dwell where Ptah is god, within the earth. In fact, he "becomes earth."[17] This is the crucial phrase in this section, since it explains (as it did also in Sec. III) the extraordinary fertility of the region of Memphis where Osiris is buried. Immediately after the interment of Osiris comes the statement that Horus ascended the throne; and with this the text ends. This section reads:

Granary of the god (Ptah-Ta-Tjenen) was the Great Throne (Memphis) which rejoices the hearts of the gods who are in the temple of Ptah, Mistress of Life (epithet of temple), where the sustenance of the Two Lands is taken care of, because Osiris floated in his† water. Isis and Nephthys perceived it. They saw him and were aghast. But

* See below, pp. 114 and 116.   † See below, pp. 190–95.

Horus ordered Isis and Nephthys to grasp Osiris without delay and to prevent him from floating away. They turned their heads in time, and thus they let him reach land.

He entered the Secret Gates (of the Netherworld?), the glory of the Lords of Eternity (the dead), in step with Him who shines in the Horizon (the sun), on the path of Re, in the Great Throne (Memphis).

He joined the court and fraternized with the gods of Ta-Tjenen, Ptah, Lord of Years.

Thus Osiris became earth in the Royal Castle on the north side of this land which he had reached. His son Horus appeared as king of Upper Egypt and as king of Lower Egypt in the arms of his father Osiris in the presence of the gods that were before him and that were behind him.

If we now consider the Memphite Theology as a whole, the most remarkable feature, besides its spiritual view of creation, is the manner in which reality and mythology are intermingled. It is true that all the personages are gods; but we have already seen in our Introduction that Egyptian art presents Pharaoh consistently as a deity, and we shall presently deal with similar inscriptional evidence. In Section II the gods Horus and Seth are contending, but the subject of their quarrel is dominion over Egypt; and we have seen that Pharaoh is occasionally called "Horus-and-Seth" to indicate that his rule marks the end of discord.* Section V, the account of creation, ends by assigning to the Creator the kingly title "Lord of the Two Lands," while the concluding Section VI is explicitly concerned with the capital, Memphis, and with the myth of Osiris. The locale of the action is, in fact, not mythological but real. It is Memphis, and, more precisely, the royal castle, the newly established seat of authority for the united country, which is the place where Osiris is interred; and the figure of Osiris is not exclusively at home in mythology either. Each king, at death, becomes Osiris (chap. 10), just as each king, in life, appears "on the throne of Horus"; each king *is* Horus (chap. 3). It is then possible that the Horus who appears at the end of the text as king of Egypt in the arms of his father Osiris (though the latter is dead and buried) is not only the god but also the king; rather, it is the royal succession as it appears upon the superhuman plane which is here referred to, and the question whether Horus and Osiris are here gods or kings is, for the Egyptian, meaningless. These gods are the late king and his successor; these kings are those gods.

There is unequivocal evidence that this is so. The embrace of Horus and the dead Osiris, with which our text ends, is realized, as we shall see (chap. 11), by a ritual in the Mystery Play of the Succession; here the new king acts in person, and the burial of his father is performed in effigy. The embrace is a true communion of spirits, involving the actual

* See above, pp. 21–22.

ruler and his deceased predecessor in a rite performed at the accession of each new king; in the same way it appears, timeless, in the Memphite Theology involving the gods Horus and Osiris. Better than any other feature of Egyptian kingship, it shows that the monarchy was conceived as a reality in the world of the gods no less than in the world of men.

It is for this reason that we find a theory of kingship implied in a cosmological text. Nature itself could not be conceived without the king of Egypt. The Memphite Theology shows this specifically; it demonstrates that the dual monarchy, centered in Memphis, realized a divine plan. The order of society as established by Menes is presented as part of the cosmic order.

Let us, then, consider of what the Egyptian theory of kingship consists. One proposition, that the king is divine, we have mentioned already. The other proposition is even more remarkable. It is clearly indicated that kingship is conceived in its profoundest aspect, on the plane of the gods, as involving two generations.

We have seen, in commenting upon the second section of the Theology, that Horus is acknowledged by the assembled gods, through Geb, not because he possesses greater power than Seth, but solely because he is the eldest son of Osiris and the legitimate heir. And in the final phrases of the text we found again that Horus and Osiris are inseparable, even at the moment when Horus appears as the ruler of Egypt, after the burial of his father. It seems that the actual occupancy of the throne creates a fusion of the powers of the late king and his successor.

This view is peculiarly Egyptian, though it is not unconnected with the more widely held belief that the king is divine. It is, therefore, important to determine the relation of the two propositions which make up the Egyptian theory of kingship.

The basic view, namely that rulership implies characteristics denied to the common man, is a conventional one. In primitive societies, and among them many in East Africa, the chieftain is also the medicine man or magician; in other words, he is believed to entertain closer relationship with the powers in nature than other men.[18] The African "rainmaker-king" is a well-known example of this type of ruler. Of the Dinka tribe it is said: "A rainmaker is buried in a cattle byre, which continues to be used (as was the royal castle of Memphis where Osiris was buried). . . . . He is said to take the food of the community into the grave, so when the next season arrives a hole is dug at the side of the byre so that the food may come out again."[19] And of the Komde: "The health of the . . . . . [Chungu] (chieftain) and the welfare of the whole community were inseparably bound up together. A Chungu in health and vigour meant a land yielding its fruits, rain coming in its season, evil averted."[20] Much farther to the west the king of Jukun is addressed as "*Azaiwo* (our guinea corn), *Afyewo* (our ground nuts), *Asoiwo* (our beans). . . . . The king of Jukun is therefore able to control the rain and winds. A succession of droughts or bad harvests is ascribed to his negligence or to the waning of his strength, and he is accordingly secretly strangled."[21] We insist on this widespread aspect of kingship in Africa to indicate the premises upon which Menes' position rested. We know that King Scorpion, who probably preceded Menes, was considered an incarnation of the god Horus; we may then assume for the predynastic period the belief that the chieftains were charged with the power of divinity. The unification increased the significance of kingship; it did not destroy any of its aspects. The superhuman associations remained valid. The uncertain services which the medicine man had given to the community became institutionalized. Kingship in Egypt remained the channel through which the powers of nature flowed into the body politic to bring human endeavor to fruition.

Now this view of kingship entailed, furthermore, two generations. If the living ruler is the intermediary between men and nature, his potency continues to profit the community even after his death. This belief is, again, widespread. The dead rulers of Uganda continue to give audiences and to advise their people through oracles. Other tribes, too, seek advice at the tombs of their dead rulers in times of perplexity and do not bury them before the succession is regulated.[22] The Kizibu know of a supreme god but actually worship the spirit of an ancient king who now rules the dead. Nyakang, the dead ruler of the Shilluk, plays a much greater part in their religious life than the supreme deity Juok and sends them rain and crops.[23] We have just seen that the rainmaker of the Dinka is supposed to take the food of the people with him in death. In Egypt the power of the buried king was seen to break forth from the earth in which he rested: plants sprouting, Nile waters flooding the banks, the moon and Orion rising from the horizon—all were manifestations of his vital power.* But it is at this point that we leave the sphere of universal primitive thought for that of peculiarly Egyptian conceptions. In Egypt the dead kings were represented by a single divine figure; each one, at death, became the chthonic god Osiris, manifest in the various phenomena which come forth from the earth after apparent death. Hence the succession of earthly rulers assumed an

* See below, chap. 15.

unchanging mythological form, Horus succeeding Osiris, at each new succession, forever.[24]

The tendency to interpret changes in unchanging mythological terms is strong in Egypt. We have found it necessary to point this out when describing Egyptian art.* We have also met it in the motif of the contending gods, Horus and Seth, who stand for all conflict and strife in nature and the state, with Horus victorious in a stable equilibrium of opposing powers. The Egyptians viewed the world as essentially static. The incidents of history, therefore, lacked ultimate reality. It is true that kings died and that one ruler succeeded another, but this merely proved to the Egyptian that the essential quality of kingship could not be the *praesens*, "this king rules"; it had to be the *perfectum*, "this king has ascended the throne," or, in mythological terms, "Horus has succeeded Osiris." Throughout Egyptian history the texts reflect a curious mood of recent achievement: "the land *has been* united; discord *has been* terminated; the king *has ascended* the throne; he *has placed* truth in the place of falsehood."†

It is on this very note that the Memphite Theology ends. The concluding phrases which show Horus in the embrace of his father, though the latter is buried and has become earth, show that death does not destroy the kings. There is a mystic communion between father and son at the moment of succession, a unity and continuity of divine power which suggests a stream in which the individual rulers come and go like waves.

* See above, p. 9.   † See below, pp. 56 and 60.

CHAPTER 3

THE KING'S PERSON: HORUS

A. HORUS, THE GREAT GOD, LORD OF HEAVEN

I T IS well in keeping with the theory of kingship, which is set forth in the Memphite Theology and which remained valid throughout the existence of Pharaonic Egypt, that the king is commonly referred to as Horus. Sometimes the name is qualified—"Horus who is in the castle"—but there is no doubt that the divinity of Pharaoh was specifically conceived as a sharing of essentials with the god Horus, even though the being of the deity was not exhausted by his incarnation in the living ruler of Egypt. It may be well to consider belief in the king's divinity in general before inquiring into its specific form.

In many texts Pharaoh is called simply "the god" (*netjer*), or "the good god" (*netjer nefer*). The Egyptians, then, shared with many primitives, with the Romans, the Japanese, and the English as late as the reign of Charles II,[1] the belief that their ruler possessed supernatural powers. We have referred to this belief as a widely observed fact at the end of the preceding chapter, but we may, for a moment, consider its foundations.

The view that the blood royal differs in some essential respect from ordinary men is both normal and reasonable. Without it one cannot account for the distinction between the hereditary monarch and a usurper or the elected head of a republic. In our parlance the usual attitude toward royalty finds expression in circumlocutions like "His Majesty" or "Your Royal Highness." The attitude originates, quite simply and directly, in the sense of awe—the experience of majesty undergone in the royal presence. And this experience is dependent on neither deliberate thought or political conviction nor the characteristics which the prince as an individual may possess. On the contrary, it springs precisely from the nonpersonal, symbolical qualities with which his office equips the monarch and which the ceremonial of the court is calculated to accentuate.

It is almost impossible for most of us to imagine the depth and directness of this, the fundamental, reaction to royalty. Modern monarchies seem to survive on the strength of tradition only, and we must turn to the primitives to observe kingship as a living force in communal life. There we find every degree of differentiation between king and commoner, from the temporary distinction of a leader in war down to the recognition of total difference which we mean when we speak of the divine kings.* The subject of the divine kings has been thoroughly investigated, but the evidence from Egypt presents problems of its own which we must now face.

Pharaoh is Horus, and of this god little enough is known. His symbol is the falcon 🦅, but we do not know whether the bird was thought in some way to be merely the god's manifestation; whether the god was embodied, temporarily or permanently, in a single bird or in the species as a whole; or whether the falcon was used as a sign referring to a much more intangible divinity. The latter possibility does not exclude the others, and modern parallels suggest, as we shall see,† that we must not expect a rigid doctrine on matters of this type but rather a fluid belief of interrelationship which may assume almost any specific form.

Horus is generally called "the Great God, the Lord of Heaven"; and texts call up a strangely compelling image. The bird has acquired gigantic proportions, as in a vision. His outstretched wings are the sky, his fierce eyes sun and moon. The speckled breast of the falcon is seen when, toward evening, the clear Egyptian sky becomes spotted with feathery clouds. And since these share the glories of sunrise and sunset, Horus is called "feathered in many hues." He is also called "wide breasted";[2] and the winds, especially the north wind, are his breath. This image is obviously of great antiquity, but it casts its spell throughout Egyptian history. The New Kingdom still uses it: "Thou art the god who came first into being when no (other) god had yet come into existence, when no name of any thing had yet been proclaimed. When thou openest thine eyes so as to see, it becomes light for everyone."[3] In Ptolemaic times the god is still addressed as "the venerable bird in whose shadow is the wide earth; Lord of the Two Lands under whose wings is the circuit of heaven; the falcon radiating light from his eyes."[4]

This visionary conception of Horus is not found in pictorial art. For art requires definiteness. It cannot well render the allusions and associations of language, poetry, and the poetical intuitions of the popular mind. Once, however, in the formative phase of Egyptian culture when experiments were common, the sky was rendered as the outspread wings of the great god (Fig. 17). The design is instructive. In the first place, we find already here, on a simple ivory comb belonging to a courtier of

* See below, p. 62.　　　† See below, p. 167.

the First Dynasty, a completely symbolical design including standard
motifs of classical Egyptian art. The great wings which render the sky
span the distance between, and seem supported by, two verticals which
have the shape of the *was* scepter, denoting "welfare." In the Old Kingdom (Fig. 19) a similar combination sometimes frames the name of the
king. The sky symbol above is then the hieroglyph *pet;* and below we
find the double-headed hieroglyph of the earth-god Akeru, a feature absent on the older comb.

The Old Kingdom design is relevant to our subject. It proclaims that
the ruler acts within a harmony between heaven and earth, which means
welfare. The design alludes at the same time to a well-known epithet
of the king, "Lord of that which the sun encircles." The wings of heaven
and the *was* scepters on the comb form so curious a combination that
we must assume them to express the same thought as the more complete
Old Kingdom framework, and that the more so since the comb, too,
shows the king's name inclosed by the design. It is written with a
snake and set in a panel crowned by the falcon,[5] exactly as on the stela
reproduced on our title-page. On the comb the god Horus is thus represented a second time, first as the Lord of Heaven whose outspread
wings are the sky, and second as incarnate in the king named in the
panel. He appears a third time, in the boat above the wings, as the sun
sailing across the sky. As such he is known from the First Dynasty to
Greek times as "Harakhte," Horus of the "Horizon" or of the "Land
of Sunrise."[6] In the clumsy parlance of modern science we say that
Horus was a sun-god as well as a sky-god; and we often forget that
the spurious precision of such terms may effectively preclude an understanding of their true significance and suggest inconsistencies which
are of our own making. Since Horus was a god of heaven, the most
powerful object in the sky, the sun, was naturally considered a manifestation of his power.

Later art used a more compact formula to express the association of
Horus with both sky and sun. It is the winged sun disk, in which the
wings stand for the expanse of the sky, as on the First Dynasty comb
(Fig. 20).[7] When the god Harakhte is depicted, he appears as a falcon
or a falcon-headed man crowned by the sun disk (Figs. 36 and 37).

The association of Horus with the sun is subsidiary to the notion of
the sky-god. That follows from the prevalence and persistence of the
imagery which we have discussed. The god's name seems suitable for a
sky-god. "Horus" does not mean "the falcon"; the bird is called *bik*, and
there are various other names for the falcon standards and symbols.
Horus (*Ḥrw*) seems to mean "the distant one."[8]

The king is an embodiment of this god. The epithet of Horus, "the Great God," appears also with the names of the kings in the Fourth and Fifth Dynasties—Snefru, Khufu (Cheops), and Sahure. Even Pepi I is called, on his coffin, "The Great God, Lord of the Horizon," and also "Horus of the Horizon, Lord of Heaven." In the tombs the dead call themselves "honored before the Great God," meaning the dead king. They also write in their tombs texts like the following: "Any noble, any official, or any man who may destroy any stone or any brick in this my tomb, I will be judged with him by the Great God." It has been shown that this judgment took place in the Hereafter;[9] yet the Great God is here, too, the king, who remained the leader upon whom the subjects continued to depend when they had joined him in death.[10] With the decline of the prestige of royalty in the troubles which actually destroyed the Old Kingdom, the epithet "Great God" was replaced by "Good God" when texts referred to the living ruler. And in the funerary texts the "Great God" envisaged was no longer the individual but the mythological aspect of each dead king—Osiris (chap. 15), who became "The Great God, Lord of the West."[11]

It remains to explain why it should have been Horus who was thought to be incarnate in the king. It is assumed by most authors (with total disregard of the religious nature of the problem) that the explanation is political, namely, that the House of Menes derived from a region worshiping the falcon-god. It is true that the city of Nekhen-Hierakonpolis, within the state of the pre-Menite chieftains, was a center of Horus worship. It is also true that in different localities differing manifestations of divine power received the main share of the people's devotion. But these so-called "local gods" were not necessarily unknown outside their chief centers of worship, nor were they all equals in the estimation of the Egyptians. If Horus, in preference to a dozen or more Upper Egyptian gods, came to be looked upon as the animating spirit of the ruler of Egypt (Frontispiece), it was because Horus was widely recognized as a supreme god. We should expect as much on the strength of the impressive image in which he was conceived. But there is more tangible evidence, too. The symbol of Horus, the falcon on its perch ⟡, may serve in the pyramid texts for the notion "god" in general, or follow, as a determinative, the name of any deity. Horus, apparently, was the god par excellence. It has even been maintained that the epithet *netjer aa*, "the Great God," which pertains to Horus pre-eminently, really means "the greatest god."[12] Finally, falcon-gods were worshiped throughout Egypt; and, though it is usual to treat these as "local gods" of independent origin and nature, it is at least as probable that they were predynastic differentiations of one and the same deity who had been worshiped as supreme by the ancestral Egyptians: πολλῶν ὀνομάτων μορφὴ μία.[13]

B. HORUS, SON OF OSIRIS

Pharaoh, then, is an incarnation of Horus the Great(est) God, Lord of Heaven. But the Memphite Theology describes how Horus, son of Osiris, ascends the throne. The question arises, therefore, whether these two gods with the same name may or may not be one.

It seems difficult, at first sight, to bring the elusive and somewhat uncanny "Horus feathered in many hues" within the family group of the Osiris cycle. The figures of Osiris, Isis, and Horus and their adventures, as told in the myth, would fit any folk tale. But this very fact should make us suspicious. Gods so strikingly human are without parallel in Egypt, and we are probably misled by the tradition that preserved their story. The fullest account derives from Plutarch, and the purely human characteristics of the main figures may be due to the enlightened age in which he wrote. The older Egyptian sources suggest, indeed, that this is so. It is true that they nowhere add up to a complete version of the myth. But the reliefs and the texts agree in giving to the members of the cycle that admixture of animal features which characterizes most Egyptian gods. Seth, the murderer, is almost always rendered by his enigmatical animal 𓁢 or as an animal-headed god 𓁛.[14] Horus appears with equal regularity as a falcon-headed man 𓁜. A relief in Seti I's temple at Abydos (Fig. 18) shows Isis as a falcon-like bird hovering over the prostrate body of Osiris, which, as the myth records, she succeeded in reviving for the posthumous conception of his son Horus. This pictorial tradition survived in Ptolemaic times; it was also put into words, and that already in the Eighteenth Dynasty. In a hymn to Osiris it is said that Isis "made shadow with her feathers and made an air current with her wings." She "erected the tiredness of the powerless one" and conceived.[15] In the tomb of Queen Nefertari of the Nineteenth Dynasty, Isis and Nephthys are shown on either side of the bier as falcons or kites wearing the hieroglyphs of their names upon their heads.[16] But the birdlike characteristics of the personages of the Osiris myth are not a late development and would, in fact, be inexplicable as such. Already in the pyramid texts, and also in later tombs, Isis and Nephthys bewailing Osiris are often called "The Two Kites";[17] the comparison was no doubt furthered by the shrill plaintive cries which the kite, *Falco milvus*, utters when circling aloft; but this poetic fantasy cannot account for the other instances just quoted. We shall see presently that

Isis has originally nothing to do with the falcon.* Horus, even when adoring Osiris, appears as a falcon-headed man. It seems, then, that the falcon Horus, god of the sky, is the same as Horus, son of Osiris, and that Isis, and occasionally Nephthys, received their birdlike character-istics through their relation to Horus.

Another feature of the Egyptian (as contrasted with the Greek) texts supports this view. In the conflict with Seth, Horus temporarily loses his eye, or is said to be wounded in the eye. This episode is always re-ferred to Horus, son of Osiris; and the conflict, though it has a most gen-eral significance, is indeed most often referred to in connection with the succession to Osiris' kingship. Yet the story is relevant to Horus the heavenly falcon whose eyes were the sun and moon. We find, in fact, that the waning moon counts as Horus' ailing eye and that the sun is attacked by clouds and thunderstorms which are a manifestation of Seth.[18] It is therefore a mistake to separate "Horus, the Great God, Lord of Heaven," from "Horus, son of Osiris," or to explain their identity as due to syncretism in comparatively late times. The two gods "Horus" whose titles we have set side by side are, in reality, one and the same. Their identity is also confirmed by an important pyramid text which addresses the king as follows: "Thou art Horus, son of Osi-ris, the eldest god, son of Hathor" (Pyr. 466a). The mother of Horus, son of Osiris, is Isis. The name of Hathor 𓉡 means "House of Horus" and refers, with obvious imagery, to her motherhood.[19] But *her* son is Horus, Lord of Heaven. And Osiris is never the husband of Hathor.[20]

Seeing inconsistencies in texts like the one we have just quoted means ignoring a very fundamental fact. Religious teachings are attempts to put into the conceptual form of language notions which cannot be entire-ly rationalized—"truths" which are sensed rather than known. The function of the king as the intermediary between humanity and the powers in nature is one of these notions which can be adumbrated but not adequately formulated in words.

Our own language disposes of many means of expression which are either totally lacking in ancient Egyptian or very poorly represented. Abstract nouns, adverbs, and conjunctions which enable us to modulate meaning were relatively little used by the Egyptian. His mind tended toward the concrete; his language depended upon concrete images and therefore expressed the irrational, not by qualifying modifications of a principal notion, but by admitting the validity of several avenues of ap-proach at one and the same time.† The king is the "sky-god" Horus; he

* See below, pp. 43–44. † See also pp. 61–62; nn. 19, 21.

is also Horus the son of his predecessor who had become Osiris at the moment of his death. The latter identification—Horus, son of Osiris— is appropriate when the king is considered in connection with his father, as heir in the legitimate line, as the incumbent of a royalty which involved (in the manner explained in the preceding chapter) two generations. But, when the avenue of approach is not the king's place in the succession, or his relationship with the ancestral spirits, or the continuity of kingship; when, on the contrary, the king is considered in the fulness of his power—then he is Horus, the Great God.[21]

The two viewpoints corresponding to "Horus, son of Osiris," and "Horus, the Great God," do not exhaust the possible avenues of approach to kingship. In polytheism the interrelations of the gods require definition. The king, even as the god Horus, must be brought in relation to other deities. Here, again, the scheme of father and son is applied; and, wherever there is a local cult, the king appears as the son of the deity. It has been thought that this relationship represents a generalization of the scheme Horus-Osiris.[22] This view is erroneous. The king is the son of Osiris, because Osiris is the deceased ruler who was normally the father of his successor. The relationship Horus-Osiris has its foundation in the physical fact of fatherhood viewed in the mythological context which we have discussed. In connection with the other gods the sonship of the king expresses a relationship of intimacy, dependence, and piety; but it is not exclusive. In other words, it is possible to find that two male gods, Atum and Monthu, address King Seti I as "our beloved son";[23] and Ramses II returns from the Battle of Kadesh to be greeted by the assembled gods with the words: "Welcome beloved son of ours!"[24] Similarly, Tuthmosis III appears as son of Atum at Medinet Habu, as son of Re at Amada, as son of Dedun at Semneh, as son of Amon, Ptah, and Hathor at Karnak. All such phrases, but especially the common "Son of Re," are subject to considerable elaboration on occasion. King Piankhi is made to say in reference to Re: "I am he who was fashioned in the womb and created in the divine egg, the seed of the god being in me. By his Ka[25] there is nothing which I shall do without him; it is he who commands me to do it."[26]

Such texts accentuate, again, the difference between the designations "Son of Re" and "Son of Osiris." The term "Son of Re" establishes a relationship with the sun-god which is equivalent to the designation Horus in that it stresses the divine nature of the king, although it does not claim identity with the god; it emphasizes that Pharaoh, "on the throne of Atum," is a distant successor of the Creator and the champion of the created order (see chap. 13). It is significant that the epithet "Son of Re" in the titulary precedes the *nomen*, the name given at birth. The combination indicated that the prince who had been known by this name up to the coronation had been recognized as the son of the Creator and therefore possessed the essential nature of a ruler.[27]

As the king could be proclaimed the son of various gods to express a relation of dependence and intimacy, so all goddesses could be addressed as his mother. But this consideration does not dispose of the problem presented by the pyramid text quoted above: "Thou art Horus, son of Osiris, the eldest god, son of Hathor." As we have said already, Osiris is never the husband of Hathor; and Hathor is not the mother of Horus, son of Osiris.

In the myth Osiris begets Horus on Isis, his sister and wife. Since the king's father and predecessor becomes Osiris at his death, we should expect the queen-mother to be Isis. This, however, is not the case, or rather, when in late texts it does occur, it is either part of a series of identifications of goddesses with the queen or a mere literary figure. It plays no part in any of the ceremonials of kingship and is thereby shown not to be a religious reality at all—this in striking contrast to the transfiguration of the dead king Osiris.

If, then, the queen-mother does not count as Isis, we must ask what Isis stands for. Her name gives us a clue. It suggests that Isis was originally the deified throne.[28] This at first startling solution has a considerable amount of evidence to support it. Ceremonial objects are very likely to become personified in Egypt. We know, for instance, that sacrifices of food and drink were offered to a standard of the god Amon.[29] We also have hymns addressed to the king's crowns.* The throne is shown by various expressions which have become established to have been an object of veneration in Egypt in early times. We have seen that Memphis was called "The Great Throne" in the Memphite Theology. The capital of a western Delta state, which the Greeks called Buto, was "Pe" in Egyptian—a word meaning seat, stool, or throne. Amon-Re was called "Lord of the Thrones of the Two Lands who commands in Karnak." Dominion over the earth is expressed by the phrase "the thrones of Geb."[30] Among the Shilluk of the upper Nile, who retain many traits recalling Egyptian usages and beliefs, the king becomes charged with the supernatural power of royalty by being enthroned on the sacred stool which normally supports the fetish Nyakang, who, like Osiris, is both a god and the ancestor of the new monarch.† In Egypt,

* See below, pp. 108–9.　　　　　　　　† See below, pp. 198–200.

too, the central ceremony of the accession took place when the ruler was enthroned and received the diadems and scepters. Thus the Egyptian might well refer to the throne, which had received a prince who arose king, as the ruler's "mother." In the same way a pyramid text states that the dead king goes to heaven to sit upon the "great throne which made the gods."[31]

The myth of Osiris and Seth, Isis and Horus, which presents religious conceptions in the guise of a narrative, described Isis as the embodiment of marital devotion and motherly love,* thus laying the foundation for the widespread veneration she found throughout the Roman Empire. But she lacks distinctive attributes when she is depicted, perhaps as a result of her origin. Like all personifications, she appears in human shape; but she wears on her head cow's horns borrowed from Hathor. In later times the two goddesses are often treated as one because both found their principal function in motherhood.[32] But in relation to the king, Isis and Hathor remained distinct. When the emphasis was laid on his divinity per se, the king was Horus, son of Hathor, suckled by the divine cow called Sekhat-Hor, "She who remembers Horus." But, viewed as the heir and successor in the royal line, the king was the son of Osiris, borne by the throne, Isis, who is therefore called his mother in this context.[33] This significance of the title "son of Isis," which occurs already in the First Dynasty,[34] is very clearly defined in a text of Ramses IV: "I am a legitimate ruler, not an usurper, for I occupy the place of my sire, as the son of Isis, since I have appeared as king on the throne of Horus."[35]

Pharaoh's human mother does not seem to have played any part in the theology of kingship. She was no more than the vehicle of the incarnation.[36] The succession of one of her sons proved that particular son —generally the eldest—to have been divine, "powerful in the egg" or "ruling in the egg,"[37] or, in other words, qualified to rule, since a god had begotten him. For, in contrast with physical motherhood, physical fatherhood was a subject of theological speculation. It was normally viewed as an element in the perennial truth that Horus succeeded Osiris. But we know of rulers of the New Kingdom who stressed their affiliation with the god Amon-Re, possibly because their claim to the throne was irregular. We have seen that the king counted as the son of Re. Hence we find reliefs in New Kingdom temples in which it is shown that Amon-Re embodied himself in the king and thus visited the queen to beget a successor.† The texts explain:

* See below, pp. 181–85.					† See below, pp. 73 ff.

Amon took his form as the majesty of this her husband, the king (Tuthmosis I). . . . . Then he went to her immediately; then he had intercourse with her. . . . . The words which Amon, Lord of the Thrones of the Two Lands, spoke in her presence: "Now Khenemet-Amon-Hatshepsut is the name of this my daughter whom I have placed in thy body. . . . . She is to exercise this beneficent kingship in this entire land."[38]

A folk tale describing how Re begot the first three kings of the Fifth Dynasty on the wife of the high priest of the Sun temple at Heliopolis suggests that a similar belief was already current in the Old Kingdom, especially since the tale describes how the goddesses Isis, Nephthys, Heqet, and Meskhent, together with the god Khnum, delivered the queen-mother. These same deities are also shown in the birth scenes of the later temples at Luxor and Deir el Bahri.[39]

The relation between the queen-mother and her consort as Horus is very rarely stressed in connection with the king's genealogy. We shall meet one possible instance at the festival of Min.* Min is identified with Horus and called Kamutef, "Bull of His Mother." This designation stresses the god's immortality through successive incarnations as due to perpetual rebirth.† Nor was it to be expected that the marital relationship of the king's parents should give rise to comment in the monuments. The king's father had been Horus; hence the king had been begotten by a god. But this matter became important only at the succession when the king's father had died and thus had become Osiris. The new king succeeded as Horus, son of Osiris.

There is a very common form of reference to the king which indicated that a god was embodied in the physical frame of Pharaoh. The word is $\vert$ (ḥm), and it is used with a possessive pronoun exactly as we use "His Majesty," "Your Majesty," in respectful circumlocution. But the usual translation with "Majesty," though it fits all uses of the word, misses the point. Ḥm originally meant "body," "physical appearance";[40] and this connotation was never lost entirely. Hence we read of an Egyptian sage replying to Pharaoh: "This is what Ipuwer said when he answered the Embodiment of the Lord of All."[41] So, also, we have to correct the renderings of the date formulas from "under the Majesty of (ḥr ḥm n) King N" or "in the lifetime of the Majesty (ᶜnḫ ḥm n) of King N" to "during the Incarnation 'King N' " or "during the lifetime of the Embodiment 'King N,' " meaning that particular incarnation or embodiment of the god which mortals know as "King N." They are not merely respectful phrases but phrases which emphasize that the earthly ruler incorporates an immortal god. The names of the individual kings serve only to distinguish the successive incarnations.

* See below, pp. 188 ff.   † See below, chap. 14, esp. pp. 168–69, 180.

C. TITULARY

The official titulary of the king of Egypt is an elaborate statement regarding his divine nature.[42] As an example, we may render the titulary of Senusert III as it appears in the cartouche at the top of Figure 20: "Horus, 'Divine of Forms'; Two Ladies, 'Divine of Births'; Horus of Gold, 'Who becomes'; King of Upper and Lower Egypt, 'The Ka's of Re appear in Glory'; Son of Re, Senusert; granted life and wealth eternally."

First, then, comes the title "Horus," which implies all that we have discussed in this chapter; it remains the simplest and most direct statement regarding the king's nature and is the oldest part of the titulary. It is followed by a name or epithet which differs in the case of each king; it defines the particular incarnation of Horus involved. This king, then, is Horus So-and-So.

Second comes the Nebty title, the two goddesses or ladies, the tutelary vulture-goddess Nekhbet of Upper Egypt, and the cobra-goddess Wadjet of Buto. This title expresses the fact that the king heads a dual monarchy and is again followed by an epithet, often the same as that which follows the Horus name.

Third is a title best translated as "Horus of Gold." Since it is written by placing the falcon over the sign for gold and the latter is also the name of Nubt-Ombos where Seth was worshiped, the title is in Ptolemaic times given a dualistic turn: Horus victor over Seth (He of Nubt). But the use of the gold sign in other combinations found in royal titles of the first three dynasties indicates that the title expresses the divinity of the king by assigning to him, Horus, the imperishable brightness which characterized the metal and also the sun.* Gold is "the flesh of the gods"; and "Re said at the beginning of his words: My skin is of pure gold."[43] Djoser, of Dynasty III, puts the whole of his name upon the gold sign.[44] And Tuthmosis III states explicitly: "(Amon) modeled me as a falcon of gold."[45] The interpretation of this title as "Horus victor over Seth" is therefore secondary.

Fourth is again a dualistic title, to be translated "King of Upper and King of Lower Egypt," literally, "He of the Sedge and the Bee." We do not know exactly what these symbols mean; but their relation to the two parts of the country is certain. The title is followed by the so-called *prenomen*, written within the cartouche, and assumed upon the accession of the king.

* See below, p. 135.

Fifth in the titulary is the title "Son of Re," followed by the *nomen* which the king had received at birth and which is now, by the combination with "Son of Re," made into a fresh legitimation.[46] It is again inclosed in a cartouche which itself proclaims the king to be ruler over "All That the Sun Encircles."

We can follow the development of the titulary during the Old Kingdom. It represents a final selection from a variety of titles and designations which had been in use and was standardized before the rise of the Twelfth Dynasty.[47] It sets the monarch apart from other men entirely. The mysterious powers in nature upon which man depends are somehow influenced by the king's actions. He shares their being; he vouchsafes their beneficial support of the community. We find even today a similar attitude prevailing among many peoples.* Some, like the Shilluk, will destroy their king when he threatens to become an imperfect link between man and the gods: "The King must not be allowed to become ill or senile, lest, with his diminishing vigor, the cattle should sicken and fail to bear their increase, the crops should wither in the fields, and men, stricken with disease, should die in ever increasing numbers."[48] It has repeatedly been maintained that the Egyptians, too, killed their king and for the same reason; but of this there is no proof at all. The Egyptians, however, did regard their king in the same manner—a bond between nature and man. Said the vizier Rekhmire in the Eighteenth Dynasty: "What is the king of Upper and Lower Egypt? He is a god by whose dealings one lives, the father and the mother of all men, alone by himself, without an equal."[49]

* See above, p. 33.

PART II. THE FUNCTIONING OF KINGSHIP

CHAPTER 4

THE KING'S RULE

ERY few administrative and legal documents of Egypt have survived; and, as a result of this scarcity, our knowledge of the functioning of kingship in Egypt is of the vaguest.[1] But there seems no
doubt that Pharaoh's predicate "god" found its correlate in his absolute
power over the land of Egypt and its inhabitants. "Private property appears early as a result of royal donations. But basically it is no more than
an exceptional transference of rights. This applies also to every personal
liberty, personal status, or rank. In theory, the king can annul these at
any time."[2] Even "justice is embodied in the god who rules the state; he
respects the tradition and the privileges of classes and regions in so far
as he approves their fairness; but in principle there is no autonomous
justice or law outside that of the Crown."[3]

This does not mean that Pharaoh is supposed to act arbitrarily. The
king lives under the obligation to maintain *maat*, which is usually translated "truth," but which really means the "right order"— the inherent
structure of creation, of which justice is an integral part. Thus the king,
in the solitariness of his divinity, shoulders an immense responsibility.
Amenhotep III strives "to make the country flourish as in primeval
times by means of the designs of Maat."[4] Maat is, naturally, personified
—a goddess, the daughter of the sun-god Re whose regular circuit is the
most striking manifestation of the established cosmic order. Thus it is
said of the king: "Authoritative Utterance (*hu*) is in thy mouth. Understanding (*sia*) is in thy heart. Thy speech is the shrine of truth (*maat*)."[5]

When, therefore, the affairs of the state suffer decline, a paradoxical
situation arises. This is well expressed by Ipuwer when he describes the
anarchy of the First Intermediate Period. (We must interpolate conjunctions to catch the logic of these phrases with their puzzled reproach to
the king.) "Hu, Sia, and Maat are with thee. (Nevertheless) confusion
is what thou dost put throughout the land together with the noise of
tumult. Behold one uses violence against another. (Yet) people conform to that which thou hast commanded."[6] Since it is the will of the

divine king which is realized, the lawless state of the land must be of his making, although the instruments of order—Authoritative Utterance, Understanding, and Truth—are with him. The king, then, is held responsible; yet, since he is divine, the community cannot act against him.[7]

It is natural that we should not find in Egypt any legal instrument by which a king could be replaced. But it is more interesting, as a proof that the supernatural character of kingship was effectively recognized by the people, that in the whole of Egypt's long history there is no evidence of any popular uprising. We do hear sometimes of intrigues of courtiers and princes; there could be competing claims among members of the royal house, which could be justified theologically as uncertainty regarding the prince chosen for the next incarnation. The people at large could not and did not interfere.

The king was truly the sole source of authority. All official actions, both in the secular and in the religious sphere, were based on power which the king had delegated. This remained true throughout Egyptian history. But a study of the titles of the Old Kingdom reveals the nonpolitical basis of this usage. The officials seem to have been originally relations of the royal house. They stand apart as a class—the Royal Kinsmen. In other words, those to whom power was delegated shared in some degree the mysterious essence which differentiated the king from all men.

It has been said that the rulers placed members of their family in high posts as a measure of security—as if the lesser branches of ruling houses were not always most fertile of pretenders and firebrands. Moreover, the system reached far out into the lower ranks of the provincial officials who could not stand in any close relationship to the ruling monarch. We know that under the Fourth Dynasty the viziers and the high priests of the great cult centers were sons or cousins of the king. The relationship sometimes forms part of an official title, too; for instance: "Chief of Nekheb of His Father"; "Chief Recitation-Priest of His Father."[8] And one wonders to what extent an archaic term *ity* was in use in addressing the king; it occurs so in the pyramid texts and seems to hang together etymologically with *it*, "father."[9]

As one of her main titles in the Old Kingdom the goddess of writing, Seshat, had "Mistress of the Archives of the Royal Kinsmen,"[10] which would have been a kind of register of nobility, for no other hereditary nobility existed, though offices were graciously allowed by the king to pass from father to son.[11] The title *sahu* ($\check{s}^c\dot{h}.w$), which is usually translated "nobles," denoted those to whom the king had granted the privilege of carrying a seal.[12] There were no classes or castes in Egypt.[13] All were commoners before the throne, except those in whose veins flowed some trace of the royal blood, however diluted. There is an exact modern parallel to this division in East Africa, among the Baganda, who have a "divine king."[14] The Royal Kinsmen would have formed a considerable class, since not only the king's own children, but all those of his brothers, and, in fact, all sired by earlier rulers as well as their descendants would belong to it and would be thought fit, because of their descent, to bear some of the authority which Pharaoh delegated. It need not astonish us, therefore, to find Royal Kinsmen even in minor posts in the provincial administration.

The delegated authority of even the highest officers in the state appears in some titles. The vizier is "Steward of the Whole Land," "Councilor of All Orders of the King." The men who have charge of mining expeditions and foreign trade missions are called "Treasurers of the God (i.e., King)." In the Old Kingdom princes generally occupied these posts. For example, Prince Meri-ib was High Priest of Heliopolis and "Supervisor of All the Buildings of the King."[15]

It is evidently consistent with the view of Pharaoh as the font of all authority that every Egyptian had a right to appeal to him, even though in practice it would be extremely difficult to gain access to the presence.[16] In fact, the king was kept at one remove from the details of government by the vizierate, which was the true center of the country's administration.[17] But important decisions were submitted for the king's approval, and the vizier was instructed to have an audience with the king each morning to report on the state of the nation. In many matters the delegation of power to the vizier enabled him to act as chief executive. It was stated explicitly in the instructions to the vizier that he, too, should hear petitions by whosoever wished to present them.[18] There was, naturally, no division between judicial and executive, or, for that matter, legislative, power, since all power was vested in the king, who alone maintained an order which was thought of as one coherent whole, established in all essentials at the time of creation.

The power of the king over his subjects did not cease with death, and we must remember that this power was experienced not as a tyranny reluctantly endured but as a relationship which established for each subject his function and place in the world.[19] There is clear evidence that, at least during the Old Kingdom, the Egyptians expected protection and guidance of their lord even in the dubious regions of the Hereafter.

Kings of the First Dynasty were buried at Abydos in the midst of great squares containing the graves of their suite. It is not necessary to assume that the court was killed at the death of its master, though a few persons actually buried in the king's tomb were no doubt killed to accompany and serve him.[20] In the graves of the surrounding squares, however, rough "tombstones" were found, which seem misnamed, since they were thrown into the tombs in many cases and therefore did not identify the occupants after burial. They rather look like rough markers of the empty graves which awaited the surviving followers of the dead king and were thrown in with the rest of the funerary equipment when the reserved brick chamber was at last occupied. By the Fourth Dynasty all traces of killings at a king's burial have disappeared, but the king's tomb, the pyramid, still heads a necropolis built in its immediate vicinity and destined for those of his followers to whom the privilege of occupancy was granted. Gathered round the throne during the king's lifetime, the hierarchy of his officials and servants, all those who in some way or other had won his esteem or served as a channel through which authority had become effective, moved with their lord and under his guidance into the afterlife.

The immense power of the king was deemed capable of sweeping later generations safely into the Beyond. Thus the mastaba tombs of these necropoleis contain sometimes the bodies not only of the servants of their builders but even of their children and grandchildren. It is obvious that in this manner the latter could also be made to enjoy the endowment made for the original occupant,[21] but we probably miss a factor when we are satisfied with this utilitarian explanation of the custom. For we have definite proof that the power of the king did not cease with his death. For instance, we find the following words addressed to the official in charge of a king's funerary monuments and referring to their eventual usurpers:

> Those who shall do anything hostile or evil to any of thy statues . . . . and other monuments, My Majesty will not permit:
>> That they or their fathers have pleasure in them;
>> That they join the transfigured spirits in the West;
>> That they be among the living (in the Beyond).[22]

Evidently the king's threats concern anybody who, in an unspecified future, may deflect the king's monuments and the income he has set aside for their maintenance to other uses. The inscription clearly implies that the dead king retains power in this world (where the usurper can "have pleasure" in his ill-gotten property) as well as in the Hereafter, where the usurper ultimately hopes to join the "transfigured spirits." We also find that ancient kings, or statues which they placed in temples, were occasionally worshiped centuries after their death.[23] It is reasonable, then, to view the coherence of court and king after death—materially expressed in the arrangement of the necropoleis—as based on a deep and lasting relationship with the monarch.

The material reviewed so far is but meagerly supplemented by direct statements. Throughout it is not the actual, but the ideal, situation which is described on the monuments;* and, as we have said, administrative documents are extremely rare. In all the temples of the land the king is depicted performing the ritual. In practice he naturally delegated his priestly function to the priests. In the papyrus containing the daily ritual of the Amon temple at Thebes the officiating priest states twice: "I am the priest. It is the king who has sent me to behold the god."[24] We also have an inscription of an official who represented King Senusert III at the celebration of the Osiris Mysteries at Abydos. Similarly, the inscriptions describe Pharaoh as commander-in-chief, and in some cases we have detailed accounts of the council of war preceding important battles. But it has been pointed out that we should be misled if we took these at their face value. They reflect an established literary form.[25] The generals advise a prudent advance. The king overrules them and decides for a bold course. The council, impressed, submits; and the king scores a great victory. This is the pattern of Kamose's attack on the Hyksos and of the Battle of Megiddo as planned by Tuthmosis III.[26] It may influence even the account of Piankhi's conquest of Egypt.[27] Only the Battle of Kadesh is reported in an unconventional manner which finds its correlate in the entirely exceptional way in which it is rendered in the reliefs. We know, in this case, something about the actual course of affairs because the king apparently insisted on the rendering of the unusual story of how he nearly lost the battle through tactical errors and the inadequacy of the Egyptian intelligence service but prevented it from becoming a disaster by his personal bravery.[28]

Even when the state embarks on a peaceful undertaking, such as a renewal of a temple or the sinking of wells on a caravan route, the king is always shown as instigator, his councilors as those who confirm his perspicacity and foresight. Thus we read how Senusert I held a crown council in which he decided to rebuild the temple of Heliopolis. The text describes, with a characteristic impersonal circumlocution in re-

---

* See above, pp. 9 and 26.

ferring to the king: "The king made his appearance with the double crown; a sitting took place in the audience-hall. One took counsel with his suite, the Companions of the Palace (Life! Prosperity! Health!), the officials of the place of privacy. One gave commands while they were heard; one took counsel in making them disclosures."[29] The last sentence characterizes the procedure as ideally conceived. In reality advice was sought. Thus a local prince of Middle Egypt prides himself that "he was called for consultation with the Privy Council (*knb.t*) without people knowing about it. The Palace (Pharaoh) was pleased with his proposals."[30] But in these meetings mere humans co-operated with a god. Such a relationship can be described only within the scope of a strict formalism in which actions and reactions conform to an accepted set of theological formulas. For this reason all deliberations preceding governmental actions appear entirely one-sided in that Pharaoh "took counsel in making . . . . disclosures." The account of Senusert I shows the king opening the meeting by saying, "Behold, My Majesty decrees a work and is thinking of a deed"; and the councilors answer: "Authoritative Utterance is (in) thy mouth, Understanding follows thee. O Sovereign (Life! Prosperity! Health!), it is thy plans which come to pass," etc. Quasi-individual traits conform upon closer inspection to this scheme.[31] Occasionally certain peculiarities, such as the bowmanship of Amenhotep II,[32] are allowed to modify the conventional features, just as in portraiture individual physiognomic traits are imposed upon the underlying pattern of the vigorous, youthful, physically perfect man and impart to it a faint flavor of individuality. Only the ruthlessly egocentric Akhenaten broke the bonds of tradition in this as in other fields. On the whole, then, the inscriptions present us with the same picture of the king as that which we found represented in art and studied in the Introduction. That picture is impersonal and unhistorical, and that for the reasons which we have already stated. No actuality, no incident of history, could ever equal the dignity of the unchangeable order of creation. Each deviation from the sanctioned norm was a blemish on the reign which might well be passed over in silence, especially since it was conceived in any case as ephemeral. It certainly was least of all deserving of commemoration in art or text. Consequently, we find in reliefs and in inscriptions the king as victor; the king as faithful guardian of the service of the gods; the king as Horus supporting (avenging) Osiris.

It is clear that we are acting in the closest harmony with the ancients when we disregard the different degrees of realization which the idea of kingship found in successive stages of Egyptian history. It would be possible, of course, to make these changes the subject of inquiry. We should then notice a shrinking of royal power at certain times, a reassertion of royal prerogatives at others. We should also find that the texts reflect a much-diminished confidence and an increasing awareness of the distance between Pharaoh and his divine father, from the end of the Eighteenth Dynasty onward.[33] But such observations are meaningless unless we understand the true nature of Egyptian kingship. The conception of Pharaoh as a god incarnate explains the historical phenomena even when they seem to deny it. For this paradox must have become almost untenable whenever the tension between the actuality of human conditions and the ideal of a static divine order became too great, as must have happened in periods of disorder or when Egypt met its equal, for instance in the Hittite Empire. Yet even then no new conception of kingship was formulated. Hence we must ignore historical changes for our present purpose. The motive force of royalty throughout Egyptian history remained the concept of kingship which we are presenting here.

If we are unable to say much about the functioning of the king, we know at least, from some unusual phrases, that the official conception of the office and its incumbent reflects accepted opinion. A famous literary work purports to be "The Instructions which the Majesty of King Amenemhet I, justified, gave when he spoke in a dream-revelation to his son."[34] The dead king addresses his successor with an epithet of the gods, "Lord of All," and then says: "Thou who hast shone forth ($ḫ^ci$) as a god, hearken to what I shall tell thee." The verb $ḫ^ci$ is written with a hieroglyph depicting the sun rising over the Primeval Hill;* it is regularly used as a term for the rising of sun and stars and for the appearance of Pharaoh at his accession, at festivals, or on the throne. The implication revealed by the connection of the word with heavenly bodies, and especially with the sun, is significant. The king partakes of the essence of these natural phenomena. A similar meaning is expressed in the same text when King Amenemhet refers to himself: "I was one who produced barley and loved the corn-god. The Nile respected me at every defile. None hungered in my years, nor thirsted in them. Men dwelt (in peace) through that which I wrought. . . . . All that I commanded was as it should be."[35] The king "produced barley," not merely in an indirect way, for instance by caring for the farmers or furthering agriculture, but through his own actions—by maintaining Maat, the right order which allowed nature to function unimpaired for the benefit of man. Hence the Nile rose effectually at the inundation so that the arable land

* See below, p. 150.

reached its maximum extent and the people prospered. We may quote in this connection another text, a song composed for the accession of Merenptah:

> Rejoice, thou entire land, the goodly time has come.
> A lord is appointed in all countries. . . . .
> O all ye righteous, come and behold!
> Truth has repressed falsehood.
> The sinners are fallen on their faces.
> All that are covetous are turned back.
>
> The water standeth and faileth not,
> The Nile carrieth a high flood.
> The days are long, the nights have hours,
> The months come aright.
> The gods are content and happy of heart, and
> Life is spent in laughter and wonder.[36]

The comparison of the two texts enhances their significance. The song might be thought to contain merely the hyperboles of a festive mood, were it not that they recur in the grim context of Amenemhet's teaching. There the beneficial influence of the king is stressed only to bring out his utter loneliness, for notwithstanding it he was betrayed. And yet, though the two texts differ in both mood and age, we find them describing regal power with the same attributes, as strong a proof as we are likely to find that the Egyptians really believed these attributes to pertain to their king. This power, then, includes the remarkable capacity to dominate and further natural processes, especially the inundation of the Nile on which the prosperity of Egypt depends. Because the king, who has established Maat, who has defeated falsehood, comes to the throne, there are abundant inundations; and the seasons—that is, the months and days and nights—follow each other in orderly procession. So the song. But the teaching of Amenemhet says practically the same thing: none was hungry, for the king made the corn grow; and the Nile, in obedience, rose to all accessible places so that they could be tilled.[37] Even as late an author as Ammianus Marcellus knew that the Egyptians ascribed plenty or famine to the quality of their king[38]—not, in a modern sense, to his quality as an administrator, but to his effectiveness as an organ of integration, partaking of the divine and of the human and intrusted with making the mutual dependence of the two a source of "laughter and wonder."

It is peculiar to Egypt that the king's influence over the inundation should be stressed above all. The connection was also expressed in ritual, at least during the Twentieth Dynasty. At the critical moment of low water, when there was not enough in the river "to cover the secrets of the Netherworld," offerings were thrown into it at Silsileh in the name of Pharaoh. With them went a copy of the "Book that Maketh the Nile Come Forth from Its Source." Two months later, at the time of "pure water," that is, when the river began to rise, the offerings were repeated.[39]

This power over natural forces is retained by the king after death. His connection with vegetation we shall discuss when dealing with Osiris; we have already met it in the Memphite Theology. And we shall meet later a curious monument proclaiming the power of a dead king over the Nile.* Obviously, then, we preclude any understanding of the ancients if we refuse to attach importance to such texts as the following, in which a certain Sehetepibre instructs his children regarding the king as follows:

> He is one who illuminates the Two Lands more than the sun disk.
> He is one who makes the Two Lands more green than a high Nile.
> He has filled the Two Lands with strength and life.
>
> The king is Ka.[40]
> His mouth is increase.
> He is the one creating him who is to be.
> He is the Khnum (former) of all limbs,
> The begetter who causes the people to be.[41]

It is significant that a common epithet of the king is *di ankh* (𓋴𓋹), which, thus written, can be translated as "giver of life" as well as "endowed with life." Both interpretations are correct,[42] the latter meaning not merely that the king is still alive but that he disposes of life in a sovereign manner and can hold death at bay. The other interpretation, "giver of life," asserts that he does the same for his subjects. Similarly, he "keeps the hearts alive" (𓏤𓋹𓄹).

These expressions, then, mean more than that gifts and appointments of the king sustain many of his subjects. It is true that this is part of his obligations. The king is not only instrumental in producing the "fat of the land"; he must also dispense it. Only then is there evidence that he functions effectively. His bounty proves that he disposes, as a king should dispose, of the earth and its produce. Hence the gods and goddesses who act as fairy godparents at the birth of Hatshepsut† pronounce that the reign will be blessed with "food" and "sustenance" among other things. Hence gifts precede and conclude the Sed festival,‡

* See below, pp. 194–95.

† See below, p. 77.   ‡ See below, pp. 82 and 88.

and token meals intervene at the climax and at the conclusion of the Mystery Play of the Succession.* But the king also keeps alive the hearts of all those subjects who do not directly partake of his bounty. For he exercises a never ending mysterious activity on the strength of which daily, hourly, nature and society are integrated. Hence, as we shall see, the incalculable risks which the interruption of the kingly power through the death of a king spells for all. Hence, also, in songs such as that celebrating the accession of Merenptah, the (to the modern mind excessive) jubilation that the crisis is left behind and a new ruler enthroned. We shall quote yet another of these poems, since we can hear in them the relief of a population which has passed through a period of acute danger and is freed from the threat of a catastrophe which we can no longer properly appreciate.

> How happy is the day! Heaven and Earth rejoice,
> For thou art the Great Lord of Egypt.
> They that had fled have come again to their towns;
> They that were hidden have again come forth;
> They that hungered are satisfied and happy;
> They that thirsted are drunken;
> They that were naked are clad in fine linen;
> They that were dirty have white garments.
> They that were in prison are set free;
> He that was in bonds is full of joy;
> They that were in strife in this land are reconciled.
> High Niles have come from their sources that they
>   may refresh the hearts. . . . .[43]

If it is by virtue of the king's intermediacy that the vital forces function in nature, man himself is not excluded from that law. The Egyptians maintained that the king's potency is felt in the very body and person of each of his subjects. They expressed this by means of a term which deserves study, the *ka*, which appeared in the Old Kingdom in proper names like the following: Kai-kher-nesut, "My Ka derives from the king."

* See below, pp. 130 and 138.

CHAPTER 5

THE KING'S POTENCY: THE KA

WHEN we attempt to describe the Egyptian's view of the human personality, the differences between his mental processes and our own become particularly disturbing. We meet a number of Egyptian terms which stand in one context for qualities while they appear in another as independent spiritual entities. "Creative Utterance" (*hu*) and "Understanding" (*sia*) are a pair of such concepts.[1] We meet them as qualities which enable the king to maintain the order of creation, Maat.* We also meet them as godlike figures standing in the boat of the sun-god. The notions "Ka" and "Ba" are of somewhat the same order. They are traditionally translated as "spirit" and "soul," and the Egyptians use them sometimes in the familiar sense which makes them appear subordinate to a larger whole, the human personality. At other times, however, they endow them with a degree of independence which seems to us meaningless. The situation is exactly reversed in the case of "shadow" and "name," which we count as extraneous to man, while for the Egyptians, as for most primitives, they partake of the essence of the person. A myth relates how Isis, the great magician, wished to complete her magical power and to that end devised a ruse to force Re, king of the gods, to confide in her his Great Secret Name.[2]

Attempts have been made to harmonize the various notions referring to man into a single picture supposed to represent man as conceived by the ancient Egyptians. Such attempts are doomed to failure because they disregard the peculiar quality of Egyptian thought which allows an object to be understood, not by a single and consistent definition, but by various and unrelated approaches.[3] It is, however, just as fatal to our understanding to fall into the opposite error and to condemn as merely confused and superficial whatever must appear to us as inconsistent. A somewhat prolonged familiarity with the pre-Greek mind makes it possible for one to appreciate its own inherent logic.[4]

It appears, then, that the connotations of most notions are, in the first place, affected by the momentary direction of the speaker's attention. What appears usually as subordinate may suddenly, under the influence

* See above, p. 51.

61

of a narrower but concentrated attention, gain the weight of an independent entity. It may even absorb the whole of which it once formed a part.

In the second place, the connotations may differ from case to case. Thus, the potency of the king, which we shall consider in this chapter, is not merely greater than, but different in essentials from, that of his subjects. This distinction is a consequence of the majesty of kingship and of the fact that the ruler is set apart from other men as a result of an experience of awe.* Thus it is said of the king of the Teutons: "The prince could achieve more than the commoner, not only because he possessed more life or richer spiritual endowment than the peasant, but because he was animated by a fundamentally different vital power."[5] The same viewpoint is found throughout the world. In Africa many Hamitic peoples, and the Bantu, under Hamitic influence, throw the bodies of ordinary people into the bush but give their chiefs an elaborate burial, since they alone are thought to survive death.[6] Some peoples, for instance the Yaos, call *mulungu*, the king, the ghost of a dead man but also "the aggregate of the spirits of all the dead; . . . . in its nature, use, and form the word does not imply personality for it does not belong to the personal class of nouns. . . . . Its form denotes rather a state or property inhering in something as the life and health inhere in the body." Besides, the word *mulungu* means "luck" or "fortune." "Even in life a man, when he meets with any piece of good luck, will be heard to say: 'That is my *mulungu*.' " On the other hand, the chief, too, is called *mulungu*, and that during his lifetime. He is so holy that his subjects endow him with a supernatural quality normally connected with the spirits of the dead.

The notion of *mulungu* is typical of conceptions found among a great many peoples, though with various shades of meaning. It is by no means an equivalent of the Ka, but the comparison is enlightening. Moreover, it indicates that, contrary to the usual procedure, we must treat the Ka of commoners and the Ka of the king separately.[7]

A. THE KA OF COMMONERS

The closest approximation to the Egyptian notion of Ka is "vital force." The qualification "vital" frees it from the precision of the natural sciences, which would, of course, be an anachronism; and the combination "vital force" may stand for a somewhat vague popular notion, without mechanistic implications. The Ka, according to this view, should be impersonal and should be present in varying strength in different persons or in the same person at different times. And we find, in-

* See above, p. 36.

deed, that the Egyptian speaks about his Ka very much as we do about "my vitality," "his will-power," etc.

The Ka of the commoner is never pictured; that is an outstanding difference between it and the Ka of the king. The Ka is written with a symbol—two arms uplifted with flat outspread hands ⊔—the whole placed upon a standard which supports symbols of divinities ⩊. The symbol is quite abstract; the Ka has never been the object of concrete imaginings as far as the ordinary man is concerned. This proves how inappropriate the usual translations, such as "spirit," "ghost," or "double," really are.

It is true that "to die" is described as "to go to one's Ka." But the Ka is never shown receiving the dead in the Hereafter; the expression, in fact, merely describes the event of death and that in a perfectly simple and coherent manner. Survival after death was taken for granted by the Egyptians, as it is by many peoples.[8] Death is a crisis during which the vital force, the Ka, leaves the body. However, since the Ka is the force of life, and since man survives death, he is bound to have rejoined his Ka in the Beyond, even though it has left his body. It is a cogent conception.

In the tomb of Queen Meresankh III we find two dates: first, the date of her death, when the body was taken for embalming in the "pure place," and, second, the date of her burial in the tomb. The first is called "the resting of her *ka*—her departure to the mortuary workshop"; the second, "her departure to her beautiful tomb."[9] The Egyptians—like many other peoples[10]—conceived of a transitional phase after death but before the ritual of interment has effected resurrection in the Hereafter. In this phase man was conceived as neither dead nor alive. It was a period of suspense during which the vital force, the Ka, "rests." In the pyramid texts the dead are called "masters of their Ka's," or even, paradoxically, "the living," since they have passed through death and reached eternal life. They may also be called "the Ka's that are in heaven,"[11] since to live, whether on earth or in heaven, presupposes the Ka, the vital force. The expression is therefore a mere example of *pars pro toto*.[12]

The characteristics of the Ka are perhaps best realized by means of a comparison with the Ba, which is often shown (in contrast to the Ka) especially in the reliefs and paintings of the New Kingdom tombs. The Ba is bird-shaped, but it has a human head and, often, human arms ⩘. It appears perched on the edge of a pond, which was included in the funerary establishment to supply refreshment, and again, drinking water poured by a goddess from a tree. (Fig. 21) The Ba represents quite clearly in Egypt that widely recognized class of apparitions in which popular imagination recognizes the dead—with thin, piping voices and flitting, birdlike movements—returning to their former haunts. The Greeks[13] and the Babylonians[14] also imagined their dead in this guise, but with the terrifying and sometimes malevolent qualities of a true specter; and of these qualities the Ba seems innocent.

"Ba" actually seems to mean "animated"—and therefore the translation "ghost" or "spirit" would be better than the conventional "soul."[15] "Ba" may, furthermore, mean manifestation, a significance easily derived from the "animated"; the Benu bird is called the Ba of Re; Orion, or the Apis bull, can be called the Ba of Osiris; and a lion-shaped amulet may be called the Ba of Shu.[16] From "manifestation" the sense may shift to "emanation," so that a sacred book is called the Ba of Re.[17] In connection with the dead man, the Ba was therefore his animated manifestation as well as his animation, pure and simple—his power to move in and out of the tomb and even to assume whatever shape he wished. Yet the Ba required the corpse, or at least a statue, in order to retain its identity. It was thought to return to the body in the grave after roaming through the fields and groves of Egypt (Fig. 22) and is often depicted hovering over the body or descending the tomb shaft to the burial chamber.[18]

By now the contrast between Ba and Ka should have become clear. The Ba is entirely personal; it is the dead man in a certain aspect. The Ba, imagined in bird-shape, is often depicted. The Ka is never depicted, is not individualized, and is a force in—and a quality of—man. The Ba represents man as animated notwithstanding the death of the body; it preserves man's identity through its lasting relationship with mummy or statue but is free from the limitations of either. It can move at will, change shape at will, visit Egypt, or fly to heaven. It possesses, therefore, great power. But the Ka *is* power.

It may be useful to introduce here yet a third concept that is, like the Ba, an aspect of the dead man. This is the *akh* 𓄿. Like the Ba, it is never mentioned in connection with the living man.[19] But, like the Ka, it is never depicted. It is written with a sign rendering the crested ibis; but it is not thought of as a bird. Its meaning, "shining, glorious," indicates that, when the dead are called *akhu*, their aspect as supernatural beings is envisaged. Their abode is heaven; and the Akh, in contrast with the Ba, does not retain any relation to the body. Yet, in contrast with the Ka, it is individualized. Food-offerings are sometimes addressed to it, and the expression "well-equipped Akh" seems to allude to the funerary establishment. We translate Akh with "transfigured spirit." It is a deceased, a transcendent, being, without earthly or material ties; and, as such, it is the most spiritualized of the various concepts of the dead.

It is clear that the Ka, Ba, and Akh are neither identical nor mutually exclusive notions. They represent different aspects of the dead, one of which, the Ka, belongs to man in this life as well as in the Hereafter. The multiplicity of these notions goes further than we can observe with other peoples with whom we are well acquainted, though in Africa it has several parallels.[20] The Semites, Greeks, and Romans distinguish but two conceptions, a life-spirit (*Lebenseele*) and a ghost or apparition (*Totenseele*).[21] The ghost is not a dematerialized soul but rather an evaporized body, appearing sometimes with the wounds by which it died. This resemblance to a living corpse gives it its frightening character.

Now it is possible to identify the Ka with the life-spirit (which the Old Testament calls *ruah* or *nephesh*) which returns to God after death (Eccl. 12:7). However, the Semites accept as normal an extinction of the individuality in death, while the Egyptians maintain that individual survival exists as Ba or Akh, but that the Ka, as vital force, supports man upon earth as well as in the Beyond. The best equivalent for the Ka is the *genius* of the Romans,[22] though the Ka is much more impersonal. But in the case of the *genius*, as well as in that of the Ka, there is the recognition of a power which transcends the human person even though it works within him. And if man believes that he will survive death, this "is not a matter of a belief in immortality but of the experience of power in its direct relation to man; and security, even in death, is only a conclusion drawn from this."[23]

The Egyptian's attitude toward the Ka is passive. He does not feel the relationship as one with a personified power, a god. For the Ka is "the experience of power in its direct relation to man." The directness is the outstanding characteristic in the relationship between a man and his Ka.

But the Ka is not confined to man; it is found throughout creation. When, in the Memphite Theology, Ptah is proclaimed the Creator from whom all the other gods derive their being, it is said that he "bequeathed his power to all the gods and to their Ka's."* Ptah henceforth works through the other gods, who are animated, like the rest of the universe, by the mysterious life-force emanating from the Creator. A little farther in the text, Ka's are mentioned again, but now as independent entities, not subordinated to gods. Immediately after the creation of living na-

* See below, p. 29.

ture is mentioned and before the creation of justice, we read that the Ka's and the Hemsut are created.

We shall ignore the Hemsut; they are rarely named and seem to be no more than the female counterparts of the Ka's.[24]

As to the plural, "Ka's," it expresses the character of an impersonal force, just as abstracts are often expressed in Egyptian by plurals.[25] When the Ka's are mentioned in this manner, the Egyptian does not commit himself to a decision about whether the vital force in nature is one and undivided, or, on the contrary, particularized, individualized. The Memphite Theology merely indicates that vital force is part of the original creation. In the phrase that describes the activity of the Ka's and the Hemsut, the verb form denotes a continuous activity: the Ka's and the Hemsut perennially create food.

We may wonder that amid lofty speculations this aspect of life, its dependence upon material sustenance, is stressed. But the Egyptians do not consider the contrast of matter and mind as absolute, nor do they adhere to our fixed estimation of their comparative values. Life depends on sustenance; the vital forces which animate the growth of animals and plants make life possible for man. In the account of creation the perennial renewal of this chain must, of necessity, be mentioned. It follows, as we have seen, the creation of living nature and precedes immediately the creation of the greatest good of civilized society—justice.

The relationship between Ka and sustenance will be found throughout the texts.[26] In the tombs the food-offerings for the dead were logically dedicated "to his Ka,"[27] and the funerary priest whose main task was to make these offerings at the proper times was called "servant of the Ka."[28] In Figure 21 the food-offerings are placed before the dead (whose seated figure is partly preserved on the right) within the Ka symbol.

In the pyramid texts we find, not Ptah, but the sun-god Atum, described as Creator; and he, too, imparts Ka to his creatures. Standing on the Primeval Hill in the midst of the waters of chaos, he created out of himself the first pair of gods, Shu and Tefnut; he vitalized them by transferring his Ka to them in that mystic embrace which we find also at the end of the Memphite Theology and in the Mystery Play of the Succession. The translation "vital force" is here particularly apt. The text addresses Atum as follows:

> Thou didst spit out Shu, thou didst spew out Tefnut;
> Thou didst put thy arms around them with thy Ka
> So that thy Ka was in them [Pyr. 1652].

The same conception makes it possible to express the pre-eminent power of a god; Geb is addressed as follows: "Thou art the Ka of all the gods; thou hast taken them that thou mayest foster them; thou lettest them live" (Pyr. 1623). Geb, the earth, produces sustenance; hence he fosters the gods, makes them live, is their Ka. Again the basic meaning of Ka appears to be "vital force."

The Ka, as an impersonal vital force, can charge any object, even if we should never conceive of it as alive. For the Egyptian it might be thought of as alive if it were effective. So we see King Seti I in his funerary temple at Gurnah embraced by a female figure who bears upon her head the symbol of the Ka in which is written her name. This name is that of the temple itself. The meaning of this curious design is clear. Just as Atum vitalized the first pair of gods, Shu and Tefnut, by putting his arms around them, imparting his Ka to them in a mystical embrace, so the dead king lives in the Hereafter through the funerary ritual daily performed in his temple. The text does not refer to the Ka but uses an image which is very prevalent in Egyptian imagery of resurrection,* namely, the mother. The words imputed to the figure of the temple are: "Behold I am behind thee. I am thy temple, thy mother, forever and forever."29

In man the Ka becomes manifest in a variety of ways which may raise doubts about the appropriateness of "vital force" as a translation. But the difficulty lies rather in the lack of congruity between our own conceptions and those of the Egyptians. For them there was something in common in the several uses of the word "Ka," just as the Yaos use the concept of *mulungu* where we would use a number of different notions.† We may turn to the teachings of Ptahhotep for some of these uses of the word "Ka." When the old sage adjures the listener to treat his son well if he proves worthy, the argument "He is thy son, whom thy Ka has begotten for thee; separate not thine heart from him."30 indicates that here the sense of the term is still "vital force." In the same text we find also sentences in which "Ka" might be translated "mood";31 but, though this free translation makes the text sound very familiar to us, we lose, perhaps, an essential subtlety, namely, the peculiarly Egyptian interpretation of ill-humor as an obstacle to the quiet flow of vital force through the person. Ptahhotep warns a messenger against paraphrasing his master's words, since common terms reportedly spoken by a nobleman will strike the recipient of the message as incongruous: "Beware of worsening words, such as might make one great man contemptible(?) to the

---

* See below, pp. 168–80.   † See above, p. 62.

other through the manner of speech of all men. 'A great man, an insignificant man,' that is what the Ka abhorreth." In a later section it is said
that all recreation should not be sacrificed to "too much care for thine
house," for "it is an abhorrence to the Ka if its time is diminished." In
our parlance: Worry is bad for one.

The word "nature" is quite often an appropriate translation for Ka.
For instance, courtiers say in their inscriptions referring to the king: "I
did what his Ka loved" or "I did that which his Ka approved." The
words may become an almost meaningless circumlocution;[32] but, when
they do not, the Egyptian expression possesses a shade of meaning which
the translation "nature" does not convey, namely, that all positive feeling—approval, joy, etc.—enhances one's vital power.

It is the Ka which makes a person into the man he is; it is through
one's Ka that one can achieve something. And so another free translation, namely, "luck, fortune,"[33] may sometimes be appropriate, for example in the epithet which certain men assumed: "The Lord of the
Two Lands made his Ka (fortune)."[34] What is lost here again—if we
translate "Ka" by "fortune"—is the feeling that the king, by his favor,
enhanced that of which his servant, thus distinguished, felt himself capable. The king "made his Ka." In retaining the term, we retain an insight into the reactions of the ancients to these royal rewards. True,
the king made the man's fortune; but he did it through that intensification of vitality which goes with success. The king was felt, not to place
his servant in favorable external conditions by his gifts and favors, but
to affect his innermost vitality so that he could achieve what had hitherto been beyond him.

This view is, again, not peculiar to Egypt. Of the Teutons it is said:

It belonged to the sailors' craft to be able to handle rudder and sail efficiently but
just as much to obtain favorable winds and to make the ship reach port. . . . . This active apprehension of life . . . . is based on the curiously naïve view of the world as a
tilting ground of wills and powers, and not as a scene of accidental happenings. Everything originating in man is viewed as one continuous line which remains uninterrupted
from the earliest stirring of the will down to the last consequence of a completed action.[35]

There is no separation between intention and execution, between capa-
bility and success. If a man is a failure, something is wrong with him, as
Job's friends maintained—on the moral plane, in his case, since they
were Jews. The primitives are of the same opinion, but they view the
defect ontologically: something must be wrong with the man. The king,
however, can undo the deficiency; the king can make a man's Ka. And
already in the Old Kingdom there are names like Kai-ni-nesut, "My
Ka belongs to the king," and Kai-nesut, "The king is my Ka."[36]

In Tell el Amarna this attitude finds the excited and hyperbolic expression which is in keeping with the spirit of that place. Not only is the king called the courtiers' Ka, but the plural, meaning food, is also brought into play:

Praises to thee, O Ua-en-Re (Akhenaten). I give adoration to the height of heaven. I propitiate him who lives by truth (*maat*), the Lord of Diadems, Akhenaten, great in his duration; the Nile-god by whose decrees men are enriched; the food (*kau*) and fatness of Egypt; the good ruler who forms me, begets me, develops me, makes me to associate with princes; the light by sight of which I live—my Ka day by day.[37]

A stela in the Cairo Museum says more concisely: "The king gives his servants Ka's and feeds those who are faithful."[38] The Egyptian, then, experiences the influence of the king in his very being, in what he feels as the center of his life's energy. It is this which he calls Ka.

B. THE KA OF THE KING

The Ka of the king is the only Ka ever shown on the monuments. It is born with the king as his twin; it accompanies him through life as a protective genius; it acts as his twin and as his protector in death. It retains the character of vital force, as the pyramid texts we have quoted in the preceding section of this chapter show. But it is personified in a manner never observed with common people, a contrast the more striking, since so many funerary usages and beliefs, originally pertaining to the king alone, were later applied to all men.

In the following text the Ka appears with the typical features which the twin assumes in folklore: it repeats the actions of the king. The association between food and vital force is once more stressed. In fact, the shared meal occurs repeatedly in the pyramid texts:[39]

Wash thyself, and thy Ka washes itself.
Thy Ka seats itself and eats bread with thee
Without surcease, throughout eternity [Pyr. 789].

Or, more vigorously expressed:

May the victuals of Teti exceed those of the year!
May the wealth of food of Teti exceed that of the Nile!
Ho, Ka of Teti! Here with it, so that Teti may eat with
thee! [Pyr. 564].

The Ka also fulfils other functions which the twin sometimes fulfils in folk tales. For instance, it goes to announce the king to the gods in heaven.[40] It is itself a god, like the Roman *genius;* we should expect that, since it is a personification of power and also since it is a twin of Pharaoh. In fact, at Deir el Bahri there is a series of square pillars showing Queen Hatshepsut in the protective embrace of varying divine couples; and one pair consists of the king of the gods, Amon, and the queen's own Ka.[41]

The treatment of the king's Ka as a twin, the personification of his vital force, while the notion remains general in every other context, cannot be explained by the unusual potency which, as we have seen, distinguishes the king from other men in the minds of most people. We need a more specific explanation of the form which the beliefs regarding the king's Ka took, once his unusual potency is admitted.

We have reason to assume that it would have been natural for the thought of a twin to arise in connection with the king. It seems that each Pharaoh was considered a twin; his "brother," however, was stillborn and passed immediately on into the Beyond, for it was the placenta, the afterbirth. Though this view may strike us as surprising, it is held, even today, by the Baganda—people who, at least in their Hamitic traits, are related to the ancient Egyptians.[42] We seem here, again, to touch upon that North and East African substratum from which Egyptian culture arose and which still survives among Hamitic and half-Hamitic people today.[43]

When a king of Uganda dies, his interest in the community which he had ruled does not cease. In a temple, constructed for this purpose, he continues to give oracles and to advise his successors. But just as the Egyptians believed that a man's ghost required a material support—mummy or statue—to function effectively, so also do the Baganda. Hence the king's jawbone is removed from his corpse and prepared, decorated, and kept in his temple. Since the king is born as a twin of the stillborn placenta and the royal person after death retains a dual character, the stillborn twin, as well as the dead ruler, requires a material anchorage for its spirit; and for this special purpose the navel cord of the newborn prince is dried and kept throughout his lifetime in a specially made and decorated container. This container with the navel cord is deposited in the temple erected after the king's death, and only when both jawbone and navel cord are present—only when the dual person of the late monarch is thus represented in the shrine—can oracles be forthcoming.

The container of the navel cord is shaped like a truncated and inverted cone and is carried by a large looplike handle. An object of identical shape is carried by one of the goddesses assisting at the birth of Hatshepsut in Deir el Bahri.[44] Since we know absolutely nothing about this object from Egyptian sources, one is inclined to explain it tentatively by reference to modern usages belonging to a group of people demonstrably related by some of their cultural, as well as by linguistic and physical, traits to the ancient Egyptians; and this attempt is the more justified, since the concomitant feature, namely, worship of the royal placenta, was known in ancient Egypt.

Early evidence of a cult of the royal placenta consists of a standard closely connected with the king and an important Old Kingdom title. A medically trained anthropologist has argued that the standard represents the placenta;[45] and its name, written in different ways, means "placenta of the king."[46] We find curious corroborative evidence in the reliefs from the Fifth Dynasty in the sun temple of Neuserre, where the standard is carried by a priest of Isis, the mother of Horus the king.[47] Inscriptional evidence is not lacking either; for the term which we translate "Royal Kinsmen" is best explained as "guardians of," or "those belonging to" the "placenta of the king."[48] The standard appears on the earliest royal monuments and remains associated with Pharaoh until the end of Egyptian history. It can be seen in our Figure 2 nearest to Narmer, and it precedes Neuserre in Figure 24. Normally it shares the honor of being carried in the closest proximity to the king with the wolf standard of Upwaut. This god is identified with the king in the Memphite Theology and replaces the god Horus in the Great Procession of the Osiris festival at Abydos.* It seems that Upwaut, the "Opener-of-the-Ways," stood for Horus—whether god or Pharaoh—in his aspect of firstborn son, i.e., "opener-of-the-body." The Upwaut standard and that thought to represent the royal placenta, the king's stillborn twin, can therefore be expected to appear together, since both would be connected with the king's birth.[49] Their close association with the monarch is particularly striking in reliefs placed in Djoser's funerary complex at Saqqara.[50] In these the representation is reduced to an austere minimum of detail, and the king is accompanied by only two standards—Upwaut and the placenta—as if they formed a counterpart to the joint appearance of jawbone and navel cord on the dais in the temples of the Baganda kings.[51]

Less conclusive evidence of the worship of the royal placenta is supplied by one name of the moon-god, Khonsu, for it is probable that this name meant "placenta of the king."[52] Khonsu has been depicted only since the New Kingdom, and the name is very rarely met before then.[53] In earlier times the moon-god was Thoth. It is quite significant that Khonsu does not figure in mythology (though the moon and Thoth do) and is altogether a colorless figure. His outstanding characteristic is the "lock of youth," which distinguishes young princes in the New King-

* See below, p. 204.

dom and which would be a comprehensible attribute for the king's twin
who died at birth. We can, with this in mind, explain the mummiform
appearance of Khonsu. Moreover, the god is occasionally depicted with
a falcon head supporting the moon disk and crescent. Yet there is no connection between the falcon and the moon unless Khonsu was the divine
"twin" of Pharaoh who embodied the falcon-god Horus. Finally, Khonsu is shown wearing the *menat* 𓎛, an ornament sacred to Hathor,
the mother of Horus and of the king (Fig. 39). If we accept the interpretation of the name of the god Khonsu and consider the iconographical
evidence just enumerated, a consistent picture emerges. Nor do we need
to wonder why the king's "twin" should have become a moon-god; the
moon was the twin par excellence—the twin of the sun.[54]

It is not known whether the belief that the placenta was a stillborn
twin was anciently held in connection with commoners.[55] Even in that
case there would be no reason why such beliefs should affect the ordinary Egyptian's conception of his own Ka. The placenta, after all, is an
individualized and definite object, the Ka an impersonal force. But in the
case of the king matters lay differently. The influence of the king's Ka
was naturally connected in the minds of all with the royal person
through whom it became manifest in the life of state and people. If the
notion prevailed that the king was born a twin, the potency of the king,
which affected every subject, was likely to become personalized, too,
and regarded as a twin, double, or genius. If the people experienced their
own Ka's passively and—as "power in its direct relation to man"—im-
personally, they experienced the Ka of the king as personified power. In
pictorial representations the individualization of the king's Ka is developed in all its consequences. In a Middle Kingdom tomb at Dahshur a
large wooden statue of a king was found bearing the Ka sign.[56] More
common is a rendering in relief, already known in the Old Kingdom[57]
and here shown on a stela of Senusert III (Fig. 20). On either side we
see the king and behind him a small figure characterized as a divinity
by its "false beard." This figure bears the Ka symbol on its head, and
between the arms of the sign appears the king's Horus name, the name
which marks the king most directly as a deity. After Tuthmosis I this
name regularly contains the epithet "Strong Bull," which is clearly
appropriate for a personification of vital force. We see, moreover, that
the figure of the royal Ka holds in one hand a pole crowned with the
head of the king and in the other a feather, the symbol of Maat. The
figure as a whole is named "The living Ka of the king who is at the head
of the palace (or sanctuary)."[58]

Sometimes the design is more abstract: The Ka symbol inclosing the king's Horus name is supported not by a divine figure but by a standard from which arms emerge (in the manner shown by the personified hieroglyphs at the bottom of our Fig. 29) to hold the staff with the king's head and the feather. This, the most common, rendering of the king's Ka shows that the notion of a double never entirely superseded the Ka's original significance as a vital force. For these renderings are obviously on a par with that of Seti I in the embrace of the figure representing his funerary temple;* they are concrete renderings of abstract ideas.

The notion "twin" prevails only in the rendering of the birth scenes of Hatshepsut and Amenhotep III. The god Khnum is shown making two identical homunculi on his potter's wheel (Fig. 23), while the goddess Hathor, the mother of Horus, appropriately gives them "life." One is the future king, the other his Ka. Next these two thumb-sucking babies are washed and presented to the gods,[59] the Ka carrying on its head its usual symbol with the king's Horus name. But after this presentation to the pantheon, the royal twin is not depicted (its materialization upon earth, as the king's placenta, was likewise ephemeral). We do find, on the other hand, the normal conception of the Ka represented in the reliefs. They actually show how the newborn infant was endowed with this remarkable force of which it was to dispose throughout its lifetime as a king. In order to understand the pictorial rendering of so abstract a notion, we must bring the texts to bear on the representations and return to the beginning of the series of panels.

We find that the queen-mother is shown there holding the infant immediately after its birth;[60] its "twin," the Ka, is not depicted. The goddess Meskhent, who presides over the scene, says:

The son (sic!) is made to be king of Upper and Lower Egypt. I surround thee with protection like Re. Life and good fortune are given to thee more than to all mortals; I have destined thee for life, luck, health, excellence, affluence, joy, sustenance, food, victuals, and all other good things. Thou wilt appear as king of Upper and Lower Egypt for many Sed festivals, while thou art living, remaining, fortunate—while thy heart is in joy with thy Ka in these thy Two Lands on the throne of Horus forever.

If we remember the various derived meanings of Ka, such as mood, good fortune, etc., the phrase "while thy heart is in joy with thy Ka" seems aptly to summarize the blessings which the goddess bestows.

The tendency toward the concrete, which characterizes mythopoeic thought in general and Egyptian thought most particularly, expresses itself at this point in a curious image: the royal child is placed in the arms

* See above, p. 67.

of twelve divinities identified as Ka's and Hemsut and is made to absorb from them the vital force, the good fortune, the power, and all the other blessings bestowed upon it. We have inscriptional evidence for the view that an immaterial endowment could be viewed as nourishment. At Deir el Bahri, Amon orders four goddesses to nurse the child Hatshepsut: "I have commanded (you) to nurse Her Majesty and all her Ka's, with all life and good fortune, all permanence, all health, all joy, and the passing of millions of years on the throne of Horus of all the living, forever."[61] Health and joy, but also the many years of the reign, are quite concretely regarded as benefits which enter the child with the milk of the nursing goddesses. It is similarly said of the king in the pyramid texts:

> The abomination of Unas is hunger, he does not eat it.
> The abomination of Unas is thirst, he does not drink it [Pyr. 131].

If it is possible in this manner to avoid hunger and thirst, it is clear that desirable conditions can be imbibed by the royal nursling.

The text, at this point, introduces an ambiguity in the interpretation of the reliefs. Amon commands that not only the queen but also her Ka's be nursed. The plural inevitably reminds us of the doctrine—known from the Eighteenth Dynasty onward—that Pharaoh had fourteen Ka's. In the reliefs we find twelve royal infants in the hands of the Ka's and Hemsut and two, in an adjoining scene, at the breasts of two cow-goddesses, the typical divine wet nurses. Yet it seems impossible to see in these infants images of the fourteen royal Ka's, for the Ka symbols identify, not the nurslings, but the nurses; and not fourteen of these, but only six. And they are not twins of the royal child, comparable with the Ka on the potter's wheel (Fig. 23), but fully grown deities. They furthermore alternate with six marked as Hemsut. Now, we have met the combination of Ka's and Hemsut in the Memphite Theology* as a collectivity representing the vital force in nature. The impersonal nature of the force is expressed by the plural in the language, but in pictorial art this device fails; twelve distinct figures are as personalized, as definite, as one or two. Nevertheless, we can still recognize the idea that is expressed in the Memphite Theology as the basis of the design. After the royal child has been blessed by the most important gods in the pantheon individually, it is shown in harmony with, and favored by, that corporate entity, the Ka's and the Hemsut, which represents the vital force in nature. We can quote a pyramid text that expresses the same idea when it describes the arrival in heaven of the late king in the fulness of his power. It speaks of "the Ka's of Unas," but in the relief

* See above, p. 29.

we discussed we could also have called the figures, loosely, the Ka's and Hemsut of Hatshepsut. In the following text we see that the first four lines allude to general forces by the contrast with the succeeding phrase which refers quite unequivocally to the single uraeus of the king's crown. This is really the goddess Wadjet who protects him.

> The Ka's of Unas are behind him;
> His Hemsut are under his feet;
> His gods are over him;
> His uraeus-serpents are over his head.
> The leading snake of Unas is at his forehead, she
> Who perceives the soul (of the enemy),
> She who excels in force of fire [Pyr. 396].

It is possible that the Ka's and the Hemsut are here, as at Deir el Bahri, brought in through association with the thought of birth, since the preceding phrases of the text mention that the Creator, Atum, made the king. What matters for us, however, is to note that in the old texts, as in Hatshepsut's reliefs, we find side by side two aspects of the Ka which to us would be mutually exclusive. Both derive from the notion "vital force."

The theory of the fourteen Ka's of the king would seem a mere systematization of the collectivity of Ka's. Names of the Old Kingdom mention a plurality of Ka's in connection with the gods: Neterkau of the First Dynasty, Menkaure of the Fourth. In the New Kingdom, Re is equipped with fourteen Ka's; but the fourteen Ka's of the king are depicted only in Ptolemaic times.[62]

If we remember that the word "Ka" stands for something which we should call abstract, but which the Egyptian tendency toward the concrete transforms into a personification or a collectivity of gods, most references to the Ka of the king become clear. For instance, we have a pyramid text in which the king's survival is insured by the identification of his person and parts of his person with various deities. It ends:

> Thy members are the twin children of Atum,
> O imperishable one.
> Thou dost not perish;
> Thy Ka does not perish;
> Thou art Ka [Pyr. 149c, d].

In another text the duplication "the king and his Ka" becomes so concrete as to suggest a bodily existence for the latter, yet the concluding phrases indicate in clear and vigorous terms that Ka is power and nothing else.

> Horus takes him (the dead King Unas) to his side.
> He cleanses Unas in the Lake of the Fox;
> He purifies the Ka of this Unas in the Lake of the
>   Dawn.
> He rubs down the flesh of the Ka of this Unas and
>   his (Unas') own. . . . .
>
> He brings Unas' Ka and (Unas) himself to the Great
> Royal Castle (of the sun-god Re). . . . .
>
> This Unas leads the Imperishable Stars;
> He sails to the Fields of Rushes (Elysium);
> Those who dwell in the Horizon row him,
> Those who dwell in the sky sail him.
> This Unas is powerful in power,
> His arms do not fail him.
> This Unas is commanding in command,
> His Ka is with him. [Pyr. 372–75].

Very significant is another pyramid text, a self-contained exuberant poem. The plural "Ka's" at the beginning stands again where we would use an abstract noun, and we may translate "vital force." The opening phrases vigorously assert that the old sacred city of Pe is one of those hallowed spots where life throbs more powerfully than elsewhere, a place (such as the Memphite Theology makes Memphis out to be) that stands in a peculiarly intimate rapport with the hidden forces of nature. It is now suggested by our text that King Teti, because he is buried at Pe, survives the crisis of death. His vitality is compared with two phenomena which are most intensely "alive," the burning flame, and the beetle-god of the rising sun, who every morning appears victorious from the darkness of night. At the same time the relevancy of these metaphors is proved by implication: the red of flame and sunrise is the color of Pe, the city of the Red Crown; and, with that multiplicity of meaning which the Egyptians love, the flame is a usual epithet for Wadjet, the cobra-goddess of Pe, who is also the "eye of the sun." Our text then continues by referring to the connection between vital force and food and ends with an appeal to an anonymous goddess, presumably Wadjet, to let the gods love and honor Teti. It is possible that the term "love" must be taken here with sexual implications as the culminating expression of that vitality which the spell glorifies:

> Ka's are in Pe; Ka's were always in Pe; Ka's will be
>   in Pe; and Teti's Ka is in Pe,
> Red like a flame, alive like the beetle-god.
>
> Be gay! Be gay! A meal for me, ye servants!

Now you should put, My Lady, the love for Teti
    and the respect for Teti,
Now you should put, My Lady, the honor of Teti
    and the charm of Teti
In the body of the gods! [Pyr. 561–62].

But even the power and effectiveness of the living king are summarized in the phrase that he is with his Ka. On this note ends a speech which the assembled gods address to their own king, Amon, after he has presented Queen Hatshepsut to them as his own daughter and the new king of Egypt.

Utterance of all the gods to Amon: This thy daughter Hatshepsut shall live. We are satisfied with her in life and peace. She is thy daughter of thy form, thy vigorous seed. Thou gavest her thy Ba, thy power, thy influence, thy magic, thy crown, (even) when she was still in the body of her who bore her. The Lowlands are hers and the mountains belong to her, everything which the heavens wrap round, everything which the sea encircles. Thou hast made her as thy female counterpart. Thou knewest the future. Thou gavest her the portion of Horus in life and the years of Seth in good fortune. . . . .

We give her dominion(?) over the lands, in peace. We give her all life and good fortune on our part; all food on our part; all sustenance on our part. She is at the head of all living Ka's together with her Ka as King of Upper and Lower Egypt on the throne of Horus, like unto Re, forever and ever.[63]

There is one more aspect of the king's Ka which we must consider. We have seen that it can be said of one god that he is "the Ka of all the gods," to express that they are dependent upon him. The king is in a peculiar way dependent upon his father, since kingship, as we have seen, is an institution involving two generations. And so we find a pyramid text in which the late king is addressed as follows: "O Osiris, Horus has supported thee; he has done it for his Ka in thee" (Pyr. 582). In connection with Osiris the expression recurs often, and we shall have occasion to quote those texts. But the king stands in the same relationship with another god whom the official titulary proclaims as his father—Re.

There is a dramatic quality in the following pyramid text which reveals that Re is the king's Ka. It opens with an emphatic warning of the dangers of the journey into the Beyond. In Egypt, as in Babylonia and in many other countries, the Hereafter is separated from the living by an expanse of treacherous water. The king's vital force has left his body and is summoning him. And it is now revealed to him that this vital force was no other than the god who begot him. That Re appears here and not Osiris is entirely logical. Osiris is the king's predecessor. Here, however, the text envisages a king who has been upon the throne for many years, who, moreover, in his death becomes Osiris to the son who will succeed him. It is the Creator, the sun-god, who now charges him to leave the earth. The text reads:

> O Unas, beware of the lake!
> O Unas, beware of the lake!
> O Unas, beware of the lake!
> O Unas, beware of the lake!
>
> Messages of thy Ka come for thee;
> Messages of thy father come for thee;
> Messages of Re come for thee:
>
> "Go, after thy days (have become full).
> Cleanse thyself, (that is) thy bones. . . . .
> That thou mayest be at the side of the god;
> And leave thy house to thy son" [Pyr. 136–37].[64]

The god is the Ka of the king. But the subjects say: My Ka belongs to the king; my Ka derives from the king; the king makes my Ka; the king is my Ka. This juxtaposition shows that an understanding of the Ka is essential for an understanding of kingship, since the relation of king, gods, and people is defined in these terms. It appears, in fact, that the Egyptians apprehended the involvement of man in nature and the mediating function of their king by means of the concept of Ka.

It will have become clear by now that there is no alternative to the somewhat laborious procedure by which we have tried, through quotations and varying context, to convey the full meaning of the term "Ka." For no translation can do justice to such a concept, since a translation inevitably carries our point of view into a field of thought that does not share our premises. Even if we translate "Ka" as "vital force" or view it as a mechanism by means of which the king is conceived to give direction to the forces of nature for the benefit of the community, these interpretations, though not entirely beside the mark, all but obliterate the specifically Egyptian features of the concept. There is no short cut to an understanding of the ancients.

CHAPTER 6

THE KING'S CEREMONIAL: THE SED FESTIVAL

AFTER the words, the acts. The ritual preserved in the reliefs of many temples expresses, no less than the texts, those thoughts of the ancients which we try to understand. For the nature of kingship in Egypt it is, above all, the Sed festival which is instructive. In the five days of its duration multifarious connections between gods and king, land and king, people and king, were woven into that elaborate fabric which held society as well as the unaccountable forces of nature by strands which passed through the solitary figure on the throne of Horus.

The Sed festival[1] is usually called a jubilee, but it was not a mere commemoration of the king's accession. It was a true renewal of kingly potency, a rejuvenation of rulership *ex opere operato*.[2] Sometimes it was celebrated thirty years after the accession, but several rulers celebrated it repeatedly and at shorter intervals. It is unlikely that a mere counting of years was the decisive factor, but we do not know on what grounds it was decided that the king's power ought to be renewed.

The date of the festival was usually the same as that reserved for the coronation, namely, the first day of the first month of the "Season of Coming Forth"—the first of Tybi.[3] The last five days of the preceding month, Khoiak, were dedicated to the Osiris mysteries; and it is remarkable that the Sed festival, in contrast to the coronation, does not refer to Osiris at all. But the difference is easily explained. At the Sed festival the king appears, not as newly ascending the throne, but as its occupant through a number of years. Consequently, it is not the succession—Horus following Osiris—which is the issue, but a renewal of all those beneficial relations between heaven and earth which the throne controls.

When it had been decided that a Sed festival should be celebrated, many preparations had to be made. Often a new temple was founded with a view to dedicating it at the feast. In other cases a "Festival Hall" was constructed within the precincts of an existing sanctuary. Great monolithic obelisks were cut at the granite quarries of Assuan and shipped downstream toward the site of the festival. If an existing temple was used, one of the great columned courts was adapted to serve as "Court of the Festival," or "Court of the Great Ones."[4] The last phrase refers to the gods who would come from other shrines to participate in the solemnities. To accommodate them, temporary shrines, called the "Houses of the Sed Festival,"[5] were erected on the archaic pattern of the reed-hut sanctuaries of prehistoric days.

The god in whose temple the Sed festival took place was by this very fact proclaimed the deity from whom the king expected most. He received especially large offerings. The obelisks were erected in his honor. It is revealing that Akhenaten's break with the Amon priesthood of Thebes occurred when he persisted in his plan to dedicate his Sed festival, not to the king of the gods, Amon, nor to Ptah, who had an old, established claim, but to the peculiar form of solar deity whose exclusive worship he wanted to establish. It is also significant that the actual blocks prepared for the Festival Hall of Akhenaten show in their reliefs the rapid changes in the formulation and clarification of his dogmas,[6] from the falcon-headed male figure of Harakhte who, notwithstanding a new elaborate epithet, retained his traditional character, to the unprecedented design of a featureless Lord of the Sun Disk sending rays down to the royal figure preaching his gospel.

In addition to the Court of the Festival, two buildings were required: the Festival Hall, where the Great Throne stood, and the "Palace," in which the king changed costume and insignia, and which, therefore, fulfilled the functions of a robing chamber.[7] The latter might be an elaborate structure, such as the small-scale palace which Ramses III built adjoining the first court of his mortuary temple at Medinet Habu. This was fitted with throne room, bedrooms, and bathrooms, so that the king could take up residence there for the duration of the festival. Tradition, however, claims for these buildings the simplicity of prehistoric architecture: "the Hall of King Unas is plaited of reeds."[8] We know shrines of this kind because hieroglyphs have preserved them, and we find them translated into stone in that extraordinary funerary establishment of King Djoser at Saqqara, where the Festival Court of the Sed festival is built as a stupendous full-scale dummy for use in the Hereafter, with doors perennially ajar. The shrines in this court are of two types, and these recur in the Dual Shrines of the Royal Ancestors, which we shall discuss presently (see Fig. 30). On the west side of Djoser's court the chapels assume the shape of the Lower Egyptian shrine; those opposite were modeled on the Upper Egyptian shrine.

The gods who came to participate in the feast were no doubt housed according to their origin from Upper or Lower Egypt.

When the preparations were completed, purification rites took place. If the temple had been newly constructed, there followed the ceremony of "Presenting the House to Its Lord." In any case, there was an illumination of the Court, the Chapels, and the Great Throne upon which the king would sit to receive homage. This "Lighting of the Flame" was also known in the necropolis and was probably an apotropaic measure. The illumination lasted for five days, ending on the eve of the festival.[9]

Thus the capital was astir for some considerable time previous to the actual celebrations. Barges with statues of the gods would arrive from all over the land, in charge of high officials and their suites. The king and his court would meet the most important among them upon their arrival and hold the hawser of the divine bark at its landing. We have some texts describing this stage of the festivities. On a stela in the British Museum a courtier states that he used the opportunity, when the priesthood of Abydos "came to see the King in his goodly Festival of Eternity," to send back with them, for erection in the necropolis, a stela which he had had made for the purpose.[10] A thousand years later the high priest of the vulture-goddess Nekhbet reports in his tomb:

Year 29 . . . . in the reign of Ramses III. . . . . His Majesty commanded that the Governor of the Residence be commissioned to bring the divine bark of Nekhbet to the Sed festival and to carry out her sacred rites in the Houses of the Sed jubilee.

Arrival at Per-Ramesse-Miamun, the great Ka of the Sun, in the year 29 . . . . month . . . . day. Reception of the front hawser of the divine bark by the king in person.[11]

The leading officials of the realm also gathered for the celebrations. They probably assumed honorific titles which in a dim past had denoted actual functions, for we find many archaic titles in the renderings of the festival, while designations of actual members of the administration, such as the vizier, the treasurer, and the judges, are absent. Yet it is certain that these men participated. The curiously primitive designations, such as "The Herdsman from Nekhen" and "The Man from Hermopolis," may disguise members of the government. Ancient official bodies, which may well have retained some religious or administrative function, appear, too. The most important is the council of "The Great Ones of Upper and Lower Egypt," consisting apparently of ten members from each of the two halves of the country; they alone were present, representing the people, at the actual coronation during the Mystery Play of the Succession.*

* See below, chap. 11.

The Royal Princes, and also the Royal Kinsmen, participated in force. In addition, some reliefs show figures designated as "men" or "subjects." They represent the crowds of onlookers who, though certainly excluded from the comparatively restricted area in the temple, watched the processions to the harbor and perhaps participated in other ways which we cannot now reconstruct. In any case the reliefs, by including these few figures to represent the populace, express the fact that it was indeed the whole community that was concerned in the celebrations. We may summarize this aspect of the Sed festival in words describing a ceremony of modern Hamites: "It involved, as well for the festivities themselves as for the preparation of the requisites, the hereditary collaboration of men and women picked from every social level and every region, however distant. And so the festival created stronger ties between the various elements of the people; it was supposed to be a large contribution to the land's fertility and the country's welfare, and in all this the part played by the king was prominent."[11a]

A. OPENING FESTIVITIES

At last, on the first day of the first month of the "Season of Coming-Forth," one of the seasonal New Year's days of the land,* the feast opened with a great procession in which the king, the statues of the gods and their priesthoods, and the secular participants took part. It seems that even at this early stage certain gifts were made to the gods. The reliefs show lists of deities with the number of cattle and sheep allotted to them. We shall see that these are not merely rewards for past services or the price for future loyalty; the king, in dispensing bounty, casts the spell of prosperity over the future and demonstrates the effectiveness of his royalty. These initial proceedings are presided over by the cow-goddess Sekhat-Hor ("She Who Remembers Horus"), the divine nurse who suckled the god-king and who is, at the same time, the protectress of cattle. The two officials directing the transfer are the "Hereditary Prince" and the Heri Udjeb, the "Master of the (King's) Largess."[12] The first is distinguished by the privilege of wearing the same archaic robe as the king, and the Heri Udjeb is an official depicted also in the tombs of the Old Kingdom[13] reading out those items on the lists of offerings which are donations of the king, the "offering which the king gives", to the funerary establishment of one of his followers. These men act on behalf of the king, and the solemnity of the occasion is shown by the fact that the sacred royal standards, which nor-

* See below, p. 103.

mally accompany the king, are carried before them when they go to inspect the cattle previous to its distribution.[14]

These initial gifts seem to reward the minor deities for their participation in the festival. The major deities are involved in more elaborate ceremonies and receive individual gifts; their priesthoods appear before the throne, carrying the symbols of the gods to pay homage to the king. And the king, in his turn, visits each of them in the shrines where they are housed, in the Court of the Great Ones.[15]

B. MAIN CELEBRATIONS

These visits to the shrines alternate with processions which come before the throne to pay homage to the monarch, and the whole of this part of the festival seems to occupy the two or three days following the opening ceremony. There is a continuous coming and going of deputations and royal processions, rich in ancient symbolism and traditional pomp. The king, enthroned, receives pledges of loyalty; then, again, he descends from the throne, and, heading processions whose composition varies according to tradition, goes to pay homage to a god or goddess in the Court of the Great Ones. Visits to the "Palace" to rest or to change dress or insignia punctuate the proceedings. Even these subsidiary actions, no more than intervals between the main events, are full of solemnity. Abbreviated renderings in the reliefs (Fig. 24) depict the king—preceded by the standard of the Royal Placenta and by a choirmaster, a fan-bearer, and a door-hinge-bearer (shown below)—being received by a master of ceremonies, a recitation priest, and courtiers, while the "Great Ones of Upper and Lower Egypt" kiss the ground before him (right-hand bottom corner), and two courtiers of the rank of "Friend" wash his feet. They pour water from a vase shaped like the hieroglyph *sma* $\frac{1}{0}$, meaning "Union" and used especially for that basic rite of the accession, the "Unification of the Two Lands." The whole of this scene merely refers to the king's entering the robing chamber called the "Palace" to change dress according to the requirements of the processional ritual and of the various acts before the throne—salutations, consecrations, donations, etc.

We may describe a few episodes about which we are rather fully informed. A deputation from the Horus city in Upper Egypt is headed by the "Herdsman of Nekhen,"[16] who is accompanied by two attendants wearing caps of wolfskin with the head and tail of the animal attached. These attributes refer to the wolf-god Upwaut, whose close connection with Nekhen, as well as with the king, we shall have occasion to study presently. The two attendants also carry a wolf-headed *user* scepter; and the warlike attributes of the god, bow and throwing stick, are carried behind the "Herdsman of Nekhen." The little procession is preceded by a master of ceremonies. At a certain distance from the throne this dignitary calls, "Back!"; and one would like to believe that at the signal those approaching performed the *proskynesis*. The foremost figures of the group are actually shown kissing the earth, while the standard-bearers remain standing; and another attendant holding a symbol meaning "herdsman" makes a gesture of acclamation. The "Master of the (King's) Largess" is present; and this suggests that gifts, probably cattle, are made to the "Herdsman of Nekhen." In fact, another scene showing this same procession on its way back from the throne includes a recitation priest who says, "Take it." If the reliefs were complete, we should no doubt be able to estimate the reward given to the "Herdsman" in exchange for his loyal address.

The princes of the blood royal join in the general homage. They are brought in on their palanquins and are shown "taking up positions on the left facing the throne" and also "going away and resuming their places."[17] Whether the queen appeared before the throne is uncertain;[18] and there must have been a number of ceremonies which escape us,[19] although the main characteristics of the celebration are clear.

Sometimes we get a glance of the detailed sequence of events, notwithstanding the damage sustained by the reliefs. For instance, we see the priest of the crocodile-god Sobek approaching the throne, near which, for an unknown reason, the standard of Anubis is now placed.[20] Two attendants (presumably on either side of the priest) carry standards in the shape of the flowers of the reeds among which the crocodile lives. A servant preceding the priest seems to offer the king a bag containing some precious substance. With him are two singers representing the two towns of Pe and Dep in the Delta. Behind the priest march two men carrying other gifts and three "prophets" waving ostrich feathers.

While this little group approaches, three men are shown running through the Court of the Great Ones. On another block of stone the priest of Sobek is shown retreating from the throne, while the three men have arrived at the shrine of the Apis bull, which is now opened. Evidently a processional visit of the king to this god is now due, or the bull is to be brought out to be led before the king's throne.

Thus, in a series of moves and countermoves, visits to shrines, and demonstrations of loyalty before the throne are woven all the varied bonds which unite the realm and the ruler, the ruler and the gods. While the ritual unfolds, the king moves like the shuttle in a great loom to re-create the fabric in which people, country, and nature are irrevocably comprised. It is this process which the texts call "assuming the protection (*šsp s3*) of the two lands."

The throne of the king is in reality one of a pair. In the hieroglyph of the Sed festival 🔲 the two thrones appear, empty, in two pavilions placed back to back. This may be merely a graphic way of combining the two royal seats, which in reality stood side by side.[21] The dual pavilion allows Pharaoh to appear as king of Upper or of Lower Egypt according to the requirements of the ritual.

C. THE DEDICATION OF THE FIELD

If the design of the king enthroned in the double pavilion could serve as an abbreviated rendering of the whole Sed festival (Fig. 25), the same function could be fulfilled by a representation of the characteristic "dance" by which a piece of land was dedicated to the gods.[22] We do not know at what point in the celebrations this ceremony took place —probably on one of the three days devoted to visits to shrines and the reception of delegates.

The word "dance" is misleading; the king crossed the piece of land in its length and breadth with a kind of fast walk which, in the graceful delineations of the reliefs, acquires for us the character of a dance step. The whole of the performance, which implied a fourfold course according to the points of the compass, was first executed by the king as Ruler of Lower Egypt with the Red Crown and then as Ruler of Upper Egypt with the White Crown. The standard of the god Upwaut accompanied the king through all the movements of the dance, being carried by a priest of the ancestral spirits of the royal house, a "Servant of the Souls of Nekhen."

In Figure 26 the procedure is clearly rendered. The king, wearing the short, stiff, archaic mantle which characterizes his appearance at the Sed festivals, enters the Shrine of Upwaut (at the left) and there anoints the standard of the wolf. He proceeds from there to the "Palace" or robing chamber and emerges dressed only in a short royal kilt with a bull's tail attached; besides this he wears a necklace and the appropriate crown and carries a flail in one hand. The long shepherd's crook which he carries together with the flail in all processions is left behind in the "Palace." In its stead he holds a small object, the *imy.t pr*, "house document," which sets out a transfer of ownership and, for that reason, takes the place of our "will," among its other functions.[23]

This curious attribute underlines an aspect of kingship which we have already discussed. The king rules essentially as legitimate heir of his predecessors and, ultimately, of the gods. On the strength of the "will" he disposes of the land and all it contains. It is thought sometimes that the "will" merely shows that the king is entitled to dispose of the field which he crosses.[24] This seems too limited a view altogether. In fact, we do not know that an actual piece of land is involved at all. It may very well be that an area was marked out in the temple court to symbolize Egypt as a whole. In view of the character of the celebrations, such a purely symbolical arrangement is very probable. The king, by crossing this "field," would dedicate it and, therewith, Egypt, to the gods and at the same time assert his legitimate power over the land. This is strongly suggested by a Ptolemaic text from Edfu which refers to the "will" as the "Secret of the Two Partners (*rḫ.wy*)"—Horus and Seth. Since their "secret" is the division of Egypt—with Horus predominant, and yet with a reconciliation between the two (see the Memphite Theology, pp. 25–27)—it is likely that the "will" concerns the land as a whole and kingship over it, not merely as a basis for some transaction such as the transfer of a field to some god or temple, but as the basic order of society which the rich and comprehensive apparatus of the Sed festival is designed to renew. To that extent the dedication of the field is the central ceremony of the festival.

The text from Edfu contains further evidence that this is the correct interpretation of the "dance." In the first place, the king states that he has received the "will" before Geb; and Geb, as we have seen, presides in the Memphite Theology and elsewhere over the conciliation of the antagonists and the final settlement of the succession. In the second place, the text is full of cosmic allusions which show that the implications of the ceremony reach a good deal further than the mere allocation of the temple lands:

To recite: "I have run holding the Secret of the Two Partners, (namely) the Will which my father has given me before Geb. I have passed through the land and touched its four sides; I run through it as I desire." (Here the quotation of the king's words ends, and the rest is legend to the design.) The Good God (the king) who runs round fast holding the Will. He runs crossing the ocean and the four sides of Heaven, going as far as the rays of the sun disk, passing over the earth, giving the field to its mistress.[25]

Crossing the field (which we assume to stand for the land of Egypt) would, then, be a ceremony of taking possession similar to the one hinted at by Amenemhet I in the teachings for his son when he says: "I trod Elephantine, I marched into the Delta. I stood upon the boundaries of the land and beheld its circuit." The "mistress" to which the Edfu text refers might be the Goddess of the Crown. Unfortunately, the abbreviated legends of the scene are not quite clear, especially in their older form. They might read: *"Gift,"* or rather *"Dedication* of the Land." The last part of the Edfu legend, anyway, refers to the king as universal ruler.

Facing the king during the "dance" we find sometimes Thoth, more often a goddess Mert, who claps her hands in accompaniment or as welcome and calls out to him, "Come! Bring ⟨it⟩!" Her significance is obscure.[26] And throughout this part of the ceremony the standard of Upwaut follows the king. Its bearer, the "Servant of the Souls of Nekhen," has even changed his costume while the king has been shedding his mantle and crook in the "Palace," and accompanies his sovereign in a skin dress instead of the usual linen kilt. In the First Dynasty a schematic rendering of the Sed festival sometimes consists of figures of the king enthroned with the crowns of Upper and Lower Egypt alternately and accompanied only by the standard of Upwaut.[27] If the association of king and Upwaut is really based on qualifications of the king as "eldest son" and therefore heir (see pp. 92–93), our interpretation of this part of the ceremony finds further support; the king asserts his dominance over the land of Egypt as lawful ruler by ceremoniously crossing the "field" that represents it, "running through it as he desires."

D. THE CONCLUDING CEREMONIES

The concluding part of the festival, like the "dance," is enacted twice; and the usages referring to the ruler as king of Upper Egypt are not merely a repetition of those which determine his acts as ruler of Lower Egypt but differ from them. This double sequence runs from a first act, when the king descends from the throne, to the last, when his royalty is announced to the four quarters of the world.

As king of Lower Egypt, Pharaoh is carried on a boxlike litter by the "Great Ones of Upper and Lower Egypt." The Upwaut standard is explicitly named as "Follower of the King of Lower Egypt." The procession moves to the chapel of "Horus of Libya who lifts his arm" and who serves as the god representing Lower Egypt, at least for Neuserre. From him the king receives the *was* (welfare) scepter ⎜ in addition to the crook ⎨ and flail ⋀ which he holds throughout this part of the ceremonies. The significance is clear: with the ritual almost completed, welfare is vouchsafed by the god. Two officials—one with the archaic title "Chief of Pe," the old city in the western Delta—place themselves on either side of the king and, in a kind of antiphonal hymn of praise, proclaim his power. They then change places and repeat the proclamation before and behind the king. Twice more the action is repeated, so that each man has spoken in the direction of the four points of the compass. The order "Silence," repeated four times, precedes each proclamation. In later times, when the actual ritual is ousted from the designs by allegorical details, the "Souls of Pe," the Royal Ancestors assigned to Lower Egypt, proclaim the king's might to the four quarters of the world.

The Upper Egyptian sequence uses a basket-shaped litter. In the temple of Neuserre it is shown as carried by the chamberlains, but in later designs, by Horus and Seth. The procession goes to the chapels of these two gods, Horus of Edfu and Seth of Ombos; and the priest of each of them gives the bow and arrows to the royal priest, the Sem, who hands them to the king. The king then shoots an arrow to each of the four points of the compass;[28] and he is, moreover, enthroned four times— each time facing in one of the four directions—upon a curious throne base, ornamented with twelve lion heads.[29] In the Bubastis reliefs two divinities place the crown upon his head at each enthronement.

Both the Upper and the Lower Egyptian ceremonies end with a return to the Court of the Great Ones for the concluding ceremony, an act of homage to deities whom we have not noticed during the earlier proceedings. They are the Royal Ancestors, the divine occupants of the Iterty, the Dual Shrines.[30] The Sem priest announces: "An offering which the king gives, of ointment, linen, victuals." The standards are conspicuous[31] and are especially designated here as "the gods who follow Horus." We shall meet them again* in this function at the Feast of Min.[32] Their prominence in the last scene of the Sed festival is, however, particularly appropriate, for they belong, not to one individual king, but to all kings; they are therefore closely associated with the Royal Ancestors and are actually kept in the Dual Shrines. The princes in their palanquins are also present. And here, in the last act of the great and complex ritual, the link between ruler and royal line is renewed, while the next generation assists at the king's appeal to the generations of his ancestors.

* See below, pp. 91 and 188.

CHAPTER 7

THE KING'S SUPPORTERS: THE ROYAL ANCESTORS

A. THE FOLLOWERS OF HORUS

Not only the Sed festival, but also the Mystery Play of the Succession, ends before the shrines of the Royal Ancestors. We cannot form an adequate idea of the nature of kingship in Egypt, nor can we understand the texts and the monuments, without a somewhat detailed knowledge of the form under which reference is made to them and the role they play. As it happens, relatively late material forms the best approach to the matter because it is both unequivocal and least alien to our own ways of thinking.

Ramses II and Ramses III show in their reliefs the great procession of the Harvest Festival of Min which we shall discuss later (chap. 15). Here statues of ancestors identified by name are carried before the king. They include Menes as the oldest of the series.[1] With them are carried the ancient standards of kingship. These, in fact, are separated from the person of the king only by the royal insignia—crook, flail, and scimitar—which symbolize, and to some extent embody, the royal power. The standards, preceding the insignia, follow in their turn the statues of the Royal Ancestors.

The texts are fortunately explicit regarding the function which the statues fulfil: "The statues of the kings of Upper and Lower Egypt, which go before this venerable god, Min-Kamutef, give life to King Ramses III."[2] Appropriately each statue carries the sign of life ♀ in its hand. Now "maintenance of life" or "giving life" is the usual term applied to that peculiar influence exercised by the gods over the king and by the king over his subjects. The reliefs and the texts can therefore be fully understood.

But the worship of the ancestors did not originally take the form which has just been described. The use of statues to represent individual predecessors is not observed before the New Kingdom. Yet the worship of the ancestors is as old as the monarchy, and it was certainly not inspired by any historical point of view such as the named statues of individual kings might suggest.[3]

The oldest form of worship of the Royal Ancestors, and a form which was never superseded, though it was elaborated in the manner we have seen, consisted in the worship of a collectivity. No single ruler was distinguished in the group; each king, at his death, became part of it. And it is curious to observe how in later times, when Egypt, perhaps under the influence of Asia, admitted the validity of a historical point of view, this collectivity of ancestors entered the historical records. The Ptolemaic historian Manetho mentions that the First Dynasty was preceded by a "manium et semideorum regnum"; and the Turin Papyrus, which is not far removed from Ramses II and III in time, gives as an equivalent of these spirits and demigods the "transfigured spirits (*akhu*), followers of Horus."

The verb *šmš*, "to follow," is ambiguous. The standards are described as "following" the king at the Sed festival, and this translation is evidently correct. The verb may also, however, mean "to worship," a semantic variation we have no difficulty in understanding.

We have seen that the god Horus was widely worshiped throughout Egypt—that Scorpion and then Menes and all the kings of the First Dynasty identify themselves with Horus. And even on the slate palettes of the late predynastic period the Horus standards play a prominent part (Figs. 27 and 28). All Egyptian kings could be called "Followers of Horus" in the sense that they were worshipers of his; but the designation was reserved for rulers of the distant past. The texts, in fact, leave no doubt that the term referred to earlier kings. An inscription of a King Ranofer, just before the Middle Kingdom, contains the phrase "in the time of your (fore)fathers, the kings, Followers of Horus."[4] Texts of Tuthmosis I and Tuthmosis III refer to them in the same manner.[5] The first mentions fame the like of which was not "seen in the annals of the ancestors since the Followers of Horus"; the other states that, in rebuilding a temple, an old plan was used and proceeds: "The great plan was found in Denderah in old delineations written upon leather of animal skin of the time of the Followers of Horus."

From these quotations it appears that "Followers of Horus" is a vague designation for the kings of a distant past. Hence the Turin Papyrus places them before the first historical king, Menes. It is also likely that the predynastic or mythical rulers whose names are preserved at the beginning of the annals of the Palermo Stone were reckoned to be "Followers of Horus." But it would seem unwise to treat the term as primarily of a historical nature.[6] For each king became at death one of the corporation of "transfigured spirits."* Each dead king became Osiris; but, with the passage of time, he lost even that restricted individuality and, as one of the "Followers of Horus"—one of the "Souls" of Pe or of Nekhen†—he merged with that nebulous spiritual force which had supported the living ruler and descendant on the throne of Horus since time immemorial.

B. THE STANDARDS

The earliest royal monuments do not name the Followers of Horus explicitly,[7] but they display a group of objects which are intimately related to the Royal Ancestors—the standards which we have seen already at the Sed festival. We noticed there that among them one, the wolf standard of Upwaut 🐺, stood out from the others, since it alone accompanied the king at the "dedication-of-the-field" ceremony. Now it is quite significant that in the pyramid texts the words "Followers of Horus" are determined precisely with this Upwaut standard and the bow and throwing stick which we met as emblems related to the god in the procession of the Herdsman of Nekhen.[8]

This standard belongs to a large class of objects consisting of some sacred symbol on a bracket at the top of a pole from which streamers hang down. These are obviously symbols of gods, but we must allow the word "symbol" more weight than we would normally ascribe to it. The symbols, by that "mystic participation" which we have discussed in the Preface, partake of the power which they represent. They are true fetishes, replete with power. This is shown by the reference in the texts of Neuserre and of the Min festival of Ramses II, where the standards are "the gods who (habitually) follow the god." It is clear that this description can refer only to the standards themselves, not to the gods they represent.[9]

We need not, then, be astonished that the predynastic monuments show standards as the actual agents of the enemies' discomfiture (Figs. 27–28). But, with the emergence of kingship, the king alone appears to act on behalf of the community; and on the maceheads and palettes of Scorpion and Narmer certain standards are shown, not as actors, but as supporters of the king (Fig. 3), exactly as they appear in the festivals of historic times. The obverse of the Narmer palette, however, shows a revealing transitional form. The main figure is, indeed, the king, who destroys the chief of the enemy. But a curious pictographic group above

* See below, p. 114.   † See below, pp. 115 and 137 ff.

the main design repeats this story by showing the symbol of Horus, active by means of a human hand which holds the "Chief of the Delta Marshes" captive.

The belief that objects can be charged with power has never left the Egyptians. A good example referring to our standards and dating from the last part of the second millennium B.C. is shown in Figure 29. There the standards are carried by animated symbols of Life or Permanence or Welfare. In between are written phrases expressing the relationship between king and standard. They are of a general nature, such as "He gives an eternity of peaceful years to King Men-maat-re (Seti I)"; and the horizontal legend above the panel contains similar beneficial spells "spoken by the gods upon their standards."

The groups of standards which are shown accompanying the king at his Sed festival, or the Feast of Min, or the Circuit of the (White) Walls on the occasion of the coronation, differ widely in composition;[10] and there is a noticeable tendency in later times to multiply protection and support for the king by accumulating a large number of divine symbols. On the late predynastic and early dynastic monuments we find the falcon, a double falcon-standard, the Seth animal, the ibis, the wolf, the Royal Placenta, and the enigmatical symbol of the god Min of Koptos. Of these, four seem to be very closely related to the king: the falcon, the ibis, the wolf, and the Royal Placenta. These, in fact, should truly count as the standards of kingship, since they appear as such from the very beginning of the First Dynasty and are shown, also, in later times, in the closest possible proximity to the king. In the cases of the placenta or twin and of the falcon, that is explicable. As to the ibis standard, we know that Thoth, though in the shape of a baboon, received special honors from the earliest kings.[11]

The god Upwaut was also closely related to the king, as we have seen, in the Sed festival (p. 87) and in the Memphite Theology (p. 26). In a "sacred conversation" of Section II of the latter, Geb calls Horus "that heir, the son of my son, the Upper Egyptian wolf, the opener-of-the-body, Upwaut ('the Opener-of-the-Ways')." And he adds, "This is a son born on the birthday of Upwaut." Upwaut is also identified with the dead king in certain pyramid texts[12] and stands for Horus in the Great Procession at Abydos (p. 204).

The wolf has even a relation to the sky, where Horus belongs, as we have seen: Upwaut is Lord of the *shedshed*, a protuberance shown in front of him upon his standard ♴, and the king is said to go to heaven upon this *shedshed*. The relation between Upwaut and Horus as gods is nowhere made explicit, but it is conceivable that Upwaut is an objectivation of some aspect of the divine king, possibly as eldest son. In any case, he belongs together with the falcon at Nekhen, as the procession of the Herdsman of Nekhen and the appearance of the Souls of Nekhen prove.

The evidence which we possess concerning Upwaut definitely disproves a popular theory that we can treat the standards and similar symbols as ensigns of districts. They are that, too; but it is an unwarranted assumption that each stands for a separate area. Nekhen, for instance, had at least two, the falcon and the wolf. And if the combination of standards habitually connected with the king had been no more than an ephemeral configuration of political power—a coalition of certain areas which once had assisted Menes—their continued use would be quite inexplicable.[13] A mechanical reference to the conservatism of the Egyptians here, as elsewhere, hides an inability to discover why certain usages continued to appeal to them while others were discontinued. If the four standards which in later times accompanied the king on festive occasions were symbols used by the house from which Menes derived, it would be understandable that they counted as the standards of kingship. This would also explain their close association with "the transfigured spirits, the Followers of Horus" in the inscriptions.

C. THE SOULS OF PE AND NEKHEN

We have seen that the outstanding characteristic of the monarchy as founded by Menes was its dualism. The ancestors were also involved in this scheme. While still called "Followers of Horus," they were also referred to as "the Souls of Nekhen" and "the Souls of Pe." Nekhen was the Upper Egyptian center of Horus worship and belonged to the original domain of the House of Menes. In the Horus temple magnificent gifts, dating from predynastic times, from Scorpion, Narmer-Menes, and so down to the Sixth Dynasty, have been found. Later this sanctuary was completely overshadowed by that of Edfu. The other city, Pe in the western Delta, was an important center that furnished many of the Lower Egyptian parallels to Upper Egyptian usages which Menes needed for the symmetrical construction of his dual monarchy. It has been maintained that Pe, too, was an ancient center of Horus worship; and while that is quite possible, especially as Horus seems to have been one of the gods recognized universally by the early Egyptians, there is no certain evidence that it was so: the arguments consist of inferences

drawn from late evidence, especially from the Edfu texts.* And it is
practically impossible to penetrate into the conditions of the period preceding Menes, just because the dualistic form which he introduced took
hold so thoroughly of every feature of kingship and state. Even the view
that Pe was a Horus center would not explain why "Souls of Pe," late
kings of a Delta state, should appear as ancestral spirits of a line deriving from the south and thus, one would expect, counting only the
"Souls of Nekhen" as its forefathers. It is obvious that the two groups
which form the "Followers of Horus" are artificially combined—that
they are part of that great stylization of political forms which made
Menes a king of Upper and of Lower Egypt and which consequently
required that he proclaim for himself a dual ancestry.

That ancestors were worshiped as "souls" in many Egyptian cities
seems likely enough. It is merely because they became the ancestors of
the Pharaohs that those of Pe and Nekhen became important in historical times.[14] But there are also "Souls of Heliopolis."[15] This term, however, may have been no more than a new collective name for the Souls of
Nekhen and Pe. That assumption would explain that Upwaut, closely
connected with the Souls of Nekhen,† is described as "Commanding
the Souls of Heliopolis"[16] and Wadjet, the goddess of Pe, as "Chief of
the Souls of Heliopolis."[17] It would furthermore explain that these souls
are called "Lords of the Dual Shrines."[18] The "Souls of Heliopolis" are
also said to assist in the king's ascent to heaven,[19] a function commonly
performed by the Souls of Nekhen and Pe; and an Abydos relief depicting the ritual equivalent of this function—the lifting-up of the king in
his palanquin—shows the Souls of Pe and Nekhen in the act, while the
text calls them the "Souls of Heliopolis."[20] All this evidence makes a
strong case for the identification of the "Souls of Heliopolis" with the
two older groups. There is also a piece of negative evidence to be considered. In vignettes of New Kingdom papyri picturing the course of
the sun (p. 159 and Fig. 37), it is adored at its rising by the Souls of Pe
and the Souls of Nekhen. There is no mention at all of the Souls of
Heliopolis; and if they were an independent group of royal ancestors,
one would expect them here if anywhere.[21]

On the monuments the "Souls of Pe" and the "Souls of Nekhen" are
clearly distinguished. The first appear as falcon-headed, the latter as
wolf-headed, men (Figs. 31 and 37). Whether or not Pe was the ancient
center of a Horus cult, falcon-headed "Souls" are appropriate for
"Followers of Horus" and ancestors of a Horus king. The wolf-headed

Souls of Nekhen belong to a town which worshiped the falcon Horus and was the religious center of the realm of the Horus king Menes and his predecessors in Upper Egypt. But this does not exclude the possibility that Upwaut was worshiped there, too. The wolf standard of Upwautwas, in fact, carried by the Servant of the Souls of Nekhen at the Sed festival (p. 83 and Fig. 26), and in the pyramid texts we find further proof of the close connection, of whatever nature it may have been, between Horus and Upwaut: Horus of Nekhen gave to the dead king "his transfigured spirits (akhu), the wolves," to serve him.[22] A late version of the same association comes from Edfu, where the Souls of Nekhen are shown carrying the god Horus, just as they carry the king at certain festivals. The text reads: "The Souls of Nekhen who introduce Horus as his heart desires, the wolf-bodies which carry the falcon."[23] Hence the outward appearance of the Souls of Nekhen need not astonish us.

We have not yet quoted evidence that the "Souls" were really the ancestral spirits of the dynasty, but their curious appearance in art allows us to do so. The Souls of Nekhen are proved to belong to the collectivity of royal ancestors called the Followers of Horus by the following epithets of a priest from Siut: "He who decked out the Souls of Nekhen, who clothed the bodies of the wolves, the gods, the Followers of Horus."[24] And Osiris, the mythological form assumed by each dead king, is one of the Souls of Nekhen, since he is described: "Adorned as a god, thy face like a wolf, Osiris!"[25] Hence we know that each king in turn joined the Souls of Pe and Nekhen at death.*

D. THE DUAL SHRINES

The Dual Shrines formed the sanctuary in which probably the standards, and certainly the images or fetishes, of the Royal Ancestors were kept. Their Egyptian name is a dualis, *iterty*; the pair consists of a Lower and an Upper Egyptian shrine, called the *per-nezer* 𓉐 and the *per-ur* 𓉥, respectively.† Figure 30 shows that both were constructed of reeds and matting, the primordial materials for building in the Nile Valley as well as in Mesopotamia. This is proof of their great antiquity. A similar structure is shown on the Hunters' Palette, which belongs to the end of the predynastic period.[26] The Lower Egyptian reed hut is a simple structure with poles at the corners and a curved roof. The Upper Egyptian hut is more elaborate; it has long eaves in front and two tall masts and is protected by a wooden palisade. The Dual Shrines in his-

* See below, pp. 114–15, 138.   † See below, n. 33.

torical times seem to have received the added protection of two upright stelae bearing the effigy of a snake and referred to as the Senut.[27]

Evidence that the objects sacred to the ancestral spirits were kept in the Dual Shrines is conclusive. In the Min procession the statues of the ancestors are called "the dead kings of Upper and Lower Egypt from the Dual Shrines." At Deir el Bahri the "Souls" are called "the gods of the Dual Shrines."[28] In the concluding rites of the Sed festival, when the Sem priest pronounces the royal offering at the Dual Shrines, the attending "prophets" invoke the ancestral spirits: "May the Souls of Nekhen give life and power." This obviously implies that the Souls are in these shrines.

Since the Dual Shrines were built of light and ubiquitous materials, they could be easily taken down and rebuilt wherever they were required—be it for the Sed festival, for the coronation at Memphis, or, perhaps, even for the Min festival in Thebes.* It is possible that their permanent location in historical times was in Heliopolis, since their occupants, the Souls of Nekhen and the Souls of Pe, were collectively called the Souls of Heliopolis. But originally the Upper Egyptian *itert* belonged to Nekhen, as is shown, not only by the name of its "Souls," but also by the relation in which it stands to the vulture-goddess who was worshiped in Nekheb, a city just across the Nile from Nekhen. Nekhbet (the vulture-goddess) is called "Mistress of the *per-ur*," and "Mistress of the *netjeri shema*," the "Sanctuary of the South." The *per-ur* is written with the same sign as the Upper Egyptian *itert* (Fig. 30), while the "Sanctuary of the South" is not; hence our conclusion that the *per-ur* is the Upper Egyptian *itert*.[29] Wadjet, too, appears in the texts as the mistress of two shrines.[30] On the Palermo Stone her shrines are placed in parallelism with those of Nekhbet.[31] The *per-ur* is parallel with the *per-nezer*, the Lower Egyptian *itert* situated in Pe. Wadjet's own shrine, parallel with the "Sanctuary of the South," was called the *per-nu*; and we suppose that it was situated in the city of Dep, adjoining Pe. But it is difficult to be certain how far back these Lower Egyptian institutions reach. For after the unification of Egypt, Pe was made to balance Nekhen as its Lower Egyptian counterpart in the dual monarchy.† In both cases we have twin cities, consisting of a settlement (Nekheb, Dep) joined to a sacred city (Nekhen, Pe).[32] As we have said already, we cannot penetrate beyond this artificial symmetry imposed on Menes' realm and cannot, therefore, decide whether a Horus cult or a cult of the chief's ancestors existed at Pe in predynastic times.[33]

* See below, pp. 188–90.   † See above, pp. 19–20.

E. THE INFLUENCE OF THE ANCESTRAL SPIRITS

We have seen that at the Feast of Min the function of the ancestral spirits was "to give life to the king." We have a similar text from the Old Kingdom where the Souls of Pe and of Nekhen appear on the doorjambs in the temple of Sahure and address the king as follows: "We give thee all life and happiness, all nourishment, all sacrifices which come out of the Nile, all good things which are in Upper (Lower) Egypt, thou having appeared as King of Upper and Lower Egypt, living unto eternity."[34] In other words, the ghostly power of the royal ancestors is not withdrawn from their descendant. They are still concerned about the well-being of their realm, and their power surrounds and supports the king. A variant of their designation, "Guardians of Pe and of Nekhen,"[35] stresses this aspect.

In the reliefs of the great temples we find the ancestral spirits, together with Wadjet and Nekhbet, the tutelary goddesses of Lower and Upper Egypt, introducing the king to the great god Amon.[36] Or they acclaim the new ruler before Amon at his accession.[37] Immediately after the enthronement the new king is taken into the per-ur and probably crowned there with the White Crown of Upper Egypt, a corresponding ceremony taking place in the per-nezer.[38] We have seen that the final acts of the Sed festival confirm the bond between ancestors and ruler; and the Mystery Play of the Succession ends with the introduction into the Dual Shrines of a group of priests serving the king's deceased predecessor.

Not only the great festivals of royalty, but its very existence, are placed under the tutelage of the ancestors. The Souls of Pe and Nekhen are shown in jubilation beside the couch on which the queen-mother gives birth to Hatshepsut.[39] They are also in evidence at Pharaoh's death, for the text which we have just quoted as spoken to Sahure is engraved upon the jambs of the "False Door" of the royal tomb, the niche which is the most sacred spot in the funerary chapel, where the world of man impinges upon the Hereafter. There the spirits welcome the king in their midst, and they are commonly believed to prepare his ascent to heaven. The Egyptian, in his concrete way, calls this "the making of a ladder." Or he conceives the Souls of Pe and Nekhen as lifting the king up. It is for this reason that they are shown carrying him in his litter in many of the reliefs depicting festivals.[40] This "making of a ladder" is described in a pyramid text which exemplifies a typically Egyptian systematization of images and concepts. As it frequently happens, the king's ascent is sanctioned by an agreement between Atum, the sun-god in heaven, and Geb, the earth-god, who has received and holds the body. Furthermore, our text co-ordinates the Souls of Pe, because they are falcon-headed, with the sky, and the wolf-headed Souls of Nekhen with the earth. This is a typical indulgence in play with pairs of opposites: the given contrast—Geb and Atum, earth (where the body is buried) and sky (where the spirit goes)—brings about the other pair of contrasts. The text also illustrates the concreteness with which the royal power is conceived. The king's magical power emanates in front of him, his glory is over him like the halo of a saint; terror goes on either side—for one dares to glance at the king only stealthily.[41]

> "How lovely to see, how pleasing to observe," so say the gods, "how this god goes forth to Heaven, how Unas goes to Heaven!
> His glory is above him; his terror is on either side; his magic goes in front of him."
> Geb has arranged for him the type of thing which had been done to him (Geb) himself (namely that)
> To him (Unas) come the gods, the Souls of Pe, and the gods, the Souls of Nekhen—the gods belonging to heaven and the gods belonging to earth.
> They make for thee, O Unas, supports of their arms; and thou mountest to heaven and climbest upon it in its name of "ladder."
>
> "Let heaven be given to him! Let earth be given to him!" Thus Atum has said.
> It was Geb who had spoken about it (with Atum) [Pyr. 476–80].

The ancestral spirits, besides helping the king in his ascent, or performing the ritual equivalent of carrying him in his litter, are usually depicted in the peculiar attitude of the hieroglyph 𓀠 for *hnw*, "to jubilate." It renders the pose of a singer, or rather of a man who beats his chest to give "a rippling, vibrating effect to the falsetto voice," a sound loved by Orientals even in our own day.[42] The presence of the ancestral spirits in this attitude—in the birth and coronation scenes of Hatshepsut and at the sunrise—demonstrates their enthusiastic approval and gives, therefore, assurance of their protection. It is the motif of protection, also, which explains their presence at the sides of the sacred barks of the gods, such as Amon.[43] They also appear at the side of the reliquary of Osiris at Abydos (Fig. 31); but here their presence is especially appropriate, for Osiris was the dead king, each dead king—the receding wraith of the recently powerful monarch joining the ancestral shades.

PART III. THE PASSING OF KINGSHIP

CHAPTER 8

THE ROYAL SUCCESSION

SINCE the Egyptians considered society under its monarch part of a divinely ordered universe, the death of a king assumed, perforce, the character of a crisis with every chance of disaster. Chaos threatened, and that, perhaps, not first and foremost on the human plane. For death is not, to most peoples, a "natural" phenomenon in the modern sense but a victory of hostile powers. The king's death showed that the powers of evil had temporarily gained the upper hand, even though the Egyptians reveal a tendency to dissimulate this by euphemistic language. The historical event, the death of a given king, was, of course, translated into a perennial mythological form: Seth had murdered Osiris.

The danger of chaos also existed in the political sphere, even though the nature of kingship in Egypt excluded the rise of pretenders that marked almost every interregnum in the Assyrian and Roman Empires. Those who were of the blood royal could assert their claims to the throne, though normally the eldest son was expected to succeed.[1] Tuthmosis III reports how he was chosen as the next ruler by an unsolicited oracle of Amon.[2] But the gods were not always so obliging, and there are indications that even in the early Fourth Dynasty princes contended among themselves. Then chaos engulfed the state.

The Egyptians had evolved a scheme which mitigated the risks of the succession and had the further advantage of conforming to the mythological pattern of "Horus appearing in the arms of his father Osiris." This scheme consisted in appointing the heir-apparent coregent with his father. The transition at the death of the old king would then, it was hoped, be entirely smooth:

> The god entered his horizon; King Amenemhet withdrew to heaven.
> He united himself with the sun disk, and the divine body coalesced with
> its sire.[3]

The coregent remained to rule alone.[4]

Almost all kings of the Middle Kingdom, and many of the New

101

Kingdom, came to the throne as coregents. Hatshepsut used the scheme of coregency as a pious fiction in her reliefs: her father, who died before her accession,[5] is shown presenting his daughter to the people as "King."

On the other hand, we know that even the practice of coregency did not prevent political unrest from disturbing the country at the old king's death. The same text, which we have quoted and which describes the peaceful retirement to heaven of King Amenemhet I, continues to tell how its hero, Sinuhe, was so frightened when he overheard the news that he fled in panic from the camp of the crown prince—the coregent—with whom he was on campaign; the crown prince hurried back to the residence without allowing his army to be informed and secured the succession as Senusert I. Another text, entitled "Instructions which King Amenemhet I gave when he spoke in a dream-revelation to his son," has been recognized as "a political pamphlet, a literary composition making propaganda for Senusert and his cause," issued after Amenemhet had been murdered during his son's absence and probably by his own chamberlains.[6]

The succession to the throne involved two stages which are not always properly distinguished. We may call them "accession" and "coronation." The coronation sealed the transfer of power to the new king; and only when this final act had been completed were the dangers of the interregnum definitely overcome. But the coronation could not take place at any time that might seem convenient. It had to wait for some new beginning in the progress of nature. For kingship, not being a merely political institution, had to conform with the cosmic events no less than with the vicissitudes of the community. Hence the coronation was made to coincide with one of the renewals of nature, in early summer and autumn. At Medinet Habu, for instance, we find one date for the accession and another for the coronation of Ramses III.[7]

In the meantime government was taken over as soon as possible by the new king. This step we call the accession. It took place at sunrise so that there might be the propitious consonance between the beginning of the new reign and the start of the new day under the rulership of Re, the father and prototype of kings. The accession of Amenhotep II is described as follows:

> King Tuthmosis III went up to heaven;
> He was united with the sun disk;
> The body of the god joined him who had made him.

When the next morning dawned
The sun disk shone forth,
The sky became bright,
King Amenhotep II was installed on the throne of his father.[8]

The three events which took place at dawn were closely related and not merely parallel or similar as we would say; the spreading light, mentioned between sunrise and accession, was part of both.

The titulary which the king assumed was drawn up in "the House of Life," a place of learned discussion and composition where religious books were compiled, interpretations given, and the program of festivals arranged.[9] The new titulary was made known by rescript to the officials throughout the land, for the oath was administered by the "life" of the king who had to be named.[10] It also seems likely that during this time the new king traveled through the land, visiting the shrines of the main gods and performing the Mystery Play of the Succession at certain towns (chap. 11). The body of the late king was meanwhile prepared for burial.

Then the moment arrived when the definitive accession to power was possible. It might be New Year's Day or some other decisive new beginning in nature's cycle. For the solar year is not a primitive concept; and within it several "New Year's Days" are possible.[11] Each significant new start, the revival of vegetation, the equinoxes or the solstices of the sun, or, in Egypt, the rise or abatement of the Nile's inundation—in short, every recurring renewal of life in nature can be counted as the beginning of a new cycle inviting man, too, to new enterprise. The vulnerability of the primitives, exposed to unpredictable natural forces, invested the periodicity of nature with a particular significance. Involuntarily, perhaps, primitive man pursues his aims in conjunction with those reliably recurring events. The harmony between nature and man thus established is felt as a powerful support of his endeavor and, perhaps, as the very condition of success.

The Egyptian calendar* started with the first day of the first month of the Season of Inundation (1 Thoth), a day originally coinciding with the beginning of the rise of the Nile. But four months later there was another new beginning: the inundation ended, the Nile returned to its bed, and the new crops were sown. The first day of the first month of the "Season of Coming Forth" (1 Tybi) was consequently celebrated as a *rite de passage* appropriate to a new beginning, although it was not the

* See above, chap. 6, n. 3.

calendrical New Year's Day. This "New Year's Day" in autumn was presided over by a snake-demon called Nehebkau, a name which can be translated as "Bestower of Dignities"[12] or as "Uniter of the Ka's"[13] (of Horus and Osiris); and we have, in both cases, an allusion to the definitive assumption of power by the new king. In the pyramid texts, moreover, we find that Nehebkau receives the newly arrived dead king among the gods or prepares him a meal or that the new arrival is announced to him and to Re.[14] This ceremony may be a heavenly counterpart of Nehebkau's function at the late king's coronation, or it may be part of his duties at the coronation of the late king's successor; for the Interment of Osiris[15] was on the eve of the coronation of a new king, on the last day of the month of Khoiak. In other words, the late king was interred (and was announced to the gods as a new arrival in the Hereafter) just before the new king was crowned.*

The festivities lasted at least five days, starting with the Feast of Sokaris on Khoiak 26 and ending on Tybi 1; and it has been suggested with good reason that the most important ceremonies repeated the celebrations with which Menes had established his sovereignty over the Two Lands. The inclusion, on Khoiak 26, of a ceremony called "Circuit of the (White) Walls" certainly points in that direction. At the moment we want merely to stress that within the year there were at least two periods during which it was fitting that a king should be crowned to reestablish the harmony between nature and society which had been shattered by the death of the previous ruler. Hence it is said of Tuthmosis I, when he indicates the date for the coronation of Hatshepsut: "He knew that a coronation on New Year's Day was good as the beginning of peaceful years."

* See below, pp. 178-79, 193-94.

CHAPTER 9

THE CORONATION

THE actual procedure of the coronation can be reconstructed in its main features from three sources: temple reliefs of the New Kingdom; pyramid texts; and the Mystery Play of the Succession, which we shall treat separately in chapter 11. In Hatshepsut's temple at Deir el Bahri the birth scenes are followed by some which refer to her accession.[1] However, these show us not the ritual procedure but rather the ideal significance of the event, serving, as do their fellows, to proclaim the legitimacy and the divine sanction of that theological monstrosity—a woman on the throne of Horus.

The series starts with two scenes concerned with Hatshepsut's presentation to the gods. First Amon and Harakhte purify her; then Amon, holding a young prince (*sic!*) on his knee, confronts the assembly of the gods. These acknowledge her as Amon's daughter and wish her well.* Next the queen is shown traveling with her father through the land, visiting various temples. On this journey, too, the gods acknowledge her.

(Each) one of the gods led another; they went around her every day and said, "Welcome, welcome, O daughter (of Amon). Behold thy law and order in the land. Thou arrangest it; thou puttest to rights what is faulty in it. . . . . We acknowledge the descendant (literally 'egg') of him who created us. . . . . Thy soul is created in the hearts of thy people (so that they say): 'She is (the) Kamutef's daughter whom the gods love.'"

On the Kamutef we shall have to speak later (chap. 14). Note that the order in the land is the king's order, just as the order in the universe is the Creator's order. The trip ends with a visit to Atum in Heliopolis.

After this the crowns are brought, and their names are made known to Hatshepsut. Next the queen is depicted crowned and in royal attire before Amon. Here, in the world of the gods, a scene is enacted which finds its precise equivalent upon earth during the Sed festival when the crown prince pays homage to the king. The prince is received by a priest, Inmutef, who stands before the throne, as the Sem priest does in

* See above, p. 77.

the Old Kingdom, acting for the king throughout the jubilee. In the reliefs Hatshepsut stands before the throne of Amon, received by an Inmutef priest who says: "Thou hast appeared on the throne of Horus. Thou leadest all the living. Thou art joyful, living with thy Ka eternally like Re." The ancestral spirits acclaim the queen here, while Seshat and Thoth, the divine scribes, take note. Thoth says: "I establish for thee then thy Crowns of [Re], and thou livest etern[ally on the throne of Horus like Re]."[2] This sequence of reliefs reflects the course of events upon a supernatural level. The brief account of Tuthmosis III's accession also separates his confrontation with the gods and the description of his effective authority.[3] And the first occurs before the fixing of the titulary and immediately after the god gives the oracle that the prince shall be king; it would normally coincide with the accession. If we also take the presentation to the gods to signify Hatshepsut's accession, her visits to the shrines of the land may be viewed as a ceremony which normally took place between the accession and the coronation; and the final scenes obviously represent the coronation itself.

The reliefs now continue to depict the equivalent in the world of men of these transcendent events, though even then they do not present a picture of actuality. In the first place, we find the fiction of coregency introduced.* Tuthmosis I has Hatshepsut placed before him upon his throne, and, putting his hands on her shoulders, he presents her to "the nobles of the king; the notables; the friends; the courtiers of the residence and the chiefs of the people." The titulary is proclaimed, and there is general jubilation. This procedure corresponds, of course, to the accession. Preparations are now made for the coronation, which will take place on the next New Year's Day; we have already discussed the significance of that choice.

The coronation is then mentioned in a curious way, not as part of the narrative, but in the very ancient form shown even on ivory labels of the First Dynasty, in which events of importance are entered in the annals of the realm. The full titulary of the queen, next the date, and, finally, the two ceremonies which mark the coronation of each king after Menes are given: "First month of the Inundation, New Year, the beginning of peaceful years, (Day) of the Coronation of the King of Upper and Lower Egypt. Union of the Two Lands. Circuit of the Walls. Festival of the Diadem."

The reliefs of Deir el Bahri devote much space to various purifications which punctuate the rites and less than we should wish to the de-

* See above, pp. 101–2 and chap. 8, n. 5.

tails of the ceremony. We see, however, that the queen is brought to the Dual Shrines, first to the Upper and then to the Lower Egyptian one, by the Inmutef and Horus of Edfu, respectively. The crowns are put upon her head by Horus and Seth, an act symbolizing that the country is truly pacified by her accession to power.

The features of the coronation represented by the reliefs are those which the ancients considered most significant; they do not allow us to visualize the procedure. We gain, however, a little more information from the pyramid texts, which suggest that the crowns were actually placed upon the king's head in the Dual Shrines. Wadjet, the cobra of Lower Egypt, and Nekhbet, the vulture of Upper Egypt, were the tutelary goddesses of those shrines and were, moreover, immanent in the Red and White crowns. The crowns, then, were objects charged with power and were, in fact, not always distinguished from the goddesses themselves, as is shown by a collection of hymns addressed to the crowns.[4] It seems that, at the coronation, the crowns were placed in the Dual Shrines and were there approached by the king. The relevant section of the pyramid texts (spells 220–22) refers to the coronation with the crown of Lower Egypt only. It opens with a hymn to this crown as a goddess. The doors of its shrine were opened, and epithets were recited; and one phrase spoken by the king indicates that the coronation, his assumption of royalty, is like a rebirth of kingly power and, at the same time, a rebirth of the goddess ("when thou art new and young"). The goddess is simply the personification of the power of royalty, "the great magician," and hence is immanent in the crown.

> The doors of the Horizon[5] are opened; their bolts are slipped.
> He comes to thee, O Red Crown;[6] he comes to thee, O Fiery One.[7]
> He comes to thee, O Great One; he comes to thee, O Magician.
> He has purified himself for thee. . . . .
> Mayest thou be satisfied with him.
> Mayest thou be satisfied with his purification.
> Mayest thou be satisfied with the words he will say to thee:
> "How beautiful is thy face, when thou art new and young."
> A god has borne thee, the father of the gods;
> He (the king) comes to thee, O Magician.
> It is Horus who has fought to protect his Eye, O Magician [Pyr. 194–95].[8]

Next comes a litany in which the king addresses the crown and which evidently aims at gaining for him the power residing in the crown. A typically Egyptian play of ideas, considered efficacious for the establishment of relations between them, appears at the end of the king's recitation. In the last line of the preceding quotation the crown is called the

"Eye of Horus." We shall discuss this important concept below.* Note, however, that the king refers back to it at the end of the litany which we are going to quote and which forms the continuation of the coronation ritual. Since the goddess of the crown is the Eye of Horus, she can be said to have come forth from the king, Horus. As a goddess she is, however, the king's mother.† Hence the king states that he has come forth from her. And it is even possible that this relationship—potentially existing with each goddess—is here felt to be pregnant with meaning; just as Isis the throne "made" the king‡ and was therefore his mother, so the crown "makes" a king-to-be a king. The king's recitation reads as follows:

> O Red Crown, O Inu, O Great One,
> O Magician, O Fiery Snake!
> Let there be terror of me like the terror of thee.
> Let there be fear of me like the fear of thee.
> Let there be awe of me like the awe of thee.
> Let there be love of me like the love of thee.
> Let me rule, a leader of the living.
> Let me be powerful, a leader of spirits.
> Let my blade be firm against my enemies.
>
> O Inu, thou has come forth from me;
> And I have come forth from thee.

It seems likely that during or at the end of the king's address the crown was placed upon his head, for the text is followed immediately by a hymn addressed to the newly crowned king.

> The Great One has borne thee;
> The Exalted One has adorned thee;
> For thou art Horus who hast fought
> For the protection of thine Eye.

The hymn which follows represents a new section of the ceremonies. It establishes the new king's relationship with the sun-god and creator Atum. He does not appear as the legitimate heir—the formula of his relationship with Osiris—but as a son who is a distant successor and patterns his rule on that of his prototype. Hence he is made to "stand" high over the land, as Atum did on the Primeval Hill when he assumed kingship over the world he was creating.§ There is a distinct allusion to creation in the way the land is described. At the same time he is, as it were, presented to the sun-god ("that Re may see thee"); and the text ends with a prayer on behalf of the new king.

* Pp. 126–27, 131.   † See above, pp. 42–43.   ‡ See above, p. 43.   § See below, pp. 152–53.

Stand (as king) over it, over this land which has
    come forth from Atum,
The spittle which has come forth from the beetle.[9]
Be (king) over it; be high over it,
That thy father may see thee,
That Re may see thee.
He comes to thee, O father of his;
He comes to thee, O Re!
    (Seven times repeated with other epithets.)
Let him grasp the Heavens
And receive the Horizon;
Let him dominate the Nine Bows
And equip (with offerings) the Ennead.
Give the Crook into his hand
So that the head of Lower and Upper Egypt
    shall be bowed [Pyr. 196–203].

It seems that at the end the crook was given into the king's hand. Here, then, we have a sample of the actual procedure during one part of the coronation. Its purpose was to transfer power from certain sacred objects to the king. A relationship was established between the monarch and the object which was the repository of the force of royalty. It is significant that the texts assume the character of an incantation, the recurring rhythm of which is likely to cast a spell over the performers and can be experienced as a compulsion effecting the transfer. A similar ceremony took place, of course, in the Upper Egyptian Dual Shrine.

The Royal Ancestors, called, as we have seen, the Gods of the Dual Shrines, were no doubt present at the solemnities; and, when the reliefs show the king emerging to begin the Circuit of the Walls, their standards are with him. At this point must have been sung the hymns which we have quoted above* and which express the profound relief of the people that the interregnum is past—that there is again a king—that the state, and also, as we have seen, nature, can be trusted to follow its accustomed and preordained course. The time, which had been "out of joint," had been "set right."

* Pp. 58 and 60.

CHAPTER 10

THE TRANSFIGURATION OF THE KING'S PREDECESSOR

BETWEEN the accession and the coronation—while the new king assumed power, issued his protocol, and visited sanctuaries throughout the land—the body and the funerary temple of his father were prepared for the interment. On the day before the coronation the burial rites were concluded by a celebration of the dead king's resurrection in the Beyond.[1]

The royal funerary ritual was inspired in part by the family relationship which placed upon the new king, as upon every Egyptian, the duty of assisting his father through the crisis of death. More important still was the enactment (and thus the realization) of the mythological pattern of kingship, the succession of Horus to the throne of the murdered Osiris. Hence the funeral of the king's predecessor, or rather his transfiguration produced or furthered by the funerary ritual, formed part of the ceremonies of the succession.

We have seen that the Egyptians recognized a period of suspense between the occurrence of death and the completion of the rites of burial.* During this period "the Ka's rested," and the dead were dependent upon the living for the termination of their inertia. The elaborateness of the funerary ritual, the accumulation of spells and incantations, and the prolonged concentration and effort required of the survivors were commensurate with the resulting achievement, the resurrection of the dead.

In the case of a dead king the usual procedure was complicated by the necessity of acknowledging the specific transfiguration which took place. If the death of the ruler, considered as an individual, called for rites of resuscitation, it indicated at the same time that the late king had become Osiris and would continue to benefit the people and to support his son and successor with all the superhuman power of which he disposed.

In the royal funerary texts these two aspects of the king's death find

* See above, p. 63.

expression. We shall begin by considering the identification with Osiris.* However, it should be realized from the start that the two aspects were not always kept apart. In fact, many spells aim at the resuscitation of the dead king as an individual by an appeal to his divine prerogatives as Osiris. Sometimes the personal aspect prevails to such an extent that the mythological forms become entirely distorted. Thus, one text makes the dead King Teti the successor to Osiris in the Hereafter, perhaps an attempt to bridge in the consciousness of the survivors the distance between the king as remembered and Osiris as whom he must now be viewed.

> Thou art on the throne of Osiris
> As successor to the Chief of the Westerners (Osiris).
> Thou hast assumed his power
> And taken his crown.[9]
> Oh, King Teti, how lovely is this, how great is this
> Which thy father Osiris has done for thee.
> He has ceded his throne to thee
> So that thou commandest those with hidden seats (the dead)
> And guidest the Venerable Ones (the dead) [Pyr. 2021–23].

Epithets given to the dead king derive from the elaboration which the figure of Osiris itself had already undergone in the Old Kingdom when these texts were written in the pyramids. All these aspects originate in the basic fact that Osiris is the dead ruler and are applied in the pyramid texts to the dead king. We shall discuss them in chapter 15 and deal here with only the fundamental conception. The dead King Unas is called "he who is in Nedyt" (Pyr. 260–61), and this amounts to a straightforward identification with Osiris, who, according to the myth, had been murdered by Seth in Nedyt, or "on the banks of Nedyt." Sometimes the ritual used at some phase of the funeral to effect the transfiguration of the dead king is still recognizable. An example is the following pyramid text, which one can imagine to have been recited at the "Neteryt" (Deification), since it presents the dead King Unas to the gods as Osiris. It starts with a litany:

> Atum, this one is thy son, Osiris, whom thou didst cause
>   to survive and live.
> He lives, and so this Unas lives;
> He has not died, and so this Unas has not died;
> He has not disappeared, and so this Unas
>   does not disappear [Pyr. 167].

Similar presentations are made to the other gods of the Ennead, who, as we shall see in chapter 15, represent a formula by which the relation

* See also below, chap. 15.

of kingship to the order of the gods is expressed. Consequently, we find Seth (who is a member of the Ennead) among the gods to whom Unas is presented as Osiris. Then follow Thoth and other gods.

Next the text addresses itself to the goddess Nut:[3]

> Nut, this one is thy son, Osiris,
> Of whom thou didst say, "He has been born to your father."
> Thou hast wiped his mouth [soiled by the earth in which
>   he had been buried];
> His mouth has been opened by his son Horus whom he loves;
> His limbs are counted by the gods [Pyr. 179].

Then the text suddenly addresses Osiris, calling him by a variety of names but retaining the refrain of the litany:[4] "He lives, and so this Unas lives," etc., until the text changes to one offering the funerary sacrifice: "In thy name 'He who is in Dep,' let thy hands be around the meal thy daughter; supply thyself with her." This now becomes the refrain, while the names with which Osiris is addressed follow one another. Yet the old litany is still appended: "He lives, and so this Unas lives." Then the sacrifice is identified as the life-giving gift, the Eye of Horus.*

> What thou hast eaten is an eye; thy body becomes filled with it.
> Thy son Horus separates himself from it for thee so that thou mayest
>   live thereby—

still with the refrain "He lives, and so this Unas lives," until the final identifying phrases to Osiris:

> Thy body is the body of this Unas;
> Thy flesh is the flesh of this Unas;
> Thy bones are the bones of this Unas.
> Thou goest, and so Unas goes;
> Unas goes, and so thou goest [Pyr. 192–93].

Another text establishing the identity of the dead King Pepi with Osiris proceeds differently—not with an incantation, but with a description of the arrival of the dead king among the gods, where several features of the Osiris myth are recognized as appropriate to him and where, finally, the sun-god confirms the identity and also the succession of the king's son to the earthly kingship.

O Pepi, thou has gone away to become a spirit—to become powerful as a god, thou on the throne of Osiris!

. . . .

Those who serve a god are behind thee; those who do homage to a god are before thee.
    They recite: "A god comes! A god comes! Pepi comes (who shall be) on the throne
    of Osiris.
That spirit who is in Nedyt comes, that power in the province of This."

* See below, pp. 126–27 and 131.

Isis speaks to thee; Nephthys bewails thee. The spirits come to thee, bowing down, and kiss the earth before thy feet. . . . .

Thou mountest to thy mother Nut; she takes thy hand and puts thee on the way to the Horizon, to the place where Re is.

The Gates of Heaven are opened for thee; the Doors of the Cool Place are opened for thee. Thou findest Re standing, waiting for thee.

He takes thy hand; he takes thee to the Dual Shrine of Heaven and places thee on the throne of Osiris.

. . . .

Thou standest (as king), O Pepi, supported (avenged), equipped as a god, equipped with the aspect of Osiris, on the throne of Him who commands the Westerners. And thou doest what he was accustomed to do, among the spirits, the Imperishable Stars.

Thy son stands (as king) on thy throne, equipped with thy aspect, and does what thou wert formerly accustomed to do at the head of the living, by order of Re the Great God.

He grows barley; he grows emmer to present it to thee.

. . . .

Thy name which is on earth lives; thy name which is on earth lasts; thou wilt not disappear; thou wilt not be destroyed in all eternity [Pyr. 752–64].

The parallelism between the dead king and his successor is nicely stressed: while the dead king does what he used to do (rule) among the dead, his son does what the dead king used to do on earth. The end of the text shows also how intimately the fate of the dead king and the continued life of the realm he ruled remain connected.

In the preceding text the Dual Shrines* are mentioned as if they were in heaven. Re introduces the dead king there and enthrones him as Osiris, thus projecting into heaven a feature of the earthly funeral. The dead king is brought into the Dual Shrines to join the ancestral spirits. This is particularly clear in the text we are now to quote. It opens with transparent references to the Osiris myth, especially the finding of the dead body by Horus and his allies, here represented by Thoth. Thoth drives off Seth and his partisans. The statement that Horus "arranged" this probably indicates some performance—mock fight or procession— during the funeral rites organized by Pharaoh for his father.

The next theme shows how the dead king, now become Osiris, is established in the Hereafter in the same manner in which his son is established on earth—in the same manner, of course, as he had succeeded his own father. We have seen in the Memphite Theology that Geb

* See above, pp. 95–96.

decides before the assembled Ennead that Horus, as son of Osiris, is entitled to the throne. Exactly in the same manner the dead king, as Osiris, is now given his legitimate place in the Hereafter; and, as a first result, Isis and Nephthys can take care of him.

Next the Royal Ancestors unite themselves with the dead king. This is important because it shows clearly that the king at his death was really made to merge with that body of spirits. That the "gods" really are the ancestral spirits is shown by the puns which are meant to effect the union. The defeat of the enemies is once more mentioned, and then the dead king is established as god by his mother, Nut. A renewed assertion of victory concludes the text. The intimate relationship between the dead king and his successor is introduced again in the statement that the dead king is the Ka of the living successor.

O Osiris-Pepi!
Horus has come to look for thee. He arranged for Thoth to make the partisans of Seth retreat before thee; and (now) he brings them to thee, all together.

He has made fearful the heart of Seth. Thou art older than he. Thou hast come forth before him (from the womb of Nut, mother of Osiris and Seth). Thy qualifications have precedence over his. Geb has examined thy qualifications; he has put thee in thy (rightful) place. Geb has brought thy two sisters, Isis and Nephthys, to thy side.

Horus has arranged for the gods (the ancestral spirits) to unite themselves with thee, to fraternize (*šn*) with thee in thy name of "He of the Senut" and not to reject (*twr*) thee in thy name of "He of the Dual Shrines" (*iterty*).

He has arranged for the gods to give thee justice. Geb has put the sole of his foot on the head of thy enemy who fears thee. Horus has beaten him.

. . . .

Nut has established thee as god because of Seth, in thy name of "god." . . . .

Horus has grasped Seth and put him underneath thee, that he may carry thee and quake under thee in an earthquake; thou art higher than he is in thy name of "He of the Risen Land" (the necropolis of Abydos).

Horus made thee recognize him (Seth)in his innermost being, and he does not escape from thee. He (Horus) has made thee grasp him (Seth) with thy hand, and he does not get away from thee.

O Osiris! Horus has supported (avenged) thee. He has done it for his Ka in thee, so that thou mayest be gracious (*hetep*) in thy name of Kahetep [Pyr. 575–82].

The immediate result of the justification of the king before Geb is that the earth, Geb's realm, does not confine the dead king any longer but allows his active parts (Ba, voice, etc.) to go forth, while remaining the repository of his body. This will make it possible for Re to transfigure the king and make him part of the corporation of ancestral spirits called here, not the Souls, but the Guardians, of Pe and Nekhen. The text on page 116 relates the events on the plane of the gods which correspond with the ritual induction of the dead king among the ancestral spirits in the Dual Shrines on earth. The description of the ritual continues, saying that the earth opens its gates when Anubis, the god of the necropolis, calls the dead king, who (after reference to another transfiguration which we shall omit) passes through the sacred region of Abydos (where the kings of the earliest dynasties were buried) and finds there an entrance to heaven.

> O Earth! Hear what the gods said, what Re will say,
> When he transfigures this King Pepi so that he may receive
> His spirithood before the gods, like Horus the son of Osiris;
> When he gives him his spirithood among the Guardians of Pe
> And ennobles him as a god among the Guardians of Nekhen.
>
> The earth speaks (in reply):
> "The Gates of Akeru[5] are opened for thee;
> The Doors of Geb are opened for thee.
> Thou leavest at the call of Anubis."
>
> . . . .
>
> When thou goest, Horus goes;
> When thou speakest, Seth speaks.[6]
> Thou goest to the Lake;[7]
> Thou approachest the province of This;
> Thou passest through Abydos (and)
> A gate in Heaven opens for thee
> Toward the Horizon.[8]
> The heart of the gods rejoices at thy approach.
> They take thee to Heaven in thy quality of Ba.
> Thou art powerful (*baty*) among them [Pyr. 795–99].

A comparison of the two texts which precede shows, as we indicated, how a ritual act could be envisaged as effective upon two planes.

The next text shows even more clearly how the Egyptians imagined their actions to be dovetailed into the invisible world of the gods. It opens with the successor's call to the dead king to partake of the sacrifices offered to him, so that, thus strengthened, he may face the opened Gates of Heaven. The ancestral spirits approach when they hear the lamentations of Isis and Nephthys bewailing their dead brother. (As we know, these lamentations formed part of the actual funerary rites.) The spirits now take up the clamor and the dance; and, at this point, the funerary proceedings pass from the earthly setting, the tomb, to the plane of the gods. For suddenly the ancestors speak the words of transfiguration, and the dead king awakens unto eternal life.

After this, the earthly celebrants once more address the dead king, calling upon him to arise, since the evil power which caused his death is vanquished and his sister and wife, Isis, has found him (as she did in the myth), so that mourning may cease in the Dual Shrines. Then a final appeal is made to the gods, the ancestral spirits, to accept the late king in their midst as one of their company.

The text opens with words spoken by the dead king's successor:

O my father, lift thyself from thy left side, turn thyself on thy right side, toward this fresh water that I have given thee.
O my father, lift thyself from thy left side, turn thyself on thy right side, toward this warm bread that I have made for thee.
O my father, the Gates of Heaven are open for thee; open for thee are the Doors of the (heavenly) Bows.

A celebrating priest (probably) continues:

The Gods of Pe have sympathy(?);
They come to Osiris upon (hearing) the voices of lamen-
      tation of Isis and Nephthys.
The Souls of Pe dance for thee;
They strike their flesh for thee;
They beat their arms for thee;
They tear their hair for thee.[9]
They say to Osiris:

"Thou art gone;
Thou art come.
Thou art awakened
(After) thou wert asleep.
Thou stayest alive."

Arise and see
Arise and hear
What thy son has done for thee,
What Horus has done for thee.
He beats him who beat thee.
He binds him who bound thee.
He puts him under his eldest daughter
Who lives in Kedem[10]—
Thy eldest sister who gathered thy flesh,
Who took thy hands, who searched for thee,
Who found thee,
Lying on thy side on the banks of Nedyt.

Mourning ceases in the Dual Shrines.
O Gods! Speak to him, bring him to you [Pyr. 1002–9].[11]

Allusions to ritual are found in the pyramid texts, as we have seen before when describing the coronation. We also find clear references to funerary rites when the dead is called upon to turn on his other side and reach for the food and drink that is offered or when his passage through Abydos is mentioned. But we do not possess a description of a royal funeral. Hence we shall continue to consider the theological aspect of the destiny of the king after death.

In the pyramid text which we have quoted on page 115, the dead king found an entrance to heaven at Abydos, the ancient burial place of the royal dead. This suggests a fate beyond his union with the ancestral spirits of the royal house, and it represents, in fact, another aspect of the king's life after death. His incorporation with the Souls of Pe and of Nekhen was a purely impersonal aspect—important for his successor and for the state: as Osiris he became one of the souls of Nekhen (Pyr. 2108a). But this thought was unlikely to satisfy the king when, during his lifetime, he pondered his future fate.[12] The personal aspect of his survival after death did not differ in essentials from the expectations of his subjects; and, though there were a great variety of views about the potentialities of life after death, they could usually be reduced to one single formula. The Egyptian hoped, after the crisis of death, to be reintegrated into the life of nature.

In an almost cloudless land like Egypt the obvious proof of the permanence of the processes of nature is found in the sky. The sun in his daily course and the stars, thought by many primitive peoples as well as by the Egyptians to be the souls or spirits of the dead, suggested immortality in the primitive sense of an endless continuation of life as it is known. And thus the desire was felt, and soon formulated, to join either sun or stars and pass with them through the sky and also through the anti-sky underneath the flat earth, emerging daily and setting daily in an everlasting joyous circuit.

At the end of the Memphite Theology it is said that Osiris, the dead king buried in the royal castle, entered the Hereafter "in step with Him who shines in the Horizon on the path of Re," that is, with the sun, rising over the Light Mountain ◌, which we translate "horizon," as is usually done.

Viewed in this manner, as a problem of individual survival, the dead king's reception by the ancestral spirits is but a station on his road to peace in the Hereafter. This is clearly expressed in the following text in which the Royal Ancestors, the Followers of Horus, purify him and give him further directions:

> Pepi has come that he may purify himself in the Reed Field;
> He descends to the Field of Kenset.[13]

The Followers of Horus purify Pepi;
They bathe him, they dry him.
They recite to him the Spell of the Right Way.
They recite for him the Spell of the Ascent.

Pepi ascends to Heaven.
Pepi embarks on this boat of Re.
Pepi commands for him (Re) those gods who row him.
All the gods are jubilant at the approach of Pepi,
Just as they are jubilant at the approach of Re,
When he emerges at the Eastern side of Heaven
In peace, in peace [Pyr. 920*b*–923].

The same notion is expressed with striking conciseness in the following text, which summarizes, in each successive phrase, one phase of the circuit: the first tells of the burial and the goal to which it leads; the second, of the finality of the transition; the third, of the underground part of the eternal circuit; and the fourth, of the emergence in the sky of the transfigured king:

Unas has been guided on the Roads of the Beetle (sun-god).
Unas rests from life in the West.
The inhabitants of the Netherworld accompany him.
Unas shines renewed in the East [Pyr. 305–6].

Rebirth through the Mother, which we shall study in chapter 14, is often combined with the motif of the circuit, generally that of the sun. But in the following text the king joins the stars, not the sun. Orion, as we shall see, embodies Osiris.

O Unas, thou art that great star, the Companion of Orion,
Which crosses Heaven with Orion
And sails through the Netherworld with Osiris.
Thou risest at the Eastern side of Heaven,
Renewed in thy time, rejuvenated at thy hour.
Nut has borne thee together with Orion;
The year has adorned thee together with Osiris [Pyr. 882–83].

In some cases, but not very often, the descent into the Netherworld is rejected as a hazard.[14] Or the dead king is identified with one of the circumpolar stars which never set: "Thou art that one star which appears at the Eastern side of Heaven and does not give itself up to Horus of the Netherworld" (Pyr. 877). But usually the Netherworld supplies a dangerous though inevitable link between the world of men and eternal life. The burial carries the king to the Netherworld, but the very fact of his being there enables him to join the cosmic circuit:

> Thou goest to the Lake and sailest upstream to the province
> of This.
> Thou passest through Abydos in this thy transfiguration
> which the gods ordered thee to be.
> A ramp is trodden for thee to the Netherworld, to the place
> where Orion is.
> The Bull of Heaven takes thy arm [Pyr. 1716–17].

Here also the old royal necropolis at Abydos counts as the proper place to enter the Hereafter. In later times the dangers which had to be overcome in the Netherworld were elaborated to such an extent that they occupy by far the largest part of the funerary papyri, which became true guides through the perils of the Beyond. But occasionally we find a similar preoccupation in the earlier pyramid texts (e.g., Pyr. 323). One short text suggests that the dead king has regained his freedom by the winning of the "snake game" (played with men on a spiral track on a board);[15] and he now joins in a truly hectic circuit:

> I have come forth from the snake game.
> I have risen as a heat wave and have returned.
> I have gone, O Heaven, O Heaven!
> I have come, O Earth, O Earth!
> I have stepped on the green Ked plant under the feet of Geb (Earth)
> (And) I walk (again) on the Roads of Nut (Heaven) [Pyr. 541].

Many problems and many accusations of inconsistency leveled at the ancients originate in our failure to recognize the dynamic quality which life after death possessed for them. We look in vain for any description of Elysian Fields in the early texts. It is true that the "Field of Rushes" or the "Field of Offerings" is named in the pyramid texts, but the designation is hardly more than a label used when reference to the place where the dead dwell becomes inevitable. The texts never enlarge upon the nature of these "fields"; their location is described in terms which are full of contradictions until we realize that the dead were not thought to inhabit a static Beyond, but to move with the sun and stars, and that the "Field of Offerings" was nothing but a name for their circuit. This, in fact, is clearly indicated by texts like the following:

> (Since he) lives who lives by order of the gods, thou shalt live.
> Thou risest with Orion in the Eastern part of Heaven;
> Thou settest with Orion in the Western part of Heaven;
> The third of you is Sothis, of pure places.
> She it is who will guide you on the beautiful roads
> Which are in Heaven—in the Field of Rushes [Pyr. 821–22].

Rising and setting, with the Dog Star as guide, the dead king moves on the beautiful roads which are in the Field of Rushes.[16] The Field of Rushes is therefore located wherever the dead are imagined to be. It may be the "Field of Kenset"[17] near the waters which the king must cross and which purify him.[18] Or the "Field of Rushes" may be another name for the Primeval Hill,* an island in the midst of those waters and pre-eminently suitable for a resurrection from death.[19] In this case the abode of the dead is, of course, located in the East.

But if the dead were imagined as circumpolar stars, they abode in the North.[20] When the land of the dead was thought of as the aim of the deceased's journey, it was located in the West.[21] In other words, it is futile to expect a given region to be consistently regarded as the abode of the dead, since they participated in the cyclic movement of nature and were not confined to either Heaven or Hades. They were in the Netherworld as well as in the night sky, and by day were in the boat of the sun. They moved in the circuit above and below the flat earth. Moreover, they were able to leave their cosmic setting and to reappear upon earth, taking the tomb as a starting-point and emerging from there as the Ba (p. 64), which retained its connection with the buried body or a statue and thus retained some of its earthly individuality.

The texts which we have quoted refer to the royal dead, and it is the survival of the kings after death with which we are primarily concerned. But the conception of man's future life as dynamic can hardly have been entertained for the kings only, and we find it mentioned in those few instances where early texts in the tombs of commoners refer to the Hereafter. We read then that the dead wish to "walk upon the beautiful roads upon which the Venerated Ones (the dead) wander." In the Sixth Dynasty, when the texts become a little more elaborate, the interment is frankly presented as a first step in joining the circuit: "The Venerated who has united himself with the earth, may he traverse Heaven and mount to the Great God."[22]

Ritual and life in the Hereafter are treated as one unbroken continuity. In these same tombs a boat journey of the dead is described as "Coming from Buto and sailing to the Field of Offerings."[23] In this "Field of Offerings" and in the "beautiful roads" we recognize features of such pyramid texts as the last we quoted. Yet there can be hardly any question of an imitation of royal models before the last part of the Sixth Dynasty. The resemblances derive from the Egyptians' basic

* See below, pp. 151 ff.

view of life after death, which affected their imaginations as regards both king and commoners.[24]

The texts referring to the royal dead are more explicit and often impressive. In the one which we shall now quote the dead king joins the sun-god-creator, Atum, almost as coregent, with the power to settle disputes in the Netherworld. This text, which in the traditional view would count as "solar" in character, starts significantly with the descent into the Netherworld, where the king can join the sun in its circuit. An initial purification was, of course, required. Sunrise appears as the birth of the sun; a midwife[25] takes the child by the head, at the horizon. The sun, continuing to ascend, passes through the "bones" of the god of the air, Shu, who is between earth and sky. The sky is reached when Nut takes the newborn child in her arms, and a second purification takes place at this entrance into a new sphere. Then the motif of the circuit is restated in a résumé in which the more neutral name for the sun, "Re," takes the place of "Atum." The movement is mentioned twice again in connection with Isis and Nephthys, the sisters of Osiris, who take care of him. Finally, the royal birth of the king is recalled, and Atum is invoked and implored to accept his son on the strength of it.[26]

> Thou throwest off thy uncleanness for Atum in Heliopolis, and thou descendest with him.
> Thou judgest the misery of the Netherworld (Naunet, anti-sky) and standest (as king) over the sites of the Primeval Waters (Nun).
> Thou "becomest"[27] with thy father Atum. The misery of the Netherworld slackens for thee.
>
> Thy head is held by the midwife of Heliopolis.
> Thou risest and openest thy way through the bones of Shu.
> The embrace of thy mother Nut receives thee.
> Thou cleanest thyself in the Horizon and throwest off thy uncleanness in the Lakes of Shu.
>
> Thou risest and settest; thou goest down with Re, sinking in the dusk with Nedy.
> Thou risest and settest; thou risest up with Re and ascendest with the Great Reed Float.
> Thou risest and settest; thou goest down with Nephthys, sinking in the dusk with the Evening Boat of the Sun.
> Thou risest and settest; thou risest up with Isis, ascending with the Morning Boat of the Sun.
>
> Thou takest possession of thy body; nobody stands in thy way.
> Thou art born because of Horus (in thee); thou art conceived because of Seth (in thee).

Thou hast purified thyself in the Province of the Falcon,
And hast received purification in the Province of the Integral Ruler,
     from thy father, from Atum.
Thou hast "become,"[27] thou art high, thou hast been transfigured.
Thou art cool in the embrace of thy father, in the embrace of Atum.
Atum, let this Unas ascend to thee; embrace him.
He is thy son, of thy body, throughout eternity [Pyr. 207–12].

The embrace is, again, that mystical act of communion and union which we have met at the end of the Memphite Theology and are now about to study in the Mystery Play of the Succession. But the meaning of the text is unmistakable. The phrase, "Thou risest and settest," repeated soothingly, casts the spell of achievement and reflects the peaceful sharing of the regular tidal movement which pervades nature.

CHAPTER 11

THE MYSTERY PLAY OF THE SUCCESSION

THE extraordinary document which we are now to consider differs from all the texts mentioned hitherto. The Memphite Theology, the story of Hatshepsut's birth and accession, and most of the pyramid texts are concerned with theory, not practice. At most we can suspect certain passages of their arguments to allude to ritual usage.

Not so the text which is now before us. This large roll of papyrus[1] is the actual "script" of a play performed at the accession of Senusert I. There is no doubt, however, that it contains elements antedating the Middle Kingdom by many centuries; the "Spirit-seekers" who play a part in it are known only on monuments of the First Dynasty, and the play, in its present form dating from about 2000 B.C., is probably but one specimen of a performance repeated at the accession of each king.

The text contains two indications as to the phase of the succession during which it was performed. In the first place, the ruler is referred to as "the king who will rule" ⥮⥮⥮. The future tense evidently suggests the time of transition after the death of the king's predecessor but before the coronation at Memphis. Secondly, it seems that the play was performed at several cities throughout the land, for, when the site of the performance is consecrated by a special type of sacrifice, this sacrifice is offered to "the god of the town." There would be no reason to avoid the proper name of this god unless the performance took place at more than one city so that the god receiving the offerings could be indicated only by a generic term. It is also clear that a propitiatory offering to the local god was indicated when the site for the performance was prepared, since the local god was the master of the territory. Now it is likely that Pharaoh traveled to a number of cities in the period of transition.[2] On this assumption we can explain that throughout the performance of the Mystery Play Pharaoh remained on board the royal barge, which served as his quarters during travel.

Actors in the play, besides the king, are the royal princes, officials, priests, and even craftsmen. The action is sometimes of a practical nature, as when the crowns or scepters which are to be used in the ceremony are brought in; but, even then, mythological allusions and parallels are adduced to sustain the supernatural significance of these acts. Actuality is never allowed to stand by itself. Throughout the play we can observe a deliberate attempt to fuse the historical event, the coronation of one particular Pharaoh, with the perennial truth that Horus succeeds Osiris. But the means by which the transcendental import of the performance is stressed occasionally seem childish to us. For the Egyptians, believing in the marvelous power of words, considered puns and word-play efficacious in establishing real relations between the objects involved. We cannot possibly do full justice here to this side of our text and to the innumerable ramifications which it establishes by these primitive means.[3] But we shall sometimes add the transcriptions of Egyptian words to our quotations to show where play on words is involved.

In addition to the actions which are indispensable for the performance, such as the bringing of insignia for the king, there are others which are symbolical or which constitute mythological situations. By the same token the localities in which the scenes are laid change rapidly. This is feasible because they are mythological localities. The medieval mystery plays, with which our text has been compared, show a similar structure. In them, too, the scene was shifted from Paradise to heaven and next, perhaps, to the field where Adam was condemned to labor after the fall. Yet there is a profound difference which must not be overlooked. The medieval mystery play represented the sacred story. But the Mystery Play of the Succession had some virtue or power in itself, though it is extremely hard in our language to render the fluid conceptions which were involved. In a way the coronation of the king in the play was no more than mimed, since it was repeated a number of times and required the definitive ceremony at Memphis to become irrevocable. Yet the play was no mere make-believe or even mere representation. It was necessary for the king to pass through its repeated ceremonies at the various cities traditionally entitled to be thus involved in establishing the religious ties which united the new ruler with his country. The performances were instrumental in establishing these bonds. The king was not properly king unless he had enacted the Play of the Succession at various cities or until he had performed "Union of the Two Lands; Circuit of the Walls; Festival of the Diadem" at Memphis, on one of nature's New Year's Days. To that extent the play was not a "play"; our categories are not congruous with those of the ancients.[4] Though the definitive act of coronation was the culminating point of the five days of solemnities at

Memphis, something changed in the world at each of the prescribed performances which preceded it; and the cumulative effect of the changes was the restoration of the harmony between cosmos and society through the accession of a new king to the throne of Horus.

It is a view alien to our way of thinking that a ceremony should be, not a token act, but an act which changes actuality—which could not be omitted or replaced by another without dire consequences. Perhaps we may approach an understanding of the pre-Greek point of view by reading the simple description of an observer who watched the installation of a new divine king of Bahima (Hamitic) stock in Africa.[5] After stating that there is much dressing and undressing of the king, with many sacred robes and insignia, he proceeds: "The chief is being initiated into the solemn mystery of the divine things; he becomes, in the process, identified with these divine things, that is: with the spirit called Imama, so that, thereafter, the crops, the birth of children and everything upon which the tribesmen depend, comes from the great spirit Imama through the medium of the chief. Therefore the chief, before he comes to power, must conform to all the ceremonies beloved of Imama."

We shall see that an outsider observing the ancient Egyptian Mystery Play of the Succession could have described it in much the same terms. We may add another common feature: both Pharaoh and the Bahima chief are brought into relation with the most important produce of nature, the chief by receiving a goatskin and three sticks of ripe grain.

The Mystery Play of the Succession presents us with an undifferentiated sequence of scenes concerned with "divine things." This absence of internal structure is a primitive feature, as we have noticed already in discussing the Memphite Theology. There is no subdivision, no emphasis, no connection between actions more closely interrelated than others, and no transition. We find a mere addition of scenes which are all equivalent from the point of view of form and through which the action progresses according to a plan and toward an aim which remain for us to discover.

Let us, then, first of all, consider the recognizable units, the separate scenes. There are forty-six of these, all built according to one and the same pattern which comprises four elements:

1. A sentence starting with "It happened that. . . . ." This sentence describes the actual occurrence at the performance.

2. A sentence starting with "This means. . . . ." Here we find an explanation of what the occurrence means in terms of mythology.

3. A sacred conversation: simple words traditionally known to have been uttered by the gods on certain occasions related to the situation.

4. Stage directions or producer's annotations to the script. There may be three or four of these, and they may interrupt the sacred conversations on the papyrus—for instance by bracketing several columns together. This did not matter since they were not to be spoken anyhow. The first of these notes or directions names the sacred person, object, or locality referred to in the scene or in the words of the gods. The second generally names the earthly equivalent of the sacred person or object mentioned in the preceding one. (Thus these notes reverse the procedure of the actual text, for the latter mentions actuality first and next its meaning in the sphere of mythology.) A final note mentions the mythological locality in which the action is supposed to take place.

We shall follow the method we adopted in summarizing the Memphite Theology and render the Mystery Play by combining into parts (in a manner which must be tentative) sets of scenes which seem to us to belong together. In a way the course of the play is obvious. The coronation is the central feature; consequently, the scenes leading up to it must be preparatory and those which follow must be complementary. But we need, of course, to understand much more specifically what the play was meant to convey or to achieve. We have distinguished six successive parts.

Part I (scenes 1–7) is concerned with the preparation of the accessories, such as the royal barge and the barges of the royal princes; and various sacrifices are made.

Part II (scene 8).—Some of the royal insignia, scepters, and a mace are brought out of a hall which is used also in the Sed festival and which bears the enigmatical name "Hall of Eating and Standing" or possibly "Hall of Eating while Standing." Here already a reference to the king's predecessor appears. Words, most of which are lost through damage to the papyrus, are addressed by Thoth to Osiris. One sentence explains the action of the bringing-out of the insignia for the new king as follows: "Horus has grown up and takes possession of his Eye." Horus is the king, but here he is emphatically represented in the light of mythology.

In the myth, Horus, born after Seth had killed Osiris, grew up to avenge his father and defeat Seth. Our play proclaims that at the coronation this change of fortune for the House of Osiris recurs. The king preparing to be crowned is Horus grown to maturity and ready to take charge of the kingdom which is his legitimate inheritance. Whatever harm he may have suffered is undone. In the myth Seth wounded or stole his Eye, but it was recovered; and with it Horus regained his full strength. Hence the Eye became symbolical of all his power and virtue. It is the "Eye of Horus" which enables the son to revive his dead father in the Hereafter (p. 112). And the symbol and seat of royal power, the uraeus on the crown, is called the Eye of Horus. In the present scene of the play Horus is said to have taken possession of his Eye to indicate the fulness of his power.

The god Thoth—represented by a Royal Kinsman who has taken one of the scepters out of the hall or container—speaks with typical Egyptian equivocation so that the words can mean "I have taken the Horus (scepter) out (of it)" or "I have fostered Horus," with a punning addition "so that he may support thee" (Osiris). The last stage direction of this scene says simply "Marching through the mountains"; and one wonders whether the king, now equipped with his insignia, had to make a processional march beyond the town where the performance took place up to the edge of the desert cliffs to establish dominion over the valley and the adjoining desert.

Part III (*scenes 9–18*).—Further preparations of barges, participants, and site are now made. The first scene represents the threshing of barley by driving bulls and male asses over it to trample out the kernels. Bread—the staple food—will be eaten at a later stage of the ceremony. Here its ingredients are won.

But in our text, as in the Memphite Theology, grain is taken as a manifestation of Osiris; and a connection with the preceding scene can be surmised. There Osiris was assured that Horus, equipped with some of the insignia of kingship, would "support" his father. Here Horus (the king) formally forbids the animals to trample the grain which stands for Osiris. They naturally do not heed his order (after all, the grain must be threshed), but Horus at least avenges his father by beating the animals that had trampled the grain. They count now, of course, as partners of the antagonist per se, Seth; and the mythological locality of the scene is therefore Letopolis, where Horus was supposed to have defeated Seth.[6] The text runs:

> It happened that barley was put on the threshing floor.
> It happened that male animals were brought to trample it.
> That means Horus avenging his father. . . . .
>
> Horus speaks to the followers of Seth: "Do not beat this my
>   father."
> (*Stage directions*) Beating Orisis; cutting up the god—barley.
>
> Horus speaks to Osiris: "I have beaten for thee those who have
>   beaten thee."
> (*Stage directions*) The followers of Seth—the bulls. Letopolis.
>
> Horus speaks to Osiris: "His spittle shall not splash thee."
> (*Stage directions*) Seth—the asses. Ascension to heaven.

The last speech of Horus with the stage directions that follow it is not relevant for us at the moment, but it gives a proper impression of the complication of our text, or rather the unbridled chains of associations and conclusions in which religious equations are likely to expand. Since the animals are partisans of Seth, Osiris must be protected. The king protects him by casting a spell protecting the barley underfoot against the animals' impurities which count as the spittle of Seth (mentioned also in other texts).[7] There is word-play between the words for "splash" and "ass" and "Seth" and "spittle," respectively. Osiris' "ascension to heaven" will, in reality, be enacted later in the play; but here it is an auspicious and symbolical interpretation forced upon the simple act of collecting the threshed barley, lifting it up, and carrying it away upon asses. By carrying it away, the asses do again what Seth, in many places in the pyramid texts (e.g., p. 114), is commanded to do; that is, they "carry one greater than themselves." Similar allusions are made elsewhere in our play: a barge carries the royal children (the barge is Seth), or a chapel is whitewashed (the chapel is Seth, the whitewash Osiris!).

We have chosen to discuss this scene in detail because it is an excellent illustration of the elements of which the Mystery Play is composed and shows with great clarity the relationship between the grain and Osiris, a point to which we shall return.

Trees or branches and other materials are now brought on board the barges. Next a libation is made over the heads of sacrificial animals probably thrown into a ditch. This is the *henket* offering, customary when new temples are founded and evidently intended here to consecrate the site where the performance of the play is to take place. The sacrifice is therefore offered to the local god, "the god of the town."

Upon the site thus consecrated the sacred Djed pillar is erected. This ceremony is part of the rites of royalty and probably serves as a symbol of rebirth and resurrection, as we shall see (chap. 15)—a symbol to be taken again in the sense imposed by primitive religion where a symbolical act achieves what it symbolizes. Thus the erection of the pillar, the concluding rite for the king's predecessor, is his resurrection in the Hereafter.

After the Djed pillar is let down again, the royal princes mount their barges. Bread and beer, the staple foods, called "the two new eyes," are given to the eyeless god of Letopolis; and a mock battle is fought. This again is a feature which recurs with the erection of the Djed pillar at Memphis (p. 179), but the two battles differ in significance. The new king's accession, as we have seen, means a conciliation, a termination of

all disharmony; the mock fight symbolizes the discord which his accession brings to an end. And the arbiter here, as in the Memphite Theology, is Geb. We shall see later, in discussing the Ennead (chap. 15),
what the significance of his role is, though we have stated already the
obvious reason for his presence—that as earth-god he is concerned with
the rule over Egypt. The text runs:

> It happened that there was fighting.
> That means Horus fighting with Seth.
> Geb speaks to Horus and Seth: "Forget!"
> (*Stage directions*) Conflict between Horus and
>   Seth. Fighting.
> Horus speaks to the Children of Horus:
> "It is you who must forget."
> (*Stage directions*) Conflict between Children of
>   Horus and Followers of Seth. Boxing.

This scene seems to end all the preparations except the preparation of
the king's person.

Part IV (*scenes 19–25*) describes how the produce of the land is brought
to the king as part of the preparation for his coronation. It culminates in
the *hetep* meal, given to the king immediately before he is crowned. The
produce of herds and fields and mines is displayed. Every one of these
products, including the wood that must be split to make furniture, is
called the "Eye of Horus," the part of Horus which sustained damage in
the fight with Seth but which healed or was restored after Seth had
stolen it. Successively there are brought before the king milkmaids,
butchers, cabinetmakers (all in pairs); the dining-table the cabinetmakers are supposed to have made; wine, carnelian; and faïence ornaments. Finally, the *hetep* meal is brought in and offered to Pharaoh.

Part V (*scenes 26–32*) represents the climax of the play, the coronation. It starts with an enigmatic ceremony in which the standards* play a
part. We also meet here dignitaries, bearing archaic titles, whom we shall
meet later in charge of the burial of the king's predecessor. They are the
Spirit-seekers.[8] The text reads: "It happened that the Spirit-seekers and
the Royal Kinsmen(?) went around the two falcon standards. That
means Thoth takes possession of the two eyes of Horus for him." The
sacred conversation merely repeats this information. The action of the
Spirit-seekers is perhaps intended to bring about the harmonious incarnation of Horus and Seth united in the one person of the king. One
thinks of the title "The Two Lords" meaning Horus and Seth.[9]

Next, two scepters are brought and also two feathers *⫴*, which

* See above, pp. 91 ff.

will presently adorn the head of the king. Again we meet a duality in keeping with Menes' conception of the rulership of Egypt. And the mythological interpretation utilizes this duality further by alluding to the conflict of Horus and Seth. When Horus was wounded in the eye, Seth was wounded in the testicles. The two scepters are equated with the testicles of Seth, and in the sacred conversation of this scene Thoth admonishes Horus to incorporate these testicles in himself to increase his power.

Next a single object is brought in—the gold headband,[10] the most essential element of the crown.

Everything is now ready for the actual coronation. At this moment a sacrifice "from the Two Regions" (i.e., from the land of Egypt as a whole) is offered; "The Great Ones of Upper and Lower Egypt" are ordered to approach, and in their presence the "Keeper of the Great Feather" fixes the crown upon the head of the monarch, who is protected throughout the ceremony by the purifying fumes of incense, senetjer, "the divine substance." After this, and as the final act of this part of the ritual, half-loaves, called "an offering which the king gives," are distributed to the Great Ones of Upper and Lower Egypt. In other words, the very first act of the newly crowned king is to distribute bounty. Out of the abundance which is to mark his reign he makes the gift which even with us has remained symbolical of all sustenance— bread. The king himself takes a hetep meal.

We have summarized these scenes in rapid succession to show their interrelation and to convey something of the dramatic values which characterize this part of the play. But we may consider them now in a little more detail.

The explanatory phrases of the text which deal with the approach of the Great Ones of Upper and Lower Egypt stress again that the duality of kingship represents conflicting powers in equilibrium. Followers of Seth are now said to be among those who attend the king, and it is again Geb who orders "the gods" to be in attendance upon Horus. The "Great Ones" represent the people of the whole of Egypt at this central ceremony; consequently, they are viewed as forming two groups, and the introduction of the motif of conciliation becomes possible. For Geb addresses them as "Children of Horus and Followers of Seth." The scene reads:

> It happened that "Come!" was said to the Great Ones of
> Upper Egypt and the Great Ones of Lower Egypt.

That means Thoth lets the gods be in attendance upon
Horus, by order of Geb.

Geb speaks to the Children of Horus and the Followers of
Seth: "Attend to Horus. Thou (O Horus) art their lord."

Before quoting the words spoken at the actual coronation, we must
note that the crown is referred to as the "Eye of Horus." This is one of
those mythological concepts which are so heavily charged with meaning
that it is almost impossible for us to grasp their full significance. We
have met the "Eye of Horus" as the source of all the good that accrues
to the dead king through the actions of his son Horus.* But it stands also
for the power in the king, Horus, and as such it is the crown, which is
the repository of that power. We have seen in a coronation ritual that
the crown is addressed as the goddess Wadjet, the uraeus, and also as the
"Eye of Horus," just as in the Mystery Play. The nexus of concepts
may once more be summarized as follows: The "Eye" of the sky-god
Horus may be the sun. The "Eye" of the sun-god Re, however, is his
"daughter," the snake-goddess Wadjet, whose fiery poison strikes death
into the god's enemies. Pharaoh's diadem was adorned with the figure
of this uraeus, since Wadjet was immanent in the Crown.[11] Therefore,
we must attempt to hear the resonance of this polyphony of meaning—
royal power over life and death, protective goddess, solar power, source
of power—when the text refers, at the most solemn moment of the
Mystery Play, to the crown of the king as "thine Eye."

The words spoken by Thoth are interrupted in the papyrus by stage
directions, but we shall quote them continuously. It must be remembered
that this is the culmination of the performance. All the elaborate preparations—of barges, of utensils, of the site, of the participants, and,
finally, of the king, to whom, then, the produce of the land is brought so
that he may partake of it and distribute it—are directed toward this
moment when the new king is invested with the absolute and divine
power of kingship by the attachment of the insignia to his person.
Thoth, the scribe of the gods, often the reconciler of Horus and Seth,
speaks while a last anointment is taking place:

Take thou thine Eye, whole, to thy face.
Place it well in thy face.
Thine Eye shall not sadden with sadness.
Take thou the fragrance of the gods (censing),
That which cleanses, which has come out of thyself.
(At this point the crown and feathers are placed upon
the king.)
Cense thy face with it so that it be fragrant through
and through.

* See above, pp. 112 and 126.

The stage directions indicate that censing continues throughout this speech of Thoth and that, at the point which we have indicated, the "Fixing of the crown by the Keeper of the Great Feather" takes place. The censing occurs here because in its fumes a divine substance permeates the king. In most countries of antiquity the gods revealed themselves, not only to sight and hearing, but also to the sense of smell.[12] The unequaled fragrance which revealed their presence issued also from the burning incense. This could be explained only by the assumption that incense partakes of the essence of the gods. At the actual coronation incense is made to "cleanse" the king, but by a quick turn of thought the notion that an external agent is employed is converted. Since the king is divine, the "fragrance of the gods" is said to come forth from his own sacred person.

Now the king stands in all his regalia, truly the ruler of the Two Lands. And his first act is a dispensation of bounty to the Great Ones of Upper and Lower Egypt, who represent the people.

The distribution of half-loaves is explained as follows: "That means Horus who counts his Eye and gives them (the gods) their heads."The last phrase is a little obscure; it recurs in the pyramid texts and very probably means that he makes it possible for the other gods—in reality the people of Egypt as represented by the Great Ones of Upper and Lower Egypt—to live. This interpretation is in keeping with the role the king plays in the consciousness of the Egyptians (chap. 5). Without him the people would be like beheaded criminals, without life and even without hope for the Hereafter, since their bodies were gravely mutilated. The king, however, gives them the very symbol of life, bread, explicitly identified with all good, the "Eye of Horus." The verb traditionally translated "counting" often means "asserting one's right to dispose of property."

The distribution of the half-loaves is, of course, a mere gesture; a real feast follows toward the end of the performance. At the point now reached the provision of sustenance is given the briefest possible form because the act "Horus succeeding Osiris," which is the basic fact of the succession, requires that immediate attention be given to the late king. After the coronation the new ruler arranges for the funeral of his father, or rather for the ritual effecting the transfiguration of the late king, making him a power in the Beyond.

Part VI (*scenes 33–46*) is concerned with the transfiguration of the king's predecessor. If we have retained the designation "Mystery Play," it is not because of resemblances with medieval mysteries which are, as we have seen, superficial, but because the scenes now to be described represent the enactment of a mystery.

We are again confronted with phenomena which defy our categories and terms. There is no question of a mere burial, nor even of the simile of a burial, repeated wherever the play is enacted. We find here, in the first place, an excellent example of those *rites de passage*[13] which—with elaborate symbolism, allusions, and precautions—guide man's personality from an earlier to a new state of life at each of the crises of birth, puberty, marriage, and death. In the second place we are faced with the mystery of communion.

In the Memphite Theology and in the reliefs of Hatshepsut, we found the new king appearing in the arms of his father—Horus in the embrace of Osiris. In the Mystery Play we deal, not with pictorial representations, but with ritual. Osiris, in the play, is the dead king whose body is to be buried. How is the embrace effected?

The answer to this question is found in a power-charged object, a fetish, in this case a stomacher called "Qeni." The king puts this object around his chest and back; the immortal parts of Osiris seem immanent in it, and the mutual embrace of Horus and Osiris is effected.

The embrace has twofold consequences: power accrues to the new king, for Osiris "is his Ka," and the divine power of kingship immanent in the late ruler is transferred to his successor. The late king, on the other hand, is "supported," at the critical moment of his transition to the Hereafter, by the vital force of his son. It is important to note the precise moment in the play when this embrace takes place. The king has just been crowned and stands in the fulness of his power. The death of the late king, on the other hand, is now to be faced as a reality: bread and beer, the products of barley, now brought to the king, are obtained through the death of the seed corn which is a manifestation of Osiris (chap. 15). Conjuring up death is fraught with danger. At this moment Osiris is therefore protected in the embrace of his living son.[14] The embrace continues while the mummy is being prepared and presumably until the moment when the dead king is "found" by priests or officials with the archaic and significant title "Spirit-seekers." It would seem that they find Osiris in the arms of his son, for from this point onward the burial takes its course. It is enacted upon the human as well as upon the supernatural plane. To the latter we reckon a short scene of the dead king's ascent to heaven. To the world of men belongs the assignment of two priestesses to his cult and the bringing of food for the induction of the Spirit-seekers into the Dual Shrines. Obviously, they convey the spirit of the late king, which they have found, to the ancestral spirits who are, as we have seen, the gods of the Dual Shrines.

A great meal, once more showing that abundance will prevail under the new king, takes place; and final purifications conclude the solemnities.

Now that we have summarized the proceedings, we must substantiate the interpretations which we have given to them and present the texts. Let us first consider the Qeni stomacher. It is known from the funerary ritual the "Opening-of-the-Mouth" (Fig. 32). A more archaic form is suggested by the determinative with which the word is written in the pyramid texts and also in our coronation play. Such objects, apparently used in actual life, are shown on the reliefs of the Old Kingdom being fabricated by herdsmen or dwellers in the Delta marshes; and, though their use is not indicated, they are of the same type as the reed capes and the reed shelters which those men manufactured.[15] Thus the Qeni stomacher, like the oldest shrines of Egypt, points back to the early times when the Nile Valley was largely swamp land and its earliest settlers used the pliable reeds to fulfil their needs for shelter and protection.

The use made of the Qeni stomacher in the "Opening-of-the-Mouth" ritual is significant; it suggests, in fact, a close parallel to the interpretation we have given of its use in the Mystery Play of the Succession. In the funerary rites of Seti I the Sem priest is shown donning the Qeni stomacher instead of his usual dress of panther skin at the moment when the finishing touches are given to the king's statue, which served as a substitute for the mummy. This statue had to undergo a dangerous treatment. It was "beaten." Possibly this means that the sculptor applied the finishing touches which established it as a true image of the king. Or perhaps the "beating" refers to the act of the "Opening-of-the-Mouth" if this was felt to be a forcible interference with the statue. In any case, this "beating" was a ceremony which could not be evaded but which was as hazardous as the making of bread and beer was for Osiris, the dead king. In the "Opening-of-the-Mouth," the Sem priest, wearing the Qeni stomacher, said repeatedly: "Do not strike my father." We have met this same theme in an earlier part of the play where barley was threshed, but there the seed corn emerged undamaged. It is only in the scene we are discussing, when bread and beer are made, that the grain must die. It is then that the stomacher is "embraced" by the king.

The "embrace" is no mere sign of affection, but a true fusion, a communion between two living spirits, *unio mystica*. In the pyramid texts it occurs once as a one-sided act in which Atum pours life (namely, his own Ka) into the gods Shu and Tefnut whom he had created.* It is similarly used when Ramses II is embraced by Ptah, who endows him with the splendor of divine life, symbolized by gold, "the flesh of the gods." Ptah spoke: "When I see thee my heart rejoices and I receive thee in an embrace of gold, I enfold thee with permanence, stability, and satisfaction; I endow thee with health and joy of heart; I immerse thee in rejoicing, joy, gladness of heart, and delights—forever."[16]

An act of vitalization as efficacious as that of Atum is mentioned in the "Tale of the Two Brothers"[17] when the elder, Anubis, found and replaced the heart in the breast of the dead Bata. At the supreme moment, when life was imparted to Bata, he did not remain passive; there was a fusion of life and a mutual act: "Thereupon one embraced the other." This is precisely what happens also in the case of Horus and Osiris. The mutual character of their embrace is made clear in the pyramid texts, where Osiris is addressed as follows:

> Thou hast closed thine arms round him, round him;
> His bones stretch themselves, his heart becomes great.
> O Osiris, move thyself to Horus; go to him; do not go
>   away from him.
> Horus has come that he may acknowledge thee.
> He has beaten and bound Seth for thee;
> For thou art his Ka [Pyr. 585–87].

Another pyramid text comes so close to the Mystery Play that we shall quote it first. We translate the third sentence tentatively, using a pregnant sense of the verb *akh* rather than accepting the usual colorless and somewhat inappropriate "It is pleasant for him near thee."

> O Osiris, this is Horus within thine arms.
> He will support thee.
> There is further transfiguration (*akh*) for him with thee
> In thy name "He of the Horizon (*akhet*) from which
>   Re goes forth."
> Thou hast closed thy arms round him, round him;
> He will not go away from thee.
>
> Horus does not allow thee to be ill.
> Horus has put thy enemy under thy feet.
> And thou livest (again).
>
> Horus has given thee his children that they may get under
>   thee—without one of them withdrawing—to carry thee.
>
> Thy mother Nut has spread herself over thee in her name
> "(She of) Shetpet." She has caused thee to be a god
>   [Pyr. 636–38].

* See above, p. 66.

Here, then, we find, after the description of the mystic embrace in the first four lines, a statement of three lines which might have been recited in exactly this form in the Mystery Play, "being ill" being a euphemism for "dying." Later in the play the Children of Horus actually carry Osiris, thereby magically effecting his ascent to heaven. The last two lines of our pyramid text imply that this ascent has been completed.

The Mystery Play, being a ritual text, is obliged to bring in many details which are interspersed among the embrace (scene 33), the carrying of the dead king by the Children of Horus (scene 37), and his ascent to heaven (scene 38) with an invocation addressed to Nut. The scene in which the Qeni stomacher plays its part (scene 33) comes first.

> It happened that a Qeni stomacher was brought by
>   the recitation priest.
> That means Horus embracing his father and turning to Geb.
> Horus speaks to Geb: "I hold in my embrace this my father
>   who has become tired. May he become quite strong again."

"To be tired" often stands for "to be dead";* the last sentence may also read "until he becomes quite strong again."

The speech of Horus is interrupted in the papyrus by stage directions which identify the Qeni stomacher unequivocally with Osiris and declare the Delta city of Pe to be the locality in which the action takes place. The scene immediately following deals, as we have said, with the bread and beer, which stand for food and drink in general and which cannot be obtained without destroying the life of the corn.

> It happened that beer was brought.
> This means Horus weeps because of his father and turns to Geb.
> Horus speaks to Geb: "They have put this father of mine into the
>   earth."
> (*Stage directions*) Osiris—loaf of bread.
> Horus speaks to Geb: "They have made it necessary to bewail
>   him."
> (*Stage directions*) Isis —Mistress of the house—beer.
>   A loaf of bread; a jug of beer.

This surely is a most remarkable scene. In the middle of a performance concerned with the accession of a new ruler, the "death" of the grain is bewailed! But perhaps we must approach the text from the opposite angle. The king bewails his father's death, but the bread and beer which serve as properties in this scene indicate that the son's loss is his people's gain. In any case, no text could illustrate better how intimately the notions of kingship and of nature's generative force were related in

---

* See above, p. 63 and chap. 5, n. 9.

Egypt. And the text contains further points of interest which are by no means obvious but which clarify the working of the Egyptian mind. For instance, the death of Osiris is inevitable; and there must, therefore, be those who cause death; but they remain anonymous and are referred to as "they." After the coronation of the king and the reconciliation of all discord, there can be no question of proclaiming Seth victorious. Moreover, there is the bread and beer, a boon to rejoice in, and the ineffable mystery that Osiris, though always dying in the grain, always revives and is at the very moment of this wailing immanent in the Qeni stomacher, "supported" in the embrace of his son. As principal mourner in the myth, Isis enters this scene also.

The next scene is concerned with woven materials almost certainly intended for the winding of the late king's body. One of the two types of mummy cloth used is called Seth, no doubt because it serves Osiris; but, once it is thus called, it must be made harmless, and so some threads are drawn out. This counts as the removal of Seth's legs. The other material, a purple cloth, is identified with Osiris. The whole scene is explained in the following words: "This means Horus speaks to Osiris when he embraces him who embraces him and who says that he (Osiris) must cling to him (Horus)."

A stage direction indicates that "the beautiful house," which is known as the place of embalming, was the locale for this performance. There is, consequently, no doubt about the main action involved, but the interpretation of the quotation can follow several lines; and it seems a mere matter of predilection which one appears most acceptable. One may take Horus' words to be spoken to the stomacher, which still serves as the repository for Osiris. Or one may assume that Horus puts on a new garment or cloth made of the purple material. Or one may think, as we do, that the purple material is used as mummy cloth but is first "charged" by contact with the king or with the Qeni stomacher worn by the king. The latter action might serve to transfer what is immortal in Osiris from the stomacher to the mummy cloth and so to the mummy.[18]

Now that the embalming of the body is completed, the Spirit-seekers start to look for Osiris. The rigid composition of our text, in which scenes of identical pattern are added one to the other, leaves open the possibility that this seeking and finding was the last part of the action described in the previous scene; in other words, that Osiris was "found" in the embrace of his son by the Spirit-seekers. It is also possible that they now "find" the "spirit" of Osiris in the embalmed mummy or in the property representing the mummy in the play. This finding might confirm the transfer of Osiris' spirit from the Qeni stomacher to the mummy cloth. The Spirit-seekers are said to be the "Children of Horus" of mythology. A vignette shows that they carry either a statue of the late king or possibly his mummy or an effigy of the mummy (the manner of carrying in the ideographic vignette need not be of consequence); and Horus, the king, addresses to them the words he used in the pyramid text quoted above, namely, "Go under him." The two phrases with which all our scenes start distinguish here with particular clarity the ritual act and its mythological interpretation:

> It happened that the Spirit-seekers carried the king's father in
>   their arms.
> That means Horus orders his children to carry Osiris.

The Spirit-seekers next make a sort of heavenly ladder and invoke the sky-goddess, the mother of Osiris, to take her child to heaven. On the human plane two priestesses, representing Isis and Nephthys, are now chosen for his cult.[19] Some of the cloth mentioned before is handed to the "Master of the (King's) Largess"* and finally given to the Spirit-seekers. It would seem that here the practical arrangements were made for the final wrapping of the mummy, the preceding dealings with the cloth having been in the nature of ritual preparations. In the midst of these arrangements there is one scene which may have a religious significance. Food is brought in, and the text seems to say that it is "for bringing the Spirit-seekers into the Dual Shrines while they kiss the earth." Is this merely to complete their services with sacrifices before the ancestral spirits of whom the late king is now one? Or are they supposed to bring with them the spirit of the late king whom they have sought and found to unite him with the other ancestral spirits? Do they do this, perhaps, by adding some object connected with the late king to the standards and other sacred objects kept in the Dual Shrines? All this remains uncertain, though the general import of the action is clear.

The performance now comes to an end with a large meal served to the notables from East and West. The commentary recalls that of the token meal following the coronation. It says: "That means Horus counts his Eye and lets the gods receive their heads," with the possible continuation (though the papyrus is damaged): "Horus speaks to Thoth:

* See above, p. 82.

'Put my Eye into their mouths so that it is acclaimed.'" This scene gathers up and brings to fruition the preparations of Part IV in which the king was invested with all kinds of produce of the land, called the "Eye of Horus." Here, in the last scene, it is available in abundance for the people. It is also likely that in this scene the two main currents of the play were felt to merge. Besides the coronation of the new king the Egyptian concept of kingship brought up at this moment the relation to his predecessor as an active and inspiring one. The festive meal cast a spell of prosperity over the reign which it had inaugurated. But it also implied reliance upon the beneficial influence which the late king, whose body was now safely interred, would exercise upon the fertility of the land.

PART IV. KINGSHIP AND THE DIVINE POWERS IN NATURE

CHAPTER 12

THE GODS OF THE EGYPTIANS

TITLES, functions, and festivals proclaim the divinity of Pharaoh. We must now consider his place in the world of the gods. We are, then, confronted by the vast and labyrinthine structure of Egyptian religion. We cannot hope to recover a complete plan. But we shall find that certain avenues of approach lead to revealing vistas into its interior.

The clue to the understanding of many individual gods, cults, and usages is lost. If divinity was power, the form in which power was recognized was a matter of personal experience which had to be accepted by the community and established by tradition; in this manner the details of the cults originated.[1] We lack the data required to reconstruct this process and thereby to explain it. "Précisément parce que le caprice de l'homme et le hasard des circonstances ont eu tant de part à leur genèse, les dieux ne se prêtent pas à des catégories rigoureuses. ... Aucune loi n'a présidé à leur naissance, non plus qu'à leur développement. ... On pourrait dire, de même, que chaque dieu déterminé est contingent, alors que la totalité des dieux, ou plutôt le dieu en général, est nécessaire."[2] We have seen, in discussing an important god like Horus, how many questions must remain unanswered;* and, in fact, the central problem, the relation between god and falcon, seems entirely insoluble. To quote another instance, if we are satisfied that the nature of the lioness explains why the goddess Sekhmet is feared as a warrior, we are left with the enigma of her Bubastite form—a Mistress of Joy.[3] The form of a deity's principal manifestation gives but a limited insight into its character. For, when power is not merely acknowledged as existing but recognized as a god, it is endowed with the attributes of personality. The throne which "makes" the king is the Great Magician Isis, but also the loving mother of Horus and the devoted wife of Osiris. Thus the name and symbol of a deity—here the throne—may come to mean very little.[4]

Current literature on Egyptian religion tends to gloss over our igno-

* See above, p. 37.

rance in essential matters. It treats the gods as counters by means of which the enormous mass of material can be ordered. This procedure is legitimate if it is remembered that the values of the counters remain unknown, a fact obscured by the spurious precision of our classificatory terms: local gods, animal gods, cosmic gods, etc.

Sometimes it is maintained that the features of Egyptian religion most difficult for us to comprehend belong to a prehistoric age whence they survive in our historical sources. But these strange features are anything but survivals. They are of the essence of Egyptian religion, demonstrably active throughout its existence.[5] Amon, who rose to prominence only in the New Kingdom, nevertheless became associated with animals, the goose and the ram, in the manner of the oldest gods in the country. The Ogdoad of frogs and snakes, supposed to have brought forth the sun from the primeval slime at Hermopolis, were honored in later times with a sanctuary and regular worship at Thebes—tributes far surpassing any paid to them in earlier days.

Another primitive feature characterizing Egyptian religion is the indefinite demarcation of the spheres of action of individual gods. We find that temples erected by Ramses II and Ramses III are dedicated to specialized forms of Amon endowed with individuality of their own and clearly distinct from the great god of Karnak,[6] though a relation exists between them. On the other hand, when one of the great gods is shown as receiving the produce of all the different districts and towns of Egypt, the personifications of these localities are all described, and sometimes depicted, as manifestations of the god who receives their offerings, and whose single nature is thus seen to pervade the whole land.[7] In fact, the tendency to particularize and to recognize gods in every field and on every occasion where power becomes manifest is counteracted by a tendency to expansion and an approach to universality which is inherent in the very notion of divine power.[8] The two tendencies are part of religious experience and are, therefore, active at all periods.

The study of polytheism is bound to present difficulties; these are aggravated by our own religious experience. No pantheon is a systematic whole, but we cannot help looking for order where there is none. Gospel, Torah, and Islam are teachings which must be transmitted, which must, therefore, be fairly consistent, and which can be so because they are concerned with the revelation of a single god. In the ancient world the ephemeral Aten cult of Akhenaten was the only religion of this type, as it was the only one to demand adherence. Normally the diversity of actuality was reflected in many unco-ordinated beliefs, each of which was appropriate to certain circumstances.

The moon, for example, could be viewed in a variety of ways: it was one of the eyes of Horus, the primeval sky-god.* Since the moon wanes, it was the Eye damaged by Seth and regained by Horus; and because the Eye counted as the most precious of Horus' possessions (especially in connection with his father),† the moon was the subject of unlimited identifications. However, it could also be viewed as a manifestation of Osiris.‡ It was the twin of the sun and was, possibly in connection with Pharaoh, personified as Khonsu, who became the child of Amon and Mut at Karnak. But the moon as time-reckoner—an aspect important already in early times—was personified as Thoth, who counted as the scribe of the gods and hence as god of wisdom, the owner of various secret books. Moreover, Thoth played a part in solar myths and the myths of Osiris. Thoth—but not Khonsu—was symbolized by the ibis and the baboon for reasons which we cannot gauge. The goddess Nekhbet also counted as the moon.[9]

If a single natural phenomenon can be viewed in so many different ways, it is evident that distinct gods are likely to differ so thoroughly that they seem connected with separate theologies, although they are members of one national pantheon. But to expect from Egypt a coherent body of religious doctrine means looking for a single tree where there is multifarious growth.

In studying polytheism, then, we can no more outline a basic doctrine than we can hope to describe in full the variety of forms in which it found expression.[10] Another approach to its understanding is possible, however. When we survey the religious texts of Egypt, we find that certain motifs recur with great frequency. They determine certain broad spheres which the Egyptians recognized as manifestations of the divine. For the theme of this book three of these spheres are of special importance: the power in the sun, the power in the earth, and the power in that class of animals which formed early man's most precious possession—cattle.

These three spheres of divine manifestation were not kept strictly separate; the recognition of power in the sun, for instance, is shot through with images and thoughts derived from the other two. On the one hand, the sun is a "golden calf borne by the heavenly cow"; on the other, he is Khepri, "he who becomes," "he who came forth (by himself)," or, more fully, "the beetle who comes forth from the earth."[11] Sometimes the powers of earth and sun are viewed as one. In a curious dialogue with Osiris,[12] Atum predicts the destruction of the world he has created and his own reversal to the shape of "a snake whom nobody

* See above, p. 37.　　　　† See above, p. 131.　　　　‡ See below, pp. 195–96.

knows," thus revealing that the secret nature of the sun-creator is one with the universal symbol of chthonic life. But this interpenetration of the three sets of concepts is what we should expect. For we are dealing, not with a systematic cosmology, but with religious experience. The mysterious forces of life which are worshiped as breaking forth triumphantly in the sun's daily rising, the earth's fruitfulness, and the fertility of the herds need not be separated by man, who is the beneficiary of them all. Nevertheless, we observe that, according to the direction in which reflection moved, images of one rather than another sphere prevailed. Thus the divine power manifest in the sun is associated primarily with creation; the divine power in cattle primarily with procreation; the divine power in the earth primarily with resurrection.

Many peoples have used solar or chthonic images or animal symbols to express their relationship with the surrounding world in religious terms. Peculiarly Egyptian is the simultaneous use of these three sets of images; their connotation of creation, resurrection, and procreation; and the religious significance attached to them. Moreover, they dominate the religious texts to such an extent that, if we add kingship (in the form Horus succeeding Osiris), it is hardly an exaggeration to say that Egyptian religious thought moved within the confines of these four concepts and that Egyptian religion, in so far as it became articulate, was circumscribed by them. All that fell outside their scope is lost to us or appears in unconnected fragments.

This applies not only to early Egyptian beliefs but also to their survival as unusual creeds; and it also applies to the popular beliefs of historic times. Thus all we know of the god Khnum can be summarized as follows: he appeared in the form of a ram, was a creator-god, and made living beings on a potter's wheel (Fig. 23). At Elephantine he was believed to guard the sources of the Nile and hence to influence the inundation. At Antinoë and Abydos, Khnum the ram was viewed as the husband of Heqet the frog.[13] Moreover, he was identified with Re, Shu Geb, and Osiris; and hymns of Greco-Roman times ascribe the qualities and achievements of these gods to Khnum, interspersing phrases to this effect with the *disjecta membra* of a more original faith which we just now summarized but cannot comprehend.[14] We are similarly at a loss when we read that the Apis bull at Saqqara is designated by the complex "Osiris-Apis-Atum-Horus in one, the great god."[15] We realize that this represents an attempt to render the complete devotion of his worshipers who recognized in their god Osiris who vanquished death,[16] Atum the creator, and Horus the most comprehensive of early cosmic gods. The detail which eludes us is, precisely, the original character and meaning of Apis.

The completeness with which the doctrines and images of power in the sun, power in cattle, and power in the earth dominate the religious texts in Egypt demonstrates their overwhelming importance, at least for the literate Egyptians. The prevalence of these conceptions transcends the chaos of local cults and entitles us to speak of Egyptian religion as a distinctive creed. If "each definite god is dependent upon many conditions while the totality of the gods, or rather the god in general is necessary," we seem to have found, in the three spheres which we shall study now, some of the characteristics which in Egypt pertained "necessarily" to the category of the divine.

CHAPTER 13

THE POWER IN THE SUN: CREATION

A. THE KING, IMAGE OF RE

IN THE Turin Papyrus and in the History of Manetho, the sun-god figures as the first king of Egypt. Whether named Re, Khepri, or Atum,[1] he is the prototype of Pharaoh; and the texts abound in phrases drawing the comparison.* Even if we allow for the flattery and the florid style of many of the documents, there remains the definite impression that these phrases were no mere figures of speech. A survey of the metaphors in Egyptian literature reached the conclusion that "with relatively few exceptions all metaphors and similes introducing the sun refer to the king."[2] The king was recognized as the successor of the Creator, and this view was so prevalent that comparisons between the sun and Pharaoh unavoidably possessed theological overtones. When we read over and over again that the king is like the sun, we remember that in the coronation ritual this thought, far from being a mere metaphor, determined the form which part of the rites assumed. Similarly the king's accession was timed for sunrise, and the same verb denoted the sun's daily appearance and the appearance of Pharaoh at public functions. Hence the vizier Rekhmire explained the closeness of his association with the sovereign in the following words: "I saw his person in his (real) form—Re the Lord of Heaven, the King of the Two Lands, when he shone forth—the solar disk (Aten), when he showed himself."[3]

And yet it would be an error to put the relation between Pharaoh and Re on a par with that of Pharaoh and Horus. The king was Horus incarnate. He was not one with the sun. At his death his "divine body coalesced with its sire," "the body of the god joined him who had made him."† The Egyptians, as we have seen, conceived kingship as an institution involving two generations. This conception is most clearly expressed in the figures of Horus and Osiris, but it lost nothing of its validity when the king was viewed as successor to Re. Here, too, the living king was not identical with his father.[4] The tendency of mythopoeic

* See below, pp. 306–9.   † See above, p. 101.

148

thought to transform resemblances into identity was counterbalanced by the conviction that Pharaoh, though divine, was distinct from his predecessor. Nevertheless, these two shared certain essential attributes; and this consubstantiality found expression in the studied similarities between royal acts and solar events in such ceremonies as accession and coronation. It could be said: "Thou art the living likeness of thy father Atum of Heliopolis (for) Authoritative Utterance is in thy mouth, Understanding is in thy heart, thy speech is the shrine of Truth (*maat*)."[5] Royal titles are usually followed by some such phrase as "endowed with life unto eternity like Re"; and we have seen that the king, like Re, possessed the untarnished brightness of gold.* The following inscription demonstrates the definite meanings which the comparisons between god and king often possess; it gives divine parallels for three royal appearances:

> Thou joinest thy palace as Atum (joins) the horizon;
> Thou sittest in thy hall as Horus upon his throne;
> Thou appearest in thy palanquin of the Sed festival as
> Re at the beginning of the year.[6]

The Sed festival took place at set times; hence the temporal qualification of the sun-god's appearance in the last line in contrast with the preceding two. It was because the Sed festival consisted in a renewal of kingship that its divine prototype was found in the renewal of Re's rule at the start of an annual cycle.

We leave the scope of comparisons altogether when we hear that the king occupies the "throne of Atum,"[7] for the sun-god had actually been the first occupant of the seat of power which each Pharaoh found at his disposal; Tuthmosis III was called "he who is upon the throne of Atum."[8] The kingly occupant of that throne referred to the rule of the Creator with two stock phrases: he prided himself with having achieved "what had not been done since the time of Re" (or "since the beginning"), or, alternately, he claimed to have restored conditions "as they were in the beginning." These two phrases are not in conflict with each other, for, in so far as the king had made innovations, he had merely made manifest what had been potentially present in the plan of creation. And both phrases illustrate the Egyptian tendency to view the world as static; the order established at the beginning of the world was considered to be normative for all times. Of this order the king was the champion.

Pharaoh's rule, then, was the image of the rule of Re. But if Re had

* See above, pp. 46 and 135.

been the first king of Egypt, he had ruled by a right which none could claim after him. The universe was his because he had made it.

The attribute of Creator was given to many gods; in fact, most temples claimed it for their deities. But though it is generally assumed that this is an original situation and that all "local gods" were viewed as creators of the universe by their devotees, this is by no means certain. In any case, we find that throughout Egypt in historical times the sun is held to be the primary source of creative energy.[9]

This view is not, of course, confined to Egypt:

> Creation does not necessarily mean the bringing forth of something out of nothing; to the eastern mind it contains the idea of regulation, of cosmos. To a large extent the material is there already and the act of creation consists in forming the chaotic material into a living organism. . . . . We found the same idea in connection with the changing of the seasons. After the chaos of summer and winter God brings forth out of the dead material the living cosmos of vegetation, a constantly repeated creation, a drama in which the cosmic and chaotic powers strive with one another, and which ends in the victory of the creative God.

> In those places where the sun is worshiped as the world creator, there, above all, emphasis is laid upon the cosmic aspect of creation. For the sun is a powerful symbol of the cosmic order; it rules the changes of day and night, of the seasons, and of the years.[10]

In the jubilant hymn on the accession of Merenptah,* these same phenomena are gratefully acknowledged as due to the accession of the proper ruler. Since Pharaoh maintains the cosmic order, his rule is truly an image of the rule of Re. We have seen how Hatshepsut was greeted by the gods with the words, "Welcome, O daughter of Amon. Behold thy law and order in the land."† "Thy" is the word that matters in this phrase.

The analogy with Re is stressed especially at the coronation, which can be regarded as the creation of a new epoch after a dangerous interruption of the harmony between society and nature—a situation, therefore, which partakes of the quality of the creation of the universe. This is well illustrated by a text containing a curse of the king's enemies who are compared with Apophis, the snake of darkness whom Re destroys at dawn. But there is a curious addition to the comparison: "They will be like the serpent Apophis on New Year's morn."[11]

The qualification "on New Year's morn" can only be explained as an intensification: the snake is defeated at every sunrise, but the New Year celebrates creation and daily renewal as well as the opening of the new annual cycle.[12] In the texts the concepts of creation, sunrise, and kingly rule are continually merged; the verb $h^{c}i$ (which marks the appearance

* See above, p. 57.   † See above, p. 105.

of Pharaoh on the throne) denotes sunrise and is written with the hiero-glyph ⌒ that depicts the sun rising over the Primeval Hill.[13] We must, then, survey in some detail how creation was imagined by the Egyptians and view in their proper context the many allusions ·to it which we have met in the texts.

B. CREATION AND CIRCUIT

According to Egyptian beliefs the sun had emerged from the primeval ocean, Nun, to begin its work of creation. Evidence that this belief was held firmly throughout the land is found in the Memphite Theology, which sets forth a different doctrine; it proclaims that Ptah, the chthon-ic god of Memphis, was the creator of the universe;* but it could do this only by underpinning, as it were, the solar creation story. Ptah could not be made a sun-god, being of the earth; but he was equated with the Eight who served at Hermopolis as a conceptualization of chaos.† The Eight brought forth the sun from the primeval waters; hence they existed before him. They were called "the fathers and mothers who made the light" or even "the waters that made the light."[14] The Mem-phite Theology could intervene at this point in the accepted account of creation and, by the identification of Ptah-Ta-Tjenen—Ptah the Risen Land—with the Eight primordial elements of chaos, establish the su-premacy of the divine powers in the earth over those in cattle and in the sun.

But these teachings never affected popular beliefs. The sun whose daily rising repeated his appearance on the First Day remained for the Egyptians the Creator. A morning song addresses him:

> Thou risest, thou risest, when thou comest forth from the
>   Ocean of Heaven;
> Thou rejuvenatest thyself again on the place of yesterday,
> Divine Youth, who came into being out of thyself.[15]

In a more didactic text the sun-god is quoted as saying: "Only after I came into being did all that was created come into being. Many are the shapes that came forth from my mouth.[16] The sky had not come into be-ing; the earth had not come into being. . . . . I found no place where I could stand."[17] The last sentence indicates what had to be the first act of the sun-god. Within the expanse of the primeval waters he created dry land, the Primeval Hill, which became the center of the earth, or at least the place round which the earth solidified.[18] Local traditions dif-fered as regards the details; but everywhere the site of creation, the

* See above, pp. 27–30.   † See below, pp. 154–55.

first land to emerge from chaos, was thought to have been charged with vital power. And each god counting as Creator was made to have some connection with this Hill. We have seen that Ptah, as earth-god, was actually declared to be the Hill itself as Ptah-Ta-Tjenen, for the notion of a primeval hill is not dependent on the belief that the Creator is a sun-god. In fact, each and every temple was supposed to stand on it—another instance of the primitive tendency to stress relationship and participation to the point of identity. This thought is applied even to temples built quite late in the history of Egypt. For in a static world, a change, an innovation, is viewed as the making explicit of what was intended (and therefore potentially present) from the very beginning. The Ptolemaic temple of Philae is inscribed: "This (the temple) came into being when nothing at all had yet come into being and the earth was still lying in darkness and obscurity."[19] And Hatshepsut states in an inscription: "I know that Karnak is the Light Mountain (horizon) upon earth, the venerable hill of primeval beginning (literally 'of the first time'), the healthy eye of the Lord of All—his favorite place which carries his beauty and encompasses his suite."[20] Sometimes, but very rarely, the king, like the sun, is called "Lord of All"; * but this inscription of Hatshepsut allows us to recognize the subtler shades of distinction between the sun and his successor on the throne of Egypt. The queen, by beautifying Karnak, honored the center from which the creation took its start. Creation had been the work of Amon-Re, but his daughter Hatshepsut, partaking of his nature, performed a creative act when building the temple, for this made manifest a hidden truth ("I know that Karnak, etc.").

The identity of the temples with the Primeval Hill amounts to a sharing of essential quality and is expressed in their names[21] and in their architectural arrangements by means of ramps or steps. Each temple rose from its entrance through its successive courts and halls to the Holy of Holies, which was thus situated at a point noticeably higher than the entrance. There the statue, barge, or fetish of the god was kept, resting upon the Primeval Hill. There is some evidence to show that the throne of Pharaoh—himself a god—also imitated the Primeval Hill.[22] It was reached by steps and was sometimes placed upon a double stairway. In writing, too, single or double flights of stairs symbolize the Primeval Hill.

Similar forms were used in funerary architecture, for the plot of ground from which creation proceeded was obviously a depository of

* See above, p. 57.

creative energy powerful enough to carry anyone who might be buried there through the crisis of death to rebirth. It is for this reason that funerary figurines appear at the top of a flight of stairs (Fig. 33). Originally this equation of the tomb with the Primeval Hill was effected by the king, the likeness of Re among men, and it found its clearest expression in the royal tombs. Even in the Nineteenth Dynasty, Seti I's cenotaph at Abydos supported the sarcophagus upon an island rising from the subsoil water which was identified with Nun; and the island was made to resemble the hieroglyph of the Primeval Hill by the addition of two antithetic dummy staircases.[23] Another architectural symbol for the Hill, the pyramid, was introduced in the Third Dynasty and modified in the Fourth. Djoser changed the superstructure of the royal tomb from the flat oblong mound, the mastaba, in use at least from Menes' days, and realized the equation of his resting-place with the fountainhead of emerging life, the Primeval Hill, by giving his tomb the shape of a step pyramid, a three-dimensional form, as it were, of the hieroglyph ⌂ for the Hill. The kings of the Fourth Dynasty substituted the true pyramid,[24] which was the specific Heliopolitan form of the Primeval Hill, the Benben.

In Heliopolis there was a place called "The High Sand"[25] which was part of the sun temple and no doubt counted as the Primeval Hill. But the first piece of solid matter actually created by Atum in the primeval ocean was also shown at Heliopolis, and one can imagine it enshrined upon this "High Sand." This first solid substance was a stone, the Benben; and it had originated from a drop of the seed of Atum which fell into the primeval ocean.[26] Immediately after this, Atum created out of himself the first pair of the gods, who then became the ancestors of all others.

A pyramid text succinctly describes these first events:

> Atum-Khepri, thou wert high as (the) Hill.
> Thou didst shine forth as Benben
> In the Benben Temple in Heliopolis.
> Thou didst spit out Shu;
> Thou didst spew out Tefnut.
> Thou didst put thine arms round them with thy Ka
> So that thy Ka was in them [Pyr. 1652–53].

The determinative, in the pyramid texts, shows a tapering, somewhat conical shape for the Benben stone, which became stylized for use in architecture as a small pyramid, the pyramidion; covered with gold foil, it was held aloft by the long shaft of the obelisk ⌡ and shone in the rays of the sun, whom the obelisks glorified.[27] In the Old Kingdom in the Sun Temple of Neuserre, a huge obelisk of masonry rose upon a base perhaps imitating the "High Sand."

Outside Heliopolis the Primeval Hill was differently conceived. At Hermopolis it was an island in a lake—which symbolized the primeval waters—and was called the "Isle of Flames" with a clear allusion to the glow of that momentous sunrise of the First Day. In the pyramid texts a curious writing of the "island of appearance (or 'of sunrise' ☉) of the earth" obviously reflects the same line of thought.[28]

The waters surrounding the Primeval Hill were, naturally, the waters of chaos; these, personified in the god Nun, were still supposed to surround the earth, an inexhaustible reserve of latent life and fertility. And the subsoil water, as well as the Nile flood, was thought to flow out from Nun. Since the Primeval Hill was the place of sunrise and creation, and hence the place of rebirth and resurrection, the waters of Nun which surrounded it became those waters of death which, in the imaginations of many peoples, separate the world of the living from the world of the dead.[29] Revealing is a pyramid text in which King Pepi calls on the ferryman to ferry him "to that Eastern side of Heaven, where the gods are born, when comes that hour of labor (Dawn)" (Pyr. 1382). It is clear that this water which the dead must cross is also the water in which they are purified and in which Re bathes before each sunrise, repeating his pristine emergence from the waters of chaos.[30]

The imagery from the solar sphere deeply affected Egyptian thought and culture, and the Egyptian always dwelt with particular pleasure upon the emergence of the sun from the waters. There was something familiar in that thought which brought the mystery and the marvel of creation closer without annihilating it. Every year, after a hot summer, when the Nile had risen and covered the parched lands and renewed their fertility by the silt which it brought, some high piece of ground would emerge from the slowly receding innundation and herald the beginning of a new season of fruitfulness. With delight, they piled image upon image for this phase of the act of creation. Sometimes the sun-god was said to have appeared as a small child, seated within a lotus flower which had been mysteriously lifted above the water. Sometimes a large egg had appeared from which the sun-child emerged; or the goose of Amon-Re had flown from it, its honking the first sound in the waste of water.[31]

The best preserved of these stories relates to Hermopolis in Middle Egypt. Here chaos had been conceptualized in eight weird creatures fit to inhabit the primeval slime. Four were snakes and four frogs or toads. They were male and female, and they brought forth the sun. They were not part of the created universe, but of chaos itself, as their names show. Nun was the formless primeval ocean, and his female counterpart, Naunet, was the sky over it. Or perhaps it would be better to say that Nun was chaotic primeval matter, Naunet primeval space. Naunet became, in the created universe, the anti-sky which bent over the Netherworld, a counterpart and mirrored likeness of Nut, just as Nun became Okeanos, surrounding the earth and supporting it. The next pair of the Ogdoad were Kuk and Kauket, the Illimitable and the Boundless. Then came Huh and Hauhet, Darkness and Obscurity; and, finally, Amon and Amaunet, the Hidden and Concealed Ones. If we allow that some of these gods, such as Nun and Naunet, represent primordial elements, the uncreated material out of which cosmos came forth, then Amon and Amaunet represent air and wind, elements sufficiently chaotic, since "the wind bloweth where it listeth and thou hearest the sound thereof, but canst not tell whence it cometh, and whither it goeth" (John 3:8). Amon could therefore be conceived in later times as the dynamic element of the chaos, the mainspring of creation, the breath of life in dead matter. But this is not the original conception,[32] which simply, by means of the Ogdoad, made the chaos more specific, more apt to be understood. On the Isle of Flames the Eight mysteriously made the sun-god come forth from the waters, and therewith their function was fulfilled.

This story was not the only one to be told. We have seen how the Egyptians admitted the validity of images which would seem to us mutually exclusive but which were acceptable to them as adequate embodiments of certain aspects of a process or situation. If, therefore, the sun is considered not primarily as the creator but as a heavenly body, it is his regular appearance and disappearance which must be accounted for. Hence it was said that the sky was a woman bent over the earth and bringing forth each morning the sun, each evening the stars. According to some versions, they pass through her body while they are invisible. More generally it is believed that at that time they pass through the Netherworld, completing a never ending circuit. But the other view, though more primitive, is obviously more in keeping with the image of the sky bearing the heavenly bodies when they appear. When the notion of world circuit prevails, that of the sky-mother may be superseded; and we find that the sun is supposed to complete his journey by boat, changing craft at dusk and dawn. Yet this notion is hardly younger than the other, for in the pyramid texts we find the sun on his journey using the most primitive craft known to man—the reed floats which are used even now by some Nubians.[33]

In addition, imagination concerned with the sun is not kept free from contamination with a different sphere of divine manifestations, that of cattle. The sun-child is suckled by a cow on the Isle of Flames; the sun is a powerful bull; the sky itself is a cow.* The ease with which these distinct spheres are made to overlap, even in pictorial art, is difficult for us to understand. So we may see the cow of heaven studded with stars and with the sun-boat sailing along her body (Fig. 34), or a woman bending over the earth upon which the sun, whom she has borne, falls down merely to take wing again as a beetle (Fig. 35).[34] Or we may read in the pyramid texts: "Thou hast sailed through the Winding Waterway . . . . as a star, sailing the Great Green (Ocean) which is under the body of Nut" (Pyr. 802). Or let us look at the "Book of Who Is in the Netherworld," which describes the nightly journey of the sun from west to east. It demonstrates with particular clarity that the daily sunrise partakes of the quality of the first sunrise, for, in the last "space" that connects night and day, Netherworld and the world of the living, we find four members of the Ogdoad present to bring the sun forth at dawn as they had done at the time of creation. The "space" in which the journey ends is called the "connecting darkness" because it corresponds to the thickness of the earth which floats upon Nun and connects the heavens with the cupola of the anti-sky:

This god comes to rest (*hetep*) in this space, the end of the connecting darkness. This great god is reborn in this space in the shape of the divine beetle Khepri. Nun and Naunet, Kuk and Kauket are present in this space in order to have the Great God reborn when he proceeds from the Netherworld and settles in the Morning Boat and appears between the thighs of Nut.[35]

Here, again, we find the image of the boat and the image of birth combined in a manner which is unacceptable to us. Even so we should not speak of confusion; in matters of so much moment for the ancients this accusation seems an absurd presumption. It is more likely that the texts, as well as representations such as the boats sailing along the body of the star-decked cow (Fig. 34) are, as it were, synthetic symbols, opening the possibility for the Egyptian to develop any particular aspect or image which the situation might require.

In fact, the course of the sun, and its culmination in the sunrise, possesses many more aspects than those covered by the images of a boating

* See below, chap. 14.

journey and birth; and each of these aspects possesses significance for the king, who appears as the image of Re in all of them.

The dramatic quality of the sun's course is acknowledged by the stories of battles which he has to fight. In Egypt, as in Babylon and Rome, the sun is *Sol Invictus*. Every sunrise is a victory over the darkness, every sunset a forcible entrance into the Netherworld where dangers crowd in upon the sun-god. The "Book" from which we have just quoted and similar papyri like the "Book of Gates" and the "Book of Apophis," recount the battles hour by hour.[36] However, these texts are only known in the New Kingdom, and the dramatics of conflict play a more subordinate part in Egypt than anywhere else, since the Egyptians viewed the world as essentially static.

The natural processes are also sacred. This is acknowledged by the repeated purifications which the sun undergoes in his circuit, the best known of which is his bathing before dawn when he rises "in his red garments."[37] We have seen how the dead king undergoes these very purifications when joining the cosmic circuit.* An account of Piankhi's visit to Heliopolis stresses the parallelism between the sun and the living king who bathed before dawn in the sacred pool (representing Nun) while preparing to adore the sun at its rising.[38]

The regularity of the sun's movements suggested (besides victory and order and immortality as rebirths without end) the thought of inflexible justice and an ubiquitous judge. Thus its behavior acquired an ethical quality. The king is judge pre-eminently as the image and representation of Re.[39] Now this thought, that the sun maintains justice, is, again, not peculiar to Egypt. The sun-god Shamash inspired Hammurabi, king of Babylon, to compose his code of laws; and an Assyrian proverb asks: "Where may the fox flee from the sun?"[40] But in Egypt the notion received a peculiar coloring from the fact that justice was part of an established order created by Re. Hence Re guards, protects, and vindicates his own work when he maintains justice. We must recall that Re's daughter is the goddess Maat—"truth, established order, right order"—by whom the gods are said "to live." Her figure is presented to them in the daily ritual —a concrete form to render an abstract idea exactly resembling the imbibing of good fortune by the royal nursling;† and the king, too, is addressed with the phrase: "Thy speech is the shrine of Maat." In fact, it is by means of the concept of Maat that the essential affinity of god and king is expressed when Hatshepsut writes:

* See above, pp. 117–18, 121.   † See above, p. 74.

"I have made bright Maat which he (Re) loves. I know that he lives by it. It is my bread; I eat of its brightness; I am a likeness from his limbs, one with him."[41] Because the king is the son of Re, "a likeness from his limbs," he lives by Maat, as part of the order of creation.

The inexhaustible significance which the sun possessed for the Egyptians as the embodiment of the divine appears in the poetry to which it gave rise.[42] We shall not quote the famous hymns of Akhenaten,[43] which appeal to our sensibilities because of the minimum of theological, and the elaboration of natural, detail. Instead we shall give a hymn from the preceding reign precisely because it brings into play so many of the themes and associations which we have discussed separately. The different names of the sun are used here to some purpose: Re was an almost neutral term for the sun; Atum, meaning possibly "the All" or the "Not (Yet?) Being," referred to the sun as demiurge; Khepri ("He Who Becomes"), appearing as a beetle, applied mostly to the morning sun;[44] while the Aten, proclaimed to be the one god by Akhenaten, was for the Egyptians in general the actual heavenly body, the orb of the sun. Harakhte, the falcon, as we have seen, referred to the ancient sky-god Horus as manifest in the most powerful object in the sky;* while Khnum, the god of the cataract region, gave shape to the formless as a potter (Fig. 23).

> Hail to thee, sun disk (Aten) of the day!
> Creator of all,
> Who made their life;
> Great falcon, feathered in many hues,
> Who came into being to lift himself;
> Who came into being by himself, without sire;
> Eldest Horus who dwellest upon Nut;
> Whom one acclaims when he shines forth
> And likewise at his setting.
>
> Thou who shapest what the earth produces,
> Khnum and Amon of men;
> Who hast taken possession of the Two Lands
> From the greatest to the smallest of that which is
>   in them;
> Patient artist,
> Great in perseverance at innumerable works;
> Courageous shepherd driving his sheep and goats,
> Their refuge, made so that they may live.
>
> Hurrying, approaching, running,
> Khepri, highly born,
> Who lifts his beauty to the body of Nut

* See above, p. 38.

And illuminates the Two Lands with his disk;
Primeval god who created himself,
Who sees what he should do; Sole Lord
Who reaches daily the ends of the lands
And views those who walk there;
Who rises in the sky in the shape of the sun,
That he may create the seasons out of the months—
Heat when he wants it, cold when he wills it.
He lets the limbs grow faint and then embraces them;
Every land prays daily at his rising in his praise.[45]

As pictorial equivalents of such hymns we figure two vignettes of a type common in papyri and on coffins of the New Kingdom (Figs. 36 and 37). They represent the sun's course in a synthetic rendering of its rising and setting.[46] The mountains, depicted with parallel lines and dots, serve for East and West. But the falcon with the sun disk, though representing the sun-god as "Horus of the Horizon," at the same time forms with his support the hieroglyph for West. The goddess of the West, offering water with her hands (Fig. 37), also appears in a pyramid text quoted below.* Among the adorants of the sun we see Isis and Nephthys, brought in from the Osiris cycle, and the Rekhyt and Henememet, representing the people. The baboons, whose chatter and animated behavior in the morning was interpreted as sun worship, represent the animal kingdom; the human-headed birds, Ba's of the dead, represent past generations; and the Souls of Pe and of Nekhen, the Royal Ancestors. The attitude which texts and designs express is that of Psalm 24:

The earth is the Lord's, and the fulness thereof; the
world and they that dwell therein.
For he hath founded it upon the seas, and established
it upon the floods.

C. THE KING, SON OF RE

The divine power which is manifest in the sun thus appears, in its fulness, to surpass all and comprise all. Even the dignity of Pharaoh appears as reflected glory. It is true that society is an inalienable part of the cosmic order and that the king functions on the plane of the gods as well as on the plane of men. But the sun represents the divine in a form which far surpasses even the divinity of kings. The pyramid texts, which stop short at no hyperbole when hymning the power of the ruler in the Hereafter, claim that he takes the place of Re only in so far as both are reborne daily by Nut in the cosmic circuit.[47] The usual relationship is

* See below, p. 169.

that which is expressed in the titulary, "Son of Re"; and sometimes the confidence of the dead ruler does not suffice for the maintenance of even that claim. He declares himself satisfied to serve Re in any manner, quite humbly as an oarsman in his boat or as its pilot, or he occupies the seat of the scribe of Re.[48] He does what Re tells him (Pyr. 491). This feeling of dependence is rather movingly expressed in one such text: King Teti, helpless in the darkness and dangers of the Netherworld, calls, not upon the brilliant ruler of the day sky, but upon the mysterious creator Atum who made the world out of the darkness of chaos and who may also bring the dead king to emerge at sunrise as a participant in the powerful circuit. The "protection" of the four goddesses may refer to the watch they kept at the bier or couch ("throne") of Osiris.[49] Notice the childlike readiness of the helpless "son" to offer some service in exchange for the help he stands in need of:

> Father of Teti, Father of Teti in the darkness!
> Father of Teti, Atum in the darkness!
> Do fetch Teti to thy side!
> He will light the lamp for thee;
> He will protect thee, as Nun protected
> Those four goddesses on that day
> That they protected the Throne [Pyr. 605–6].

The distance between Pharaoh and the sun-god can best be measured if we turn to certain texts from the New Kingdom when the solar doctrine gained a profounder significance than it had ever had before. This became possible by substituting the deity Amon-Re for Re. This is usually considered a mere trick of priestly syncretism intended to add glamour to the god of the capital Thebes. In reality it was a truly creative thought which realized the potentialities of a combination of the concept of the creator-sun with that of Amon, the "breath of life," "the hidden one," who, as one of the Eight of Hermopolis, was part of uncreated chaos.[50]

We have seen how theological speculation had at an early age apprehended chaos as four pairs of deified concepts. One of them, Amon, occupied an exceptional position; he was recognized as a god of some importance already in the Old Kingdom,[51] and as a personification of the wind he represented a dynamic element. Just as Ptah could, by being equated with the Ogdoad, be considered the First Cause, the divine person from whom the sun was an emanation, so, among the figures of the Eight, Amon could be viewed as the First Cause, especially since, as breath, unseen, he could be apprehended as the basis of all life. Hence the phrase: "Amon, the venerable god who came into being first; he is that breath which stays in all things and through which one lives forever."[52] The same thought is expressed in the Luxor temple in a design in which Amon holds the sign of life toward King Amenhotep III with the words: "My beloved son, receive my likeness in thy nose."[53]

The theological argument establishing Amon as the First Cause takes into account that the Creator is the sun, Atum: "Amon who came forth from Nun. He leads mankind. Another of his forms is the Ogdoad. The begetter of the Primeval Gods giving birth to Re. He completed himself as Atum."[54] And Amon is really felt to combine the characters of sun and wind: "To thee belongs what thou seest as light, what thou passest through as wind."

In the old terms, which incorporate established Egyptian beliefs, it is said:

Amon who came into existence at the beginning. None knoweth the form of his emergence. No god came into being before him. There was no other god with him that he might tell his shapes. He had no mother for whom his name was made. He had no father who begot him and who said: "It is I." Shaping his own egg. Force, mysterious of births, creating his beauties. Divine god, coming into existence by himself: all gods came into being after he began to be.[55]

Thus the god who had been the invisible dynamic element of chaos, the wind, became the source of light and order and power, not unlike the Hebrew *ruah elohim*, the "breath of God," which "moved upon the face of the waters." As has been well said, Amon is not only *deus invisibilis* but *deus ineffabilis*.[56] He is also the god to whom the poor can pray: "Thou art Amon, the Lord of him who is silent, who cometh at the voice of the humble man."[57] He is felt throughout nature:

He lives in what Shu uplifts (the clouds) to the end of the circuit of the sky. He enters into all trees and they become animated, with branches waving . . . . he raises heaven to furor and the sea to revolt, and they become (again) peaceful when he comes to peace. He brings the divine Nile to a flood when his heart suggests it . . . . one hears his voice, but he is not seen while he lets all throats breathe; he strengthens the heart of her who is in labor and lets the child which comes forth from her live.[58]

Amon, then, was a universal god, while Pharaoh's godhead was of a different order. He was but the son; his power derived from his almighty father.[59]

CHAPTER 14

THE POWER IN CATTLE: PROCREATION

A. EGYPT IN AFRICA

WESTERNERS, whether modern or Greek, are baffled by the worship which so civilized a people as the ancient Egyptians accorded to animals. The deification of cattle is obviously part of this complex of beliefs. But if we treat it as such, the custom submerges in that vast sea of the incomprehensible; yet it is possible to salvage and understand it to some extent.

Egyptian zoolatry confronts us with one general and many special problems. The first consists in the proposition that the divine can be manifest in animals. We have stated in discussing the god Horus that our evidence does not suffice for a correct appraisal of the relationships which were believed to exist between this god and the creatures connected with his cult. The special problems are presented by the particular cults. These pose the question why in each case a given animal or species was singled out and why the cult, the myths, and the beliefs show the characteristics which we can observe. We have mentioned above* why such specific problems are mostly incapable of solution; these cults and all that pertains to them are the outcome of a historical development which we cannot reconstruct for lack of data.

The cattle cults of Egypt,[1] however, differ from all the other animal cults in that they can be approached in two ways, in addition to the usual approach through religious documents. One takes as its starting-point writings which are not primarily religious, or at least not primarily concerned with the worship of cattle. The other seeks a way to understanding by starting from modern observations of an attitude toward cattle which resembles that of the ancients.

Egyptian texts of the most varied nature abound in metaphors, appraisals, and other expressions which relate to cattle. The king is "a strong bull"; a queen-mother is called "the cow that hath borne a bull";[2] the sun is "the bull of heaven"; the sky is a huge cow. A moralizing

* P. 143.

treatise states, most unexpectedly: "Well tended are men, the cattle of God."[3] It is curious that scholars view such images as purely poetical without connecting them at all with the cults of Hathor, Apis, Mnevis, etc.—to us equally strange. Yet both groups of phenomena obviously derive from the same root. They show that cattle played an altogether extraordinary role in the consciousness of the Egyptians. This led, on the one hand, to religious veneration, and, on the other, to the spontaneous production of cattle images and cattle similes whenever some unusual observation required figurative speech for adequate expression.

The profound significance which cattle evidently possessed for the ancient Egyptians allows us to bring an entirely fresh kind of evidence to bear on the problem. For some modern Africans, related to the ancient Nilotes,[4] display a similar attitude toward cattle; and these living adherents to a point of view so utterly alien to us open our eyes to possibilities which our own experience could never have suggested.[5] In the life of the Hamites and half-Hamites, cattle play an enormous part.[6] Nowadays these people are economically dependent upon their herds. But it is generally acknowledged that this is a consequence and not the cause of the esteem in which cattle are held.[7] Generally cattle are not killed for meat; and, though milk is a staple food, there are many taboos connected with it, and it is ceremoniously served to the chiefs.[8] Though some of these people, like the Banyoro, know the principles of stock-breeding, they do not breed with a view to producing better milch cows but are guided by other considerations. Among some Nilotes, for instance, the aim is to increase the length of the horns.

The economic dependence on cattle seems, then, to be a secondary feature among those tribes. The prestige of the herds and the emotional value attached to them led to a neglect of other forms of food production. We have here a typical example of that "partial exploitation of the environment" which is a characteristic of many primitives[9] and which distinguishes these Africans from the ancient Egyptians, who, from early predynastic times, possessed a balanced economy in which agriculture, hunting, and fishing, as well as stock-breeding, played their parts. This difference between the economies of the modern and the ancient inhabitants of northeastern Africa is characteristic of the contrast between people who have drifted into a backwater and people who are truly primitive in the sense that they are pristine and rich in unrealized potentialities.

The contrast reflects itself in the religious sphere.[10] We shall see in the next chapter that the Egyptians recognized divine power in the earth and in the vegetation which it brought forth as well as in the animals which lived upon it. An occasional indication, such as the epithet of Min, "he who has created the vegetation to let the herds live,"[11] suggests the existence, in Egypt, of an attitude of mind such as we find among the Masai, who hold grass sacred and use it in many rites because it is the food of their cattle.[12] In Egypt cattle were recognized as outstanding, but not the sole, embodiments of the mysterious forces of life which man calls divine. Nevertheless, the similarities with modern Africa are unmistakable. "Among the Bayankole . . . . when a king dies, his body is wrapped in the hide of a newly killed cow, after the royal corpse has been washed with milk . . . . and even the cattle are made to participate in the mourning. Cows are separated from their calves so that both make a melancholy lowing."[13]

We find this very feature in the royal funerals described in the pyramid texts, where the dead king has, of course, become Osiris:

> Heaven speaks (in thunder); the earth is shaken, because of
>   terror of thee, Osiris, when thou makest ascent.
> O yonder milch cows, O yonder nursing cows, go round him;
>   bewail him; praise him; keen him—when he makes ascent.
> He goes away to heaven amongst the gods, his brothers [Pyr. 549–50].

Again, in modern Africa:

> The attitude of herdsmen toward their cattle is one of extreme solicitude; the care and affection lavished on the herds is one of the most impressive aspects of their culture. Religious and magical concepts associate cattle with life beyond the grave, with burial rites, and with the sacrificial use of meat, milk, and blood. . . . . At the head of a social system which is founded on pastoral pursuits, the office of king or chief has sacred functions, and official rain-makers are the principal priests. Special status depends on the ownership of cattle. . . . . In the legal system cattle are important as tribute, for payment of taxes and as compensations.[14]

Even here we meet several features which can be paralleled in Egypt. But the abstract terms of the summary fail to convey the peculiar attitude of mind upon which these usages are based. This appears from certain more specific descriptions of the relation between man and beasts.

> Among the Dinka there is a well defined initiation ceremony at which the father of the young man presents his son with a bull, and it is no exaggeration to say that the youth attaches himself so strongly to this animal that the process called by psychologists "identification" takes place. He will pass hours singing to and playing with his bull; he will be known to his associates by the name of his bull; and the death of the latter is a true bereavement.[15]

In Uganda "men become warmly attached to their cows; some of them they love like children, pet and talk to them, and weep over their ailments. Should a favorite cow die, their grief is extreme and cases are not wanting in which men have committed suicide through excessive grief at the loss of an animal."[16] In the same region "a chief will frequently bemoan the loss of one of his cows with more genuine and heartfelt grief than he would display if he lost a wife or a child."[17]

"Among the Nuer, Dr. Evans Pritchard notes that a man may dance with his arms upheld so as to mimic the horns of his beast, the left bent forward in front of his brow, the right curved upwards. As he shuffles forward he calls out the name of his *macien*."[18] The *macien* is a bull with artificially deformed horns, a feature of especial importance to us. Among the Suk in Kenya such bulls are called *kamar;* and there they play a part, not only in the private lives of their owners, but in the life of the community. "Before a raid the *kamar* are collected, bedecked with ostrich-feathers, and taken to the river, where the warriors assemble, and dance round them, brandishing their spears and vaunting their bravery. A captured *kamar* is slaughtered and eaten ceremonially."[19]

Ancient Egypt, at least during the Old Kingdom, knew and valued its *kamar* or *macien*. In the tombs they are depicted among the bulls or oxen brought to the dead man (Fig. 38). Since the Dinka and the Nuer use different modes of deformation, it is surely remarkable that both are found in the Old Kingdom tombs. The entirely nonutilitarian character of the "improvement" excludes independent development, and its occurrence in Egypt and modern Africa must be due to a common attitude underlying the usage and to a continuous tradition in maintaining it. In Egypt the habit was discontinued in the Middle Kingdom.[20] But in the New Kingdom we find that Negroes, bringing tribute from Nubia, include some of their most valuable animals with deformed horns (Fig. 38).[21] This is extremely important, for it disposes of the argument that we are dealing here with a usage which Africa derived from Egypt. Egypt discontinued the deformation of the horns of its cattle in the Middle Kingdom before it had subjugated Nubia. Negroes from the South provide us with proof of the survival of the custom outside Egypt in the second millennium B.C., and thus supply an intermediate stage between the third millennium, when Egypt retained this heritage of its prehistoric African origins, and modern times, when remnants of the Hamitic substratum of Egyptian culture still continue it.[22]

On this African background certain curious traits in Egypt gain remarkable relief. At Badari cattle burials were found, dating from the Old Kingdom.[23] In the Mystery Play of the Succession we find that milkmaids and butchers are the first of all those who bring the produce of the land to the new king.[24] Bakers are not mentioned, although the *hetep* meal, to judge by the sign with which it is written, consisted of bread. One wonders whether we have here a trace of the very ancient prestige of the produce of cattle.

Cattle seem to have served originally as a measure of wealth. At the Sed festival of Neuserre the gods received presents of cattle, and the cow-goddess Sekhat-Hor presided over the ceremonies in the early stages. Throughout the Old Kingdom there seems to have been a biennial census of cattle, sheep, and goats for tax purposes,[25] though in later times the yield of the fields was taxed. To what extent practical considerations and, to us, a strange appraisal of cattle intermingle in these practices it is hard to say. But the African background which we have indicated does explain the extraordinary role which cattle play demonstrably in the spiritual life of the Egyptians.

We may, in the first place, recall the ease with which figurative language in Egypt assumes forms which the modern cattle-keepers of East Africa would appreciate.[26] There is the astonishing sentence: "Well tended are men, the cattle of God." The upper part of the skull, where crowns and other insignia are worn, and even the forehead, are named and written with a pair of cattle horns ⊍. A verb "to be joyful" is determined 𓄿 with a cow turning round to a calf at her side. Meskhent, the goddess who presided over childbirth, has as her symbol the bicornate uterus of a heifer 𓉔.[27] The notion "innumerable" is expressed, as with us, by the term "as the sand on the shore," but also by "as the hairs of cattle."[28] Again we face a more balanced and cultured development of a habit which, among savage peoples, for instance among the Suk, goes to extremes. In Suk "if an adjective stands by itself, the noun it qualifies is always understood to be cow. Again, in Suk, even the skin of an ox has a different name to the skin of any other animal; and the verb to drink, if the fluid be milk, is different from the word meaning to drink any other liquid, while an ordinary gourd has a name different from that of one used to collect milk."[29] If this seems an altogether extreme development, we must remember that in Egypt the word "leader" or even "owner" calls up the image of a bull with his herd. Osiris is called "Bull of the West," or "Bull of Abydos";[30] Seth, characterized by a strikingly nonbovine animal 𓃣, is "Bull of Nubt";[31] and, in the pyramid texts, a snake is called "Bull of the Forelock"[32] and the ferryman of the Hereafter, "Bull of the Gods."[33] The same usage survives in Africa today where the Nilotic Lango call the leader of the combined warrior-formations "Bull of the Host"[34] and where the divine king (Mugabe) of Ankole is called "the leading bull" or "the leading bull of the herd."[35]

If we turn to more purely religious phenomena, we find in the cults of the sacred bulls the most obvious sign of cattle worship.[36] It is generally assumed that they represent primitive cults, originally unconnected with the great gods with whom they were related in historic times. But the assumption may well be unfounded. That relationship is expressed by a significant title in the case of both the Apis bull of Memphis and the Mnevis bull of Heliopolis. The bulls are the "heralds" of the gods. Their full titles were "the living Apis, the Herald of Ptah, who carries the truth upward to Him-with-the-lovely-face (Ptah)" and "the Herald of Re, who carries the truth upward to Atum." It has been pointed out that this sounds as if the bulls were the earthly representatives of their respective gods and kept them informed about what happened upon earth.[37] Conversely, the bulls gave oracles in which they acted, as it were, as heralds on behalf of the gods.

Let us compare with this fully developed and established religious form the more fluid and uncertain forms of primitive religion.[38] We know that the Shilluk worship their first king, Nyakang, as a god. He is referred to as father, ancestor, or ret (king) and is incarnate in a fetish-like object and also in the living ruler. But he is also yomo (wind or spirit) and lives among his people whom he protects and to whom he shows himself in various forms. Everything which shows a somewhat royal character in the animal world is considered to embody Nyakang temporarily or to be in his service, to remind the Shilluk of their king and their duties. When a bull turns out to be exceptionally fine, it must necessarily have been chosen by Nyakang to be his vehicle, so that such animals are not merely sacred to Nyakang, but actually embody him, though not completely or exclusively or continuously. Therefore, they can be killed only for sacrifice. It is clear how these indefinite beliefs could have formed the basis of the theological structures which we find in the cults of Apis, Mnevis, and Buchis. In Egypt a series of distinct markings are required for the identification of the sacred animal, while an impression of majesty suffices for the Shilluk. However, it is also clear that in both cases the sacred animals did not embody their respective gods completely or exclusively.

In addition to the well-known cults of the three bulls we have named, there were a number of other cattle cults, notably in the Delta, but also in Upper Egypt.[39] Moreover, the cult of the goddess Hathor, who was conceived in the form of a cow, was very widely spread throughout

Egypt and that from very early times. We have shown that the deformation of bulls' horns survived as late as the Middle Kingdom. But already in the predynastic period—the Gerzean to be precise—we find amulets in the shape of bulls' heads[40] and also palettes showing a cow's head combined with stars.[41] Here, then, at a very early age indeed, we have that interpenetration of the two spheres of religious imagery which we noticed in passing when discussing the power in the sun.

B. SUN AND SKY

Having discussed both the solar sphere of Egyptian religion and the sphere connected with cattle, we may attempt an explanation of their relationship. We have stated repeatedly that the Egyptians rendered account of natural phenomena by the simultaneous use of diverse images. The conception of the sun as Creator, Atum, "the All," or the "Not yet Being," did justice to the unfathomed power and the cosmic order which he exemplified but omitted an aspect which impressed itself deeply on the Egyptians—so deeply, in fact, that it determined their expectations for the world to come. This was his daily disappearance and reappearance, which, since night carried an evil connotation and was hostile to life, was felt as an ever renewed resurrection—rebirth. The sun was born at dawn, the stars were born at dusk. Here, where the concept of procreation obtrudes itself, the images of cow and bull are at hand; and they serve, almost inevitably, as the expression of the Egyptians' thought. In one of the hymns with which the priests greeted the sun at its rising we read:

> The gods extend their hands to thee,
> Thy mother Nut has borne thee.
> How beautiful art thou, Re-Harakhte!

And again:

> Hail to thee, Great One
> Who came forth from the Heavenly Cow.[42]

The cattle images, brought in with the thought of birth, obtain a wider significance in the solar context, since the sun's circuit represented life after death.* But the loftiness of this conception did not diminish the concreteness of the imagined process of rebirth. The Egyptians insisted that, where there is birth, there must have been conception. The god or the king, to be reborn, must beget himself upon the

---

* See above, pp. 119–22.

mother-goddess. The god (or the king) possessed the miraculous power to achieve this; he was a bull, and this image signified not only a "leader" but a dominating male, an embodiment of virile fertility. The correctness of this view is proved by the fact that "bull" and "pillar" are interchangeable in many locutions;[43] "pillar" is used in them with a naïve and natural phallic symbolism which is, in fact, familiar to psychoanalysis. It figures as *pars pro toto*. Hence the following words, spoken by the Goddess of the West at the approach of the setting sun: "There comes the one whom I bore, whose horn shines, the anointed pillar, the Bull of Heaven" (Pyr. 282*c*). The sun will enter the West to be reborn in the Netherworld; he will then pass through the Netherworld and be reborne by Nut in the sky. But the sun makes his entrance by impregnating these goddesses. Thus Amon-Re is called "He who begets his father," a paradoxical formula for the line of thought we have just described and which we find expressed, simply and directly, in the following pyramid text: "O Re, impregnate the body of Nut with the seed of that spirit that must be in her" (Pyr. 990*a*).

Re and Nut are neutral, descriptive terms for sun and sky. But we recall that a queen-mother was called "the cow who bore the bull"; and Amon is called the "Bull of the Four Maidens,"[44] just as Geb, the earth-god, was the "Bull" of the sky-goddess Nut.[45] And similarly the sun becomes a great wild bull, the sky a cow, the rising sun a calf born each morning.[46] In a hymn to the sun this last image enters as follows:

> The Imperishable Ones adore thee.
> They speak to thee:
> "Hail to thee! Hail to thee, thou calf . . . .
> Which came forth from the Ocean of Heaven."
> Thy mother Nut speaks to thee and stretches
>   out her hands to greet thee:
> "Thou hast been suckled (by me)."[47]

Here again we meet allusions to distinct images. The Ocean of Heaven recalls the view that the sun rose from Nun. The calf is born of a mother who can stretch out her hands—a coalescence of the notions under discussion with the image of Nut bent over the earth (Fig. 35). Nut, like Isis, is depicted with cows' horns if she is shown among other gods.[48] In a pyramid text she suckles her child—the dead king, Osiris—and is credited with two arms but is also called "with long horns" (Pyr. 1344*a*). The Hermopolite cult of the Ihet cow represents a similar coalescence of images. She was supposed to have suckled the young sun upon his emergence from the primeval waters,[49] although the creation story in which his appearance from Nun is related does not allow for such a feature at all.

Images, however, lead a somewhat independent life and may flourish far beyond their original meaning. We find that in a text in which rebirth is not explicitly mentioned the late king spreads terror in the Hereafter by appearing as a dangerous bull rampaging among the "herd" of the stars: "Ho there, thy meadows are terrified, O Iad star, before the pillar of the stars, when they have seen the Pillar of Kenset (the land of the dead),* the Bull of Heaven, how the herdsman of cattle was overwhelmed by him" (Pyr. 280).[50]

In another text the notion of the sun as the Bull of Heaven is elaborated in a manner which strikes us as comical: King Teti, having to cross the waters which separate the dead from rebirth, acts like a peasant fording a stream with his beasts:

> Greetings, Re, who passest through heaven,
> Who sailest through Nut.
> Thou hast crossed the Winding Waterway.
> Teti has caught thy tail, because Teti is really
>   a god, the son of a god [Pyr. 543].[51]

Elsewhere the late king as son of Re attempts to establish his relationship with the heavenly family by calling himself a calf—and a golden one, at that—thus sharing the sun's substance:

> Pepi comes to thee, O father of his!
> Pepi comes to thee, O Re!
> A calf of gold, born of heaven,
> The soft one[52] of gold, formed by the
>   Hesat-cow [Pyr. 1028–30].[53]

The interpenetration of solar images and those connected with cattle can now be understood. The Egyptian was deeply preoccupied by the problem of life after death. He found one of its solutions in rebirth through the mother. He saw, at the same time, eternal life in the circuit of sun and stars. The coexistence of thoughts and images derived from both these solutions did not disturb him; each was adequate to a specific approach to so complex a problem. The sun as creator of the established order was the source of his own and of all existence: "Joining his seed with his body to create his egg within his secret self."[54] But rising as the perennial victor over darkness, evil, and death, the sun is reborn in the sky at every dawn: "Thou art beautiful and young as Aten (the sun disk) in the arms of thy mother Hathor."[55]

* See above, p. 117.

C. THE KING AND HATHOR

The king often appears as a strong bull in the monuments as well as in the texts (Figs. 2 and 28). Narmer-Menes and even earlier kings appear as bulls trampling down enemies or destroying fortresses. We should not need to see more in these pictures than metaphors carried rather further than a Western artist would think permissible, if it were not for the peculiar significance of cattle images in ancient Egypt, where, in fact, the king was viewed as the son of a cow-goddess, Hathor or Nut.

The king is primarily "Horus," and Hathor is the mother of Horus. Her name means "the house of Horus." In Egyptian, "house," "town," or "country" may stand as symbols of the mother. For instance, a vizier addressed his mother as "great city, country from which I came forth."[56] Psychoanalysis again is in keeping with this naïve imagery, since it also explains these symbols as images of the mother from whom the child came forth and to whom, in the infantile regression of psychosis or in the fantasies of immortality, it may want to return.[57] The latter trend, as we have seen, takes form in the accounts of the sun's rebirth; and we shall presently meet it in texts concerned with the king's resurrection.

Since Hathor's name proclaimed motherhood as her principal function, we can understand why the Egyptians imagined her as a cow; when depicted in human shape, she wears cow horns and the sun disk on her head ⅍. On objects dedicated to her service, like the sistrum ⍦, she is represented by a full-face head of a woman with cow's ears (Fig. 2). Hathor's embodiment was not the domesticated cow but the wild animal, living in the marshes. A statue from Deir el Bahri shows her parting the stalks of papyrus with her head,[58] and the marshes counted so definitely as her home that even her epiphany at a man's tomb in the western desert is incongruously depicted amidst a clump of flowering papyrus (Fig. 39). The emblem of the god Ukh, who sometimes counted as her husband and who was impersonated by a bull in rites at Meir,[59] consisted of a papyrus flower crowned with feathers ⍦. Papyrus was sacred to Hathor because it formed the natural setting in which the goddess chose to manifest herself, and the picking of papyrus was a ceremony carried out in her honor.*

It is more difficult to understand the connection which existed between Hathor and trees. The association was old[60] but remains obscure.[61] In later times men recognized her in the goddess who offered

* See below, p. 177.

refreshment to the dead from the trees planted near their tombs (Fig. 21). But this may have been a secondary association due to the identification of Hathor with the Goddess of the West, who is not well differentiated from either Hathor or Nut. In fact, these three goddesses are but three different aspects of the Great Mother in her peculiarly Egyptian, non-Asiatic, character.[62]

The role played by Hathor in the funerary rites in the Theban necropolis is explained partly by the presence of her temple at Deir el Bahri and partly by the transference of beliefs of immortality from kings to commoners. For Hathor was originally the mother, not only of Horus the Great God, Lord of Heaven, but also of his incarnation Horus the King. Pepi I puts "Son of Hathor of Denderah" instead of the usual "Son of Re"[63] in his titulary, a replacement which shows that the relation with Hathor was conceived in more specific terms than the "sonship" which the king assumed in relation to all deities. The Hathor cow is shown suckling the newborn king in the reliefs at Luxor and Deir el Bahri.[64]

Now the earliest association of a king with a mother conceived as a cow is found on the same monument which shows him as a "strong bull." The upper corners of the palette of Narmer-Menes (Figs. 2 and 3) consist of heads of the goddess, with horns and cows' ears; and the king, in the large representation on the reverse, wears, hanging from his girdle, appendages which also show the head of the goddess. Djoser in the Third Dynasty, who left us the earliest Hathor-head columns, was wearing the same appendages in one of his statues.[65] Menkaure appears with Hathor in a number of statuary groups.[66]

Two objects used in the cult of Hathor, the rattle (sistrum) ☥ and the *menat* necklace ☥ (cf. Fig. 39), are also closely associated with the king in various ceremonies. At an audience in the palace, the princesses, when they make their appearance, are equipped with these objects, which they present and hold out toward the king.[67] The words with which they accompany the action are: "May the Golden One (Hathor) give life to thy nostrils. May the Lady of the Stars unite herself with thee." The last title reminds us of the slate palettes of predynastic times which show a cow's head studded with stars, and the motif of union with the mother-goddess will occupy us presently. The *menat* necklace is also worn by Khonsu,[68] who, as we have seen, was originally the placenta or "twin" of the king. The appropriateness of the god's association with an ornament sacred to Hathor, the divine "mother" of the king, is obvious.

The mingling of the falcon and cattle images in the relationship of Horus and Hathor is not due to syncretism.[69] It recurs in the case of the war-god Monthu of Thebes, who was conceived as a falcon but was also manifest in the Buchis bull.[70] The royal titulary shows it, too, for after Tuthmosis I the name which is crowned with the falcon and is called the Horus- or Ka-name regularly includes the epithet "strong bull." The palette of Narmer (Figs. 2 and 3) illustrates how little the ancients were disturbed by this simultaneous use of the two images. It shows the king's victory three times: once as a man destroying the enemy chief with his mace, once as the Horus falcon holding him in subjection with a rope passed through his nose, and once as a "strong bull" demolishing enemy strongholds. Each of these images is valid if the appropriate avenue of approach is chosen.

In certain contexts Hathor did not count as the mother of Horus the king. If the historical actuality of the reign was envisaged, the king's mother was Isis, the Great Throne; for at the accession it had become manifest that the king who was enthroned was Horus. The specific significance of the king's relation with Isis is clearly expressed in the words which Ramses II addressed to his deceased father: "Thou restest in the Netherworld as Osiris, while I shine as Re for the people, being upon the Great Throne of Atum, as Horus son of Isis."[71] If, on the other hand, the king's origin was considered, not from the point of view of legitimacy (for then he was Horus son of Osiris) or from that of actuality (for then he was Horus son of Isis), but from the point of view of his faculties and potentialities—his divinity, in short—then he appeared in the fulness of his power, the embodiment of that great cosmological figure who embraced sky, sun and moon, clouds and wind in one exuberant image, Horus the son of Hathor.* The simultaneous validity of these views of the king is, again, a primitive feature and not the product of the syncretism of later times. It is a perfect parallel for the simultaneous validity of the falcon and bull images relating to the king. These were employed throughout Egyptian history but were used already on the Narmer palette. Similarly, we find the epithet "Son of Isis" already in the First Dynasty, while the Narmer palette proves by its designs that the king's close relation with Hathor existed at the same time.

The modern African evidence† exemplifies the spontaneous and compelling force with which the cow presents itself as a mother-image to people standing in the peculiar relation to cattle which we have de-

* See above, p. 37.   † See above, pp. 162–68.

scribed. And so we find this mother-image intruding (to our way of thinking) in the pyramid texts when the king appears as the son of the vulture Nekhbet of El Kab. This goddess, as the White Crown of Upper Egypt, counts as his mother* and is shown in the mortuary temples of the Old Kingdom nursing him after his rebirth.[72] We read:

> Thy mother is the Great Wild Cow, living
>   in Nekheb,
> The White Crown, the Royal Headdress,
> With the two tall feathers,
> With the two pendulous breasts.
> She will suckle thee,
> She will not wean thee [Pyr. 729].

Here is a truly mythopoeic "concrescence"; the thought of crown and headdress calls up the two feathers 𝕝 which are the main insignia at the coronation.† Feathers are in keeping, moreover, with the vulture of Nekhbet; but, being a pair, they also call forth the thought of the breasts of the goddess who, in the form of a woman, suckles the king. None of these images has any relation to that of the cow; but, since motherhood is the issue, the latter imposes itself. The same coalescence of the images of cow and vulture occurs elsewhere when Nekhbet is called "the Great Wild Cow . . . . with spreading pinions";[73] in yet another place her anthropomorphic form prevails but is combined with that of the cow: "The Great Wild Cow who is in Nekheb . . . . with long hair."[74]

The representations of the mother-goddess in these texts and reliefs form an integral part of the tombs in which they appear, for the mother-image fulfils a distinct function in the Egyptian beliefs of life after death. It does not bear witness to the king's divine origin, but it holds out a promise of immortality. This is unambiguously expressed in a text which starts with the king's assertion that he knows his mother, and which then develops into a dialogue between the king and the goddess of El Kab:

> My son Pepi, so she said,
> Take my breast that thou mayest drink, so she said;
> So that thou livest (again), so that thou becomest
>   small (again), so she said;
> Thou wilt go forth to heaven like the falcons;
> Thy pinions will be like those of geese, so she said
>   [Pyr. 910–13].

The last two verses, promising the king ascent to heaven (and, incidentally, introducing the image of the bird), show beyond a doubt that

---

* See above, pp. 107–8.   † See above, pp. 129–32.

the divine mother is concerned, not with the king's birth, but with his rebirth after death. And the earthly parentage of the king is disclaimed with vigor, for such parentage would imply mortality. The son who officiates for the dead king, for instance, is made to say:

> Ho there! Ho there!
> I make this "Ho there!" for thee, my father,
> Because thou hast no fathers among men,
> Because thou hast no mothers among men.
> Thy father is the Great Wild Bull;
> Thy mother is the Young Cow [Pyr. 809].

In our quotation both parents appear in the guise of cattle. Whether we must think of the sun-god as the Great Wild Bull, or whether nothing so specific is intended, we cannot decide. The images used for sun and king are the same in the matters of birth and rebirth. This is particularly clear as regards the union with the mother which serves to explain the sun's daily reappearance and serves also as an image realizing the king's desire for immortality. We have quoted the text referring to Re: "O Re, impregnate the body of Nut with the seed of that spirit which must be in her" (Pyr. 990a). And now we read regarding the king: "It was sore for the body of Heaven under the fury of the divine seed which had to be in her. See, Teti, too, is a divine seed which must be in her" (Pyr. 532).[75]

There is no need to view this text as an adaptation to the king's purposes of notions originally applicable to the sun, although it is true that the dead desire to join in the cosmic circuit.* We have seen in the preceding chapter that the divinity of the sun-god is of an order different from that of the king. Of the mother-goddesses through whom immortality is reached, Nut is the mother of Osiris, the dead king, while Hathor is the mother of the living king, Horus. It remains a moot point whether the king expects rebirth through Nut because he joins the cosmic circuit (and is therefore reborn daily with the sun) or whether his hopes are based on a binding association of the ideas of mother and birth and require a return to Nut as mother of Osiris. It is really futile to press for a decision whether the solar or the Osireian aspect of Nut is relevant here: our very doubts prove the inner logic of Egyptian beliefs. Whatever the latitude and variety of details, in these last matters Egyptian religion presents us with a cogent system.[76]

The thought that rebirth is the only way to immortality has suggested to the Egyptians a curiously static scheme in which the sarcophagus

* For quotations, see above, pp. 118–22

chamber or the coffin is identified with Nut. Thus the dead king is actually put to rest in the body of his mother, and rebirth is assured. We
must divert our attention from the cattle images to illustrate this solution. It found pictorial expression in the Eighteenth Dynasty, when
royal usages were increasingly adopted by commoners; we find, then,
that the insides of coffins, or of coffin lids, were covered with a large
figure of Nut with open arms in which the dead rested. The Greek authors preserve stories which are only explicable if we remember these
coffins and at the same time allow for the fact that Nut, as the mother,
often assumed the shape of a cow (Fig. 34). Herodotus informs us that
the daughter of Menkaure was buried in a statue of a cow made of gilt
wood;[77] Diodorus states that Isis collected the bones of Osiris and put
them into a wooden cow covered with fine linen.[78] But already in the
pyramids of the kings of the Fifth and Sixth Dynasties the burial in the
mother's body was expressed, not pictorially, but by means of texts
which were written on the walls of the sarcophagus chamber to bring
Nut down to the king. These texts represent the first stage of a development which ends with the identification of Nut and the coffin in the
pictorial devices we have just described.[79] In fact, they appear on the
six inside surfaces of the coffin of King Teti of the Sixth Dynasty. One
of them reads:

> Thou hast been given (handed over) to thy mother
>   Nut in her name "grave";
> She has enfolded thee in her name "coffin";
> Thou hast been brought to her in her name "tomb"
>   [Pyr. 616d-f].

The texts which cast a spell bringing the mother-goddess to the dead
king are not abstract but, on the contrary, rich in those feelings and associations which the concept of "mother" evokes in man:

> O Pepi, one comes; and thou wantest not.
> Thy mother comes, and thou wantest not.
> Nut—and thou wantest not.
> The protectress of "the Great One"[80] and
>   thou wantest not.
> The protectress of the fearful, and thou
>   wantest not [Pyr. 827].

Sometimes it is the stellar, not the solar, circuit which the king seeks
to join. This is the case in the following hymn addressed to Nut:

> Great one, who became Heaven,
> Thou didst assume power; thou didst stir;
> Thou hast filled all places with thy beauty.
> The whole earth lies beneath thee.

> Thou hast taken possession of it.
> Thou enclosest the earth and all things (on it)
>   in thy arms.
> Mayest thou put this Pepi into thyself as an
>   imperishable star [Pyr. 782].

Notice that there is not merely poetic indulgence in images here: Nut has inclosed "the earth and all things," including the dead king, in her arms. The situation requires only a last action by the goddess, and rebirth is certain. Our text, as a matter of fact, is preceded by another which states quite simply and directly: "Mayest thou transfigure this Pepi within thee that he may not die" (Pyr. 781*b*).

This relationship with the mother is entirely passive, but we also find traces of a more active attitude. Instead of waiting for the protective mother to take her child to herself, the son acts. He enters her, impregnates her, and thus is borne again by her.[81] Hence the designation of Amon-Re: "He who begets his father" and the corresponding epithet of his spouse at Thebes, the goddess Mut (the name means simply "mother") who is called "the daughter and mother who made her sire."[82] This is the typically paradoxical form which all theology is obliged to give to intuitive religious insights.

The same notion is expressed in a pyramid text which we shall quote. It starts appropriately with the most impressive act of fertilization known to the Egyptians—the Nile flood. However, this motif does not serve solely to cast an auspicious spell of fecundity; it is germane to the subject since the king has power over the Nile.* The Nile flood is viewed here as the strongest one—the prototype of all later inundations —when the earth had emerged from "the Lake." The power in Unas is the immortal power of kingship. A further allusion—to the reconciliation of discord—adds proof of his power. After this the union with the mother is proclaimed.

> It is Unas who flooded the land
> When it had emerged from the Lake.
> It is Unas who pulled up papyrus.
> It is Unas who reconciled the Two Lands.
> It is Unas who will be united with his
>   mother, the Great Wild Cow [Pyr. 388].

There is one phrase in this text which we have not explained. It is stated that Unas pulled up papyrus. This is a ritual act performed in honor of Hathor.[83] The reference to this rite in our text serves as a prelude to the projected union.

* See above, pp. 57–59.

Papyrus and rebirth through the mother are also connected in the rite of raising the Djed pillar ꕺ, an artfully contrived column of papyrus stems.[84] Texts corroborate our view that the Djed pillar represents a mother-goddess, notably Hathor, pregnant with a king or god. A late text calls Hathor "the female Djed pillar which concealed Re from his enemies."[85] It should also be remembered that Hathor was worshiped in trees even in early times.[86] In the myth of Osiris as related by Plutarch, the god was likewise concealed in a pillar: Osiris' body, thrown by the murderer Seth into the Nile, floated to Byblos, where a tree grew round it. The tree became a pillar in the palace of the local prince, and Isis found it and recovered the body.[87] The story of a pillar recovered by a goddess may well be a rationalization of an earlier belief that a pillar was identical with a goddess, as the epithet of Hathor suggests. Yet another late author, Firmicus Maternus, describes the hollowed fragment of a tree trunk containing a figure of Osiris probably made from moist earth and grains.[88] The important point for us is that this tree trunk is said by him to be used in the Isis cult. In Denderah the coffin of Osiris is shown inclosed in the branches of a tree.[89] This seems a merely pictorial variant, possibly adopted for greater clearness. In any case, the symbol of tree or pillar for the goddess containing the god seems well established in Egypt, and there is clear evidence that this god was Osiris. Inside coffins of the New Kingdom the Djed pillar is painted with eyes and holding the scepters and wearing the crown of Osiris (Fig. 40). Sometimes the figure is wrapped round with the wings of Nut, Osiris' mother (Fig. 41)—an explicit reference to his rebirth. Such designs are exactly equivalent to the texts which appear on Old Kingdom coffins, for in both cases the arrangements aim at bringing the dead man within the maternal body; and parturition is assumed to follow. The difference between the two usages (in their original application to a royal funeral) might be described as one of viewpoint: the body in the coffin (which is Nut) is considered from the standpoint of the survivors; it is the dead king Osiris. The body in the reeds of the Djed pillar is viewed (as the late king was during his lifetime) as Horus the son of Hathor. But the two points of view are not clearly distinguished, and, indeed, why should they be? In both cases the dead king returns to the source of his being and is born anew.

The "raising of the Djed pillar" is depicted in a tomb of the New Kingdom.[90] The pillar appears here, too, with eyes, scepters, and crowns which show that it contains Osiris. But the ceremony also contains unmistakable references to Hathor. While the king and some

royal kinsmen are pulling the rope that raises the pillar, sixteen princesses hold the *menat* necklace and shake the sistrum, Hathor's symbols. Below men are shown using papyrus stems, pulled in the marshes,
as weapons in a mock fight between inhabitants of Pe and Dep, the twin
Delta cities. Now mock fights are common in ritual performances; they
provide a means for the community to partake in a cosmic event which
is conceived as the overcoming of resistance. But in our tomb painting
the ceremony has a very specific connection with the account of a mock
fight which Herodotus (ii. 63) reports as taking place in the Delta city
of Papremis. An annual festival centered round a visit which the god
Ares (Horus)[91] paid to his mother, and it is indicated that the god's
purpose was incestuous intercourse with her. We have good Egyptian
evidence regarding this tradition. In a magical papyrus we read:

> Isis is faint upon the water.
> Isis rises upon the water.
> Isis' tears fall upon the water.
> See, Horus violates his mother;
> And her tears fall upon the water.[92]

At Papremis some of the people had made a vow to fight for Horus,
and, when the statue of the god neared the temple of the goddess, her
priests, assisted by some of the inhabitants, opposed the approaching
procession with force. It is precisely such a situation that seems to be
hinted at in the painting showing the erection of the Djed pillar, for
some of the men who are engaged in the mock fight with papyrus stems
call out, "I take Horus," as if choosing sides. On this occasion the son
who approaches his mother with a view to union is the late king.[93]

One may well ask: "Why this sadness of Isis in the song we have
quoted above, and the resistance symbolized by the mock fights at
Papremis and at the erection of the Djed pillar, if an incestuous union is
the accepted form in which the periodicity of the sun's appearance and
reappearance, and also the resuscitation of the king are expressed?"
The answer lies in the preponderance of the thought of death over that
of rebirth. However gladly man would believe in unhampered rebirth
after death, yet the thought of death brings fear. The dangers and uncertainties which no beliefs about man's future state can overcome are
objectivated into opposition on the part of the mother-goddess, which in
its turn is put to nought in the mock fight. The battle both expresses and
overcomes the uncertainty.

A second question which may well be asked is how a relationship applicable to the sun in its course and the king in death can be transferred

to the god Horus. But the notion of a god who begets himself on his own mother became in Egypt a theological figure of thought expressing immortality. The god who is immortal because he can re-create himself is called Kamutef, "bull of his mother." That this term really deserves the drastic interpretation which we claim for it is amply proved.[94] We have referred at the beginning of this chapter to parallel expressions; for example, Geb is called the "bull" of his spouse Nut, and Amon the "bull of his mother, who rejoices in the cow, the husband impregnating with his phallus."[95] There are more detailed, but equally clear, theological elaborations, especially when we deal with the triad of father, mother, and son, which in later times became established in most of the Egyptian temples. At Karnak we find Khonsu as the son of Amon-Re and Mut, and the goddess is called "Mut the resplendent serpent who wound herself round her father Re and gave birth to him as Khonsu."[96] We shall presently describe a festival in the course of which the mystery of the Kamutef took place (chap. 15) and the god renewed himself through Pharaoh. Here we must only note once more that the Egyptians, pondering the problems of immanence and transcendence, of mortal kings sustaining an immortal order, found their means of expression in the spontaneous imagery of the African cattle-keepers.

CHAPTER 15

THE POWER IN THE EARTH: RESURRECTION

A. OSIRIS, SON OF GEB AND NUT

THE power in the earth is recognized by most men but is conceived in different forms. "Mother Earth" of the Greeks, Babylonians, and many modern peoples was not known in Egypt.[1] There the earth was a male god—Ptah or Geb. In the figure of Ptah the power in the earth was envisaged as supreme.[2] We have found this view expounded in the Memphite Theology (chap. 2). It remained characteristic of the teachings of Memphis at all times and is found in several important texts. Ramses II calls himself "King (ity), Son of Ta-Tjenen, like Atum."[3] A hymn from the end of the second millennium expresses it with the same allusions to the emergence of the earth out of a primeval ocean that we found in the Memphite Theology; for the "lassitude" of the land is its inaction under inundation, and this is but a repetition of that first state when the earth was covered by the waters of chaos:

> Thou hast stood (as king) on the land during its lassitude
> From which it recovered only afterwards
> When thou wert in thy shape of Ta-Tjenen,
> In thy manifestation as the Unifier of the Two Lands.
> What thy mouth created, what thy hands shaped (viz. the land),
> Thou hast taken it out of the primeval waters.[4]

The first phrase of the quotation shows that the Primeval Hill, which in the solar context was the first product of the Creator's activity, is here considered the very embodiment of the Creator, Ptah-Ta-Tjenen, "Ptah the Risen Land."

The figure of Geb would seem to possess the same potentialities as that of Ptah. Geb stands, in the first place, simply for the earth. Barley is grown "on the ribs of Geb," and the harvest is "what the Nile causes to grow on the back of Geb."[5] The same veneration of the powers in the earth which proclaims Ptah the First Cause addresses itself sometimes to Geb; we have quoted a pyramid text which states him to be the Ka of the other gods.* He is sometimes called "the father of the gods," and it

---

* See above, p. 67.

is possible that at some time and place he was worshiped as the Creator.[6] Yet in our sources indications of his supremacy are rare. Even in the theology of the Old Kingdom, Geb usually appears as part of the Ennead, among whom Atum, the sun-god, is the primary source of creative energy. But it is not Geb's dependence on the sun which is stressed but his power which supports the next generation of gods, including Osiris.

With the figure of Osiris, the dead king, we are by now familiar. When we consider him in his theological context, his relationship with Geb appears of fundamental importance.[7] Nut, the sky, and Geb, the earth, are his parents. As we have seen in the Memphite Theology, Geb adjudicates the rulership of Egypt when the throne has been left vacant by the death of Osiris. For the king of Egypt, Horus, is "the seed of Geb."[8] Thus, the accession of Tuthmosis I can be described in these words: "He has seated himself upon the throne of Geb, wearing the radiance of the double crown, the staff of royalty; he has taken his inheritance; he has assumed the seat of Horus."[9]

It is important for us to realize that this genealogy—Geb, Osiris, Horus—is not an empty theological formula but represents an acknowledgment of the power in the earth and its relation to kingship. It is part of a curious mythological figure—the Ennead or Nine Gods of Heliopolis—which looks at first sight entirely artificial.[10] Far from being an accidental combination of deities who happened to have found recognition in the city, this grouping represents a concept pregnant with deep religious significance.

At its head stood the creator-sun, Atum. Then followed the divine pair whom Atum created out of himself—Shu and Tefnut, air and moisture. The children of this couple followed. They were Geb and Nut, earth and sky; and their children, Osiris and Isis, Seth and Nephthys, were the last four gods of the Ennead.

There is clearly a profound difference between the last four deities and the preceding five. Atum, Shu and Tefnut, Geb and Nut represent a cosmology. Their names describe primordial elements; their interrelations imply a story of creation. The four children of Geb and Nut are not involved in this description of the universe. They establish a bridge between nature and man, and that in the only manner in which the Egyptians could conceive such a bond—through kingship. Osiris[11] was the mythological form of the dead ruler forever succeeded by his son Horus. The sister and wife of Osiris was Isis, the deified throne;*

* See above, pp. 43–44.

but she was completely personified and consequently able to assume a definite character in mythology. She was the loving mother of Horus and the faithful companion and supporter of Osiris. Nephthys' name means "Lady of the House," and she was conceived as the spouse of Seth. But in mythology she appears almost exclusively in connection with Osiris, whom she and Isis succor and bewail. She resembles the trusted friend or servant in the classical tragedy. Seth, finally, is the antagonist per se;* but this role endows him with certain characteristics of his own. He becomes the god of the desert and the Asiatics in opposition to the fertile land of Egypt; the god of thunder and clouds in opposition to the sun; even the god of the earth in opposition to Horus, the god of the sky, and the sun's protagonist, in opposition to the sun's enemy Apophis.[12] Above all, he is the opponent of Osiris and of Osiris' legitimate heir, Horus. We may call Isis, Nephthys, and Seth satellites of Osiris, for their whole *raison d'être* seems to have consisted originally in their relationship with him and with his son, whatever secondary features religious imagination may have added to this groundwork.

Thus the Ennead was formed out of the five cosmic gods and Osiris with the three gods of his circle. Here we hold the clue to its meaning; it was a theological concept which comprised the order of creation as well as the order of society. It is peculiar to the Egyptian concept of kingship that it envisaged the incumbent of that office as part of the world of the gods as well as of the world of men. If Osiris was the son of Geb and Nut, he was also the dead king in Egypt. And if Horus, the living king,[13] stood outside the Ennead, he was yet the pivot of this theological construction. Horus lived perennially in each king. Hence each king at death receded before his successor and merged with Osiris, the mythological figure of "king's father"; the power that had been guiding the state sank back into the earth and from there continued its beneficial care of the community, shown in the abundance of the harvest and the inundation. Egyptian views of great antiquity, rooted in African beliefs, find expression in this conception of the dead king's future life.†

But this view disregarded the ruler as a person. It did not remove the threat of annihilation which faced each individual king. Osiris, however, was the son not only of Geb, the earth, but also of Nut, the sky. This relation promised personal resurrection through rebirth. It could be said:

Thy mother Nut is spread over thee. . . . . She causes thee to be a god. . . . .
She protects thee from all evil in her name ("she of) the Great Sieve."[14] Thou art the eldest of her children [Pyr. 638].

* See above, pp. 21–22.　　　　　　　　† See above, pp. 33–35.

Osiris, the son of Nut, found immortality through rebirth and was thereby enabled to join the circuit of sun and stars. The remarkable coherence of Egyptian beliefs appears here again. The parentage of Osiris seems to involve him in two mutually exclusive destinies until we remember that the Egyptian hoped for a future life in unison with the great cyclic movements of nature which seem eternal.* In the circuit of the heavenly bodies, which passes through the Netherworld as well as through the sky, we have a concept to which the thoughts of "Osiris become earth" and "Osiris reborn in heaven" can be subordinated. The obscurity which remains when it is thus claimed that part of man is absorbed by nature while his individuality is somehow preserved is not greater than that in other accounts of the mystery of man's life after death. In any case, we have objective evidence that the view just set forth was indeed the one to which the Egyptians adhered. For the Memphite Theology, in its final section, ascribes precisely this twofold destiny to Osiris: "He entered the Secret Gates, the Glory of the Lords of Eternity (the dead) in step with Him who shines in the Horizon, on the path of Re, in the Great Throne (Memphis). He joined the court and fraternized with the gods of Ta-Tjenen, Ptah, Lord of Years."† It is obvious that "Osiris joining the court of Ta-Tjenen, 'The Risen Land' " is the mythological form of a belief which is expressed quite directly in the phrase "Thus Osiris became earth" which immediately follows our quotation. It is equally evident that the first sentences describe Osiris' joining the sun in its ciruit.

We have dealt with the personal aspect of the dead king's destiny in which both his mother Nut and his father Geb played a part (chaps. 10, 13, and 14). However, the community was more concerned with the other aspect—the manifestation of the power of the son of Geb in whatever came forth from the earth after apparent death: the annual vegetation after drought, the inundation after the diminution of the Nile, the rising of heavenly bodies after a period of disappearance. Osiris was not, like Ptah, the god of the earth, who, in the eyes of his devotees, *was* the earth, supreme master of all the unaccountable forces which it contains, and, in fact, on the strength of that, master of the universe and its Creator. Osiris, as we shall discern, was of lesser degree. He was the dead king. But since kings were divine, since the power they embodied was of the essence of nature itself, since Osiris was the son of Geb and Nut, his life could not end; his death was transfiguration. His power was

* See above, pp. 117–22.

† See above, p. 31.

recognized in that life which breaks forth periodically from the earth, everlastingly renewed. Hence Osiris was the god of resurrection.

Among the great gods of Egypt, Osiris was exceptional. No province of nature was entirely his. He was immanent in the earth, but not its personification. He participated in the solar circuit, but was not its master. The Nile had its own god, Hapi, and the grain its goddess, Ernutet.[15] Even the power of generation, the sheer fertility of plants and animals, was represented by another god, Min. Osiris was life caught in the spell of death. Hence he was not a "dying god" but—if the paradox be permitted—a dead god. There is no evidence that his death was represented in ritual; at every ceremony Osiris appeared as a god who had passed through death, who survived in the sense that he was not utterly destroyed, but who did not return to life. His resurrection meant his entry upon life in the Beyond, and it was one of the inspiring truths of Egyptian religion that, notwithstanding his death, Osiris became manifest as life in the world of men. From his grave in the earth or in the depleted Nile, from the world of the dead, his power emanated, mysteriously transmuted into a variety of natural phenomena which had one common feature: they waxed and waned.

B. OSIRIS IN THE GRAIN

The annual sprouting of vegetation from the soil is the most striking manifestation of the forces of rebirth and growth immanent in the earth; and Osiris is viewed as reappearing in the grain in the earliest texts which we possess, as well as in those of all succeeding periods. In the Memphite Theology it is the interment of Osiris at Memphis which makes the surrounding region into the granary of Egypt. In the Mystery Play of the Succession there are two distinct scenes in which Osiris is identified with barley. In the "Contendings of Horus and Seth," Osiris answers Re: "Wherefore shall my son Horus be defrauded, seeing that it is I who make you strong, and it is I who made the barley and the emmer to nourish the gods, and even so the living creatures after the gods, and no (other) god nor any goddess found himself (able) to do it."[16] Similarly it is said of Osiris in the Ptolemaic temple of Denderah: "Who made the corn from the liquid that is in him to nourish the nobles and the common folk; ruler and lord of food offerings; sovereign and lord of victuals."[17]

In the Ptolemaic temple of Philae ears of grain, watered by a priest, are shown to grow from the supine body of Osiris.[18] In tombs of the Eighteenth Dynasty and later an anthropomorphic figure consisting of earth and seeds was placed on a bier, and the figure was watered for a week so that the seeds were brought to germination. Thus the resurrection of the god (with whom the dead were all identified at the time) actually took place within the tomb.[19] The temple ritual of the Ptolemaic period included the preparation of "Osiris beds" or "gardens" in several of the main sanctuaries and there, again, the sprouting of the grain signified the resurrection of the god.[20]

It was not only in the official cult that Osiris was felt to arise in the grain; in late times, at any rate, the view was firmly established in popular beliefs. This is testified by several Greek and Roman authors. Thus Plutarch states, referring to the Egyptians: "When they hack up the earth with their hands and cover it up again after having scattered the seeds, wondering whether these will grow and ripen, then they behave like those who bury and mourn."[21]

At the harvest time the god in the grain died yet again. The first ears of corn were cut with wailing, and Isis was invoked. However, when the harvest was completed, the grain winnowed, and the seed corn gathered, the rebirth in the sprouting grain of the next season was anticipated and taken for granted. Late classical authors state that Isis collected the scattered limbs of Osiris in a winnowing basket, and such a basket was carried in the processions of the Isis cult throughout the Roman Empire. Since the child Dionysus was also "awakened" in a winnowing basket by the wild dances of the Thyriades on Mount Parnassus, we might doubt the Egyptian origin of the significance of winnowing. But we have a pyramid text which seems to contain this motif. It is a curious text which acknowledges the identity of the dead king and Osiris in the emphatic manner in which its first phrase is constructed. The middle part consequently refers to the beneficial features of the Osireian ritual of interment. But the text vigorously combines the king's ineluctable identity with Osiris and his desire for personal survival. He is the grain but mounts to heaven in the clouds of chaff which rise when the grain is winnowed.[22] The king's personality is not confined to the seed corn which must die in the earth to produce next year's harvest. This is the motif binding the opening line with the jubilant conclusion; we omit a few theological allusions:

> *Osiris* is Unas in the mounting chaff!
> His loathing is the earth;
> He has not entered Geb to perish.
> He is not sleeping in his house (tomb) upon earth
> So that his bones may be broken.

His hurt is driven out!
He has purified himself with the Horus Eye.
His hurt is driven out
By the Two Kites of Osiris (Isis and Nephthys).

. . . . Unas is up and away to heaven;
Unas is up and away to heaven
With the wind, with the wind! [Pyr. 308–9].

In this text we find an acknowledgment of the identification with Osiris but an evasion of the chthonic implications, and resurrection is achieved, as it were, by a short cut. We remember that in the Mystery Play of the Succession, when bread and beer, the products of barley, are brought in, "Horus speaks to Geb: They have put my father in the earth . . . . they have made it necessary to bewail him."* It is understandable that the king, when pondering his own imminent death, would not choose this aspect of his future life to dwell upon.

We must probably explain in the same way a curious discrepancy between popular and official religion in Egypt, if the usages of the peasants of Greco-Roman times, quoted at the beginning of this section, go back to preclassical antiquity. In that case, the connection between Osiris and the grain was acknowledged at every stage of the farmer's labor, but it played little part in the official calendar. This stands in striking contrast to the preponderant role allotted there to the vicissitudes of that other manifestation of Osiris, the Nile. As we shall see, these dominated the festivals of the official year. Obviously the harvest could not be neglected; the state had to participate in it and thereby establish harmony with the progression of nature through the seasons. Therefore, the king went each year at harvest time to cut a sheaf of grain and to dedicate it to a god. But this god was not Osiris. For the harvest could only mean death to a deity whose power was immanent in the earth and manifest in the grain. The grain was cut, and the earth lay bare under a strengthening sun, waiting for the flood waters which were not to be expected for another two or three months. A harvest festival centered around Osiris would have been bound to take place in a minor key. The Babylonians, as we shall see, could have entertained such a thought.† All we know of the Egyptians shows that they would have found it distasteful. They did not readily admit the shadow side of life, not only, perhaps, on hedonistic grounds, but also because, in their static conception of the world, grief had no permanence. To the Baby-

* See above, p. 136.
† See below, pp. 281–85.

lonians uncertainty was of the essence of life, and to deny anxiety would have been as unrealistic to them as predominance of distress to the Egyptians.

The harvest festival, then, was dedicated, not to Osiris, but to Min ∤—the god who personified the generative force in nature, the abundant power of procreation in men, beasts, and plants. The god's statue was, from the earliest times, the figure of an ithyphallic man, and it was accompanied in processions and in chapels by a box of lettuce plants.[23] Moreover, Min was a rain god, "opener of clouds,"[24] and related to the African complex of beliefs regarding cattle through his association with a white bull and the epithet "he who has created the vegetation, letting the herds live."[25] Further, his shrine was crowned with a pair of bull's horns.[26] The name "Festival of the Stairs of Min" establishes a relationship with the concept of the Primeval Hill, which, as a center of creative force, was appropriately thought of as the place where the god took his stand.

At this harvest festival[27] the king went in procession, accompanied by the white bull, the queen, the standards, the statues of the ancestors, and also the statue of the god, which was carried on the shoulders of a body of priests hidden except for their heads by great decorated hangings. Perhaps the god's statue was carried to the fields, where a temporary shrine for him may have been erected. At any rate, the king cut a sheaf of emmer which seems to have been offered to the white bull. Up to this point the procedure has been deduced from the texts and reliefs without great difficulty. The offering of grain to the bull can only be explained by surmise; perhaps it was an apotropaic rite. Since the first fruit of the harvest served to strengthen the embodiment of fertility, the bull, the danger that the cutting-down of the grain would cast a spell of sterility was averted. The succeeding rites are obscure. It is possible, though there are only hints to this effect, that the king and queen had intercourse at this point.[28] At any rate, a priest invoked the mystery of the Kamutef—an epithet given to Min more regularly than to any other god: "Hail to thee, Min, who impregnates his mother! How mysterious is that which thou hast done to her in the darkness."

The mystery is that of conception and rebirth. But was it merely Min as the personification of fertility in general who was renewed in the union with his mother at the festival? Or was it, at the same time, the god in Pharaoh who prepared the renewal of his incarnation by begetting an heir? Hatshepsut was called "the daughter of the Kamutef," and it was said that Amon became one with Tuthmosis I when she was begotten.* In the Festival of Min the sacrifice immediately preceding the ceremony of the sheaf was offered up to "his (the king's) father, Min-Kamutef; to the Ka of the king; and to the Royal Ancestors." If we remember that the Ka represents the vital force, this series of three invocations may well concern the continuation of the royal line.[29] The divinity who is incarnate in the king is Horus, but we have seen that in certain aspects Pharaoh appeared as Upwaut,† and there is no reason to deny that Min, too, may have been thought to animate the king in certain circumstances. Min was definitely viewed as a form of Horus, as the text of the festival implies when it states that "Min issues orders together with his father Osiris." Already in the Middle Kingdom, Min was called "son of Osiris, born of the divine Isis"[30]—epithets which identify him unmistakably with Horus, the ruling Pharaoh. The pyramid texts connect Min with the Dual Shrines,[31] and theophoric names of princes of the Fourth and Fifth Dynasties are composed exclusively with the elements Re, Horus, and Min.[32] It is clear from these facts that Min was more intimately connected with kingship in early times than any other god except Horus, and we might have expected as much. Min personifies the fertility of fields, beasts, and plants, and Egyptian kingship insured the benefits of nature's abundance for society. Min, then, might be an aspect of Pharaoh. It would be consistent with this line of thought if the continuation of the royal line were achieved at the Festival of Min, where the god was one with Pharaoh as Amon had been one with Tuthmosis I in the conception of Hatshepsut. There is, in fact, a text expressing the most intimate relation which can be conceived as existing between the king and the god: "Thy (Min's) heart united with the king as the heart of Horus united with his mother Isis when he violated her and turned his heart toward her."[33]

In addition to these indications, there is a general consideration which would lead us to expect an act affecting kingship to form part of the ritual of the Feast of Min: we need such an act to balance the cutting of the sheaf of emmer which stamps the feast as a harvest festival. In any case, the concluding rites of the whole ceremony are such that the interpretation as a harvest festival is inadequate. The final scene shows the king returning from the shrine of Min crowned with the double crown and holding in his hands some ears of the grain which has been cut and consecrated. Two priests hold bulls' tails, and some references to "Souls of the East" remain obscure. But at the same time four birds are released to carry the following proclamation to the four corners of

* See above, pp. 44 and 105.   † See above, pp. 26, 71, 92, and 204.

the earth: "Horus the son of Isis and Osiris has assumed the Great Crown of Upper and Lower Egypt; King Ramses III has assumed the Great Crown of Upper and Lower Egypt."

At the coronation a similar release of birds seems to have proclaimed the king's accession,[34] but of this there could be no question at the Feast of Min. The message could convey only something that happened at the annual celebration. It could not announce that the king had ascended the throne, but it might have announced that the god Min-Har-Nakht (Min-Horus the Vigorous) had assumed the crown during the festival by becoming one with King Ramses III. We can only surmise what the texts do not state explicitly. But it is clear that the festival led to a reaffirmation of the harmonious interlocking of nature and society in the person of the sovereign. Thus the state celebrated the reaping of the crop with the worship, not of Osiris, but of a deity whose exuberant fertility was immune against the depredations of the reapers upon the earth's growth.

C. OSIRIS IN THE NILE

Osiris was manifest in the grain, for the seemingly dead seeds sprout and grow because of the vital forces of the earth. An equally mysterious and momentous phenomenon, which may be understood as the effect of chthonic forces, is the annual flood of the Nile which gives new vitality to the parched, denuded fields.[35] The water of the inundation which carries the silt was called the "pure water" or the "young water," and it is this water that was thought to be brought by Osiris or to emanate from him or to take its power from him, so that Osiris might even be identified with it: "Horus comes to recognize his father in thee, rejuvenated in thy name 'young water' " (Pyr. 589). Vitality emerging from the earth, either in plant life or in the water of the Nile, was a manifestation of Osiris, son of Geb.[36] The place where the Nile broke forth from the depths had been identified by the early Egyptians with the weird granite rocks, the rapids, and the whirling currents of the cataracts at Assuan. Therefore, a libation was poured for the dead king to return to him what had come forth from him:

> O Osiris Pepi! Take to thyself this libation (*ḳbḥw*) which is poured for thee by Horus, in thy name "who came forth from the cataract (*ḳbḥw*)."
> Take to thyself thy natron (*nṭr*) that thou mayest become divine (*nṭry*). Thy mother Nut has caused thee to be a god (*nṭr*) because of thine enemy, in thy name "god (*nṭr*)."
> Take to thyself the outflow that has come forth from thee [Pyr. 765].

Ramses IV says in his hymn to Osiris: "Thou art the Nile . . . . gods and men live from thy outflow."[37] A pyramid text says: "The watercourses are full, and the channels overflow because of the purifications which come forth from Osiris" (Pyr. 848).

This same thought is elaborated in all kinds of ways. Osiris is equated with every known body of water—the Aegean Sea, the Ocean, the Bitter Lakes, etc.[38] Concrete imagining goes so far as to equate the inundation with the liquids running from his decaying corpse (Pyr. 788, 1360). These secondary developments do not, however, obscure the plain sense of the majority of the texts, that Osiris is manifest in the life-giving waters rising from the earth when land and people need them most. Even in Plutarch's days this view of Osiris was valid; he states: "On the nineteenth of Athyr they descend to the water in the night. The stolists and priests bring a casket which contains a gold vessel. Into this they pour sweet water and the crowd which is present raises the cry: 'Osiris is found.' "[39]

This "finding" of Osiris in the Nile plays an important part in both myth and ritual. It is common in the pyramid texts,[40] which generally locate it on the banks of Nedyt—a site at Abydos. In the Memphite Theology, Horus was "put in the place where his father was drowned," and later the body of Osiris was seen by Isis and Nephthys while it floated down the Nile and was "found" and interred at Memphis. In this scene the regal and cosmic features of Osiris cannot be disentangled. If the fertilizing power of the inundation was conceived as an emanation from Osiris, the vivid picture of the god floating down with the rising waters of the flood is wonderfully suggestive. At the same time Osiris appears as the late ruler whose interment in the royal castle explains the fertility of the land around Memphis.

The motif of the drowning of Osiris (which also occurs in the pyramid texts)[41] is in itself ambiguous. It may be simply the most concrete image in which the fertilizing power of the flood can be combined with an anthropomorphic figure: the power of the earth to bring forth fruit disappears when the water in the Nile recedes to a few deep channels in its bed. Osiris is lost in the shrunken river, drowned, possibly thrown into it by the hostile Seth, the god of the hot desert. When the summer has progressed a little, the waters begin to rise—without any visible reason, for the heat continues. But fertility returns with the flood; Osiris is "found," in the Nile, or on the "banks of Nedyt." An alternate explanation of the motif of Osiris' death by drowning starts from the premise that Osiris is pre-eminently inherent in the earth; by this approach his "drowning" may be the image for the disappearance of the fields underneath the water of the inundation, even though the latter emanates from Osiris himself.[42] This last view seems less likely than the former to be correct, since it would imply that the "finding" of Osiris consisted in the emergence of the fertilized lands from the receding flood, while the other interpretation gives a precise mythical counterpart for the ritual recorded by Plutarch. In another pyramid text (Pyr. 1011-15) Osiris appears as a personification of the Nile in parallelism with Geb as the personification of the earth. Just as the dead king is lifted to heaven by Geb when he enters the earth (as a corpse), so Osiris will lift him to heaven if he should fall into the Nile. And in the damaged Scene 4 of the Mystery Play of the Succession "fish and birds are ordered to search for Osiris," an order which, again, points to his being in the Nile. It is even possible that Osiris was at one point in the play represented by eight jars filled with Nile water.[43]

While the relation of Osiris to vegetation remained alive in popular usages and in the festivals of kingship, his association with the Nile flood was recognized by the main seasonal celebrations which followed the rise and fall of the river. The New Year was meant to coincide with the rise of the Nile; the great celebrations at the end of the month of Khoiak coincided with the Nile's subsidence and the emergence of the fertilized fields. When the Nile was at its lowest, Isis and Nephthys were said to bewail Osiris.

It is likely that this event was celebrated by the people, since the fearsome scarcity of the water upon which they depended would inevitably call up the specter of famine and urge participation by some rite. We have only a late reference to the Season of Inundation, however, when Pausanias, showing that mythology can be interpreted as sympathetic magic, says: "The Egyptians say that Isis bewails Osiris when the river begins to rise; and when it inundates the fields they say that it is the tears of Isis."[44] The tradition may, of course, be ancient. The state also acted in the annual emergency, at least in the Twentieth Dynasty. We know from inscriptions on the rocks of Silsileh that Ramses II and Ramses III threw sacrifices into the river at this critical time and also a scroll of papyrus which contained either an order to the Nile to rise or a contract proffering gifts in exchange for its rise.*

Also roughly about this time the Great Procession took place at Abydos. It seems that the Egyptians were anxious to assist at the festivities and that the bodies of their dead were sometimes taken there at about this time.[45] The celebrations took place upon a lake, as we know from the inscription of Neferhotep.[46] This lake is also mentioned in the

* See above, pp. 58–59.

pyramid texts. The god Osiris was aboard a ship, and opposition against him was overcome on the waters of Nedyt.* This setting and the date of the festival (the time of the rising inundation) make it tempting to suppose that the Great Procession "found" Osiris as the sweet water of the mounting flood in the manner related by Plutarch. Of this, however, there is no proof, though the pyramid texts state that Osiris was "found" on the banks of Nedyt.

In the Great Procession and in other festivals possibly connected with the rising Nile,[47] the accent was naturally upon victory and the renewal of life. In the autumn, when the great river subsides, other festivals were held; and these, too, were dedicated to Osiris. On the last day of the Season of Inundation (30 Khoiak) the "Interment of Osiris" was enacted. Plutarch's account seems misleading.[48] In Pharaonic times these celebrations apparently possessed none of the lugubriousness which their name suggests, nor was there reason for grief. If the recession of the Nile flood showed the diminution of the god's power in one sphere, it was merely as a prelude to an increased display of his vigor in another. For almost at once the freshly sown grain would start to sprout in the drying fields.

Perhaps we must reckon with the possibility that the name "Interment of Osiris" referred, not to the disappearance of the water of the inundation, but to the sowing of the grain. The phrase is preserved in certain calendars (such as the one at Denderah) which also mention the feast of "hacking up the earth" eight or eighteen days earlier. This is a long interval to leave between two activities which would normally follow each other immediately, and so we remain uncertain as to the precise meaning of the "Interment of Osiris," in so far as it was not a rite of royalty. The Ptolemaic calendars were certainly not concerned with popular rites but with certain symbolical priestly acts;[49] yet one would expect these to have originated in celebrations of the people as a whole. Plutarch's report that the peasants sowed with a mournful mien as if burying someone would also support the interpretation of the "Interment of Osiris" as the sowing of the grain, if we could be sure that the tradition is old. But the official celebrations of a season which in Egypt is one of liberation and expectancy were altogether in a happy vein; they culminated in the erection of the Djed pillar as a symbol of the god's resurrection. The Denderah calendar shows the following entry for the last day of the Season of Inundation: "Raising of the Djed-pillar in Busiris, the day of the Interment of Osiris."[50]

* See below, pp. 203–7.

We have discussed the raising of the Djed pillar in its connection with kingship,* but it was an annual event, as was the "Interment of Osiris." Both rites were performed as regular periodic celebrations in which the community actively expressed its concern over the vicissitudes of a god whose "resurrection"—the rising Nile or the growing grain—was a prerequisite for its own welfare during the coming year. Moreover, these recurring celebrations of the revival of Osiris' power in the earth obtained added significance if, in the preceding year, a king had died. Then the god honored yearly by the people's celebration was actually present in their midst in the form of the dead body of the later ruler. The "Interment of Osiris" gained an altogether exceptional actuality in the concluding rites of the royal funeral. The revival of the forces of nature were never more intimately related to the hope of resurrection; the expectancy and promise of prosperity, always inherent in the season, were never more vividly experienced, than when the erection of the Djed pillar was followed by the festivities of the new king's coronation.

We have quoted songs† which demonstrate that the coronation was greeted by the people with a sense of relief and with expectations explicable only if we remember that the accession of a new king was an event of transcendent significance. When we now approach this same celebration through the religious festivals and inquire how it would affect the annual feasts of Osiris, we can appreciate once more the consistency and inner logic of Egyptian beliefs. The community participated in the great natural crises of the year—the turning-points in the annual cycle of the Nile, the sowing and ripening of their crops—by festivals centering round the mythological figure of a divine king, Osiris. The realities of kingship—its beginning in a new reign, its renewal in the Sed festival, its reassertion in the Feast of Min—were made to coincide with those same "New Year's Days." When, therefore, death imparted actuality to the formula of Horus succeeding Osiris, the rites of the succession, celebrated on the dates of the Osiris festivals, were not experienced as a combination of the ceremonies of royalty with those of the god, but the two coalesced into a single celebration which was exceptional only in that the underlying conception of a society functioning within nature by means of its king was realized with rare intensity.

We possess a small monument on the death of Tuthmosis III which throws vivid light on the peculiar moods of these celebrations. We must remember that this king had altered the face of Egypt profoundly: he had given it an Asiatic empire, had erected buildings throughout the

---

* See above, pp. 178–80.   † See above, pp. 58 and 60.

land, and had organized its administration effectively. Moreover, he had ruled for fifty-four years. In other words, at his death, a situation arose which many of his subjects had never known; they saw the country without his strong hand at the helm. His death took place about March 14,[51] in the most critical period of the year, with the harvest being removed from the fields, the Nile so low that "there was not enough water to cover the secrets of the Netherworld."[52] Osiris was dead. It was not certain what the inundation would amount to. In fact, the inundation was not due for another three months.

This situation explains the issue of small scarabs with the following reassuring inscription: "Tuthmosis III is in heaven like the moon. The Nile is at his service. He (Tuthmosis III) opens its cave to give life to Egypt."[53] The name Osiris is avoided, since it is obviously desired to refer to the late ruler. If our conjecture as to the period of the issue is correct, the reference to his strong personality was the most important feature of the text. But the implications are so outspokenly Osireian in character as to be unmistakable. "The Nile is at his service." Moreover, he lets it come forth from its cave, from the earth, the domain of Osiris. And, finally, the king is said to be in heaven, not like Re, but like the moon; and the moon is another form in which Osiris becomes manifest. In the temple at Denderah it is said: "He (Osiris) awakes from sleep (of death) and he flies like the benu bird and he makes his place in the sky as the moon."[54]

D. OSIRIS IN ORION AND THE MOON

We have seen that Osiris "becomes earth" but is not a "god of the earth"; he is a god of the manifestations of life which come forth from it. Osiris, if we must use these inexact terms at all, is a "god of grain" and a "god of the Nile." But anything which seems to come forth from the earth may be considered a manifestation of Osiris. And, though it may seem paradoxical to us, this applies to all heavenly bodies. The stars rise at the horizon, and so do the sun and the moon, so that Osiris is even called "he of the horizon from which Re goes forth." But the more usual heavenly representative of Osiris is Orion. We have met this equation before,* and we may quote yet another text in which it is said of the dead king: "Lo, he has come as Orion. Lo, Osiris has come as Orion" (Pyr. 819c). The near-by dog star, Sothis, is Isis. The actual position of the two in the sky is reflected in a Ptolemaic text in which Isis addresses Osiris as follows: "Thy sacred image, Orion in

* See above, pp. 118–19.

heaven, rises and sets every day; I am Sothis following after him, and I will not forsake him."[55]

There is no denying that to us this spreading net of associations and identifications seems to destroy the significance of the symbols involved, and the limit of the meaningful is well passed when we meet in New Kingdom texts such compounds as "Osiris-Apis-Atum-Horus in one, the Great God."* But if we disregard such extremes, we shall find that much that appears senseless at first sight is not without meaning. Moreover, the primitives, far from sharing our passion for precise definition and distinction, appreciate each relationship which can be established between seemingly disparate phenomena as a strengthening of the fabric of understanding in which they attempt to comprehend the world. The heavenly associations of the chthonic Osiris in particular appear appropriate. There is, first, a similarity between Osiris, who overcomes Seth and death, and the heavenly bodies, victorious over darkness and over those unknown powers which cause their occasional disappearance. The waxing and the waning of the moon show particularly close similarities to the vicissitudes of Osiris, who succumbs to his enemy to be revived by Isis; who dies in the grain and wastes away in the waters of the Nile to recuperate mysteriously after set intervals.[56] Moreover, the moon is widely believed to influence the germination of seeds and to affect animal fertility.[57] In late times crescent-shaped figures of moist earth and seeds were made as soon as Osiris, as Nile water, was "found."[58] And in the Osiris hymn of Ramses IV we read: "In the days of which it is said that Nut was not yet pregnant with thy beauty, thou didst live nevertheless in the shape of gods and men and mammals and birds and fishes. Lo, thou art the moon on high; thou becomest young at will and agest at will."[59]

In addition to the similarity between the fate of Osiris and the fates of the heavenly bodies in their courses,[60] there is another concept which permits their comparison. That is the cosmic circuit, which comprises the Netherworld of Osiris and the sky in one continuous series of movements. In fact, we read: "A ramp is trodden for thee to the Netherworld, to the place where Orion is." There the deceased joins the cosmic circuit. If the daily reappearance of the sun and stars assumed the character of a resurrection, it was not illogical to recognize that a force, so similar as to suggest identity, animated the heavenly bodies, the growth of the crops, and the emergence, after drought, of the waters of the Nile. Hence a blessing like the following, spoken to a king: "I

* See above, p. 146.

grant thee that thou mayest rise like the sun, rejuvenate thyself like the moon, repeat life like the flood of the Nile."[61]

E. OSIRIS, KING OF THE DEAD

If many natural phenomena can be interpreted as resurrections, the power of resurrection is peculiarly Osiris' own. The divine figure of the dead king personified the resurgence of vitality which becomes manifest in the growing corn, the waxing flood, the increasing moon. But Osiris was not characterized by sheer vitality such as Min possessed; his was the gift of revival, of resurrection. For the king had to die to enter the earth and benefit man as a chthonic god; the seed corn had to die to bring forth the harvest; the Nile had to recede to bring forth the flood.

Osiris, then, defeats death. Therefore, he could gain a significance which surpassed even the Egyptian's concern about the integration of society and nature. His fate might be construed as a promise of future life for all. But, for this to be possible, it was necessary that the barrier which separated king and commoners as essentially different be weakened. This happened in the First Intermediate Period, when the disintegration of the Old Kingdom brought about a decline of kingship and a dissolution of established traditions. All kings survived in the Beyond as Osiris; the people, lacking guidance, usurped the royal prerogative in their anxiety and aspired to an Osireian burial in the hope of gaining resurrection.* From that time onward, we find that Osiris, the dead king, is adored as the prototype and savior of the common dead.

In the following pages we shall discuss this aspect of Osiris. It prevails in the majority of extant monuments. But it was not new. It was as little a reinterpretation of the god's original character as the chthonic aspect which we have studied in its various manifestations. Both aspects pertained to Osiris because he was a dead king, ruling the powers immanent in the earth,† and also the dead.

OSIRIS, CHIEF OF THE WESTERNERS

Osiris was resurrected, but he did not resume his former existence, i.e., he did not reascend the throne. The work of Seth was not undone entirely, for Seth, too, had his recognized function in the existing order. Osiris was resurrected to a life in the Beyond; his figure appears

---

* See below, pp. 207–10.　　　　† See above, pp. 33–35.

wrapped in mummy cloth. He is the "Chief of the Westerners," the king of the dead.

The epithet "Chief of the Westerners," however fitting, seems originally not to have referred to Osiris. Whatever the poorer people may have believed, the men of the Old Kingdom who left us records relied on the king whom they had served in this world to guide them into the Beyond. The figure of Osiris did not at first replace that of the individual monarch in this respect. Hence it is understandable that Osiris does not seem to be mentioned in the great temple of Abydos before the Middle Kingdom. The earlier inscriptions, some of which reach back to the beginning of the monarchy, name "Khentiamentiu," the "Chief of the Westerners."[62] This god is depicted as a dog or jackal couchant 🐕, in the manner of Anubis, with whom he is often identified.

But the fact that Osiris absorbed Khentiamentiu (a process already completed when the pyramid texts were written,[63] though the temple texts of the Old Kingdom ignore it) does not mean, as is often maintained, that Osiris was a god of the dead in the sense that the jackal-god was. The difference between the two is too great. The jackal knows the ways of the desert: he guides the dead into the cemeteries in which he is master. The Egyptians had several gods of this type; they were the lords of the necropoleis. Anubis, moreover, became the god of the burial rites—of mummification—as well as of the tombs. Hence these deities are gods of the dead in a much more restricted sense than Osiris.

It is, of course, significant that Osiris early should have been identified with a necropolis god. But Osiris did not merely preside over the funeral rites or the grave. Since he was a dead king, he was the leader and protector of the dead; he was also their prototype because he had reached eternal life through death. Mortals might follow him in the Hereafter and find life.

It is true that Osiris is at first invoked alongside Anubis. But this is a perfectly understandable combination; the jackal-god was called upon because the dead entered the grave. But at the same time an appeal was made to the leader who had preceded the dead in the Hereafter. Since Osiris was, and always remained, the mythological figure with whom each succeeding ruler merged at his death, men looked to him for guidance in death.

NYAKANG

In order to imagine with sufficient vividness the role which such a figure may play in the spiritual life of a people, we should consider for

a moment a very similar god worshiped by the Shilluk, modern Nilotes who are related to the ancient Egyptians. We have referred above* to Nyakang, who, like Osiris, counts as a former king. Like Osiris, too, he is credited with having given to his people the elements of culture. Both are permanently concerned with the well-being of their people and influence it from Beyond. "Even before the millet is reaped the people cut some of the ripening ears and thrust them into the thatch of the sacred hut. Thus it would seem that the Shilluk believe themselves to be dependent upon the favor of Nyakang for the rain and the crops"[64]— just as Osiris brings the inundation and the crops to the Egyptians. The supreme god of the Shilluk is not Nyakang but Juok, just as Amon-Re is acknowledged as superior to Osiris. Like Osiris, Nyakang is a single god with whom successive rulers coalesce. But at this point the peculiarly Egyptian view of kingship presents a more complicated picture than the Shilluk concept provides. Though Osiris is said to be the Ka of Horus, and the two unite in the mystic embrace of the ritual of succession, the living king in Egypt is not identical with Osiris but becomes Osiris at death. Nyakang is the equivalent of both Horus and Osiris in this respect. He is a former king, but he is incorporate in each successive king or *ret*, though he has an independent existence outside this incarnation.†
He is therefore immortal and is the Ka of both king and people, as the Egyptians would say. We may gain an impression of these beliefs with a certain directness in the following story: "When a missionary asked the Shilluk as to the manner of Nyakang's death they were filled with amazement at his ignorance and stoutly maintained that he never died, for were he to die all the Shilluks would die also."[65]

For our present purpose the most interesting feature of Shilluk beliefs is the opportunity they offer for studying a mythological figure who combines human and divine, historical and religious, features, and who, moreover, is credited with individuality while absorbing the personalities of successive rulers. It is difficult for us to understand these beliefs. We observe that each Pharaoh had an individual funerary cult; each *ret* of the Shilluk at death receives a shrine which is kept up. Yet Osiris was worshiped throughout Egypt, and we find a number of sites claiming his tomb, or, in the tradition which has come down to us, part of his body. In the Shilluk country, too, there are a number of tombs of Nyakang; yet these "are in fact cenotaphs; for though spoken of as his tombs it is well known that he is not buried in any of them."[66]

The Shilluk and the ancient Egyptians thus confront us with the doc-

* Pp. 43 and 167.   † See above, p. 114 and 133–39.

trine that a succession of individuals embodies the same divine being, yet they do not disregard the individuality of each separate ruler. The Egyptians, as we have seen, admitted the existence of this paradox by envisaging a twofold destiny for their ruler after death: as Osiris "become earth" the dead ruler lost his separateness, but as Osiris son of Nut he gained individual rebirth in the Hereafter. These views form the theological correlate to the existence of temples for the state worship of Osiris alongside royal tombs and temples.

BUSIRIS

The comparison of ancient Egyptian and Shilluk beliefs makes some problems connected with Osiris less embarrassing, since we can at least propose a solution by analogy. This applies, for instance, to the fact that even in early texts Osiris seems related to more than one site. Most important among these is Busiris, a site in the eastern Delta whose Greek name, quoted just now, means "House of Osiris." Osiris is habitually called "Lord of Busiris," and the epithet even precedes "Lord of Abydos." It has therefore been assumed that Osiris was originally at home in the Delta, especially since the god of the Busirite region, Andjeti, was (alone among the early symbols) of human shape and appeared with feathers ⫴, crook ⌇, and flail ⋀, as did Osiris. It is, therefore, widely believed that Osiris derived these attributes from a deified Delta king.[67]

It may well be that Osiris was at an early date connected with Busiris, but the argument which we have just summarized and which maintains that the cult of Osiris spread from Busiris to Upper Egypt lacks cogency and cannot be maintained in the face of evidence to the contrary. We may recall that feathers, crook, and flail are no more than the early attributes of rulership and that it would be easy to invert the usual theory and to suppose that a southern conqueror, such as Scorpion, subjected part of the eastern Delta prior to the reign of Menes and thus earned the title "*Andjeti* ('He of the Andjet district') who commands in the eastern provinces";[68] he might even have given to the subjected region the unusual standard in the shape of an early king.[69] This theory would find support in the fact that Andjeti's headgear includes a long streamer hanging down at the back—an ornament which is characteristic for Min and Amon, two gods of undoubted Upper Egyptian origin. But we set little store by this kind of hypothetical reasoning and would rather insist on other considerations.

Each great chieftain of the predynastic period who had become a legendary figure would tend to be regarded as Osiris once the country had been united under a Horus king. For those who lived under Pharaonic rule and accepted the cosmological views which we have described in the preceding chapters would find the predynastic conditions incomprehensible and would interpret traditions relating to the great chiefs of the past as concerned with Osiris.[70] A situation still met with in Africa would thus acquire its peculiarly Egyptian character. The Yaos, for instance, inhabit land formerly occupied by the Anyanya. These buried their chiefs on hilltops, and the Yaos continue to worship these "'gods of the land' along with their own ancestors and look upon them as *genii loci* of particular hills."[71] It is likely enough that in Egypt, too, some venerated tombs of predynastic chieftains survived the unification of the country. However, they would have become shrines, not of local gods, but of Osiris, for a dead king always became Osiris. In this way an apparently ancient tradition would have connected Osiris with a number of shrines, and this assumption, in turn, could explain the strange fact that several sites in Egypt claimed to possess his body, or part of it. For the story that Seth dismembered the body of Osiris and that Isis buried the parts where she found them—that is, at the fourteen, sixteen, or forty-two sites claiming Osiris relics—can hardly have been an original Egyptian belief. It is only known from late authors who stood under the influence of the myths of Dionysus and Adonis, and it disregards the Egyptians' conviction that the preservation of an undamaged body is the first requirement for life in the Hereafter.[72] The pyramid texts abound in spells in which Isis and Nephthys, Horus or Nut, "unite" the members of the dead Osiris; they nowhere hint at an earlier wilful dismemberment. The gods repair the normal results of decay—the dislocation which one finds in burials without mummification, where rats and jackals add to the confusion and damage following the dissolution of flesh and tendons. The myth of dismemberment sounds like a rationalization of the fact that many places claimed the tomb of Osiris; but it cannot explain that fact.

Busiris possessed one of these and was connected with Osiris already in the Old Kingdom. But we could only accept the view now current that the Osiris cult emanated from Busiris if we were prepared to leave a number of facts unexplained which become understandable if Abydos in Upper Egypt was the original center of the worship of Osiris.

ABYDOS

The most important of the Osiris relics, the head, was assigned to Abydos by tradition; and it was there that later times recognized the tomb of Osiris in the grave of one of the kings of the First Dynasty and

that the Great Procession took place. From the Middle Kingdom onward, Abydos was the main center of the Osiris cult. We may well ask
what were the grounds for this association of an unimportant town in
Upper Egypt with the cult of the god. There is considerable, though circumstantial, evidence to suggest that the association was an original
one. It seems that Osiris (as the dead king) was acknowledged and worshiped by the house from which Menes derived and which owned the
province of This where Abydos lies. If this is true, the worship of
Osiris, not as a god of the dead, but as the mythological form of the
dead ruler, was already established at Abydos before the rise of Menes.

We do not maintain that the worship of Osiris at Abydos was unique
in all respects. On the contrary, we have attempted to show that the
figure of Osiris represents ideas concerning kingship which were deeply
rooted in Egypt and possibly in the Hamitic substratum of Egyptian culture. Just because the dead chiefs were considered, throughout Egypt,
to continue to influence the forces of nature, the worship of Osiris as a
dead king could be accepted throughout the land once the country had
been united under Menes. One would expect, however, that the specific forms which that worship assumed (such as the Great Procession)
and the name under which the dead kings were worshiped (Osiris)
would derive from the region whence the royal house came. And this
is precisely what the evidence seems to suggest.

This evidence is found in the Memphite Theology—which was probably composed soon after the unification of the country—and in certain
features of the Osiris festivals, celebrated at Abydos in historic times.
The Theology takes for granted the multifarious connections between
Osiris as the buried ruler, grain, and the Nile, so that it must deal with
old established views; it treats them more summarily than the new teachings concerning Ptah which are carefully argued and set forth step by
step.

Now these new teachings contain certain features which seem to
point to the region of Abydos. This region, of which This was the political center, was known as "The Great Land," "great" standing again
for "greatest" in the sense of "oldest" and alluding to the Primeval
Hill.[73] The same applies to the epithet of the god Ptah, namely Ta-
Tjenen, "the Risen Land"; and not only this phrase but also the manner
in which the god is represented shows resemblance to the Abydene usages. Ta-Tjenen wears two feathers upon the horizontal horns of an ex-
tinct species of ram, *Ovis longipes palaeoaegypticus*, and, since this crown
is also worn by Andjeti, it is usual to consider it Lower Egyptian. But

this argument is not sound, and the crown seems, on the contrary, to belong to the region of This. The two feathers appear on the standard of the province 🏛 and also on the standard of Abydos 🏛 (Fig. 4). Moreover, they are worn by the local god of This, Onuris; the falcon-god of Hierakonpolis-Nekhen 🦅, as a beautiful gold head shows;[74] and the god Min of Koptos 🏺, from whom Amon derived them. And Nekhen and Koptos fell within the territory dominated by Menes and his house.[75]

The attributes which Ta-Tjenen seems to have assimilated from this region draw our attention to a possible connection with Abydos presented by the main teachings of the Memphite Theology. We have seen that the most novel feature of this theology consists in its claim that the earth, and not the sun, was the First Cause. It is clear that this doctrine may owe something to a creed which assigned great influence to the dead king "become earth"—a creed such as we may postulate for Abydos if Osiris really originated there. Now the founder of Memphis came from the same region, and this adds likelihood to the supposition that similarities between the dogmas for the Ptah temple in the new capital and Abydene beliefs should be explained as derivations by the younger from the older site. This applies to such symbols as the feather crown, to names like "The Great Land," and to the general fact that a chthonic god is endowed with supreme creative power.

THE GREAT PROCESSION

The distinctive feature of the cult of Osiris at Abydos was the Great Procession. It was an eminently local festival; people came from all over the country to take part in it. Such festivals have a strongly traditional character, and it is significant that the Great Procession, held at a site where early kings were buried, apparently retained throughout historical times certain features of the royal funerals. Moreover, Osiris counted as one of those early kings—or, rather, he represented each one of them.

The Great Procession is described by one Ikhernofret, who went, under Senusert III, to represent the king at the festival:

> I arranged the Procession of Upwaut when he went to champion (avenge, support) his father.
> I repelled those who rebelled against the Neshemet boat and overthrew the enemies of Osiris.
> I arranged the Great Procession and accompanied the god on his way.
> I caused the divine boat to sail, and Thoth guided the journey.
> I adorned the boat named "He who shines forth in Truth, the Lord of Abydos" with a deckhouse and put on him (Osiris) beautiful jewelry when he went to the locality of Peqer.

I directed the path of the god to his tomb in Peqer.
I championed Unnefer (Osiris) on that day of the great conflict and
   overthrew all his enemies on the banks of Nedyt.
I made him embark in the ship. She carried his beauty.
I made the hearts of the deserts of the East great for joy and brought
   jubilation to the hearts of the deserts of the West when they saw
   the beauty of the Neshemet boat.
She landed at Abydos and brought Osiris, the Chief of the Westerners,
   the Lord of Abydos, to his palace.[76]

The mood is characteristic for a cult which celebrates a resurrected
god; yet the rites described by Ikhernofret would seem appropriate to
the cult, not of a "dying god," but of a dead king. There is, in the first
place, no question of a return of Osiris to the land of the living. In this
respect the contrast with the "suffering god" of Mesopotamia is complete. The performance did not possess the character of a passion play,
and it is a mistake to suppose, as is often done, that the death of the
god, though never mentioned, was enacted.[77] Neither in this text nor in
any other ritual is there a hint that the dreadful event of the god's death
takes place before the participants. On the contrary, the premise from
which all the rites take their cue is that Osiris is dead—a victim to be
avenged, supported, or championed, but one who abides throughout the
proceedings in the Beyond.

In the second place, it is striking that Horus is not mentioned in
Ikhernofret's text. Horus is par excellence the avenger of his father; the
statement is a commonplace in texts referring to the god as well as in
royal texts. The omission is unaccountable and perhaps a matter of
names only; it seems that Horus appears in the guise of one of the participants. If we consider the celebration as the performance of a myth,
there is no room for such a supposition. For in mythology, and hence in
the cult of Osiris as a god, Horus alone appears. But this very fact suggests that the Great Procession is concerned not with the myth of
Osiris in its late form but with the myth of royalty and the rites of
royalty in which the figures of Horus and Osiris had originally their appointed places. And, in fact, another god plays the part of Horus in the
performance. We find Upwaut as the main avenger of Osiris in the
text of Ikhernofret, and Upwaut may, as we have seen,* stand for
Pharaoh, the earthly embodiment of Horus. The opening of the inscription becomes understandable only if we assume that it referred originally to a royal rite. If Upwaut represents Pharaoh in his aspect of eldest
son, it makes sense to say that the wolf-god "went to champion his

* See above, pp. 26, 71, 87, and 92.

father." But in mythology, and hence in the cult, no relation with Up-waut plays any part at all. The supposition that Upwaut referred orig-inally to the king receives support when we read on a Middle Kingdom stela, "The Great Ones and Nobles kiss the earth before Upwaut when he completes the run of This,"[78] for this description, which probably refers to the Great Procession,[79] seems to describe the court's assisting in a ritual in which the king takes part as Upwaut rather than in a purely religious performance.

A pyramid text* which shows parallels with the inscription of Ikherno-fret confirms the view that the Great Procession reflects the burial of a dead king, for it plainly deals with a royal interment and yet opens with phrases which can be read as a summary of the Great Procession. It states that the king, Horus (but Upwaut under certain circumstances), comes to look for his father and that Thoth, who also assisted with the boat journey at Abydos, repels the enemies when they "rebel against the Neshemet boat."

According to the stela of Ikhernofret, the Great Procession ended when Osiris was brought, not to his "temple," but to his "palace"; and we are reminded that the dead kings of Uganda give audiences as in their lifetimes in the buildings where their remains are kept. King Nefer-hotep knows that "the pylons of thy (Osiris') temple are the gates (leading to) the Field of Rushes." Moreover, the description which this Neferhotep, a king of the Thirteenth Dynasty, gives of his activ-ities at Abydos and his participation in the Great Procession is cast en-tirely in the terms of royalty.

My Majesty is the supporter (avenger) of his father Osiris. I will form (literally "beget") him . . . . just as My Majesty has seen it in the books, how he shone forth as King of Upper and Lower Egypt, in his coming forth from the body of Nut.

I am his son, his supporter, his image which came forth from him, the Chieftain in the Great Hall of his father, to whom Geb gave his heritage with the approval of the Ennead.

I am in his great office which Re gave (to me). (I am) an excellent son who forms (literally "begets") the one who formed (literally "bore") him.[80]

This text could be taken as describing the establishment of the funerary cult of a dead king by his son. Moreover, the insistence on the "form-ing" of the god, the making of statues, finds a parallel in the attention which even the short inscription of Ikhernofret pays to the making of statues, palanquins, a deckhouse, and adornments for the god. It has been rightly stressed that these features seem to form an essential part of the celebrations at Abydos,[81] and they recall, of course, the elaborate preparations of funerary equipment at the royal funerals.

* See above, p. 114.

The maneuvers of the boats took place on the lake at Abydos which represented the waters separating the world of the living from the world of the dead,* and the dead king on his journey was assisted in overcoming the danger which the waters symbolized by means of mock battles.[82] We have met a mock fight at the erection of the Djed pillar, another ritual of Osiris' resurrection in the Hereafter.

We are once more reminded of funerary usages when we read that toward the end of the Great Procession Osiris embarked on a "ship." The word used is *wrt*. This "ship" was used in the funerals of the Old Kingdom and depicted in some tombs.[83] It was, in reality, a ship-shaped sledge upon which the coffin was placed so that it might be dragged to the necropolis in the desert. It is significant that in Ikhernofret's inscription the "desert-dwellers," the dead in the necropolis (depicted in one of the reliefs showing the *wrt*), rejoiced at the sight of Osiris after he "embarked" on the *wrt*. In Abydos, at the end of the festival, the figure of Osiris placed in the Neshemet boat was apparently dragged back through the desert from the "tomb in Peqer." For while the dead were buried in their tombs and the ceremony ended there, the statue of the god was returned to its temple. Nevertheless, the locality of Peqer preserved the character of an ancient royal grave. It is depicted as a mound upon (or around) which trees are planted,[84] and these features are, at Abydos, incorporated in a cenotaph which King Seti I built, surrounded by tree pits going down to the level of the subsoil water (the outflow of Osiris.)[85] The trees around the cenotaph, like those on the mound of Peqer, illustrate the ancient African belief that the dead king lives again in all life that proceeds from the earth. Thus the place to which the procession moved, as well as the name of the "ship" which carried the god, recall a royal funeral; and even the designation "Great Procession" (*pr.t ꜥꜣ.t*) meant "Great Mourning" in late times; the decree of Kanopus gives *mega penthos* as its equivalent.[86]

The funerary prototype of the Great Procession can be deduced from the most distinctive feature of the locality where it was celebrated. Kings actually were interred at Abydos during the First and Second Dynasties. The magnificent valley in the western cliffs in front of which these kings are buried probably gave rise to the tradition that the entrance to the Netherworld was there. We have found this belief in several of the pyramid texts which we have quoted,† and it may explain the presence of an early royal cemetery at this spot. The alleged tomb of Osiris would naturally be located in this necropolis if he was—as we

---

* See above, pp. 115, 119, and 154.   † See above, pp. 115 and 119.

believe—the mythical ancestor of the House of Menes. In keeping with this view is the fact that Osiris appears in the pyramid texts as one of the Upper Egyptian royal dead, a wolf-headed "Soul of Nekhen."[87] These texts would preserve, then, a most ancient tradition when they refer to Osiris as that "spirit who is in Nedyt . . . . that power in the province of This."

THE KING OF THE DEAD

Now if Osiris was originally a mythological figure expressing the Egyptian conception of kingship, it remains to explain in more detail than we have done so far* how this dead chieftain, worshiped because the community viewed its leader as an intermediary between man and nature, became a god with whom every Egyptian identified himself in death and in whom he placed reliance for his personal salvation.

This change, one of the most profound which the otherwise fairly stable religion of Egypt underwent, can be followed in detail. Its starting-point is the worship of Osiris as the dead king who continues to be powerful even in death. But his general beneficial activities as Osiris "become earth" did not, as we have seen, supplant the more personal bonds which had connected him with his followers. Hence the great squares of graves surrounding the tombs of the kings of the First Dynasty and the corresponding arrangements of the necropoleis of the Fourth and Fifth Dynasties. It is obvious that the king who in life had "kept the hearts alive" could lead his faithful subjects through the crisis of death into an orderly Beyond. In those days men based their own expectations for life in the Hereafter upon their former relationship with the deceased monarch. But, with the weakening of kingship toward the end of the Old Kingdom, the reliance upon individual rulers was no longer justified. The anarchy of the First Intermediate Period, while defying understanding,† destroyed Egyptian complacency. It has been shown that the disillusionment of this age led to searching inquiries into ultimate values and ethical standards which up to that time had been implied and taken for granted rather than proclaimed.[88] In any case, while the individual kings lost authority so that they could not even maintain dominion over the whole of Egypt and the claim that their power extended beyond the grave seemed altogether preposterous, the traditional figure of Osiris, the dead king resurrected in the Beyond and living in the varied life that went forth from the earth, was not af-

* See above, pp. 54, 110, and 120.

† See above, p. 51.

fected by the turmoil. Since the Egyptians could conceive order only in terms of kingship, they now saw the Hereafter under the guidance of Osiris. While the state was disintegrating and Pharaoh disqualified, the dead king, in his most general form, became king of the dead:

> They are all thine, all those who come to thee,
> Great and small, they belong to thee,
> Those who live upon earth, they all reach thee,
> Thou art their master, there is none outside thee.[89]

It may be objected that the development we have outlined could apply only to those who had been in the more or less immediate surroundings of the ruler and who now transferred their allegiance from his person to his prototype. But these people set the tone for the rest of Egypt. The earliest identification of a commoner with Osiris occurs toward the end of the Sixth Dynasty.[90] The smaller officials and the burghers, in so far as they could own tombs substantial enough to come down to us, show the new allegiance to and identification with Osiris from the Middle Kingdom onward. We have spoken just now of the identification with Osiris, which was, in fact, the central feature of the funerary cult of Egypt after the Old Kingdom. It is a peculiar innovation, but it can well be understood. When confidence in the living ruler as a champion of his followers here and in the Hereafter was shaken, Osiris was not entirely adequate as a substitute. He was a passive figure, not an aggressive leader likely to keep back the hostile powers lurking in the Beyond. A change of attitude toward the king of the dead was therefore to be expected.

Now the people knew the cult of Osiris as a service rendered by his son Horus, the living ruler. Every Egyptian was similarly dependent upon his son for the funerary service which insured his safe entrance and blessed existence in the Hereafter. To this extent Osiris did resemble the common dead, and for the mythopoeic mind resemblance easily becomes identity. Hence the identification of all the dead with Osiris was less preposterous than it would seem at first sight, granted that the essential difference between royalty and commoners had become blurred as a result of the political developments during the First Intermediate Period. The royal origin of Osiris was glossed over in the popular funerary cult; dependent upon his son, he became the ideal prototype of the blessed dead—their divine king who had himself savored death, whom one should imitate, and to whom one could appeal for support on the dreadful journey "to the West." In this function, in the popular funerary cult, Osiris shows little trace of the complexity which his character originally possessed. His resurrection in vegetation, Nile flood, Orion, or the moon was sometimes referred to, but the notion possessed no great significance in relation to commoners; it was bound up with the peculiar conception of kingship which prevailed in Egypt. The people took part in the public festivals which celebrated the god's manifestation in natural phenomena, but their more personal relationship with him was confined to the overwhelming problem of individual blessedness in the Hereafter. Since this was achieved by identification with a blameless god, there could be no question of a development of ethical values to take the place of the qualities of a nature-god which had become atrophied in the king of the dead.[91]

Identification with Osiris led to a desire to imitate as closely as possible the means by which he had achieved the transition from life through death unto rebirth. This means was perfectly well known: it was the royal rite of burial. Thus a process set in which continued unchecked: the usurpation of royal prerogatives and funerary usages by the common man. In the Middle Kingdom we find painted within his coffin objects which he may need in the Hereafter. Among them are crowns, scepters, and other insignia of royalty.[92] A little later, and especially in the New Kingdom, this vulgarization of the royal rite goes so far that we find figures wearing the crown of Lower Egypt carried in the funerary procession of any well-to-do Theban, while the mourners, or possibly hired performers, bear titles which had been reserved for the highest officials of the state in the time of the pyramid-builders.[93]

The new doctrine imparted an unprecedented significance to the place of burial; it was thought an advantage to be buried at Abydos, the oldest royal cemetery, or at least to be represented there by a cenotaph or a funerary stela. It is even possible that the boat trips to Abydos depicted in tombs from the Fifth Dynasty onward were undertaken or supposed to be undertaken to provide the deceased with a semblance of burial at that hallowed site. It was particularly advantageous if he could be there to take part in the Great Procession which celebrated Osiris' resurrection. Thus the burial of the commoner assumed the forms of the Osireian—that is, the archaic royal—burial.

It may be well to emphasize that the identification of the dead with Osiris was a means to an end, that is, to reach resurrection in the Hereafter. The same applies to the materialistic features which are so in evidence when we read funerary inscriptions. They do not betray an exclusive preoccupation with material well-being or mere hedonistic expectations for life after death. The Egyptians could not conceive of any

life which would do without the requirements of the life they knew.*
Although the supply of food and other commodities takes such a large
part in the funerary texts and predominates entirely in the equipment of
the tomb with paintings and reliefs (for even the scenes from daily life
depict food and other necessities in the process of being produced), all
this great apparatus is no more than a preparation for the afterlife and
not its essence. In the last instance the Egyptians' desire, though it took
many forms, could always be reduced to the wish to join in the joyful
circuit of sun and stars and seasons, to become one with the unchanging
rhythm of nature.

We have quoted accounts of the circuit in chapter 10. We have seen
that the dead were usually supposed to join it in the Netherworld and
that Abydos is sometimes specifically mentioned as an auspicious start-
ing-place. In any case, the dead went to the West. Osiris was the "Chief
of the Westerners." The sun seems to enter the earth in the West, and
so do the stars. And since the stars are the lights of night, and night
belongs to the Netherworld, because life belongs to day, the word *dat*,
"Netherworld," is written with a star ⊗;[94] the stars are inhabitants
of the Netherworld, and consequently they obey Osiris: "The firma-
ment and its stars obey him, and the Great Gates are open for him.
There is jubilation for him in the southern sky and adoration for him in
the northern sky. The imperishable stars are under his regimen."[95]

This text furthermore suggests that Osiris, being the master of the
stars, was also conceived as lord of the circuit, for the acclamation of
stars in the northern and southern parts of heaven represents a demonstration on either side of the circuit road which runs from east to west
through the sky and from west to east through the Netherworld. Amon-
Re is acclaimed in just the same way.[96]

OSIRIS AND RE

Osiris, as ruler of the Netherworld, appears sometimes as a true
Pluto, a king of Hades, corresponding to Re in heaven. "(Osiris), he
who appeared upon the throne of his father (Geb), like Re when he
ariseth in the horizon, that he might give light to him who was in the
darkness."[97] And yet Osiris was not really considered an equal of the
Creator—not because of his chthonic character, for we have seen that
in the person of Ptah the power in the earth could be acknowledged as
fully equal to that in the sun or in cattle—but because he remained, always, a somewhat ambiguous figure. It was never forgotten that he was

* See above, p. 66.

a dead king, even if his worshipers treated him as one of the Great Gods. If, for instance, in a love charm, Re-Harakhte and the Seven Hathors were called upon to further the lover's suit and the latter wished to add weight to his prayer by threats, it was not to those gods, but only to Osiris, that he dared to refer: "If you (the gods) do not make her come after me, then I will set (fire) to Busiris and burn up (Osiris)."[98]

The mythological texts also distinguish sharply between Osiris and the Great Gods, especially Re. There is a fascinating text in which Osiris interviews Atum with all the anxiety which an Egyptian might feel about his destiny in the Hereafter. Atum is characterized as the sovereign power, and he reassures his interlocutor, who answers with a mixture of continued concern and gratitude.[99] Sometimes the contrast takes a folkloristic turn which is grotesque.[100] One text starts with an acclamation of Osiris who has succeeded to the throne of Re. Osiris put on the crown of Re "that the gods might fear him"; but the sorcerer's apprentice could not cope with the master's magic. "Then Osiris became ill in the head because of the heat of the diadem of Re which he wore." Re "came home" and found Osiris "sitting in his house with his head swollen by the heat of the diadem." Re then had to draw off blood and pus to cure Osiris. Even the great hymn which Ramses IV set up in Abydos to honor Osiris, and which starts with the assertion that he is more mysterious than other gods (he who is Moon, Nile, and King of the Netherworld), acknowledges that Re is the undoubted ruler; Osiris is allowed to share his throne. "When Re appears daily and reaches the Netherworld to govern this land and also the (other) countries, then thou (Osiris) also sittest there like him. Together you are called 'The United Soul.' "[101]

As we know Osiris, he is purely a figure of thought, but of speculative mythopoeic thought—a figure concretely imagined and of manifold significance. Together with Horus he is the bearer of the peculiarly Egyptian concept of kingship as an institution involving two generations. As a dead king he is a force in nature, and as a buried king he is seen more especially in the emergence from the earth of renewed life. The myth of Osiris treats these various aspects as episodes in a narrative, a form congenial to naïve imagination and normally assumed by mythopoeic thought. If reflection, distinguishing the various aspects of the god, stood in danger of destroying the unity of the Osiris figure, the myth counteracted that centrifugal tendency effectively by translating them into adventures of a single divine person and of his relatives, Isis, Horus, and Seth. But the Osiris myth is secondary to the fundamental idea that Pharaoh is the intermediary between society and nature. This is well shown by the fact that references to the myth in the pyramid texts are of a most cursory nature, in contrast to the full and repeated discussions of the relationship of Osiris with Geb, Nut, and Horus.

The Horus king is truly king because he is the "seed of Geb" and succeeds Osiris. On the theological plane this is expressed by the "justification" of Horus, Geb adjudicating dominion to him as Osiris' heir with or without explicit reference to his lawsuit with Seth in the "House of the Prince" at Heliopolis.[102] On the human plane the figure of Osiris played a predominant role in the texts and royal rituals of succession and coronation, while gaining significance for the commoner as a king of the dead.

It seems futile to inquire whether there are historical foundations for the myth and person of Osiris—in other words, whether there ever was a king whose achievements and fate contributed to the story of Osiris. All understanding of this most Egyptian of the gods is made impossible if one starts an inquiry whether the concept of Osiris as a dead king or that of Osiris as a cosmic god is original. They are not and have never been distinct but are two aspects of one and the same conception, a conception of immemorial antiquity in Egypt—that the king is a god who establishes a harmony between society and nature, whose beneficial power is felt even from beyond the grave.

Fig. 17.—Ivory Comb with the Name of King Djet
of Dynasty I (Cairo)

Fig. 18.—Isis as a Falcon Conceiving Horus on Osiris' Bier (Abydos)

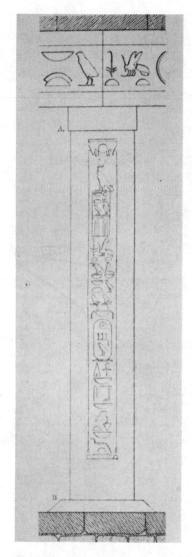

Fig. 19.—Column from the Mortuary Temple of King Sahure

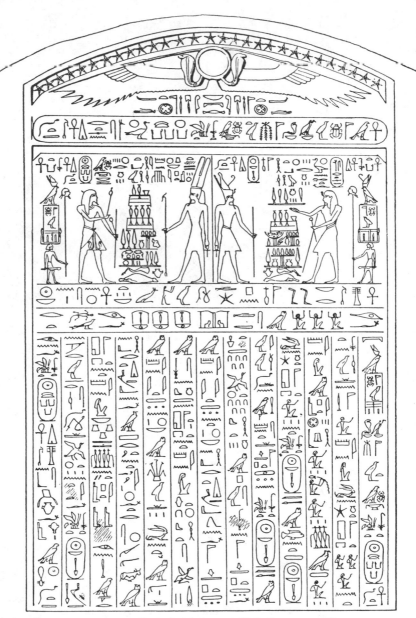

Fig. 20.—Stela of King Senusert III

Fig. 21.—Tomb Relief Showing the Dead Man Finding Refreshment in the Garden of His Tomb (Thebes)

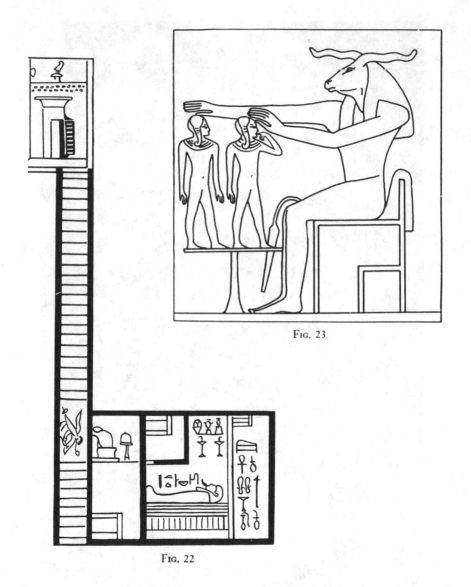

FIG. 23

FIG. 22

FIG. 22.—THE BA DESCENDING THE TOMB SHAFT TO GO TO THE MUMMY

FIG. 23.—THE GOD KHNUM FORMING THE FUTURE KING AND HIS KA ON THE POTTER'S
WHEEL (LUXOR)

Fig. 24.—Foot-washing of Neuserre on His Way to the Robing
Chamber or Palace of the Sed Festival (Abu Gurob)

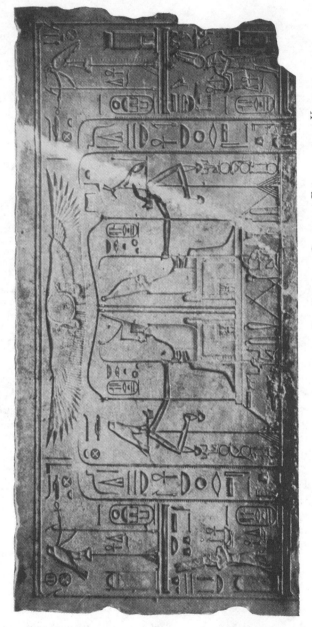

Fig. 25.—Abbreviated Rendering of the Sed Festival: Senusert Enthroned as King of Upper and of Lower Egypt (Medamud)

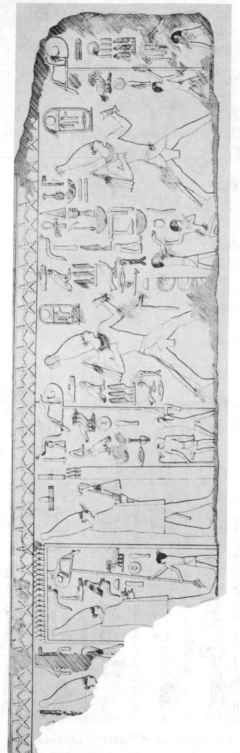

Fig. 26.—Neuserre "Dedicating the Field" at the Sed Festival (Abu Gurob)

Fig. 27.—Fragment of the Lion Palette (Ashmolean Museum)

Fig. 28.—The Bull Palette (Louvre)

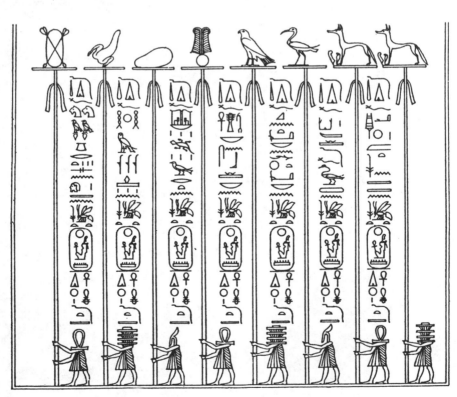

Fig. 29.—The Standards of Royalty (Abydos)

Fig. 30.—The Dual Shrines (Saqqara)

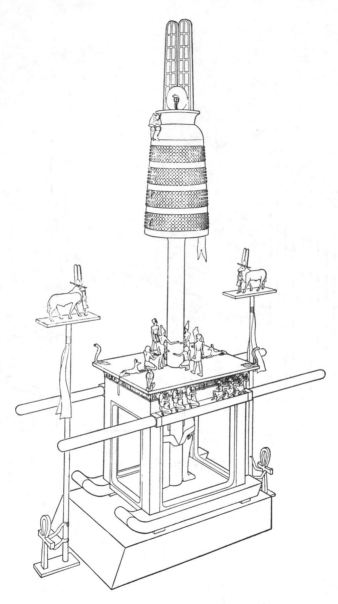

Fig. 31.—A Reconstruction of the Reliquary of Abydos

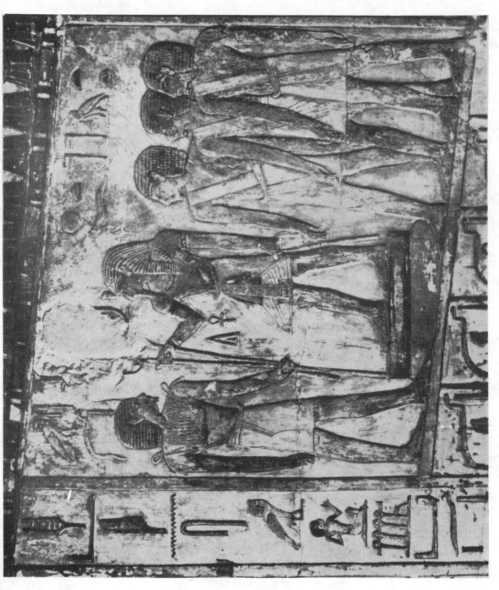

Fig. 32.— The Sem Priest Wearing the Qeni Stomacher at the Ceremony of "Opening-the-Mouth" before a Statue of Seti I (Thebes)

FIG. 33.—THE DEAD MAN UPON THE PRIMEVAL HILL (FLORENCE)

Fig. 34.—The Heavenly Cow and the Sun in Its Boat (Thebes)

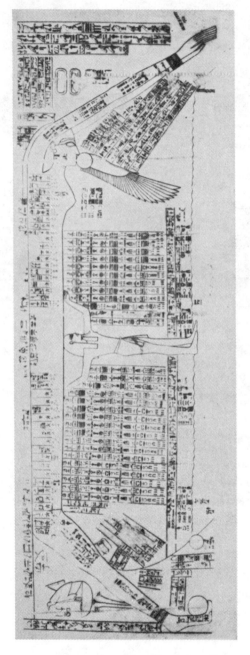

Fig. 35.—Nut Supported by Shu, and the Sun in Its Course (Abydos)

FIG. 36.—ADORATION OF THE SUN AT ITS RISING AND SETTING BY
DEITIES AND MEN, LIVING AND DEAD (BRITISH MUSEUM)

Fig. 37.—Adoration of the Sun at Its Setting by the Souls of Pe and Nekhen, the Baboons, and the Dead Man (Sheikh abd el Kurna)

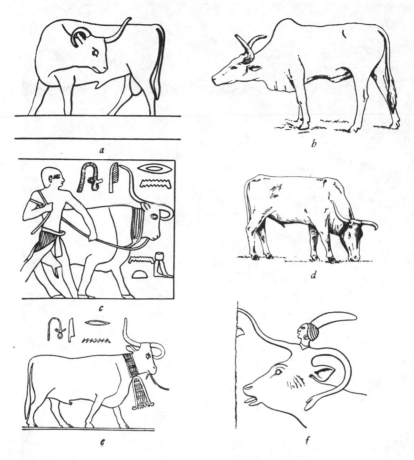

FIG. 38.—CATTLE WITH ARTIFICIAL DEFORMATIONS OF THE HORNS, IN
TOMBS OF THE OLD KINGDOM (*a, c, e*), AT LUXOR (RELIEF OF TUT-
ANKHAMON, *f*), AND AMONG THE DINKA (*b*) AND NUER (*d*)

Fig. 39.—Epiphany of Hathor among Papyrus in the
Western Desert at Thebes (British Museum)

Fig. 40.—Painting in a New Kingdom Coffin Showing Osiris in
the Djed Pillar Protected by Horus (Leiden)

Fig. 41.—Painting in a New Kingdom Coffin Showing Osiris in the
Djed Pillar Wrapped Round by the Wings of Nut (Leiden)

BOOK II. MESOPOTAMIA

PART V. THE FOUNDATIONS OF KINGSHIP

CHAPTER 16

THE HISTORICAL FORMS OF KINGSHIP
IN MESOPOTAMIA

A. MESOPOTAMIAN BEGINNINGS AND PRIMITIVE DEMOCRACY

IN MESOPOTAMIA, as in Egypt, kingship emerged at the beginning of historical times. But its roots were more deeply imbedded in Africa than in Western Asia. Behind Pharaoh we can discern a primitive conception of a chieftain endowed with power over natural forces, a "rain-maker king." But in Mesopotamia monarchical rule had no such foundation, and kingship remained to some extent problematical. It arose under the pressure of circumstance in a community which originally had not acknowledged authority vested in a single individual.

It has recently been established[1] that the oldest political institution in the country was the assembly of all free men; that they left power to deal with current matters in the hands of a group of elders; and that in times of emergency they chose a "king" to take charge for a limited period. The assembling and interpretation of these scattered but unequivocal traces of "Primitive Democracy" enable us for the first time to understand the nature and development of Mesopotamian kingship.

We must note, in the first place, that the original articulation of Mesopotamian society was local rather than tribal. In other words, habitat rather than kinship defined one's social affiliation. However, the elders, who dealt with current affairs, seem to have been not only influential members of the community but heads of families, for they are designated in Sumerian by the word *abba* ("father"). In the elders we seem, therefore, to have a connecting link between Primitive Democracy and the primordial organization of society in families and clans. But while a social order based on kinship does not, as a rule, contain features which prevent it from spreading over large areas, Primitive Democracy was unsuitable for such expansion because it carried with it the autonomy of each separate locality and entirely lacked organs through which to exercise conjoint authority. Moreover, it entailed some of the disadvantages of freedom. Often it must have been difficult to get the assembly to act, since voting and submission by all to the will of the majority were unknown. The issues were clarified through general discussion—"asking one another," as the Babylonians expressed it.[2] Communal action required unanimity, and this could be reached only by means of persuasion. Hence the need for action and leadership fostered a parasitical growth of personal power which ultimately destroyed the original system of government.

The change which we have just described was completed before the end of the Early Dynastic period. We cannot know with certainty when Primitive Democracy flourished in its pure form; the Proto-literate—preceding the Early Dynastic—period[3] has left us some semipictographic tablets on which the signs for "elder" and "assembly" occur.[4] Hence, the system existed in Proto-literate times, and there is no inherent improbability in the claim that it derived from a yet earlier, prehistoric age.

The prevalence of a political system based on the autonomy of each separate locality, while it is unfavorable to the development of political unity, need not destroy an awareness of national cohesion. The politically divided Greeks were well aware of a common descent and a common culture and possessed that "sense of kinship" which we find among similarly disunited savages.* The early inhabitants of Mesopotamia expressed their consciousness of solidarity in the figure of the god Enlil. In a Sumerian poem the memory of a golden age is evoked in the following terms:

> In those days there was no snake, there was no scorpion, ...
> There was no lion, there was no wild dog(?), no wolf,
> There was no fear, no terror,
> Man had no opponent.

> In those days the land Shubur (East), ...
> Discordant Sumer (South), the land of the "decrees of princeship,"
> Uri (North), the land having all that is needful,
> The land Martu (West), resting in security,
> The whole universe, the people in unison(?),
> To Enlil with one tongue gave praise.[5]

Enlil was a national—and not merely a local—god. For this reason the city of Nippur, which contained his main shrine, enjoyed a prestige for which there is no historical or political foundation. The usual explanation postulates a period of which all trace is lost and during which Nippur was the seat of hegemony in the land. But this construction seems

* See above, p. 17.

redundant. We know that Enlil was universally venerated in Sumer, and the prestige of Nippur may well have been a simple reflection of the esteem in which its god was held. Important events of man's past were localized at Nippur. There in the sacred area, Dur-anki, "the bond of heaven and earth," was "the place where flesh sprouted forth," the spot where Enlil had split the crust of the earth with his pickax so that "the vanguard of mankind" could "break through" and populate the land.[6] If Enlil's shrine was founded when the plain was first settled, it would be understandable that the early inhabitants of southern Mesopotamia should have called their country after the center where the national god was worshiped. Both *Sumer* and *kalama* (the land) can be derived from dialectical variants meaning "the region of Nippur."[7] The influence which a religious center may exercise while remaining entirely devoid of political power can be studied in the case of Delphi. The sanctuary of Apollo was held in reverence by all the Greeks, and its authority was acknowledged even by their neighbors. It seems that the Enlil shrine at Nippur occupied a similar position in Early Dynastic Mesopotamia. In both Greece and Mesopotamia a sanctuary symbolized and sometimes saved a national unity which the political institutions were unable to embody.[8]

In Mesopotamia, as in Greece, the character of the land encouraged separatist and centrifugal tendencies. The small settlements of early times appeared lost in the boundless plain. They remained isolated units, each surrounded by drained or irrigated fields and separated from the next community by a wilderness of marsh or desert. We have tangible evidence of the scattered nature of the settlements in large deposits of sand which was blown in from the empty spaces during periods of depression or neglect and which we find, accumulated sometimes to a depth of several meters, in our excavations.[9] With the increase in population and the improvement in equipment which the large-scale use of metal brought about, the fields of neighboring settlements became contiguous. Henceforth conflicts were bound to arise. The wars between Lagash and Umma illustrate this well,[10] and they show that it was impossible to merge the separate city-states into a political unit for any length of time. Now one city and then another found itself able to subject its neighbors and to dominate the land. But within a few generations, if not sooner, the enforced unity disintegrated.

Mesopotamia is in no sense a geographical entity. Even the powerful Assyrian kings wasted the substance of their people in futile attempts to reach natural limits within which their dominion might remain safe and stable. The plain of the Euphrates and Tigris merges into the limitless deserts of Arabia, and the foothills of its eastern borders rise gradually toward the mountain chains of Persia and Armenia. There are no boundaries from which power may recoil to concentrate at the center. In this respect Mesopotamia contrasts sharply with Egypt, which is clearly defined (except in the south) by immutable frontiers. A native chieftain extending his conquests in the Nile Valley was bound to reach a point where he had to realize that all the land which he could dominate was in his power; beyond he might raid but not conquer. At such a moment the concept of a single united country, a kingdom of Egypt, must have taken shape. But we cannot imagine a concatenation of physiographical and political factors which would give rise to the notion "king of Sumer" or "king of Mesopotamia."

The amorphous character of their land conspired with the deficiencies of their political institutions to impede the unity of the people of Mesopotamia. We have already indicated the weaknesses of Primitive Democracy. Mesopotamian kingship was introduced to meet emergencies with which the existing organs of government were unable to cope. In early times, when peril threatened, the assembly elected a king to whom it delegated its power. Even as late as Akkadian times assemblies felt themselves entitled to adopt this procedure:

> In the "Common of Enlil," a field
> belonging to Esabad, the temple of Gula,
> Kish assembled
> and Iphurkish, a man of Kish,
>
> . . . .
> they raised to kingship.[11]

The power of the king was great. The term *lugal*, "king," means literally "great man." But it is also used to designate the master of a slave or the owner of a field. Hence we may infer that the community put itself completely into the hands of its ruler. It was understood, however, that his power would not outlast the emergency. The office of kingship was a *bala*, a word meaning "return" or "reversion" to origin;[12] and the source of the king's authority was his election by the assembly. Hence the great power assigned to a single leader was meant to be exercised for only a short time. In practice, however, the ills of the state could not be cured by such intermittent appointments. The need for quick and resolute action which they fulfilled became a permanent need as soon as the settlements ceased to be small and isolated. The formation of cities and city-states increased the opportunities for conflict between separate groups. The requirements of drainage and irrigation made each community dependent upon the co-operation of its neighbors. The necessity for the inhabitants of an alluvial plain to import vast amounts of raw materials such as wood, stone, and metals imposed the duty of safeguarding the passage of these materials. Hence the elected kings or certain officials who could exercise quasi-royal powers* were forced to remain continuously on the alert; and, consequently, kingship lost its temporary nature.

The change through which kingship became a permanent institution was furthered also by the character of its incumbents. We may suppose that the leaders chosen would have been elders whose wisdom qualified them for the task, or young men with the dash and valor of warriors. Both types are well described in ancient texts—though we have to go to the Old Testament to find a complete portrait of an elder. We know that many Palestinian cities were governed by an assembly and elders, and it has been pointed out[13] that Job's status before catastrophe overtook him was precisely that of an elder in a Primitive Democracy. We must remember that the assembly did not vote and that, consequently, action could be taken only when, at the crucial hour of decision, the multitude was swayed by one counsel. A leader able to bring about consensus under those conditions must have possessed exceptional wisdom, strength of character, and command of language. He must have enjoyed a position in which his authority was neither imposed nor challenged but accepted as natural and beneficial:

> When I went forth from my gate up to the city,
> And prepared my seat in the square;
> Young men saw me and withdrew,
> And old men arose and stood;
> Princes stopped talking,
> And placed their hands upon their mouths;
> The voice of the nobles was silent,
> And their tongues clove to their palates.
>
> For when the ear heard, it called me happy;
> And when the eye saw, it testified for me:
> That I delivered the poor who cried for help,
> And the orphan, and him that had no helper.
> The blessing of him that was ready to perish
>   came upon me,
> And the heart of the widow I made glad.
> I put on righteousness, and it clothed me;
> Like a robe and a turban was my justice.

* See below, pp. 221–23.

> For me men listened and waited,
> And kept silence for my counsel;
> After my speech, they did not reply,
> And my word dropped upon them.
> They waited for me as for the rain,
> And opened their mouths as for the spring rain.[14]

It may be assumed that such a man, if temporarily equipped with kingly power, would step down as soon as the emergency was past. But often the circumstances called, not for a leader of Job's type, but for a younger man who was qualified specifically to assume leadership in war. Ideally, such a man would respect the prerogatives of the assembly and the elders, and it is significant that such a relationship is described in the Epic of Gilgamesh, which purports to reflect a situation of great antiquity. Gilgamesh is permanent king of Erech; but when he is about to take action which may involve the city in a war he scrupulously consults the assembly as well as the elders.[15] These, in their turn, show great affection for their young king and impart fatherly advice. It is clear that such a relationship, if it existed in reality, would have presented a most precarious balance of power, which would have been upset if the war leader were at all inclined to dominate. This is exactly the situation which we find described in the Babylonian Epic of Creation, which tells how the gods, threatened by the powers of Chaos, appealed to Marduk, one of the youngest and most vigorous among them, to be their leader against the host of Tiamat. Marduk replied:

> If I am to be your champion,
> vanquish Tiamat, and save you,
> then assemble and proclaim my lot supreme.
> Sit down together joyfully in Ubshu-ukkinna,
> let me, like you, by word of mouth determine destiny.
> So that whatever I decide shall not be altered,
> and my spoken command shall not (come) back (to
>   me), shall not be changed.[16]

In these words we hear distinct tones of ambition and threat. Marduk is not merely indicating to his interlocutors that the calling of the assembly is the correct procedure. He is declaring in effect that his co-operation can be bought only at the price of absolute power: his command shall not be changed.

No doubt the assemblies of the early Mesopotamian cities often found themselves confronted by just this situation. Those best fitted to take charge in an emergency must have enjoyed the exercise of power and have been the least willing to relinquish it at the end of their term of office. We have seen, moreover, that the end of a crisis can but rarely have meant that the underlying causes had been removed. Small wonder, then, that personal ruie became established in all the cities of Meso-potamia.

B. THE TEMPLE COMMUNITY

Only a minority of Early Dynastic rulers bore the title *lugal*. There were other officials besides the elected king who were in a position to seize power while fulfilling the people's need for leadership. They were the high priest (*sangu mah*) and governor (*ensi*) of the city-state.

We have hitherto dealt with the secular aspects of the early settlements. But the feeling that man depends upon the gods pervaded the whole of Mesopotamian life, and each settlement centered round one or more temples. If power was vested in the assembly of free men, that power depended upon the sovereign will of the gods. The same group of people who constituted themselves in an assembly with its elders for po-litical purposes formed a socio-religious organization which we call the temple community.[17]

The temple community showed a strongly democratic character. Since it projected its sovereignty in its god, the members were all equal in his service; and this service entailed so large a part of normal life that we may speak of a theocratic communism. Resources and labor were pooled; tools and raw materials were supplied from a common store; harvests, herds, and the products of handicrafts were at the disposal of those who had assumed executive function on behalf of the community and appeared as the stewards of the god. Thus the Mesopotamian gods symbolized not only the divine powers which man recognized but also the communities themselves. How else can we explain the fact that the god owned the land and its produce, that high and low willingly under-took the annual work on his fields, dikes, and canals, and that the most moving account of the destruction of a city takes the form of a lament by the city-goddess?[18]

The land owned by the community (in the guise of its god) was di-vided into three parts. Some of it, *kur* land, was parceled out to provide sustenance for the members of the community who cultivated it. The sizes of these allotments differed considerably, but even the smallest contained almost an acre—enough to keep a man, and possibly a small family. Another part of the land—in one case, for instance, one-fourth of the total—was reserved for the god. This was called *nigenna* land, and its produce was stored in the temple. All members of the com-munity, irrespective of their rank or function, were obliged to cultivate this land and to undertake *corvée* on the dikes and canals insuring its irrigation. The implements and teams of oxen and asses used for these communal tasks were kept in the stables and storehouses of the temple; they were evidently owned by the community as a whole. Grain for sowing was also supplied by the temple. Not only the produce of the fields, but implements, ritual equipment, and animals needed for sacrifices or rations for the people were likewise temple property. Furthermore, members of the community acknowledged the obligation to exercise their special skills in the service of the god. Metalworkers, stonecutters and carpenters, boatmen and fishermen, gardeners and shepherds, all worked for a certain time, or produced a certain amount of work, for the temple. Yet all these men were primarily agriculturalists who worked the *kur* land allotted to them. Those who had special skills exercised them not only for the community but also for private trade and barter. Thus individual enterprise found a certain scope. In fact, a third type of temple land (*urula* land) was rented out for cultivation by individuals.

Our insight into the functioning of the temple community is derived from the texts, but the excavation of the Temple Oval at Khafajah[19] has given a singular concreteness to the historical reconstruction (Fig. 42). We notice how the people lived around their shrine which towered above the houses, a focal point toward which the streets converged. The storehouses surrounded the inner court and the platform of the sanctuary. The building on one side of the outer court between the two inclosure walls was probably occupied by the high priest who directed the affairs of the temple community. He supervised in person the fixing of the boundaries of lands and fields. He also supervised the allotment of land and assigned individual tasks in the *corvée* on the *nigenna* lands and the canals.

The city or city-state as it is known to us through the Early Dynastic documents was a complex organism comprising several temple communities. The tablets from Lagash mention twenty shrines;[20] the section of the Early Dynastic city at Khafajah which was excavated contained two large, one medium-sized, and two small temples.[21] As an example of the size of individual communities we may mention that that of the Baba temple at Lagash comprised some 1,000–1,200 souls and owned about 6,000 acres of land.[22] The total population of the city-states can be computed only in a general way, but it would seem to vary from, say, 10,000 to 20,000 people.[23]

Just as the temple community was viewed as the estate of a god, so also was the city as a whole owned by a deity, the city-god. This god owned one of the largest temple communities, and his high priest was governor (*ensi*) of the city, charged with the integration of its component parts. The individual communities lost some of their independence in the merger which brought the city-state into being, and it was apparently the duty of the governor to assign shares in the communal tasks to each of the temple communities, while the high priest of each of these subdivided them among the members. Moreover, the governor dealt with matters of irrigation and trade which may be said to have constituted the field of foreign policy.

Certain peculiarities in the organization of the governor's estate made it well-nigh impossible for the community to control him. For instance, he derived most of his income and provisions from the *nigenna* land of each temple.[24] Since these fields were cultivated as a *corvée* by members of the communities, it would have been hard to say at any moment to what extent this obligatory labor was serving the temple—and thus the community as a whole—and to what extent it was merely enriching the governor.

The governor differed from the king in that he was a permanent, not a temporary, official. Yet, like the king, he found himself wielding great power. It was necessary that he should do so if the community were to flourish. But the demarcation line between justifiable initiative and illegal aggrandizement must often have been hard to draw. Urukagina of Lagash, at the end of the Early Dynastic period, describes certain abuses to which he put an end. For instance: "The oxen of the gods plowed the onion-plots of the governor, for the onion-plots and the cucumber-plots of the governor were situated in the good fields of the gods."[25] Such abuses were the natural consequence of the equivocal origin of Mesopotamian rulership. It had come into being to answer a need which the organs of Primitive Democracy were unable to fulfil. The government of the compound and expanding city-states called for more vigorous leadership than an assembly of free men or a body of elders was able to give. The king, the high priest of a powerful temple, and the governor of the city-state were in a position to fulfil that need. By Early Dynastic times one or the other of these functionaries had established himself as a ruler in each of the Mesopotamian cities.

C. DESIGNATIONS OF THE RULER AS EVIDENCE OF
UNBROKEN TRADITION

Our bland reference to a "Mesopotamian" form of kingship stands in need of justification. It may well be questioned whether a political institution was likely to retain a distinct character throughout the series of spasmodic alternations between anarchy and centralization which formed the history of Babylonia and Assyria. The final answer to such doubts should be found in the following chapters. The fact that we can illustrate our points by quotations from different periods of Mesopotamian history demonstrates the lasting validity of a well-defined conception of kingship. It is true, however, that another conception is also represented in our sources; and we shall give here a preliminary justification of our treatment of the one as characteristic, of the other as non-typical and even anomalous. The contrast is easily demonstrated when we survey the designations of the Mesopotamian ruler.

THE DIVINE DETERMINATIVE

The names of a number of kings are preceded in the texts by the determinative of divinity. This usage is narrowly circumscribed in its incidence. The first king to be thus distinguished was Naram-Sin of Akkad; and the custom was followed by all kings of the Third Dynasty of Ur except the first. After the fall of that dynasty, the kings of Isin, and occasionally a ruler of one of the other city-states into which the country had been redivided, assumed the sign of divinity in their inscriptions. We notice it, for instance, with a few kings of Eshnunna.[26] Rim-Sin of Larsa took it in his twenty-third year,[27] but his great opponent, Hammurabi of Babylon, never used it. Shamsuiluna, and after him a few Kassite rulers, were the last to style themselves gods. Neither the Assyrians nor the Neo-Babylonians renewed the custom.

Here, then, is a striking contrast with Egypt. In the Nile Valley a god was king at all times and inevitably; in Mesopotamia we find that less than a score of rulers, between 2300 and 1500 B.C., appear, in the writing of their names, to have laid claim to divinity. There can be no question in Mesopotamia of kings who differ necessarily and in essence from other men, and the precise implications of the determinative remain problematical. We shall see that most of the evidence commonly adduced as proof of the deification of kings does not, in fact, bear on this problem (chap. 21). Yet one rite in which the kings of Isin and Ur took the part of a divine bridegroom substantiates the orthographic use and perhaps explains its origin, as we shall see.

Art expressed deification much more rarely than orthography and ritual. Naram-Sin also left us pictorial evidence to show that his superhuman nature was taken seriously (Fig. 43). This is found on his stela of victory. The king wears the horned crown of the gods; he outstrips all

other figures in size, a differentiation usual in Egyptian but not in Mesopotamian art, and that for the very reason that the Mesopotamian king,
in contrast with Pharaoh, was not essentially different from men (see
the Introduction). The whole composition of the stela emphasizes
Naram-Sin's divinity in a striking manner. Below him the soldiers are
ascending the mountain, the rhythm of their steps repeating his stride.
On the right the defeated enemies, collapsing and fleeing, form the an-
tithesis of the Akkadian army. The king stands alone above this agita-
tion; near him is the unscaled summit of the mountain, above are the
great gods.

Not the least astounding feature of the stela is its uniqueness. No
other Mesopotamian monument expresses in formal language the divinity of kings. This fact alone vitiates the argument that the Akkadians
qua "Semites" introduced the notion of divine kingship in Mesopotamia;[28] moreover, the usage flourished most in the "Sumerian" south
and disappeared almost with the "Semitic" First Dynasty of Babylon,
while it was quite unknown among the "Semitic" Assyrians. But the
deification of kings is not "Sumerian" either;[29] the oldest Sumerian texts
ignore it. They reveal, as we have seen, the prevalence of Primitive
Democracy.

The limited occurrence of the deification of kings is an anomaly
which we cannot fully explain. In our particular field of inquiry it indicates the basic complexity of Mesopotamian culture—a compound in
which certain elements could remain somewhat distinct. This is not to
say that Mesopotamian culture lacked integration or coherence. On the
contrary, it possessed a pronounced character of its own, unusually resistant to historical accident. This point deserves to be stressed, since
the histories of Greece and of Islam have had an unfortunate influence
on the historiography of the ancient Near East. The earliest civilizations
of Egypt and Mesopotamia were truly autochthonous, and it becomes
increasingly clear that movements of populations and foreign influences
have but occasionally disturbed, and not even always modified, the deep-
rooted cultural continuity in those lands. An exception, however, is the
displacement of Sumerian by Akkadian as the spoken language of Mesopotamia in the second half of the third millennium B.C. It has been
shown that these two tongues were the vehicles of profoundly different
spirits.[30] Yet the contrast between "Semites" and "Sumerians" does
not present an answer to any Mesopotamian problem but is a problem in
itself[31]—and one vastly more complex than is generally realized. It has
been shown that the ascendancy of the Akkadians under Sargon was ex-

perienced neither as a racial conflict nor as a shift from native to foreign rule,[32] and attempts at correlating certain elements of Mesopotamian culture with Sumerian-speaking or Semitic-speaking elements of the population have not been very successful, for a resistant cultural fabric comprised both. Since, however, widely different mentalities contributed to that fabric, we must be prepared to find here and there peculiar designs which are not always consistent with the main strands. These special formations remain of limited occurrence; the deification of the king is one of them.

King and governor.—We have seen that the earliest terms for ruler, *lugal* ("king") and *ensi* ("governor") originally denoted different offices. But in Early Dynastic times this distinction had been obliterated, and the two titles marked a difference in the extent of a ruler's power. The *ensi* usually ruled a small city-state, though the title was sometimes retained even when its bearer had subjected a considerable area. The title *lugal*, as a rule, denoted extensive dominion and might be assumed by an *ensi* after the conquest of foreign territories or relinquished when these were lost again. The distinction in the significance of the two terms was well illustrated when a subject of Enannatum I used the term *lugal* in speaking of "his king Enannatum," but dedicated a macehead "(for the life of) Enannatum, *ensi* of Lagash," using the correct title.[33] He evidently differentiated between the official position of Enannatum and the power which the latter, as his sovereign, had over him.

In some cases tradition played a part in the titulary of a local ruler. The ruler of Kish was always called "King of Kish"—be it because Kish had a permanent king, as Erech had in the Epic of Gilgamesh, or because Kish had long exercised the hegemony in Babylonia. That the title was well established is illustrated by the phraseology used by Eannatum in describing his capture of the city of Kish as a favor granted by the goddess Inanna:

> To Eannatum, Governor of Lagash
> Inanna, because she loved him,
> has given the kingship of Kish
> (along) with the governorship of Lagash.[34]

The title "King of Kish" possessed such great prestige that Mesannipadda of Ur, after his conquest of Kish, used it in preference to his own. It was also used by Sargon of Akkad, who dominated the whole of Mesopotamia. In fact, it is the first in a series of titles demonstrating the continuity of the Mesopotamian traditions of rulership, for it appeared in an archaic form even in the titulary of the late Assyrian kings.[35]

The other title, *ensi*, and its Akkadian form *ishakku*, also survived the Early Dynastic period and continued to express rulership over a single city or city-state under the sovereignty of a god. But the political connotations of the title varied according to the constellation of power in the land. Under the strongly centralized government of the Third Dynasty of Ur the *ensi* was simply a civil servant, appointed by the king of the land and sometimes shifted from one city to another at the pleasure of his royal master.[36] But sometimes descendants of a native dynasty who had submitted to Ur continued to rule as its vassals. This ambiguity in the meaning of the title *ensi* continued to exist under the dynasties of Isin, Larsa, and Babylon. Conversely, when a subjected ruler regained his independence (while he might continue to style himself "governor"), he proclaimed his election to have been an act of the city-god rather than of his overlord.[37] And, again, we must note a survival of this conception to the very end of Mesopotamian history. The kings of Assyria used the designation "Governor of Assur" in their titulary; thus they retained the modest rank of a ruler exercising stewardship for the city-god in whose temple they had received their insignia (chap. 17).

King of the Land.—At the end of the Early Dynastic period, Lugal-zaggesi introduced a new title, "King of the Land." It is the first title we meet in which the conception of rulership over the entire country is distinguished from rulership over a city-state. In this respect it marks an advance in political thought. Actually, Lugalzaggesi's dominion did not differ from that exercised before his time for longer or shorter periods by the rulers of Kish, Ur, or Lagash. He, too, started as the governor of a single city; and it was in accordance with custom that the national god, Enlil, was credited with having sanctioned his nation-wide rule. But Lugalzaggesi went further than his predecessors when, in the inscription we shall quote, he acknowledged rulership over Mesopotamia to necessitate ascendancy over the predatory populations of the neighboring regions. This is shown in the interplay of the terms *kalama* and *kurkur*, the first of which means "the land" (viz., of Sumer), while the other denotes foreign countries or inhabited lands in general:

> When Enlil, king of all countries (*kurkur*)
> had given the kingship of the land (*kalama*) to Lugalzaggesi;
> when he (Enlil) had directed the eyes of the nation (*kalama*) to-
> wards him

and had laid all countries (*kurkur*) at his feet;
and when he had subjected unto him (everything) from East to
   West—

On that day he (Enlil) pacified(?) for him the roads from the Lower
   Sea (the Persian Gulf)
along the Tigris and Euphrates to the Upper Sea (the Mediterranean).[38]

King of the Four Quarters.—The political ideas which Lugalzaggesi
expressed were upheld by Sargon of Akkad, who defeated him and
ruled in his stead. Sargon expressed his conception of kingship in a new
title which had somewhat more distinctly religious implications than
"King of the Land." He called himself "he who rules the Four Quarters," and his son Naram-Sin assumed the title, "King of the Four
Quarters," which had hitherto been applied to certain gods—Anu, Enlil, and Shamash (Utu), the sun-god.[39] The king so styled was potentially the earthly ruler of Creation, a paraphrase which contains the same
religious overtones as the title itself. The Assyrian kings used an exact
equivalent, *shar kishati*, "King of the Universe." Both this title and its
older equivalent carry the connotation of sanction, recognition, or even
election, by the gods. But they do not imply that he was divine.

King of Sumer and Akkad.—The Third Dynasty of Ur continued the
titles which we have discussed but added to their number "King of Sumer and Akkad." The dynasties of Isin, Larsa, and Babylon brought no
significant change in the titulary; and there is, therefore, no need to discuss them.

THE ASSYRIAN TITLES

The shift of the center of gravity from Babylonia to Assyria during
the second millennium B.C. presents a considerable break in continuity.
The cultural center of the country had been in the south. Early Dynastic
civilization had moved upstream along the two rivers and has been
found well established in Mari on the Euphrates[40] and at Assur on the
Tigris.[41] The temple at Brak in the Habur plain[42] suggests that a similar expansion had taken place in the Proto-literate period. Up to the
middle of the second millennium B.C. the political power likewise centered in the south. Therefore, the question arises whether the political
supremacy of Assyria introduced concepts of rulership which were at
variance with those which had existed before. This seems not to have
been the case. We shall see that the titulary continues to use traditional
designations and, moreover, that rulership developed in the north on
much the same basis as it did in the south. For Primitive Democracy was
known in the north and, in fact, survived there for a thousand years
after it had been superseded in southern Mesopotamia. Just as the as-

sembly (*ukkin*) had originally possessed sovereign power in the communities of the south, so the Assyrian communities knew a council (*puhru*) which is named in the oldest Assyrian sources and in those of the colonies sent out by Assur to Cappadocia.[43] All these documents date from the beginning of the second millennium B.C. Besides the council, they name a prince (*rubu*) whose function one would imagine to have resembled that of the *ensi* in the south. In fact, he bears the same title in relation to his city-god, namely, "governor" (*ishakku*).

A change came with the reign of Shamsi-Adad I in the eighteenth century B.C. He referred to his predecessors, not as "princes," but as "kings."[44] He also used the title "King of the Universe" (*shar kishati*), which we have met as an equivalent of "King of the Four Quarters." At the same time he placed himself in line with the oldest Mesopotamian tradition by styling himself "appointee of Enlil."

These titles have far-reaching implications. They are not mere imitations of southern usage. They proclaim that the unprecedented position which the north occupied under Shamsi-Adad I was not in conflict, but in line, with the immemorial traditions of the south. From the earliest times Enlil had assigned kingship over "the land" in accordance with the decree of the assembly of the gods. The king now served notice that, not one of the old cities of the south, but his own city of Assur—which lacked all prestige of history or tradition—had been selected by the gods to become the seat of sovereignty in Mesopotamia.

Shamsi-Adad's action can be explained in two ways. He probably came from the middle Euphrates region,[45] a district which by Early Dynastic times was included in the domain of southern Mesopotamian culture; and he may have wanted to shape his authority in accordance with the southern traditions with which he was familiar. On the other hand, a case can be made for an ancient connection between Enlil and the city of Assur. The Assur temple and its component parts bear Sumerian names which resemble those of Enlil's sanctuary at Nippur.[46] Assur's spouse is said to have been Ninlil,[47] the female complement of Enlil; and Tukulti-Ninurta I explicitly called Assur "the Assyrian Enlil," or simply "Enlil."[48] If Enlil was the god originally worshiped at Assur, the title "appointee of Enlil" would be on a par with "beloved of Tishpak" at Eshnunna and with similar formulas proclaiming the relation between ruler and city-god. Hence the alternative with which Shamsi-Adad's title faces us can be formulated also in another way: did Enlil appoint the king in his (Enlil's) function as city-god or in his function as national god of Sumer?

The material favors the latter view. The Early Dynastic remains found at Assur do not mention Enlil, and the similarity of names used in the Assur sanctuary to those at Nippur may be due to an Assyrian policy of justifying pretensions based on newly acquired power by means of ancient traditions. In any case, we cannot doubt that Shamsi-Adad's title had the programmatic significance which we ascribed to it, since he also styled himself "King of the Universe." The occurrence of the title "appointee of Enlil" further supports our view. Shamsi-Adad's ambitions were soon destroyed by Hammurabi. But when Eriba-Adad finally threw off the suzerainty of Babylonia in the fourteenth century B.C., the title was reintroduced; and from then on, until the time of Sennacherib, the Assyrian rulers retained it.[49] Eriba-Adad's son, Assur-uballit I, styled himself "King of the Land of Assur, King of the Universe," as Shamsi-Adad had done.

Thus the powerful masters of the Late Assyrian empire formulated their sovereignty in terms entirely in keeping with Babylonian tradition. As we have seen, they used the secular titles "King of Assyria" and "King of the Universe" as well as the religious titles "Governor of Assur" and "Appointee of Enlil." The convergence of northern and southern usage was complete when Tukulti-Ninurta I named himself "King of the Four Quarters of the World."

CONCLUSIONS

The continuity of tradition in the royal titulary throughout the time of Mesopotamia's independence contrasts sharply with the short-lived use of the divine determinative. It justifies our treatment of Mesopotamian kingship as a valid concept which was not materially affected by historical changes, for the titles of even the latest periods are intimately related to those of early times. It remains for us to determine the nature of this concept. We shall afterward (chap. 21) return to the problem of the deification of certain kings, which is a collateral phenomenon. In the traditional Mesopotamian titulary every trace of deification is absent. The titles are impressive enough, and so are many Assyrian epithets, such as "Lord of Lords," "Prince of Princes," "King of Kings."[50] They stress the power of the king, but they never set him apart. They do not contain a hint that his nature differs essentially from that of other men. The Late Assyrian emperor who struck terror in the hearts of people from Egypt to Armenia had more in common with the Sumerian *lugal* who gloried in the subjugation of a neighboring city than with the "Living Horus" on the throne of Egypt.

CHAPTER 17

THE MAKING OF A KING

IN HISTORICAL times the Mesopotamian, no more than the Egyptian, could conceive of an ordered society without a king. Yet he did not regard kingship as an essential part of the order of creation. According to Egyptian views, the universe was the outcome of one single creative process, and the activity of the creator had found its natural sequel in the absolute rule which he exercised over the world he had brought forth. Human society under Pharaoh formed part of the cosmic order and repeated its pattern. In fact, Re, the creator, headed the lists of the kings of Egypt as the first ruler of the land who had been succeeded by other gods until Horus, perpetually reincarnated in successive Pharaohs, had assumed the legacy of Osiris.

In Mesopotamia the theological aspect of kingship was less impressive; the monarchy was not regarded as the natural system within which cosmic and social forces were effective. Kingship had gained universal acceptance as a social institution, but nature did not appear to conform to a simple scheme of forces co-ordinated by the will of a ruler.

It is true that Anu and Enlil were habitually styled "King of the Gods" and that words derived from their names (*anutu, enlilutu*) denoted kingship. Yet it is peculiar that there should have been two kings: Anu, the aloof heaven, personifying the majesty of kingship, and Enlil, the violent storm-wind, its executive power.[1] The matter becomes clearer when we observe that the texts usually describe the gods, not under the absolute authority of these kings, but rather following their guidance. The gods made decisions after general discussion, and Anu and Enlil derived their exceptional positions from the fact that they were the leaders of the assembly.

The title "king" has a less strict meaning in Mesopotamia than it has in Egypt. We have seen that a "governor" of Lagash might be called "king" by his subjects. In the same way, city-gods like Ningirsu of

231

Lagash, who never appear as "kings" among the gods, are constantly called so by their liegemen upon earth. Neither among the gods nor among men did the title "king" denote the summit of a rigid hierarchical pyramid which was acknowledged as the only possible structure of society—for the memory of a kingless period in the past was never lost.

THE ORIGIN OF KINGSHIP AMONG THE GODS

The Mesopotamian myth of beginnings knew neither single origin nor single authority. The primeval chaos contained two elements, sweet water and salt water—the male Apsu and the female Tiamat. This couple brought forth a multitude of gods whose liveliness disturbed the inertia congenial to Chaos. So Chaos rose to destroy its progeny. In this conflict the older gods proved inadequate, and a young deity was chosen king. After his victory he created the world as we know it.

The violence and confusion depicted in this story are poles apart from the serene splendor of the Egyptian creator rising from the primeval ocean on the first morning to shape the world he was to rule. In the Mesopotamian epic the actual creation forms, not the beginning, but the end of the narrative. On the other hand, the Egyptian, who viewed the universe as an immutable order, could not conceive anything preceding the establishment of his static world. For him the act of creation stood truly at the beginning. It was said to have occurred amid a stagnancy of water, an immeasurable potential of fertility, Nun. At Hermopolis chaos had been conceptualized in an Ogdoad of which Nun was one. But hardly anything could be said about these eight gods, since neither action nor order was possible before creation. When the Ogdoad is called "the waters that made the light,"* we must remember that mythopoeic thought habitually expresses itself in narrative form[2] and that, consequently, such phrases mean no more than that the sun emerged from the waters of chaos. The Egyptians, positing an Ogdoad of deities named "Darkness," "the Boundless," and so forth, merely rendered with the concreteness to which mythopoeic thought is prone a chaos such as Milton conceived:

> . . . . a dark
> Illimitable Ocean without bound,
> Without dimension, where length, breadth and height
> And time and place are lost.[3]

Nothing could occur in this chaos until the miraculous appearance of the creator heralded the first act of all—creation—and the beginning of his reign.

* See above, p. 151.

The Egyptian and Mesopotamian views of creation were, then, diametrically opposed. The contrast between them is thrown into relief by certain resemblances which are, perforce, of a secondary nature. Common to both is the description of the starting-point in negative terms. The first lines of the Babylonian Epic read:

> When on high the heavens had not (yet) been named,
> And below the name of firm ground had not (yet) been thought of. . . . .

And we read in the pyramid texts:

> When heaven had not yet come into existence,
> When men had not yet come into existence,
> When gods had not yet been born,
> When death had not yet come into existence . . . . [Pyr. 1466].

This negative description of creation is by no means confined to the ancient Near East. In fact, the most obvious way of introducing an account of creation is to emphasize the absence of all familiar phenomena. In the Sumerian myths we find this purpose served by phrases like "the wolf did not snatch away lambs," or "eye disease did not say, 'I, Eyedisease.' "[4] Both sentences mean: this familiar phenomenon did not yet exist. Elsewhere this piling-up of negatives shows a more ambitious purpose. In the Rigveda, for instance, it constitutes an attempt to escape from the tendency toward the concrete which characterizes mythopoeic thought and to conceive the act of creation without a material substratum.[5] Egyptian and Mesopotamian thought were never aware of bondage to the concrete, and the second similarity between the creation myths of the two countries consists precisely in an agreement about the nature of the material substratum. It was held to be water. Now the belief that the world emerged from a primeval ocean has been one of those most widely held throughout the world, among all kinds of peoples and at all periods. The reason is a simple one: the universe is viewed as endowed with life; and the emergence of life, whether of plants or of animals, is preceded by water—be it rain, the floods of rivers inundating fields, or the outflow of the amniotic liquid.[6]

A third resemblance between the Egyptian and Mesopotamian creation stories consists in the fact that they reflect certain natural features of their respective countries. But it is a mistake to see in the contrast of physiographical conditions the basis of the difference between the myths. The Mesopotamians could have built from their material—had they been so inclined—a story as serene as that of Atum's appearance in Egypt. In fact, the first section of the Epic of Creation, which reflects the Mesopotamian scene, lacks precisely the destructive nihilism, the anxiety, and the violence which dominate the central and major portion of the poem. It depicts in mythical terms the curious conditions which prevail even today in the southern part of the country where civilization arose.[7] There, in the lagoons at the head of the Persian Gulf, the waters of Euphrates and Tigris mingle with those of the sea and deposit their silt. The contrast of land and water is blurred; men, moving in boats, pitch their tents on the reeds which grow from the marsh bottom, beating them down to form a shallow mattress upon the slime. Hence Ea, the god of water, was originally called Enki, the Lord of Land. And so we read in the Epic of Creation that Apsu, sweet water, and Tiamat, salt water, were intermingled in the primeval chaos. Next

> Lahmu and Lahamu appeared, and they were named;
> Increasing through the ages, they grew tall [I, 10–11].

The names of this, the second couple in chaos, have been interpreted as meaning "silt."[8] At the edges of the watery waste, all round the horizon, a deposit of mud slowly mounted, forming a great double circle—the beginning of earth and sky: the earthly horizon *kishar* and the heavenly horizon *anshar*.

> Anshar and Kishar (then) were formed, surpassing them;
> They lived for many days, adding year unto year.
> Their son was Anu, equal to his fathers [I, 12–14].

With Anu we have reached the head of the Mesopotamian pantheon, but not yet creation. Before the extant universe could be said to exist, it was necessary that the solid disks formed by a continuing process of deposition out of the silt circles, Kishar and Anshar, should be separated. This separation was the act of creation, and it was originally ascribed to Enlil, the storm-wind.[9] Again we observe a parallel with Egypt, where Shu, the god of air, was said to have lifted the sky from the earth. But we do not know the details of this myth in Mesopotamia;[10] in the extant version Marduk has displaced Enlil. And Marduk made the sky and the earth from the two halves of Tiamat's body. It is unlikely that the older story gave a more peaceful account of creation, for Enlil was the god of the storm, and the Mesopotamian myths impart to the gods characters which, for all their plausibility, express the nature of the peculiar element in which the god is manifest. Enlil, consequently, appears as moody, impulsive, and passionate.[11] We must, however, discount this version of the epic and consider the one which is preserved and in which Marduk is the creator. This last term has, of course, to be taken in a somewhat restricted sense. For we have seen that all the gods and much else existed and that many events had taken place before

Marduk created heaven and earth. The Mesopotamians saw the world in perpetual flux, and even the creation of the existing universe was not an absolute beginning. Creation was but an episode in a larger story which was known as far back as the joint existence of Apsu and Tiamat.

The battles of the gods against Chaos moved from a promising start to a crisis which forced them to subordinate themselves to a king. The first threat of Tiamat and Apsu was countered by the destruction of the latter when Ea "cast a spell upon the waters." (Note that the victor was not a king but a magician.) The reaction of Chaos was terrifying. Its powers gathered (using the forms of Primitive Democracy), and prolific Tiamat spawned a numerous brood of monsters to strengthen their ranks:

> Angry, scheming, restless day and night,
> they are bent on fighting, rage and prowl like lions.
> Gathered in council, they plan the attack.
> Mother Hubur—creator of all forms—
> adds irresistible weapons, has borne monster serpents,
> sharp toothed, with fang unsparing;
> has filled their bodies with poison for blood.
> Fierce dragons she has draped with terror,
> crowned with flame and made like gods,
> so that whoever looks upon them shall perish with fear,
> and they, with bodies raised, will not turn back their breast.[12]

The gods stood aghast. Even Anu, the embodiment of authority, was helpless

> . . . . when Anu approached and saw the mood of Tiamat
> He could not stand before her and turned back.
> He went in terror. . . . .[13]

We have now reached the crisis of the conflict. Note that the story has so far proceeded without assigning any significance whatsoever to the concept of kingship. Only at this point in the emergency was Marduk asked to take charge. He accepted on the conditions which we have discussed.* Consequently, the gods imparted their collective power to their elected king, and after due preparations the battle was joined:

> The Lord raised up the floodstorm, his mighty weapon.
> He mounted the chariot, the irresistible, terrifying cy-
>   clone. . . . .
> For his clothing he wore armor that inspires fright;
> His head was covered with frightening radiance.
> The Lord set out and pressed toward her,
> Toward the place of raging Tiamat he set his face.

* See above, p. 220.

He held between his lips a talisman(?) of red clay;
An herb to destroy the poison he grasped in his hand.
Then they crowded around him, the gods crowded around
    him;
The gods, his fathers, crowded around him, the gods
    crowded around him![14]

These excited phrases introduce the description of Marduk's victory.
His election was justified, and his kingship was made permanent while
the gods intoned a magnificat proclaiming his fifty names.

Since our copy of the Epic of Creation was written in Late Assyrian
times, it shows that throughout Mesopotamian history the kingship of
the gods was believed to have originated, not as a natural concomitant
of an orderly society, but as the product of confusion and anxiety. This
genesis of kingship among the gods followed the pattern of its inception
among men. The same rule holds good in Egypt, where the origin of
kingship was made to coincide with that of the universe because personal rule had existed in Africa since time immemorial.

However, the ruler of the Mesopotamian gods differed from the human ruler in one respect: in the ideal world of the gods the limitations of
kingship were maintained. It is true that the Epic of Creation ends in a
glorification of Marduk, but this is understandable, since the text was
recited annually in the Marduk temple in Babylon. Other gods, too,
were hymned as mighty rulers in their own shrines by their devotees.
Yet it is significant that the very phrases in which the gods proclaim their
submission to Marduk (words which might *mutatis mutandis* have
been spoken in many an early assembly of the city-states) exalt the
power of his "word" or judgment in their deliberations:

Thou, O Marduk, art our champion;
We gave thee kingship, power over all things.
Take thy seat in the council; may thy word prevail.
May thy weapon not yield, may it smite thy foes.
Grant breath of life to lord(s) who put (their) trust in
    thee.
But if a god embraces evil, shed his life.[15]

In the Mesopotamian view the assembly of the gods remained the *fons
et origo* of divine decrees. In a text dealing with the destruction of Ur,
it is said to have decided the ruin of the leading city of the land; in the
"Song of Ishtar and Saltu,"[16] it is credited with having curbed Ishtar's
warlike propensities; at every New Year's festival, at the critical turn
of the seasons, it was thought to decide what would be the destiny of
mankind.* Two thousand years after it had been superseded by mon-

* See below, pp. 331–33.

archy in human society, Primitive Democracy was believed to survive among the gods.

THE ORIGIN OF KINGSHIP UPON EARTH

The origin of kingship among men was also bound to be a subject of speculation in Mesopotamia, and it is evident that the secular and historical explanations which we have given in the preceding chapter would have been meaningless to people who regarded human destiny as the outcome of divine decrees. The Mesopotamians asserted that in the earliest times, and again after the Flood, "kingship had descended from heaven." This remarkable formula combines the awareness that kingship had not always existed with the fact that it represented the only known form of government in historical times. Moreover, the phrase indicated that the office, and not the office-holder, was of superhuman origin. The majesty of kingship, the awe and sanctity of him who symbolized the community and represented it before the gods, was acknowledged as it was in Egypt. But while the Egyptians saw Pharaoh as a god, the Mesopotamians viewed their king as a mortal endowed with a divine burden. "Kingship descended from heaven,"[17] as if it were something tangible. In fact, another text, placing kingship in exact parallelism with the insignia of royalty, suggests that it was somehow inherent in crown, tiara, and staff:

> They (the gods) had not yet set up a king for the beclouded people
> No headband and crown had (yet) been fastened . . . .
> No scepter had (yet) been studded with lapis lazuli . . . .
> . . . .
> Scepter, crown, headband and staff
> Were (still) placed before Anu in heaven
> So that there was no counseling of its (i.e., kingship's) people.
> (Then) kingship descended from heaven.[18]

The first line of the quotation intimates that the people were lost, lacking all direction, moving, as it were, in a fog, because there was no king. But the specific power of kingship existed from the first; it was immanent in the royal insignia, and these were in heaven, before Anu, the god who personified authority and from whom, therefore, all order ultimately emanated. When kingship had been brought down to earth, Enlil and Inanna sought "a shepherd of the people," but there "was no king in the land. Kingship (descended from heaven) and Enlil bethought himself (to institute a king.)"[19] In these early texts the basic conception of kingship in Mesopotamia is clearly expressed: Royalty was something not of human origin but added to society by the gods; the king was a mortal made to carry a superhuman charge which the gods could remove at any time, to bestow it upon another.

THE CHOICE OF THE GODS

We do not know by what means the gods conveyed whom they had chosen for the throne. Omens, dreams, and the pragmatic proof of success were accepted at different times as indications of their choice. The texts use many different phrases instead of describing a formal ritual of divine election as is often thought.[20] They name gods with whom the new ruler stood in a particularly close relationship, and these are described as concurring explicitly with the choice of the assembly by some gracious act. For instance, Eannatum, an Early Dynastic ruler of Lagash, called himself one "whose name was called to mind by Enlil; endowed with strength by Ningirsu; envisaged by Nanshe in (her) heart; truly and rightly suckled by Ninhursaga;* named by Inanna."[21] But on another brick of the same Eannatum these actions are divided somewhat differently among the various deities. He is a ruler "endowed with strength by Enlil; truly and rightly suckled by Ninhursaga; whose name was called to mind by Ningirsu; envisaged by Nanshe in (her) heart."[22] Gudea calls himself:

> Shepherd envisaged by Ningirsu in (his) heart; steadfastly regarded by Nanshe; endowed with strength by Nindar; the man described(?) by Baba; child borne by Gatumdug; endowed with dignity and the sublime scepter by Ig-alima; well provided with the breath of life by Dunshagar; he whom Ningiszida his god has made to appear in the assembly with (proudly) raised head.[23]

The later texts continue to use similar expressions, but they also introduce others.[24] The king was, as before, said to have been singled out by a god's glance: "When Shamash . . . . with radiant face had joyfully looked upon me—me, his favorite shepherd, Hammurabi."[25] Or in a text of Shalmaneser III of Assyria: "When the great lord Assur, in the steadfastness of his heart, had singled me out by his dazzling gaze."[26] Or in Esarhaddon's phrase: "In the gladness of their hearts the gods, lifting their eyes to me, had chosen me to be truly and rightly king."[27]

Sometimes the king is said to have been predestined to rule,[28] and one meets phrases which recall the Egyptian view of kingship but which sound almost like mockery when applied to rulers so harassed by fear of the gods' changing favor. Assurbanipal stated of himself: "Assur and Sin have pronounced (my) name for rulership since time immemorial."[29]

* See below, pp. 299–301.

And Nabonidus said that "Sin and Ningal determined that he should rule when he was still in his mother's womb."[30] Other rulers emphasize the discrepancy between their status in youth and the position which they ultimately occupied and which could, therefore, be explained only as a result of divine election. This was no doubt the purpose of the "birth legend of Sargon of Akkad," who is described as the son of a priestess, set out in a reed basket and found and brought up by a gardener.[31] A similar tendency underlies the following verses which Assurnasirpal II addressed to Ishtar:

> I was born amid mountains which no one knew
> I did not recognize thy might and did not pray to thee.
> The Assyrians did not know of thy godhead and did not
>   pray to thee.
> But thou, O Ishtar, fearsome mistress of the gods,
> Thou didst single me out with the glance of thine eyes;
>   thou didst desire to see me rule.
> Thou didst take me from among the mountains.
> Thou didst call me to be a shepherd of men.
> Thou didst grant me the scepter of justice.[32]

Sargon was not of royal descent, but Assurnasirpal II was the son of King Shamsi-Adad IV. We could desire no clearer proof that even in Late Assyrian times divine election and not descent was regarded as the source of the king's authority.

The reasons which prompted the gods' choice are sometimes indicated, and they are quite surprising; they betray a concern with the welfare of the people for which the theological tenets we are considering do not provide a basis. For man was specifically created as the servant of the god* and did not, therefore, have a claim to their sympathy. But the gods mercifully desired that their people should enjoy just rule; in other words, if the living faith of the Mesopotamians comprised a feeling of utter dependence upon the gods, it also sustained the conviction that the gods had decreed justice as the foundation of society. In the text of Assurnasirpal II, Ishtar equips the king with the "scepter of justice." Hammurabi is more explicit. He declares to be called by Anu and Marduk "to make justice appear in the land, to destroy the evil and the sinful, to prevent the strong from oppressing the weak."[33] The same motivation appears in late texts, last of all in an inscription of the very ruler who ended the independence of Mesopotamia while modeling his kingship on Mesopotamian prototypes. Cyrus, the Persian, said: "(Marduk) reviewed the totality of the lands, and having seen them, he searched for a just king, a king after his own heart, whom he could

* See below, p. 332.

guide by the hand. He pronounced his name 'Cyrus of Anshan' and he signified his name for kingship over all."[34]

The gods might call a man to rule over a city or to rule over the land. Early rulers, as we have seen, were not concerned with "kingship over all" nor yet with kingship over the land, but with rulership over a city. An early text reflects the original division of the country among many city-states by describing how kingship, when it had been created, was assigned to several cities at once.[35] But in historical times a much more complex situation prevailed. Rulership over the country had become an ideal which men attempted to realize even though the central government had for the time being succumbed to the centrifugal force of particularism. Often it would be impossible to know to what type of dominion the gods had called the man of their choice, for rulership over the land was always an extension of rulership over a city. Every local ruler might aspire to hegemony, and his relation with the world of the gods did not differ from that of an overlord of the whole of Mesopotamia. Let us consider these two relationships.

As one would expect, the call to rulership over a city issued from the city-god.[36] He acted, however, in agreement with the divine assembly. A text of Gudea gives us a clear impression of the hierarchical relationship of city-ruler, city-god, and the pantheon at large. Enlil, the leader of the divine assembly, initiated the execution of his decree by instructing Ningirsu to withhold the annual rise of the Tigris at Lagash as a sign to the inhabitants that something was required of them. Ningirsu did this, and he furthermore ordered his temple Eninnu to "manifest its powers" in a manner we cannot reconstruct—perhaps by omens:

> On a day when destinies were being determined in heaven
>   and upon earth,
> Lagash held her head high in pride of her great powers.
> Enlil looked deliberately upon Lord Ningirsu:
> "Let the proper occurrences fail to take place in our city!
> Let the 'heart' fail to overflow!
> Let the 'heart of Enlil' fail to overflow!
> Let the 'heart' fail to overflow!
> Let the high flood, filled with brilliance and awesomeness,
> Let the good waters not be brought down in the 'heart of
>   Enlil,' that is (to say) in the Tigris!"
>
> To the house (temple) its owner (Ningirsu) called out,
> And (the temple) Eninnu began manifesting its powers in
>   heaven and on earth.
>
> The governor—being a man of understanding—took notice.[37]

A similar hierarchical order was acknowledged in an older inscription of Lagash in which Entemena gives the history of a boundary dispute between Lagash and the neighboring city of Umma. Enlil was said to have determined the boundary between the estates of the respective city-gods, Ningirsu and Shara. On the human plane this decision was given effect by Mesilim, the king of Kish, probably the most powerful ruler in the land at that time.

> Enlil, the king of all countries, the father of the gods, established the boundary for both Ningirsu and Shara by his unalterable command. And Mesilim, King of Kish, measured the fields and set up a stela in that place at the command of his god Sataran.
>
> Ush, Governor of Umma, repeatedly transgressed the agreement. He tore out that stela and moved it into the plain of Lagash.
>
> The warrior of Enlil, Ningirsu, at his (Enlil's) just command, did battle with Umma. At Enlil's command he clapped (his) *shushkallu* net down on it (s people) and lined up their burial mounds in the plain at that place.[38]

Note that Enlil did not address himself to Mesilim directly but that the king's personal god transmitted the order. Our text goes on to relate that a later ruler of Umma had not respected the boundary; Entemena had defeated him and now represented his victory as an achievement of the god of Lagash. This obviously leaves unsolved the thorny problem of the god of Umma's part in the course of events; another text frankly admits that the ruler of Umma acted "by command of his god."[39]

Thus the conflicts between city-states were viewed as conflicts between their divine owners. The human victor could speak with a certain complacency of the justice of his cause, as Entemena did. The loser faced an insolvable moral problem if he was convinced of being without guilt. Such was the case with Urukagina of Lagash when he was conquered by Lugalzaggesi of Umma and Erech:

> The man of Umma, after he destroyed Lagash, committing a crime against Ningirsu —the hand which he laid upon it (Lagash) shall wither! There was no crime on the part of Urukagina, King of Girsu (in Lagash).
>
> Let that crime be on the head of Nidaba, the (personal) goddess of Lugalzaggesi, the Governor of Umma.[40]

The men of Lagash felt that the causes of the calamity which had overtaken them transcended human relationships. The conviction that rulers, as well as ordinary men, were tools in the hands of the gods allowed them, if not to explain, then at least to express their helplessness and perplexity.

When rulership over the land as a whole had become well established, a new theological concept was introduced. For now an explanation was needed, not merely of the occasional success of individual rulers, but of the centuries of predominance which cities such as Akkad, Ur, or Babylon enjoyed. The assembly of the gods was credited with assigning temporary rule of the land to one city after another. The earliest embodiment of this view is probably the Sumerian king list,[41] which was drawn up when the Dynasty of Akkad had definitely established rulership over the whole land. The list combined the older historical traditions of the separate city-states and expressed its new concept in an old form when it opened with the statement: "When kingship was lowered from heaven, the kingship was in Eridu," or when it summarized the First Dynasty of Ur: "four kings reigned its 177 years," or when it continued: "Ur was smitten with weapons; its kingship was carried to Awan."[42]

But if one city profited as a result of the divine decree which gave it the leadership of the land, another city suffered eclipse; and its inhabitants were no more able to account for their misfortune than the subjects of Urukagina of Lagash had been. There was no reason why they should explain it as a result of their own shortcomings rather than of decisions which altogether transcended the sphere of man in their motivation.[43] Yet they felt the need to account for the ineffectualness of their city-god on whom they had relied for help and whose estate was now ravaged. Conflicts between gods could be postulated to explain wars between city-states, even though man could not presume to explain how the gods could transgress a decree of Enlil. But changes in the rulership of the land could not be due to conflicts between individual gods, since these changes were approved by unanimous decision at the highest level in the divine assembly. Man imagined, however, that the deliberations of the assembly sometimes reached a dramatic tension which induced individual gods to concur with actions to which they objected at heart. A text dealing with the destruction of Ur describes how Nanna (Sin), the city-god, joined in the unanimous pronouncement of the gods: "Let it be!" When the city was in ruins, he bitterly regretted that action. But the decree could not be annulled:

> Enlil answered his son Sin concerning it:
> The deserted city, with throbbing heart, weeps bitterly;
> Sobbing thou passest the day in it.
> (But), Nanna, through thy own submission thou didst accept the "Let it be!"
> By the verdict, by the word (of) the assembly of the gods,
> By command of Anu and Enlil . . . .
> Was the kingship of Ur . . . . carried away.

Since olden days when the country was founded
Have the terms of kingship been constantly changed;
As for its (Ur's) kingship, its term has now been changed
for a different term.[44]

B. THE ACCESSION

The Mesopotamian king derived his authority from divine election, but we do not know how the choice of the gods was recognized. We do know that in Assyrian times the death of a king more often than not called forth several pretenders to the throne who did not even require the qualification of royal descent. The most that could be said for it was this: the gods in assigning hegemony to a particular city—to start under a king whom they chose and to last through several generations—might be credited with the intention of appointing that king's descendants to succeed him. The argument was not conclusive, and its weakness is proved by the disturbances that occurred at the beginning of almost every new reign. Once more the contrast with Egypt is illuminating; there the inflexible rule of an established order became operative at the death of Pharaoh and supplied the country with its next king. In Mesopotamia each succession was essentially an *ad hoc* solution.

The Late Assyrian kings attempted to smooth the transition from their reigns to those of their successors by an equivalent of the Egyptian institution of coregency.* In Assyria the king inquired of the gods whether they desired one of his sons to succeed him;[45] and if they answered favorably, the heir apparent was installed. The crown prince was not always the eldest son, and the solemn oath of allegiance sworn at his investiture did not prevent his brothers from contesting the succession at their father's death. But officially the problem of the succession was solved once a prince had been inducted in the "House of Succession" or "Palace of the Crown Prince,"[46] hence Assurbanipal adored the Ishtars, saying: "From the House of Succession (they) have magnified my kingship."[47] Esarhaddon's account of his installation as crown prince is characteristic:

I was the younger brother of my adult brothers. (Yet) my father who begat me exalted me in the assembly of my brothers at the command of Assur, Shamash, Marduk, Nebo, Ishtar of Nineveh, and Ishtar of Arbela, saying: "This one is my successor." He questioned Shamash and Adad through oracles. They replied to him in the affirmative: "It is he who should be thy successor." Honoring this important pronouncement, he called together the people of Assyria, great and small, as well as my brothers born in the paternal house. Before the gods Assur, Sin, Shamash, Nebo, Marduk, the gods of

* See above, pp. 101–2.

Assyria, the gods who inhabit Heaven and Earth, he made them swear to respect my primacy. In the month of Nisan, on a propitious day, according to the august will of the gods, I entered gladly in the House of Succession, the awesome place of royal destinies.[48]

In the House of Succession the crown prince was initiated in the craft of kingship. He took an active part in the government, representing the king in official celebrations, carrying out special missions, and supervising religious festivals. He was therefore in the best possible position to take over when the king died.

It should be emphasized that in Mesopotamia the funeral rites of a king were in no way connected with his successor's accession. The reason is that the relationship between the two had little theological significance. In Egypt kingship involved two generations,* and the burial and transfiguration of Osiris were part of the celebrations at the succession of Horus. In Mesopotamia the king arranged for the funeral of his predecessor as a simple act of piety. A Late Assyrian account of a royal funeral—the only account that has come down to us—describes how the body was lying in state, decked out with the regalia and surrounded with the various objects which were to be interred with it:

> (In the) tomb, place of mystery,
> on the Royal Esplanade,
> I made him goodly rest.
>
> The sarcophagus, the groove for its cover,[49]
> I sealed its opening with solid bronze.
> I established its spell (against robbers and demons)
>
> Equipment of gold and silver
> fitting for a tomb
> (and) the royal insignia which he (my father) loves,
> I exhibited in the light of the sun.
>
> I put all this in the tomb,
> with my father who begot me.
>
> I offered sacrifice
> to the divine rulers, the Anunnaki,
> and to the gods who inhabit the earth.
>
> The channels complain
> and the watercourses respond.
> Of trees and fruit
> the face is darkened.
> The orchards weep
> and what was green. . . . .[50]

The last lines suggest that nature, too, mourned; and we know from other texts that the people gathered to bewail their late ruler.[51] But no-

* See above, pp. 33–35.

where is there any suggestion that these rites were related to the ceremonies of the accession.

The accession of the new king was formally sealed by the ritual of coronation. To view such solemnities as purely symbolical distorts the significance which they had for the ancients.[52] For them the first contact between the new ruler and the royal insignia was but the outward sign of a union in which the unchanging powers of kingship took possession of his person and made him fit to rule. Because the insignia of kingship were charged with these powers, they were divine. The primitive awareness of a confrontation with power brings with it an imputing of personality.[53] Consequently, the inanimate object in or through which power becomes manifest is perceived as a god. We remember that in Egypt at the coronation the throne which made a prince king became the mother-goddess Isis.* The crowns of Upper and Lower Egypt were also goddesses and the "mothers" of the king. A Sumerian text[54] similarly treats the royal insignia as goddesses, "Lady of the Crown" and "Lady of the Scepter."

The king received the insignia in the temple of the city-god who disposed of kingship during the period for which the assembly had decreed the ascendancy of the city in the land. While in the mythical time before "kingship descended from heaven, scepter, crown, tiara, and staff *were placed before Anu* in heaven," the proper place for the insignia after the introduction of kingship was the temple of the city-god. The Sumerian text which describes a coronation in Erech states that the "Lady of the Scepter" and the "Lady of the Crown" stood on a "throne dais." An Assyrian text which we shall quote presently describes their supports as "seats." Such seats are commonly depicted supporting symbols of the gods, and notably the crowns of Anu and Enlil (Fig. 44, upper left-hand corner). In shape the "seats" resemble altars.

We shall now quote first the description of the coronation ritual in Erech. The ceremony took place in Eanna, the temple of Ishtar (Inanna), the mistress of Erech:

> He (the ruler) entered into Eanna.
> He drew near the resplendent throne dais.
> He placed the bright scepter in his hand.
>
> He drew near the throne dais of Nin-men-na
>   ("Lady of the Crown")
> He fastened the golden crown upon his head.

* See above, p. 43.

> He drew near to the throne dais of Nin-PA
> ("Lady of the Scepter")
> Nin-PA, fit for heaven and earth. . . . .
>
> After she had discarded his "name (of)
> smallness,"
> She did not call his *bur-gi* name
> But called his "name (of) rulership."

Though the expression "*bur-gi* name" remains unexplained, the translator suggests that the last phrases describe a change of the ruler's name during the coronation. This supposition has much in its favor. One of the phrases in which divine election is described claims that a god has "pronounced the name" of the chosen ruler. That formula may well mean, pregnantly, that the god proclaimed the throne name by which his favorite was henceforth to be known.*

In Egypt, where the king was born to the purple, the throne name, together with the rest of the titulary, could be made known throughout the country immediately upon his accession.† In Mesopotamia the new name was given at the coronation when the choice of the gods became effective in the world of men. The "name of smallness" is presumably the name which the new ruler bore before his accession, and this interpretation finds support in the fact that the Sumerian word for "king," *lugal*, means "*great* man."

The Assyrian description of a coronation[55] does not mention change of name; otherwise the ritual resembles those of earlier times. The king went to the temple of the god Assur, where the royal insignia rested upon "seats." (It is interesting that the Assyrian kings were crowned, not in Calah or Nineveh, the capitals of the empire, but in the ancient city of Assur from which the empire took its rise.) The king on his portable throne was carried to the temple on the shoulders of men, while a priest going in front beat a drum and called out: "Assur is king! Assur is king!" This phrase emphasized that the new ruler—as yet uncrowned, and hence not "king" in the fullest sense of the word—was on his way to the god who was the depositary of kingship in Assyria.[56] The king entered the temple, kissed the ground, burned incense, and mounted the high platform at the end of the sanctuary where the statue of the god stood. There he touched the ground with his forehead and deposited his gifts: a gold bowl with costly oil, a *mina* of silver, and an embroidered robe. He then arranged Assur's offering-table while priests set those of the other gods. Next followed the last preparations for the coronation.

---

* See above, p. 238.   † See above, p. 103.

The text is damaged here, but it seems likely that the king was anointed with the oil brought in the gold bowl. The account then continues: "The crown of Assur and the weapons of Ninlil (Assur's spouse) are brought," and they were put on "seats" at the foot of the platform before the god. However, the central ceremony of the coronation is preserved in one text. The priest carried crown and scepter, still on the felt cushions which supported them when lying on their "seats," and brought them to the king. Then, while crowning the king, he said:

> The diadem of thy head—may Assur and Ninlil, the lords of thy
> diadem, put it upon thee for a hundred years.
> Thy foot in Ekur (the Assur temple) and thy hands stretched
> towards Assur, thy god—may they be favored.
> Before Assur, thy god, may thy priesthood and the priesthood
> of thy sons find favor.
> With thy straight scepter make thy land wide.
> May Assur grant thee quick satisfaction, justice, and peace.[57]

After the priest had spoken, the great dignitaries present at the ceremony pronounced prayers; and, upon the return of the procession to the palace, they gathered before the throne to do homage to the king. They presented gifts, deposited their badges and other insignia of office before him, and placed themselves in an irregular fashion, avoiding the order of precedence of the ranks they had just relinquished. It is clear that this usage was intended to allow the new ruler to choose his advisers to his own liking; but in Assyrian practice changes in the administration must have been made in an earlier or a later phase of the new reign, for the ritual of the coronation states simply: "The king then says: 'Everyone resumes his office.' The dignitaries take up their badges and their order of precedence."

We cannot but be struck by the simplicity and sobriety of this Assyrian ritual, especially if we remember the tone of its Egyptian counterpart. The very odor which characterized the gods emanated from Pharaoh when the feathers were bound upon his forehead, and the goddesses of the crowns were reborn in the union with his divine person.* It may be an accident that we have no Mesopotamian equivalents of the song which celebrated Pharaoh's accession, for in Mesopotamia, too, the opening of the new reign must have been an occasion of rejoicing, if only because man greets every new beginning with new hope. But for the ruler and those near him sobriety was the appropriate mood. The gods, in choosing the king, had given him signal proof of their favor; but the task which he now faced was hazardous in the extreme.

* See above, pp. 107–8 and 131–32.

The coronation, though it made him capable of ruling, did not diminish the gulf which separated him from the gods. Great as his power was relative to that of his people, he remained subject to the inadequacies of man in relation to nature. Nature was the realm of the gods, and the Assyrian king stood outside it, a servant of its masters, while Pharaoh was himself one of these. In Egypt, Hatshepsut could say—referring to *maat*, the "truth" or ruling principle of cosmic order—

> I have made bright Truth which the god loves. . . . .
> I eat of its brightness. I am a likeness from his limbs,
>   one with him.

But the Mesopotamian king was not conscious of such superhuman resources within him. When confronted with one of those disquieting portents which were never absent for long and which were so hard to interpret, he could only pray:

> In the evil eclipse of the moon which took place in the month
>   of Kislimu, on the tenth day;
> in the evil of the powers, of the signs, evil and not good,
> which are in my palace and my country,
> I fear, I tremble, and I am cast down in fear!
> . . . . At thy exalted command
> let me live, let me be perfect and let me behold thy divinity!
> Whenever I plan, let me succeed!
> Cause truth to dwell in my mouth![58]

Pharaoh's acts were divine revelations, acclaimed by the people and inspired, admired, and supported by the other gods. But the Mesopotamian king was obliged to grope his way through omens and oracles. It was with full knowledge of the burden which royalty imposed upon the new king that the priest prayed at the height of the coronation ceremony: "May Assur grant thee quick satisfaction, justice, and peace!"

PART VI. THE FUNCTIONS OF THE KING

CHAPTER 18

GOVERNMENT

A. ADMINISTRATION OF THE REALM

SINCE the administrative functions of the Mesopotamian kings have been studied fully, we shall recall only the most important of them. Our sources of information are collections of laws and other official documents, as well as part of the correspondence of Hammurabi and other kings of his dynasty and of the Late Assyrian Empire. In the Babylonian letters the king appears as a remarkably informed executive "in active control of even subordinate officials stationed in distant cities of his empire . . . . we . . . . see him investigating quite trivial complaints and disputes among the humbler classes of his subjects, and often sending back a case for retrial or for further report."[1]

The king's decision was sought in connection with all events of importance, and he supervised energetically the carrying-out of his orders. Many lawsuits were settled by his decisions: the relevant documents were traced in the palace archives or transmitted to the court, and the parties (or, in general, the culprits) were summoned to Babylon and brought there under escort to be judged. Taxes were energetically collected; if postponement of payment was granted until after the harvest, reminders were sent out at the proper time. Rents were collected. The large herds of the royal domains, the sheep-shearing, and so on were kept under supervision. Arrangements were made for delivery of wood from the marshes in the South. Ships were furnished for transport. The *corvées* of the serfs were strictly controlled, but care was taken that nobody was pressed into service who was not obliged to render it by his social status; and the specific rights of the different social classes, such as the merchants, were carefully guarded. Attempts by local assemblies, elders, or judges to annul land rights were checked. Strong action was taken against bribery. Besides all this there was the never-ending care for the maintenance and extension of the canals . . . . and for the intercalation and other measures required for the cult.[2]

The letters of the Late Assyrian kings show a similar concern with the details of government in all its aspects.

B. INTERPRETATION OF THE SUPERHUMAN

It would be a mistake to consider the Mesopotamian king as merely an administrator. His office combined personal power and servitude in a curious manner. This is strikingly documented by letters which certain

Assyrian kings addressed to the god Assur and in which they reported to him—as a vassal to his overlord—the course of their military campaigns.[3]

The king's duties were threefold: the interpretation of the will of the gods; the representation of his people before the gods; and the administration of the realm. This division is somewhat artificial, for the king, as representative of the people, interpreted the will of the gods. And his administrative acts were based on his interpretations. To some extent the three aspects of royalty are present wherever a king rules under divine sanction, but the manner of their combination and the weight attached to each distinguishes kingship from one country to another.

The relative importance of the three functions may change somewhat in the course of time even in the same country. In the documents from the Dynasty of Akkad and the First Dynasty of Babylon, the religious functions of the king are much less in evidence than in those from Late Assyrian times when the ruler styled himself *sangu* or "priest," as he had done in the Early Dynastic period.[4] But at all times the king stood at the head of the clergy and appointed the high priest.[5] Naturally, the gods were consulted before the appointment was made. A text in which Nabonidus of Babylon describes the installation of his daughter as High Priestess of Nanna (the moon-god) at Ur insists on the king's methodical piety:[6] Nanna had provided an omen by darkening his heavenly body, the moon, on the thirteenth day of the month Elul; and this was interpreted as a sign that a "divine bride," a high priestess, had to be installed. "I, Nabonidus, the shepherd who fears his (the god's) divinity, honored his command and obeyed (it)." The king then relates how strongly he was affected by the demand for a divine bride. He visited the sanctuaries of Shamash and Adad, the "Lords of Oracles," and asked them to confirm his interpretation: "I repeated it, and I inspected the portent, and they gave me a more favorable oracle than before." Nabonidus then suggested various members of his family, but each was rejected until he proposed his daughter. And she proved acceptable to the god.

This text illustrates two of the methods by which the gods could communicate with their servant the king. They could send signs: Nabonidus observed that the moon was darkened on a certain day; Gudea noticed that the Tigris failed to rise at Lagash. They could also answer questions by means of oracles. Dreams were a third method of communication. But neither portents nor oracles nor significant dreams were viewed as miraculous interruptions of a natural—and therefore meaningless—

course of events. Our concepts of the "natural" and of "natural law" did not exist; the life of nature was the life of the gods and hence full of significance; the movements of the constellations and the planets, changes in the weather, the behavior of animals—in short, all normal and recurring phenomena—involved divine activities and betokened divine intentions no less than extraordinary occurrences like eclipses, earthquakes, or plagues.

Although the king was charged with interpreting the will of the gods, he was not supposed passively to await their communication. Even significant dreams were more likely to come to him when he took the initiative to go and sleep in a temple. His duty was perpetual observance. In Assyrian times this duty was delegated to a large body of priests and soothsayers who sent daily reports to their royal master. We shall quote some examples of these:

To the king my lord, your servant Balasi: Greetings to the king my lord. May Nabu and Marduk bless the king my lord.

As to what the king wrote, "Something is happening in the skies: have you noticed?" —As far as I am concerned, my eyes are fixed. I say "What phenomenon have I failed to see (or) failed to report to the king? Have I failed to observe something that does not pertain to his lot?" As to the observation of the sun, of which the king my lord wrote,—this is a month for the observation of the sun, twice do we observe it: on the 26th of Marheshvan (and) on the 26th of Kislev, we make our observations. Thus we make the observation of the sun during two months. As to that eclipse of the sun, of which the king spoke, the eclipse did not take place. On the 27th I shall look again and send in (a report). For whom does the king my lord fear misfortune? I have no information whatsoever.[7]

To the king of countries my lord, your servant Bel-ushezib. May Bel, Nabu and Shamash bless the king my lord.

An eclipse occurred, but was not visible at the capital (Assur); it passed by. The capital, the royal city, where I dwell, was overshadowed with clouds; we do not know whether the eclipse occurred or not. Let the lord of kings send to Assur, to each and every city, (including) Babylon, Nippur, Erech and Borsippa; undoubtedly it was visible in (some one of) these cities. Let the king procure a reliable (report). . . . . The omens associated with an eclipse in the month of Adar and in the month of Nisan (invariably) come (true). I shall send (an account of) it all to the king my lord. The king should not neglect the lustral incantations for the eclipse (which) are performed to compensate for any sin (which may have been committed). The great gods dwelling in the city of the king my lord, (caused) the sky to be overshadowed (with clouds and) did not allow the eclipse to become visible, saying, "Let the king know that this eclipse is not (directed) against the king and his country." Let the king rejoice.[8]

This letter is clear. It is necessary to send to other cities for the details of the eclipse, but it can be said already that the state is not threatened by the dread event, since the gods took the special precaution to veil it from the capital. Another report on an eclipse was written on an unfavorable day; hence the writer omitted to invoke the gods in greeting. But he had to explain the omission so as to avoid giving the impression that he was lacking in respect:

To the king my lord, your servant Nabu-ahe-erba: Greetings to the king my lord.
It is a day of mourning, I have not sent a blessing. The eclipse moved from the East (and) turned entirely toward the West. Jupiter (and) Venus disappeared within (the zone of) the eclipse until they were released. For the king my lord it is a good sign: the evil (thereof) involves Amurru. Tomorrow I shall send to the king my lord a written report on the eclipse.[9]

Amurru was the western neighbor of Assyria, and, since the eclipse progressed toward the west, the evil it portended was thought to move in that direction. Such an observation might be interpreted as an encouragement by the gods to wage war against the west.

Even matters of the greatest importance to the king personally could be decided without consideration of his opinion or wishes. For instance, he could be forbidden by those who read the signs to receive a visit from the crown prince.

To the king my lord, your servant Balasi: Greetings to the king my lord. May Nabu and Marduk bless the king my lord.
Concerning the crown prince, with reference to whom the king wrote me: "Is the planet Mars brilliant?" Mars will be brilliant until the month of Iyyar, (its) brilliance is increasing. In case he (i.e., the crown prince) should suffer harm by appearing before the king when Mars is brilliant, we should be held accountable for (it), is it not so? He shall not return to Assyria; nor shall he go into the sacred area(?). No one shall go into the inner palace before the king for it (would be) sin. If, in this month, it is not agreeable to the king, in the month of Nisan—at the beginning of the year, when the moon completes the days (of the month)—(then), in the month of Nisan, (the crown prince) may appear before the king.[10]

In the following letter the king appears a true slave of the ritual. It was apparently written when clouds or fog prevented the observation of the moon, and hence the proclamation of the new month, even though Jupiter had been visible:

To the king our lord, your servants Balasi (and) Nabu-ahe-erba: Greetings to the king our lord. May Nabu and Marduk bless the king our lord.
The king our lord is gracious. A day has gone by since the king began fasting and has not eaten a morsel. "Until when?" is his inquiry. Today the king should eat no food, the king is a beggar. At the beginning of the month the moon will be seen. (The king says:) "Release me! Have I not waited (long enough)? It is the beginning of the month. I want to eat food, I want to drink wine!" Now, is Jupiter the moon? Later, for a whole year, the king may ask for food. We have pondered the matter and we have prescribed. We have written accordingly to the king.[11]

The letters to the king which we have discussed so far have dealt with natural phenomena which presented themselves for observation and did not depend on human initiative in any way. These phenomena would, in fact, have escaped notice but for the perpetual vigilance with which Mesopotamian society watched nature in the hope of stealing a march on fate and forestalling catastrophe by a timely recognition of divine intentions. However, the gods also suffered themselves to be questioned. The most usual method consisted in an inspection of the liver of a sheep. Before the animal was slaughtered, the question addressed to the gods was whispered into its ear. It was then killed, and the answer was indicated by the conformation of the animal's liver. The following letter is concerned with such an inspection:

> To the king my lord, your servant Adad-shum-usur: Greetings to the king my lord. May Nabu and Marduk bless the king my lord.
> All is well with the officials of the rear palace. Concerning the gall-bladder about which the king my lord wrote, "Is it bent(?)?"—The firm lobe of the liver(?) was bent(?). The gall-bladder had dropped underneath. This position is not favorable. What should be above was placed below. During two days a fluid flowed out (of it). It is a good sign. May the king be of good cheer.[12]

The following quotation shows that the gods sometimes gave answers which made additional inquiries necessary. In this particular case these inquiries had to be made at the last moment. The question was obviously whether repairs to the temple roof might usefully be undertaken. The month was favorable, but certain specific unfavorable signs seem to have been observed. The beginning of the letter is lost; the remainder reads:

> Perhaps it is not good to send the men up onto the roof of the temple. Verily in the morning some plan can be devised after observing (the flight of) a bird or some other omen. As to the roof of the Marduk temple, of which the king my lord spoke, it is a good time to build it: the month of Elul is propitious (for doing so), and the second day is propitious for divination. Let it be done at once.[13]

The gods communicated with the king most directly in dreams. One Assyrian text relates how a crown prince had monstrous dreams, the meaning of which remains obscure to us.[14] But a clear account of dreams which served as a means of communication between the gods and the king is preserved by Gudea of Lagash.[15] We have described how the gods conveyed to Gudea that Eninnu, the temple of Ningirsu, should be rebuilt.* Gudea brought sacrifices, and during the night Ningirsu (whom Gudea called his "king") appeared in his dream:

> And the lord Ningirsu—when Gudea saw his king
>   in the middle of the night—
> Spoke to him concerning the building of his house.
> Upon Eninnu, the powers of which are great, he made
>   him look.

Gudea acted in a significant manner on the revelation of Ningirsu's wishes; there was no joy or pride at being honored by a direct communi-

* See above, p. 240.

cation from the god. His one dominant emotion, here as in similar texts, was fear that he might misunderstand the message and be the cause of his lord's displeasure. In his perplexity he decided to ask advice from the goddess Nanshe:

> Gudea, his heart beclouded,
> Was pondering the command;
> Go to, I must tell it to her. Go to, I must tell it to her!
> May she stand by me in these things!
> I am a shepherd; the princeliness of a shepherd has been
>   entrusted to me;
> (Yet) I do not know the innermost (meaning) of that which
>   the middle of the night brought me;
> I must take my dream to my mother.

Gudea then sailed up a canal through his city-state of Lagash, first past another sanctuary of Ningirsu and then past one belonging to the goddess Gatumdug. In both he offered sacrifice and prayed for assistance. Arrived at his destination, he unfolded to the goddess Nanshe the terrifying vision at which the previous phrases had only hinted.

> In the dream, the first man—he was boundless like heaven,
> Was boundless like the earth.
> According to his head and crown he was a god,
> According to his wings he was the divine Imdugud bird,
> According to his lower parts(?) he was a flood wave.
> Lions were lying on his right and left.
> He commanded me to build his house.
> I did not know what exactly he had in mind.
>
> Daylight rose for me upon the horizon,
> And the first woman—whoever she may or may not have
>   been—
> Coming out ahead, prepared a razed (building) plot.
> She held a stylus of gold in her hand;
> She placed a clay tablet with the stars of heaven (on it)
>   on (her) knee
> And consulted it.
>
> The next—a warrior—wore horns(?).
> He (She) held a tablet of lapis lazuli
> And began to set down on it the plan of a house.
> Before me stood a silver basket;
> A brick mold of silver had been prepared (in a square),
> And a typal brick had been put in the mold for me;
> Into the . . . . trough standing before me
> A birdman was constantly pouring clear water,
> And a donkey stallion on the right of my king
> Continued to paw the ground for me.

The goddess Nanshe explained the dream, identifying the figures as Ningirsu and other deities and the stallion pawing the ground as Gudea, impatient to start the work required of him. Moreover, she added significant advice: Although Gudea is preparing to honor Ningirsu by rebuilding his temple, he will do well to pacify the god. He should construct a new war chariot and offer it—complete with a team of donkey stallions, quivers, and a standard—while Ningirsu's beloved drum is being sounded. When these gifts are offered "to the gift-loving warrior, thy master, the lord Ningirsu . . . . , he will accept from thee (even) thy softly spoken demand as if it were one loudly spoken. The umbrageous heart of the lord, of Ningirsu, the son of Enlil, will be soothed (and friendly) toward thee; and he will reveal to thee the plan of his house." Nanshe's advice reveals again the fear which was so strong an element in Mesopotamian, as it was in Hebrew, religiosity; the *mysterium tremendum* outbalanced the *mysterium fascinosum* when the Mesopotamian confronted his gods.

Gudea, on his return to Lagash, acted on the advice of the goddess. He made the gifts, and yet doubts remained. Again he sacrificed, burned aromatic herbs and wood, and addressed Ningirsu:

> My king Ningirsu—lord of the awesomely rising waters,
> Trusty lord, seed spawned by the Great Mountain (Enlil),
> Hero who hast no superior (?)—
> Ningirsu, thy house I shall build for thee;
> But I have not my specific orders.
> O warrior, thou hast announced what (will be) seemly;
> But, O son of Enlil, lord Ningirsu,
> I do not yet fully understand it.

The answer came in a dream:

> For the second time to the sleeper, to the sleeper,
> He (appeared) standing at (his) head, prodding him with
> a sword.

The god first revealed himself in a series of impressive and terrifying epithets. Then he promised Gudea a return of the intercepted flood waters of the Tigris as soon as the work on the temple was begun.

> When, O trusty shepherd Gudea,
> Thou shalt have started for me (work) on Eninnu, my royal
> abode,
> I will call up in heaven a humid wind.
> It shall bring thee abundance from on high
> And the country shall spread its hands upon riches in thy
> time.
> Prosperity shall accompany the laying of the foundations
> of my house.
> All the great fields will bear for thee;
> Dikes and canals will swell for thee.

Where the water is not wont to rise,
To high ground it will rise for thee.
Oil will be poured abundantly in Sumer in thy time.
Good weight of wool will be given in thy time.

Then follows a list of the materials from which the temple is to be built. Hence Gudea could call the people together to start the work.

Gudea's detailed description of the preliminaries to his building operations forms a parallel to the Assyrian letters which we quoted above. The Mesopotamian ruler was obliged to interpret the will of the gods, his masters. But no duty could be more exacting, and the risks involved were immense. For, while it was difficult to avoid misunderstanding the commands, mistakes brought down the calamity of divine anger upon the ruler and his people. In the Assyrian letters we watch a large body of officials laboring, in co-operation with their king, to elucidate the gods' intentions. In Gudea's text we meet a simpler situation: the king is shown striving, with endless patience, devotion, and humility, by prayer and by cajoling, to obtain the divine guidance without which all his efforts were bound to miscarry.

C. REPRESENTATION OF THE PEOPLE

The king chosen by the gods was responsible to them for the behavior of his subjects; conversely, he could appeal to the gods on their behalf. The latter duty is rarely stressed in the inscriptions, for these tend to emphasize the king's election and to give to his relationship with the gods a purely personal character. But occasionally in the texts the king appears as the representative of the people. For instance, Utuhegal, a king of Erech who had succeeded in driving away the Gutium (a mountain people who had overrun the country during the last years of the Dynasty of Akkad and pillaged it for over a century), acted specifically on behalf of the people of Mesopotamia. This is shown by the second line, and by the end of our quotation.

Enlil—Gutium, a viper of the mountains . . . . ,
The one which had carried the kingship of Sumer off to
    the mountains;
Had filled Sumer with banditry(?);
Had robbed the one who had a spouse of his spouse;
Had robbed the one who had a child of his child;
Had established brigandage(?) and violence in the land—
Enlil, king of all countries,
To destroy its name,
Unto Utuhegal,
The mighty man,
King of Erech,

King of the Four Quarters,
Did the king whose orders are not to be gainsaid,
Did Enlil, the king of all countries,
Give commission.

To (the goddess) Inanna, his (Utuhegal's) Queen, he
    went in.
He greeted her:
"My Queen, Lioness of Battle, fighting with all countries,
Enlil has given me commission to return the kingship of
    Sumer into its hands.
Be thou my helper!"[16]

Utuhegal presents himself here as the representative of the autochthonous population which had been suppressed by the foreigners; and Enlil, for once, appears concerned, not with the power of the king, but rather with returning "the kingship of Sumer into *its* hands."

Another example of the representative role of the king appears in an earlier text which complains of the overthrow of Urukagina and refers to the hostile people as well as to their ruler. The tradition of the popular assembly also kept alive the notion that the king represented the people. But this function was particularly important when the king had to answer for the people's behavior before the gods. Gudea "made the city kneel and the country bow down"[17] upon the completion of the temple and while Ningirsu was on his way to occupy it.

In Assyrian times the responsibility of the king for the actions of the people as a whole was stressed to an unusual degree.[18] The king was manipulated almost like a talisman—or he became the scapegoat, charged before the gods with all the sins of the community. Hence his time was largely taken up with penitence and prophylactic magic. We have quoted letters imposing a fast upon the king at the end of a month and his humble prayers when an eclipse of the moon predicted evil. Other examples could be cited in profusion; they are all of the first millennium, and they may well represent an unprecedented development of features playing but a subordinate role in earlier times. We may note the treatment to which the king had to submit after an earthquake: Offerings were made in the morning to Anu, Enlil, and Ea; and, when various recitations had been completed, "(the king) shall make obeisance. He shall have himself shaved (completely). Thou shalt enclose the hairs of his body in a *lahan-sahar* vase, and thou shalt deposit this vase at the enemy's frontier."[19]

A somewhat mechanistic point of view determined the relation between threatening danger and prophylactic action. Against each specific danger to which society was exposed, the gods had provided a specific expiatory rite.[20] As an example of this attitude we shall quote a letter written when the king inquired whether the particular month in which omens of an earthquake were observed was so unfavorable that the danger had to be taken seriously. If so, the king had to submit to a ritual shaving in which all the body hair was removed; and the Assyrians were as hirsute as the modern Armenians, while their razors were of bronze or iron. The king, impatient with the burden imposed upon him, had apparently asked the wise men to put an interpretation on the omens that would free him from the ceremony. Answered the priest:

> To the king my lord, your servant Balasi: Greetings to the king my lord. May Nabu and Marduk bless the king my lord.
> Concerning the interpretation of the name about which the king my lord wrote me, "The king with his authority is he of no account? What can the wise men do?" The interpretation of the names of the months is after this fashion: one is unlike the other. Each receives its interpretation in order. The one whose interpretation is of least account indicates a disturbance of the earth: in it(?) there will be an earthquake. What is the ceremony that should be performed for an earthquake? Your gods will cause it to pass away. Ea made (the earthquake), Ea will release (us from it). (For) whoever made the earthquake has also provided the lustral incantation against it. In the time of the fathers (and) grandfathers of the king, there was no earthquake: I, because I was of no account, have not seen earthquakes. That (same) god will give wisdom to the king, saying, "Let him spread out his hands (in prayer) to god. Let him perform the proper lustral incantations; it will surely pass away."[21]

The meaning of the evil portent which the king is to counteract by the proper ritual is indicated in another text: "If the soil shakes—attack by the enemy. The foundation of the land will not be stable. If the soil is displaced, there will be instability in the whole land. The land will lose its reason."[22]

The rites of penitence and conciliation not only entailed discomfort but interfered seriously with the business of government. We have, for example, a letter in which it is prescribed that the king shall pass seven days in a reed hut like the ones used by those who were seriously ill, submitting to purifications all the time.[23] Sometimes his time could be saved by performing rites over his mantle while he attended to other business. The daily cult of the gods, for which the king was responsible, was left to the priests, who acted as his representatives except on the none-too-rare occasions when his presence was imperative. Moreover, his participation in acts of government was subject to the continuous observations of the soothsayers and to the peculiar quality—the exact, favorable or unfavorable, nuance—which pertained to each day in the year and was carefully noted in calendrical lists. We have met references to this aspect of the days in several letters quoted above. To indicate the complexity of the rules, let us recall[24] that the number six should stand for Adad and that consequently the sixth, sixteenth, and twenty-sixth days of each month were sacred to him. Since Adad, as the god of the thunderstorms, could release forces of destruction, a liturgy of contrition, including a confession of sins, had to be recited on those days by the king. However, five months were unsuitable for the recitation of such a liturgy for various reasons, and in those months it could be omitted. But in each month there were from six to nine other days which were potentially dangerous and upon which no serious business should be taken in hand. As an example we quote:

> Dangerous day. The Shepherd of the Great Peoples (i.e., the king) shall not eat meat roasted upon coals nor bread baked in the ashes. He shall not change the clothes of his body. He shall not put on clean vestments. He shall not sacrifice.
> The king shall not mount his chariot. He shall not speak as ruler. In the place of mystery, the divination priest shall not speak a word. The doctor shall not touch a patient.
> This day is unsuitable for the realization of one's wish.[25]

Thus each day and month possessed certain good or evil potentialities the totality of which formed a framework of predictable junctures; within this framework the unusual portents on the earth or in the sky became significant. The initiates, watching these signs continuously, calculated the balance of the forces to which the state seemed to be subjected at any one time.

The king, however, was not merely guided through this intricate network of hostile or favorable influences; he was made to modify them by his own actions. For the very fact that the gods had chosen the ruler of the state made him a talisman, mystically connected with the powers in nature and with every part of the universe. He "bore the taboo (*ikkibu*) of Bel, Sin, Shamash, and Adad."[26] Hence he was capable of affecting the threat of danger. In Assyrian times the king consented when necessary to forego his role as steersman of the state and to become its rudder, manipulated by those who watched the portents, in order that all might remain afloat upon the waves of the unknown.

CHAPTER 19

THE SERVICE OF THE GODS

A. THE PERILS OF SERVICE AND THE SUBSTITUTE KING

THE dogma of divine election which formed the foundation of kingship in Mesopotamia gave rise to contradictory feelings. It was a source of both pride and anxiety, but the latter predominated, at least in the texts. Uncertainty characterized the Mesopotamian's relations with his gods. If omens indicated that a national misfortune was imminent or that his king was threatened by danger, he found himself in a dilemma. Perhaps the king had served the gods ill so that his continuation in office imperiled the welfare of the state. On the other hand, it was also possible that the gods intended the people to protect their chosen servant; in the absence of proof that they had rescinded their decree of election, the people did not dare to replace him. The king was a divine pledge in the hands of man. And, when the threat of danger assumed unusual proportions, a substitute was installed in the hope that the royal person might be saved.

This particular practice is the most striking of many more or less similar rites, all of which introduce a person or object to replace the ruler for a limited time. In Assyria "substitution" was resorted to, not only to protect the king, but also to make greater use of his supernatural endowment than would otherwise have been possible. Some ceremonies, for instance, were performed with figures of the king;[1] on other occasions his mantle did service. For example, when omens portended an earthquake and the king had submitted to purifications, had made a confession before Anu, Enlil, and Ea, and had recited propitiatory prayers accompanied by lamentations of the *kalu* priest, then the same lamentations and prayers were recited in the other cities of the realm over his mantle.[2] The practice of substitution derives from the "mystic participation" which characterizes mythopoeic thought[3] and which betrays an inability, not to think clearly, but to abstract from the world of perceptions. Since the sight of the king's mantle was able to evoke some of the emotions—say, loyalty or awe—which his person would call forth, the presence of the garment was felt to produce some of the effects which the king's own attendance would have produced.

In other circumstances substitution served as protection. When a magic spell was cast over the enemy before battle, the king did not take part in the ceremony so that he would not involve his person in the risks which the manipulation of magic necessarily entailed. Hence "a royal eunuch named by the same name as his master . . . . put on the dress of the king" and pronounced the proper formulas before the gods.[4] In this and similar cases the substitution was a preventive measure. The substitute exposed himself to great dangers, but, if all went well, he emerged unharmed. The expression "May I go in the king's stead"[5] envisages this kind of substitution; this sometimes worked mechanically, without taking the will of either the king or his subject into account. For instance, when there was a dangerous portent, like the eclipse of sun or moon, but there were at the same time favorable circumstances, such as the presence of the royal planet Jupiter in the sky, then the king was protected, and the text states: "In his place, this year, a grandee or a commoner will die."[6] If, however, dangerous omens accumulated, and there were no signs that the person of the king was in any way protected, a substitute king was appointed. He reigned for one hundred days, and he was then destroyed in the hope that he would carry away with him the disasters which had threatened the real king. We shall quote from letters written by an official to a Late Assyrian king:

The substitute king who arrived on the fourteenth toward sunset, who on the fifteenth spent the night in the king's palace, and in whose presence an eclipse took place—he entered Akkad on the night of the twentieth without mishap. He has stayed there. I made him recite the litanies on the tablets before Shamash. He has taken upon him all the portents of heaven and earth and he governs all countries. May the king my lord take notice.[7]

The substitution had to be complete in order to be effective. Hence it is stated that the substitute "governs all countries." In fact, a royal chronicle records that when a king of Isin, to avoid disaster to his house (no doubt predicted by omens), installed a gardener as substitute king and then died, the substitute retained his power:

That the dynasty might not end, King Irra-imitti made the gardener Enlil-bani take his place upon his throne and put the royal crown upon his head. Irra-mitti died in his palace because he had swallowed boiling broth. Enlil-bani who was upon the throne did not relinquish it and was installed as king.[8]

Even if this entry contains as much folklore as history,[9] it is significant that it could be believed. It may refer to a substitute king who, like the royal eunuch in the Assyrian ritual, was not necessarily killed after fulfilling his function. But for this very reason it might be interpreted as proof that death could not be averted from the king unless the substitute underwent it in his stead. We know, at any rate, of a Late Assyrian substitute who was killed together with a lady of the court whom the king had put at his disposal, no doubt to increase the verisimilitude of his rulership.[10] The victim, Damqi, had apparently been chosen by a prophetess in a trance: "A prophetess cried out these ritual phrases; she said to Damqi . . . . : 'You will take upon you kingship.' Next, in the assembly of the land, the prophetess said: 'This weapon, a present which my lord has indicated, I place in your hands.' " We may assume that the weapon was a symbol of royalty, like the "weapons of Ninlil" at the coronation. The letter continues: "Damqi, the son of the superintendent of Akkad, governs the lands of Assur and of Babylon and the totality of the lands." The rest of the letter hints at Damqi's death ("he has met his fate") and describes his funeral, ending with the reassurance that all evil has now been averted.

He, Damqi, and his lady of the court, as is proper, have taken upon themselves (the part of) substitute for the king my lord and of Shamash-shum-ukin. For their (the king's and prince's) deliverance, he has met his fate. We have built a tomb. He and his lady of the court have been prepared and laid out for burial. Their bodies have lain in state. They have been buried and bewailed. A holocaust has been made. Numerous rites of atonement have been performed completely. . . . . May the king my lord take notice. . . . . The ceremonies of expiation which have been undertaken are completed. May the heart of the king my lord be entirely at peace. The Akkadians were afraid. We have reassured their hearts.

It is certain that measures of such severity were taken only in exceptional cases when the threat to the royal person was overwhelmingly strong.[11] It is possible that some of the more elaborate Early Dynastic tombs at Ur contained the bodies of the royal substitute and his court.[12] However that may be, we should stress how well the institution of the substitute king illustrates the nature of Mesopotamian kingship. As the representative of the people, the king was threatened by every evil omen of importance. But his person was immensely precious because his election by the gods constituted a pledge of their support. Hence, when disaster seemed imminent, he was, as it were, temporarily withdrawn from his function; and a substitute was exposed to the danger or was sacrificed as the victim the supernatural powers seemed to require.

It is significant that the institution of a substitute king is unknown in Egypt. Where the king is a god incarnate, we may find that he is destroyed when physical disability seems to interfere with the effectiveness of the incarnation,* but the notion that a man could effectively take

* See above, p. 47.

the king's place would be sacrilegious. Thus the institution of the substitute king accentuates the essential difference between the monarchs of Mesopotamia and a divine king.

B. THE JOYS OF SERVICE AND THE STATE FESTIVALS

The importance attached by the ancients to the ideas which we are discussing in this volume is clearly shown by the care and the riches which they expended on festivals of a politico-religious nature. Public life reached its highest intensity in the course of these celebrations. In Mesopotamian cities all business activity was interrupted more than once during each month in order that the people and their ruler might devote themselves, for two or three days at a time, to honoring the superhuman powers which affected the life of the community.

We pointed out in the Introduction that these festivals, for all their exuberance, possessed a degree of seriousness which it is difficult for us to imagine. They represented participation by the community in cosmic events which would appear to us to be entirely independent of human action. For the ancients could not abstract from emotional reality;[13] they did not recognize impersonal natural laws; the change of seasons, storms, blight, or flood had an individual character in the precise time, place, and circumstance of their occurrence and, moreover, stood in a particular relation to their victims. Hence a "will" was felt to assert itself in every event of this kind; and society, being so deeply affected, felt the need of some action on its part, either to further a change that was beneficial or to deflect or modify a menace. From this point of view most ancient celebrations become understandable. Although we shall discuss some of them in detail in the next chapter, it is necessary to settle certain general matters as a preliminary to the detailed discussions.

We are often unable to explain why the festivals assume specific forms. For instance, it is understandable that the completion of each of the moon's phases was celebrated in Mesopotamia, as in other countries where the moon is recognized as the manifestation of a divine power. But we can no longer explain why at Lagash the new moon feast in "the house of the new light" should have been celebrated in the "holy city" of the mother-goddess Baba. Nor do we know why in later times this same feast should have entailed sacrifices to past rulers: Gudea, Shulgi, and Shu-Sin.[14] Here again we are confronted by the outcome of a historical development which we cannot trace to its source.*

We know that the king officiated at the important festivals. In Assyri-

* See above, pp. 143–45.

an times, for instance, he spent the night of the new moon in the temple sacrificing to Marduk and Ishtar and again, at daybreak, to Shamash and Sin. The inscriptions describe only the actions of the royal officiant. But occasionally we catch a glimpse of the populace; for instance, a text is preserved describing what should be done at Erech—then a provincial city, not a capital—at the feast following full moon.[15] In the Anu temple the statues of the gods and goddesses were to be taken from their sanctuaries and placed in the court. Libations were to be made and hymns sung; a torchlight procession through the temple precincts was to be held; food was to be offered. But note this, also:

> The people shall light fires in their houses; they shall offer food to Anu, Antu, and all the gods . . . . ; they shall say the same prayers as specified above. The guards of the city shall light fires in the streets and at crossroads. The gates of Erech shall not be closed(?) until dawn. The guards shall place posts on the right and the left of the gates, and they shall keep fires burning in the gates until dawn.

Again we cannot explain why the celebration should have assumed this particular form, but such a description as we have quoted suggests a background of vague popular ritual from which the precise acts of the king stand out in relief. As the religious leader of his subjects, the king expressed a concern and a devotion which animated the people as a whole.

The gods showed their satisfaction by singling out the king for their favors. The royal inscriptions underline this fact *ad nauseam*, but it also found expression in ritual. On certain occasions the gods moved in solemn procession to the king's palace, where they were enthroned and entertained as honored guests. We know of this custom as early as the Third Dynasty of Ur.[16] Later Adad-nirari I mentions a palace chapel "in which is the throne where every year the god Assur my lord takes his seat."[17] And Sargon of Assyria writes about his newly founded residence at Khorsabad: "After I had completed the construction of the city and my palaces, I invited the great gods who dwell in Assyria into their midst in the month of *Tashritu*. I held their dedication feast."[18]

Esarhaddon, too, invited the gods to his palace.[19] The visits of the gods to the king, and of the king to the temples, objectivated the bonds which existed between them. We have described a similar coming and going of gods and king at the Sed festival in Egypt. And yet similar forms cloak profound differences. In Egypt the king mingles with the gods, his equals (Fig. 14), to such an extent that we find (in the mystery of the Kamutef at the Min festival,* for instance) that the god and king

* See above, pp. 188–90.

are indistinguishable. We shall see (chap. 21) that in Mesopotamia, in certain exceptional circumstances, some kings acted the parts of gods. But normally the world of the gods was closed to man; and when an artist had to depict the king of Assyria, at the height of his power, receiving the approval of his god (Fig. 45), he could but visualize a gesture thrust forth from an impenetrable cloud.

C. THE REWARDS OF SERVICE AND THE BUILDING OF TEMPLES

The relationship between the king and the gods is well illustrated by the ceremonies connected with the erection or restoration of temples. No greater service could be rendered to a god than the building of his house. When, in the Epic of Creation, Marduk had defeated Chaos, created an ordered cosmos, and saved the gods from destruction, they exclaimed:

> Now, O Lord, who has brought about our deliverance,
> What shall be the sign of our gratitude before thee?
> We will build a shrine. . . . .[20]

Man, too, honored his gods by building or embellishing their dwellings upon earth. It was natural that he should expect to be blessed with good fortune in return. Said Esarhaddon:

The earlier temple of Assur, which Shalmaneser, son of Adad-nirari, king of Assyria, a prince who lived before me, had built, fell into decay. . . . . That temple,—the place of its site I did not change, but upon gold, silver, precious stones, herbs, (and) cedar-oil I established its foundation walls (and) laid its brickwork. I built and completed it, I made it magnificent to the astonishment of the peoples. For life (lit., my life), for length of days, for the stability of my reign, for the welfare of my posterity, for the safety of my priestly throne, for the overthrow of my enemies, for the success of the harvest(s) of Assyria, for the welfare of Assyria, I built it.[21]

In both Egypt and Mesopotamia the size and magnificence of the temples were staggering, and the rulers of both countries prided themselves on the construction and endowment of shrines. Yet the spirit in which they were built in the one country differed profoundly from that in the other.

We quoted above (p. 55) the beginning of a description of a crown council in which Senusert I announced his intention to rebuild the temple at Heliopolis. The decision was made by the king in the fulness of his power:

I will establish the offerings of the gods and I will make a work, namely a great house for my father Atum. . . . . I will nourish his altars upon earth, I will build my house in his neighborhood. My beauty shall be remembered by means of his house: the pyramidion is my name and the lake is my monument. Such is the eternity which profitable deeds have made.[22]

This text is exceptionally detailed, but even the shortest Egyptian build-ing inscription is direct and free of doubt: "Amenemhet I: he made it as his monument for his father Amon-Re, Lord of Thebes, making for him a shrine of pink granite, that he may thereby be given life forever."[23] Hatshepsut showed more exuberance when she had the temple of Speos Artemidos inscribed as follows:

> Hear ye, all ye people. Ye people as many as ye are! I have done this according to the design of my heart. . . . . I have restored that which was in ruins, I have raised up that which was unfinished. . . . . I have commanded that my titulary abide like the mountains; when the sun shines its rays are bright upon the titulary of My Majesty.[24]

Pharaoh built "according to the design of his heart"; but when Nabo-nidus discovered a foundation brick in the temple at Larsa he said:

> I became fearful and afraid. I said to myself: The wise king Burnaburiash built the temple and made Shamash the Great Lord dwell therein. I will rebuild(?) that temple. . . . .
> I lifted my hand and [prayed to the Lord of Lords]: O Lord, Supreme God, Prince Marduk, without thee no dwelling is found nor its plan designed. Who can do anything without thee? O Lord, by thy exalted command, let me do what is agreeable to thee.[25]

When Esarhaddon succeeded Sennacherib, the destroyer of Babylon, the reconstruction of the sacred city was of immediate concern to the king. He states:

> At that time I, Esarhaddon, king of the universe, king of Assyria, who waits for Assur's command, object of the desire of the great gods—thanks to the wide understand-ing, the breadth of vision, which the Master of the gods, the prince Nudimmud (Ea) granted me, through the insight which Assur and Marduk "opened up" in my under-standing, for the restoration of the (images) of the great gods, with upraised hand, (with) supplication and prostration before Assur, king of the gods, and the great lord Marduk, I implored their divinity: "With whom, O ye great gods, creators of gods and goddesses, do you send me on (this) difficult mission to an unknown place,—a mission of restoration, with people who are not loyal, who do not know their own minds, who have been foolish since days of old. O ye creators of gods and goddesses, build the struc-ture with your own hands, the abode of your exalted divinity. Whatever is in your hearts, so let it be done, without any deviations from the command of your lips."[26]

We have quoted both texts somewhat fully to bring out the differ-ence in the circumstances facing Nabonidus, who repaired the ravages of time, and Esarhaddon, who repaired the furious destruction wrought by his predecessor; yet the similarity in their attitudes is striking. A king might be eager to grasp the opportunity of honoring the gods, but he was, above all, aware of the enormity of the proposition that man should offer residence to a deity. Nabonidus became "fearful and afraid"; Esarhaddon approached the gods "with supplication and prostration." But Pharaoh, on the other hand, states with total unconcern: "Behold, My Majesty decrees a work and is thinking of a deed."

The attitude of Nabonidus and Esarhaddon is characteristic for the Mesopotamian rulers of all times. The continuity of culture is clear in this respect, also. Two thousand years before Nabonidus, Gudea of Lagash was confronted with the task of rebuilding a temple. He, too, felt weighed down by his responsibility and "his heart was beclouded."* But Gudea styled himself "a man of understanding," just as Esarhaddon boasted of his "wide understanding" and "breadth of vision"; both merely prided themselves on having interpreted correctly the will of the gods. Nevertheless, they went to great lengths to eliminate misunderstandings. For here was danger indeed. It could not be doubted that honoring the gods was meritorious. But what if the gods had at a certain time purposefully caused the ruin and disgrace of their shrines? We have seen how the desolation of cities could be ordained with total disregard of the behavior of the inhabitants.† When the brickwork of a temple had disintegrated and could not be restored by running repairs or when lightning struck the temple at Assur or a fire destroyed the temple at Eshnunna, "the gods and goddesses who dwelt therein flew off, like birds, and went up to heaven."[27] When Babylon was destroyed, the gods decided that it should remain deserted for seventy years; and when Marduk took pity on his people, even he could not undo that decision. But by a magnanimous trick, by holding the Book of Destiny upside down so that the numeral seventy appeared as eleven, he reduced the period of distress.[28] If the decay of the sanctuary was considered punishment from the gods and the existing of a well-functioning shrine a sign of their good will, then the rebuilding of a temple could not be started lightly. Imagine a man's presuming to begin the work before the divine interdict had expired! This indeed would be *hubris* and a certain cause of calamity.

In Egypt this problem was never envisaged. In fact, Egyptian religion ignored the theme of the wrath of God. The state felt secure under the guidance of the living Horus, the son of Re. But in Mesopotamia no one, not even the king, shared the divine counsels; and it was unavoidable that men should wonder whether the gods intended indeed to bestow upon a city the boon of a new divine dwelling.

PREPARATIONS

When the gods had sent a sign that a temple should be rebuilt, many oracles were sought to avoid misunderstanding. We have described Gudea's procedure in detail.‡ Later rulers acted similarly. Nabonidus, for

* See above, p. 256.   † See above, p. 242.   ‡ See above, pp. 256–57.

instance, states: "I visited the shrines of Shamash, Adad, and Nergal for the purpose of building that temple."[29] In other words, he built only after having consulted three divinities. Throughout the preparatory work, continuity with the past was sought; and it was considered an exceptionally favorable omen if the gods themselves revealed remains of earlier structures as a pattern for the work. The accidental discovery in Sippar of a clay plaque showing an ancient cult statue of Shamash was treated as a direct encouragement from the god by Nabu-apla-iddina,[30] for instance. This desire to discover historical precedents for the work they were preparing to undertake is quite characteristic for the Mesopotamians. The view that conformity with usages of the past does not stand in need of justification is widely held among primitive people,[31] and the Egyptians, as well as the Mesopotamians, acknowledged the past as normative. But they did so for different reasons. Since Egypt viewed the universe as essentially static, changes merely made explicit what had been potentially existing since creation. Hence, even newly built temples derived their sanctity from the fact that the gods had preordained their erection on that particular spot.* We have seen that the unfolding of these potentialities was in itself a creative act, appropriately undertaken by the Son of Re. The Mesopotamians did not view the cosmos as static, but they relegated its dynamism to the world of the gods. Hence, the gods had to take the initiative in all matters of moment; and, even after they had made their will known, the rulers felt that they had to rely upon divine guidance. Gudea begged Ningirsu to disclose the specifications of the temple which he knew should be built. Esarhaddon adjured the gods: "Build the structure with your own hands, the abode of your exalted divinity." Hence, the extraordinary significance of a portent which revealed a pattern tried and approved by the gods in the past. It happened, for instance in the reign of Nabonidus, that "by the order of Marduk . . . . the four winds approached, the [violent] tempests; the sand dunes with which that city and that temple were covered over were blown away and Ebarra, the awe-inspiring dwelling, became [visible]."[32]

There is not, in Mesopotamia, reference to a primeval plan, an order established at the time of creation. For the Mesopotamian the world was in flux, the gods were "determining destiny" each New Year's Day; and thus he could never postulate the past as an absolute norm as the Egyptian did. His past was a historical and an empirical past; certain acts of man, certain arrangements for the temple, had proved acceptable.

* See above, p. 152.

It was safe to go back to those patterns whenever it was possible. It was imperative to do so when the gods had actually assisted in their rediscovery.

When Pharaoh built, he could say without contradiction: "It was according to the ancient plan. Never was done the like since the beginning (of time)."[33] When Nabonidus built, he stated that the foundations were "put on top of the ground-plan, not projecting or receding one finger's width."[34]

This attitude toward the plan of an earlier period was naturally strengthened by the knowledge that occasionally the gods indicated in detail how temples should be built. Whenever, therefore, the plan of the original building was discovered, it was possible to suppose that its particulars had received divine sanction. If the original plan remained unknown, the earliest plan that could be recovered was made to provide guidance. When Nabonidus described his rebuilding of the Larsa temple only forty-five years after Nebuchadnezzar had renewed it, he made much of the fact that the latter had been satisfied with recovering the building inscription (and, hence, the foundations) of Burnaburiash, while he, Nabonidus, had discovered that of an earlier king, Hammurabi. Nabonidus made it a rule to search for building inscriptions and foundation deposits in his reconstruction work. These deposits, besides disclosing the measures and materials used in the earlier building, also showed the appropriate size of brick.[35] We shall see that the molding of the first brick was the central ceremony of the rites of reconstruction; and it has been suggested that each temple possessed a tradition which determined the size of the bricks to be used in its construction.

When the omens had been extensively consulted and the details of plan and elevation had been established, the site had to be cleared of debris, after which it was purified. This initial stage of the procedure was entirely in a minor key. The ever present doubt about whether the will of the gods was properly understood prevented demonstrations of confidence and joy; and the damage which the old building had sustained, be it through neglect, an act of an enemy, or an act of the gods, was a source of sorrow, since it showed the weakening of the bond between the gods and the community. There were prescribed "lamentations" appropriate to "assuaging" the hearts of the gods.

> (What to do,) when the walls of a temple fall in ruin, in
>   order to demolish them and to build a new temple . . . . :
> In a favorable month, on a propitious date, in the night,
> A fire shall be lit for Ea and Marduk, and a sacrifice shall
>   be made for them.

The *kalu* priest[36] shall sing a lament; the singer shall sing
a doleful plaint.
In the morning, three installations (for sacrifices) shall be
erected on the roof of the temple (in honor of) Ea, Sha-
mash, and Marduk. . . . .
The *kalu* shall make music with his flute before Marduk.
Then he shall sing: "Ezida . . . . weeps for itself!" . . . .
The *kalu* shall lift his hands and bow down before (the god).
Dolefully he shall recite a psalm of penitence and shall cry:
"Woe!"[37]

And Assurbanipal states: "With sadness and weeping I laid my hands
to (the reconstruction of) that which the foe had destroyed, in joy I
finished it."[38]

After the debris had been cleared away, the site was purified: "By
means of the act of exorcism, the wisdom of Ea and Marduk, I purified
that site,"[39] states Nabopolassar. Gudea described these purifications
again in great detail. Not only the temple site, but the whole city, was
cleansed; and the measures went far beyond the removal of actual and
ritual impurities. They aimed at the creation of a favorable atmosphere,
a general feeling of good will. A kind of civic peace was imposed:
mothers did not scold their children; masters did not punish their servants; there were no lawsuits; persons under a sexual taboo were driven
out of Lagash.[40] Great pyres of aromatic wood purified the city, which
remained in a state of religious exaltation: "During the day there were
prayers, during the night oraisons." Gudea once more consulted the
oracles while vast quantities of costly stones, wood, and metal were
brought into the city from foreign lands. And so the central feature of
the celebrations was reached.

THE MOLDING OF THE FIRST BRICK

When at last the production of bricks for the new temple could be
taken in hand, the mood of the celebrations changed completely. The
tentative questioning of the gods, the mournful occupation with the
relics of past misfortune or neglect were left behind; and all attention
was centered on the positive achievement of rebuilding. However, this
happy change required that the first brick for the new building be well
and truly formed, and the nature of the material makes the extraction of
a perfect brick from its mold by no means a foregone conclusion. Consequently, the successful molding of the first brick assumed the significance of a last ordeal, the final answer to the question whether the gods
would accept the labor of their servant. On Early Dynastic seals a man
is shown measuring a plano-convex brick against a rod held by an enthroned deity (Fig. 47). A relief of the same period shows Ur-Nanshe

of Lagash carrying on his head a basket with clay for the molding of the first new brick (Fig. 46). Down to Late Assyrian times the rulers are depicted in this position, either on stelae[41] or in small bronze figures[42] buried in the foundations of the temples they rebuilt. For the molding of the first brick was always carried out by the king in person. As an example of the texts of the first millennium B.C. we may quote Nabopolassar: "I bent my neck for Marduk, my lord; and, girding up the robes of my royalty, I carried bricks and clay upon my head."[43]

The ceremony of making the first brick is described well by Gudea. His text betrays a lyricism which should warn us that the crowning scene of the rites entailed more than the display of a brick of dried mud to the people and the rays of the sun. He had passed the preceding night in the temple, thus protecting himself against a possible pollution by the profane and, at the same time, making himself available if the gods wished to communicate with him once more in his dreams. In the morning "the pure head-pad, the sacred mold, he. . . . . He went with uplifted head. The god Lugal-kur-dub went before him; the god Ig-alima followed him. Ningiszida, his (personal) god, held him by the hand."[44]

Ur-Nammu, too, is shown on his way to the ceremony carrying builders' tools and led by gods (Fig. 13). When the procession reached the site of the temple, a libation was made. Water and probably butter and honey were poured into the brick mold. Aromatic wood was burned to drive away all impurities and evil spirits. Then followed the molding: "He lifted on to his head the pure head-pad. He brought the mold. Gudea put clay in the mold. He did all that was needful."[45] The clay was allowed to dry during the rest of the day and the night. At dawn of the following day the mold was broken while fires of aromatic wood burned again. The first brick was lifted out: "The sun-god was overjoyed with the brick which he (Gudea) had placed in the mold."[46]

The brick was shown to the people too—a sign that the period of trial was past and that the gods had accepted the service which was offered to them. The text reads like a paean:

> Out of the mold he lifted the brick:
> Like a pure crown lifted toward the sky, he lifted the brick.
> He brought it to his people.
> Like unto the holy warrior Babbar[47] was that brick which he
>   had lifted up toward the temple;
> Like unto the cow of Nanna.[48]

With the successful molding of the first brick the turning-point in the long series of building ceremonies had been passed. The next phrases of Gudea's account refer to the continuation of the building to which he devoted himself:

> Like a young man who is founding a house, he let no pleasure
> come before him.
> Like a cow who turns its eyes to its calf, he brought all his
> love to bear on the temple.[49]

The detailed arrangements mentioned in the remainder of the text need not detain us. It is interesting that the completion of the work from this point onward is described as due to direct participation by the gods. This again illustrates the great significance of the molding ceremony. The building had been planned upon the gods' initiative. Up to the molding of the first brick the king had striven continually to interpret their intentions and to make the necessary arrangements. But afterward the work proceeded smoothly and without raising problems or doubts. Figure 48 shows an Akkadian cylinder seal depicting the gods with their distinctive crowns, mixing mud, carrying mortar up ladders, and throwing bricks up to others who are at work on top of the temple.

New Year's Day, the beginning of a new cycle in nature, was chosen for the dedication. On that day the god was brought to the completed dwelling, where his spouse awaited him.[50] Their union inaugurated a new cycle of prosperity for the community to which the gods had returned (chap. 21); there was a determination of destinies while the city was again hushed in a sacred peace. And this time it implied more than a mere avoidance of unpropitious acts and disturbing feelings. It seems that the everyday rules of society were suspended, as if their imperfection were acknowledged and an attempt were to be made to live by the laws of the gods:

> That day when the king (Ningirsu) entered the temple
> (And) for seven days,
> The servant competed with her mistress,
> The domestic was on a par with his master.
> In the town the mighty and the humble slept side by side;
> An evil tongue changed its words to good ones.
> All evil was driven out.
> He (Gudea) paid heed to the laws of Nanshe and Ningirsu,
> Left not the orphan at the rich man's mercy,
> Left not the widow at the mercy of the strong.
> The house which had no son—
> Its daughter became its heir.
> Days of righteousness dawned for him,
> And on the neck of lawlessness and of rebels he set his foot.[51]

Gudea's enchanting evocation is beclouded by the melancholy resignation of the opening phrase, "That day . . . . and for seven days." After so short an interval everyday life, with its wrongs and its uncertainties, took its course again. But in the meantime the "destiny" of the city and its people had been determined.

PART VII. KINGSHIP AND THE DIVINE
POWERS IN NATURE

CHAPTER 20

THE GODS OF MESOPOTAMIA

A. COSMIC POWERS AND SOCIAL JUSTICE

THE theme which recurs with but slight variation throughout the preceding chapters does not constitute the whole of Mesopotamian religion. We have seen the king acting as servant of the gods and the gods directing human affairs. But the Mesopotamians did not imagine deities to be exclusively preoccupied with man. The great gods were natural powers; and if their interest in man centered in his service, man's concern with the gods sprang largely from his desire to live in harmony with nature. These words suggest to us a contemplative ideal and a purely personal mood. But for the ancients to live meant to act; when they were aware of a harmony between life and nature, they knew that society did not set out upon its enterprises in hazardous isolation but that it was carried forward by a current of immeasurable potency.*

In Egypt the alignment of society with nature was assumed to be perfect because a divine mediator ruled the land. The death of Pharaoh showed that the harmony was temporarily disturbed, but the coronation of his successor restored the normal equilibrium. In Mesopotamia the concord was, on the contrary, felt to be unstable; and the community united on numerous occasions, and notably at each New Year, in an effort to strengthen or restore it. We shall see that the New Year's festival opened with rites of atonement which prepared the people for a participation in the change of fortune which certain gods experienced at the turn of the season; the final act was a "determination of destiny" by the gods. It is characteristic for Mesopotamian religiosity that the celebration should have culminated in a decision beyond the control of man. Even though nature revived, it was by no means certain that society was going to reap the fruits of this regeneration in increased prosperity. In Egypt it was unthinkable that nature and society should follow different courses, for both alike were ruled by *maat*—"right, truth, justice, cos-

* See above, p. 103.

mic order."[1] The gods existed by *maat*, and Pharaoh's speech was "the shrine of *maat*"; what was right came to pass, in nature as well as in society. In Mesopotamia, too, the gods had decreed justice as the order of society. They desired their elected ruler to be a just king and persecuted injustice wherever it occurred. But the Mesopotamian did not presume that the gods themselves were bound by any order which man could comprehend; Mesopotamia knew no prophets who revealed the motivation of the divine will. The order of justice decreed for society was not a universal order; cities were known to have been ruined although their rulers and their people were not convicted of injustice.*

> What seems praiseworthy to one's self is but contemptible before the god(s),
> What to one's heart seems bad is good before one's god;
> Who may comprehend the mind of gods in heaven's depth?
> The thoughts of god are like deep waters, who could fathom them?
> How could mankind, beclouded, comprehend the ways of gods?[2]

We accept the polarity between the sphere of man and the divine sphere—a polarity which dominates Mesopotamian religion—more readily than the Egyptian belief in society's capacity of being faultlessly integrated with the divine. In the ethical sphere, too, we are revolted by the Egyptian belief that the dead, confronting judges in the Hereafter, got away with reciting a long list of sins which they claimed never to have committed. "I knew no wrong" is the leading theme of the "Declaration of Innocence" in the Book of the Dead.[3] On the other hand, we accept the Mesopotamian counterpart of this text in which attempts of the dead to whitewash themselves are shown to fail miserably.[4] Hence there is a tendency to overrate the similarities between the Mesopotamian and the Judeo-Christian viewpoints. It is true that the Mesopotamians lived under a divine imperative and knew themselves to fall short of what was asked of them. But they did not have "The Law." The will of God had not been revealed to them once and for all, nor were they sustained by the consciousness of being a "chosen people." They were not singled out by divine love, and the divine wrath lacked the resentment caused by ingratitude. The Mesopotamians, while they knew themselves to be subject to the decrees of the gods, had no reason to believe that these decrees were necessarily just. Hence their penitential psalms abound in confessions of guilt but ignore the sense of sin; they are vibrant with despair but not with contrition—with regret but not with repentance. The Mesopotamian recognized guilt by its conse-

* See above, pp. 241–43.

quences: when he suffered, he assumed that he had transgressed a divine decree. He confessed, in such a case, to be guilty, although he declared:

> I do not know the offense against the god,
> I do not know the transgression against the goddess.[5]

When a fault had been committed, through whatever cause, the gods struck automatically.[6] Hence the desire to expiate "the offense which I know and the offense which I do not know; which I have committed in negligence, as a crime, in carelessness or in contempt."[7]

Such a desire was not sufficient to alleviate the punishment; it was necessary to know which specific rule one had transgressed,[8] since specific penances had been prescribed by the gods for the expiation of each of them. We have met an instance of this belief in the correspondence of an Assyrian king: "Ea made (the earthquake), Ea will release (us from it). (For) whoever made the earthquake has also provided the lustral incantation against it." Thus everything pertaining to human guilt was likely to assume a mechanistic and gloomy aspect. For a chosen people conformance with the will of God can be a source of joy. For the Mesopotamians the divine decrees merely circumscribed man's servitude. Religious exaltation fell, for them, outside the sphere of ethics; it sprang from the awareness that they lived in conformity with the rhythm of divine life. This is what we have called "living in harmony with nature"—for in nature the life of the gods was manifest.

There is an essential difference between a belief that gods are immanent in nature and an allegorical use of personified natural forces. We obliterate that difference when we speak of solar or chthonic deities, gods of the sky or of water, and so on. These terms, used for convenience, direct our attention, not to the divine figure, but to the province of nature in which he is most commonly manifest. But religious feeling is aroused by the devotion addressed to the god who reveals himself and not to the natural phenomenon. Anu was heaven, but also "the force which lifts (the universe) out of chaos and anarchy and makes it into an organized whole. . . . . The force which ensures the necessary voluntary obedience to orders, to law and custom in society, to the natural laws in the physical world, in short the world order."[9] Enlil, manifest in the storm, was the power who enforced the decrees of the divine assembly; who, in a passion of fury, sent the Flood to destroy mankind; who sustained all legal authority by force, in particular the rightful ruler of the city or the land. Ninhursaga, the "Lady of the Mountain," was Mother Earth: "the lady who gives birth," "the fashioner of all wherein is breath of life," "the mother of all children." Ea, water, was anciently called Enki, "Lord of the Earth," because water is of the earth from which it wells up if it is not inextricably mixed with it, as in the marshes of the south.* There, at Eridu, was Ea's main shrine. Ea was personified intelligence, knowledge, especially magical knowledge; for "the ways of water are devious. It avoids obstacles rather than conquering them, goes around and yet gets to its goal. . . . . It flows out over the field, irrigating it, and then trickles away and is gone."[10] A similar richness of meaning characterizes the second generation of gods —Sin, the power in the moon; Shamash, the power in the sun; Adad, the power in thunder; and the many-sided goddess Ishtar, manifest in the planet Venus.

The belief that the gods were immanent in nature was not confined to the pristine age of Mesopotamian religion. It is true that the Sumerian myths, as a recent interpretation shows,[11] excel in unfolding a story in such a way that each divine actor appears endowed with a comprehensible character while yet reflecting the nature of the element which was his principal medium of manifestation. But we have equally decisive proof for a persistence of the belief in the immanence of the gods in late periods. This evidence is found in the "An-Anum list."

The earliest Mesopotamian documents include attempts to present knowledge systematically. For this purpose the scribes used a simple tool—a word list in which the entries were grouped in a recognizable order.[12] They never gave up using this device and actually overtaxed its capacity for conveying meaning. The Sumerian king list, for instance, was intended to give a retrospect of the parallel histories of the city-states. But the scheme of a continuous list of dynasties and kings confused the issue to such an extent that its true nature was almost unrecognizable once the tradition had been lost; and it has, in fact, only recently been recovered.[13] The same scheme, that of a list of names, was used to give a methodical survey of the pantheon. It is called "An-Anum" because this equation of the Sumerian and Akkadian designations of the god of heaven heads the enumeration of the gods. But Anu's name is followed by his genealogy, given under the guise of a series of names so that the character of the text as a whole is homogeneous throughout. The creation story implied by the names tallies with that in the Epic of Creation;† but the various stages of the process are not described in the manner of the Epic; they are simply indicated by a succession of divine names—Apsu and Tiamat, Lahmu and Lahamu, etc. There are twenty-

* See above, p. 234.   † See above, pp. 232–37.

one of these in all, summarized by a separate entry in the list as "the twenty-one parents (forefathers) of Anu." These primeval figures were not worshiped; they were not members of the pantheon. Their inclusion in the list was most inappropriate if that document was merely intended to be a catalogue of the gods. Consequently, we must assume that it was not. By opening their list with a succinct story of creation, the authors indicated that they were not merely assembling names of divinities but that they were accounting for the whole hierarchy of divine powers extant in the universe. Thus their work assumed the character, not of a catalogue, but of a cosmology; and the ancient belief that the gods were immanent in nature was once more affirmed.

B. THE SUFFERING GOD

In Mesopotamia, as in Egypt, we are faced with the task of comprehending a polytheistic religion. We must, once more, distil from an immense variety of divine manifestations the essence which constitutes the concept "divinity"—"the god in general who is necessary." We found that in Egypt the concepts of creation, procreation, and resurrection were expressed in symbols and co-ordinated with one another in a manner which was distinctly Egyptian. Moreover, they dominated the whole of Egyptian religion (in so far as it became articulate) to such an extent that we were entitled to see them as essential elements of a distinctively Egyptian religiosity. In Mesopotamia these three concepts provided neither a focal point for religious feeling nor the impetus to religious speculation. In a world in flux, creation is but an episode and not the lasting foundation of existence, as it is in a static universe. Procreation was endowed with a religious significance in Egypt because of its relation with rebirth after death and with the solar and stellar circuit; in Mesopotamia it had no connection with either. Resurrection, finally, was not even a tenet of Mesopotamian religion, which held that man's inescapable fate was death—at best a quasi-annihilation or a wraithlike lingering in limbo, otherwise torture through thirst and dust and evil demons. If in Egypt the reality of death was almost denied, and in any case hidden under the elaborate rituals proclaiming belief in survival, in Mesopotamia it was known that even the life of nature stood in danger of extinction. And many deities were believed to succumb to it temporarily.

The contrast between the Egyptian and Mesopotamian viewpoints indicates also where the operative ideas of the latter are to be found. We discern a conception of fate which often became a sense of doom and a conception of suffering gods in which the richness as well as the cruelty of existence found expression. The feeling of uncertainty, of a change for the worse which may at any moment destroy man's happiness, is amply illustrated in our earlier chapters. If most of the quotations given so far have referred to the king, we must remember that he too was a mortal. Penitential psalms and prayers in which the petitioner is a commoner are similar in spirit to those employed by the king.[14] We need not, then, enlarge on the Mesopotamian conception of fate but may turn to that of the suffering god.

Summer in Mesopotamia is a burden hardly to be borne. Vegetation withers, the hot dust hurts eyes and lungs, and men and beasts, losing resilience, submit, dazed, to the protracted scourge. In such a country the notion of creation is not connected with the sun. The generative force of nature resides in the earth. For even water is of the earth; the sky is too rarely clouded, too cruel during five exhausting months for the blessing of moisture to be associated with it. Water belongs to the wells and ditches of the earth; and in spring Ningirsu brings it down in black clouds from the mountains.[15]

One single rhythm flows through the life of nature and of man, quickening when the autumn rains bring relief, slowing down somewhat under the severities of winter, expanding marvelously in the brief enchanting spell of spring. The gods who are in nature must partake of this movement of ebb and flow, and a remarkable number of them were believed to suffer imprisonment or injury. This applies first and foremost to the gods in whom natural forces were personified. These bore Sumerian names which are mostly epithets; and a study of their iconography, and of the conditions in which their monuments are distributed through the ruins, shows that a single conception underlies the figures of Ninurta or Ningirsu, Ninazu, Ningiszida, Tammuz, Tishpak, Abu, and several others.[16] These gods are not altogether without distinctive features, but their particularities are best explained as a result of differentiation. It is only to be expected that different aspects of the basic conception would be emphasized in certain localities at the expense of others, so that the different cities ultimately worshiped related but not identical gods.[17] Yet the awareness of their basic identity was still alive in Akkadian times, as is proved by the promiscuous use of their attributes in the pictorial art of the period; and the equations of gods with one another, which we find in Assyrian lists like "An-Anum" and which are usually explained as the product of syncretism, may very well be due, in many cases, to a clear realization that a single divinity was indicated

by the several names. In the case of the gods whom we have just enumerated the underlying unity is especially clear; all of them personify
the generative force in nature. Moreover, they may be considered typical in that the notion of the divine in Mesopotamia seems to have some
connection with the periodic decline and renewal of natural life. This
would explain that even the powerful Enlil and Anu, the epitome of
authority, are said to have been captives in the realm of death.[18]

The suffering god finds a counterpart in the mourning goddess. She,
too, was known by many names and epithets—Ninhursaga, Mah, Nin-
mah, Nintu, or Aruru;[19] and even the many-sided Inanna-Ishtar partook
of the character of the Great Mother, who suffered the bereavement of
both mother and bride through the death of the god and who went to
search for him and liberated him, sometimes with the help of his son.

In the myth of the suffering god and the mourning goddess the complex of feelings which characterizes Mesopotamian religiosity could
find adequate expression: the anxiety inherent in an uncertain destiny;
the sorrow that life is transitory and death unrelieved by hope; the exultation that life knows abundance. In the next chapter we shall describe
the celebrations which formalized those feelings. Here we must elucidate the significance of the dual symbol of the dying god and the mourning goddess who was his mother and his bride.

There can be no doubt that the relationship claimed to exist between
god and goddess was a multiple one; the following lines indicate it by
their emphatic parallelism. The goddess mourns the loss

> of the husband, laid to rest, of the son laid to rest;
> of the husband who is dead, of the son who is dead. . . . .

And later:

> when the good husband—husband-brother—went away;
> when the good son—son-brother—went away. . . . .[20]

In accordance with the view embodied in the last verses, the goddess is
sometimes called the god's sister. Our quotations show, however, that
we are misled if we take these terms too literally. They indicate that the
relationship between god and goddess is extremely close and more comprehensive than any known to man. The term "son" expresses the dependence of the god upon the goddess; yet the goddess loses in him not
merely one of her children but one who can be replaced by no one else
and whom she needs as a woman needs her husband or her favorite
brother.

The clue to an understanding of their relationship lies in the Mesopotamian view that life comes forth from a goddess, that the universe was conceived rather than begotten: the source of life is female. In the Epic of Creation, Tiamat, primeval chaos, is called "the mother of the deep who fashions all things." In another text the goddess Nammu "gave birth to heaven and earth";[21] and the standard version of the An-Anum list elucidates once more the Mesopotamian view of the world. Like the Epic of Creation, it describes the genesis of the universe by listing successive generations of divine couples, each of which represents a stage in the process. This is a common way of giving an account of creation. It survives among many modern peoples and was also used by Hesiod. In Egypt we find the same device represented by the Ennead of Heliopolis, a list of nine gods implying a creation story. Atum "was alone" and begot upon himself Shu and Tefnut (air and moisture), the parents of Geb and Nut (earth and sky), who in turn brought forth Osiris and Isis, Seth and Nephthys. In the Babylonian list the creation story which we have discussed is summarized by an entry as "the twenty-one parents of Anu." The uneven number finds its explanation in the view that life originates in the female: one parent, the goddess Antu, is not matched by a male complement. The Mesopotamian view is therefore diametrically opposed to that of the Egyptians, who ascribed the creation exclusively to male deities—Re-Atum, Ptah, or Khnum. The mother-goddesses, like Nut or Hathor, merely reproduced life within the established creation. Once again we find the Mesopotamian viewpoint more congenial than that of the Egyptians: "For the earth bringeth forth fruit of herself; first the blade, then the ear, after that the full corn in the ear" (Mark 4:28).

Throughout the ancient world, in Syria, Anatolia, and Greece, Mother Earth was the source of all life. In these countries, as in Mesopotamia, the seasonal decline of nature was represented by the loss of a child—Adonis, Attis, or Persephone—which the Great Mother suffered. For if the female principle is taken seriously as the First Cause, the male principle must of necessity derive from it, and the god is, in this view, the child of the goddess. In Syria, Anatolia, and Mesopotamia this was indeed the case; but the parallel of Persephone shows that the young deity is not, in the first place, distinct from the parent in sex but represents a different aspect of natural life.[22] The goddess personifies nature's prolific fertility; in the guise of Tiamat this threatened existence itself, but as the Great Mother it guaranteed recovery from the annual injury which the loss of the child-god symbolized. Sometimes—in Greece and in the Levant—the young god represents the brief spring, a sudden blooming of indescribable loveliness which withers in a few weeks. Adonis and Persephone in particular derive the pathetic features of their character from this aspect of nature. But the Mesopotamian "dying god" had a more general character. He stood for the vital force in plants and animals and counted, moreover, as the husband of the goddess. For the Mesopotamians, although they viewed the goddess as the source of life, could not think of birth without conception. Tiamat needed Apsu as her complement; and the mother-goddess celebrated annually her wedding with the god who was also her son.

The question may be raised whether the god's liberation and resurrection, or, alternatively, his marriage with the goddess, stood for the revival of natural life. The answer is the same as that which had to be given when we faced similar complexities in Egyptian mythology, namely, that the question is inappropriate, since it confronts conceptions of the ancients with a modern view of causality. Separate images, which seem mutually exclusive to us, elucidated for them distinct aspects of the phenomena which concerned them. Nature revived; the vegetation re-emerged; the god was found, liberated, resurrected. But, also, nature promised to bear fruit again; the goddess had wed the god, and there would be issue.

There is no Mesopotamian parallel for the divine pair of Eleusis, Demeter and Persephone, nor is Tammuz at all like Adonis, a youth "dead ere his prime." The suffering god of Mesopotamia was a mature and virile figure. Sometimes the "son" aspect was almost obliterated, especially in the case of aggressive city-gods like Marduk and Ningirsu;[23] the goddess then counted as consort rather than mother. But even in those cases the original relationship transpires in the rite which most clearly reveals the significance of the gods in nature. At the sacred wedding it was the goddess Baba, and not the impetuous Ningirsu, who dominated;* and such evidence as we have from Ur and Erech suggests the same for the procedure in those cities.

We have noticed that even the greatest male deities like Anu and Enlil became powerless and dependent upon others during a recurring stage of their existence. This is also true of some of the city-gods, although these symbolized not only the divine powers upon which a given community depended but also the community itself. Yet these gods never became wholly detached from nature. Down to the latest periods they possessed a cosmic as well as a social aspect. In Mesopotamia a basic and indestructible unity comprised the life of man, the existence of soci-

* See below, chap. 21, n. 7.

ety, and the ebb and flow of natural life. The texts are quite explicit in this respect and do not betray any consciousness of a discrepancy between the heroic character of such gods as Enlil and Marduk and their helplessness during their "imprisonment." In one text the god is simply referred to as *lillu*, "the feeble one."* It is difficult for us to accept this feature as an original trait of the gods in question; we are likely to postulate "syncretism," especially in the case of Marduk, who seems to have close relations with the sun (and solar deities are almost always heroic and invincible).[24] Yet the evidence of his captivity is at least as old as the time of Sargon of Akkad. On a famous seal in the British Museum (Fig. 50) the god who is liberated from the mountain of death is explicitly characterized as a sun-god, for he carries the saw, and rays issue from his shoulders. Marduk's name is written with signs which may mean "young bull of the sun"[25] and which are interpreted in the Epic of Creation as "divine child of the sun."[26] Yet Marduk was not, in the first place, a sun-god; for his festival falls, not at one of the critical points in the sun's circuit, the solstices, but in the spring.[27] And, on the other hand, the most typical example of the suffering god of nature, Tammuz, appears continuously in the hymns as a "hero," the "strong one," the "manly one," etc.

Perhaps the best aid to an understanding of the Mesopotamian god is a reminder that the combination of heroism and temporary defeat is also found in the case of a dying god with whom we are familiar and who appears in medieval art and poetry, not only as Christ the King, but as the noblest of warriors. We quote a few lines from an Anglo-Saxon poem, "The Dream of the Rood," "in which the Cross of Christ, speaking in the first person, recounts in passionate language its own experience and testimony of the crucifixion:

> "Then the young hero, that was God Almighty, stripped
>   himself,
> Strong and steadfast; bold in the sight of many
> He mounted the high cross, that he might redeem mankind. . . . . "[28]

In the theme of this book the suffering god is of special importance, for it is only with this god, who depended on the Great Mother and who knew impotence and defeat, that at certain times and on certain solemn occasions a Mesopotamian king was identified.

EXCURSUS: TAMMUZ, ADONIS, OSIRIS

The suffering god of Mesopotamia, who enters the Netherworld and revives with the vegetation, recalls Osiris. We should not feel obliged

* See below, p. 321.

to refer to this resemblance were it not customary to treat the two gods as variations of an established type, "the dying god," which is also represented by Attis, Adonis, and Dionysus and by many "spirits of the corn."[29] We cannot ignore this viewpoint because it challenges one of our basic assumptions. We have maintained that only the precise analysis of the specific forms in which a creed has found expression can reveal its nature and that classificatory terms are likely to obscure essentials. We must, therefore, make a digression at this point and inquire whether the introduction of a category "the dying god" to comprise Tammuz, Adonis, and Osiris contributes to our understanding.

The "dying god" of the *Golden Bough* is a mortal, a king in whom a god or spirit of fertility is incarnate, and who dies a violent death. Frazer describes divine kingship and fertility cults, the sacred marriage and the scapegoat, and a number of other institutions, without defining their interrelations and their differences. He feels that somewhat similar motives gave rise to all of them and hopes "to prove that these motives have operated widely, perhaps universally, in human society, producing in varied circumstances a variety of institutions specifically different but generically alike."[30] We question that the generic features are the most significant; to emphasize them, or to direct our inquiry toward them, seems to us risking a distortion of historical reality by the schematism of abstractions. The evidence discussed in the present work demonstrates that neither Egypt nor Mesopotamia knew "divine kingship" in the Frazerian sense, although many phenomena in those countries recall chapters from the *Golden Bough*. We shall now consider as a test case three gods to whom Part IV of the *Golden Bough* is devoted; and, even when we thus restrict the scope of our comparisons, we shall find that the "specifically different" is far more significant than what seemed to be "generically alike."

One must start by conceding that it is possible to recount a myth of a dying god which contains features common to the myths of Egypt, Mesopotamia, and Syria. His story would run like this: The god was killed by an enemy in the guise of a boar (Adonis) or symbolized by the boar (Osiris, Marduk). Moreover, the god's body floated upon the water, or he was said to have drowned (Osiris, Tammuz), or his blood stained the water of a river (Adonis). His death brought about the stagnation of all natural life; a goddess bewailed him and set out to retrieve him. The god was found and liberated, sometimes with the aid of his son (Osiris, Marduk, Enlil). With his resurrection nature, and especially all vegetation, revived.

The hero of this story is clearly not the "dying god" as conceived by Frazer. He is not incarnate in a human being and is not killed ceremoniously but dies in the course of the normal rotation of the seasons. But the story is fairly detailed, and the problem which it raises can be formulated as follows: Does it represent a basic creed which the three countries shared but which appears in each of them complicated by insignificant accretions? Or is our story no more than an abstract, of little or no value, since it lacks the features which distinguish each of the actual myths and which impart to them their peculiar significance?

Whether an abstract or a basic creed, the reconstructed story certainly presents a theme known in Egypt as well as in Asia. The god with whom it deals personifies plant life, and the story of his death and resurrection reflects its annual ebb and flow. Hence it is said that the god was "found"; there is an element of the unpredictable in his resurrection because the return of nature's vitality lies beyond the scope of human planning. Yet the community cannot passively await a revival upon which its very existence is dependent. Hence a ritual "search" is undertaken, and society's concern with the god's fate is expressed by processions, laments, and other appropriate rites. Mourning and search are presented in the personification of myth as the part of a goddess; the image of a bereaved mother or wife imposes itself where the withering and sprouting of plant life inevitably calls up human analogies. If these natural phenomena possess a strong emotional appeal, if in particular the annual rebirth of nature affects man deeply in many lands, it is not merely because his own life depends on it but also because it is an image of his fate and hope—whether that hope concerns personal resurrection, as in Egypt, or a survival in one's descendants, as in Mesopotamia. It is no doubt due to this peculiarly personal appeal which the three gods possessed that we find their worship represented, not only by temple rituals, but also by widespread popular observances of which vague echoes can be found in our sources. But when it is said that the cult of these gods belongs to popular rather than to official religion, the statement requires qualification. It holds good for Adonis, who had not, as far as we know, a temple of his own and was worshiped in the shrine of the great goddess at Byblos.[31] It is probable that Tammuz was similarly worshiped in the shrine of Inanna-Ishtar in Erech, and the wailings for Tammuz which Ezekiel observed in Jerusalem (Ezek. 8:14) belong also to the sphere of popular religion. But such public laments did not constitute the whole of the cult of the suffering god in Mesopotamia, and Tammuz is only one of his many names. In one guise or another he was quite often the object of an official cult. As Tishpak, for instance, he was the city-god of Eshnunna. Even Assur and Marduk seem to have been specialized forms of "Tammuz." In Egypt the popular cult of Osiris came into being in historical times and was demonstrably a derivate of the official cult of a god who represented in an unchanging mythological guise the predecessor of the ruling monarch.

It is due to Osiris' character as a dead king that he ranked below the sun-god, and thus yet another resemblance between Osiris, Tammuz, and Adonis loses its cogency. It is true that Tammuz and Adonis also rank below the greatest gods of their respective pantheons, but that is due to their character as "son"; they are dependent upon the Great Goddess. We touch here upon a fundamental contrast between Osiris and the Asiatic gods. Osiris is emphatically not dependent, and is not a child of the goddess who succors him. Osiris is the son of Nut, an aspect which is stressed in the funerary texts, since it contains a promise of rebirth through the mother to eternal life. But in the myth Osiris is sought and found by Isis, his sister and wife, who in this respect resembles the Asiatic mother-goddesses. But she differs from them in her total dependence upon the god; Osiris dominates Isis. When she conceived Horus after Osiris' death, when she had "erected the tiredness of the powerless one,"* the mystery of unquenched vitality was evidently not in the goddess but in the god who begot Horus.[32]

In the son of the suffering god, too, the differences between Egypt and Asia outweigh the superficial similarities. Adonis was never conceived as progenitor. Horus "supported" or "avenged" Osiris, but not in the manner in which Nabu or Ninurta, the sons of Marduk and Enlil, aided their captive fathers.[33] In Mesopotamia the son temporarily took charge while his parent was incarcerated; once Marduk, Enlil, and Assur were set free, they led the battle against chaos and death; and they scored the victory, Nabu or Ninurta acting merely as their agents to terminate their temporary subjection. In Egypt, on the other hand, Osiris did not return to his throne. Horus was his legitimate successor. A mysterious, lasting, and mutual relationship persisted between the two. Osiris, in fact, was not a "dying" god at all but a "dead" god. He never returned among the living; he was not liberated from the world of the dead, as Tammuz was. On the contrary, Osiris altogether belonged to the world of the dead; it was from there that he bestowed his blessings upon Egypt. He was always depicted as a mummy, a dead king,

* See above, p. 40.

though *qua* king a god—a complex but characteristically Egyptian, nay, African, figure.

Even in their basic relation with plant life the gods show profound differences: Adonis personified the spring vegetation; Tammuz the generative force, not only of plants, but also of animals; while Osiris brought forth the grain and did so as part of the function which the dead king fulfilled in the natural economy of his people. Both Osiris and Tammuz were believed to suffer when the grain was threshed. This is unequivocally expressed in the Egyptian Mystery Play of the Succession and somewhat less clearly in a text referring to Tammuz.[34] It was still believed in medieval times when Tammuz worshipers survived at Harran.[35] Texts from Ras Shamra prove that the belief was also held in Syria, although not demonstrably within the scope of the Adonis cult, which is known to us only from late sources.[36] The doctrine follows directly from the connection between every one of these gods with plant life and cannot count, therefore, as a specific feature which they have in common beyond the general character just indicated.

Vegetation cannot appear without water; and we may therefore view the mastery over water, claimed for Osiris, Tammuz, and Adonis, as the consequence of their mastery over vegetation. But neither in Syria nor in Mesopotamia do we find a parallel for the very specific relationship which existed between Osiris and the Nile. In the Tammuz hymns water appears simply as an accessory of the god's power. Hence the goddess can be said "to rejoice in him who comes forth from the river."[37]

The motif of drowning and the bringing of the inundation mentioned in connection with Tammuz recall Osiris; but we should expect them in connection with any god whose power is manifest in the re-emergence of vegetation.* Tammuz "drowned" because the vegetation disappears when the waters dwindle in the rivers and canals in the heat of summer. When he is reborn and the plants revive, spring or autumn rains proclaim his power at the same time. Hence the annual cycle of nature is summarized in the following manner in the life-history of the god:

> When young he lay in a sinking ship,
> When adult he lay immersed in the grain.[38]

But in Egypt the Nile flood was a manifestation of Osiris' power because it was believed to rise from the earth, his domain.

If we move from mythology to the actual usages of the cult, we find a detailed resemblance between Osiris and the Adonis rituals in the use

---

* See above, pp. 191–92, and quotation on p. 31.

made of germinating seeds. Our problem here is to determine the antiquity of the usage in Syria and in Egypt and to decide whether it was originally at home in one or in both of these countries. The "Adonis gardens" consisted of seeds—sown in pots or baskets—which germinated and wilted quickly. These were thrown into wells or into the sea—we do not know why.[39] But the rite seems to be part of the wailings for Adonis, and the emphasis was on the fact that the young plants had wilted. The "Osiris beds," on the other hand, were not allowed to wilt in the sight of man. They were of two kinds:* Heaps of earth, in the shape of a mummy and sometimes covered with mummy cloth or cartonnage, were placed on a bier; they contained seeds which were watered for a week. When these germinated, they were placed in the tomb, serving as a spell of resurrection. They belonged, therefore, to the funerary ritual. But a second type of "Osiris beds" was used in the temples, at least in Ptolemaic times. These consisted of molds of gold or silver filled with earth and seeds, which were watered for nine days and buried on the day of the "interment of Osiris," the last day of the last month of the season of inundation (Khoiak).[40] The general character of Adonis and Osiris suffices to explain the rite. Note that, on the one hand, the "Adonis gardens" wilted and that, on the other, the use of the "Osiris beds" in the funerary rites has no parallel in Syria, although it was known in Egypt from the Eighteenth Dynasty onward. Finally, the use of "Osiris beds" in the temple cult is not certified in Pharaonic times at all and has no demonstrable relation with any popular celebration of an event or critical transition in nature but only with the revival of the god in the temple.† The possibility exists that the use of germinating seed in the Ptolemaic temples was derived from the cult of Adonis, which had been established in Egypt at least since the days of Theocritus, in the third century B.C.[41]

We touch here upon a most important element in the comparisons which can be made between Egyptian and Asiatic cults—the influence of the Greeks. They, too, knew "the old Mediterranean ritual of sorrow with its periodic wailing for a departed divinity, hero or heroine," expressing "the emotion of natural man excited by the disappearance of verdure, by the gathering of the harvest, or by the fall of the year."[42] The Greeks have not only identified Egyptian gods with their own but have used the Egyptian material creatively for their own ends. The spread of the cult of Isis throughout the Roman Empire is the outstanding example of an adaptation in which the original features disappeared

* See above, pp. 185–86.   † See above, chap. 15, n. 49.

almost completely. Most, if not all, of the information on Egyptian religion which classical authors offer is disfigured from the Egyptian point of view. Even the oldest Greek source exemplifies the peculiarly Greek tendency to transmute every borrowed trait into an expression of Hellenic thought; Herodotus (ii. 59) equated Isis with Demeter. Moreover, the Greeks were settled in Lower Egypt, and while we know that the Fayum and Alexandria had a curiously hybridic culture, we do not know whether the Greeks found Asiatic beliefs established in those parts or whether they themselves introduced them there. As a result of this uncertainty, the most definite link between Asia and the Osiris myth remains entirely problematical. This is Osiris' connection with Byblos as described in classical sources.[43] His body and coffin had floated there; they were found by Isis after they had been made into a pillar in the palace of the local ruler and were claimed by her and taken back to Egypt. But Isis was said to have behaved at Byblos exactly as Demeter was believed to have done under very similar circumstances at Eleusis. In Roman times Adonis was said to be really Osiris.[44] But of all these Byblite connections Pharaonic sources know nothing at all, although Egypt had traded with Byblos since the beginning of historical times and identified its Great Goddess, the "Lady of Byblos," with Hathor.[45] It is for this reason that we may have to discount the whole of the Byblite connections of the Osiris myth as a late elaboration. Another feature of the story was perhaps introduced at the same time. In the myth there is an obvious duplication: Seth not only murdered Osiris but later got his enemy's body and dismembered it. We have discussed already the unlikelihood that this story originated in Egypt in early times and have found a possible explanation for it;* an alternative explanation would derive it from the equation of Osiris and Dionysus, which prevailed in late times. Dionysus, too, became manifest in a pillar,[46] while Osiris was connected in early times with the Djed pillar; however, this was not a wooden column but a bundle of papyrus.

Whatever features the Greeks may have added to the original Osiris myth, they treated most cavalierly a trait which was of the greatest importance to the Egyptians. This was the royalty of Osiris. For the Greeks Osiris' character as a dead king was quite meaningless. To the Egyptians it was his outstanding characteristic.[47] We have seen that all other aspects of the god were derived from it (chap. 15). Yet the Greek accounts totally obscure these Egyptian beliefs. Nor is there an equivalent for Osiris' royalty in Asia. Adonis was a youth, never a

* See above, pp. 200–201.

king. Tammuz occurs in the Sumerian king list, but in connection with the legendary Second Dynasty of Erech.[48] He follows the god Lugal-banda (a Tammuz-like figure) and precedes the semidivine Gilgamesh. Since Inanna, a form of the Great Mother, was worshiped at Erech, Tammuz was at home there, too; and the list seems to link its earliest historical tradition with the world of the gods in the approved fashion of myth. Royalty plays no part in the cult of Tammuz and is not character-istic for the god as he is depicted in the hymns. In this respect the con-trast with Osiris is complete.

In comparison with the deep-rooted differences between the three gods, their "generic alikeness" dwindles to insignificance; they personi-fy the life in vegetation but that in a manner which is peculiar in each case. Curiously enough, however, there remains a common element in their myths which calls for an explanation; and it, too, belongs entirely to the area of the specific. Osiris' and Tammuz' enemies were embodied in boars, and it was a wild boar which slew Adonis.[49] We are not de-pendent on classical sources for these statements. Plutarch's story that Seth found Osiris' body in its coffin on a boar hunt and Herodotus' re-port that pigs were sacrificed to Osiris only gain authority when we find in the Book of the Dead that Seth had been incarnate in a boar on a certain occasion;[50] and the same myth is alluded to in the pyramid texts.[51] It has even been suggested with some probability that the enig-matical animal which represents Seth might be a long-legged type of pig.[52] At the Babylonian New Year's festival a boar symbolized the enemy and was killed before the captive god could be liberated.* We have seals of the third millennium to prove the antiquity of this prac-tice, and in Egypt the enemy of Horus and Osiris was known as a pig about the same time.

The impersonation of the god's enemy by a boar seems too odd and too specific to be viewed as an accidental resemblance between the myths of the three gods. Furthermore, it has been maintained that the names of Osiris and Assur, and the epithet "Asaru" borne by Marduk, may be derived from a common root.[53] One might, then, tentatively ad-vance the hypothesis that some features in the cult of the three gods go back to a remote past, before the Hamitic and Semitic languages had developed from their common root, before the track of the Atlantic storms had shifted northward, and when a belt of habitable lands stretched from Africa's west coast to the Persian Mountains. Adonis represents the wild vegetation (upon which the nomad depends) rather

* See below, chap. 22, n. 41.

than the grain.[54] Tammuz and the related Mesopotamian gods are all intimately related with flocks and herds as well as with plant life. The Egyptian as well as the Mesopotamian "Lady of Births" uses the uterus of a heifer as her emblem.[55]

But we need not dwell here upon these hazy possibilities of a common origin, since we are concerned, not with the history, but with the significance, of the divinities who are grouped together as "dying gods." Whether resemblances in their mythology and cult are due to independent parallel growth or derive from a common root; whether a "god of plants and animals" was worshiped before people moved from the desiccating highlands into the drying marshes of the river valleys, we do not know. But even if a few features in cult or myth—a designation, an animal symbol—should be survivals from a distant common past, the gods as they confront us in the religions of the ancient Near East express profoundly different mentalities. And it is through the "specifically different," not through the "generically alike," that we may understand them.

CHAPTER 21

THE DEIFICATION OF KINGS

THE texts and usages which we have examined hitherto bear witness to a single conception of rulership: the Mesopotamian king was a mortal charged with the crushing burden of leading mankind in its servitude. Although his divine election endowed him with a potency surpassing that of ordinary men (chap. 18), it did not approximate him to the gods.

But we must now consider certain usages in which the polarity between the human and the divine appears as suspended or destroyed. We have seen that certain kings used the divine determinative before their names, but this graphic device is not alone in suggesting that deification of kings was known in Mesopotamia. It is true that not all the documents which would at first sight seem to indicate deification will be found to bear on the problem.[1] Several of them are, in fact, consistent with the normal Mesopotamian estimate of the king. But a few texts establish beyond a doubt that occasionally a fusion of humanity and divinity took place in the person of certain Mesopotamian rulers; this was the case when a goddess had chosen a king to act as her bridegroom.

A. THE UNION OF KING AND GODDESS

The renewal of nature in the spring was conceived as the marriage of the mother-goddess with the liberated god.[2] Their union took place in nature but also in their temples—residences erected by their orders in the cities of man. The change in nature and the temple ritual both constituted the divine union, and we may think of them as two parallel, inseparable, and equivalent events. For our present theme it is of importance that, at certain times and in certain places, the king was made to play the part of the divine bridegroom in the ritual.

The appearance of the king as a god is most clearly described in a hymn which glorifies Ishtar as the evening star. Her bridegroom bears an epithet of Tammuz, yet he is actually King Idin-Dagan of Isin. The poem begins by exalting Ishtar's power and continues:

To guard the life-breath of all lands. . . . .
To perform the rites correctly on the day the moon is invisible,
Has on New Year's day, the day of observances,
A couch been set up for my lady.
Grass and plants . . . . cedar they purify there,
Put it for my queen on that couch.
On its . . . . the blanket is arranged for her,
A blanket delighting the heart, to make the bed good.[3]

Next follows a realistic account of the censing and lustration of both the goddess and the king of Isin and of their physical union. The king's name, and Ama-ushumgal-ana ("Great Ruler of Heaven"), an epithet of Tammuz, are used alternately when reference to the bridegroom is made; and this wilful confusion of god and king—"fusion" is a more appropriate term—continues when the emergence of the couple from the bedchamber is described.

Around the shoulders of his beloved bride he has laid his arm,
Around the shoulders of pure Inanna he has laid his arm.
Like daylight she ascends the throne on the great throne dais;
The king, like unto the sun, sits beside her.
Abundance, pleasure, wealth are ranged before her,
A sumptuous meal is placed before her.
The black-headed people are(?) ranged before her.
. . . . music . . . . singers. . . . .
The king has reached out for the food and drink,
Ama-ushumgal-ana has reached out for the food and drink.
The palace is in fest(ive mood), the king is glad,
The people are passing the day in abundance.

Thus the king of Isin acted the part of the god, in contrast with Egypt, where a god took the part of a king in the sexual act.[4] The distinction is important, even though in practice in both places we find a king incarnating a god. In Mesopotamia a king was exalted beyond human comprehension; in Egypt a king who was never human realized the ineffable mystery of his own rebirth as Kamutef, "Bull of his Mother."

We are free to speculate as to the manner in which the goddess was represented in the Mesopotamian ritual, since there is no information available on this point.

The purpose of the rite—"to guard the life-breath of all lands"—is in keeping with what we know of the New Year's festival: the union of the god and goddess vouchsafed prosperity for the year to come and was followed by a banquet which cast the spell of abundance which the rite, objectivating the seasonal forces, attempted to insure.

There is no evidence that the king of Isin impersonated other phases of the annual cycle of the suffering god; and the part he took in the sacred marriage becomes a little easier to explain when we notice a peculiar characteristic of that ceremony: the bride was the active partner, and the king who impersonated the bridegroom remained her obedient servant. For in the sacred marriage the dependence of the god upon the goddess is strongly emphasized. Texts from Isin leave no doubt that the initiative was ascribed to her. An apostrophe to one of the kings reads: "(O Enlil-bani), the goddess Inanna, coming from Eanna (her temple) has gladdened thy heart. On her sacred couch, with majesty, she has approached thee."[5] King Ishme-Dagan said of himself: "I am he whom Inanna, Queen of Heaven and Earth, has chosen for her beloved husband."[6] In all these phrases the goddess is the active partner. She appears so even in the sacred marriage of Baba with the domineering Ningirsu.[7] Again, in the Epic of Gilgamesh, it is Ishtar who invites the king of Erech to become her husband.[8]

Perhaps we hold here the clue to the problem of the deification of kings in Mesopotamia. It may well be that only those kings were deified who had been commanded by a goddess to share her couch. In a general way the kings who use the divine determinative before their names belong to the same period as the texts mentioning the marriage of kings and goddesses; and we have seen that some kings adopted the determinative, not at the beginning, but at a later stage of their reigns.* If we assume that they did so on the strength of a divine command, we remain within the normal scope of Mesopotamian thought, while the view that a king should have presumed of his own accord to pass the barrier between the human and the divine conflicts with everything we know of Mesopotamian beliefs.

Our assumption seems to find support in a text known as "The Deification of Lipit-Ishtar."[9] It shows how this king was deified—as a prelude to a sacred marriage with Ishtar—by being fused with Urash, a fertility god.[10] The text consists of a song cycle, and its construction suggests that it was actually recited as a ritual of deification to prepare the king for his exalted function. The first song relates how Anu appointed Lipit-Ishtar as king of the land. The ruler is called "child of Enlil," a term which would serve as a first approximation of the king to the divinity in which his person was to be absorbed; moreover, Anu is said to have acted in the assembly of the gods gathered "to determine destiny." This shows that at Isin, as at Lagash, Babylon, and other cities,

* See above, p. 224.

the ritual of the sacred marriage formed part of the New Year's celebrations. In the second song Anu addresses Lipit-Ishtar directly:

> The black-headed people—driven like sheep—shall go
>   in their yoke the straight (path) for thee,
> O Lipit-Ishtar, the foreign countries—thou shalt be
>   their king, far (and wide).

The next two songs resemble the first two, but they are addressed,
not to the king, but to the god Urash. Urash was one of the sons of
Enlil, and this explains the term "child of Enlil" applied to the king in
the first pair of songs. But now it is said of Urash: "Ishtar is thy lover;
may she prolong thy life." The wish contained in the last half of the
verse is a curious one to address to an immortal. But it can be understood if the songs belonged to the ritual which centered round King
Lipit-Ishtar. Even if the words were ostensibly addressed to the god
Urash, it was the king (now identified with Urash) to whom they were
spoken.

The rest of the text contains many phrases which would apply to
Lipit-Ishtar as well as to Urash; Anu promises Urash a victorious
reign, the power to champion justice "like the sun-god," etc. The aim
of the text is clearly to treat Lipit-Ishtar and Urash as one and the same.
The two songs concerned with the god copy those which had been addressed to the king in that the first in each pair describes Anu's favor
and the second uses direct speech.

The songs to Urash are followed by two antiphons, after which the
goddess Ishtar is introduced in the text with a paean of praise spoken
by herself:

> My father has given me heaven, has given me the earth;
> I am mistress of heaven,
> Is there a single deity who is my equal?

Other allusions in this song are very obscure. But the construction of the
song cycle suggests that it was recited just before the king entered into
the presence of the goddess; merging with the god Urash he was raised,
as it were, to her level. The text of Idin-Dagan shows that he remained
there during the banquet which followed the sacred union.

The question now arises whether the rite could have affected the
status of the king permanently. We cannot be certain of this, but it is not
impossible that the deification of kings as expressed by the use of the
divine determinative derived from the role they had played in the sacred marriage. The rite was not confined to Isin. References of the kings
of Ur (see below) indicate that it followed the same pattern there.

Deification did not, perhaps, outlast the ritual in early times; but, in any case, it is worth noting that precisely at Ur and at Isin, where kings acted as the divine bridegroom and used the divine determinative, the rulers were credited with an influence on the prosperity of the land far exceeding that for which the usual Mesopotamian terminology allowed. Enlil-bani was called "he who produces abundance of grain"; Lipit-Ishtar was chosen by Anu, Enlil, and Ninlil "so that there should be a wealth of grain in Isin"; Idin-Dagan had been charged by Enlil with "the task of feeding the people with excellent food and of making them drink sweet water."[11] These phrases, and similarly extravagant epithets accorded to Shulgi,* may have found their justification in the ritual fusion of these kings with the divine bridegroom. The expressions remind us of those which described Pharaoh's power over the course of nature. But the comparison does not go beyond appearance. In both Egypt and Mesopotamia the king was instrumental in furthering the natural processes, but the character of that instrumentality differed. In Mesopotamia the goddess claimed a service which the king rendered; in this respect at least the deification of the king during the ritual—inevitable under the circumstances—was in keeping with the prevalent Mesopotamian view that the king was the chosen servant of the gods. Pharaoh, on the other hand, was never deified. He was divine in origin and essence, one of the powers whose acts reverberated in the hidden depths of nature as well as in the world of men. Pharaoh was a god, but a hymn to a king of Ur states: "O Shulgi, thou art created for the pleasure of Inanna."[12] The Mesopotamian king, even when taking part in the sacred wedding, did no more than put the greatest natural force of which man disposes at the service of his divine mistress.

B. THE KING AS "SON" OF THE GODS

Although some Mesopotamian rulers named deities as their fathers or mothers, they did not, in doing so, pretend to godliness. When we refer back, once more, to Egypt, we find that Pharaoh could appear as the son of any god or goddess but that he counted specifically as the child (in the literal sense) of certain deities. As far as physical existence was concerned, Pharaoh had been begotten by Amon-Re upon the queen-mother. As regards his divine potency, he was Horus, the son of Hathor. As the legitimate successor to the throne (a notion with cosmic implications), he was Horus the son of Osiris and Isis, the grandson of Geb, the earth.

* See below, p. 311.

In Mesopotamia we do not find equivalents for the unchanging, precisely defined relationships which connected Pharaoh with Amon-Re and Osiris, with Hathor, and with Isis. Only the general formula which makes it possible for Pharaoh to appear as the son of any god or goddess recurs in Mesopotamia. In both countries, moreover, we find that the king can appear as the child of a number of gods at one and the same time. Gudea calls himself the son of Ninsun, Nanshe, or Baba—three goddesses who, though similar in essentials, had become so much differentiated in the course of time that we cannot assume that Gudea used their names as synonyms. The same ruler is also the son of the goddess Gatumdug, whom he addresses as follows:

> I have no mother; thou art my mother.
> I have no father; thou art my father.[13]

The unrealistic projection of both parents in one divine person accentuates the figurative meaning of the expressions. In Mesopotamia, as elsewhere, the terms of parentage are used in connection with the deity to express both intimacy and dependence. Hence it is possible for Hammurabi, in the preamble to his code, to call himself "son of Sin" (II, 13–14), "son of Dagan" (IV, 27–28), and "brother of the god Zamama" (a "son of Enlil" [II, 56]), while in yet another text he is the son of Marduk.[14] Assurbanipal was equally far removed from any naturalistic interpretation of kinship when he said: "I knew not father and mother; in the . . . . of my goddesses I grew up."[15] And in other texts he names as his mother sometimes Ninlil, sometimes Belit of Nineveh, and sometimes Ishtar of Arbela.[16] For earlier times we have Lugalzaggesi's epithets: "son born of Nisaba, fed by the holy milk of Ninhursaga."[17]

If the king felt justified in using the terms of kinship with certain gods to express his feeling of dependence and love, the gods on their part are said sometimes to have taken an active interest in the ruler from the very moment of his conception. Assurbanipal addressed Ninlil as follows: "I am thy servant Assurbanipal whom thy hands have formed without father and mother—whom thou, Queen, hast caused to reach maturity."[18] The gods appear even more clearly as protectors distinct from the human parents when the king declares: "I (am) Assurbanipal, offspring (i.e., creature) of Assur and Belit, the oldest prince of the House of Succession, whose name Assur and Sin, the lord of the tiara, have named for the kingship from distant days, whom they formed in his mother's womb, for the rulership of Assyria."[19] When it is said that the gods form the royal child in the womb of its mother "with their hands,"[20] it is clear that they are distinguished from his physical parents.[21] The Mesopotamian king was a mortal marked—and to some extent changed—by divine grace.

One passage in Eannatum's Stela of the Vultures seems to contradict the evidence adduced here and to establish a god and goddess as the physical parents of the ruler of Lagash.

Ningirsu implanted the seed of Eannatum in the womb and Ninhursaga bore him.

Over Eannatum Ninhursaga rejoiced; Inanna took him on (her) arm and named him "Worthy of the Eanna of Inanna of Ibgal." She set him down on Ninhursaga's knee for her, and Ninhursaga suckled him.

Over Eannatum, the seed implanted in the womb by Ningirsu, Ningirsu rejoiced. Ningirsu laid upon him his span, laid upon him his cubit even (up to) five cubits, (making him) five cubits and one span.[22]

If we accept the prima facie meaning of this text, the epithet "fed with the sacred milk of Ninhursaga" becomes significant. But Eannatum never claimed divinity in his texts; on the contrary, he named his earthly father and grandfather.[23] Therefore, we face a dilemma: we either accept this text at its face value, in which case it conflicts with orthography and represents an inexplicable deviation from the usual conception of kingship, or admit that, in view of the overwhelming evidence to the contrary, the literal interpretation cannot be correct. The text may then have a ritual or symbolical meaning which escapes us. As a mere guess we might suggest that it refers, not to the actual birth of Eannatum, but to his ritual "birth" as a god fit to be Inanna's bridegroom. For in another text[24] Eannatum is called "the beloved husband of Inanna," and in the text we are discussing Inanna declares him worthy of her. However that may be, the numerous other texts in which Mesopotamian kings are called the "sons" of gods or goddesses do not imply that they are divine.

C. THE KING WORSHIPED IN TEMPLES

As far as we know, the Mesopotamian kings who were deified were worshiped only in the shrines of cities which they dominated as overlords, not in the cities where their authority as earthly representatives of the city-gods had its basis. Their worship appears, then, to have been an instrument of policy. In Egypt the divinity of Pharaoh implied that rebels or external enemies were always misguided wretches doomed to destruction:

There's such divinity doth hedge a king,
That treason can but peep to what it would,
Acts little of his will (*Hamlet*, Act IV, scene 5).

In Mesopotamia the king's divinity was given a political connotation in one period only—during the Third Dynasty of Ur. At Tell Asmar

(Eshnunna) the local ruler, dependent upon King Shu-Sin of Ur, dedicated a temple of which his overlord was the god. This is clearly stated in the inscription on its pivot stones:

> For the divine Shu-Sin, mentioned by name by Anu, beloved of Enlil, the king whom Enlil thought of in his holy heart for the shepherdship of the country and of the four quarters, mighty king, king of Ur, king of the four quarters, his god—Ituria, governor of Eshnunna, his servant, has built his temple.[25]

This inscription is explicit in that Shu-Sin of Ur is called the god of Ituria; and the building in which it was found, a complete temple built for the worship of Shu-Sin, shows that the expression carried its full meaning. Moreover, there is curious corroborative evidence in the subsequent history of the building. As soon as Eshnunna had become independent from Shu-Sin's successor Ibi-Sin, the last king of the dynasty, the temple built by Ituria was secularized and made a part of the palace of the local rulers. These now called themselves servants, not of an earthly overlord, but of the city-god Tishpak.[26] Thus the kings of Ur who used the divine determinative before their names deliberately put themselves in the place of the city-gods of their vassals; these were therefore compelled to give public expression to their subjection in worshiping the kings of Ur. Temples dedicated to these god-kings have not been discovered outside Eshnunna, but we know from inscriptions that they existed in Lagash, Umma, and Drehem.[27] They give substance to an epithet of Hammurabi—"god of kings."[28] But neither Hammurabi nor (as far as we know) any other king before or after the Third Dynasty of Ur went to such lengths in proclaiming his suzerainty. It has sometimes been thought that the Late Assyrian kings set themselves up as gods to be worshiped by subjected peoples because they erected stelae with their own images throughout the empire. It has been rightly pointed out, however, that there is no inscriptional evidence for this assumption and that the kings themselves appear upon these stelae in the act of worshiping the great gods.[29] Hence the stelae do no more than proclaim that the kings' suzerainty was sanctioned by the gods. And, as we have said already, even the king of Ur was not worshiped in a temple of his own city. He might be a god in Eshnunna; but at Ur he was the servant of the city's owner, the moon-god Nanna.

D. THE WORSHIP OF ROYAL STATUES

It is certain that royal statues were set up in temples and received offerings, but this does not imply that the kings thus honored were divinities. For the manner in which their sacrifices were listed differed significantly from the formula used for offerings to the gods. Up to Shu-Sin's reign offerings to statues of gods were entered as follows: *To the god X*; offerings to royal statues, on the other hand: *To the statue of King Y.* This distinction was made even when the statue depicted a king who wrote his name with the sign of divinity, and it made no difference whether the king was alive or dead. Under Shu-Sin a change was introduced to the effect that kings who used the determinative of divinity before their names were treated as gods; offerings to their statues were listed: *To Y.*[30] In other cases the differentiation was maintained, indicating that the existence of a statue and the making of offerings to it did not imply that the king was worshiped; the continuation of the offerings long after the lifetime of the king does not prove worship either.[31] It was considered ethical not to neglect the institutions of earlier rulers, and each hoped that his own arrangements would in their turn be respected by his successors. Gudea inscribed one of his statues with a list of offerings due to it and then continued: "A (future) ruler who would cancel them (viz., the offerings) or who would obstruct the decisions of Ningirsu—his (own) established sacrifices shall be canceled and his (own) orders shall be obstructed."[32]

The important point to observe is that the offerings were not made to the king at all but to the statue. In the listings of offerings it is the statue that stands in parallelism to the god; the statue is the recipient of the offerings in the one case as the god is the recipient in the other. Hence the statue, not the king, is treated as a divinity in these inscriptions. Now there is no doubt that the Mesopotamians viewed a statue as an entity endowed with power independent of the person whom it represented. Gudea, for instance, gave a formal message to one of his statues: it had to recount to Ningirsu, in whose temple it was placed, the manner in which Gudea had celebrated the completion of the temple. The relevant passage reads:

> Gudea, giving instruction to the statue (said):
> "Statue, say to my king. . . . ."[33]

The phraseology recalls the opening sentences of letters which, in turn, reflect the original custom of sending a messenger; nothing could illustrate better the treatment of the statue as an independent entity, a true mediator between king and god. It was to plead the case of Gudea before the statue of the city-god and remind him of services rendered. Its function resembled that of the personal gods who also acted as intermediaries between man and the great gods and appear upon the monuments introducing their protégés to other deities and interceding on their

behalf (Fig. 13). It is revealing for the nature of kingship in Mesopotamia that the kings, like all other men, had their personal gods, who
were more accessible than the great gods and were willing to approach
these when necessary. Conversely, when the great gods had chosen a
prince to be king, the city-god informed the appointee's personal god of
the decision;[34] and the personal god of a king was held responsible for
the latter's transgressions. A man was in the "shadow" of his personal
god, an expression indicating that the god's protection was extended
over him as over a client; this protection implied willingness to press the
client's rights in the law courts and to lend authority and power to the
verdict in favor of that client, so that it could be executed.[35] In the following text the personal god of Entemena is asked to render the same
service which the statues were intended to perform:

> Entemena, Governor of Lagash, endowed with the scepter by Enlil, endowed with
> intelligence by Enki (Ea), envisaged in the heart of Nanshe, great governor of Nin-
> girsu, a man who grasps (the meaning of) the commands of the gods—may his (per-
> sonal) god DUN- . . . . stand before Ningirsu and Nanshe until far-away days (praying)
> for the welfare of Entemena.[36]

The parallelism between statues and personal gods, and the fact that the
statues received offerings, indicate that they were considered divinities.
The argument of the ancients which led to this conclusion can be reconstructed without difficulty. The statue, placed before the god, perpetually recalled the donor to him. Hence, being effective, it had power.[37]
Since it did not decay, it was immortal. In both respects it partook of
divinity. Power, however, means life; and life requires sustenance.
Hence the statue received regular offerings of food and drink so that it
could maintain its friendly service.

In the beliefs connected with statues, the Egyptian and Mesopotamian points of view are similar if compared with our own but differ significantly if compared with one another. Common to both is the belief
that food and drink should be offered to an inanimate object in order to
sustain the power with which it was charged.[38] Thus in the temple of
Karnak a statue of King Tuthmosis III with hands uplifted took the
king's place, to consecrate the offerings made to the god. It was decreed
that "after the majesty of this august god (Amon) (was) satisfied with
his offering," a specific amount should be given to the statue.[39] Obviously, these offerings did not sustain the king but the statue, or more particularly its "life," its power to consecrate the royal gifts before Amon. In
both Egypt and Mesopotamia, "life" was first imparted to the statue by
an "opening-of-the-mouth" ceremony.[40] It was true in both countries

that the erection of a statue did not imply that its owner was considered to be a god[41] even though the statue itself was effective beyond the scope of man. Yet the two countries differed in the degree of dissociation which they allowed between the statue and the person represented. In Egypt the dissociation went less far than in Mesopotamia, and the offerings made before a tomb statue were actually offered to the Ka of the dead man (chap. 5). I am not aware of an Egyptian text which would match Gudea's exhortation to his own statue. Although temples and sacred objects were personified in Egypt,* as well as in Mesopotamia, the Mesopotamians displayed a certain agility of thought which allowed them to acknowledge the characteristics and functions of an object as such and yet to personify it as a deity. This procedure is excellently illustrated by lists like "An-Anum," which show a sequence of the great gods, each followed by all the members of his family and household. Among the deities composing the suite of Anu, for instance, we find some whose names show that they were simply objects used in the cult. One of these is the god Ninshubur, called a vizier and a doorkeeper of Anu. But as one of his Sumerian names we meet Ig-galla, which means "the great doorleaf." This is no allegory. Ig-galla is, quite concretely, the great wooden door swinging in the gate of the shrine. At Lagash, it is called Ig-alima, "the door of the bison."[42] But this door is, at the same time, a minor god, a member of Ningirsu's household. When Gudea, the earthly steward of Ningirsu, came into the temple on the morning after the god's entry, to organize the estate and its personnel, he made the following arrangement: "For the Lord Ningirsu he had his (Ningirsu's) beloved son Ig-alima . . . . perform his duties as the great door in Girnun." These duties are specified in the text: Ig-alima had to decide who was to be admitted to the presence of his master—the task of the oriental doorkeeper to this day. He admitted "the just—the evil people he restrained." When his master went out, he handed him his scepter. It is interesting that Ig-alima is said also to have given Gudea his scepter. We may estimate the concreteness with which the personification of the door was imagined when we read that Ig-alima accompanied Gudea in the solemn procession on the occasion of the molding of the first brick for the new temple.†

In the Late Assyrian An-Anum list in which Ig-galla, "the great doorleaf," appears as a name of Anu's vizier, we find that the latter has a son called Hedu. This word simply means "lintel, arch," or possibly "doorframe." This part of the door, then, was also felt to be charged

* See above, pp. 67, 107.					† See above, p. 273.

with divine power and to be a separate entity; the connection with the doorleaf was considered to be that of son with father.

This discussion of the personification of a specific group of power-charged objects illustrates the peculiar fluidity which the concept of divinity possessed in Mesopotamian, as it does in primitive, religion. It could crystallize and attach itself to any object in which power became manifest.[43] In this manner the royal statues acquired a certain degree of divinity, but this quality was quite independent from the kings whom they represented. It was the statue which received offerings, not the king; and neither the existence of statues nor the fact that sacrifices were made to them proves that the kings were worshiped as gods.

E. THE KING IN PERSONAL NAMES

In personal names a royal name sometimes takes the place of that of a god, but personal names reflect popular beliefs rather than authoritative theology; and the term "god" may be used a little more loosely by the people than by the official scribes. Since great differences of power existed, since a divine hierarchy was known, since each man knew a personal god who served as an intermediary between him and the great gods, and since even sacred objects acquired a divine personality, little was needed to surround the king, in the eyes of his subjects, with the aura of an unsought divinity.[44] In the same way subjects of Early Dynastic rulers might address an *ensi* or governor with the title *lugal*, "king." Even Hammurabi, who never used the determinative of divinity, nevertheless called himself a "god of kings" in respect to his vassals (Code, II, 55). Small wonder that his subjects, in contrast with the official scribes, occasionally wrote his name as if he were a god. This happened especially in oath formulas, when the parties swore by certain gods, and by the king, to insure that these powers would act if the oath were broken. In this context the effective power of the king was foremost in the mind of the writer, and his name was linked with those of gods.[45]

A similar trend of thought can account for the appearance of the king's name as an element in personal names.[46] We find even personal names like *Sharru-ili*, "the king is my god," or *Rim-Sin-ili*, "Rim-Sin is my god."[47] Others, like "The King is My Life"[48] or "With the King is Life,"[49] recall Egyptian names; but in Mesopotamia these usages are restricted to a comparatively short period: personal names composed with a royal instead of a divine name are not found after the First Dynasty of Babylon.[50] And the popular beliefs expressed in them do not find support in rituals and official texts. In Egypt, on the contrary, similar beliefs are in complete accordance with the official inscriptions and, in fact, with Egyptian theology. This contrast is of the greatest significance, and it recurs consistently.[51] We may, for instance, consider a stanza from the Babylonian poem, "I Will Praise the Lord of Wisdom":[52]

> The day of divine worship was happiness to my heart,
> The day of the goddess' procession was profit to me,
>   yea, riches!
> Homage to the king was my joy,
> Music for him was dear to me.
> I taught my country to keep the commands of God,
> I instructed my people to honor the goddess.
> The majesty of the king I put on a par with God,
> And I made the people learn respect for the palace;
> I knew indeed that this is pleasing to God.

Homage to the king follows worship of the gods and is clearly subsidiary to it. Respect for the king was instilled in the people because it pleased the gods (since the king was their appointee). Can one imagine an Egyptian explaining why the king should be honored, or taking credit for having equated the Majesty of Pharaoh with the gods?

F. THE KING AND THE POWERS IN NATURE

Although the mechanics of magic allowed the Mesopotamian king to exert some pressure, the natural processes remained under the control of the gods; and the king could only attempt to bring about favorable conditions by retaining the divine favor. The indirectness of his influence upon nature is amply illustrated by our quotations. But the sources are likely to be misinterpreted. The literary style of the ancient Near East is often repetitious. It achieves richness and variety by elaborate imagery. But metaphors can be understood only if their frame of reference is fully grasped. Consequently, we must attach a different significance to similar-sounding phrases in Egyptian and in Mesopotamian texts, for they imply a different theological aspect of kingship. If we survey the usual Mesopotamian expressions which seem to suggest that the king had power over nature, we shall find that, with but a very few exceptions, they remain within the bounds of Mesopotamian theology.

In Mesopotamia, as in Egypt, the ruler is often compared with the sun. Hammurabi stated in the preamble of his law (Code, V, 4–9): "I am the sun of Babylon who causes light to rise over the land of Sumer and Akkad." The deified Amar-Sin calls himself "a true god, the sun of his land."[53] If in the translation of Hammurabi's epithet we have used "sun" rather than "sun-god," while the Akkadian *Shamshu* may mean either, we have done so precisely because we consider these expressions to be metaphors. Moreover, the qualifications "of his land," "of Babylon," agree better with the translation "sun" than with the notion implied in the English "sun-god." In Egyptian texts of the New Kingdom we find similar expressions. However, these do not occur in older inscriptions but appear when Pharaoh's rightful dominion over the whole earth had been challenged by strong Asiatic peoples. Tuthmosis III is called "Ruler of Rulers, Sun of All Lands"; Seti I, "Re of Egypt and Moon of All Lands," or "King of Egypt, Re of the Nine Bows"— the latter being the traditional formula for foreign peoples.[54] These expressions are unusual in Egypt, where the normal way of comparing Pharaoh with the sun is based on the intimate relation between prototype and successor, progenitor and offspring.* The fact that purely metaphorical comparisons between king and sun could arise even in Egypt adds force to the translation "sun" (rather than "sun-god") in Hammurabi's text. Moreover, if the expression "sun of Babylon" were not understood as a metaphor, it would be not only difficult to explain its use by Hammurabi, who never claimed divinity, but impossible to explain why the Late Assyrian kings often styled themselves "sun of the totality of mankind."[55] Quite often the metaphorical character of this and similar uses of the word "sun" is unmistakable. It is so when Ur-Nammu of Ur is said to have been "predestined by Enlil to rule the land like Utu himself."[56] Even the deified Lipit-Ishtar uses the comparison with the sun quite clearly as a metaphor† without claiming identity; and Hammurabi states, a little before the quotation we have given, that Anu and Enlil, when they chose Marduk as ruler over all men, also named him "to make legislation appear in the land, to destroy the evil and the wicked, so that the strong should not harm the weak, so that I should appear like the sun to the black-headed people and make light the land, and create well-being for mankind" (Code, I, 32–48).

In dealing with Egyptian beliefs, we have described how the sun quite universally appears to be symbolical of order and hence also of the order of justice; and in this respect the king could be viewed, in Mesopotamia as elsewhere, as an image of the sun-god. Hence the prayer "may Ur-Ninurta, like Shamash, rule the country for many years,"[57] which re-

* See above, pp. 148–50.

† See above, p. 296.

sembles the words spoken nowadays in Westminster Abbey before the enthronement of the king of England, when the archbishop prays that God may establish his throne in righteousness, that "it may stand fast for evermore, like as the sun before him, and as the faithful witness in heaven."[58]

When the Mesopotamian king was compared with the sun, the essential distinction between the earthly prince and the sun-god was not ignored; and the same qualification applies to a number of phrases which were applied to the ruler as well as to the gods.[59] None of these expresses an identity; all merely proclaim that, from the point of view of the subject, the king seems godlike. Hence we read in the prayer of an ill-fated Babylonian:

> May the god who rejected me help me!
> May the goddess who [resented me] have pity on me!
> May the shepherd, the sun of men (the king), who
> is like a god (be gracious to me)![60]

In this derived sense the comparison of the king with the sun is common throughout the ancient Near East, but only in Egypt is there a precise theological concept implied in the view that the king is the image of the sun upon earth.

We found in Book I that the function of Pharaoh in the cosmic and social orders appeared in a new light whenever we shifted our standpoint and regarded him in relation, not only to the creative power of the sun, but to the procreative power of nature symbolized by cattle images or to the powers of life and resurrection immanent in the earth. In Mesopotamia no such variety of aspects existed, and the conception of kingship was correspondingly simpler than it was in Egypt. This was not due to a greater simplicity of the Mesopotamian pantheon—far from it. But all differences between the gods were insignificant in comparison with the one characteristic they had in common: they were absolute masters, and man was created to serve them. The king, therefore, stood in one and the same relationship with all the gods. He was their chosen servant. We have seen that, as such, he maintained the harmony between society and nature; and it could be said of him, as it was of Pharaoh, "the king is he who maintains the life of his country."[61] But, as we have pointed out above, his instrumentality in procuring "life" was less direct than Pharaoh's. The Mesopotamian king was not at one with the gods, inspired by their will, executing their counsels in his own divine decisions. He could maintain the natural harmony only by watching over the service of the gods and attuning the life of the community to such por-

tents as were vouchsafed him as revelations of the divine will. His faithful service was rewarded by abundance, so that he could call himself the
"husbandman" of his land.[62] Assurbanipal said:

> After Assur, Sin, Shamash, Adad, Bel, Nabu, Ishtar of Nineveh, queen of Kidmuri,
> Ishtar of Arbela, Urta, Nergal, and Nusku had caused me to take my seat, joyfully
> upon the throne of the father who begot me, Adad sent his rains, Ea opened his foun-
> tains, the grain grew five cubits tall in the stalk, the ear was five-sixths of a cubit long;
> heavy crops and a plenteous yield made the field(s) continuously luxuriant, the orchards
> yielded a rich harvest, the cattle successfully brought forth their young,—in my reign
> there was fulness to overflowing, in my years there was plenteous abundance.[63]

This hymn of prosperity is preceded by the statement that Assurbanipal
was king "by order of the great gods whose names (he) called upon, ex-
toling their glory."

The Mesopotamian kings interpreted the welfare of their country
as proof that they had not disappointed the gods who elected them.
Only in this very indirect manner can the king be said to have "produced
a plenteous abundance" or to have created "the well-being of mankind."[64] Hence we find him asking for benefactions of which Pharaoh
disposed in full sovereignty. Sargon of Assyria prayed:

> O Ea, lord of wisdom, creator of all things, to Sargon, king of the universe, king of
> Assyria, viceroy of Babylon, king of Sumer and Akkad, builder of thy abode—open
> thy fountains; let his springs send forth the waters of plenty and abundance; give water
> in abundance to his fields. Quick understanding and an open mind decree for him; pros-
> per his work; let him attain unto his desire.[65]

It is significant that Sargon follows up his prayer for abundant water—
the everlasting preoccupation of the Mesopotamian—with a prayer for
"quick understanding and an open mind"—attributes, not of the self-
sufficient, divine king, but of the servant of the gods. Entemena, Gudea,
and other rulers lay claim to the same attributes. If, then, as a great exception, we find a phrase which ascribes power over nature to the king,
we have two alternatives: we may view it either as a hyperbole or, if
the king in question acted as a divine bridegroom, as a reflection of his
temporary elevation for that act. In its baldness the following verse—
supposing that it renders the Sumerian adequately—certainly ascribes to
the king of Ur powers such as only gods possessed: "Shepherd Shulgi,
thou who hast water, shed water."[66] But the line is damaged, and it
stands in direct contrast to the prayer of Sargon of Assyria; it is this
prayer, not the verse, that voices the common Mesopotamian view. In
hymns addressed to kings of Isin—who, like Shulgi, were chosen by a
goddess as husbands—we have found phrases which go far in ascribing

to them an influence on the course of nature, but never so far as the one just quoted. In any case, imagery possesses associative and emotional value which may, by itself, account for some of these similes. We may, for instance, quote from other Shulgi hymns:

> Shulgi, the King, the gracious Lord, is a date-
> palm planted beside a watercourse.

> Thou art a cedar, rooted beside abundant waters,
> (giving) pleasant shade.[67]

We also read in Jeremiah: "Blessed is the man that trusteth in the Lord . . . . for he shall be as a tree planted by the waters" (17:7-8), and the same image appears in the First Psalm. Moreover, we can parallel the verses addressed to Shulgi with an Egyptian poem addressed to Thoth. Now this god had no power over, and no connection with, water; and he was never symbolized by a palm tree or any other plant. But an Egyptian scribe addressed the divine patron of his craft as follows:

> O thou great dom-palm, sixty cubits high!
> Thou who bearest fruits with kernels;
> There is water in the kernels!
> O thou who bringest water to distant places
> Come, save me who am silent.
> Thoth, thou sweet spring for a man thirsting
> in the desert,
> Closed for him who talks, open for him who
> is silent.[68]

The associative progression is clear: the palm, the fruits with water, the water that solaces the thirsting, the solace for the silent sufferer of injustice. The starting-point remains obscure until we remember how easily the oriental poet translates a mood of gratitude and worship into images evoking the perennial benefactions of moisture and shade. We cannot prove, of course, that the lines addressed to Shulgi are the result of the same poetic process; but we prefer that assumption to the literal acceptance of a statement which ascribes to him powers normally reserved for gods alone.[69]

After what we have said above,* it is clear that the king who "bears the taboo of the gods" possesses superhuman power of a sort. The ambiguity, the unsolved problem of how to regard a king who, though a mortal, yet stands apart from other men, is not peculiar to Mesopotamia. Superhuman power may appear to be the natural concomitant of

---

* Pp. 261 and 299-302.

an office which invests its incumbent with the dignity of a symbol. How serious was Samuel Pepys when he wrote in his diary on the nineteenth of July, 1662: "In the afternoon I went upon the river: it raining hard upon the water, I put ashore and sheltered myself while the king came by in his barge, going towards the Downes to meet the Queen. . . . . But methought it lessened my esteem of a king that he should not be able to command the rain." The Secretary of the Admiralty wrote without thought of readers; perhaps he noted, not quite frivolously, the complex reactions of his own mind upon the spectacle of social and natural powers at odds. It is precisely from such reactions that theologies and political theories take their rise.

CHAPTER 22

THE NEW YEAR'S FESTIVAL

A. THE SIGNIFICANCE OF THE CELEBRATIONS

IN MESOPOTAMIA the New Year's festival appears as the confluence of every current of religious thought, as the expression of every shade of religious feeling. If most of the ancient festivals served to establish that harmony with nature which was indispensable to a fruitful social life (chaps. 19 and 20), if the continual tending of that harmony was the main task of the king (chap. 18), if man's unqualified servitude to the gods found some compensation in his ability to participate in their periodic changes of fortune (chap. 20), then the New Year's festival must be considered the most complete expression of Mesopotamian religiosity.

Yet a discussion of the festival, especially as celebrated at Babylon in late times, may strike the reader as irrelevant to our theme. We catch only occasional glimpses of the king—praying, leading a procession, performing acts of sympathetic magic. In older sources, which give us a less complete account of the proceedings, the king looms larger. But we notice throughout a difference from the festivals described in Book I. There could never be any doubt that the Egyptian ceremonies should be considered in a study of kingship. Even in those which were not primarily concerned with the king's person—the raising of the Djed pillar, or, to some extent, the harvest festival of Min—Pharaoh appeared as the moving spirit who imparted to the rites such virtue as they possessed. The share of the Mesopotamian king in the celebrations was more modest. The main actors were the gods. Yet the participation of the king was essential; at Babylon, for instance, certain important rites were not performed unless the king was present in person. But he moved on a lower plane, representing the community in a concourse of forces which sprang from beyond the range of human will or understanding.

The New Year's festival could be held in the autumn as well as in the spring. We translate Sumerian *zagmuk*, which means "beginning of the year," and the Akkadian *akitu*, which has an uncertain meaning, "New

Year's festival," because these feasts are essentially what the modern term indicates—festive celebrations of a new beginning in the annual cycle. But, as we have indicated already, in the Near East nature offers two starting-points within the solar year—the one at the end of winter, the other at the end of the even more deadly summer. In Egypt, where the inundation made the difference between famine and prosperity, New Year's celebrations were co-ordinated with the Nile; they could take place in the early summer, when the river began to rise, and in autumn when the waters receded from the fertilized fields. But in Mesopotamia the rains were important; in Babylon the Akitu festival was celebrated in spring, in the month of Nisan; in Ur and Erech the festival took place in the fall as well as in the spring, in Tishri and in Nisan. The transcendent significance accorded to seasonal changes is emphasized by the elaborate commemoration of the creation which formed part of the New Year's festival. The recital of the gods' victory over chaos at the beginning of time cast a spell of accomplishment over the hazardous and all-important renewal of natural life in the present.[1] This association is preserved in

the link which Jewish tradition lays between the creation of the world and the New Year's festivities in Tishri and Nisan, both of them the beginning of a new harvest. . . . . . The treatise of Rosh Hashshana quotes from the story of creation the words: "Let the earth bring forth grass, the herb yielding seed etc." It is then asked: "In what month did this happen?" The answer is: "In Tishri, the time of rainfall." And it is not by accident that on the same page of the Talmud the same thing is said of Nisan, for then, also, come forth the new shoots. And again it is in accordance with this conception that Rabbi Eliezer says: "In Tishri was the world created," and Rabbi Josua: "In Nisan was the world created." Both months, Tishri and Nisan are indeed months of rain.[2]

The people expressed their concern with the seasons at yet another time; in May and June, when the stifling heat settled over the plain, suspending all agricultural pursuits and exhausting man and beast, the populace gave expression to its misery and anxiety by ritual wailings which seem not to have been part of any temple service, though many temple hymns and songs reflect their mood. The stagnancy of natural life and the dubiousness of its rebirth was given mythological expression. In each city the bereaved goddess gave herself up to laments in which the people joined:

> The wailing for him who is far away—(for) he may not
>   come!
> The wailing for my (own) son who is far away—(for) he
>   may not come!
> For my Damu, who is far away,
> For my *guda* priest, who is far away,

(The wailing) to the holy cedar where (his) mother bore
   (him),
The wailing (issuing) from Eanna[3] above and below—
   (for) he may not come!
The wailing of the lord's temple—(for) he may not come!
The wailing of the lord's city—(for) he may not come!
That wailing is truly a wailing for the bean-pods: the
   garden-beds(?) may not give birth to them.
That wailing is truly a wailing for the grain: the furrow
   may not give birth to it.
Is truly for the perished spouse, the perished child: the
   . . . . may not give birth. . . . .
That wailing is truly for the mighty river: it may not
   give birth to its waters.
That wailing is truly for the . . . . field: it may not give
   birth to the . . . . grain.
That wailing is truly for the marshes: they may not give
   birth to the fishes.
That wailing is truly for the canebrakes: the old reeds
   may not give birth to (new) reeds.
That wailing is truly for the forests: they may not give
   birth to the. . . . .
That wailing is truly for the desert: it may not give birth
   to the. . . . .
That wailing is truly for the vineyards(?): they may not
   give birth to the sweet vine(?).
That wailing is truly for the garden-beds: they may not
   give birth to the *lassu* plants and the cress(?).
That wailing is truly for the palace: it may not give birth
   to enduring life.[4]

Even if the state ceremonies ignored wailings for Tammuz in early
summer, the mood with which the New Year's festival opened agreed
with that of the popular celebrations. For the Mesopotamians attuned
themselves to the prevailing state of nature when preparing to celebrate
the great *rite de passage* which would lead nature and society to a new
period of fruitfulness. The god who was the hero was absent. In the
popular celebrations the agitated wailers complained that he had died.
The official rites avoided this hyperbole; they declared that he was held
captive in the mountain of the Netherworld. But this misfortune, this
temporary "death" of the god, was not enacted.[5] The supposition that
an accident of discovery has robbed us of its description is not merely
unfounded but actually falsifies the character of the New Year's celebrations. The Akitu festival (like many of the rituals which retained
something of their original spirit) was conceived as an interplay of nature and society. The god had become impotent in the realm of nature,
and there was no need for man to enact his discomfiture. In fact, for

those who believed in the efficacy and the "reality" of symbols and mimed actions, the thought of enacting such a disaster must have seemed perverse. We have seen in the manipulations with the Qeni stomacher what precautions were taken in Egypt when the funerary ritual or the Mystery Play of the Succession made it necessary to introduce the death of Osiris into a performance.* In Mesopotamia, when the New Year's festival began, the bare fields and the penned flocks made the god's fate all too evident.

In order to establish a harmony with nature at the opening of the great rite of the renewal of life, man attuned himself to this desolation. We know from the prophet Ezekiel (8:14), as well as from native sources such as hymns, that the demonstrations of grief reached a high pitch of emotion. This strength of feeling, the realization of utter bereavement, was of the essence of the celebration; without it the feast could have no virtue. For feelings thus aroused, and intensified by being shared, are potent beyond the experiences of daily life. Therefore, when the ritual reached its turning-point, when the mood changed from desolation to rapture at the "discovery "or the "liberation" of the god, the very violence of feeling created the conviction that something marvelous had been achieved, the god resuscitated, salvation found. The Tammuz hymns show their strongly emotional character by their composition. They are incantations, repeating again and again either the beginning of a verse or its end, while the remaining words are variants on a theme, not conveying information but forming, as it were, a series of exclamations by means of which the song moves forward. This type of song is still known in the Near East, and its effect—hypnotic or exciting—is very marked. The Tammuz hymns do not tell the story of the god's suffering but enumerate its consequences upon earth or the reaction of the goddess. Toward the end they often show an unheralded reversal of mood, implying the god's return or liberation, and then jubilation suddenly takes the place of lament. For instance, the hymn from which we have already quoted a few lines (p. 283) ends with these words:

> Where there was no more grass, they graze;
> Where there was no more water, they drink;
> Where there were no more stables, a stable is set up;
> Where there were no more hurdles for the flocks, they
>   are plaited.
> Where there was no more reed shelter, they rest in its
>   lee.[6]

* See above, pp. 133–37.

Another hymn, allegedly recited by the goddess, describes how the river no longer brought water, the grain failed to germinate, and the cattle suffered when the god was away. Then follows, with an implied "but":

> He has done, my brother, he has done marvels!
> . . . .
> The flood wets the quay; he has done marvels!
> . . . . in his course, he returns to his place!
> He is announced at the gate of the land; he returns to his place!
> He approaches the gate of the land; he returns to his place.[7]

The miracle of renewal which the hymns celebrate also dominated the ritual. It was expressed by various archetypal acts, each with its own peculiar associations, yet all conveying the message that life rises triumphantly from its bondage. This motif provides the overtones even for simple performances like the sacred procession or the boat journey of the god. These ceremonies served the practical requirements of the rites, but they also represented the achievement of a successful change in that the gods were carried over a significant route and returned safely to their shrines. To that extent even the rites "participated" in the victory over hostile and chaotic forces which took place in nature and set the tone for the festivities. The mock battles, the finding of the god, the sacred marriage possessed, besides their specific significance, a general relevance to the main theme of the celebrations. The festival could, therefore, without loss of meaning, comprise all or only a few of these performances. The motif of battle, for instance, is duplicated in Babylon and Assur: first, the god whose captivity was revealed by the desolate state of nature was liberated by his son; next he defeated the hostile powers which had compassed his impotence and were now arrayed against him. On the other hand, the battle is totally absent from Gudea's text, although the omission does not prove that it did not take place, since his description is incidental to the dedication of a new temple and may not describe the celebrations in full. It is also quite possible that the festival took a somewhat different course at different places and at different times. Yet its tenor was always the same, and its main features formed a consistent whole and not a syncretistic conglomerate as is often assumed.[8] The inner logic of the Babylon celebration appears in its calendar which we propose to reconstruct as follows:

Nisan 1– 4: Preparations and purifications.
Nisan   5: Day of Atonement for the king; the populace "descends" to the suffering god. Increasing commotion in the city during the "search" for Marduk.

Nisan   6: Several gods arrive by barge at Babylon, among them Nabu, the son and avenger of Marduk, who takes up residence in Ezida, his chapel in the Marduk temple.

Nisan   7: Nabu, assisted by other gods, liberates Marduk by force from the "mountain" of the Netherworld.

Nisan   8: First Determination of Destiny. The gods assemble and bestow their combined power on Marduk who thus obtains a "destiny beyond compare."

Nisan   9: Triumphal procession to the Bit Akitu under the king's guidance. This represents the participation of the community in the victory which is taking place in nature and renews Marduk's destruction of Chaos.

Nisan 10: Marduk celebrates his victory with the gods of the Upper- and Netherworlds at a banquet in the Bit Akitu and returns to Babylon for the consummation of his marriage that same night.

Nisan 11: The Second Determination of Destiny. The gods assemble to determine the destiny of society in the ensuing year.

Nisan 12: The gods return to their temples.

We shall presently see the evidence for this reconstruction. It gives a more complete picture of the festival than we obtain anywhere else. Gudea's text, as well as the texts from Isin,* centers on the sacred marriage. But the differences between these traditions are not confined to their scope alone. The Isin texts stress the extraordinary role of the king as divine bridegroom. The Babylonian texts, as well as those from Assur and Erech, show most clearly the communal aspects of the celebrations. Gudea does full justice to these aspects; but, in addition, with an astonishing directness, he depicts the gods as natural forces. All sources agree in presenting the king as instrumental in procuring for the community the boon of a harmonious integration with nature.

B. THE FESTIVAL AT BABYLON AND ASSUR

RITES OF ATONEMENT

During the first five days, the rites within Esagila (Marduk's temple in Babylon) reflected the somber mood of the holy season. Each morning before sunrise the high priest, after a ritual washing, entered the temple alone and prayed to Marduk and to other gods. Afterward the other priests commenced their daily tasks. Typical of the mood of those days is the "Kyrie Eleison" sung before dawn on the second day and called "The Secret of Esagila":

> Lord without peer in thy wrath;
> Lord, gracious king, lord of the lands;
> Who made salvation for the great gods;
> Lord, who throwest down the strong by his glance;
> Lord of kings, light of men, who dost apportion destinies!

* See above, pp. 296–98.

O Lord, Babylon is thy seat, Borsippa thy crown;
The wide heavens are thy body.
O Lord, with thine eyes thou piercest the Universe;

. . . .
With thine arms thou takest the strong;

. . . .
With thy glance thou grantest them grace,
Makest them see light so that they proclaim thy power.

Lord of the lands, light of the Igigi,[9] who pronouncest
    blessings;
Who would not proclaim thy, yea, thy power?
Would not speak of thy majesty, praise thy dominion?
Lord of the lands, who livest in Eudul, who takest the
    fallen by the hand:

Have pity upon thy city, Babylon;
Turn thy face towards Esagila, thy temple;
Give freedom to them that dwell in Babylon, thy wards.[10]

On the evening of the fourth day, the Epic of Creation in its entirety
was recited in the temple, for each New Year shared something essential with the first day when the world was created and the cycle of the
seasons started. A recital of that triumphant achievement increased the
power of all favorable forces to overcome the hazards which had led to
the incarceration of the god of natural life. This is said explicitly in a
commentary on the New Year's feast which refers to the Epic (as is
usual) by its opening words, *Enuma elish* ("When on high"). The commentary states: "Enuma Elish, which is recited and which they sing
before Bel (Marduk) in the month of Nisan; it is because he was
bound."[11] In later stages of the festival, Marduk's battle with Chaos was
actually represented in the ritual; but on the evening of the fourth day
the recital of the Epic was only an interlude in the general preparation
for the atonement.

The Day of Atonement was the fifth of Nisan, and the king appeared
as the main actor in its ritual. In the morning the high priest again offered prayers of appeasement, this time to Marduk as manifest in
heavenly bodies:

The white star (Jupiter) which brings omens to the world
    is my lord;
    My lord be at peace!
The star Gud (Mercury) which causes rain is my lord;
    My lord be at peace!
The star Gena (Saturn), star of law and order, is my lord;
    My lord be at peace![12]

Then the temple was purified. Offerings and incantations continued.
Craftsmen equipped the chapel of Nabu (Marduk's son who was to ar-

rive on the morrow) with an offering-table and a gold canopy from the treasury of his father. While these preparations were going on, the king entered Marduk's shrine. He was escorted into the chapel by priests who left him there alone. The high priest emerged from the Holy of Holies where the statue of Marduk stood. He took the king's scepter, ring, scimitar, and crown and put them upon a "seat" before the statue of the god. Again he approached the ruler, who was standing deprived of the signs of royalty, and struck his face; then he made him kneel down to pronounce a declaration of innocence:

> I have not sinned, O lord of the lands,
> I have not been negligent regarding thy divinity,
> I have not destroyed Babylon. . . . .

The high priest replied in Marduk's name:

> Do not fear . . . . what Marduk has spoken. . . . .
> He [will hear] thy prayer. He will increase thy dominion . . . .
> heighten thy royalty. . . . .[13]

The high priest then took up the insignia and gave them back to the king, striking his face once more in the hope of drawing tears—which were counted a favorable omen and proof of the god's good will.

What is the meaning of this painful scene? It is clear that by his penance and confession the king cleansed himself of the taint of past sins and thus became fit to officiate in the succeeding rites. It is also clear that his renewed investiture with the insignia of royalty signified a renewal of kingship. At the coronation, too, the insignia had been placed upon seats in front of the god* before the king had received them together with the power of royalty. But, in addition, the humiliation of the king brought him into harmony with the conditions under which the great ceremony of renewal started. Though communication with Marduk was still possible in Esagila, in the outer world the god had "disappeared." The people were disturbed; nature appeared lifeless. Now the king, too, was robbed of his splendor, of the protection of the royal insignia, and reduced to a minimum of power which corresponded to the low ebb in the life of nature, to the "captivity" of the god and also to the state of chaos preceding creation.[14] Five days of sacrifice, atonement, and purification culminated in the king's degradation and reinstatement. The preparatory rites were completed; the scene was set for the arrival of the avenging son, Nabu, who would defeat the powers of death.

* See above, p. 245.

THE LIBERATION OF THE CAPTIVE GOD

While the measured rites which we have described occupied the priests at the great shrine of Marduk, the populace entered upon a different kind of performance which ultimately filled the town with commotion. We learn about these popular activities from a commentary in which they are listed in no other order, it seems, than that in which they were remembered at the time of writing. This document explained the ritual acts of the people in terms of mythology, for the benefit of a priestly school.[15]

The commentary opens with a damaged statement about "Marduk who was confined in the mountain." This expression is the Mesopotamian formula for the "death" of a god[16] and characterizes the point from which the festival took its start. We have already pointed out that the word "death" in this context is misleading and have spoken of the "suffering god." Other Babylonian texts dealing with a similar situation elucidate the connotation of the term. A myth relates how Ishtar had rashly decided to descend into the Netherworld.[17] There she was held captive by the forces of death—as Marduk was—and was wounded and struck with illness. Although she was entirely powerless, her life was not taken. Similarly, it is said of Marduk at the New Year's festival:

> (Into the house of bondage) from the sun and light
> They caused him to descend.[18]

And again: "When the gods bound him he perished from among the living."[19] We have an excellent description of the condition in which the Mesopotamians imagined a god caught in the "mountain," the world of the dead, to be. In a Sumerian text a Tammuz-like god, Lillu, "the weak one," is bewailed by a goddess and answers her from his "house of bondage":

> Deliver me, O my sister, deliver me! . . . .
> O sister, do not reproach me: I am no longer a man enjoying sight.
> . . . . the place where I rest is the dust of the mountain.
> I rest amid evil ones.
> I sleep in anxiety, I bide among enemies.
> O my sister, I cannot lift myself from my resting place.[20]

The god's "death" is not death in our sense, nor in the sense of the ancient Egyptians. Like the human dead, he suffers thirst; and he is in the dust, bereaved of light and exposed to hostile demons. Yet he lives, although he is temporarily overcome by the miseries of the land of the dead.

The ritual of the New Year's festival effected the resuscitation of the god by bringing him the assistance of which he stood in need. Just as the sister "descended" to Lillu, as Ishtar "descended" to Tammuz, so the people "descended" to the imprisoned god. They could not go to him where he was, in the Netherworld; but they evoked a mood of despair by their wailings and laments. When the people had "descended" in this way, the ritual effected a reversal of mood, and the god was brought forth triumphantly to the world of the living.

The thought that death is vanquished at the beginning of the New Year survives in the religions which originated in the Near East, because it carries conviction through the harmony which it establishes between the visible and invisible worlds. A hymn of the Eastern Church contains the words "The Almighty awakens the bodies (at Epiphany) together with the spirits"; and it is said that Christ writes our names in the Book of Life. In the Talmud, too, the raising of the dead is linked with the rainstorms, which, in turn, are connected with the New Year. "Thou art the Almighty unto eternity, O Lord, who causeth the dead to arise; Thou art mighty to redeem, who causeth the wind to blow and the rain to fall."[21] Again: "Rabbi Joseph answers: 'That the mention of rain is connected with resurrection, it occurs because this is like unto that.' " And again: "God hath three keys, of rain, of birth, of rising of the dead." In Moslem theology the same relation is acknowledged: "Then rain will come down from heaven and mankind will germinate, just as the grains germinate."[22] It is clear, therefore, that the complexities of the New Year's festival in Babylonia are due not to syncretism, but to a chain of connections which were suggested to early man by the natural conditions under which he lived and which consequently retained their validity for his descendants. The seasons of spring and autumn bring rain and the victory over death. The god is liberated from the mountain.

In the ancient cities there must have been traditional settings for the activities of the populace during the holy season. The commentary on the Babylonian festival mentions a "house on the edge of the mountain wherein they question him."[23] This mountain is known in judicial texts as a place of ordeals,[24] and our quotation refers to Marduk, who was questioned upon entering the Netherworld as Ishtar had been at her descent to Hades. Moreover, someone is said to have "ridden" to the mountain[25] and someone else to have gone to a gate which counted as the gate of Marduk's grave.[26] A number of classical authors knew of a "Tomb of Bel" in Babylon, and they describe it in such a manner that there can be little doubt that they refer to the ziggurat or temple tower of Marduk, called Etemenanki (Fig. 49).[27] Somewhere in its inclosure there must have been a place which counted as the "gate" of Marduk's tomb, but we do not believe that a separate monument represented the tomb itself. Rather would it have been the ziggurat, the massive temple tower, which stood for the "mountain," as a symbol of the earth, the Netherworld, or the place of sunrise. We know that many of these towers bore names characterizing them as mountains,[28] but we do not know how these differing concepts were related with the temple and its ziggurat. On the seals the liberated god is shown emerging from the mountain (Fig. 50), and the destruction of his enemy by his son and a goddess takes place near it (Fig. 51). The classical references to the "Tomb of Bel" make it very probable that the ziggurat counted as Marduk's temporary tomb, even though no passages led into its solid brickwork. On this assumption we can understand Marduk's epithet: "whose grave in the place of wailing nobody approaches."[29]

In the meantime, the population of the town was subject to increasing disturbances. The commentary states: people "hasten in the street; they seek Marduk (saying), 'Where is he held captive?' "[30] We assume, then, that much of the commotion centered round the temple tower. We also read that a number of symbolical figures performed certain acts which often remain incomprehensible to us. But thanks to the Tammuz hymns we recognize the goddess who in her sorrow seeks the god, and, when she has found him, stays at his side. Her acts clearly represent, on the mythological level, the acts and feelings of the people:

The Enchanter who goes before Beltis of Babylon—that is the messenger; he weeps before her . . . . saying: "They have taken him unto the mountain." She goes down(?) saying: "O my brother, O my brother."[31]

(The gate of the . . . .)-s to which she goes—that is the gate of the grave; she goes there seeking him.[32]

Beltis of Babylon who binds an *atu* garment on her back and a *sipu* of wool on her face . . . . (that is because she with her hand wipes away) the blood of the body which was poured out.[33]

The goddess who tarries with him has descended (to seek) for his welfare.[34]

The commotion also spread outside the city and involved the Bit Akitu (the festival building), which, a few days later, was to be the goal of the victorious procession of the resurrected god. But in the early stages of the celebration the chariot of Marduk, without its master, was sent careening along the road to this building,[35] a sign of the confusion prevailing when the Lord of Babylon had disappeared. Perhaps even a mourning goddess was sent down the processional road, for the following line mentions "the dazed goddess who from the city goes, wailing. . . . ."[36]

The people, in the meantime, wanted to have a more active part in the tragedy which concerned them so vitally: "After Marduk went into the mountain the city fell into a tumult because of him, and they made fighting within it."[37] We do not know whether the fights of the populace to which the last quotation refers took place in the night of the fifth of Nisan or whether they accompanied Nabu's triumphal entry into Babylon and his battle with the enemies of Marduk on the sixth or seventh. But we know that on the sixth many barges with statues of the gods from Nippur and Erech, Cutha and Kish,[38] converged upon Babylon; and Nabu arrived from neighboring Borsippa that same day. The commentary is quite explicit: "That is he who comes (to seek) after the welfare of his father who is held captive."[39] Possibly there was one great procession from the quays to the temple under the direction of the king, who is mentioned as being present and pouring out a libation before the gods. In Assur the role of the king was more impressive than it was in Babylon. In the north, the protagonist of the gods was not Nabu but Ninurta; and the king himself represented the divine hero, standing in the royal chariot in the procession[40] or being carried out of the Assur temple with a golden tiara as "Ninurta who has avenged his father."

Some incidents which took place while the procession was moving from the landing place to the temple are mentioned in the commentary on the feast at Babylon.[41] It seems unlikely that the actual liberation of Marduk could have been enacted on the same day that the gods arrived. Moreover, we have the seventh of Nisan to account for. Unfortunately, we do not know at all how the liberation was represented. The commentary refers to it as follows: "The 'door with aperture' as they call it; that means that the gods confined him; he entered into the 'house' and before him one locked the door. They bored holes into the door and there they waged battle."[42]

On cylinder seals of the middle of the third millennium the liberation of the god from a mountain is shown (Figs. 50 and 51). The liberator is a god with a bow—Ninurta—and a goddess is in attendance. These seal designs, however, show not the rite but the myth; hence they depict a real mountain. Sometimes the goddess "tarrying" (kneeling) with the captive god is shown inside, while another god destroys the vegetation above ground.[43] These seals prove the antiquity, if not of the usages, then of the myths which are reflected in the ritual but are

not included in the Epic of Creation.[44] But such illustrations of myth do
not teach us what form the corresponding acts in the ritual assumed.

THE FIRST DETERMINATION OF DESTINY

After Marduk's liberation, the statues of the gods were brought together in the Chamber of Destinies, to "determine destiny." This ceremony took place on the eighth of Nisan and again on the eleventh.[45] The
two gatherings differed in significance, but both took place in part of the
temple called Ubshu-ukkinna, a name designating the place of assembly
of the gods in the Epic of Creation and elsewhere. This assembly was
traditionally thought to take place in Nippur.* The gathering of the
gods on the eighth of Nisan corresponds, therefore, with the first "Determination of Destiny" in the Epic of Creation in which Marduk was
elected king of the gods and given absolute power. The rites of the New
Year's festival lacked the dramatic vivacity of the dialogues in the Epic
but possessed an elaborate formalism. A text from Erech[46] describes
how the statues of the gods were arranged in order of precedence for the
assembly. The king acted as chief chamberlain or master of ceremonies.
Carrying a shining wand or staff, he summoned each god in succession
to leave his chapel and, "taking his hand," guided the deity to the appropriate position in the great hall where the gods faced their leader.

The corresponding scene in the Epic gives the meaning of this ceremony.

> They made a princely dais for him.
> And he sat down, facing his fathers, as a councilor.
> "Thou art of consequence among the elder gods.
> Thy rank is unsurpassed and thy command is Anu('s).[47]
> Marduk, thou art of consequence among the elder gods;
> Thy rank is unequaled and thy command is Anu('s).
> From this day onward shall thy orders not be altered;
> To elevate and to abase—this be within thy power.
> What thou hast spoken shall come true, thy word shall
>   not prove vain.
> Among the gods none shall encroach upon thy rights!"[48]

With these words the gods put all the power of which they dispose in
the hands of Marduk. In the manner of the ancients we must conceive
this transfer of power as concretely affecting the god's nature, and,
since one's nature is one's destiny, Marduk's destiny is now declared
to be unequaled; he actually commands the consolidated power of all
the gods. The Epic goes on to describe how, immediately after the

* See above, pp. 217 and 220.

speech we have quoted, an experiment was made with a robe to test whether power had indeed been successfully transferred to Marduk:

> They placed a garment in their midst
> And said to Marduk, their firstborn:
> "O Lord, thy lot is truly highest among gods.
> Command annihilation and existence, and may both come
> true.
> May thy spoken word destroy the garment,
> Then speak again and may it be intact."
> He spoke—and at his word the garment was destroyed.
> He spoke again, the garment reappeared.
> The gods, his fathers, seeing (the power of) his word,
> Rejoiced, paid homage: "Marduk is king."[49]

This, then, was the meaning of the assembly of the gods on the eighth of Nisan: they were to confer upon Marduk their combined power so that the liberated god, thus strengthened, was ready to lead the battle against the powers of chaos and of death.

We know that a hush of reverence dominated the city while the gods assembled, in order that evil influences caused by thoughtless acts or words could be avoided. A similar mood prevailed in Lagash when Gudea molded the first brick of his new temple and later again when the gods "determined destiny." In connection with the New Year's festival of late times there is an entry for the eighth of Nisan in a calendar of lucky and unlucky days: "Show no enmity at all."[50]

THE PROCESSION TO BIT AKITU

When the Late Assyrian kings recorded their annual visits to Babylon, they gave as the purpose of their coming participation in the ceremony which we are now to describe. Sargon, for instance, wrote: "Into Babylon, the city of the lord of the gods, joyfully I entered, in gladness of heart, and with a radiant countenance. I grasped the hand(s) of the great lord Marduk, and made the pilgrimage to the 'House of the New Year's Feast'" (Bit Akitu).[51] The gods, too, came to Babylon "to take the hands of Bel"[52]—"to lead him in the procession to Bit Akitu."[53] The king was privileged to give the signal for departure:

> Come, go forth, Lord, the king awaits thee!
> Come, go forth, Our Lady, the king awaits thee!
> The Lord of Babylon goes forth, the lands kneel
> before him.
> Sarpanitum goes forth, aromatic herbs burn with fragrance.
> By the side of Ishtar of Babylon, while her servants
> play the flute,
> Goes all Babylon exultant![54]

Another text typifies the procession in a single flash: "All the gods who go with Marduk to the House of Prayer—it looks like a king with the assembled host!"[55] The military simile is appropriate. For the procession —which went northward through Babylon, left by the Ishtar Gate, and continued in boats across the Euphrates to the Bit Akitu—represented the victorious army of the gods who, on the eve of Creation, went out against Tiamat and destroyed her forces. It was this very scene that Sennacherib had depicted upon the copper doors which he made for the Bit Akitu of Assur; but his own figure appeared there "standing in Assur's chariot." (We must remember that, in the north, Assur took the place of Marduk.)

Sennacherib then describes the gate designs as follows:

A figure of Assur, going to battle against Tiamat, carrying the bow, on his chariot holding the "weapon of the storm" (abubu), and Amurru, who goes with him as charioteer, according to the command revealed by Shamash and Adad in omens at the sacrifice, I engraved upon that gate, (besides) the gods who march in front and the gods who march behind him, those who ride in chariots and those who go on foot. . . . (and) Tiamat and the creatures (that were) in her.[56]

If the divine host and the monsters of Chaos appeared on the doors of the Bit Akitu, there must have been a relation between the myth of the battle and the rites connected with this building. A marginal remark on the tablet summing up what the gates showed reads as follows:

The victorious prince, standing in Assur's chariot;
Tiamat and the creatures of her inside.

"The victorious prince" can hardly refer to anyone but Sennacherib; and the suggestion that the king of Assyria personified Assur in the procession is confirmed by the concluding sentences of the text in which the depicted gods are listed by name. At the head of the list we read: "Image of Assur, going to do battle with Tiamat, image of Sennacherib, King of Assyria."

In Babylon the king seems not to have represented Marduk but to have played the more modest part of master of ceremonies. But what happened at the Bit Akitu? And are we entitled, on the strength of Sennacherib's inscription and the close relation between the Epic of Creation and the New Year's festival, to assume that the battle against Tiamat was mimed? There is no evidence to show that it was; and, in fact, the little evidence we have is against the assumption, at least in Babylon. It may well be that at this point, again, the ritual observances and the actuality of nature were felt to interlock. Just as the "death" or "captivity" of the god was a datum in actuality from which the celebrations started, so the victory of the god may have been felt to realize itself in nature, while man, with the pomp and exultation of the great procession, participated in the effort. The departure of all the gods from the city and their return after one or two days supplied the break and the new beginning in the city's life which the season demanded if a harmony between society and nature were to be established. It is significant that the king was considered indispensable to the realization of that harmony. When, in Assyrian times, the king could not come to Babylon, the New Year's festival was celebrated on a reduced scale within the Marduk temple, and the procession to the Bit Akitu did not take place. A chronicle states: "(that year) the king did not come to Babylon. Nabu did not come to Babylon. Marduk did not go forth; the Akitu festival did not take place; sacrifices were (only) made in Esagila and Ezida."[57]

This procession was considered so important that every detail of its start and completion was watched carefully and possessed the significance of an omen for the year which was beginning. It seems, therefore, that the procession itself, and not a mock battle, represented Marduk's victory in the cult. This view is supported by a commentary which enumerates various acts of what is usually called "sympathetic magic" —acts which are evidently parallel to phases of the victory as related in the Epic. For instance: "The king smashing a hariu pot with a weapon: that is Marduk who subjected Tiamat."[58] It is true that the word "Tiamat" in this much-damaged text is not certain, but enough is preserved to show that this type of act was performed by the king and others. It is said, for instance, that a fire was kindled before the goddess, and a sheep thrown upon it: "The sheep which is put on the brazier, which the flames devour: that is Kingu who is burned in fire!"[59] It is clear that we cannot expect a mock battle if the various phases of Marduk's victory over Tiamat and her host are represented by a series of symbolical acts apparently executed by the king and the priests, possibly at the Bit Akitu.

Two conclusions must be drawn, however. In the first place, Marduk's victory over Chaos was celebrated—and that, for the mythopoeic mind, means "realized once more"—at the New Year's festival. This follows, not only from the connection between creation and the New Year which we have discussed,* but from an explicit epithet of Marduk:

* See above pp. 150 and 313–18.

"The Lord who sits in the midst of Tiamat at the Akitu festival." This is a clear reference to the Epic of Creation, where it is said that Marduk splits Tiamat's body to make heaven and earth out of the two halves:

> The lord rested, to look at her dead body, (to see)
> How he might divide the colossus (and) create wondrous
>   things (therewith).
> He split her open like a mussel(?) into two parts.[60]

But this simile is not the only one used. In the Assyrian ritual for the New Year we read: "The pigeon which is thrown is Tiamat. It is thrown and cut into two halves."[61] And on an Akkadian seal cylinder Marduk actually stands in Tiamat, who is represented by two wings rising on either side of him (Fig. 52).

In the second place, it is certain that the Bit Akitu was the place where the Creator's victory over Tiamat was celebrated. Only this assumption makes the figures on the bronze doors of Sennacherib appear relevant. Moreover, we have an inscription of Nebuchadnezzar in which he calls the building "the temple of the sacrifices of the exalted New Year's festival of the Enlil of the gods, Marduk; the dwelling of the joy and exultation of the gods of the Upper- and Netherworlds."[62] Now these gods, the Igigi and the Anunnaki, are mentioned in the Epic of Creation as rejoicing in Marduk's victory. It is also certain that a great banquet was held in the Bit Akitu. This is most easily explained as a celebration of the victory. It has even been suggested that the word *akitu* refers to this banquet;[63] and on Early Dynastic reliefs (like Fig. 46) which we believe to refer to this festival[64] the banquet is the main theme.

If the victory over Tiamat was achieved on the ninth of Nisan (on the eighth the gods met in the Chamber of Destinies), the great banquet may have fallen on the tenth. This is also suggested by a stela of Nabonidus: "In the month of Nisan, on the tenth day, when the king of the gods, Marduk, and the gods of the Upper- and Netherworlds take up their abode in the House of Prayer (Bit Akribi), the House of the New Year's festival (Bit Akitu) of the Lord of Justice."[65]

We should repeat here that we are best informed about the festival at Babylon but that it was celebrated in all or most of the cities in the land;[66] and we know of a number where a Bit Akitu existed. This building was always situated a little outside the city. That of Babylon was mentioned about 1700 B.C., when King Ammizaduga sent out summonses to attend a sheep-shearing to be held there.[67] That of Erech is known in late texts; that of Assur has actually been excavated.[68] It was built about two hundred meters outside the city walls, and its outstanding characteristic was the richness of the gardens which surrounded it. Even the courtyard was filled with regularly spaced trees and shrubs. On either side there were porticoes, an unusual feature in Mesopotamian temples. The enormous "cella," twenty-five by one hundred feet, extends over the whole width at the back and may well have served as a banqueting hall. All around the building were elaborate gardens, carefully watered. They remind us of the fact that the god was not merely a conqueror of Chaos but also the personification of the life of nature. It is this aspect of the complex figure of Marduk or Assur that is especially stressed by the following phase of the celebrations.

THE SACRED MARRIAGE

The union of a god and goddess was in the last instance neither an act of the cult nor a symbol, but an event in nature the immediate consequence of which was the restoration of the fertility of fields, flocks, and men, after the stagnancy of winter or summer. The feeling of the objective reality of this restoration was probably never lost. It is vividly present in a text of Gudea: Ningirsu entered his temple "like a rumbling storm," "like a bird of prey descrying its victim."[69] The goddess "approached his black side," "entered between his black arms," the blackness alluding to the dark rain clouds in which Ningirsu was manifest.[70]

The purely ritual aspect of the sacred marriage was discussed when we described the occasions on which a king acted the part of the divine bridegroom. Its more usual form, without the participation of the king, is well described in a letter to an Assyrian king in which the details of the wedding of Nabu are listed:

> To the king my lord, your servant Nergal-sharrani: Greetings to the king my lord. May Nabu and Marduk bless the king my lord.
> Tomorrow, (that is) on the fourth (of Iyyar) toward evening, Nabu and Tashmetum will enter the bedchamber. On the fifth, they shall be given of the king's food to eat, the (temple) overseer being present. A lion's head (and) a torch(?) shall be brought to the palace. From the fifth to the tenth (both) gods (will stay) in the bed chamber, the (temple) overseer staying with them. On the eleventh Nabu will go out, he will exercise his feet; he will go to the (hunting) park; he will kill wild oxen; then he will go up and dwell in his habitation. He will bless(?) the king and . . . . I have written to the king my lord (in order that) the king my lord may know (about it).[71]

Of Marduk, too, it is said that "he hastened to the wedding."[72]

It is likely that the sacred marriage took place in Esagila and not in the Bit Akitu.[73] We know that Nabu, Ningirsu, and Inanna of Isin celebrated their weddings in the temple; and it is, on the face of it, likely that a ceremony having the significance which we ascribed to the sacred marriage should take place in the midst of the community.[74] In any case, we know from a late text that there was a "room of the bed" in Esagila.[75] And Herodotus describes the temple on top of the tower of Babel as follows (the towers in this account are really the seven tiers of the temple tower [see Fig. 49]):

> In the last tower there is a great shrine; and in it a great and well-covered couch is laid, and a golden table set hard by. But no image has been set up in the shrine, nor does any human creature lie therein for the night, except one native woman, chosen from all women by the god, as say the Chaldaeans who are priests of this god.
> These same Chaldaeans say (but I do not believe them) that the god himself is wont to visit the shrine and rest upon the couch.[76]

It is quite possible that the chamber for the marriage of the god and goddess was not the same as that which Herodotus saw on the top tier of the temple tower. But the matter is of no great importance for us here. The sacred wedding with the goddess took place in a room or building called *gigunu*. Ninlil, as the spouse of Enlil, is called "(she) who embellishes the *gigunu*."[77] And it is said of Ishtar and Anu: "They abode together in the *gigunu*, the chapel that is the seat of joy."[78] Whether or not this *gigunu* was the bedchamber which Herodotus described, it is certain that it formed part of the temple complex; and the sacred marriage, therefore, took place, not at the Bit Akitu, but after the god's return from there. The most likely date for the sacred marriage would then be the evening of the tenth, after the return from the banquet at the Bit Akitu.[79]

Whatever acts may have been performed in the cult, the sacred marriage signified the end of the period during which life in nature had been suspended. Now god and goddess united; the male forces, awakened, fertilized the Great Mother from whom all life came forth.

THE SECOND DETERMINATION OF DESTINY

It is usual for early man to counteract the hazards of change by appropriate *rites de passage*. But the mood of the Babylonians at the beginning of the year was peculiar. They not only felt uncertainty as regards the future but feared that their own inadequacy and guilt might have incurred divine wrath. Perhaps society was precluded from enjoying the fruits of the union of god and goddess. Nature revived, but man remained to be judged. On the twelfth of Nisan the gods assembled once more in the Chamber of Destinies.

Judaism, in a similar way, combines judgment with the beginning of the year. The Talmud states that "destinies" are "determined" at the beginning of the New Year:

The books are opened at New Year: that of the utterly godless, that of the truly righteous and that of the intermediate ones. The truly righteous are written down and immediately stamped unto life: the utterly godless are written down and immediately stamped unto death: the intermediate ones are in an intermediate state from New Year (1 Tishri) till the day of atonement (10 Tishri).[80]

We have described the rites of atonement with which the Babylonian New Year's festival opened. But if it could be hoped that failures, errors, and defilement could be robbed of their evil consequences, it yet remained for the gods to decide whether the renewal of society, coinciding with nature's rejuvenation, would be blessed.

The anxiety which finds expression in this as in so many other details of the New Year's festival is characteristic for the Mesopotamians. The Egyptians were subject to doubt and fear in relation to their own personal destinies, especially as regards their survival after death; but they had the most complete confidence in the fate of their society. Their static world did not offer the possibility of a truly new start, and they knew neither a day of atonement nor a determination of destiny. Yet the combination of these two concepts with the New Year is of the greatest significance:

In cosmology this idea means: victory over chaos with its demoniac powers and establishment of cosmic order; in theology: accomplishment of the judgment of mankind. Each new period begins thus, with the establishment of order, with the settlement of destinies, with judgment. And every New Year is a day of judgment.[81]

In the Epic the creation of mankind was decided upon in this second meeting, which took place after Marduk's victory when he had formed the universe but not its human inhabitants. Marduk said:

Arteries I will know and bring bones into being.
I will create *lullu*, "man" be his name;
I will form *lullu*, man.
Let him be burdened with the toil of the gods,
    that they may freely breathe [VI, 5–8].

The crafty Ea carried out the design, significantly forming man from the blood of Kingu, the rebellious leader of the forces of Chaos.

They bound him (Kingu), held him before Ea,
Condemned him, severed his arteries.
And from his blood they formed mankind.
Ea then imposed toil on man and set the gods free.[82]

Both quotations explain the creation of man as a result of the wish of the gods that some being should serve them. This, then, was man's destiny, and happiness was possible only if he lived out his destiny. We may assume that the gods, when they met on the twelfth of Nisan, determined the fate of society during the ensuing year with reference to the service which it had rendered the gods in the past;[83] even so, the gods were not bound by any obligation toward their creatures, and we have seen how the fall of Ur was decreed without taking the merits of its population into account.*

The determination of destiny was the last act of the gods at the New Year's festival. On the next day, the twelfth of Nisan, the visiting deities returned to their cities; and the business of plowing and sowing and trading for the new crop was taken in hand.

* See above, pp. 242–43.

EPILOGUE

EPILOGUE

THE HEBREWS

THE ancient Near East knew a third kind of king. In addition to the god incarnate who was Pharaoh and the chosen servant of the gods who ruled Mesopotamia, we find a hereditary leader whose authority derived from descent and was originally coextensive with kinship. This is a more primitive kind of monarchy, a product rather of nature than of man, based on the facts of consanguinity, not on any conception of man's place in the universe. Yet it was the equal of the Egyptian and Mesopotamian institutions in that it formed an integral part of the civilizations in which it occurred. For the type of rulership we are now to discuss is found among people who acknowledged kinship above every other bond of loyalty and whose coherence derived from a shared nomadic past rather than from what they had achieved as a settled community. It is found, significantly, in the peripheral regions of the ancient Near East where autochthonous civilization was feeble. Palestine and Syria, Anatolia and Persia, were overrun by foreign peoples on many occasions, and, furthermore, the newcomers succeeded in taking charge. In this respect the contrast between the peripheral regions and the centers of the ancient Near East is striking. Foreigners could rise to power in Egypt, but on condition that they were completely assimilated. When large groups of immigrants—Amorites, Kassites, Aramaeans—were absorbed by Mesopotamia, they insinuated themselves in the traditional fabric of Mesopotamian culture which henceforth determined their behavior. But the peripheral regions lacked cultural individuality, and once immigrants had asserted their power their mastery was complete. The Philistines and Hebrews put their stamp on Palestine; Hittites, Mitanni, Medes, and Persians on other peripheral regions.

The position of these new arrivals was anomalous. They brought with them hereditary tribal institutions, such as rulership based on descent. But settling in civilized lands, they faced problems for which their nomadic existence had not prepared them. When Cyrus conquered

Babylon, for example, he assumed a cultural heritage which could not be accommodated within the traditional forms of Persian life. The Persian king was *primus inter pares*,[1] the head of the principal of seven dominant clans, and ruled the nation in continual consultation with the leading clansmen. But after the conquest of Babylon, Cyrus found himself the center of an immense apparatus which set the Mesopotamian ruler apart and insured his proper functioning as an intermediary between society and the divine powers. Although our knowledge of the Achaemenian kingship is very slight, Greek sources show that its original simplicity was lost when it became burdened with the dignity of "King of the Lands." In the ruins of Pasargadae, Persepolis, and Susa we have material proof that kingship under Cyrus the Great and Darius I was given a setting for which there were no Persian precedents and in which the Mesopotamian ingredients are clearly recognizable. If the pillared halls of the Achaemenian palaces had prototypes in the vast tents of nomadic chieftains, the walled artificial terrace, the monstrous guardians at the gates, the revetments of sculptured stone slabs, and the panels of glazed bricks derived from Babylon, Assur, and Nineveh, even though they were executed by craftsmen from all over the empire and transfused with a spirit demonstrably Persian.[2]

The same process, on a smaller scale, took place in Anatolia when the Indo-European-speaking Hittites founded their empire. The artistic antecedents of the buildings at Boghazkeuy are as yet obscure, but the royal titulary betrays its derivative nature. Royal names were written under the winged sun disk as in Egypt. The Hittite king called himself "the Great King, beloved of the god So-and-So" as was done in Mesopotamia. He also applied to himself the circumlocution, "My Sun," no doubt in the belief that this was Egyptian usage, since the Asiatic vassals addressed Pharaoh as their sun. Yet the power of the Hittite king was closely circumscribed by a council of nobles which could even sit in judgment over him under certain circumstances. Similar conditions can be observed in Mitanni and in the smaller Syrian states; a native chieftainship was given additional splendor by titles, symbols, and paraphernalia which were derived from Egypt and Mesopotamia and which were never wholly meaningful outside their country of origin.

Our knowledge of Hittite, Syrian, and Persian kingship is so incomplete that we cannot pass beyond generalities. But we know more about the Hebrew monarchy. This was also based upon descent but possessed a peculiar character of its own which makes it an effective foil for the material we have discussed in this book; for the Hebrews, though in the Near East, were only partly of it. Much is made nowadays of Canaanite and other Near Eastern elements in Hebrew culture, and a phenomenon like Solomon's kingship conforms indeed to the type of glorified native chieftainship which we have characterized in the preceding paragraph. But it should be plain that the borrowed features in Hebrew culture, and those which have foreign analogies, are least significant. In the case of kingship they are externalities, the less important since they did not affect the basic oddness of the Hebrew institution. If kingship counted in Egypt as a function of the gods, and in Mesopotamia as a divinely ordained political order, the Hebrews knew that they had introduced it on their own initiative, in imitation of others and under the strain of an emergency. When Ammonite oppression was added to the Philistine menace, the people said: "Nay; but we will have a king over us; that we also may be like all the nations; and that our king may judge us, and go out before us, and fight our battles" (I Sam. 8:19–20).

If the Hebrews, like the Mesopotamians, remembered a kingless period, they never thought that "kingship descended from heaven." Hence the Hebrew king did not become a necessary bond between the people and the divine powers. On the contrary, it was in the kingless period that the people had been singled out by Yahweh and that they had been bound, as a whole, by the Covenant of Sinai. It was said in the Law: "Ye are the children of the Lord your God: . . . . and the Lord hath chosen thee to be a peculiar people unto himself, above all the nations that are upon earth" (Deut. 14:1–2). Moses said to Pharaoh: "Thus saith the Lord, Israel is my son, even my firstborn: and I say unto thee, Let my son go, that he may serve me" (Exod. 4:22–23). For the service of God was part of the Covenant, which the people must keep even though it imposes a moral obligation which man's inadequacy makes forever incapable of fulfilment: "Now therefore, if you will obey my voice indeed, and keep my covenant, then ye shall be a peculiar treasure unto me above all people: for all earth is mine: And ye shall be unto me a kingdom of priests and an holy nation" (Exod. 19:5–6).

The conviction of the Hebrews that they were a chosen people is the one permanent, as it is the most significant, feature in their history. The tenacity of the Hebrew struggle for existence in the sordid turmoil of the Levant was rooted in the consciousness of their election. This animated the leaders of the people, whether they were kings like David and Hezekiah, or prophets opposing kings in whom belief in the unique destiny of Israel had been compromised. But this intimate relationship between the Hebrew people and their god ignored the existence of an earthly ruler altogether. Hebrew tradition, vigorously defended by the great prophets and the post-Exilic leaders, recognized as the formative phase of Hebrew culture the sojourn in the desert when Moses, the man of God, led the people and gave them the Law. Kingship never achieved a standing equal to that of institutions which were claimed—rightly or wrongly—to have originated during the Exodus and the desert wandering.

The antecedents of Saul's kingship were known. The settlement in Canaan left the tribal divisions intact, and the Book of Judges shows the varying ranges of power to which individual chieftains might aspire. Abimelech made himself king after he "slew his brethren, the sons of Jerubbaal, being threescore and ten persons" (Judg. 9:5). His power was founded on force, was challenged by Jotham, and was in turn destroyed by force: "And when the men of Israel saw that Abimelech was dead, they departed every man unto his place" (Judg. 9:55).

The tribesmen recognized the bond of blood alone, and it was exceedingly difficult to envisage a loyalty surpassing the scope of kinship. Nevertheless, when the separate tribes were threatened with extinction or enslavement, Saul was made king over all. Samuel anointed Saul, thereby expressing Yahweh's approval of the initiative of the people who had in any case sought advice from the seer. But royalty received little sanctity from this involvement. It is true that David shrank from buying personal immunity at the price of laying hands "upon the Lord's anointed" (I Sam. 24:10); but such scruples are perhaps more revealing for David's character than for the esteem in which kingship was held among the Hebrews. And the tragic sequel of Saul's history proves how little Yahweh's initial approval protected office and officeholder. In fact, once kingship had been established, it conformed to the tribal laws which treat relatives as one, for better or for worse. Saul's "house" was exterminated by David (II Sam., chap. 21) on Yahweh's orders. David's "house" was promised lasting dominion by Yahweh through the mouth of the prophet Nathan (see below). It is very significant that in actual fact the Davidian dynasty was never dethroned in Judah. But David belonged to Judah; and when Solomon died and his son Rehoboam was ill advised and refused to alleviate the burdens imposed by Solomon's splendor, ten of the tribes refused to acknowledge him: "So when all Israel saw that the king hearkened not unto them, the people answered the king, saying, What portion have we in David? neither have we an heritance in the son of Jesse: to your tents O Israel: now see to thine own house, David" (I Kings 12:16). No voice was raised to decry the rejection of David's grandson as an impious act. On the contrary, even David, Yahweh's favorite, had been confirmed in his rulership by the elders of all the tribes who, in accepting him, began by acknowledging their consanguinity:

Then came all the tribes of Israel to David unto Hebron, and spake, saying, Behold we are thy bone and thy flesh. . . . . So all the elders of Israel came to the king to Hebron; and King David made a league with them in Hebron before the Lord: and they anointed David king of Israel [II Sam. 5:1, 3].

In the light of Egyptian, and even Mesopotamian, kingship, that of the Hebrews lacks sanctity. The relation between the Hebrew monarch and his people was as nearly secular as is possible in a society wherein religion is a living force. The unparalleled feature in this situation is the independence, the almost complete separation, of the bonds which existed between Yahweh and the Hebrew people, on the one hand, and between Yahweh and the House of David, on the other. Yahweh's covenant with the people antedated kingship. His covenant with David concerned the king and his descendants, but not the people. Through Nathan, Yahweh promised David:

I will set up thy seed after thee. . . . . I will be his father, and he shall be my son. If he commits iniquity, I will chasten him with the rod of men, and with the stripes of the children of men: But my mercy shall not depart from him, as I took it from Saul, whom I put away before thee. And thine house and thy kingdom shall be established for ever before thee: thy throne shall be established for ever [II Sam. 7:12–16].

Only in later times, when this promise was made the foundation of Messianic expectations, did the people claim a share in it. As it was made, it was as simple and direct a pledge to David as the earlier divine promises had been to the Patriarchs (e.g., Gen. 15:18–21). It committed Yahweh solely to maintain the greatness of the House of David. It can be argued that this implied the greatness of the Hebrew people, or at least of Judah; but the conclusion is not inevitable. Nowhere else in the Near East do we find this dissociation of a people from its leader in relation to the divine; with the Hebrews we find parallelism while everywhere else we find coincidence. In the meager information about Hebrew ritual it has been attempted to find indications that the king fulfilled a function not unlike that of contemporary rulers. But even if we take an exceptional and apparently simple phrase, "[Solomon] sat on the throne of the Lord as king, instead of David, his father" (I Chron. 29:23), we need only compare this with the corresponding phrases "throne of Horus" or "throne of Atum"* to realize that the Hebrew

* See above, p. 149.

expression can only mean "throne favored by the Lord," or something similar. The phrase confirms what the account of Saul's elevation and David's scruples showed in the first place—namely, that there is interplay between the king's person and sanctity, as there was a connection between the king's fate and the national destiny. But these relations were not the nerve center of the monarchy, as they were in Egypt and Mesopotamia, but rather cross-currents due to the religious orientation of Hebrew society; and their secondary nature stands out most clearly when we consider the functions of the Hebrew king.

The Hebrew king normally functioned in the profane sphere, not in the sacred sphere. He was the arbiter in disputes and the leader in war. He was emphatically not the leader in the cult. The king created the conditions which made a given form of worship possible: David's power allowed him to bring the Ark to Jerusalem; Solomon's riches enabled him to build the temple; Jeroboam, Ahab, Manasseh, and others had idols made and arranged for "groves" and "high places" for the cult of the gods of fertility. But the king played little part in the cult. He did not, as a rule, sacrifice; that was the task of the priests. He did not interpret the divine will; that, again, was the task of the priests, who cast lots for an oracle. Moreover, the divine intentions were sometimes made known in a more dramatic way when prophets—men possessed—cried, "Thus saith the Lord." These prophets were often in open conflict with the king precisely because the secular character of the king entitled them to censor him.

The predominant accusation of the prophets against the kings was faithlessness to Yahweh, a "seduction" of his chosen people (e.g., II Kings 21:9–11) so that they followed the ways of the gentiles. Said the prophet Jehu in the name of Yahweh to Baasha, king of Israel: "Forasmuch as I exalted thee out of the dust, and made thee prince over my people Israel; and thou hast walked in the way of Jeroboam, and hast made my people Israel to sin, to provoke me to anger with their sins" (I Kings 16:2). Such accusations recur with monotonous regularity throughout the Books of Kings. Most rulers "did evil in the sight of the Lord"; and we cannot discuss Hebrew kingship without considering this evil which seems to have attached to it. If the kings seduced the people, we must admit, in the light of the Egyptian and Mesopotamian evidence, that they offered the people something eminently desirable. The keeping of Yahweh's covenant meant relinquishing a great deal. It meant, in a word, sacrificing the greatest good ancient Near Eastern religion could bestow—the harmonious integration of man's life with the life of nature.

The biblical accounts stress the orgiastic joys of the Canaanite cult of natural powers; we must remember that this cult also offered the serene awareness of being at one with the universe. In this experience ancient oriental religion rewarded its devotees with the peace of fulfilment. But the boon was available only for those who believed that the divine was immanent in nature, and Hebrew religion rejected precisely this doctrine. The absolute transcendence of God is the foundation of Hebrew religious thought. God is absolute, unqualified, ineffable, transcending every phenomenon, the one and only cause of all existence. God, moreover, is holy, which means that all values are ultimately his. Consequently, every concrete phenomenon is devaluated. We have discussed elsewhere this austere transcendentalism of Hebrew thought, which denied the greatest values and the most cherished potentialities of contemporary creeds, and have offered an explanation of its origin.[3] Here we must point out that it bereft kingship of a function which it exercised all through the Near East, where its principal task lay in the maintenance of the harmony with the gods in nature. And so we observe—now for the third time—the inner logic and consistency of ancient Near Eastern thought. We have described the peculiar nature of Hebrew kingship, starting from its relation to the people and their past; it would have appeared with the same characteristics if we had taken our stand on Hebrew theology. The transcendentalism of Hebrew religion prevented kingship from assuming the profound significance which it possessed in Egypt and Mesopotamia. It excluded, in particular, the king's being instrumental in the integration of society and nature. It denied the possibility of such an integration. It protested vehemently—in the persons of the great prophets—that attempts by king and people to experience that integration were incompatible with their avowed faithfulness to Yahweh. To Hebrew thought nature appeared void of divinity, and it was worse than futile to seek a harmony with created life when only obedience to the will of the Creator could bring peace and salvation. God was not in sun and stars, rain and wind; they were his creatures and served him (Deut. 4:19; Psalm 19). Every alleviation of the stern belief in God's transcendence was corruption. In Hebrew religion—and in Hebrew religion alone—the ancient bond between man and nature was destroyed. Those who served Yahweh must forego the richness, the fulfilment, and the consolation of a life which moves in tune with the great rhythms of earth and sky. There were no festivals to celebrate it. No act of the king could promote it. Man remained outside nature, exploiting it for a livelihood, offering its first-fruits as a sacrifice to Yahweh, using its imagery for the expression of his moods; but never sharing its mysterious life, never an actor in the perennial cosmic pageant in which the sun is made "to rise on the evil and on the good" and the rain is sent "on the just and the unjust."

Kingship, too, was not, for the Hebrews, anchored in the cosmos. Except by way of contrast, it has no place in a "study of ancient Near Eastern religion as an integration of society and nature." The Hebrew king, as every other Hebrew, stood under the judgment of God in an alien world, which—as the dying David knew (II Sam. 23:3-4)—seems friendly only on those rare occasions when man proves not inadequate: "He that ruleth over men must be just, ruling in the fear of God. And he shall be as the light of the morning, when the sun riseth, even a morning without clouds; as the tender grass, springing out of the earth by clear shining after rain."

Fig. 42.—An Early Dynastic Temple at Khafajah

FIG. 43.—THE STELA OF VICTORY OF NARAM-SIN (LOUVRE)

Fig. 44.—Boundary Stone (*kudurru*) with Symbols of the Gods (Louvre)

FIG. 45.—THE BROKEN OBELISK OF AN ASSYRIAN KING (BRITISH MUSEUM)

Fig. 46.—Ur-Nanshe Carrying Clay To Mold the First Brick for a New Temple (Louvre)

FIG. 47.—A GOD MEASURES THE PLANO-CONVEX BRICK HELD BY THE BUILDER
OF A TEMPLE: A SEAL IMPRESSION FROM TELL ASMAR

FIG. 48.—GODS BUILD A TEMPLE WHILE THEIR ENEMY IS DESTROYED
AN AKKADIAN SEAL IMPRESSION

Fig. 49.—The Temple Tower Esagila and the Marduk Temple Etemenanki
at Babylon: A Reconstruction

FIG. 50.—A GOD IS LIBERATED FROM THE MOUNTAIN: AN AKKADIAN
SEAL IMPRESSION (BRITISH MUSEUM)

FIG. 51.—THE ENEMY OF THE GODS IS DESTROYED BY A GOD AND GODDESS UPON
THE MOUNTAIN IN WHICH A GOD IS HELD CAPTIVE (BAGHDAD)

FIG. 52.—MARDUK IN TIAMAT AND MARDUK ON HIS MOUNTAIN BEFORE
EA: AN AKKADIAN SEAL IMPRESSION (BAGHDAD)

NOTES

NOTES

NOTES TO INTRODUCTION

1. A. J. L. Wensinck, "The Semitic New Year and the Origin of Eschatology," *Acta Orientalia*, Vol. I (1923).

2. A useful term employed by Miriam Schild Bunim, *Space in Medieval Painting and the Forerunners of Perspective* (New York, 1940).

3. The relative insignificance of historical facts is shown by the ease with which they got copied whether they are relevant or not. Ramses III carried the names of conquered towns over from the funerary temple of Ramses II when he used the latter's designs as a basis for his own. We find even in the Old Kingdom that the Libyans who appear as the victims of Pepi II's conquests bear the same personal names as those who appear in the temple reliefs of Sahure two centuries earlier (see Jéquier, *Pepi II*, p. 14).

4. *Studies Presented to F. Ll. Griffith* (London, 1932), Pl. 31.

5. H. H. Nelson *et al.*, *Medinet Habu*, Vol. I (Chicago, 1932), Pl. 35. Breasted, in *Studies Presented to F. Ll. Griffith*, pp. 267–71, sees in the Egyptian relief the prototype of the Assyrian versions. Bruno Meissner, in *Beiträge zur altorientalischen Archäologie* (*Mitteilungen der Altorientalischen Gesellschaft*, Vol. VIII [1934]), holds the opposite view, because the chariots were Asiatic originally. There is, however, no demonstrable artistic influence either way. The knowledge of the horse-drawn chariot derives from Asia; but Meissner confuses the issue by claiming artistic dependence on the strength of the proved derivation of the actual objects depicted. The art of Egypt and Mesopotamia presents us with a different aspect of the horse and chariot. The Asiatic rendering on the "standard" from Ur, the gold bowl from Ras Shamra, and the reliefs of the Assyrian kings always shows the laboring draft animal. The Egyptians evolved their own formula of a prancing, hollow-backed, noble creature, and this rendering is found as early as the reign of Amenhotep II (Tomb of Userhet; Wreszinski, *Atlas zur altägyptischen Kulturgeschichte*, Vol. I, Pl. 26*a*). The Mycenaeans, on their rings, give yet another version of the motif. It would seem that a lion attacking the royal chariot from behind would occur so rarely as to require a common origin for this motif when it is found in Egypt and in Assyria, but perhaps we are mistaken in the premise. The Assyrian king "hunted" within a square of soldiers forming a wall with their shields. If the Egyptian king hunted with beaters in the plain, a similar situation might arise; in either case hunter and game would turn round within a limited space, and so the motif might enter into the art of the two countries independently.

6. Breasted, *Ancient Records*, II, 865 (revised by J. A. Wilson).

7. It remains uncertain whether the figure had a human head or a bird's head, since it is incomplete (Borchardt, *Sahure*, I, 33; II, Pl. 8 and p. 21; *Neuserre*, pp. 46 ff.).

NOTES TO CHAPTER 1

1. G. M. Morant, "Study of Egyptian Craniology from Prehistoric to Roman Times," *Biometrika*, XVII (1925), 1–52.

2. Kees, *Götterglaube*, p. 122, is led astray by the archeologists' habit of speaking of a "culture" when referring to a merely local variation of a widely spread civilization. Hence he finds archeological corroboration for his view of Egyptian religion as a conglomerate of entirely unrelated local cults. It is precisely this view which conflicts with the archeological evidence when properly interpreted, for the predynastic remains from widely separated sites are remarkably homogeneous. Tasian, Badarian, and Amratian are three successive stages of a single culture covering the Nile Valley and surrounding regions, though not the Delta. In the Gerzean this culture continues in many respects; Semainean is now eliminated altogether.

The most recent description of predynastic civilization in its various phases is found in the Introduction of A. Scharff's *Die Altertümer der Vor- und Frühzeit Ägyptens* ("Mitteilungen aus der ägyptischen Sammlung," Vol. IV [Berlin, 1931]). See also W. M. Flinders Petrie, *Prehistoric Egypt* (London, 1920). Both are subject to the corrections of Helene J. Kantor, "The Final Phase of Predynastic Culture, Gerzean or Semainean?" *JNES*, III, 110–46.

3. Amratian proper is found in Egypt and Nubia and on the Red Sea coast; it shows certain features later known in Libya (Scharff, "Vorgeschichtliches zur Libyerfrage," *ZÄS*, LXI, 16 ff.). But the Badarian phase of predynastic civilization, which develops into Amratian, is represented in the Libyan Desert west of Abydos (*Man*, 1931, No. 91) and even as far south as the third cataract, four hundred miles west of the Nile (*JEA*, XXII [1936], 47–48). The Delta proper remains a blank, in this as in other respects.

4. The basic proof that features of an ancient African civilization survive today and that, consequently, resemblances between modern Africans and ancient Egyptians are not always emanations from Egypt is supplied by certain Masai arm rings. These are identical with two found in a grave of between 3000 and 2700 B.C. which almost certainly contained not an Egyptian but a foreigner from Punt or Somaliland. See *Studies Presented to F. Ll. Griffith*, pp. 445–54. To the literature there quoted should be added: Wilhelm Hölscher, *Libyer und Ägypter* ("Ägyptologische Forschungen," herausgegeben von Alexander Scharff, Heft 4 [New York, 1937]), and Marianne Schmidl, "Die Grundlagen der Nilotenkultur," *Mitteilungen der Anthropologischen Gesellschaft* (Wien), Vol. LXV (1935). A second argument in favor of a Hamitic substratum's being responsible for similarities between Egypt and modern Africa is the fact that these features were found in an early period in Egypt but discontinued there, while they survived somewhat longer on the upper Nile and are found today among certain savages (see below, chap. 4, n. 20).

Linguistic comparisons allow us to call this East and North African substratum of ancient Egypt "Hamitic." It is true that ancient Egyptian also shows resemblances to the Semitic languages, and these seem to be of two varieties: common features derived from a period before Hamitic and Semitic groups were differentiated and the influence of developed Semitic tongues (Ernst Zyhlarz, "Das geschichtliche Fundament der hamitischen Sprachen," *Africa* [London], IX [1936], 433–52; "Ursprung und Sprachcharakter des Altägyptischen," *Zeitschrift für Eingeborenensprachen*, XXIII [1932–33], 1 ff.; XXV [1934–35], 161 ff.). Zyhlarz considers ancient Egyptian a language which is essentially Hamitic, containing two separate Hamitic strains and one recognizable Semitic strain. He thinks that it developed as a "Verkehrssprache" in the manner that the French of "Ile de France" spread over France and "Hochdeutsch" over Germany. Sethe, *Urgeschichte und älteste Religion der Ägypter*, p. 64 with n. 1, also considers Egyptian a mixture of languages. The important point for us is to note the difference in the relations of ancient Egyptian culture with Hamitic and Semitic civilizations, respectively—using these two linguistic terms for brevity's sake. The material and spiritual culture of ancient Egypt differs throughout from the ancient civilizations of Semitic-speaking peoples and shows striking similarities to that of the Hamites and half-Hamites of Africa. Some of these we shall discuss in this book. From those quoted in *Studies Presented to F. Ll. Griffith*, we may recall here that differences in hairdress between the elders and warriors of the Masai explain peculiarities of Pharaoh's coiffure; that predynastic slate palettes show a peculiar type of circumcision still used by the Masai; and that only the Masai and the ancient Egyptians count the day after the last visibility of the moon as the first day of the new month. But other members of the East African group are also involved. A peculiar type of simple bow is known in ancient Egypt and among the Masai, Somali, and Bahima. The curious habit of wearing a dagger or knife stuck in a bracelet on the upper arm is found in early Egyptian graves (Scharff, *Die archäologischen Ergebnisse des vorgeschichtlichen Gräberfeldes von Abusir el-Meleq* [Leipzig, 1926], p. 49), on the mummies of King Kamose and some of his contemporaries, and among Nubians, Bisharin, Tuaregs, and Berbers. See also below, pp. 70–71, 162–68.

On the whole, I have avoided adducing West African features and confined myself to modern peoples who show affinities to the ancient Egyptians in language or in physique or both. But Hamitic influence is found in Africa well beyond these limitations (see C. G. Seligman, *The Races of Africa* [rev. ed.], p. 96; and W. D. Hambly, *Source Book for African Anthropology* [Chicago: Field Museum, 1927], map of African linguistic groups opposite p. 288).

For the climate, fauna, and flora of predynastic and Pharaonic Egypt and its present equiva-

lent on the White Nile in the Sudan, see Percy E. Newberry, "Egypt as a Field for Anthropological Research," *Smithsonian Report, 1924*, pp. 235–59. See also Passarge's work quoted
in n. 18 below.

5. In current literature all the stress is laid upon "original" differences and subsequent
"syncretism," especially in religious matters. The existence of an Egyptian religion is thus
implicitly denied. We prefer, therefore, to explain the differences as indicated in the text,
unless evidence to the contrary exists. See also below, pp. 39–40.

6. Sethe, *Urgeschichte*. Sethe reconstructed the "Urgeschichte" with one single principle:
whenever a god was recognized throughout Egypt, he assumes his city to have been the capital of the country or of a large part of it, at one time or another. Others, such as Junker, *Onurislegende*, p. 64 *et passim*, had maintained that each cult "spread" when its adherents subjected their neighbors to their rule, but Sethe constructed an elaborate history of prehistoric
times. He admits in his Preface the purely hypothetical character of his work, but his impressive mastery of the sources has gained general acceptance for his views. Sethe's "persön-
liches Vorstellungsbild. . . . . Wer es nicht glauben will, mag es nicht glauben" (*Urgeschichte*,
pp. 2–3) has by now become "Dem üblichen Verlauf in der ägyptischen Religionsgeschichte
entsprechend . . . ." (Junker, *Die politische Lehre von Memphis* [*Abhandlungen der Preussischen Akademie, Phil.-hist. Klasse*, No. 6 (1941)], p. 62). Kees alone ("Kultlegende und
Urgeschichte," *Nachrichten von der Gesellschaft der Wissenschaften zu Göttingen*, 1930, pp.
345–62) opposed Sethe's views, but his own are equally inadequate. His admirable familiarity
with the sources is combined—and that wilfully (Foreword to *Totenglauben*)—with ignorance
of comparative religion; hence the unreality which adheres to his discussions and the baseless-
ness and triteness of his generalizations (e.g., *Totenglauben*, pp. 31 and 38, and his treatment
of myth and of the relation between primitives and natural phenomena and similar problems
in *Götterglaube*). Neither rationalization nor belief in the unlimited envy and competition
of ancient priesthoods are valid guides to an understanding of the ancients. No reality in religious life corresponds with a phrase like the following, which is typical for Kees: "In älterer
Zeit war dagegen der Königsgott Horus das Machtziel des Min" (*Götterglaube*, p. 200).
Kees's work, like Sethe's, has enriched our knowledge of innumerable details of Egyptian
cults but not our understanding of Egyptian religiosity. Both scholars ascribe great influence
to Heliopolis; but, while Sethe postulates a predynastic kingdom centered in that city, Kees
assigns its influence to the Fourth and Fifth Dynasties. Neither believes, as we do, that its
influence was based, not on political developments, but on the quality of its theologians and
their sustained preoccupation with and formulation of beliefs which had been held in one form
or another by most of the Egyptians since a distant past.

Recently Gardiner, in "Horus the Behdetite," *JEA*, XXX, 23–26, destroyed another prop
of Sethe's reconstruction by showing that Horus of Edfu was not originally at home in
Damanhur, nor in any other site in the western Delta, but rather in a swamp-surrounded
Behdet in the extreme northeast of the Delta, which could not possibly have been (*ibid.*, p.
59) the capital of the postulated Lower Egyptian state. Gardiner does not prove that Horus
of Edfu came from this place; on the contrary, he shows that Lower Egyptian Behdet adopted
southern gods in historical times and thus may have adopted Horus from southern Edfu,
where the god was already established by the Third Dynasty (*ibid.*, p. 32). The argument
that Horus came to Upper Egypt from the north seems to have no other foundation than the
god's role in symbolical representations of the Two Lands. Kees, *Götterglaube*, pp. 426–29,
has once more insisted on the fallacy of this argument. We must add that one has no right to
project the meaningful symmetry of Menes' dual monarchy back into the period before unification was an accomplished fact. But, once the pair Horus and Seth was used to symbolize
the Two Lands, Horus had to stand for Lower Egypt, since Seth's two sanctuaries, at
Ombos and at Su, were in the South. In the Memphite Theology, to which Gardiner appeals
(*op. cit.*, pp. 24–25), Seth appears as god of the South, but Horus does *not* appear as the in-
digenous god of Lower Egypt (see below, pp. 26–27). Note also that one has no right to
read in titles of the First Dynasty (e.g., Gardiner, *op. cit.*, p. 59 with n. 4) "Horus the
Behdetite" for "Horus." See also *ibid.*, p. 48, n. 4.

7. Seligman, *op. cit.*, pp. 83–84.

8. *Ibid.*

9. We designate the creator of a unified Egypt "Menes" because Egyptian tradition knew
him by that name. It is a moot point, however, whether any king of the First Dynasty—and

if so, which —was known to his contemporaries as Menes. The sign *mn* occurs in connection with several rulers. W. B. Emery, *Hor-Aha (Excavations at Saqqara, 1937-38* [Cairo, 1939], pp. 4–7), marshaled the evidence which can be adduced in favor of an identification of Aha with Menes. V. Vikentiev, *ASAE*, XXXIII (1934), 208 ff., XXXIV (1935), 1 ff., and XLI (1942), 276–95, objects cogently to this view. But the occurrence of the *mn*-sign with more than one king proves little for or against any identification; it merely aids to explain how the name Menes became the traditional designation for the founder of the First Dynasty. Drioton and Vandier (*L'Egypte*, pp. 162–63) survey the problem clearly and concisely and conclude that the identification of Narmer with Menes is the most acceptable hypothesis. Petrie, *History of Egypt* (10th ed.), I, 6; Sethe, *Urgeschichte*, pp. 177–78; and B. Grdseloff, *ASAE*, XLIV (1945), 279 ff., adopt the same attitude.

In view of the fluid usages of archaic writing we attach particular importance to the circumstantial evidence. Narmer is one of the kings whose name is associated with the sign *mn* on seal impressions (Petrie, *The Royal Tombs of the Earliest Dynasties*, Part II [London, 1901], Pl. XIII, No. 93), and his palette (Figs. 2 and 3) shows this ruler conquering an enemy in the Delta (see H. Ranke, "Eine Bemerkung zur Narmer Palette," *Studia Orientalia* [Helsingfors, 1925], pp. 167–75). He also appears there with the crown of Upper and the crown of Lower Egypt, and as the symbolical representative of his country. Hence we know from contemporary monuments that Narmer achieved what tradition viewed as the work of Menes; and he has, therefore, to our mind, the best claim to be regarded as the founder of Pharaonic Egypt.

10. J. E. Quibell and F. W. Green, *Hierakonpolis*, Vol. I (London, 1900), Pls. XVII, XIX, XX, XXV, XXVI*c*.

11. A. H. Gardiner, *The Admonitions of an Egyptian Sage* (Leipzig, 1900). Also Erman-Blackman, *Literature*, pp. 92 ff.

12. This subject deserves special study. A tendency to comprehend the world in terms of pairs of opposites seems to be Hamitic. Meinhof, *Die Sprachen der Hamiten*, p. 20, n. 1, *et passim*, observes it in the linguistic and social fields. The Egyptian language retains a *dualis*, but, characteristically, not for any two objects but for those which are conceived as a pair (Sethe, *Von Zahlen und Zahlworten bei den alten Ägyptern* [Strassbourg, 1916], p. 97). An example of dualistic conceptions which the ancient Egyptians (p. 70 below and chap. 5, n. 55) probably shared with the Baganda is the notion that man is born a twin. The tendency to dualistic elaboration is marked in Egyptian religious texts. In certain scenes of the Mystery Play of the Succession (p. 128 below), almost any two objects used in the ritual become symbolical for pairs of opposites. The same tendency is apparent in the far-reaching relevancy accorded to the antagonists per se, Horus and Seth. It is clear that to a mentality thus inclined the conception of Egypt as consisting of Upper and Lower Egypt united in harmony must have had a powerful appeal.

13. See below, pp. 21–22. The most striking evidence of the Egyptians' conception of totality as duality is provided by the name of the hall wherein the dead were judged in the Hereafter, and possibly also the name of the Judgment Hall of the vizier. Its name was "The Hall of the Two Truths" (!) (Sethe, *Die Einsetzung des Veziers*, p. 27; C. J. Bleeker, *De beteekenis van de Egyptische godin Maat* (Leiden, 1929), p. 60, n. 2; Sethe, *Kommentar* I, 399–400).

14. Kees, *Götterglaube*, pp. 178–79. The material adduced there shows the modern postulate of a pre-Menite Lower Egyptian state with its capital at Buto to conflict with the evidence from the Delta.

15. Independent of modern hypotheses about pre-Menite kings, there are ancient traditions which refer to them. Here the analogy with the Babylonian king list is instructive. It has been shown by Thorkild Jacobsen, *The Sumerian King List* (Chicago, 1939), that in Mesopotamia, where unity was an ideal, but division the rule, local dynasties which ran parallel in time were forced into the scheme of a single line holding sovereignty by divine sanction. It has also been shown that in Egypt during the confused intermediate periods between the Old, Middle, and New Kingdoms, simultaneous "dynasties" ruled which were enumerated in succession in the historical lists, just as was done in Mesopotamia. We assume that the Egyptians had a similar attitude toward the predynastic chieftains. Memories of great rulers survived and were acknowledged but were understood in the terms established by the founding of the united monarchy. Hence we find that the Turin Papyrus mentions

kings of the North and of Memphis as rulers between the dynasty of the gods and the "Followers of Horus" (see below). In Manetho these kings are called Memphite and Thinite (as if to indicate that they represent a projection backward of early dynastic conditions) and appear between the rule of the gods and the "manium et semideorum regnum" (Ed. Meyer, *Ägyptische Chronologie* [Berlin, 1904], pp. 115-23, 203-4). On the fragment of the annals which is preserved in the Palermo Stone, names of kings with the Red Crown and others with the Double Crown precede the First Dynasty (Breasted, "The Predynastic Union of Egypt," *Bulletin de l'Institut Français d'Archéologie Orientale* [Cairo], XXX [1930], 709-24). All this material may well represent traditions apprehended in the forms of historical times, and it does not prove the hypothesis that a unified realm, or a unified Lower and a unified Upper Egypt, preceded the unification of the country under Menes. If it is objected that we know nothing of the Delta in early times, we can see in this fact only an additional reason to avoid postulates such as a pre-Menite kingdom of Lower Egypt. See also pp. 200-1 below.

16. Sethe, *Beiträge zur ältesten Geschichte Ägyptens* (Leipzig, 1903), p. 29 and n. 8; Borchardt, *Sahure*, II, 116, and n. 8.

17. In the badly damaged Section IV of the Memphite Theology (discussed in our next chapter), Isis reconciles Horus and Seth (ll. 28*b*–31*b*) and insists that they be henceforth at peace. Normally, she champions Horus, but in the passage under discussion she seems to appear as the throne who "made" the king (see below, pp. 43–44). The Memphite Theology is concerned with the nature of kingship; and in the person of the king (once he is crowned) Horus and Seth are at peace.

18. See also pp. 115 and 121 below for pyramid texts which ascribe certain qualities to a king because he embodies both Horus and Seth. Pyr. 848–51 describe the purification of the king at his entrance into the Hereafter as the purifications of Horus and Seth. The best description of the physical conditions in early Egypt is found in S. Passarge, *Die Urlandschaft Ägyptens und die Lokalisierung der Wiege der altägyptischen Kultur* ("Nova Acta Leopoldina," N.F., Vol. IX, No. 58 [Halle (Saale), 1940]).

19. Kees, most recently in *Götterglaube*, pp. 194–99, 410–20, has shown that the conquest of Menes was never conceived as a conflict between the followers of Horus and Seth and that notably the myth of Edfu may not be viewed as reflecting ancient political antagonisms (see n. 6 above). But Kees, too, misses the point of the relationship between the two gods, since he sees in their conflict a mere rivalry between two Upper Egyptian deities, in accordance with his general view of Egyptian religion as a battle for hegemony between local priesthoods. Already Maspero, *Etudes de mythologie*, II, 251, and especially W. B. Kristensen, in *Theologisch Tydschrift* (Leiden) XXXVIII (1904), 233–53, have stressed that Horus and Seth formed a pair of antagonists, irrespective of geographical and political contrasts. Kristensen states, in *Het Leven uit den Dood* (Haarlem, 1926), pp. 19–20, that Horus and Seth represent the divine and demoniac powers in the world and that the world is divided between them, "not in a cosmographical but in a cosmological sense." See below, chap. 15, n. 12.

20. A combined and restored plan of the royal tombs at Abydos appears at the end of G. A. Reisner, *The Development of the Egyptian Tomb down to the Accession of Cheops* (Cambridge, Mass., 1936), after W. M. Flinders Petrie. *The Royal Tombs of the First Dynasty*, Vols. I and II (London, 1900, 1901). See also Petrie, *Tombs of the Courtiers and Oxyrhynkhos* (London, 1925).

21. This tradition, which Herodotus records, has been proved to be most probably correct by Sethe in *Beiträge zur ältesten Geschichte Ägyptens*, pp. 121–41.

22. So also Sethe (*ibid.*). The name might be thought to suggest white limestone, but this material was only introduced for building purposes by Djoser of Dynasty III. The walls of Menes must have been of brick, which may have been whitewashed; but the name is unlikely to refer to this common treatment.

23. This title seems especially significant if we compare it with other "royal titles" of divinities: "Amon-Re, Lord of the Thrones of the Two Lands, Commanding in Karnak"; "Atum, Lord of the Two Lands, of Heliopolis." The simplicity of Ptah's title and the use of the term *nesut*, "king," but also specifically "King of Upper Egypt," would be easily understood if the title derived from the time of Menes.

24. See below, p. 152. Even temples founded in the Eighteenth Dynasty or in Ptolemaic times are stated to have been built on a place chosen by the gods for this purpose from the very beginning.

NOTES TO CHAPTER 2

1. The significance of the text was first pointed out by Breasted. After further study by Erman, Sethe recognized the obscure "sacred conversations" and thereby found the key to an understanding of the document as a whole (*Dramatische Texte*, pp. 1–80). H. Junker, *Die Götterlehre von Memphis (Abhandlungen der Preussischen Akademie, Phil.-hist. Klasse,"* No. 23 [1939]) and *Die politische Lehre von Memphis (ibid.,* No. 6 [1941]), has further elucidated certain details; but his most important new proposals for an interpretation of the text seem to us entirely out of tune with Egyptian thought. The Memphite Theology is a most remarkable document by any standard. The extant copy dates to the eighth century B.C. It is a granite block upon which an ancient work, presumably written on a leather roll, has been copied by the order of King Shabako. The text says: "My Majesty copied this book anew in the temple of Ptah-who-is-to-the-South-of-his-Wall. My Majesty had found it as a work of the ancestors. It had been devoured by worms. It was unknown from beginning to end." Sethe (*op. cit.,* pp. 2–5), taking up Erman's view that Shabako's original dated from the Old Kingdom, finds philological grounds to ascribe the original composition of the text to a yet earlier period, namely, to the First Dynasty, and points out how well its contents agrees with this view. Junker maintains that the text was written down in the Fifth Dynasty, but the "internal evidence" which he quotes as proof that it could not go back to a document of the First Dynasty (*Götterlehre*, pp. 6–10; *Politische Lehre*, pp. 13–20, 61–72) consists of speculations about the political situation which we consider quite unwarranted. In chapter 15 we shall find further evidence in support of the view that the main outline of the text was composed at the beginning of Pharaonic times. Junker's two essays were kindly put at my disposal while this book was going to press by Professor R. J. Forbes of Amsterdam. At the same time I received Maj Sandmann Holmberg, *The God Ptah* (Lund, 1946), in which all the material relevant to Ptah has been studied. Mrs. Holmberg (*op. cit.,* pp. 23, 51, 267) also rejects Junker's views.

2. A similar lack of structure marks the "Mystery Play of the Succession" (see below, p. 125) and the cosmological text of H. O. Lange and O. Neugebauer, *Papyrus Carlsberg No. 1* (Copenhagen, 1940), p. 15, sec. 11, and p. 65, where the disposition of the subject matter is shown to be well thought out but in no way indicated by the scribe in the arrangement of his text. This lack of literary structure is a correlate to the scarcity of conjunctions, which, as De Buck points out, is one of the main difficulties in translating Egyptian texts; sentences are added to one another without their interrelation's being made clear (see *Jaarbericht Nr. 7: Ex Oriente Lux* [Leiden, 1940], p. 299).

3. We prefer Sethe's emendation to Junker's; it presupposes less.

4. Pp. 87, 204–5. The distinction of the animals of Upwaut and Anubis as wolf and jackal or dog is conventional and based on Greek onomastics; the Pharaonic monuments and the skeletal remains do not confirm it (see chap. 3, n. 16, below, and C. Gaillard, "Les animaux consacrés à la divinité de l'ancien Lycopolis," *ASAE*, XXVII [1927], 33–42).

5. Junker's translation (*Götterlehre*, pp. 23–24; *Politische Lehre*, pp. 31–32) disregards the story which is concluded by this passage, namely, that the land became united by the decision of Geb, not through any action on the part of Horus. The awkwardness of Sethe's translation (which we follow) consists in the long title of Ta-Tjenen which appears as the "Great Name" of "This Country"; the view that the land of Egypt is essentially identical with the chthonic god whom the Memphite Theology magnifies recurs throughout the text. But in the present passage it obscures the continuity of the argument which runs: Geb gave the whole land to Horus; hence Horus stood as king over it, and the two crowns grew out of his (Horus') head. The final phrase restates once more that the Two Lands are now united under the single rule of Horus. Junker's view that in this passage Ptah stands for Horus or is presented as identical with Horus is quite untenable. The text establishes that Ptah is the supreme god. Ptah is therefore called "King of Egypt" *qua* creator; the same applies to Atum or Re in solar theology (below, pp. 148 ff.). But Horus' kingship is of an entirely different order; he rules as heir to Osiris and is, in the very passage under discussion, acknowledged as legitimate heir by Osiris' father Geb. He is specifically king of Egypt, while the creator is king of Egypt because he is king of all that he has made.

6. Similar views are found in later hymns acclaiming Amon-Re: "The Eight Gods were thy first form" (*ZÄS*, XLII [1905], 30, 34).

7. Of the three possible translations which have been proposed, we prefer Erman's because it renders the meaning and intention of the text exactly. Sethe's (*op. cit.*, p. 47) "The gods who took shape in Ptah" expresses a modern view about the text, namely, that it was an attempt to combine the recognized gods of Egypt with Ptah. This view may be historically correct; but, since it suggests that there were gods before Ptah, it is diametrically opposed to that which the text propagates, namely, that the existing gods are but manifestations of Ptah. Junker's translation (*Götterlehre*, p. 17), "Die Götter die in Ptah Gestalt haben," though better, likewise fails to express the point which the text makes—that Ptah is *fons et origo* of every god and of all else.

Note that the eight equations include male as well as female deities and that Ptah is described even in late texts as conceiving as well as begetting (Sethe, *op. cit.*, p. 48). But there is no reason to call Ptah a bisexual god (as Kees does in *Götterglaube*, p. 163, where he speaks of "immanenter Doppelgeschlechtlichkeit"). The distinction of sex may be immaterial in a creator; the sun, for instance, is called the "father and mother" of its creatures (Davies, *The Rock Tombs of el Amarna*, IV, 28). The identification of Ptah with Nun is more common than the others (Stolk, *Ptah*, p. 24; Holmberg, *The God Ptah*, pp. 115 ff.), since Nun often stands alone for chaos, the world having emerged from a watery waste according to the Egyptian view; moreover, Ptah, as god of land, was manifest in the Primeval Hill which emerged from Nun, another reason why Nun could be viewed as a form of Ptah, namely, Ptah before he became manifest in his most characteristic form, as land.

8. The Ka is the vital force (see below, p. 62, where this passage is further discussed). Several translations are again possible, and we follow Sethe's, since Junker's (*Götterlehre*, pp. 40 ff.) implies a priority of Atum, and this view is precisely the one against which the text militates, maintaining, as it does, that Atum was the first objectivation of Ptah's spirit.

9. Here following Junker (*ibid.*, p. 49) in his translation of *ḥr šb₃*, "wegen der Lehre dass, aus der Erwägung dass," but not in his treatment and interpretation of the passage.

10. The Hemsut are the female counterpart of the Ka's (see chap. 5).

11. The last paragraph of the quotation gains pregnancy if we remember that the Ennead (and therewith the universe which the nine gods animate) is viewed by the Egyptians as a body of which the separate gods are the members (Sethe, *op. cit.*, p. 49). We reject Junker's supposition (*Götterlehre*, pp. 68–74) that the text reached us in a garbled state so that theological doctrines are wrongly interspersed with fragments of a "Naturlehre." We have demonstrated elsewhere (*Speculative Thought*) that mythopoeic thought cannot be "abstracted" from the imagery in which it finds expression; and the interplay of the references to Ptah and the heart and tongue render adequately the thought of his all-pervading power.

12. By Sethe, *op. cit.*, p. 60, and by J. A. Wilson in *Speculative Thought*.

13. Our interpretation seems to be supported in particular by ll. 56–57 of the Memphite Theology, which may be paraphrased as saying: "In this manner the gods, including Atum and his Ennead, were created; but do not forget that their being was called forth and is now sustained by an uttered thought, a 'divine word,' of the Creator Ptah." We may interpret the addition of "all divine words" to "all things" in our quotation as a similar reminder of ultimate causes. Peculiarly Egyptian is the systematic application of the belief in the creative power of words to theology, but not the belief itself; for this is almost universal in primitive religion. See Van der Leeuw, *Religion in Essence and Manifestation*, pp. 403 ff., and L. Dürr, *Die Wertung des göttlichen Wortes im Alten Testament und im antiken Orient* (Leipzig, 1938).

14. The last sentence after Junker, *Götterlehre*, p. 66.

15. See also Sethe, *op. cit.*, p. 39.

16. We shall discuss then (chap. 15) the confusion which exists as regards the relationship of Osiris with Abydos. As a god of the common dead he was not known there before the end of the Old Kingdom. But as the mythological form of the deceased ruler he was worshiped at Abydos under the First Dynasty and probably earlier. We consider the prevalent view that Osiris originated in the Delta most improbable.

17. Sethe (*op. cit.*, p. 76) adduces some evidence that *ḥpr m t₃* may be translated as "got into the earth," but this deserves consideration only if the normal translation "became earth" is senseless. Far from being so, it is essential for an understanding of the character of Osiris and of the meaning of this part of our text.

18. One would expect this subject to be studied by Tor Irstam, *The King of Ganda: Studies in the Institutions of Sacral Kingship in Africa* ("Ethnographical Museum of Sweden Publications," New Series, No. 8 [Stockholm, 1944]). However, it was not. He has collected a very large number of facts; but, since the significance of each of these can be estimated only when the cultural context in which they belong is known, they pose many more questions than they solve if they are presented in isolation. Irstam's conclusions are, furthermore, vitiated by his reliance on Baumann, Schilde, and others, who consider that sacral or divine kingship came to Africa from western Asia, an opinion which is untenable in view of the evidence which we present in Book II of the present work.

19. C. G. Seligman, *Egypt and Negro Africa: A Study in Divine Kingship* (London, 1934), p. 22.

20. *Ibid.*, p. 28.

21. *Ibid.*, p. 38.

22. P. M. Küsters, "Das Grab der Afrikaner," *Anthropos*, XVI–XVII (1921–22), 919.

23. Frazer, *The Golden Bough*, Part IV, Vol. II, pp. 166–74.

24. This is the common form. But in view of the reproach of inconsistency, so often leveled at Egyptian thought, we must insist that we are not dealing here with a tenet of an alleged "Osireian" religion; for the same conception of kingship reappears in other forms when the nature of Pharaoh is approached from another direction. Considered as the son and successor of the first king, Re, Pharaoh at death "coalesces with his sire" (pp. 101–2 below); and the relation with the new king, his son, in this solar context is the same as the one we described in our text. Again, the Theban formula which includes Amon expresses the same idea, for the dead king, son of Amon(-Re), becomes a form of the god Amon, or, as Dr. Nelson puts it, "the Osirid king was identified with the Amon of his (mortuary) temple" (*JNES*, I, 127–55, esp. pp. 151–52). The filial relationship, in whatever form, reduced the singular, historical event, the death of an individual king, to the unchanging mythological formula best known as "Horus succeeding Osiris."

NOTES TO CHAPTER 3

1. Curing scrofula, "the king's evil," by the monarch's touching the patient was reintroduced at that time.

2. E.g., Pyramid Text 1048*c*. These are henceforth quoted with *Pyr.* followed by the number of the paragraph, after Sethe's definitive edition, *Die altägyptischen Pyramidentexte* (4 vols.; Leipzig, 1908–22), and *Übersetzung und Kommentar zu den altägyptischen Pyramidentexten* (quoted hereafter as "*Kommentar*"), of which four volumes were available at the time of writing.

3. A. Moret, *Le rituel du culte divin journalier en Egypte* (Paris, 1902), p. 129.

4. H. Junker, *Giza*, II, 49.

5. The ♀ sign may be interpreted in two ways, both giving a form to the king's designation which is usual in later times. It may combine with the falcon above the king's name either as "the living Horus" or as "Horus of the Living" (i.e., the god of men).

6. The word usually translated "horizon" means, really, "Land of Light" or "Mountain of Light." It is the place of sunrise, originally conceived quite concretely as mountains to the east of the Nile Valley; and it retained its significance as an existing region at the eastern edge of the earth (see Charles Kuentz, "Autour d'une conception égyptienne méconnue," *Bulletin de l'Institut Français d'Archéologie Orientale*, XVII [1920], 121–91). We consider Kuentz's view of Harakhte untenable, however.

7. Schäfer, *Weltgebäude der alten Ägypter*, pp. 113 ff., was the first to see the importance of the ivory comb and to interpret it correctly. Gardiner, *JEA*, XXX (1944), 46 ff., has recently discussed the winged disk and summarized the main views as to its meaning. Sethe, *Urgeschichte*, pp. 127 ff., reversed the story of its origin by explaining it as a "coat-of-arms" invented for a united Egypt. However, the ivory comb demonstrates that the symbol was not an artificial compound, that it had antecedents in the natural imagery of early religion, and that it retained its original character as a symbol of Horus. But it was given a dualistic interpretation, first, because it symbolized the god who was incarnate in the king of Upper and Lower Egypt, and, second, because of the nature of the design. One finds, for instance, a uraeus with a red crown on one side of the disk balanced by another with a white crown.

Gardiner (pp. 49 ff.) sees in the winged disk a symbol of "the king's actual person." The symbol could be so used because it represented Horus (though not at first necessarily the Behdetite). But it was certainly not the inclusion of the disk which made it possible for the design to denote Pharaoh, for Pharaoh was not one with Re (above, chap. 2, n. 24, and below, chap. 13) in the manner in which he embodied Horus. The winged disk, by this line of argument, seems again primarily connected with the falcon and not with the sun; the wings, and not the disk, are its most important component. Hence we find the epithet "feathered in many hues" as part of the full description of the winged disk in Pharaonic texts.

In Figure 20 there is a piling-up of symbols which is not uncommon in Egypt. Above the winged disk we find the sky depicted a second time, now in the form of the hieroglyph *p.t*, curved to fit the stela and studded with stars. The same hieroglyph depicts the sky once more above the figures of the king and the gods.

8. Junker, *Giza*, II, 51. Kees (*Götterglaube*, pp. 40–45) suggests that the name Horus was secondary in many places where the falcon-gods had been worshiped under other names originally. These names sometimes survive in historical times and are mostly epithets; hence they may or may not have applied to a single god. Even if a heavenly god in the shape of a falcon was worshiped by the ancestors of the Egyptians, it is likely that different aspects of this deity were stressed at the different localities in which his cult became established; whether the name "Horus" was part of the primeval tradition or spread in historical times, as Kees thinks, we cannot decide. If one admits that, in view of the physical and archeological homogeneity of predynastic Egypt, a corresponding community of beliefs must be postulated (it cannot be proved, of course), the manner in which the name "Horus" came to designate the falcon-god throughout the land loses importance. See also n. 21 below.

9. Gardiner and Sethe, *Egyptian Letters to the Dead*, pp. 11–12.

10. See pp. 53–54. J. S. F. Garnot has carefully studied the texts referring to "Le tribunal du grand dieu sous l'Ancien Empire égyptien," *Revue de l'histoire des religions*, CXVI (1937), 26–34. His objections against the identification of "the great god" with Pharaoh are valid in the case of the *living* king. They do not invalidate the identification of "the great god" with the *dead* king.

11. Gardiner and Sethe, *op. cit.* Most of the arguments adduced by Breasted, *Development of Religion and Thought in Ancient Egypt*, pp. 170–71, and Kees, *Totenglauben*, pp. 31 ff., to show that Re was called "the great god" are vitiated by the fact that the sky-god Horus, too, had a solar aspect. Sometimes, however (e.g., Pyr. 1471c), Re is certainly intended; but then the epithet seems to be used somewhat loosely, as is usual in later times. See also H. Jacobsohn, *Die dogmatische Stellung des Königs in der Theologie der alten Ägypter* ("Ägyptologische Forschungen," Heft 8, herausgegeben von Alexander Scharff [Glückstadt, 1939]), pp. 55 ff.

12. Junker, *Giza*, II, 47 ff. Junker unfortunately postulates a sky-god of universal nature with whom the falcon-god Horus would have coalesced. There is no evidence for this complication (see also Anthes in *OLZ*, XL [1937], 218 ff.); and the very nature of Horus, as revealed in the texts which we have discussed, shows Junker's assumption to be gratuitous. In *Die Götterlehre von Memphis* and in *Der sehende und blinde Gott* (München, 1942), Junker claims that the universal god is hidden under the designation *Wr*, "the Great One," and that this god was syncretistically combined, not only with Horus, but also with Atum. However, the term is not a name but an epithet, meaning "the greatest and eldest," and is also given to other gods, such as Ptah and Osiris. See Kees, *Götterglaube*, p. 172, and n. 4 and our next note. The great age and universal appeal of the falcon sky-god in Egypt is proved by the extraordinary spread and ramifications of the eye-motif which derives from him. The Sun Eye and the damaged Moon Eye play an even more preponderant part in the mythology and ritual of the ancient Egyptians than we can demonstrate in the scope of this book (see below, pp. 112, 126, 131).

13. The term "supreme god" carries obvious qualifications when used in the context of polytheism. The dynamic character of power explains why many deities show a tendency to universalism (see chap. 12, n. 8). But it is a far cry from this admission to the claim of an original monotheism as advocated by W. Schmidt (*Der Ursprung der Gottesidee*) or even to the modified claim of R. Pettazzoni ("La formation du monothéisme," *Revue de l'histoire des religions* [1923], pp. 193–229; "Allwissende höchste Wesen," *Archiv für Religionswissenschaft* [1930], pp. 209–43) that heaven itself was everywhere the first om-

niscient, omnipresent god. One may be prepared to admit that the evidence indicates a general human inclination to look to the heavens as a seat of superhuman power; but generalizations about a "Hochgott" vitiate one's understanding from the very start. They probably led Junker to the theory refuted in the preceding note. They explain neither the peculiar Egyptian beliefs about Horus nor those about Re; and they ignore Osiris, just as they lead, e.g., to an interpretation of Shilluk beliefs (E. O. Widengren, *Hochgötterglauben im alten Iran* ["Uppsala Universitets Årsskrift," No. 6 (1938)], pp. 357–58) which lays the accent misleadingly on the *deus otiosus*, Juok, because he is in the sky, and ignores the preponderantly important beliefs regarding Nyakang. See below, p. 199, and also our chap. 12; and (on Juok) C. G. Seligman, in *Fourth Report of the Wellcome Tropical Research Laboratories at the Gordon Memorial College, Khartoum* (London, 1911), Vol. IVB, *General Science*, p. 220.

14. Dr. Harold H. Nelson has drawn my attention to a few exceptions to this rule. In renderings of the Ennead as a body and on three blocks in Karnak (one from the granite shrine of Hatshepsut, one in the Hypostyle Hall, and one in the Khonsu temple), Seth is anthropomorphic and only identifiable by legend.

15. H. Kees, *Lesebuch*, p. 28, No. 41 (Stela Louvre C 286). Kees, *Totenglauben*, p. 194, and Sethe, *Kommentar*, III, 175, point out that Pyr. 632 implies the posthumous conception of Horus.

16. Nina de Garis Davies, *Ancient Egyptian Paintings* (Chicago, 1936), shows Nephthys in Pl. XCIII. Other reproductions are listed in B. Porter and R. L. B. Moss, *Topographical Bibliography*, I, 45, Tomb 66, under 2. Mrs. Davies writes in the text volume (p. 181): "The bird . . . . is drawn exactly like the falcon of Horus, but is proved both by its color and by the generic name *edjret* usually given to it to be a kite." In fact, in their paintings the Egyptians did not distinguish these birds any more than they did wolf, jackal, and dog (see chap. 2, n. 4, above, and also G. Bénédite, "Faucon ou Epervier," *Monuments Piot*, XVII [1909], 23–28; Th. Hopfner, "Der Tierkult der alten Ägypter" [*Denkschriften der Wiener Akademie der Wissenschaften, Phil.-hist. Klasse*, Vol. LVII, No. 2 (1914)], p. 107). See also below, chap. 14, n. 69.

17. See A. H. Gardiner and N. de Garis Davies, *The Tomb of Amenemhēt* (London, 1915), p. 49, n. 2; Pyr. 1280.

18. Sethe, *Sonnenauge*, p. 17.

19. H. Junker maintains that Hathor could not have been the mother of Horus, since Horus was a universal god. But this term is of doubtful validity (n. 13 above), and the multiplicity of approaches often discussed in this book (see also *Speculative Thought*, chap. i) explains the coexistence of imaginative conceptions which we should think mutually exclusive. Junker's argument (*Der sehende und blinde Gott*, p. 40, lower half) consists of ingenious but unproved suppositions crowned by the conclusion that the Egyptians are guilty of "Verwirrung" (*ibid.*, p. 41). We prefer to accept the Egyptian texts while abandoning Junker's suppositions; the confusion is then also disposed of. For example, Junker sees a "Vermischung der Auffassungen" (*ibid.*, p. 41, n. 1) in Brugsch, *Drei Festkalender*, Pl. IV. Here Horus of Edfu counts as spouse of Hathor, as is usual in late times. If we want to understand how this view could have arisen if she counted originally as his mother, we need merely refer to the mystery of the Kamutef (see chap. 14 below). The text states, moreover, that Hathor is pregnant with the Horus child, which is "inside her body; inside her a house of Horus is being prepared, hence her name is Hathor (House of Horus)." Now here is not confusion but clear and graphic evidence that a goddess called Hathor was originally the mother of Horus, for the image which the Egyptians explain in the text is only appropriate of the pregnant mother, not of the spouse. The use of this image for the mother can be corroborated. See below, p. 171.

20. A. Rusch, "Die Stellung des Osiris im theologischen System von Heliopolis," (*AO*, Vol. XXIV (1924), interprets Pyr. 466 as proof that Osiris was sometimes the husband of Hathor, since he does not understand that two distinct aspects of the king are envisaged in that text. His study well exemplifies the unrealistic and sterile nature of the fashionable "explanation" of religious phenomena by postulated developments in other spheres such as politics.

21. In this chapter we develop the several aspects of the king as Horus on the basis of Pyr. 466*a*, in order to demonstrate the peculiar nature of Egyptian theological texts. But the reader should not assume that this one text constitutes the evidence upon which the inter-

pretation is based. Throughout this book will be found the evidence that the Egyptian attempted to express religious insight by formulating, side by side, separate avenues of approach which we should call mutually exclusive but which he did not intend to be combined in a more comprehensive conception. Thus the god Horus was not thought to be absorbed by his incarnation in Pharaoh; he continued to exist independently, being powerfully manifest in nature. Hence the king, "Horus of the Living," could worship the cosmic god Horus. In later times complex theological situations of this type are rendered in art: Ramses II is shown adoring a statue of a falcon-headed sun-god named "Ramses, the Great God, the Lord of Heaven" (see Scharff, in *ZÄS*, LXX, 48 ff.). For the king making offerings to a statue of himself see our chap. 21, D, below.

Pyr. 466a is interpreted differently by Sethe, *Kommentar*, II, 269; he attempts a rationalization of the text by considering it a discussion of descent rather than a theological statement. But it is gratuitous to emend the text into "Horus the eldest son of his parents" when we know "Horus the eldest (i.e., greatest) god" as described in Section A of this chapter. Pyr. 301, to which Sethe refers, is similarly obscured by the elaboration which he proposes. There, too, we find a clear statement of three distinct aspects of kingship set side by side: (1) Unas is heir to Geb, who disposes of kingship as god of the earth and father of Osiris (see p. 26); (2) Unas is heir to Atum, who was the first king and the prototype of royalty (see chap. 13); (3) Unas is on the throne of Horus the eldest, greatest god as embodiment of that god. The three statements cannot be made to appear consistent in the modern sense by any emendation, but they are perfectly clear if viewed as complementary and find a parallel in a similar pronouncement regarding Ramses II which we quote below (p. 173). The various aspects of the god Horus may well have developed into quasi-independent deities if they received varying emphasis at the different localities where Horus was worshiped (see n. 8 above and pp. 144–45 below). For example, at Letopolis, Haroëris, "the elder Horus," preserved the character of the great self-sufficient god, while the son aspect practically disappeared. This latter aspect was, on the other hand, important in the funerary cult or wherever Horus was worshiped in connection with Osiris, as at Abydos. For Kees (*ZÄS*, LXIV, 104–7), the eldest Horus or Horus the Great God is "a merely theological figure of cosmic origin," invented with the express purpose of making a variety of local falcon-gods important enough to stand comparison with Re. Hence Kees views the identification of this god with Horus, son of Isis, as a paradox; and he enumerates a number of passages which, he thinks, betray confusion, syncretism, or an "allzufrühe Verschlingung der Mythenkreise." But most of these passages make good sense once we grasp that the Egyptians could express distinct aspects of a god or king by independent and complementary images; the difficulties are simply created by Kees's erroneous viewpoint. A convenient list of the seven aspects of Horus which were sufficiently separated for the Greeks to name them as distinct gods is given by Roeder, "Horos" (art.), in *Pauly-Wissowa*, Vol. XVI.

22. Moret, *op. cit.*

23. Kees, *Opfertanz*, p. 69.

24. This and many other examples are listed by Hugo Müller, *Die formale Entwicklung der Titulatur der ägyptischen Könige* ("Ägyptologische Forschungen," Heft 7, herausgegeben von Alexander Scharff [Glückstadt, 1938]), pp. 65 ff. Dr. Harold H. Nelson draws my attention to Mariette, *Abydos*, Vol. I, Pl. 28, where the king says of himself: "He made (this) as his monument for his fathers, the gods who are in the Temple of Men-maat-re."

25. A form of oath; for the Ka see chap. 5.

26. Breasted, *Ancient Records*, IV, 850 (revised by J. A. Wilson).

27. The inclusion of the title "Son of Re" as a regular part of the king's protocol was perhaps due to the theological difficulty presented by a change of dynasty. When a new ruler was not the actual son of his predecessor, actuality was at variance with the established formula "Horus, the son of Osiris." The title "Son of Re," however, based the king's fitness as a ruler on the undoubted freedom of the god to beget a successor wherever he wished. It is significant that the tale of Papyrus Westcar allegedly relates events contemporary with the introduction of the title "Son of Re" in the protocol: a seer is described as predicting to Cheops that his grandson will be succeeded by three children whom Re has begotten on the wife of a Heliopolitan priest; these were to become the first three kings of the Fifth Dynasty. The extinction of a royal line could thus be explained as due to a deliberate choice of the god, while the ancient formula of an automatic succession of Osiris by Horus left no such

loophole. A similar appeal to the god's free decision was implied in Hatshepsut's justification of her own succession to the throne, although she was a woman (see below, p. 44).

28. So also Sethe, *Urgeschichte*, p. 85.

29. "OIC," XVIII, 48. See also Spiegelberg, "Der Stabkultus bei den Ägyptern," *Recueil de travaux*, XXV, 184–90. Even the royal "false beard" and the two royal sunshades were worshiped as gods (Sethe, in Borchardt, *Sahure*, II, 97, and Gardiner, *JEA*, XXX, 29–30).

30. Pyr. 317c; *Urk.*, IV:82, 16; 180, 11; etc. J. E. Gautier and G. Jéquier, *Mémoire sur les fouilles de Licht* (Cairo, 1902), p. 34, Fig. 31.

31. Sethe, *Urgeschichte*, p. 85, quoting Pyr. 1154b and Pyr. 1153h. The throne is charged with *baraka*, "holiness," which is also the power of kingship (see Westermarck, in *Man*, 1908, No. 9). See also chap. 1, n. 17, above.

32. Isis had acquired these characteristics already in the Eighteenth Dynasty, as, for instance, a stela in the Louvre shows (Kees, *Lesebuch*, p. 28, No. 41).

33. Kees, *Götterglaube*, p. 151, explains the combination of Isis and Osiris simply by stating that Isis was "brought in" from a town in the neighborhood of Busiris and was "a suitable spouse." Since the frog Heqet counted as spouse of the ram Khnum, and anthropomorphic Ptah was wedded to the lioness Sekhmet, the argument seems a little weak.

34. Petrie, *Royal Tombs*, Vol. II, Pl. II, Nos. 13, 14; W. B. Emery, *Ḥor-Aḥa* (Cairo, 1939), pp. 4–5.

35. Mariette, *Abydos*, Vol. II, Pls. 54–55, ll. 13–19, after Kees, *Lesebuch*, p. 42, No. 70.

36. C. E. Sander-Hansen, *Das Gottesweib des Amun* (Copenhagen, 1940), has shown that the function of queen-mother possessed theological significance in the Eighteenth Dynasty: the title "spouse of the god" was given (probably posthumously) to the ancestress of the dynasty, Aahhotep, the mother of Aahmes, its first king. The title descended from mother to daughter, and the princess thus distinguished married the future king her brother. Sometimes the rule had to be relaxed, and a half-brother, not the son of the "spouse of the god," married the princess. When an heir was born, the mother received the title "mother of the god" in addition to "spouse of the god" (*ibid.*, p. 20). The continuity was broken after Mutemuya, the queen of Tuthmosis IV and mother of Amenhotep III, perhaps because no daughter was born. Thus the institution, although not abolished, lost its original significance, which had been that it established a hereditary succession, not only in the male line in the son of Amon-Re who ruled Egypt, but also in the female line in the receptacle of the divine seed. This theological conception is best understood in connection with the mystery of the Kamutef (pp. 177–80).

37. Moret, *Royauté*, p. 66, n. 2, has enumerated some of the places where the expression is used. See also below, p. 77, the speech of the gods to Amon concerning Hatshepsut.

38. Translation by Dr. J. A. Wilson of *Urkunden*, IV:219–21. See also Ptah's words to Ramses II: "I am thy father .... I assumed my form as the Ram, Lord of Mendes, and begat thee in thy august mother" (Breasted, *Ancient Records*, Vol. III, par. 400).

39. Moret, *Royauté*, pp. 66–67, has seen this connection and, furthermore, recalls Maspero's conclusion that similar beliefs underlie an account of the divine origin of Alexander the Great.

40. See J. Spiegel, "Die Grundbedeutung des Stammes *ḥm*," *ZÄS*, LXXV, 112–21. Gardiner's objections (*JEA*, XXIX, 79) are not decisive; the circumlocution does indeed "avoid direct reference to (the king's) sacred person," and the absence of the determinative for limb can be due to an early dynastic origin of the phrase.

41. A. H. Gardiner, *The Admonitions of an Egyptian Sage* (Leipzig, 1909), p. 15, l. 13.

42. The significance of the titulary has been studied by Moret, *Royauté*, chap. 1, and by G. J. Thierry, *De religieuze beteekenis van het Egyptische koningschap* (Leiden, 1913). The historical development of the titulary is described by Müller, *op. cit.* (n. 24 above).

43. *JEA*, IV, 249.

44. Müller, *op. cit.*, pp. 54 ff.; Kees, *Götterglaube*, p. 412.

45. Breasted, *Ancient Records*, II, 145.

46. This *nomen* sometimes assumes the characteristics of a family name: the Eleventh Dynasty uses "Antef" and "Mentuhotep"; the Twelfth Dynasty, "Amenemhet" and "Senusert"; and the Eighteenth Dynasty, "Amenhotep" and "Tuthmosis."

47. The designation "Pharaoh," meaning "the great house, the palace," is a circumlocution of the type of "The Sublime Porte" for the sultan of the Ottoman Empire.

48. B. Z. and C. G. Seligman, *The Pagan Tribes of the Nilotic Sudan* (London, 1932), p. 90. Many instances of the usage among other African peoples can be found in C. G. Seligman, *Egypt and Negro Africa: A Study in Divine Kingship* (London, 1934).

49. Gardiner, "The Autobiography of Rekhmire," *ZÄS*, LX, 69.

NOTES TO CHAPTER 4

1. In chapter ii of our forthcoming *Ancient Egyptian Religion: An Interpretation*, we have dealt with the function which Pharaoh fulfilled in the state more fully than was possible in a book entitled *Kingship and the Gods*.

2. Kees, *Kulturgeschichte*, p. 42.

3. Ed. Meyer, *Geschichte des Altertums*, I, 2, 192.

4. C. J. Bleeker, *De beteekenis van de Egyptische godin Maat* (Leiden, 1929), p. 33; after Mariette, *Karnak*, p. 35. Cf. *Recueil de travaux*, XXIX, 162–63. Bleeker is a pupil of W. B. Kristensen; and it was the latter who was the first to interpret *maat* as a concept with cosmological as well as ethical implications; e.g., *Het Leven uit den Dood*, pp. 70 ff.

5. A. H. Gardiner, *PSBA*, XXXVIII, 50. See also Spiegelberg, "Die ägyptische Gottheit der 'Gotteskraft,' " *ZÄS*, LVII, 145–48, and below, chap. 5, n. 1. For their relation with the basic views of the Memphite Theology, see J. A. Wilson, *Speculative Thought*, pp. 54–59.

6. Gardiner, *Admonitions*, p. 84.

7. Those readers who have not had the experience of watching the social effect of spiritual forces may find an entirely different terminology relevant to the relationship between king and people. They are referred to N. S. Timasheff, *An Introduction to the Sociology of Law* ("Harvard Sociological Studies," Vol. III [Cambridge, Mass., 1939]), and especially to Part III (pp. 171–94): "A social group in which the power phenomenon appears as a polarized group consisting of two correlated elements: the active (dominators) and the passive (subjects)" (p. 172). "From the introspective viewpoint, the basic factor in the consciousness of individuals in a power structure is a disposition to carry out suggestions coming from (willed by) the dominators" (p. 177). "Every power structure is an historical fact. It arises under certain circumstances as the result of forces which completely explain its structure in the early stage" (p. 185).

8. Kees, *Kulturgeschichte*, pp. 185 ff., and Erman-Ranke, *Ägypten und ägyptisches Leben im Altertum* (Tübingen, 1923), pp. 92 ff.

9. Kees, *Götterglaube*, p. 179 with n. 2.

10. Borchardt, *Sahure*, II, 76, n. 7, 77, 97. Jéquier, *Pepi II*, pp. 18–19, objects to this translation because Royal Kinsmen are shown in subordinate positions, assisting at certain rites; but we have seen that they are also found in subordinate posts in the government. In both cases, no doubt, we meet people who derive some privilege from a very remote relationship with the royal house.

11. It is significant that the biographies of Old Kingdom officials who lived under more than one king do not describe their lives as continuous careers in the service but acknowledge their successive ranks as separate distinctions received from Pharaoh. See, e.g., Breasted, *Ancient Records*, Vol. I, pars. 256–63; also pars. 293–94, 307–15, 320–24, etc. See *ibid.*, pars. 375–85, for royal appointments in quasi-hereditary offices.

12. Kees, *Kulturgeschichte*, p. 186 with n. 4.

13. The division into castes which classical authors claim for Egypt is part of the disintegration of the traditional Egyptian social order following the usurpation of the crown by the High Priest of Amon. See Ed. Meyer, "Götterstaat, Militärherrschaft und Ständewesen in Ägypten" (*Sitzungsberichte der Preussischen Akademie, Phil.-hist. Klasse* [1928]), pp. 495–532.

14. J. Roscoe, *The Baganda*, p. 86. Only two classes are recognized: the blood royal and the commoners. Roscoe's study of the dignitaries and their functions, their different relations with the person of the king, and, in fact, his whole sketch of the native kingdom of Uganda, is most instructive reading for an Egyptologist. Among the Shilluk, too, the princesses are not allowed to marry because marrying a prince would be incest and marrying a commoner, desecration. Among the Barundi, who are also ruled by a divine king of Hamitic stock, "the

king transfers the leadership of parts of his sultanates to some chiefs, almost in every case relatives (brothers, uncles, cousins), members of the royal family (*baganwa*)" (Georges Smets in *Man*, 1946, No. 6, p. 14).

15. In later tombs the titles seem less reliable, and the purity of structure of the official-dom, the blood-bond between ruler and officials, is lost. A similar loss of prerogatives and distinctions of old standing can be observed in the funerary usages. As is well known, the en-trance of the dead into the Hereafter and their position there are described in the texts from the Middle Kingdom onward in terms which in the pyramid texts still apply exclusively to the king. In the Theban tombs of the Eighteenth Dynasty we find in the funerary rites par-ticipants who bear titles reserved for the highest officials of the Old Kingdom (see p. 209). Just so we find notables of the Middle Kingdom flaunting dignities and titles which repre-sented high distinctions in the Old Kingdom. The local princes acted as the chief priests of the local gods. (One, at Meir, went so far as to claim Sed festivals for himself.) And they also gave themselves a title which is translated "Hereditary Prince," literally "mouth of the people," and which was reserved for royal princes in the Old Kingdom.

The Middle Kingdom restored the old distinctions to some extent. The vizier Mentu-hotep, of the Twelfth Dynasty, calls himself a "Hereditary Prince by order of the Two Lords" (the king, Horus-and-Seth).

16. An excellent example of oppression of a poor man and of his difficulties in finding re-dress is given in the narrative connecting the complaints of "The Eloquent Peasant," Fried-rich Vogelsang, *Kommentar zu den Klagen des Bauern* (Leipzig, 1913), and Erman-Blackman, *Literature*, pp. 116–33.

17. For the latest treatment of the inscriptions of the vizier Rekhmire see Norman de Garis Davies, *The Tomb of Rekh-mi-rēᶜ at Thebes* ("Metropolitan Museum of Art, Egyptian Expedition Publications," Vol. XI [New York, 1943]). See also Kees, *Kulturgeschichte*, pp. 88 ff.; Peet in *JEA*, X, 125.

18. Breasted, *Ancient Records*, Vol. II, pars. 666–70.

19. See above, n. 7.

20. This problem has been studied carefully by G. A. Reisner, *The Development of the Egyptian Tomb*, pp. 117–21 (see also Index, "Sati burial"). In the Sudan, as late as the Mid-dle Kingdom, many dependents, especially women, were buried alive with the head of the family (Reisner, *Excavations at Kerma* ["Harvard African Studies," Vol. V (Cambridge, Mass., 1923)]). This recalls the burial of the king of Banyoro "in a grave lined with the living bodies of his wives and retainers" (Seligman, *Races of Africa*, p. 213) and of the king of Uganda (Roscoe, *op. cit.*), as well as of chiefs of the Zande and Nyam-Nyam (Reisner, *Kerma*, p. 72). The distribution in time of this usage provides an exact parallel to that of the deformation of the horns of cattle which we discuss below (p. 165). These customs, na-tive to Africa, are known in predynastic times in Egypt (Reisner, *Kerma*, pp. 73–74, dis-cusses multiple predynastic burials), but are discontinued in Pharaonic times while surviving in the barbaric regions of the Upper Nile somewhat longer, notwithstanding Egyptian in-fluence. They are still retained by certain modern Africans deriving from the old Hamitic substratum.

21. Normally the endowment of lands went with the gift of a tomb, and workers were added to supply the necessary offerings. Thus a graduation of favors was possible. The follow-ing line, for example, appears in an inscription in which an official addresses King Sahure: "It is a command which thy Ka, beloved of Re, has ordered, that there should be given to me a stela of stone" (Sethe, *Urk.*, I: 38; *PSBA*, XXXVIII, 50). Deserving individuals some-times received, not complete tombs, but false doors or offering tables made in the royal workshops, or special gifts to be included in the sacrifices. Or they were merely allowed to put up certain inscriptions. This happened in the case of the priest Rawer, who was acci-dentally struck when the king swung a scepter at some ceremony. Rawer was indemnified by the king's having the event cut in stone to be placed in his tomb (Selim Hassan, *Excava-tions at Gizeh, 1929–30* [Oxford, 1932]).

22. Raymond Weill, *Les décrets royaux de l'Ancien Empire égyptien* (Paris, 1912), No. 34; Sethe, *Urk.*, I, 304–5 (translated by J. A. Wilson).

23. Erman, in *ZÄS*, XXXVIII, 114 ff.

24. A. Moret, *Le rituel du culte divin journalier en Egypte* (Paris, 1902), pp. 42–43, 55.

25. A. de Buck, *Het typische en het individueele by de Egyptenaren* (Leiden, 1929).

26. Latest translation by R. O. Faulkner in *JEA*, XXVIII (1942), 5.

27. Breasted, *Ancient Records*, Vol. IV, esp. pars. 822, 824, 835. The meaning of the first (822) is disclosed by Gardiner, *JEA*, XXI, 219 ff.

28. Breasted, *A History of Egypt*, pp. 427–35. See the reliefs in Wreszinski, *Atlas zur altägyptischen Kulturgeschichte*, Vol. II, Pls. 16–25 (Abydos); Pls. 63–80 (Luxor); Pls. 92–106 (Ramesseum); Pls. 170–74 (Abu Simbel). For the latest treatment see Chalres Kuentz, *La bataille de Cadech* ("Mémoires de l'Institut Français d'Archéologie Orientale" [Cairo, 1928]).

29. After A. de Buck, in *Studia Aegyptiaca*, "Analecta Orientalia," XVII, (1938), 48–57.

30. Rudolf Anthes, *Die Felseninschriften von Hatnub* (Sethe, *Untersuchungen*, Vol. IX [Leipzig, 1928]), Graphito 25. Translated by J. Spiegel, *Die Erzählung vom Streite des Horus und Seth* (Glückstadt, 1937), p. 75. The inscription naïvely shows the added prestige which the consultation gave to the prince in his own circle: "He was a confidant of the king; the princes of Upper Egypt came to him (*viz.*, to beg his good services)."

31. Alfred Hermann, *Die ägyptische Königsnovelle* ("Leipziger ägyptologische Studien," Heft 10, herausgegeben von W. Wolf), has studied such stories from this point of view (see esp. pp. 8–20).

32. Schäfer, *OLZ*, 1929, pp. 234 ff.; *ibid.*, 1931, pp. 89 ff. and 697; *ASAE*, XXVIII (1928), 126; *ibid.*, 1937, pp. 131 ff.

33. The differences find expression in art as well as in the texts. In the Old Kingdom, the gods bring bound captives to Pharaoh (Borchardt, *Sahure*, Vol. II, Pl. 5); in the New Kingdom, Pharaoh destroys enemies before the impassive gods (our Fig. 5). As regards texts we may compare, for instance, the following inscription of Seti I in the temple of Wadi Abbad (*JEA*, IV, 245) with the text of Pepi II which we have quoted on p. 54. Both are concerned with the preservation of the king's monuments and institutions by future generations. Yet the difference in spirit is remarkable:

". . . . came His Majesty to adore his fathers, all the gods, and said:

" 'Hail to you, great gods who founded heaven and earth at your good pleasure! Ye shall shew me favour, to all eternity, ye shall perpetuate my name forever, inasmuch as I am serviceable, am of good to you, am watchful over the matters that you wish.

" 'Therefore shall ye tell those who shall come, kings, officials and people, to confirm for me my deeds. . . . . Speak yourselves, and your word shall be acted on, for it is ye are the lords. I have spent my life being staunch to you to seek my betterment with you. Cause my monuments to endure for me, my name being perpetuated upon them.' "

One should remember, of course, that Seti I was the great restorer of empire, cults, and temples after the upheaval of the Amarna episode and that the hereditary succession was shattered by a sequence of three kings none of whom was of royal birth—Ay, Haremhab, a general, and Seti's father, Ramses I, also a general. See also below, p. 117, and chap. 10, n. 12.

34. The translation in Erman-Blackman, *Literature*, pp. 72 ff., should be corrected after R. O. Faulkner in *Studies Presented to F. Ll. Griffith*, pp. 69–73; A. de Buck, *Mélanges Maspero*, Vol. I, 2 ("Mémoires de l'Institut Français d'Archéologie Orientale," LXVI, 846–51), and B. Gunn in *JEA*, XXVII, 2–6.

35. Translation revised by J. A. Wilson.

36. *Literature*, pp. 278–79.

37. I am omitting, here as elsewhere, statements which sound to us like the flattery of courtiers, though the ancients may well have found a greater percentage of fact in them than we do. In the present context, for instance, we could quote from the Kubban Stela of Amenhotep III: "If thou thyself shouldst say to thy father, the Nile, the father of the gods: 'Let water flow forth upon the mountains!' he will act according to all that thou hast said" (translation by Dr. J. A. Wilson, in *Speculative Thought*, p. 80).

38. J. Frazer, *The Golden Bough*, Part I, Vol. I, p. 354.

39. Ch. Palanque, *Le Nil aux temps pharaoniques*, pp. 72 ff., 87. A. Moret, *La mise à mort du dieu en Egypte* (Paris, 1927), pp. 10 ff. Stern, in *ZÄS*, XI (1873), 129 ff.

40. Vital force. See chap. 5.

41. Erman-Blackman, *Literature*, pp. 84–85.

42. G. van der Leeuw, *Religion in Essence and Manifestation* (New York, 1938), p. 214.

43. Erman-Blackman, *Literature*, p. 279. Spiegelberg, in *OLZ*, XXX (1927), 73–76, points out that this song was written down in Year 4 of Ramses IV; but in form and contents it reflects the mood of the accession so closely that Adolf Erman in his *Literatur der alten Ägypter* quotes it as an example of an accession hymn. See also De Buck in *Bibliotheca Orientalis* (Leiden), I (1944), 67.

NOTES TO CHAPTER 5

1. Studied by Gardiner in *PSBA*, XXXVIII (1916), 43–54, 83–95. We must remember that such concepts are not purely descriptive as they would be with us. *Hu*, for instance, does not mean a command given in an authoritative tone of voice but a command possessing an inherent power which forces obedience. As an example of personification we may quote Gardiner's explanation that *hu* is sometimes called "Hu, the son of the Ka's of Urt-Hiqe." Now Urt-Hiqe, "Great in Magic," is a designation of the cobra-goddess Wadjet on the crown of Pharaoh. "The Ka's of Urt-Hiqe" would, accordingly, be the various attributes or aspects of royal authority, the outcome or " 'son' of which, Hu . . . . might be conceived to be."

2. See G. Roeder, *Urkunden zur Religion des alten Ägypten* (Jena, 1915).

3. See *Speculative Thought*, pp. 13–14, 16–17; also our Index under "Multiplicity of approaches."

4. See Ernst Cassirer, *Philosophie der symbolischen Formen*, Vol. II: *Das mythische Denken* (Berlin, 1925); Lucien Lévy-Bruhl, *Les fonctions mentales dans les sociétés inférieures* (Paris, 1910) (*How Natives Think* [New York, 1926]). Lévy-Bruhl defined the difference between modern and mythopoeic thought clearly, but he went too far (see *Speculative Thought*, chap. i). When we speak occasionally of "pre-Greek" or "primitive"—instead of mythopoeic—thought, we do not mean to suggest that the Egyptians and Mesopotamians must be viewed as modern savages or that the myth-making tendencies died with the Greeks. See, e.g., below, chap. 11, n. 4. But, however irrational modern man may be in reasoning or reactions, he nevertheless attaches authority to "scientific" thought alone. It is the absence of this norm which puts primitive and pre-Greek thought beyond our understanding unless we allow for the difference and adapt ourselves to its consequences.

5. V. Grönbech in Chantepie de la Saussaye's *Lehrbuch der Religionsgeschichte* (Tübingen, 1925), II, 559 ff. See also Fritz Kern, *Kingship and Law in the Middle Ages* (Oxford, 1939), p. 14: "The special claim to lordship possessed by the noblest kin among the folk always rested upon some distinctive inner virtue—a virtue which could be seen in the beaming eye of a prince of the royal blood."

6. Carl Meinhof, *Afrikanische Religionen*, p. 62. Hofmayr, in *Anthropos* (1911), pp. 120 ff., reports that only the ancestors of the great chiefs and the king of the Shilluk were the objects of a cult. Sir Henry Johnston, *The Uganda Protectorate*, II, 832, reports the same for the Masai.

7. G. Steindorff, in *ZÄS*, XLVIII, 152–53, and Kees, *Totenglauben*, p. 68, have seen that the Ka of the king must be distinguished from that of commoners.

8. Egypt produces exceptionally clear evidence of this belief in the form of letters written by living people to dead relatives. These deal with everyday matters in the settlement of which the addressee is requested to assist. In one case a dead mother is asked to arbitrate between her sons, one being also dead, the other still alive. In another letter a man is asked to "awake" his ancestors and with their help to right the affairs of his widow and small son, the defenseless victims of some avaricious relatives. These letters are private documents free of official doctrine or make-believe. They are the spontaneous expressions of people in trouble. They show how the survival of the dead was assumed as a matter of course by the Egyptian because the dead were involved in that indubitable reality, his own anguish, expectation, or resentment. See Gardiner, in Brunton, *Qau and Badari*, I, 76 ff.

9. *Bulletin of the Museum of Fine Arts* (Boston), XXV, 74 and Fig. 18; see J. A. Wilson, in *JNES*, III (1944), 202, n. 5.

10. "It is not death but ritual which opens up the way to future life. The moment when the ghost sets out upon its way is not the moment when the body dies, but that at which it is committed to the ground with due observances" (John Layard, "The Journey of the Dead," *Essays Presented to C. G. Seligman*, p. 118). This statement, referring to the people of Malekula in Melanesia, would also apply to the ancient Egyptians. They, too, believed that those

who did not obtain proper burial would not reach eternal life or at least would be condemned to a most distressing form of existence in the Hereafter. The expression "to be tired," meaning "to be dead," may therefore be more than a euphemism. It corresponds to the "resting of the Ka" of Queen Meresankh.

11. Pyr. 1220d.

12. Van der Leeuw (ZÄS, LIV, 62) errs, therefore, if he concludes that the Ka exists outside the body during man's lifetime, as an "external soul."

13. See, e.g., Georg Weicker, Der Seelenvogel in der alten Literatur und Kunst (Leipzig, 1902).

14. Frankfort, in Archiv für Orientforschung, XII (1937–39), 134–35.

15. Just as one may speak of a certain man's ghost, although the man is dead and exists, henceforth, only as a ghost, so Egyptian funerary texts speak of a man's Ba. This has induced some to think of the Ba as a part of man and not as the dead man in a certain aspect, namely, as manifest to the living. This error, and the inability to recognize the Egyptian "multiplicity of approaches," explains the lack of clarity in the otherwise useful article of Eberhard Otto, "Die beiden vogelgestaltigen Seelenvorstellungen," ZÄS, LXXVII (1943), 78–91, which reached me while this book was in press.

16. Kees, Totenglauben, p. 407.

17. Gardiner, JEA, XXIV (1938), 157 ff., esp. p. 168.

18. The Ba is discussed in its proper context, the Egyptian beliefs of life after death, in chap. iv of our forthcoming Ancient Egyptian Religion: An Interpretation. See also Ranke, ZÄS, LXXV, 133, and Kees, Totenglauben, p. 60, who observe that the Ba is practically never mentioned in private tombs of the Old Kingdom. This is due to the absence of pictures or descriptions of the Hereafter in those tombs. Such representations are not common in private tombs before the Nineteenth Dynasty. In the Old Kingdom the texts and decorations of such tombs provide the apparatus which fulfils the requirements for a desirable life after death (see also below, chap. 10, n. 22, and pp. 152–53, 209). Dr. J. A.Wilson has pointed out to me one mention of the Ba in a tomb of the Old Kingdom: Sethe, Urk., I:186, 14.

19. The conversation of the "man weary of life" (Erman-Blackman, Literature, pp. 86–92), in which a man discourses with his Ba, does not invalidate our view, since the speaker, on the point of committing suicide, hovers on the brink of death; it is there that his Ba confronts him.

20. This may have roots in that substratum of African culture which survives today, but our evidence is not conclusive. The best authorities on the Hamites and half-Hamites write about the Shilluk: "Every living man has both wei and tipo, the former signifying 'breath,' 'life,' the latter 'shadow,' 'image,' as in water or in a mirror. We have already referred to the cen of one dying in anger and malevolence: a surviving malevolent element or ghost; and there is a word aneko meaning 'ghost,' i.e., the spirit of one dead. There may also be an element winyo (lit.: 'bird') of whose functions we can predicate nothing" (B. Z. and C. G. Seligman, The Pagan Tribes of the Anglo-Egyptian Sudan, p. 103). There are obvious resemblances here to the ancient Egyptian beliefs as to the Ka, shadow, image, and Ba; but they are not specific enough. Outside Africa even more complex views of man's nature prevail. It is said that primitive man "has never fallen into the error of thinking of it [the Ego] as a unified whole or of regarding it as static," but that, on the other hand, the primitive, like the Egyptians, commits the "error" of the "concretization of ideas" (Paul Radin, Primitive Man as Philosopher [New York, 1927], pp. 259 and 264). I am unable to judge whether the Maori, Dakota, and Batak views which Radin describes could be understood, in the manner of the Egyptian concept, as separate and unrelated aspects of man; but, in any case, they illustrate once more that our concepts are not congruous with those of the primitives.

21. See the excellent study of Walter F. Otto, Die Manen oder von den Urformen des Totenglaubens (Berlin, 1923).

22. Ibid., pp. 59–63.

23. See Van der Leeuw, Religion in Essence and Manifestation (New York, 1938), p. 296.

24. See Sethe, Dramatische Texte, pp. 61–63.

25. The plural is not common in connection with nonroyal persons. An unusual phrase from an inscription in the tomb of Ptahhotep says of the dead man: "His hand is grasped by his forefathers and his Ka's" (Sethe, Urk., I:189). Dr. Wilson has given me two further instances of the use of this plural: Sethe, Urk., I:190, and Firth and Gunn, Teti Pyramid Ceme-

teries, I, 230; II, Pl. 24*A*. To us this particular instance suggests personification rather than abstraction. But see below, pp. 74–76.

26. Erman-Grapow, *Wörterbuch*, V, 91–92, give many examples in which "Ka," and especially the plural, "Kau," must be translated "food."

27. Sometimes offerings are specifically destined for the Ka of a god. Dr. H. H. Nelson has drawn my attention to an interesting sculptured block of a structure of Hatshepsut. It was found by M. Chevrier some years ago, with many of its fellows, built into the third pylon at Karnak. The queen is offering food and other gifts to Amon, who is worshiped under many names in many temples and somehow present in all of them. The text states that the offerings are for "Amon in every place wherein his Ka is" (See *Biblical Archaeologist*, VII [1944], 49).

28. J. Spiegel, "Die Grundbedeutung des Stammes *ḥm*," *ZÄS*, LXXV, 118–19, shows that the original meaning of the term was "reviver of the (dead) body" and that the interpretation "servant of the Ka" is secondary, though established by the Middle Kingdom. See also chap. 11, n. 8, below.

29. H. H. Nelson, in *JNES*, I, 131, and Fig. 5. This personification was not unusual. The pyramids, for instance, were also personified (see C. Wilke, in *ZÄS*, LXX, 56–83).

30. Erman-Blackman, *Literature*, p. 59, sub. 12.

31. Gardiner, *Egyptian Grammar*, Glossary, and also in *PSBA*, XXXVII (1915), 257.

32. Erman-Grapow, *Wörterbuch*, V, 87–88.

33. Cf. *mulungu*, p. 62, above.

34. Gardiner, *Egyptian Grammar*, p. 172, n. 12.

35. V. Grönbech, in Chantepie de la Saussaye's *Lehrbuch der Religionsgeschichte* (Tübingen, 1925), II, 557.

36. H. Junker, *Giza*, II, 158; H. Jacobsohn, *Die dogmatische Stellung des Königs in der Theologie der alten Ägypter* (Glückstadt, 1939), pp. 60–61.

37. N. de Garis Davies, *The Rock Tombs of El Amarna*, I, 49. Compare also the text of our p. 29.

38. Cairo, No. 20538.

39. See also Pyr. 162 and 1357.

40. Pyr. 815–16.

41. Lepsius, *Denkmäler*, III, 34*b*.

42. A. M. Blackman, in *JEA*, III, 199–206.

43. See above, chap. 1, n. 4.

44. Naville, *Deir el Bahari*, Vol. II, Pl. 51. The object does not occur in the birth scenes of Amenhotep III at Luxor. Dr. Nelson has been so kind as to verify this on the spot for me. The goddess depicted by A. Gayet, *Le temple de Louxor* ("Mémoires de la Mission Archéologique Française au Caire," Vol. XV [Paris, 1894]), represents Selket; and the object on her head is the scorpion, not the *hes* vase. Gayet's drawing is incorrect (*ibid.*, Pl. LXX, Fig. 199).

45. C. G. Seligman and M. A. Murray, in *Man*, 1911, No. 97.

46. Blackman, in *JEA*, III, 235 ff. For a long and inconclusive discussion of the whole matter, see Von Bissing, "Untersuchungen zu den Reliefs aus dem Re-Heiligtum des Rathures," I (*Abh. der Bayer. Akademie, Phil.-hist. Klasse*, Vol. XXXII, No. 1 [München, 1922]), 37–46.

47. Von Bissing–Kees, *Re-Heiligtum*, II, Blatt 16, Stone 39.

48. Sethe, in Borchardt, *Sahure*, II, 76–77.

49. It could likewise be explained that an object closely resembling the standard of the royal placenta appears attached to the front of Upwaut's standard in the pyramid texts Ⳟ.

W. Stevenson Smith, *A History of Egyptian Sculpture and Painting in the Old Kingdom*, p. 137 and Pl. 30, has published early reliefs—probably of the Third Dynasty—and has pointed out that the standard of the placenta and the object on the standard of Upwaut are rendered identically, the surface being in both cases covered by small incised dots. This is a strong argument in favor of the identification. Against it is the straight cut-off back of the last-named object and its name, *shedshed*, which is of unknown meaning but differs from the word for placenta. Neither objection is decisive. Upwaut is called the "Lord of the Shedshed," and the dead kings are said to go to heaven upon it (Pyr. 539–40, 800*a*, 1036*a*). We shall see (pp.

174 ff.) that the king desired to enter the body of the goddess Nut in order to be reborne by her, and there are indications (Sethe, *Kommentar*, III, 11–12, and Erman-Grapow, *Wörterbuch*, IV, 566, 14) that these texts may possibly convey that the king entered the body of the mother-goddess by means of sympathetic magic, using an object which had come forth from her.

50. Firth and Quibell, *The Step Pyramid*, Vol. II, Pls. 17 and 41.

51. It may be that in Egypt, too, the belief that the placenta was a stillborn twin found expression in funerary usage. At Saqqara, Djoser was buried under the Step Pyramid, but a second tomb was placed under the southern inclosure wall of the area. Ricke has shown (*Bemerkungen zur ägyptischen Baukunst des alten Reichs*. I, 70) that both the Step Pyramid and the southern tomb are parts of architectural layouts with strictly parallel features. The southern tomb can be compared with the so-called "queen's pyramid" which stands in the southern part of the pyramid inclosures of the Old Kingdom. Jéquier has shown (*Douze ans de fouilles dans la necropole memphite*, pp. 43–44) that these small structures cannot have been tombs of queens. They might have been tombs for the placenta of the king, as Lauer suggested (*La pyramide à degrés*, I, 111–12). Lauer prefers to think them burial places for the intestines, but there is no evidence either way. It is perhaps significant that the southern tomb of Djoser's complex was finished before the Step Pyramid.

52. Blackman, "The Pharaoh's Placenta and the Moon-god Khons," *JEA*, III, 235–49.

53. Dr. J. A. Wilson has drawn my attention to some Middle Kingdom occurrences (H. Ranke, *Personennamen*, I, 271, 4, 12, 13) and to Pyr. 402a, where a god *ḥnsw* (with soft *s*) occurs who might be the same as Khonsu, though this name uses the sharp *s̆*. Sethe, *Kommentar*, II, 157, is actually of this opinion, too. The word *ḥnśw*, with sharp *s̆* like the god's name, occurs in medical texts with the meaning "swelling, tumor, or abscess," which can well be explained if we accept the etymology given in the text connecting the god's name with the placenta.

54. Van der Leeuw, in *JEA*, V, 64.

55. In the case of the Baganda, not only the king's placenta, but that of every man, is considered a stillborn twin. Consequently, everyone carries the dried navel cord in a bag on his person, and definite taboos prevail; for instance, only certain people may eat fruit from the tree under which a man's placenta is buried (Frazer, *The Golden Bough*, Part I, Vol. I, pp. 195–96). If similar usages obtained in ancient Egypt, we should almost certainly not know about them, since they would remain within the scope of unwritten folklore. But the belief that the placenta is a stillborn twin is found in modern Egypt and may be a survival. The Fellahin call the placenta *el-walad-et-tani*, the "other" or "second" child; and this is not a mere manner of speaking, for women treat it in certain circumstances as they would treat a dead child. Just as a woman tries to lure the spirit of the dead child into her body again so that she may conceive once more, she tries also to capture the spirit of the "other child," the placenta (W. Blackman, *The Fellahin of Upper Egypt*, p. 63, cf. p. 67). This usage shows that the modern Egyptians, like the Baganda, credit the placenta with a spirit; and this belief is the more suggestive of an ancient survival since it is not general in the Arab world. In Iraq, for instance, the placenta is sometimes played up as a twin; but this is known to be a trick and aims at deluding the evil spirit Qarina by offering her a substitute for the baby (E. S. Drower, *Iraq*, V, 110). Other peoples also believe that the newborn child's future is dependent upon the treatment given to the placenta. See E. S. Hartland's introduction to the article on "Birth" in *Hastings Encyclopedia of Religion and Ethics*, II, 639; Frazer, *The Golden Bough*, Part I, Vol. I, pp. 182–200.

56. J. de Morgan, *Fouilles à Dahchour*, Pl. XXXIII, where the arms of the Ka sign on the head are omitted! Borchardt, *Statuen und Statuetten*, Vol. I (*Catalogue général* [Cairo, 1911]), No. 259.

57. Borchardt, *Sahure*, Vol. II, Pl. 46; Jéquier, *Pepi II*, Pls. 36, 41, 61.

58. *ZÄS*, XLVIII, 157. It is significant that the Ka of the king bears the king's Horus name, the name that pertains to him as a god. Divinity is of his essence; his vital force is the vitality of a god. A very unusual representation of the royal Ka (kindly brought to my attention by Dr. Richard A. Parker) appears in a building of Taharqa at Karnak. E. Prisse d'Avennes, *Monuments égyptiens*, Pl. XXXIV, shows the Ka with hieroglyphs for "life" about the mouth or neck, full-face, and ithyphallic. The last-mentioned feature agrees with the view expressed in the quotation from Ptahhotep on p. 67 and n. 30.

59. Gayet, *op. cit.*, Pl. LXVII.

60. Naville, *Deir el Bahari*, Vol. II, Pl. LI. Text after Sethe, *Urk.*, IV:227.

61. Naville, *op. cit.*, Pl. LIII (translation revised by J. A. Wilson). The four divinities are the two tutelary goddesses of Upper and Lower Egypt, i.e., the vulture Nekhbet and the cobra Wadjet, and, furthermore, the scorpion Selket and the cow Hesat.

62. Gardiner writes, in *PSBA*, XXXVIII (1916), 83: "In the Graeco-Roman temples the king is often represented standing before the particular deity of the place, and leading into the presence of that deity a line of male figures with offerings, upon whose heads the sign *ka* is conspicuously shown. Each *ka* has the name of an attribute attached to it, and since there are usually fourteen of them, and since it is known from New Kingdom texts that Rē͑ was credited with fourteen *kas*, it is clear that these *kas* or 'attributes' of the king must be identical with those of the Sun-god whose son and heir Pharaoh was.

"The meaning of the temple-scenes here described is now apparent: the king seeks to honour the god whom he is visiting by presenting to him the first-fruits and the material output of his inherited kingly virtues." See also Alan W. Shorter, *Catalogue of Egyptian Religious Papyri in the British Museum* (London, 1938), pp. 60, 69–70. The epithets of these Ka's can usually be considered as manifestations of the Ka as vital force. They recur in the Ka or Horus names of the kings of the Old Kingdom, and many of them can be found in the speech of the birth-goddess at Deir el Bahri. The dogma of the fourteen Ka's of the king (and of Re, for that matter) thus appears as a theological elaboration of the basic idea of the Ka which we have formulated. Dr. Richard A. Parker has informed me that offerings to Ka's of Re are depicted in the temple of Ramses III at Medinet Habu; six figures are preserved. See also n. 27 above.

63. Sethe, *Urk.*, IV:244–45. The epithet "at the head of the living Ka's," may mean "at the head of all the living," but also "at the head of all the preceding kings" (see Jacobsohn, *op. cit.*, p. 54).

64. For the translation of the middle part see De Buck in *Studies Presented to F. Ll. Griffith*, p. 58.

NOTES TO CHAPTER 6

1. The name is not satisfactorily explained. Various theories are summarized in Von Bissing–Kees, *Untersuchungen*, pp. 96 ff. We are inclined to indorse a suggestion made in 1904 by Professor Margaret A. Murray (*The Osireion at Abydos*, p. 34). She drew attention to the god Sed, named on the Palermo Stone (Schäfer, *Ein Bruchstück altägyptischer Annalen*, p. 21) and in the titles of the Old Kingdom (Murray, *Index of Names and Titles of the Old Kingdom* [London, 1908], p. 30). The god's name is determined by the Upwaut standard complete with *shedshed* and mace 𓌉 . If Sed were an ancient form of the god Upwaut, his name could appropriately designate a feast of the rebirth of kingship, for Upwaut (p. 92 below) was probably a divine form of Pharaoh in his aspect of eldest son and plays a prominent role in the Sed festival.

2. The texts (e.g., at Abydos, translated by Moret, *Royauté*, p. 256) leave no doubt that kingship is renewed at the Sed festival. The Rosetta Stone, which calls the king κύριος τρια-κονταετηρίδων, proves the existence of a tradition connecting the festival with a thirty-year period; and the practice of several kings (Pepi II, Senusert I, Tuthmosis III, Amenhotep III, Ramses II, Ramses III) suggests that it was normally celebrated for the first time thirty years after the king's accession. But this period was not essential, for, after the first celebration, the Sed festival was celebrated again at two-, three-, or four-year intervals until the king's death. Moreover, some kings celebrated it before their thirtieth year (e.g., Pepi I in his eighteenth year, Ranebtaui Mentuhotep in his second year), while others, who did not reign for thirty years, celebrated Sed festivals nevertheless (Dedkare, Amenhotep II, Seti II, Psammetichos II). The assumption that the celebration took place thirty years after the admission of the king to coregency (Sethe, *ZÄS*, XXXVI, 64, n. 3) is contradicted by the known facts of the reign of Ramses II and by the two celebrations of the Sed festival by Tuthmosis IV, whose mummy shows that he could hardly have been more than twenty or twenty-five years old when he died. See Moret, *Royauté*, pp. 256–61, who also quotes the older literature, and Breasted, in *ZÄS*, XXXIX, 55–61.

It seems that thirty years, or, in a more general way, "a generation" (Edouard Naville, in *PSBA*, VII, 135), was the normal time to elapse between a king's accession and the celebration of the Sed festival but that certain symptoms (the nature of which we cannot guess) might at any time indicate to the ancients that a renewal of kingship was due. It is possible that the king's health may have been one of the symptoms; but the widespread belief that the Sed festival was a modification of an earlier custom which required that the incarnation of the god be replaced by a more perfect man as soon as the present king showed signs of senility or illness projects into Egypt an East African custom (p. 33 above) which may have been adhered to, of course, but for which there is no evidence at all. There is, moreover, no relation between the Sed festival and Osiris, since the festival renews existing kingship and is not concerned with the succession. The depiction of a Sed festival of Osiris on a late coffin (G. Möller in ZÄS, XXXIX, 71 ff.), besides being confused in the rendering of details, refers to Osiris as a dead king celebrating a ceremony of kingship in the Hereafter.

3. The Egyptian year consisted of three seasons of four months each. The first was Akhet, the "Season of Inundation"; the second was Peroyet, the "Season of Coming-Forth" (originally of the fields from the flood and also, perhaps, of the sprouting plants from the earth); the third was Shomu, the "Season of Deficiency" (of water). The first season started with the rise of the Nile, in June or July. We are not concerned here with the intricacies of the Egyptian calendar, or, as we should say, calendars, since several were in use concurrently. We are concerned with the peasant's year, in which the festivals were celebrated in harmony with the seasons—a harmony which in certain cases, like the Harvest Festival of Min, must always have been maintained and which seems in Pharaonic times to have been more or less rigidly maintained in the case of all festivals which had not become mere temple observances. For the problems of Egyptian time-reckoning and the absence of astronomical data for the third millennium, see O. Neugebauer in "Acta Orientalia," XVII (1938), 169–95, and in JNES, I, 396–403; A. Scharff, in Historische Zeitschrift, Vol. CLXI, pp. 113–31; H. E. Winlock in Proceedings of the American Philosophical Society, Vol. LXXXIII, No. 3 (1940). For the date of the Sed festival see Gardiner, JEA, XXX (1944), 30, n. 4.

4. An inscription on the second pylon suggests that the second court of the temple of Medinet Habu was the "Festival Hall." See U. Hölscher, "The Mortuary Temple of Ramses III" (The Excavation of Medinet Habu, Vol. III ["OIP," Vol. LIV]), p. 8, with Nelson's remarks in n. 24. Granite obelisks are not known from the Old Kingdom, but some kings, e.g., Neuserre, seem to have built or embellished a sun sanctuary on the occasion of their Sed festivals; and an obelisk of masonry was the main feature of such a sanctuary (see Von Bissing-Kees, Re-Heiligtum, III, 49).

5. Basic for our understanding of the Sed festival are the reliefs from the temple of Neuserre: Re-Heiligtum, Vols. II (1923) and III (1928), and especially the text of Herman Kees in the last volume. See also Von Bissing–Kees, Untersuchungen.

Jéquier, Pepi II, Vol. II, has subjected the fragments of reliefs which he discovered to a most careful scrutiny and thus succeeded in restoring the scenes. Throughout the temple the king is shown moving among the gods as an equal. The dance of the Sed festival, which was to be repeated four times, is depicted four times in the couloir. It is not certain that the festival is depicted in the antichambre (Pls. 46–60). There Pepi II is shown confronting the gods of the land, who stand near their shrines, while bullocks are slaughtered and the Sem priest officiates. Gardiner, JEA, XXX, 30, has noted that the date of the Sed festival (tepi renpet) appears in a fragment of text (Pl. 50). But the king does not wear the short stiff robe which is his customary garb on that occasion, or the Red, White, or Double Crown. Instead he wears the kilt and headcloth which are his usual attire. Moreover, the text mentions his Ka (Pl. 50), and, since the Sem priest functions in the funerary rites as well as at the Sed festival, it would seem possible that the reliefs of the antichambre go together with those of the sanctuaire and represent the king in the Hereafter received by all the gods of the land, including the Souls of Nekhen and Pe. The appearance of the king between Nekhbet and Anubis above the North Door (Pl. 54) supports this view, since Anubis is a god of the dead.

A later and more confused, but important, series of reliefs is published by Edouard Naville, The Festival Hall of Osorkon II (London, 1892); the reliefs at Soleb are not fully published. But see Breasted in AJSL, Vol. XXV (1908), and Wilson in JAOS, LVI (1936), 293–96. Many other reliefs refer to the Sed festival in more or less schematic ways (see also below, chap. 14, n. 90). The earliest is the macehead of Narmer-Menes (Quibell, Hierakonpolis, Vol. I, Pls. XXV–XXVIB). This macehead shows the three enigmatical curved signs which appear with scenes of the Sed festival. The ivory tablets of early kings, such as that studied by Vikentiev in *ASAE*, Vols. XXXIII–XXXIV, cannot be proved to depict the festival.

6. See H. Schäfer, "Die frühesten Bildwerke Königs Amenophis des IV," *Amtliche Berichte aus den Preussischen Staatssammlungen*, XL (1919), 221–30; Henri Asselberghs, in *ZÄS*, LVIII (1923), 36–38; F. Ll. Griffith in *JEA*, V (1918), 61–63; H. Schäfer, in *Sitzungsberichte der Preussischen Akademie der Wissenschaften*, *Phil.-hist. Klasse*, 1919, pp. 447–84.

7. Kees, *Kulturgeschichte*, p. 182, points out that in the Ptolemaic temples it bears the old name of the royal robing chamber, *per duat*, "House of the Morning," that is, of the morning toilet. Herbert Ricke, *Bemerkungen zur ägyptischen Baukunst des alten Reichs* (Zurich, 1944), I, 89–96, has ingeniously interpreted Temple T of Djoser's complex at Saqqara, accepting Firth's suggestion that it was the robing chamber for the Sed festival.

8. Pyr. 130*a*.

9. See J. A. Wilson, "Illuminating the Thrones at the Egyptian Jubilee," *JAOS*, LVI (1936), 293–96.

10. A. M. Blackman, "The Stela of Nebipusenwosret," *JEA*, XXI, 1–9; as a *quid pro quo*, the owner of the stela showers blessings on the obliging priesthood.

11. Gardiner, in *ZÄS*, XLVIII (1910), 47 ff., an inscription agreeing with a note in the Turin papyrus.

11*a*. Georges Smets, "The Structure of the Barundi Community," *Man* (1946), No. 6.

12. See Gardiner, *JEA*, XXIV, 85–89: ". . . . bearer was the official presiding over the king's table, who saw to its supplies, and who catered for the wants of his guests. The title itself strictly refers only to the last-named function. . . . . Since the royal gifts extended not only to the courtiers and officials of his entourage, but also to the gods and to the dead, it is clear that the chief holder of the title . . . . must have been at the head of a large organization." Wilson, *JNES*, Vol. III (1944), translates "the Master of the Reversion" and explains: "the 'reversion' is the flow of goods, by the king's grace, from temples to tombs." Drioton-Vandier, *L'Egypte*, p. 179, assign to his care "ce qui est relatif aux terres arables." Kees, *Kulturgeschichte*, p. 39, shows that his office was connected with the cattle census and suggests that it, together with that of the superintendent of the fields, represented what we should call the Ministry of Agriculture. On the form of the title see Gardiner, *JEA*, XXIV, 84, n. 3.

13. Junker, *Giza*, II, 65.

14. Von Bissing–Kees, *Re-Heiligtum*, Vol. II, Pl. 6, blocks 13, 14.

15. Gardiner (*JEA*, XXX, 28–30) has recognized that fragmentary scenes from the funerary temples of Sahure (Borchardt, *Das Grabdenkmal des Königs Sahure*, Vol. II, Pl. 19) refer to the Sed festival. As in the funerary temple of Pepi II (see n. 5 above), the gods stand before their temporary shrines, the "houses of the Sed festival"; they receive offerings and in return give "life and prosperity" to the king. In the Middle Kingdom gateways from Medamud (Remy Cottevieille-Giraudet, *Rapport sur les fouilles de Médamoud [1931]*: *Les monuments du Moyen Empire* ["Fouilles Institut Fr. Arch. Or.," Vol. IX (1933)], Pls. I, V) similar scenes appear on the doorjambs. At Bubastis the gods appear in their shrines, and in each of these a small kneeling figure of the king offers a sacrifice (Naville, *The Festival Hall of Osorkon II*, Pls. VII, XII, XXIX, XXXI). These various methods of abbreviation render the main ceremonies which we are describing after the detailed representations of Neuserre.

16. Von Bissing–Kees, *Re-Heiligtum*, Vol. III, Pl. 13, block 229 and p. 34.

17. *Ibid.*, Pl. 14, block 246. The princesses seem to go on foot (*ibid.*, Vol. II, Pl. 3); hence the figure in the palanquin on the Narmer mace is unlikely to be a princess, as Newberry maintains (*Smithsonian Report, 1924*, p. 447). His references to fire-lighting and races run are fanciful.

18. She is given unwarranted prominence in the older literature on the Sed festival. The evidence is slight. The queen appears with Osorkon II in the Twenty-second Dynasty. Before that date we have no evidence beyond the reliefs of Amenhotep III at Soleb (Lepsius, *Denkmäler*, III, Pls. 84–86). There the queen accompanies the king. The gems of Amenhotep III (*JEA*, Vol. III [1916], Pl. XI) may not render a real situation at all but present an allegorical design. They show Queen Ty holding the year-stick before Amenhotep III, who is enthroned in the double shrine of the Sed festival. We know nothing of the role of the queen of Egypt at the festival.

19. There is evidence, for instance, that at some point in the proceedings the king hunted a white (or Upper Egyptian) female hippopotamus with a harpoon. See Von Bissing–Kees, *Re-Heiligtum*, III, 30 ff.

20. *Ibid.*, Vol. II, Pls. 4, 5.

21. At the southern end of the west side of the Court of Djoser at Saqqara there are two chapels with steps which one could imagine to lead up to a throne. This arrangement is also depicted on the Narmer macehead. However, there is also a base in the court with two small flights of steps leading up to it; and this might be a throne base, too. See J. Lauer, *La pyramide à degrés*, pp. 130–53, Pls. LV–LIX. "Temple T" would be the "Palace" or robing chamber used at the celebration.

22. It is understandable that pictorial references to the Sed festival choose either the double pavilion or the "dance" of the Dedication of the Field as their themes; of these two abbreviations, the double pavilion has the advantage of giving an admirably symmetrical design, for instance for the decoration of lintels above doorways. To this end the king is shown simultaneously enthroned with the Red Crown in one pavilion and with the White Crown in the other. The narrative renderings of the procedure, such as we have from the temple of Neuserre, show that this is no more than a decorative device.

23. On the "house document," see Erwin Seidl in *The Legacy of Egypt*, ed. S. R. K. Glanville, p. 199 with n. 1: "an accurate translation of this word has not yet been found." and Alexander Scharff and Erwin Seidl, *Einführung in die ägyptische Rechtsgeschichte bis zum Ende des Neuen Reichs* ("Ägyptologische Forschungen," Heft 10 [München, 1939]), pp. 22 ff., 57 ff. Although the translation "will" is not correct in all cases, nothing would be gained by replacing it in our discussion by the meaningless "house document." The function of the document is clear in the context of the Sed festival. See also Kees, *Opfertanz*, pp. 142–45.

24. Kees, *Opfertanz*, chap. iv, corrected in his *Re-Heiligtum*, III, 7.

25. Kees, in *ZÄS*, LII, 68 ff.

26. Headdress or inscriptions sometimes characterize the goddess as the Upper or Lower Egyptian Mert, and Jéquier, *Pepi II*, p. 20, points out the similarity of her name to the common designation of Egypt, *ta meryt*, "the beloved Land"; he therefore suggests that there is a pair of Mert goddesses personifying the two parts of Egypt, "bénéficiaires de la course royale." Jacobsohn, *Dogmatische Stellung des Königs*, p. 47, speaks of Mert as a "goddess of love" on the strength of her name and her association with music. But that does not suffice to stamp the "dance" over which she presides a fertility rite. Nor is her title "mistress of the gold house" an indication that the dance is concerned with an enrichment of the temple treasury (Kees, *Re-Heiligtum*, III, 7). For one thing, the statues were not only made but submitted to the "Opening-of-the-Mouth" ritual in the "gold house." Mert is discussed by Kees, *Opfertanz*, pp. 103–9, and Eberhard Otto, *Studia Aegyptiaca*, I ("Analecta Orientalia," Vol. XVII) (Roma, 1938), pp. 25 ff. Thoth is connected with the dance by Den-Wedimu (W. B. Emery, *The Tomb of Hemaka* [Cairo, 1938], p. 64, Fig. 26), Djoser (Firth and Quibell, *The Step Pyramid*, Vol. II, Pl. 16), and Sahure (Borchardt, *Sahure*, Pl. 25 and p. 104). See below, chap. 7, n. 11.

27. Petrie, *Royal Tombs*, Vol. II, Pl. XV, No. 108.

28. This is shown in Lepsius, *Denkmäler*, III, 36b, and Moret, *Royauté*, p. 105, Fig. 21. Seligman, *Egypt and Negro Africa*, pp. 15 ff., points out that this ceremony closely resembles the ceremony of "shooting the nations" performed at the coronation of the king of Kitara (Unyoro). On this occasion the king shoots arrows in the directions of the points of the compass. Seligman notes that at several places in Africa a reinvigoration of kingship is celebrated, but the details of the performances differ from those observed in Egypt in every respect except for the shooting of arrows.

29. It is depicted in the reliefs (Kees, *Re-Heiligtum*, Vol. II, Pl. 23, and Naville, *Festival Hall of Osorkon II*, Pl. II); and an original in limestone was found in the colonnade of Djoser's Complex at Saqqara. See Borchardt, in *ASAE*, XXVI, 100, and Firth and Quibell, *The Step Pyramid*, Vol. II, Pl. 56.

30. Toward the end of the Sed festival references to the Ancestors appear occasionally. In the Upper Egyptian ceremony, Neuserre is carried by courtiers; but afterward, when he leaves the shrine of Seth of Ombos to go to "the Court of the Great Ones" for his sacrifice at the Dual Shrines, he is carried by "the Guardians of Nekhen." This, as we shall see, is another name for the "Souls of Nekhen," who, with the "Souls of Pe," stand for the Royal

Ancestors as a group (chap. 7). At Karnak, Tuthmosis III is shown carried by the "Souls of Pe" in the final scenes (Von Bissing–Kees, *Re-Heiligtum*, Vol. III, Beiblatt A), just as Seti I appears at Abydos carried by "the Souls of Pe and the Souls of Nekhen" (Mariette, *Abydos*, Vol. I, Pl. 31*b* and Moret, *Royauté*, p. 247).

31. Kees, *Re-Heiligtum*, Vol. II, Pls. 18, 21.

32. See Sethe, *Urgeschichte*, p. 156, n. 2, against Kees in *Nachrichten von der Gesellschaft der Wissenschaften zu Göttingen, Phil.-hist. Klasse*, 1927, pp. 196 ff.

NOTES TO CHAPTER 7

1. H. H. Nelson *et al.*, *Medinet Habu*, Vol. IV: *Festival Scenes of Ramses III* ("OIP," Vol. LI), Pls. 196–217. Ramses II shows fourteen ancestors in one scene and nine in another; Ramses III shows seven, but there is no reason to believe that the statues depicted represent anything but a convenient selection. In both cases the statue of the living king is carried as well. Perhaps this feature is meant as an anticipation of the future, since the reliefs are shown in the mortuary temples of these kings.

2. *Ibid.*, Pl. 203, l. 2.

3. Occasionally an earlier ruler was chosen by one of his successors as a special object of worship. So Tuthmosis III built a shrine at Semneh, a fortress in Nubia, to Senusert III, who had first subjugated the region. Other instances are discussed by Erman in *ZÄS*, XXXVIII, 114 ff., and by Jacobsohn, *Dogmatische Stellung des Königs*, pp. 40 ff., 59. These, of course, have nothing to do with the worship of the ancestors as a collectivity.

4. Petrie, *Koptos*, Pl. 12, No. 3.

5. Sethe, *Untersuchungen*, III, 6.

6. As Sethe does, *ibid.*, pp. 11–13; *Urgeschichte*, p. 156, n. 1.

7. In the annals on the Palermo Stone the "Following of Horus" is listed every other year during the First and Second Dynasties. The words are determined with a ceremonial boat and may indicate a festival, but Borchardt, *Die Annalen und die zeitliche Festlegung des Alten Reichs*, p. 32, n. 1, and Kees, in *Nachrichten von der Gesellschaft der Wissenschaften zu Göttingen* (Göttingen, 1927), p. 206, and *Kulturgeschichte*, p. 46, insist that the expression indicates a tax levied to maintain ("serve, follow") the Horus king and his court and officials.

8. See above, p. 83, and Pyr. 921*a*, 1245*c*.

9. Dr. Seele points out to me that the Ramesseum text actually uses "gods" where the text of the Feast of Min of Ramses III at Karnak has "standards."

10. The standards shown in the reliefs are discussed by Von Bissing–Kees, *Untersuchungen*, pp. 24–59.

11. This follows from the material discussed by Kees, *Nachrichten von der Gesellschaft der Wissenschaften zu Göttingen* (Göttingen, 1929), pp. 57–64, as well as from the magnificent figure of Thoth's baboon dedicated by Narmer-Menes (A. Scharff, *Altertümer der Vor- und Frühzeit Ägyptens* ("Mitteilungen aus der ägyptischen Sammlung" [Berlin, 1929]), Vol. II, Pl. 19.

12. Sethe, *Dramatische Texte*, p. 31. Upwaut has been studied by E. Otto (see "Die beiden Länder Ägyptens in der ägyptischen Religionsgeschichte," "Analecta Orientalia," XVII [1938], 11–16, 19). There is no justification for seeing in the two wolf-standards on the Bull Palette symbols of the Upper and Lower Egyptian Upwauts rather than a combination on a par with that of falcon and ibis, for example.

13. The view we reject is held by Kees (*Götterglaube*, pp. 188–94). It is also rejected by Sethe (see above, chap. 6, n. 32). Some of Sethe's arguments, however, are not valid—namely, those based on his unproved assumption that two established kingdoms existed in Upper and Lower Egypt, respectively, before the days of Menes and that these kingdoms had been preceded by a unified state with its capital at Heliopolis (see above, chap. 1, n. 6). Kees's further claim that the gods were conceived as "feudal lords" (*Götterglaube*, p. 127) is unjustified; this is clearly shown by a comparison with Mesopotamia (Book II below), where the relation between the city gods and the people can rightly be described as that between a lord and his retainers and serfs. It is one thing to acknowledge that a bond existed between a community and its god and another to define the nature of that bond.

14. In coffin texts (spells 154–60) and in the Book of the Dead, several groups of "souls" occur: of Hermopolis, of the New moon feast, of East and West, and also of Pe, Nekhen,

and Heliopolis. These latter show no trace of the original meaning with which we are concerned but have simply become part of the mumbo-jumbo of the late funerary texts. The early Egyptian writing of the plural with the triple word sign has been misunderstood, hence the "souls" appear in these texts as triads of gods. See Sethe, *Untersuchungen*, III, 17–18; *Urgeschichte*, pp. 105–6; and, for the texts, "Die Sprüche für das Kennen der Seelen der heiligen Orte," *ZÄS*, Vols. LVII–LIX.

15. They are mentioned at Deir el Bahri but also on the Palermo Stone, Rev. 2, No. 2; Rev. 4, No. 3; Rev. 5, No. 2.

16. Kees, *Opfertanz*, p. 253.

17. Pyr. 1305*a*.

18. Pyr. 1262*b*.

19. Pyr. 1089.

20. Kees, *Opfertanz*, pp. 68 ff., discussing Mariette, *Abydos*, Vol. I, Pl. 29, and Calverley-Gardiner, *The Temple of King Sethos I*, Vol. II, Pl. 36.

21. Kees, *Götterglaube*, p. 280, states that the Souls of Pe and Nekhen cannot be royal ancestors because one would not expect them, then, in a presumably Heliopolitan context where they appear to the exclusion of the Souls of Heliopolis. But this argument is based on his acceptance of Sethe's imaginary "kingdom of Heliopolis" as a historical reality, so that there would be dead kings of Heliopolis as a separate group of ancestors. He proposes to see in the "Souls" "representatives of the assembled gods of the two halves of the country," but the evidence which we have discussed militates against that view. Moreover, Egypt, in contrast with Mesopotamia, did *not* know a divine assembly as a regular institution.

22. Pyr. 1294*a*, 2011*d*.

23. Sethe, in Borchardt, *Sahure*, II, 103.

24. Sethe, *Untersuchungen*, III, 8, 16, 20.

25. Pyr. 2108*a*.

26. Often illustrated, e.g., Jean Capart, *Les débuts de l'art en Egypte* (Brussels, 1904), Pl. I.

27. Kees, in *ZÄS*, LVII, 120 ff.

28. Naville, *Deir el Bahari*, Vol. III, Pl. LX.

29. Sethe remarked that some graffiti at El Kab (Nekheb) mentioned officials of the *per-ur*, but, since Nekhen was situated just across the Nile, these inscriptions do not vitiate our conclusion. See Sethe, *Kommentar*, IV, 189, *ad* Pyr. 910*b*.

30. Gardiner, *JEA*, XXX (1944), 27, n. 3.

31. Palermo Stone, Rev. 2, 2; Rev. 3, 1.

32. See already Ed. Meyer, *Geschichte des Altertums*, I, 2, pars. 198–99.

33. Gardiner, *JEA*, XXX (1944), 27, has proposed a new translation of *iterty*, namely, "the Conclave of Upper (or Lower) Egyptian deities"! He bases this on the gathering of these gods at the Sed festival, but it cannot account for the relation between the *iterty* and the "Souls" or Royal Ancestors at the Min festival, at the Mystery Play of the Succession, and in Pyr. 1262*b* and similar texts.

34. Borchardt, *Sahure*, II, 40, 102.

35. E.g., Pyr. 795 (see below, p. 115). In the temple of Neuserre the "Guardians of Nekhen" carry the Upper Egyptian king in his litter, but the onlookers call out, "May the *Souls* of Nekhen give life."

36. Nelson *et al.*, *Medinet Habu*, Vol. IV, Pl. 235.

37. Naville, *Deir el Bahari*, Vol. III, Pl. 60. Similar reliefs depicting the accession of Ramses II are published in *JEA*, Vol. XX (1934), Pl. III, 3.

38. Naville, *Deir el Bahari*, Vol. III, Pls. 63 (left side) and 64. The relief is damaged where the Upper Egyptian shrine was presumably mentioned.

39. *Ibid.*, Vol. II, Pl. 51.

40. E.g., at Abydos (see n. 20) and at Karnak: Von Bissing–Kees, *Re-Heiligtum*, Vol. III, Beiblatt A. See also Sethe in Borchardt, *Sahure*, II, 103.

41. So Sethe, *Kommentar*, II, 293.

42. H. E. Winlock, *Bas-reliefs from the Temple of Rameses I at Abydos*, p. 53. Here is further evidence that the "souls" were ancient kings. The verb *hnw*, in one of its occurrences, has as its determinative a man in the usual attitude beating his breast but wearing the Red Crown of a Lower Egyptian king. At Deir el Bahri (Naville, *Deir el Bahari*, Vol. III, Pl. 60) three

groups of souls are shown instead of the usual two groups, but there is no evidence that the third group belongs to Heliopolis. Their connection with shrines also falls outside the usual scheme: the wolf-headed figures are "lords of the divine palace," the falcon-headed figures, "lords of the Upper Egyptian (sic) Dual Shrine," and the human-headed figures, "lords of the Lower-Egyptian Dual Shrine."

43. Nelson et al., Medinet Habu, Vol. IV, Pls. 229, 231.

NOTES TO CHAPTER 8

1. The changes of dynasties took place, in all likelihood, through association of an outsider with a princess of the blood royal; or, after times of confusion, a new line might see in its success in unifying the country proof that the gods were truly working through it. We know extremely little of the actual changes of dynasty because they were glossed over in the official records for the sake of the ideal continuity. Thus the Turin Papyrus does not indicate a break in the line of Menes before the Sixth Dynasty (see above, chap. 3, n. 27). All preceding kings count as ancestors of the monarch irrespective of his true descent. We have seen that all kings back to Menes appear as the Royal Ancestors at the Min festivals of Ramses II and Ramses III (p. 89). To quote a very specific instance, we find King Sebekemsaf in the Thirteenth Dynasty completing a porch at Medamud "in continuation of what had been done by his father Senusert III." Senusert III was not even of the same house as Sebekemsaf. See R. Cottevielle-Giraudet, Fouilles de Médamoud (1931), "Fouilles de l'Institut Français d'Archéologie Orientale du Caire," Vol. IX, p. 6.

2. Sethe, Urk., IV:156; Breasted, Ancient Record , II, 140

3. Thus begins the story of Sinuhe.

4. While the institution of coregency is easily understood as a political expedient, it is difficult to explain its theological significance. I am not aware of evidence bearing on this matter. The accession formula "Horus in the arms of Osiris" did not apply until the old king had died. The coregent may have been in the position of a new ruler in the transitional period between accession and coronation, a phase we shall discuss presently. The prince sometimes became coregent when he had "reached the years of discretion." See De Buck in "Analecta Orientalia," XVII, 55, n. 26, translating the new sphinx-stela of Amenhotep II (ASAE, Vol. XXXVII, Pls. I, II, l. 11): "His Majesty was crowned as king as a beautiful youth, when he had come of age and when he had completed 18 years."

5. Naville, Deir el Bahari, Vols. II–III, Pls. 56–64. W. F. Edgerton, The Thutmosid Succession ("SAOC," No. 8), has shown that Tuthmosis I probably died before Hatshepsut assumed power. Officially she was regent for young Tuthmosis III, her nephew and husband, the son of her half-brother, Tuthmosis II, who had made the boy coregent. And it is interesting that a biographical inscription of an official, Ineni, reports the death of Tuthmosis I and II and the accession of Tuthmosis III as a child but recognizes only Hatshepsut's de facto powers, not the claim of being the legal successor which her reliefs and inscriptions are intended to demonstrate. Ineni's inscription (Breasted, Ancient Records, Vol. II, pars. 108, 116, 118, 341) runs: "The king (Tuthmosis I) rested from life, going forth to heaven, having completed his years in gladness of heart. The hawk in the nest (appeared as) the King of Upper and Lower Egypt, Aa-kheper-en-re (Tuthmosis II). He became King of the Black Land and Ruler of the Red Land, having taken possession of the Two Regions in triumph.

"He went forth to Heaven in triumph, having mingled with the gods. His son (Tuthmosis III) stood in his place as King of the Two Lands, having become ruler upon the throne of the one who begat him. His sister, the divine consort Hatshepsut, settled the (affairs) of the Two Lands by reason of her plans."

6. A. de Buck, in Mélanges Maspero, I, 2, 847–52. Also Gunn, in JEA, XXVII (1941), 2 ff.

7. Nelson et al., Medinet Habu, Vol. III ("OIP," Vol. XXIII), Pl. 152, l. 553; Pl. 163, l. 1191. Dr. Keith C. Seele points out to me that Ramses III erased the coronation date from his calendar and replaced it by a Feast of Victory (ibid., Pls. 162, 163, 164). His accession, on the other hand, was celebrated all through his life and even after his death in the reign of Ramses X (ZÄS, LXXII, 114). This is easily understood: if a choice had to be made, the accession was more important than the coronation, since the latter merely completed the transfer of power which had taken place at the death of the king's predecessor. Under special cir-

cumstances the distinction was apparently disregarded: Dr. Černý has established that Ramses IV was crowned on the day of his accession, which was also the day his predecessor Ramses III was murdered (ZÄS, LXXII, 109–18). See n. 15 below.

In *The Coregency of Ramses II with Seti I* (Chicago, 1940), p. 29, Dr. Seele distinguishes between accession and coronation in the case of kings who had been coregents; his use of those terms differs from ours.

8. Sethe, *Urk.*, IV: 895, 17—896, 8. Brugsch, and especially De Buck, *Oerheuvel*, pp. 89–90, have recognized the significance of this passage.

9. Gardiner, in *JEA*, XXIV (1938), 175–76.

10. One copy of a rescript announcing the accession of Tuthmosis I has been preserved (Erman, in *ZÄS*, XXIX, 116–19).

11. M. P. Nilsson, *Primitive Time-Reckoning* (Lund, 1920), pp. 45–108, 266–77; Wensinck, *Acta Orientalia*, I, 158–59.

12. A. W. Shorter, in *JEA*, Vol. XXI.

13. Gardiner, in *JEA*, II, 123–24. See also Sethe, *Kommentar*, II, 42; Kees, *Totenglauben*, p. 293.

14. Pyr. 340b; 346a; 356a, b; 361a; 1708c, d.

15. For the significance of the combination of the annual Osiris festivals with the rites of the dead king see below, p. 194. Brugsch, *Thesaurus*, V, 1125, argues that the coronation always took place on 1 Tybi because it followed the interment of Osiris. At Edfu the first of Tybi is the day of accession and the coronation of the god Horus. We know, however, from Hatshepsut's inscription, that 1 Thoth was an alternate possibility. We must assume that the majority of dates preserved in inscriptions were accession dates, referring to the actual assumption of power by the new king, since they are spread all through the year.

NOTES TO CHAPTER 9

1. See above, pp. 73–74. Cf. Naville, *Deir el Bahari*, Vols. II–III, Pls. 56–64; Sethe, *Urk.*, IV: 242–65. Sethe, *Dramatische Texte*, p. 4, points out that the orthography of the texts of Hatshepsut retains traces of very great antiquity. Junker, *Die Götterlehre von Memphis*, p. 13, errs in dating the texts after the introduction of the title "son of Re" in the Pharaonic protocol; the texts are dependent not upon a solar relationship but upon the concept of the Kamutef for which the immemorial identity of the king with Horus suffices.

2. A similar series of reliefs depicted Ramses II's accession: *JEA*, XX (1934), 18–19 and Pl. III.

3. In Breasted, *Ancient Records*, Vol. II, the oracle is described in par. 140; the confrontation with Amon-Re in pars. 141–42; the titulary in pars. 143–47; the establishment of effective rule in par. 148.

4. A. Erman, "Hymnen an das Diadem der Pharaonen" (*Abhandlungen der Preussischen Akademie, Phil.-hist. Klasse* [1911], No. 1). See above, pp. 67 and 92, for inanimate objects believed to be replete with power.

5. See above, chap. 3, n. 6.

6. Or possibly we should read "Neith." The goddess Neith of Sais always appears with the Red Crown, and there are traces that *bity*, the title of the Lower Egyptian king, is connected with Sais. (Sethe, *Urgeschichte*, pp. 67–68, and Von Bissing-Kees, *Untersuchungen*, p. 48). The Red Crown is found on a predynastic pot (Wainwright, in *JEA*, IX, 26–27).

7. The word *nezert* ("flame") identifies her with the goddess Wadjet, the uraeus, whose poison is a flame. And the name hangs together with that of the Lower Egyptian Dual Shrine, the *per-nezer* (see Sethe, *Kommentar*, I, 102).

8. There are further theological speculations implied in the text if we believe that the "father" of the crown is not merely called "father of the gods" to add to the stature of his daughter but that the title refers to Geb, who often bears it (Sethe, *Kommentar*, I, 105), and who is appropriately the father of snakes which emerge from the earth. The crown-goddess is then the sister of Geb's son Osiris, as is explicitly stated in Pyr. 309a. So Hugo Müller, *Die formale Entwicklung der Titulatur*, pp. 39–41. E. Otto, in "Analecta Orientalia," XVII (1938), 20–25, has studied various speculations to which the two crowns and the goddesses personifying them gave rise.

9. The evidence given in chap. 12, n. 26, and the fact that the various fluids of the body

are not always sharply distinguished make it possible that *neshesh*, "spittle," might stand for "semen." The "beetle" refers to the sun-god as Khepri (see p. 148 below).

NOTES TO CHAPTER 10

1. The last day of Khoiak was listed as "the Burial of Osiris" at Busiris and Denderah (*JEA*, II, 123). Dr. Richard A. Parker has put at my disposal his translation of a text from Denderah (Mariette, *Dendérah*, Vol. IV, Pl. 77) which shows that the interment of Osiris was enacted on Khoiak 24–30, with great jubilation in anticipation of his resurrection on the last day of the month. The preparation of the mummy is described in detail. Finally, "he awakes from sleep, and he flies like the *benu* bird, and he makes his place in the sky as the moon." Unfortunately, purely ritual interests predominate in these late texts. See chap. 15, n. 49, below.

2. Dr. J. A. Wilson points out that Sethe's "received" is a restoration and that Hayes, *Senwosret-ankh*, col. 513, has *ḥnp*, "carried off" or "stolen."

3. Dr. Wilson has also indicated that the uncertainty in Sethe's edition about Nut's being mentioned is removed by the text in Jéquier, *Le monument funéraire de Pepi II*, Vol. I, *Le tombeau royal* (Cairo, 1936), l. 715 to Pyr. 179*a*.

4. The litany-like character of this long text may explain the incongruence of second and third persons here.

5. Akeru is an earth-god.

6. Here again the king is identified with Horus and Seth (see above, p. 21).

7. The "Lake" must have been an expanse of water at Abydos used in connection with the Osiris mysteries. The description of Ikhernofret mentions that the enemies who rebelled against the Neshemet-boat of Osiris were defeated (Schäfer, "Die Mysterien des Osiris in Abydos unter König Sesostris III," in Sethe, "Untersuchungen zur Geschichte und Altertumskunde Ägyptens," IV); but Neferhotep (Pieper, "Die grosse Inschrift des Königs Neferhotep in Abydos," in *Mitteilungen der Vorderasiatisch-Ägyptischen Gesellschaft*, Vol. XXXII [1929]) explicitly mentions the lake immediately before this conflict is described (see below, p. 206).

8. See above, chap. 3, n. 6.

9. "Beating of the flesh" and undoing and tearing the hair are actions of mourners, as the tomb paintings show. In this way the "souls" take up the theme of the earthly funeral, continuing the procession, as it were, in the Hereafter, until they then suddenly speak the five short sentences of transfiguration.

10. The allusion is obscure.

11. In the funerary ritual the scene described in this text is enacted; the dead man is actually welcomed by dancers, called Muu, who represent the inhabitants of the Hereafter. See Emma Brunner-Traut, *Der Tanz im alten Ägypten* ("Ägyptologische Forschungen," No. 6 [Glückstadt, 1938]), pp. 43, 53–59. The Muu wear sometimes high reed crowns, sometimes plants on their heads; some of them are connected with Pe. But recognizing the religious importance of Pe does not mean accepting the imaginary "history" of predynastic times constructed by Sethe (see chap. 1, n. 6, above), although this is done by the two authors who have dealt with the dance of the Muu—Junker, in *Mitteilungen des Deutschen Instituts für Ägyptische Altertumskunde in Kairo*, IX, 1940, 1–39, and J. Vandier, in *Chronique d'Egypte*, 1944, pp. 35 ff.

12. The two aspects of the king's survival after death find a parallel in the ways in which he regarded his monuments and institutions. His decisions were spontaneous and creative acts, motivated by considerations which mere humans could not comprehend and realizing a divine order. But he also wished his name—the name of the mortal incarnation of Horus—to survive by means of monuments. See below, p. 268, and chap. 4, n. 33.

13. Kenset is an ancient name for Nubia; originally it probably designated the weird and mysterious cataract region near Assuan, at the southern limits of Egypt, where the Nile breaks through a granite barrier. In this wild region and in the boiling and whirling currents among the rocks, the Nile was thought to emerge from the Netherworld. Hence it was a place where the dead underwent purification when entering the Netherworld or Hereafter. They were purified "in the waters of Kenset" or "near the field of Kenset." Re is the "bull of Kenset," for the land of the dead may also be projected into the sky. For references see Sethe, *Kommentar*, I, 317–18, and *Sonnenauge*, p. 15.

14. The doctrine of the king's transfiguration at death sometimes presented difficulties even to the Egyptians—hence a small number of pyramid texts which do not identify the dead king with Osiris. One can explain them, as we have done in the text, by the inability of some survivors to think of their dead monarch, known hitherto as Horus, as Osiris, and by the desire to insure him an individual survival. In the latter case a distinction between dead king and Osiris was insisted upon, Osiris appearing as a true Pluto (see below). This distinction gives rise to texts which have been interpreted as signs of hostility to Osiris on the part of the worshipers of Re. But it is totally misleading to introduce theories of conflicting religious schools, such as a "religion of Osiris" and a "religion of Re" (e.g., Breasted, *Development of Religion and Thought*, pp. 140–41; Kees, *Totenglauben*, pp. 90 ff., 205 ff.). The evidence upon which they are based shows no more than that different aspects of the Hereafter were differently stressed; it does not annul the evidence of the homogeneity of Egyptian culture at all periods or of its strong continuity. Many of the texts adduced to prove antagonism between the cults of Re and Osiris can be explained quite well without that assumption. For instance, if Pyr. 2175 warns the dead king against the roads of the West, another and older version (Pyr. 1531–32) warns him against the roads of the East; and both texts are merely concerned that the dead join the cosmic circuit in the best possible manner. Other alleged instances of antagonism lose their relevancy when considered in context; so, in Pyr. 145–46 (Breasted, *op. cit.*, pp. 139–40), which is part of a long mythological act in which dualism plays a preponderant part, the king appears as Horus-and-Seth (Pyr. 141*d*). See also Sethe, *Kommentar*, I, 16–38, esp. 19.

Pyr. 1236–37 stress that the king in the course of his cosmic circuit enters and leaves the land of the dead *and is not retained there:* "No god can retain him." Pyr. 349–50 conveys the same view, Osiris being named as a true king of the dead alongside another necropolis god. Here, then, there is an opposition, not between theologies or priestly schools, but between two conceptions of the late ruler who appears as the unchanging image of the dead king, Osiris, or as an individual, recently dead, and thought of as surviving death individually. The moment this distinction is felt at all, Osiris is likely to appear as the personification of death. Another contrast, related to the one just discussed, is that between the dead ruler and the ordinary dead: "Thou approachest the gates which repel the (ordinary) people" (Pyr. 655*b*). But the common dead are thought to be in the charge of Osiris. They are addressed: "Ye who are under the direction of Osiris" (Pyr. 1236*b*), but to the king is said: "Thou art not among them" (Pyr. 251, for example). Here, again, the "antagonism" to Osiris is but apparent and due to the specific context. Other texts quoted to prove the existence of conflicting schools of thought merely stress the dead king's immense power, even over gods (e.g., the "Cannibal Text" [Pyr. 393–414]).

The matter has been further confused by the fact that scholars have overlooked the significance of the circuit which connects Osiris, and not only Re, with the sky (see below, pp. 195–97 and p. 210). It is, moreover, erroneous to separate the night sky from the thought of death. Since day and light pertain to life, darkness and night sky pertain to death and are thought of as part of the Beyond. In the "watches" (Junker, *Die Stundenwachen in den Osirismysterien nach den Inschriften von Dendera, Edfu und Philae* [Wien, 1910]), Isis and Nephthys keep watch with Osiris all through the night; but at daybreak he leaves them, for the night is the time of the dead. In the coffin texts we read: "Bastet .... is there to guard thee until the earth brightens and thou descendest into the Netherworld" (Lacau, *Textes religieux*, No. 21, quoted by Kees, *op. cit.*, p. 401). See further, for the correlation of night and death in Egyptian texts, C. E. Sander-Hansen, *Der Begriff des Todes bei den Ägyptern* (Copenhagen, 1942). Kees, *op. cit.*, p. 92, wrongly ranges the night sky alongside the day sky as the opposite of the Netherworld and of death.

These examples may suffice to show that one should make a stand against the atomized rendering of Egyptian religion which tends to become fashionable as a result of the legitimate and very necessary investigation of special problems.

15. See Ranke, "Das altägyptische Schlangenspiel" in *Sitzungsberichte der Heidelberger Akademie der Wissenschaften*, Vol. XI; Pieper, in *ZÄS*, LXVI, 16 ff.

16. See Sethe (*Kommentar*, IV, 69), who urges that the grammar of Pyr. 822*c* requires our interpretation but rejects it as unintelligible. In Pyr. 2062*c* the "Roads of Heaven" and the "Roads of the Field of Offerings" are also identical.

17. See p. 117 above, with n. 13, and p. 170 below. Also Pyr. 920*b, c*; 1245*a, b*.

18. See pp. 117–18, 121, 154.

19. See pp. 152–54 and Pyr. 542a, 265a.

20. Pyr. 749 states that the "Reed Field" and the "Field of Offerings" are inhabited by the Imperishable Stars. Pyr. 100c and d locate the place of the dead, therefore, "on the east side of heaven in its northern region."

21. See also Pyr. 1080.

22. See Junker, *Giza*, II, 41 ff., 57–59. The view that at any time the ancient Egyptians' speculations about life after death were confined to thoughts about a proper interment (so, for instance, for early periods, Kees, *Totenglauben*, *passim*) is untenable, since it does not explain the elaborate preparations and funerary rites. These prove that detailed views about life in the Hereafter existed and that measures were taken to meet its requirements. The tomb, down to the Middle Kingdom, merely furnished the necessary apparatus, *realiter* or *in effigie*, and did not depict or describe the Hereafter. We agree with Junker that the texts refer to both interment and afterlife, but we insist also that the first is viewed as merging into the latter without sharp boundary. See also n. 23.

23. It is characteristic that the rendering of these boat journeys appears to us to be full of ambiguities. We want to decide whether they present ritual or an imagined event in the Hereafter. The Egyptian did not need to be unequivocal in distinguishing these, since an imagined event acquired a measure of reality, at least effectiveness, by the very fact that it was depicted. For our dilemma (which is decidedly ours alone), see, for instance, Gardiner and Davies, *The Tomb of Amenemhēt*, pp. 47–48.

24. The Egyptian beliefs concerning the Hereafter have been treated somewhat more systematically in my forthcoming *Ancient Egyptian Religion: An Interpretation*.

25. Dr. J. A. Wilson points out to me that sometimes Nut bears this title also (Pyr. 823d).

26. It is curious that the text ends with an appeal to Atum, since all that precedes takes Atum's intimate relation with the dead king for granted. But this feature recurs often and seems peculiar to the Egyptian mind. On p. 116 we find a final appeal to the gods of the Dual Shrines, after the warm reception which they granted the dead king has been described in detail. Such closing phrases sound like a docket summarizing the meaning of the preceding text.

27. *Kheper*, "to become," seems the typical verb for the progress and the changes of the sun in its circuit.

NOTES TO CHAPTER 11

1. Published as the second part of Sethe, *Dramatische Texte*. The roll of papyrus measures 2.15 by 0.25 meters and is covered with 139 vertical columns of cursive writing. At the foot of the columns are sketchy vignettes showing some action described in the text above.

2. We remember that Hatshepsut visited a number of sanctuaries in the suite of her father after her accession had been assured but before she was crowned. One wonders whether this account renders actual events or whether it is a mere interpretation (aimed at strengthening her claim of legality) of visits which were obligatory between accession and coronation. The Middle Kingdom rulers who were elected coregent were exactly in the position described (probably untruthfully) by Hatshepsut. For them, too, a period of initiation may have separated accession and coronation.

3. The following objects, for instance, are all identified with Osiris: a tree; barley; bread and beer; water; the Qeni stomacher; a divine chapel. The following, on the other hand, are called "the Eye of Horus": oil; wine; eye paint; incense; raisins; faïence; carnelian; textiles; the two feathers of the king; the two scepters; the diadem; the two falcon standards; two plaques with baboons; a food table; the king's ship.

4. Similarly: "When we turn to the medieval coronation, we must bear in mind that we are moving in a world that has become completely strange to us," and that because "we have degraded symbols into tokens and have adopted the habit of sundering form from content" (Percy E. Schramm, *A History of the English Coronation* [Oxford, 1937], pp. 10–11 *et passim*).

5. *Man*, 1935, No. 59; *ibid.*, 1939, No. 21.

6. Letopolis is one of the places where Osiris had been vindicated (Book of the Dead, Sethe, *Urk.*, V: 119).

7. Pyr. 261a–b; 1628c.

8. We are retaining this translation of the title *sekhen akh* (see Sethe, *Dramatische Texte*, pp. 193, 217), though Spiegel, *ZÄS*, LXXV, 118–19, makes it probable that the original meaning was "reviver of the *akh*," parallel to the *hem ka*. This title is always translated "the servant of the ka." But the sign read *ka* was originally *sekhen* and the title, therefore, originally *sekhen hem*, "reviver of the (dead) body." The term *sekhen* meant something more specific than our "reviving." It indicated the action by which the dead man was restored to life in the Hereafter, possibly by means of the "embrace" which we discuss below (pp. 133–37), since the sign shows two curved arms. The official called *sekhen akh* actually carried the dead king in his arms (p. 138).

9. See above, p. 21. Dr. J. A. Wilson points out that this idea finds support in the abbreviation of the title *Nebuy*, "The Two Lords," to two falcon standards, a usage observed as late as the Eighteenth Dynasty (Sethe, *Urk.*, IV: 138, 3) and even, as Dr. Seele points out to me, under Ramses III (Nelson *et al.*, *Medinet Habu*, Vol. IV, Pl. 229, l. 33). These standards serve as the determinative of *Nebuy* in earlier times, e.g., Pyr. 593*b*.

10. The text indicates that a circular object of gold is brought in; but Sethe's translation "ring" is apt to be read as "finger ring," and such rings were not, as far as we know, part of the regalia. But the gold diadem is known to have been its essential component and was, moreover, called for at this point in the ceremony.

11. J. Spiegel, *Die Erzählung vom Streite des Horus und Seth*, p. 85, has seen that the Eye represents the crown in this tale too. It has become ownerless through the death of Osiris and is presented by Thoth (as in our Mystery Play) to the supreme god in Heliopolis, while the child Horus presses his claims to the throne.

While the various meanings of the Sacred Eye in the funerary and coronation rituals are interrelated in the manner we have described, there is some confusion in mythology. On the one hand, it is said that the Eye (the sun) is sent out and fetched back by an ambassador of the sun-god—Thoth, Onuris, or Shu—"after it has thrown down the enemies of his (Shu's) father Re." This Eye can deal death with its searing heat, yet it is indispensable (Sethe, *Sonnenauge*). On the other hand, there is the beneficial moon waning at intervals; it is the Eye of Horus, torn out or damaged by Seth, and it must be recaptured or healed.

12. So Lohmeyer, "Der göttliche Wohlgeruch" (*Sitzungsberichte der Heidelberger Akademie* [1919]).

13. A. van Gennep, *Les rites de passage* (Paris, 1909).

14. It is, again, an indication of the Egyptians' concrete way of thinking that the well-being of the dead in the Hereafter was dependent on descendants who were actually possessed of life (see p. 110). The food-offerings are merely instrumental to the survival of the dead. The essential feature of the funerary cult is the absolute dependence of the dead upon those who possess the secret and the substance of life. The formula regulating the relations of dead and living in the funerary cult (which also applies to Horus and Osiris) is: The quick revive the dead; the dead support the living.

15. See Jéquier in *Bulletin de l'Institut Français d'Archéologie Orientale*, XIX (1922), 257–60.

16. Breasted, *Ancient Records*, Vol. III, par. 401.

17. The "Tale of the Two Brothers" appears in Erman-Blackman, *Literature*, pp. 150–61. It is used as an example of the distinctive imagery and reasoning of Egyptian theology, not without justification, by H. Jacobsohn, *Die dogmatische Stellung des Königs*.

18. In the daily ritual of the temple when cloth of this same purple material is given to the god, it is said, "One god joins himself to the other." See A. Moret, *Le rituel du culte divin journalier* (Paris, 1902), p. 188.

19. See R. O. Faulkner in *JEA*, Vol. XXII, for a late ritual in which these priestesses play a part.

NOTES TO CHAPTER 12

1. The basic experience is beautifully illustrated in an example quoted by Van der Leeuw, *Religion in Essence and Manifestation*, p. 37: A West African Negro is on an important expedition when he suddenly stumbles over a stone. He cries out, "Ha! are you there?" and takes the stone with him. The stone had, as it were, given a hint that it was powerful; hence the Negro strengthened himself by taking possession of it. This is the pattern of many

experiences which in their turn may give rise to cults. First there is an emotional tension which makes man receptive to signs of a supernatural order. (In our example the importance of the expedition created this favorable atmosphere.) Then there is the sudden impact of a power which makes itself felt in the outside world. Finally, this power is brought into some relation with the individual involved in the experience. If he succeeds in making his community acknowledge the validity of his experience, a cult will be established. This happens, for instance, in the following case: An Ewe Negro finds a piece of iron, goes home, and falls ill. The priests declare that a divine being is manifest in the iron and demand that the village henceforth worship it (ibid.). See also Speculative Thought.

2. Henri Bergson, Les deux sources de la morale et de la religion (Paris, 1934), pp. 202–13.

3. In the funerary temple of Neuserre (Borchardt, Neuserre, p. 94, Bastet appears as a lioness; in that of Sahure (Borchardt, Sahure, Vol. II, Pls. 35–36), the head is lost; but the titles of the goddess are the same as in the other relief. In late times, when the goddess appears as a cat, she often carries a lion mask in one hand. Sethe, Urgeschichte, pp. 19–20, enumerates a variety of goddesses, including a hare, who became lionesses and were identified with Sekhmet.

4. This question has been studied further in my forthcoming Ancient Egyptian Religion: An Interpretation. It has been shown there that in the case of Isis and the throne, and of cosmic phenomena and human problems, we have to deal with correlations in the strictest sense of the word.

5. When Eberhard Otto, Beiträge zur Geschichte der Stierkulte in Ägypten (Leipzig, 1938), p. 5, decrees that no animal cult can have been introduced after the anthropomorphic conception of gods had become familiar to the Egyptians, he implies that distinct types of divinities succeeded one another and formed, as it were, phases in a historical development of Egyptian religion. The same postulate underlies Sethe's Urgeschichte. But this view ignores the living reality of Egyptian, as of all primitive, religion which recognizes gods as personified powers but does not hold that a single embodiment limits their scope (p. 167 below). They may be conceived in human as well as in any other form in which they are felt to manifest themselves. See the first chapter of my Ancient Egyptian Religion: An Interpretation.

6. JNES, I, 132 ff. See above, chap. 5, n. 27.

7. Gardiner, in JEA, XXX (1944), 35.

8. For an excellent study on this subject see A. Bertholet, Götterspaltung und Göttervereinigung (Tübingen, 1933).

9. Sethe, Urgeschichte, p. 160; Kommentar, IV, 173 (Pyr. 900a).

10. The one has been attempted by Heinrich Brugsch and W. B. Kristensen, the other by Sethe and Kees. Kees, "Grundsätzliches zur Aufgabenstellung der ägyptischen Religionsgeschichte," Göttingische gelehrte Anzeigen, 1936, pp. 49–61, assumes naïvely that his rather banal approach (see chap. 1, n. 6, above) shows that he "will sich . . . . zur Denkweise eines andersgearteten Volks mit andersgearteter Logik bequemen." His method, he maintains, follows directives first formulated by Maspero, Etudes de mythologie et d'archéologie égyptiennes, II (1893), 183–278, 337–93. But Maspero never lost sight of the fact that the Egyptians shared a common creed as well as a common language and a common material civilization (e.g., ibid., pp. 261–62). We have attempted here, and in Speculative Thought, to describe the "andersgeartete Logik" of the Egyptians and to understand their religion by tracing in the pages which follow the main avenues of their mythopoeic thought. We have, moreover, described their main religious preoccupations in Ancient Egyptian Religion: An Interpretation. There we have furthermore attempted, not to formulate a "basic doctrine of Egyptian religion," but to show that Egyptian beliefs are less incoherent than is commonly alleged; for they appear to be rooted in a single basic conviction—hardly explicit but of all-pervading importance—that the touchstone of significance is changelessness.

11. So clearly in the inscription on the large granite beetle erected by Amenhotep III in Thebes (Spiegelberg, in ZÄS, LXVI [1931], 44–45).

12. This dialogue forms part of chap. 175 of the Book of the Dead (see Kees, Lesebuch, p. 27, No. 40). In Götterglaube, p. 216, n. 6, Kees points out that Anthes (Die Felseninschriften von Hatnub [Leipzig, 1928], Graffito No. 26) also refers to the primeval snake which survives when everything else is destroyed at the end of time.

13. Kees, Götterglaube, pp. 62 and 335.

14. The material has been collected and discussed by Ahmad Mohammed Badawi, Der

Gott Chnum (Glückstadt, 1937). See also Kees, *Lesebuch*, p. 19, No. 25, and, for late theological speculations connected with Khnum, Kees, *Götterglaube*, pp. 436–43.

15. Otto, *op. cit.*, p. 32, of the Nineteenth Dynasty! See *ibid.*, pp. 23–31, for various theological speculations which found expression in this compound name. We do not exclude their relevance but have merely given the simplest formulation of the ideas which went into the compound.

16. The preoccupation with survival after death was almost an obsession with the Egyptians. Consequently, the figure of Osiris who had known both life and death gained preponderant importance in their religious life. By the time our sources throw light on the daily cult in the temples, the ritual is shot through with symbols and ceremonies which were originally relevant to Osiris only; but this is a secondary development. The daily ritual of the Amon temple in the New Kingdom is published by Moret (*op. cit.*), who believed that from the first the Osireian funerary rites set the stage for the cults of all gods. W. B. Kristensen recognized as Egyptian the thought that eternal life can be reached only through death and thus explained many symbols of Egyptian and other ancient religions (see his bibliography in *Jaarbericht No. 5: Ex Oriente Lux* [Leiden, 1938], pp. 284–86). He would consider the coming-forth out of death of spontaneous life the basic manifestation of the divine and would presumably consider the three spheres which we have distinguished (p. 145) as subsidiary. We admit that the Egyptians were predominantly concerned with the mystery of life, but this forms the pivot of the processes of creation and procreation no less than of that of resurrection; we consider that the latter was viewed as parallel rather than as basic to the two others and that Kristensen relies too much on Osireian and funerary documents. For the distortion of Egyptian beliefs in classical sources see below, pp. 291 ff.

NOTES TO CHAPTER 13

1. Attempts to treat Re and Atum, not as different aspects of a single god manifest in the sun, but as two deities who were originally distinct, rely on purely hypothetical constructions and must do so since the earliest texts do not allow the distinction to be made. This applies to Sethe, *Urgeschichte*, pp. 94–95, as well as to Junker, *Der sehende und blinde Gott*, pp. 29 ff., 39, *et passim*. Sethe states that the sun's old nontheological name was Re but that he was identified at Heliopolis with a local god Atum, who was not, however, like the old local gods "natürlichen Ursprungs," but a product of theological speculation. Junker (*op. cit.*) makes much of the different relations of Re and Atum with Nut, the sky, which can, however, be more easily explained as a consequence of the usual Egyptian multiplicity of approaches (see Index). It is significant that Atum's name is never combined with that of any other god but Re.

2. H. Grapow, *Die bildlichen Ausdrücke des Ägyptischen* (Leipzig, 1924), p. 30.

3. *ZÄS*, LX, 68.

4. See chap. 2, n. 24.

5. Kubban Stela, ll. 17–18; Blackman, in *JEA*, XI, 202, n. 5.

6. Mariette, *Abydos*, Vol. I, Pl. 51, 40 ff., after De Buck, *Oerheuvel*, p. 97.

7. Also "throne of Re" or "throne of Amon." References in De Buck, *Oerheuvel*, p. 98.

8. Sethe, *Urk.*, IV: 291, 10. The fact that the phrase is followed by the formula "like Re" is due either to the tendency of separate aspects of one god to become independent (see above, p. 144) or to the appropriateness with which it can be appended to an epithet of the king in other contexts.

9. It is usual to ascribe the universal recognition of the power of the sun in Egypt to the ancient political influence of Heliopolis. It seems to us that Heliopolis was a center where *common* Egyptian beliefs were effectively elaborated. Religious phenomena cannot be treated as the by-products of developments in other spheres. If it is said that the worship of Re became prominent in the Old Kingdom because the Fifth Dynasty derived from Heliopolis, we must remember that as early as the Second and Third Dynasties names compounded with Re, such as the epithet "Golden Sun Disk" (instead of "Gold Falcon"), occur and that the Ennead seems to appear on reliefs of the Third Dynasty (*Mitteilungen des Deutschen Instituts für Ägyptische Altertumskunde*, IV, 6–14). The sun disk worn by Seth and Geb in these reliefs suggests, in any case, that they were depicted as members of the Ennead of Atum. The

political development, the accession of the Fifth Dynasty, cannot be made responsible for the solar theology or for its wide acceptance. It was part of the common heritage of the Egyptians, a correlate in the religious field of the unity which is so clearly observed in the fields of linguistics, archeology, and physical anthropology.

10. A. L. J. Wensinck, in *Acta Orientalia*, I (1923), 174.

11. Erman-Ranke, *Ägypten und ägyptisches Leben im Altertum*, p. 170.

12. This is a typical instance of mythopoeic participation (see *Speculative Thought*). The view that New Year's Day is the anniversary of creation is fairly common. See Wensinck, *op. cit., pp.* 168–69, who quotes, for instance, the Jewish liturgy of the New Year: "Today is the beginning of thy works, the memorial of the first day."

13. So De Buck, *Oerheuvel*, pp. 63–71. Also Sethe, *Kommentar*, III, 18–19.

14. Sethe, *Amun*, pp. 52, 61.

15. Scharff, *Ägyptische Sonnenlieder* (1922), p. 31.

16. Here we meet the same theory of creative utterance which formed a fundamental element in the Memphite Theology, written more than one thousand years earlier (see above, chap. 2).

17. The Book of Apophis; see Roeder, *Urkunden zur Religion des alten Ägypten* (Jena, 1915), p. 108; and H. Grapow, "Die Welt vor der Schöpfung," *ZÄS*, LXVII (1931), 34 ff.

18. This subject is thoroughly investigated by De Buck, *Oerheuvel*. See also Wensinck, "The Ideas of the Western Semites concerning the Navel of the Earth," in *Verhandelingen der Koninklijke Akademie van Wetenschappen* (Amsterdam, 1916).

19. Junker, *Das Götterdekret über das Abaton*, p. 9.

20. Sethe, *Urk.*, IV: 364.

21. Cities in which great sanctuaries stood referred to these beliefs in their names. Memphis was called "The divine emerging primeval island," Thebes "The island emerging in Nun which first came into being when all other places were still in obscurity," Hermonthis "the high ground which grew out of Nun" or "the egg which originated in the beginning" or "the seed of the Great Soul (Amon-Re-Atum)" (De Buck, *Oerheuvel*, pp. 72–84; Sethe, *Amun*, pp. 117–18).

22. De Buck, *Oerheuvel*, p. 99.

23. Frankfort, *The Cenotaph of Seti I at Abydos* (London, 1932).

24. The only theory which accounts satisfactorily for the evidence, including the architectural development, is the one which starts from the concept of the Primeval Hill and is thus able to account for both the step pyramid (and possibly the recently discovered step mastabas at Saqqara) and the true pyramid. This approach was first found, as far as we are aware, by W. B. Kristensen, *Het Leven uit den Dood* (Leiden, 1926), and De Buck, *Oerheuvel*. Earlier authors had interpreted the pyramid as closely related to the sun without finding the true key to the problem; so Breasted, *Development of Religion and Thought in Ancient Egypt*, pp. 15, 70–78; and Moret, lastly in "L'influence du décor solaire sur la pyramide," in *Mélanges Maspero*, I, 624–36.

25. H. Ricke, "Der hohe Sand in Heliopolis," *ZÄS*, LXXI (1935), 107 ff.; De Buck, *Oerheuvel*, pp. 25 ff.

26. The evidence that the *benben* stone was viewed as solidified seed of Atum is conclusive. A late text from the Khonsu temple is unequivocal. This temple is called Benent; and this name ("seed") is explained in the following text in the usual Egyptian manner by establishing relations through word-play. It says about Amon-Re: "He is the god who begat (*bnn*) a place (*bw*) in the primeval ocean, when seed (*bnn.t*) flowed out (*bnbn*) the first time (i.e., at creation) . . . . it flowed out (*bnbn*) under him as is usual, in its name 'seed' (*bnn.t*)" (Sethe, *Amun*, p. 118). Then follows a reference to "the high ground which arose out of the primeval ocean" so that we are dealing here with a late Theban parallel to the Heliopolitan *benben* referred to in our pyramid text. In fact, the Theban text identifies the Khonsu temple with the Primeval Hill. This is usually done with important temples, as we have seen.

In perfect agreement with the text from the Khonsu temple is another text in which the four male members of the Ogdoad become a black bull, the four females a black cow, for the purpose of creating the sun; but the Primeval Hill is envisaged when the outflow of the seed of the bull in the Great Lake of Hermopolis is mentioned (Sethe, *Amun*, pp. 84–85). For in this lake was the "Isle of Flames," the Primeval Hill of that locality.

The root *bn* and its duplication *bnbn* are connected with various outflows, including those of a sexual nature (see *Wörterbuch*, I, 456 ff.).

27. The pyramidion on top of the obelisk is called *bnbnt*, and the *bnbn* stone had originated as a drop of seed of Atum or of a bull (see n. 26); hence it is likely that the obelisk did not serve merely as an impressive support for the stylized *benben* stone which formed its tip but that it was originally a phallic symbol at Heliopolis, 𓊽𓊽, the "pillar city." Pillar and bull are often interchangeable in Egyptian imagery (see p. 169 below); and a bull, Mnevis, was worshiped at Heliopolis. In a variant of Pyr. 792 the determinative "obelisk" stands for "pillar," and in Pyr. 1178*a*, "It is Pepi who belongs to the two obelisks chosen by Re and belonging to the earth," the obelisks carry a bull's head in their name. A bull's head is attached to the pillar in one of the symbols depicted by Osorkon II (Naville, *The Festival Hall of Osorkon II*, Pl. IX, 9).

28. Sethe, *Kommentar*, III, 18–19. Curious evidence that the Primeval Hill in any form was *ipso facto* charged with vital power comes in the so-called "Cannibal Text" in the pyramids, where the dead king increases his potency by incorporating into himself other gods. It is said of him that he "ate their intestines after they had filled their stomachs with magic on the 'Isle of Flames' " (Pyr. 397). It is a result of a development of this view of the Primeval Hill as a place of burial and resurrection (because it is a center of vital force) that in the coffin texts the dead are said to dwell there or come from there (Kees, *Totenglauben*, pp. 294, 334).

29. See also Kristensen, *De plaats van het zondvloed verhaal in het Gilgamesh epos* (*Mededeelingen der Koninklijke Akademie van Wetenschappen, Afd. Letterkunde*, Vol. V [Amsterdam, 1916]). In the pyramid texts these waters are variously called "The Winding Waterway," "The Lake of a Thousand Waterbirds," "The Lake of Rushes" (the "Isle" is then the "Field of Rushes"), "The Lake of the Fox," or "The Lake of Those at the Dawn."

30. See above, pp. 69, 117, and 121, for purification texts. In the cosmological text, Lange and Neugebauer, *Papyrus Carlsberg No. 1*, chap. A I, l. 8 (p. 16; cf. pp. 22–23), the sun is stated to rise from water.

31. Erman, *Religion*, p. 62.

32. Hence our argument is not affected even if Wainwright (in *JEA*, XVII, 151 ff.) is right in denying that Amon belonged originally to the Ogdoad.

33. Pyr. 337, 926; Sethe, *Kommentar*, II, 27 ff. Cf. *JEA*, IV, 174.

34. The winged beetle is shown beside Nut's knee in our figure. Next to the great design of Nut as a woman stands a "Dramatic Text" which adds yet another image to those we have discussed. Since Nut swallows the stars at dawn to bear them again at dusk, she is called "Sow who eats her piglets" (*ibid.*, p. 83), and she is, in fact, occasionally represented as a sow (Grapow, in *ZÄS*, LXXI, 45–47).

35. Sethe, in *Sitzungsberichte der Preussischen Akademie*, 1928, p. 8.

36. On these see Grapow in *ZÄS*, LXXII, 12 ff.; also De Buck, *Oerheuvel*, pp. 38–39, and Charles Maystre and Alexandre Piankoff, *Le livre des portes* ("Mémoires de l'Institut Français d'Archéologie Orientale," Vol. LXXIV [Cairo, 1939]).

37. See above, n. 30.

38. Breasted, *Ancient Records*, Vol. IV, par. 870.

39. Breasted has insisted on the moral influence which the beliefs concerning Re had in Egypt (*Development of Religion and Thought in Ancient Egypt*, pp. 170 *et passim*). Cf. Joachim Spiegel, "Der Sonnengott in der Barke als Richter," *Mitteilungen des Deutschen Instituts für Ägyptische Altertumskunde in Kairo*, VIII (1939), 201–6.

40. Luckenbill, *Ancient Records of Assyria and Babylonia*, Vol. II, par. 523.

41. Breasted, *Ancient Records*, Vol. II, par. 299.

42. A fine collection of these poems is published by Scharff, *Ägyptische Sonnenlieder*.

43. See Erman-Blackman, *Literature*, pp. 288–91.

44. See above, n. 1, and chap. 12, n. 11. The several names of the sun-god are sometimes substantialized into separate personages, e.g., in *The Contendings of Horus and Seth*.

45. After Scharff, *Ägyptische Sonnenlieder*, pp. 56–57, revised by Dr. J. A. Wilson after British Museum, *Hieroglyphic Texts from Egyptian Stelae, etc.*, Part VIII, Pl. XXI, and p. 24.

46. Schäfer, in *ZÄS*, LXXI, 17–19; also Sethe, "Altägyptische Vorstellungen vom Lauf der Sonne" (*Sitzungsberichte der Preussischen Akademie* [Berlin, 1928]), and De Buck, in

Jaarbericht No. 5: Ex Oriente Lux (Leiden, 1938), pp. 305 ff. W. B. Kristensen, in *Jaarbericht No. 2: Ex Oriente Lux*, pp. xv ff., esp. p. xx, has demonstrated that East and West, as places of transition between night and day, can be treated as interchangeable and thus give rise to a confusion which, in its turn, underlies the controversy between Sethe and Schäfer.

47. Pyr. 703–5, 1686–88.

48. Pyr. 367–68, 490–91, 922, 954–55. Sethe, *Kommentar*, II, 387–88, lists a number of places where the dead king acts as court official of Re.

49. Sethe, *Kommentar*, III, 124. The four goddesses are Isis, Nephthys, Neith, and Selket, who are in charge of the canopic jars which inclose the intestines of the dead.

50. This development is brilliantly studied by Sethe, *Amun*. It would seem that the universal devotion commanded by Amon-Re was due not to the political position of Thebes but to the unprecedented religious significance which the combination of the features of Re and of Amon possessed.

51. *Ibid.*, p. 73, with reference to Pyr. 1540*b*.

52. *Ibid.*, p. 78.

53. *Ibid.*, p. 92.

54. Gardiner, in *ZÄS*, XLII, 34.

55. *Ibid.*, p. 33.

56. Sethe, *Amun*, p. 90. Sethe also points out that Plutarch and Diodorus state that the Egyptians called Zeus (Amon) *pneuma theon*.

57. Gunn, in *JEA*, III, 81 ff.

58. Sethe, *Amun*, pp. 97–98.

59. It would be wrong to view such lofty ideas as characteristic of only the latter part of Egypt's history. The Memphite Theology, an ancient work, is as profound as the texts concerning Amon, even though it is less explicit and less congenial to us. But the universalism which the Memphite Theology propounds did not find acceptance outside the circle of Ptah's devotees, for it ran counter to the fundamental Egyptian belief that the sun was the primary source of creative energy. The universalism of the New Kingdom, on the contrary, did affect Egyptian religion profoundly; for it succeeded, by its combination of Re and Amon, in giving a deeper significance to ingrained Egyptian beliefs.

We do not hold that similar universalistic beliefs could be found before Pharaonic times. We are inclined to consider the profundity of the Memphite Theology a manifestation in the field of thought of that efflorescence of cultural life which found political expression in the unification of the country under Menes. It would seem, rather, that in predynastic times the universality of the divine was comprehended by the recognition of a limitless number of divine powers.

NOTES TO CHAPTER 14

1. Rams and sheep sometimes take the place of bulls and cows, e.g., Pyr. 252*b*, *c* (see below, n. 46).

2. Stela of Piankhi, ll. 158–59; Breasted, *Ancient Records*, Vol. IV, par. 883.

3. "The Teaching of Merikare" (see Erman-Blackman, *Literature*, p. 83). So also in the Amon hymn in Cairo: "O Re who is adored in Karnak . . . . who watches when all men are asleep and seeks what is beneficial for his *cattle*, Amon . . . . Atum, Harakhte; 'Praise unto thee'—so they all say—'Honor unto thee, since thou weariest thyself for our sake'" (Kees, *Lesebuch*, p. 5 [No. 11]). See also *ZÄS*, LXIV (1929), 89–90.

4. See above, chap. 1, n. 4.

5. This enormous increase in possibilities of explanation is the main value of introducing anthropological material. Its danger lies in the temptation to force analogies and to forget that each culture is an integrated whole so that, contrary to Engnell, Hocart, Wainwright, Widegren, and others, a "divine king" or a "sky-god" means totally different things in different cultures. The fallacy of comparing isolated traits or using type labels is well demonstrated in Ruth Benedict's *Patterns of Culture* (Boston, 1934) with the motto "In the beginning God gave to every people a cup of clay, and from this cup they drank their life" (a Red Indian proverb). We have diminished the danger of misinterpretation by confining our comparisons to modern peoples representing the substratum of ancient Egyptian culture (see chap. 1, n. 4, above). It will be noted, moreover, that we have not used anthropological data to fill the gaps in the evidence from ancient Egypt but that our interpretation of the latter is self-con-

tained and only receives relief through the analogies provided by surviving Hamites and half-Hamites.

6. For a comprehensive study see M. J. Herskovits, "The Cattle Complex in East Africa," *American Anthropologist*, XXVIII (new ser., 1926), 230–72, 361–88, 494–528, 633–64.

7. Hambly, *Source Book for African Anthropology*, I, 349 ff. Striking evidence of the non-economical significance of cattle in East Africa is given by Georges Smets in *Man* (1946), No. 6. He demonstrates that the economy of the Barundi is based on agriculture, but that rank, prestige, and actual power derive from the ownership of cattle alone.

8. Carl Meinhof, *Die Religionen der Afrikaner in ihrem Zusammenhang mit dem Wirtschafts-leben* (Oslo, 1926), p. 75. See also n. 24 below.

9. R. U. Sayce, *Primitive Arts and Crafts* (Cambridge, 1933), pp. 27 ff. Sometimes there are indications that exclusive concentration on cattle-keeping is a recent development (see Sir Harry Johnston, *The Uganda Protectorate* [London, 1902], II, 796–97).

10. If Hermann Baumann, *Schöpfung und Urzeit des Menschen im Mythus der afrikanischen Völker* (Berlin, 1936), p. 3, rightly distinguishes the mythology of the agriculturalists as concerned with "soil, body, soul, life and death" from that of the hunters and cattle-keepers as concerned with "wood, water, heaven and its bodies, animals and 'Kraftstoff' "—then ancient Egypt is less one-sided than the modern primitive African cultures in this as well as in other respects, for both groups of problems play equal parts in its mythology.

11. Gauthier, *Les fêtes du dieu Min*, p. 235.

12. Herskovits, *op. cit.*, pp. 517–18.

13. Hambly, *op. cit.*, p. 350.

14. *Ibid.*, p. 359 (sources are given on the preceding page).

15. Seligman, *Races of Africa* (rev. ed.), p. 172. For the emotional value of cattle for the Bari see B. G. and C. G. Seligman, *Pagan Tribes of the Nilotic Sudan*, p. 244; for the Nuer, *ibid.*, p. 320.

16. J. Roscoe, *The Northern Bantu* (Cambridge, 1915), p. 104.

17. Johnston, *op. cit.*, II, 741–42. Nor are feelings alone affected by the loss or acquisition of cattle: among the Barundi the borrower of cattle "becomes the liege of the donor" and, "in some cases, the recipient is considered a near relative, even a son of the donor and marriage impediments ensue from the assimilation." (Smets, in *Man* [1946]. No. 6.)

18. Seligman, in *Studies Presented to F. Ll. Griffith*, p. 461.

19. *Ibid.*, p. 462.

20. Two instances occur in Middle Kingdom tombs: P. Newberry, *Beni Hasan*, Vol. I, Pl. XIII, and A. M. Blackman, *The Rock Tombs of Meir*, Vol. I, Pl. XI.

21. From the Luxor temple of Tutankhamon. The beasts are playfully decorated with Negro heads between the horns, while the tips of the latter are equipped with model hands; the effect is that of the donors' acclaiming the king to whom tribute is brought.

The cattle of the Negroes in Gardiner and Davies, *The Tomb of Ḥuy* (London, 1926), Pl. 30, show the same embellishments. It was an expression of the same spirit which induced the Nubians to pay that part of their tribute which had to be in gold, not merely in bulk, but in elaborate vases with centerpieces of trees and animals. See Schäfer, "Altägyptische Prunk-gefässe mit aufgesetzten Randverzierungen," in Sethe, *Untersuchungen*, Vol. IV.

22. In view of the evidence summarized in chap. 1, n. 4, above, the interpretation which we have given is indicated (see also above, chap. 4, n. 20). Seligman suggested that the custom spread from Egypt to the rest of Africa, because he considered the Negroes as given to it instead of the Hamites; and at the time of writing he accepted Junker's thesis ("The First Appearance of the Negroes in History," *JEA*, VII [1921], 121–32) that no Negroes lived near Egypt in the Old Kingdom. In *Races of Africa* (rev. ed.), pp. 54 ff., he disproves Junker's theory; but the presence of the Negroes is in any case irrelevant if the existence of a Hamitic substratum of Egyptian civilization is recognized. For it is then highly probable that it is the Hamitic, and not the Negroid, strain in the Nilotes which is responsible for the custom which they share with the Egyptians of the Old Kingdom. But Seligman has unfortunately retained the prejudice that resemblances between ancient Egypt and modern Africa are due to influences emanating from Egypt, even though he admits our inability to explain it (see his *Egypt and Negro Africa* [London, 1934], p. 18). Seligman recognizes the Hamitic substratum (*ibid.*, pp. 55–70), which, in fact, has become tangible largely as a result of his researches.

23. G. Brunton and G. Caton Thompson, *The Badarian Civilization* (London, 1928), pp. 91 ff. Cf. a cemetery of cattle found in the Eastern Desert in the Bisharin country and described by G. W. Murray in *JEA*, XII (1926), 248–49.

24. Scene 19. See above, p. 129. Just as many cattle-keepers refuse to kill cattle for meat, so they often forbid women to care for the sacred animals. But this injunction is not general. With the Masai, for instance, the women milk the cows (see Johnston, *op. cit.*, pp. 812 ff.). On the sacred character of milk see, e.g., Seligman, *Races of Africa* (rev. ed.), pp. 107, 161, 213, and *Journal of the Royal Anthropological Institute*, XLIII (1913), 654.

25. Sethe, *Beitrage zur ältesten Geschichte Ägyptens*, pp. 75–79. It may be accidental that other methods of counting capital (land, gold) are already known in the Second Dynasty, while the biennial census is not known until the Fifth Dynasty. In any case, this is no reason why the census should not be considered to go back to more ancient times (see Ed. Meyer, *Ägyptische Chronologie*, p. 186, n. 2.

26. "Words which denote types of beauty come from cattle terms and it is a high compliment to a friend, a wife or a lover, to name an animal after this person" (E. W. Smith and A. M. Dale, *The Ila-speaking Peoples of Northern Rhodesia* [London, 1920], p. 127).

27. Gardiner, *Grammar*, p. 457, No. 45. See the illustration of the organ in *Kemi*, Vol. II (1929), Pl. III, and *Journal of Experimental Zoology*, XXIII (1917), 423. For a Mesopotamian parallel see *JNES*, III (1944), 198 ff.

28. Grapow, *Die bildliche Ausdrücke des Ägyptischen*, pp. 80–81.

29. Seligman, *Races of Africa*, pp. 160–61.

30. Sethe, *Kommentar*, I, 306.

31. Petrie, *Naqada and Ballas*, p. 68. Once, on the stela in M. Mogensen, *La collection égyptienne de la glyptothèque Ny Carlsberg*, Pl. 103, No. 706, Seth not only is called "Bull of Nubt" but is actually depicted with a bull's head! He stands in the prow of the sun-boat, is winged, and attacks Re's enemy Apophis with a spear. The stela appears to belong to the Nineteenth Dynasty.

32. Pyr. 444*b*.

33. Pyr. 925*c*.

34. R. Thurnwald, *Die menschliche Gesellschaft*, I, 232.

35. M. Fortes and E. E. Evans Pritchard, *African Political Systems* (Oxford, 1940), pp. 136, 157.

36. See Eberhard Otto, *Beiträge zur Geschichte der Stierkulte in Ägypten* (Leipzig, 1938). This is a careful work, but it suffers from a wholesale acceptance of Sethe's "reconstruction" of Egyptian prehistory.

37. Erman in *Sitzungsberichte der Preussischen Akademie* (Berlin, 1916), p. 1149.

38. See P. W. Hofmayr, "Religion der Shilluk," in *Anthropos*, 1911, p. 123. We follow this description. See also Seligman, *Pagan Tribes of the Nilotic Sudan*, p. 86.

39. Otto, *op. cit.*, pp. 6 ff.

40. Petrie, *Prehistoric Egypt*, Pl. IX, 1–5.

41. Petrie, *The Labyrinth, Gerzeh and Mazghuneh*, Pl. VI, 7; Quibell and Green, *Hierakonpolis*, Vol. II, Pl. LIX, 5.

42. A. Scharff, *Ägyptische Sonnenlieder*, (Berlin, 1922), pp. 80–87.

43. Sethe, *Kommentar*, I, 317. Sethe, however, accepts an allegorical interpretation which we reject.

44. Sethe, *Amun*, p. 84.

45. Pyr. 316*a*.

46. It is possible that the ram is an equivalent for the bull in the portrayal of the sun on his nightly journey. In the "Book of Gates" and the "Book of Who Is in the Netherworld," for instance, the sun is depicted as a ram or a ram-headed man. The image was perhaps intended to suggest the virility which enabled him to leave the region of the dead by impregnating the mother-goddess; the sun is figured with a ram's head when approaching the Goddess of the West. Schäfer, *ZÄS*, LXXI, 16, explains this as an anticipation of his nightly form. Kees, *Götterglaube*, p. 81, suggests that the ram became a symbol of the sun-god in the First Intermediate Period, perhaps at Herakleopolis, where the ram Harsaphes was worshiped. This is quite possible, but the wide distribution of the ram cults suggests that ram and bull were more or less equivalent personifications of virile gods from very early times, as one would expect. A ram crowned with a sun disk appears in rock engravings in the Sahara Atlas (Frobenius

and Obermaier, *Hadschra Maktuba*, Pls. 37, 38, 93, 94, 108; Frobenius, *Kulturgeschichte Afrikas*, Pl. 19 and pp. 118–19). Their date is uncertain. See F. R. Wulsin, *The Prehistoric Archeology of Northwest Africa* ("Papers of the Peabody Museum," Vol. XIX, No. 1 [Cambridge, Mass., 1924]), pp. 116–23.

47. Scharff, *op. cit.*, p. 39.

48. Dr. Nelson has drawn my attention to a few rare exceptions where Nut appears without horns, e.g., Calverley, *Abydos*, III, 14.

49. Sethe, *Amun*, pp. 33, 50. The mother-image becomes a source of confusion when we read, "Ihet, the great one, who bore Re," ignoring the Ogdoad entirely.

50. Sethe, *Kommentar*, I, 318, insists that the hieroglyph shows an ox, not a bull. This makes no sense, since the castrated animal is not fierce. Moreover, no Egyptians, who, even in the early periods had artificial genitals molded to their corpses (see G. Elliot Smith, *Egyptian Mummies*, p. 74; W. M. Flinders Petrie, *Deshasheh*, p. 15; and C. M. Firth and J. E. Quibell, *The Step Pyramid*, I, 102, No. 7), would accept this identification. Either the sculptors of the hieroglyphs did not distinguish consistently between ox and bull or the phallus is purposely omitted to rob the animal of its dangerous character in accordance with similar mutilations which occur throughout these texts (Lacau, "Suppressions et modifications de signes dans les textes funéraires," *ZÄS*, LI [1901], 1–64). See Sethe, *Kommentar*, I, 218, where another text is quoted in which the sense requires "bull," not "ox."

51. In another text, where the same situation is depicted (Pyr. 547), Re is explicitly called "bull" or "ox." See also Pyr. 201*a*.

52. Suggested by Dr. J. A. Wilson.

53. The Hesat cow is here the heavenly cow; in Heliopolis she counts as the mother of the Mnevis bull (Otto, *op. cit.*, p. 35).

54. A. H. Gardiner, "Hymns to Amon from a Leiden Papyrus," *ZÄS*, XLII (1905), 24–25. See also the quotation on p. 151 above.

55. Hymn of Haremhab (Scharff, *op. cit.*, p. 58).

56. Sethe, *Urgeschichte*, p. 120, n. 2. See also above, p. 67, for the funerary temple's appearing as the king's mother.

57. C. G. Jung, *Wandlungen und Symbole der Libido* (Leipzig, 1912), pp. 200, 209.

58. Naville, *The Eleventh Dynasty Temple at Deir el Bahari*, Vol. I, Pls. XXIX–XXXI.

59. W. Wreszinski, "Der Gott Wḥ," *OLZ*, 1932, pp. 521–23; Blackman, *op. cit.*, II, 25.

60. Sethe, *Urkunden*, I: 80, 16.

61. See above, pp. 143 ff., and below, p. 178. For Sethe (*Urgeschichte*, pp. 14, 27, 47), Hathor simply replaces local tree-goddesses. But in this, as in most of his "explanations," he does not touch on religious matters at all. With all the ingenuity—but also the remoteness from reality—of a chess-player, Sethe plots series of moves: when the local falcon-fetish Horus became a sun-god, his mother Hathor the cow "almost automatically had to become" a sky-goddess and thus she was equated with Nut (*ibid.*, p. 22). It is worth remembering that these pawns meant a great deal to the Egyptians. Kees, *Götterglaube*, pp. 83–89, argues in much the same way as Sethe. As to the relation between mother-goddess and tree, it is unequivocally expressed in the texts and rites (see below, pp. 178 ff.). Jung, *op. cit.*, finds the *tertium comparationis* in the "Umschlingung," quoting the Denderah relief where the body of Osiris is shown wrapped round by the branches of a tree (Mariette, *Dendérah*, Vol. IV, Pl. 66).

62. See below, pp. 283 ff. Cf., e.g., *JEA*, III, 86, for a text referring to the Goddess of the West as the Lady of Mercy who succors her devotee.

63. See above, p. 42; cf. Hugo Müller, *Die formale Entwicklung der Titulatur der ägyptischen Könige*, pp. 71–72.

64. Gayet, *Louxor*, Pl. LXVI, Fig. 192; and Naville, *op. cit.*, Vol. II, Pl. LIII. Hathor is depicted either as a cow or as a woman with cow's horns. On early monuments (the Narmer palette) she is shown full face with cow's horns and ears; on sistra and on capitals of columns she is shown full face without horns but with cow's ears.

65. *ASAE*, XXVI (1926), 177–84.

66. G. A. Reisner, *Mycerinus* (Cambridge, Mass., 1931), pp. 109–10.

67. Gardiner, "Notes on the Story of Sinuhe," *Recueil de travaux*, XXXIV, 72 ff.

68. E.g., on the well-known statue in Cairo, *Le Musée égyptien*, Vol. II (1907), Pls. I, II, pp. 9 ff. The *menat* is also shown very clearly in the relief of Haremhab's pylon, *ibid.*, Fig. 3, or in Keith C. Seele, *The Coregency of Ramses II with Seti I and the Date of the Great Hypostyle Hall at Karnak* (Chicago, 1940), Fig. 9.

69. Kees, *Götterglaube*, p. 37, blandly states that Hathor was originally a female falcon. He finds no better authority for this claim than the name of the city Atarbechis mentioned by Herodotus (ii. 41), but note that Herodotus describes this city as a center of *cattle* worship. We have shown that in ancient Egypt the thought of motherhood gave rise to the image of the cow as a matter of course, and the combination of falcon and cattle images will be seen to occur already in the First Dynasty. Kees's claim is no more than the postulate of a rationalism which has been baffled by Egyptian religion since the days of Plutarch. Compare the combination of the cow and vulture images in the goddess Nekhbet (p. 174 below).

70. See Otto, *op. cit.*, pp. 41, 47, 49, where the explanation is sought in "Kulttopographie." Monthu appears as a bull in Medamud, and the king is called "Bull of Monthu" under Tuthmosis III (*ibid.*, pp. 45–47).

71. After Breasted, *Ancient Records*, Vol. III, par. 272. Notice how in one sentence Ramses II represents himself in three aspects. He shines for the people like Re, the neutral designation of the sun-god. He is on the throne as Atum, the sun-god as the creator, who was also the first king of the universe so that the throne, as the seat of power, may be said to have been essentially Atum's. Finally, the king qualifies himself as the successor of his father by referring to his enthronement; he calls himself Horus the son of Isis (the throne). There is no question of a thoughtless piling-up of epithets, which is all that modern interpreters often see in these texts.

72. Borchardt, *Sahure*, Vol. II, Pl. 18 and p. 93; Jéquier, *Pepi II*, Pl. 32.

73. Pyr. 1566*a;* in Pyr. 389 Sethe's interpretation claims the association of the images of woman, cow, and vulture, but the text itself is not unequivocal on this point.

74. Pyr. 200*d.* A similar coalescence of the images of cow and woman occurs with Nut, mother of the sun (see above, p. 169).

75. Pyr. 1416*c* has "Nut" instead of "heaven."

76. In learned texts Nut stands, not for the whole sky, but approximately for the zodiacal belt. Beyond her is limitless and chaotic darkness ("darker than the darkness of the Netherworld"). These are uncreated regions unknown to sun and gods and spirits (Lange and Neugebauer, *Papyrus Carlsberg No. 1*, pp. 16, 26, 28, 66). When Nut is taken in this restricted sense her relation with the solar circuit is, of course, even closer. When Junker, *Der sehende und blinde Gott*, p. 38, declares that his hypothetical "Allherr" rules the realms of outer darkness as well as the existing universe, he follows an entirely un-Egyptian line of thought. The fact that the sun, the Creator, is said explicitly not to know those regions indicates that they stand for the uncreated, for nothingness, a notion too abstract to be rendered by Egyptian thought in a way which would not to us suggest a certain concreteness. To me it seems remarkable how well *Papyrus Carlsberg No. 1* conveys the notion of nonexistence.

77. ii. 129–32. Here, as elsewhere, the question whether the story is true is less important than the fact that it could be told and believed, for this shows that it must have contained familiar, or at least acceptable, motifs.

78. i. 85. Plutarch (*De Iside et Osiride* 39, 52) mentions a figure of a cow in connection with Osiris rituals, but we cannot be sure of its significance; it may have been simply a symbol of Isis and not an image of a "mother" within whom the dead god was inclosed to be reborn.

79. So.W. B. Kristensen, in *Mededeelingen der Koninklijke Akademie van Wetenschappen, Afd. Letterkunde*, Vol. V, Part II (Amsterdam, 1916). A. Rusch has collected and discussed these texts in *Die Entwicklung der Himmelsgöttin Nut zu einer Totengottheit (Mitteilungen der Vorderasiatisch-Ägyptischen Gesellschaft*, Vol. XXVII [1922]). The book is somewhat marred by Rusch's belief that the cult of Osiris arose in the later part of the Old Kingdom.

80. "The Great One" alludes to Osiris; but it is, at the same time, involved in a wordplay. In the related text, Pyr. 638*c* (see p. 183), we read: "She protects (*ḥnm*) thee from all evil in her name [she of] the Great Sieve (*ḥnm.t*)." Sethe suggests (*Kommentar*, III, 186) that this refers to heaven as a sieve through the holes of which the stars appear. This is a mere fantasy; and it seems more appropriate, since the goddess Nut is involved as the mother, to recall that nowadays the women in Egypt lean on a great round sieve when bearing down

in labor and that such a large circular sieve may be depicted in the birth scenes of Hatshepsut (Winifred Blackman, *The Fellahin of Upper Egypt*, p. 63). The connection with Nut, who daily bears the sun and stars, and (it is hoped), the king, would be natural. Against Junker, *Die Götterlehre von Memphis*, p. 29, and *Der sehende und blinde Gott*, pp. 37 ff., it must be said that Nut is never the spouse of Atum. When Nut is called *wr.t*, "the great one," in such pyramid texts as we have quoted (e.g., Pyr. 782), and when Atum is called *wr*, we have by no means a pair like Amon and Amaunet, since the latter are names which express the affinity of the deities who bear them, while *wr* and *wr.t* are mere epithets, not peculiar to either Atum or Nut. "The Great One" is also used for Horus, Ptah, and Osiris (Kees, *Götterglaube*, p. 172 with n. 4). Atum and Nut never occur together as *wr* and *wr.t* or, for that matter, in any other manner.

In our translation of this text we have followed Gardiner's rendering in *Egyptian Letters to the Dead*, p. 112, except for the phrase just discussed. Sethe has shown (*Kommentar*, III, 185) that "the protectress of 'The Great One' " (*ḥnm.t wr*) is an older version than "the Great Protectress" (*ḥnm.t wr.t*).

81. See above, p. 169 and also chap. 5, n. 49. Here again there is complete agreement between Egyptological and psychoanalytical material. C. G. Jung maintained thirty years ago that the motif of incest, which plays so great a part in subconscious symbolism, is by no means to be taken in the literal sense (as was often done by the Freudian school) but serves often as an image of the desire for immortality (*op. cit.*, pp. 216, 341, 349, 392–93).

82. Sethe, *Amun*, p. 30.

83. Sethe, in *ZÄS*, LXIV, 6–9; Balcz, *ZÄS*, LXXV, 75, 32–38; Junker, *Vorbericht Giza*, 1924, Pl. 4 (*Anzeiger Wiener Akademie der Wissenschaften* [1927]).

84. Schäfer in *Studies Presented to F. Ll. Griffith*, pp. 429 ff. His view is now confirmed by two ivories of the First Dynasty found in a tomb at Heliopolis. See Zaki Yusef Saad, in *ASAE*, XLI (1942), 407 and Pl. 39. The name of the Djed pillar suggests a connection with Busiris (Djedu) in the eastern Delta where papyrus abounded; but Sethe, *Dramatische Texte*, p. 156, points out that the Old Kingdom seems to ignore the association; it may therefore be secondary and caused by, rather than explaining, the similarity of the names. Kees, *Götterglaube*, p. 129, confuses essentials and incidentals when he puts the identification of the Djed column and Osiris on a par with that of the column and Seth in the Mystery Play of the Succession. In the play objects used in the ritual are continually invested *ad hoc* with symbolical meanings (see above, chap. 11, n. 3), and the Djed pillar is once equated with Seth just as, in another scene, a barge or a chapel are so viewed, because each is "carrying one who is greater than himself"—a phrase commonly used in the pyramid texts of Seth (see above, pp. 114, 128). But this identification with Seth has no validity outside the ritual context in which alone it occurs. On the other hand, we are unable to treat as derivative the coherent ritual involving the dead king, Hathor, and the erection of the Djed pillar. The fact that the ceremony was originally localized in Memphis (Sethe, *Dramatische Texte*, p. 156) corroborates our belief that the rite—and hence the association of Osiris with the Djed column—is an original feature of the Thinite monarchy.

85. Sethe, *Sonnenauge*, p. 33. The substitution of Re for Osiris or Horus need not occupy us here.

86. Above, p. 171. Sethe, *Urgeschichte*, pp. 14 ff.; Erman, *Religion*, p. 31. It is even possible that this complex of ideas explains why the tomb of Osiris at Abydos is called *peqer*, or *gate of peqer*, while *peqer* is written as if it were the name of a tree or tree trunk, as Schäfer, in *ZÄS*, XLI (1904), 107–11, has shown. It may also be due to the emergence of the tree from the earth or tomb. See, for a parallel, Seligman, *Pagan Tribes*, p. 87.

87. The Greek text makes an erica grow a trunk fit to be used as a pillar; see Sethe in *ZÄS*, XLV (1908), 12 ff.; XLVII (1910), 71–72.

88. Gressmann, *Tod und Auferstehung des Osiris*, p. 9; Frazer, *The Golden Bough*, Part IV, Vol. II, pp. 108.

89. Mariette, *Dendérah*, Vol. IV, Pl. 66.

90. Until the war the scenes depicted in Tomb No. 192 were only known from diagrammatical sketches in Brugsch, *Thesaurus*, V, 1190 ff. I have not had the opportunity of studying the recent publication by Ahmed Fakhry in *ASAE*, XLII (1943), 449–508. Kharuef, the owner of the tomb, was "Steward of the Great Royal Wife Ty"; and in this capacity he assisted at the Sed festival and the raising of the Djed pillar which preceded it.

91. Ares stands for Anhur (Onuris) (see Leiden Papyrus U, re-edited by U. Wilcken in *Mélanges Nicole* [Geneve, 1905], 582, II, 11, 14–16, translated by G. Maspero, *Les contes populaires de l'Egypte ancienne* [4th ed.], pp. 306–10); and Onuris, the god of the province of This, is a form of Horus, especially in his aggressive aspect. See Junker, *Onurislegende*.

92. After H. O. Lange, *Der Magische Papyrus Harris*, p. 62.

93. The ritual contains some perplexing features. It is inconceivable that any Egyptian could exclaim, "I choose Horus" in the presence of Pharaoh and not mean the living king. Does the design really reflect the abstruse theology of the rite to the extent of naming the dead king "Horus" because he is resurrected in a pillar representing Hathor, the mother of Horus? Other explanations are possible. The exclamation may refer to the living Pharaoh, for Horus the king may be the leader of Osiris' partisans, as Upwaut was in the Great Procession of Osiris at Abydos (see below, p. 203). Or perhaps we wrongly connect the mock battle with the erection of the Djed pillar; the relief also depicts the "Circuit of the Walls" with cattle and asses, a ceremony which, according to the inscriptions, took place on the day of the raising of the Djed pillar. Hence the scrimmage with papyrus stalks may have been a separate ceremony connected with the king. If this is true, we can cite a close parallel from the modern Sudan. When Mr. P. P. Howell assisted at the installation of a new king of the Shilluk in 1944 (*Man* [1944], No. 117, and more fully in a forthcoming number of *Sudan Notes and Records*), he noticed more than one quasi-conflict between the king-elect and Nyakang, the god who becomes incarnate in the king at the coronation (see below, p. 199). Immediately before the last-named ceremony there was a mock battle between two groups of Shilluk, those from the north forming Nyakang's army, while southerners flocked to the king-elect. "After an exchange of messages the king-elect . . . . marched forward to join battle with Nyakang. Millet stalks—which were used to represent spears—began to fly through the air and with wild war cries the two armies met. In this fight the king was captured by Nyakang and carried off to his shrine at Fashoda." In the shrine the coronation took place. This mock battle is a *rite de passage* in which awe for the divine anticipates and overcomes opposition to the desired incarnation of Nyakang in the king by a ceremony in which the initiative passes to the god.

So the mock fight need not have taken place while the king was erecting the Djed pillar; the appearance of the two scenes side by side on the wall does not prove their simultaneous performance. In the Abydos mysteries, too, the mock fight precedes the "finding" or resurrection of the god (see below, p. 203). Another apparent difficulty is that the Osiris myth leaves no room for a union between Osiris and Nut, or Horus and Hathor. But, then, the myth ignores the mother-image altogether and is concerned with the relation between Osiris and Isis; this may be due to the late tradition which preserved the myth for us, since the pyramid texts are very insistent upon the relationship between the dead king and the mother-goddess.

94. Helmuth Jacobsohn, *Die dogmatische Stellung des Königs in der Theologie der alten Ägypter* (Glückstadt, 1939). The author has given a summary of his view: "Einige Merkwürdigkeiten der altägyptischen Theologie und ihre Auswirkungen," in *Studie materiali di storia delle religioni*, XVI (1940), 83–97.

95. Grapow, *op. cit.*, p. 78.

96. Sethe, *Amun*, p. 30. Kees has not understood the concept of the Kamutef (*Götterglaube*, p. 350). Hence he quotes the epithet of Mut as an illustration of "immanent bisexuality" (*ibid.*, p. 163) and thinks that Horus and Min in their function of Kamutef merely committed acts of violence (*ibid.*, p. 184). Yet it appears even from the Ptolemaic story of Shu, Geb, and Tefnut (Naville and Griffith, *The Mound of the Jew and the City of Onias* [London, 1890], pp. 71–73, Pls. 24–25) that the union of a god (in this case Geb) with his mother was part of the renewal of divine rule, even though in this story, as in "The Contendings of Horus and Seth," a mythical subject is obscured by being presented in the guise of a folk tale.

NOTES TO CHAPTER 15

1. A. Dieterich, *Mutter Erde* (2d ed.; Leipzig, 1913); G. van der Leeuw, *Religion in Essence and Manifestation*, pp. 91–100; and below, chap. 20.

2. This (for Egypt unusual) conception can best be understood as a result of two causes. In the first place, Ptah seems to have been the *genius loci* who became a main god when Menes founded the new capital for united Egypt but who retained his chthonic character. In the

second place, the House of Menes traditionally worshiped the powers of the earth in the form of Osiris; and there were, moreover, certain features in the sun cult which stressed the association of the earth with the process of creation (see above, pp. 151–54, 195–97). See below, pp. 201–3, for the influence of Abydene symbols on the cult of Memphis.

3. See *ASAE*, XXV, 34–35. In the "Contendings of Horus and Seth" (Gardiner, *Papyrus Chester Beatty, No. I*), Ptah counts as the father of Osiris (p. 13, No. 1, l. 2) and as Creator (p. 25, No. 15, ll. 5 ff.). Martinus Stolk, in *Ptah* (Berlin, 1911), quotes an Edfu text (*Rochemonteix, Edfu*, II, 37) and *Papyrus Golenischeff* and *Papyrus Hood* referring to Ptah as Creator. Even in Abydos, in the temple of Seti I, Ptah is called "he who has created Maat (cosmic order)." In *The God Ptah*, chap. 4, Maj Sandmann Holmberg has discussed many texts which proclaim Ptah the Creator of the Universe.

4. W. Wolf in *ZÄS*, LXIV, 17–44.

5. Sethe, *Urk.*, IV: 146, 14.

6. So Sethe, *Urgeschichte*, pp. 58–62.

7. The relationship of Osiris with Nut and Geb usually remains unexplained and is, in fact, inexplicable on the current assumption that the Ennead represents a medley of gods which an ambitious priesthood succeeded in claiming for Heliopolis at some hypothetical phase of predynastic development.

8. E.g., Pyr. 466*b*.

9. Breasted, *Ancient Records*, Vol. II, par. 70.

10. So Sethe, *Urgeschichte*, p. 99; Kees, *Götterglaube*, pp. 148 ff. The designation "Ennead" came to stand for a combination of gods irrespective of their numbers; for instance, a Theban "Ennead" counted fifteen members; an Abydene one, eleven (see Kees, *op. cit.*, pp. 150–51). The Heliopolitan Ennead was the prototype of these other formations and should therefore not be treated on a par with them; it is a priori likely that the orignal had a significance which the imitations lacked.

11. Sethe, *Urgeschichte*, p. 79, interprets the name of Osiris as a term of affection "seat of the eye," that is, "object upon which the eye rests continuously and (by implication) lovingly," a term equivalent to our "apple of the eye." Dr. J. A. Wilson objects to this interpretation on the grounds that Egyptian *wśîr*, ⌡◁; Assyrian *uśîru;* Aramaic *ausri;* Coptic *ûsire, ûsiri, ûser;* Greek Ὄσιρις and the writings ⌡◁ and ⌡ agree in showing an initial *w* which shows no connection with ⌡ "place, throne" (Isis; Assyrian *eśu;* Aramaic *asi;* Coptic *ese*, etc.; Greek Ἶσις), so that the normal writing of Osiris' name might be a graphic pun on a word of unknown meaning. He reminds me, moreover, of the fact that *ś.t* before a part of the body means "the activity of that member" (*PSBA*, XXXIV [1912], 261, n. 14), in our case "sight," so that, even if the name meant "seat of the eye," it need not have been a term of affection.

12. Seth is often included in the crew of the sun boat (Kees, *Götterglaube*, p. 237); and this proves yet again that he was considered not to be essentially evil but rather to personify the element of strife and conflict which is discernible in the universe. Once the sun's enemy had become the great snake, Seth, in opposing it, decided the battle in the sun's favor. For Seth as chthonic god in opposition to Horus see Pyr. 143–44; for Seth as wind-god in the coffin texts see Kees, *Totenglauben*, p. 320; and for other identifications with natural phenomena see Kees's article "Seth," in *Pauly-Wissowa*, cols. 1909–10. In the funerary temple of Pepi II, Seth leads the Royal Ancestors, the Souls of Nekhen (Jéquier, *Pepi II*, Pl. 50 and p. 43).

13. He is sometimes called "the tenth god" (see Sethe, *Urgeschichte*, p. 101). But if Sethe says that Horus is excluded as representative of the present because the last four gods of the Ennead represent the past of the country as it fell within human memory (*ibid.*, pp. 98–99), one must object that the last formula might apply to Osiris, but certainly not to Isis, Nephthys, and Seth; and, furthermore, that in this manner one forces upon Egyptian thought a contrast which is alien to its view of the world as unchanging, in general, and to its conception of kingship in particular. See above, pp. 34–35.

14. See above, p. 176, and chap. 14, n. 80, for evidence that this epithet suggests the motif of rebirth. Our quotation continues that given on p. 135. It is followed by a reference to Osiris' other parent, Geb, who symbolically counteracts the decay which the king's body would normally undergo in his realm, the earth, by restituting Osiris' head. Geb also lets the wise

Thoth cure the evil of death which adheres to the king. Sethe, *Kommentar*, III, 186, interprets the "giving of the head" to mean that Geb leaves Osiris free to pass from the earth to the sky. This theme exists in the pyramid texts, but in the form of a conversation or agreement between Geb and Atum. See, e.g., above, p. 115.

15. On Ernutet (Renenutet) see Kees, *Götterglaube*, pp. 56–57.

16. *Papyrus Chester Beatty No. I: Description of an Hieratic Papyrus, etc.*, by Alan H. Gardiner (London, 1931), 14, 11–12, pp. 24–25. Gardiner refers to coffin texts and spells from the Book of the Dead, where Osiris is identified with the corn-god Nepri.

17. A. M. Blackman, in *Studia Aegyptiaca*, "Analecta Orientalia," XVII (1938), p. 2.

18. I. Rosellini, *I monumenti dell' Egitto e della Nubia*, Vol. III: *Monumenti del culto* (Pisa, 1844), Pl. 23; or R. V. Lanzone, *Dizionario di mitologia egizia*, Pl. 261.

19. For a good example from the tomb of Amenhotep II, see Daressy, *Fouilles de la vallée des rois* (*Cat. gén.* [Cairo, 1907]), Pl. VII, No. 24061. See also Gardiner and Davies, *The Tomb of Amenemhēt*, p. 115, and instances quoted by Frazer in *The Golden Bough*, Part IV, Vol. II, pp. 90–91.

20. See below, n. 49.

21. *De Iside et Osiride* 70.

22. This translation is not certain, but it accounts for the determinatives and the affinities of the word better than "dust storm" (see Sethe, *Kommentar*, I, 376–77).

23. L. Keimer, in *ZÄS*, LIX, 140 ff., points out that this is the only plant having a milky juice which was cultivated in Egypt. This might have been interpreted in the manner of sympathetic magic as influencing the flow of either milk or semen. Nowadays the Egyptians believe that the eating of much lettuce is conducive to rearing a large family.

24. Gauthier, *Les fêtes du dieu Min* (Cairo, 1931), p. 194. See H. Jacobsohn, *Die dogmatische Stellung*, p. 17, with n. 10, for the possible title "rainmaker-king" for Min.

25. Gauthier, *op. cit.*, p. 235.

26. *Ibid.*, pp. 143–52; Petrie, *Athribis*, Pl. XX; Jéquier in *Bulletin de l'Institut Français d'Archéologie Orientale*, VI, 35–38.

27. The Feast of Min is mentioned already in the tombs of the Old Kingdom (Junker, *Giza*, II, 60–61). The Ramessid reliefs and texts are published by H. H. Nelson *et al.*, *Medinet Habu*, Vol. IV, Pls. 196–217. For a discussion see Gauthier, *op. cit.*, and Jacobsohn, *op. cit.*, pp. 29–40.

28. Gardiner was the first to recognize the character of the festival. He adduced the evidence without actually drawing the conclusion which we have formulated somewhat tentatively (*JEA*, II, 125). Jacobsohn (*op. cit.*) did suggest that the king becomes Kamutef at the feast. In addition to the more weighty grounds given in our text above, we may point out some further evidence which possibly corroborates this view. The queen is the only female figure in the first part of the procession and may well, therefore, be the "Shemayt," an untranslatable female title designating a person who recites a spell seven times just before the king cuts the grain. In doing so, she "goes around" him. The verb *phr* which is here translated "goes around" occurs also as "winding around" in the epithet of Mut concerned with the Kamutef mystery which, we suppose, may have taken place at this point in the Min festival. Mut, as we have seen, is called the "snake who wound around her father Re and bore him as Khonsu" (p. 180).

29. Since the Min festival was celebrated annually, we might speak of "the expansion of the royal line"; but each prince was a potential heir. In our view the festival institutionalized the coalescence of god and earthly progenitor which was the prerequisite for the birth of a crown prince.

30. Erman-Blackman, *Literature*, p. 137 (Stela Louvre C 30). For Isis as the mother of Min see Kees, *Götterglaube*, Index, "Isis in Koptos."

31. Pyr. 256*a*, 1928*b*, *c*, 1998*a*.

32. Sethe, *Urgeschichte*, pp. 166–67.

33. H. O. Lange, "Ein liturgisches Lied an Min," *Sitzungsberichte der Preussischen Akademie der Wissenschaften* (Berlin, 1927), pp. 331–38.

34. Moret, *Royauté*, pp. 104–5.

35. A late song of Osiris describes the god with concrete, plastic images as god of the earth, of the plants, of the Nile ("the Nile comes from the sweat of thy hands"), and as "the father and mother of men" (Erman, *ZÄS*, XXXVIII [1900], 30–33).

36. The inundation demonstrated the power immanent in the earth. Hence it could also be ascribed to Ptah: "The canals are filled with water anew, and the earth is flooded with his (Ptah's) love" (Gardiner and Davies, *Ancient Egyptian Paintings*, Vol. II, Pl. 70; cf. *JNES*, IV [1945], 184).

37. Kees, *Lesebuch*, p. 16, No. 21.

38. Pyr. 628. Osiris, therefore, may appear in the function of Nun, the primeval waters, since these were also underneath the earth and, as the original font of all that exists (and thus of immeasurable fertility), were also recognized in the waters of the inundation. We meet here again a multiplicity of approaches, which leads to results which are at first sight confusing. The common function of Nun and Osiris leads to the peculiar situation that Osiris can be identified with the waters from which the sun rises in the morning and may hence appear as the "father" of the sun. See below, n. 101.

39. Plutarch (*De Iside et Osiride* 39) places this feast in the month of Athyr; and Frazer (*op. cit.*, Part IV, Vol. II, pp. 86–87, 91 ff.), discussing the influence of the fixed Alexandrian calendar upon the shift of the festivals from their proper relationship with the seasons, supposes that Plutarch refers to the same celebrations that fell in Khoiak in earlier times—a view also held by others, e.g., R. Kittel and M. P. Nilsson. But Plutarch's account does not fit the description of these festivals, nor does it reflect Egyptian conditions in general. It may well refer to an Alexandrian usage or to one prevailing in the towns of the Delta. When he mentions the lengthening of nights and the falling of leaves, we are certain that he refers to an autumn festival; but it is the Greek from the northern shores of the Mediterranean, rather than the Egyptian, who would consider these somber portents; nor would the Egyptian describe either our autumn or our winter season as a period of "denudation of the earth." On the contrary, the crops grow and ripen in these seasons. If, therefore, the festival described by Plutarch was not peculiar to the Greeks in Egypt, or at least to the Delta, it is most likely to have found its place originally in the period from March to June, during the low Nile, and perhaps more especially at the end of this period, so that the "finding of Osiris" as water would coincide with the beginning of the inundation. In Hellenistic and Roman times we must count with the influence of the Adonis cult. See below, p. 291. The dates of the Egyptian Adonis and Osiris festivals are considered in relation with one another by G. Glotz, "Les fêtes d'Adonis sous Ptolémée II," *Revue des études grecques*, XXXIII, esp. 214–20, but his conclusion differs from ours.

In cap. 52, too, Plutarch implies that Osiris is to be found in water. At the winter solstice a cow (symbol of Isis) is carried seven times around the sun temple; and this ceremony, Plutarch says, is called the quest of Osiris, because Isis desires water. Note that Apuleius (*Metam.* xi. 9 ff.), describing an Isis procession in one of the harbor towns of Corinth, mentions as the most sacred object carried there a small gold jug. It may have contained water, or it may have been a survival of Egyptian rites such as Plutarch describes in cap. 39. For a proper appreciation of these Hellenistic Osiris festivals during or after the winter solstice see Eduard Norden, *Die Geburt des Kindes* ("Studien der Bibliothek Warburg," Vol. III [1924]), esp. pp. 33–40.

40. E.g., Pyr. 584, 612, 1008 (see p. 116), 1255–56, 1799, 2144.

41. Pyr. 24, 615*d*, 766*d*.

42. The last-named explanation is Bonnet's (*Zeitschrift der Deutschen Morgenländischen Gesellschaft*, LXXXI [1927], 185). He speaks rightly of a contrast between a "god of the Nile" and a drowned victim of the river, refuting the usual "explanation."

43. Sethe, *Dramatische Texte*, p. 107.

44. *De phocis* x. 323.

45. Kees, in *Totenglauben*, p. 354, points out that the calendar of Ramses III names the twenty-second of Thoth for the Great Procession; and it seems that in Gardiner and Davies, *The Tomb of Antefoker*, Pl. XVIII, the dead Senet goes to Abydos to take part in the Great Procession. See also above, chap. 10, n. 23.

46. See above, chap. 10, n. 7. Herodotus ii. 171 mentions that in his time the Mysteries of Osiris at Sais were performed on a lake.

47. One suspects some connection with the Nile in the case of the mysterious Uag feast, which was celebrated with wine; one had to sail upstream and arrive at Abydos, going downstream, on the day of the celebration (Kees, *Totenglauben*, pp. 354–55). Osiris is "Lord of

the wine at the Uag feast" (Pyr. 819c–820, 1524a). Dr. Richard A. Parker's researches in the lunar calendar indicate that the Uag feast fell within the early weeks of the inundation.

48. See above, n. 39.

49. The Ptolemaic inscriptions of the temple of Denderah list the celebrations in the various temples of the land, but they are concerned with the ritualistic elements of the performances rather than with their significance. For these texts the "Interment of Osiris" consists of the burial of certain figures made of earth and seeds on the eighteenth of Khoiak, the day of "hacking up the earth." There is no demonstrable connection with a sowing festival or with popular celebrations of any kind. For these Ptolemaic rites see H. Junker, "Die Mysterien des Osiris," in *Internationale Woche für Religionsethnologie*, III (Tilburg, 1922), 414–26; V. Loret, "Les fêtes d'Osiris au mois de Khoiak," *Recueil de travaux*, III, 43–57; IV, 21–33; V, 85–103; Mariette, *Dendérah*, Vol. IV, Pls. 65–90. A tomb in Thebes dating to the reign of Tuthmosis III refers to the eighteenth of the month as "the day of the moistening of the barley and spreading a bed for the Osiris Neferhotep," i.e., for the owner of the tomb (Gardiner and Davies, *The Tomb of Amenemhēt*, p. 115). Again the day is considered only in its significance for the funerary ritual of making the Osiris bed, not in relation with agricultural activities. We seem to lack evidence that the sowing of grain was connected with Osiris in Pharaonic times. See also below, p. 291.

50. Gardiner, in *JEA*, II, 123. In this important review of Frazer's *Adonis, Attis, Osiris*, Gardiner not only emphasized the complex and problematical character of Osiris but also attempted to co-ordinate the religious festivals of Egypt with the seasons.

51. L. Borchardt, *Die Mittel zur zeitlichen Festlegung von Punkten der ägyptischen Geschichte* (Cairo, 1935), p. 87.

52. Palanque, *Le Nil aux temps pharaoniques*, pp. 72 ff.

53. Drioton, in *Egyptian Religion*, I, 39 ff.

54. Translation by Dr. Richard A. Parker. See above, chap. 10, n. 1.

55. *Mélanges Maspero*, I, 340: 4, 11–12. (Dr. Wilson kindly drew my attention to this text.) For older periods see Pyr. 632.

56. Plutarch, *op. cit.*, cap. 43, records the Egyptian belief that there was a definite correspondence between the phases of the moon and the rise of the Nile.

57. For Egypt we have the explicit statements in *ibid.*, caps. 8, 42, 43.

58. Plutarch, *op. cit.*, cap. 39.

59. Kees, *Totenglauben*, pp. 209–10, where, however, the connection between Osiris and the moon is "explained" as a product of Heliopolitan speculations.

60. A quite exceptional similarity of the fate of Re with that of Osiris, the victim of Seth, is alluded to in Pyr. 285, where it is said that Re is "bound" during the night and liberated at dawn.

61. Piehl, *Inscriptions hieroglyphiques*, Vol. II, Pl. 4, quoted by De Buck, *De godsdienstige beteekenis van den slaap* ("Mededeelingen en Verhandelingen: Ex Oriente Lux," No. 4 [Leiden, 1939]).

62. Petrie, *Abydos*, II, 47, and Eduard Meyer in *ZÄS*, XLI (1904), 97–104. Even so it can hardly have been accidental that the main god of Abydos was the "Chief of the Westerners" at a site which was of no political importance (the city of This was the capital of the province of the same name), but derived all its significance from the presence of the royal tombs. In other words, it seems possible to us that the figure of the jackal and the title "Chief of the Westerners" applied to the royal ancestor Osiris in Thinite times. We have seen that the wolf Upwaut also stood for the Horus king of Hierakonpolis in a certain aspect, apparently that of the eldest son of his predecessor (see above, pp. 26, 87). Kees, *Götterglaube*, p. 330, n. 1, lists Old Kingdom tombs in which "Khentiamentiu, Lord of Abydos" is a parallel to "Osiris, Lord of Busiris"; this may mean that either one or two gods are referred to. From the Sixth Dynasty onward the identity of the two is clearly expressed in the phrase "Osiris Khentiamentiu, Lord of Abydos."

63. See above, p. 111; also Pyr. 759b and 1666a.

64. Frazer, *op. cit.*, p. 166. Frazer, too, compared Nyakang and Osiris, but on grounds which we do not consider to prove much. See also P. P. Howell in "The Installation of the Shilluk King," *Man* (1944), No. 117, and more fully in a forthcoming issue of *Sudan Notes and Records*.

65. D. Westermann, quoted by Frazer, *op. cit.*, p. 163.

66. Seligman, *Pagan Tribes*, p. 77.

67. So Junker, *Die Onurislegende*, p. 64; Sethe, *Urgeschichte*, pp. 64–66, 80–83; Kees, *Totenglauben*, p. 197. In *Götterglaube*, p. 117, last paragraph, Kees states the current view succinctly, and every sentence contains an unproved hypothesis. The whole elaborate construction thus presented becomes superfluous if one interprets the available evidence to indicate that Osiris originally belonged to Abydos and the Thinite dynasty. The evidence for this interpretation is given in the sections on "Abydos" and "The Great Procession" of the present chapter.

68. Sethe, *Urgeschichte*, pp. 64–65.

69. Other signs of southern influence on the Busirite nome should be looked for. Griffith has pointed out (*PSBA*, XXI [1899], 277) that Ptahhotep's estate in the Busirite nome contains the name of *Nekhen*, the Egyptian name for Hierakonpolis, located a little south of Abydos on the east bank of the Nile. The name of the estate is "Osiris of Nekhen," if one corrects Quibell, *Ramesseum*, Pl. XXXIV, upper row, fourth from right, after Dümichen, *Resultate der archäologisch-photographischen Expedition*, Pl. XV, No. 14; and N. de Garis Davies, *The Mastaba of Ptahhetep and Akhethetep*, Vol. II, Pl. XVII, No. 368, and p. 37.

70. See above, chap. 1, n. 15.

71. Alice Werner, *The Mythology of All Races*, Vol. VII: *African* (Boston, 1925), p. 117.

72. See the interesting parallel of the "Apotheosis by Drowning" which Kees has shown (*Studies Presented to F. Ll. Griffith*, pp. 403–5) to be a late form of the belief. We have quoted a few of the many texts mentioning the counting or gathering of the limbs of Osiris (above, p. 112). Wainwright, in Petrie, *The Labyrinth, Gerzeh and Mazghuneh*, pp. 14–15, has collected evidence from graves which might be interpreted as showing wilful dismemberment of bodies. However, if it had been the custom to equate the dead with Osiris as mutilated by Seth, some regularity in the procedure should be observable. Yet the cases quoted show every conceivable irregularity in the disposal of the bones and remain a small minority of the many thousands of graves which have been investigated. One is, therefore, obliged to view them as the results of accidents caused by marauding animals, grave-robbers, etc., after which the bodies were piously reburied by unknown hands. See also Brunton, *Qau and Badari*, I, 48, whose negative conclusion is based on an extensive series of observations of actual graves. Frazer, *op. cit.*, pp. 97–102, quotes many instances of dismemberment, none of which proves anything in relation to Osiris if one does not start from the assumption that he is a corn-god. The older Egyptological literature, under the spell of the myth, refers often to dismemberment—e.g., Moret, *Rituel*, pp. 73 ff., and Eduard Meyer, *Geschichte des Altertums*, I, 2³, 63–64.

73. Junker, *Onurislegende*, p. 65; Sethe, *Urgeschichte*, p. 183.

74. Quibell, *Hierakonpolis*, Vol. I, Pl. XLI.

75. The arguments regarding this crown are as inconclusive for a Lower Egyptian origin as are those regarding Andjeti's for a Lower Egyptian origin of Osiris. Yet the association of the feather crown with Andjeti is considered by most authors sufficient grounds to dub it Lower Egyptian! The treatment of Abd el Monem Joussef Abubakr, *Untersuchungen über die ägyptischen Kronen* (Berlin, 1937), is merely begging the question. He states that the feathers and horns represent Lower Egypt in the combination of the *atef* crown. Note that his statement that Wadjet crowns Neuserre with this crown on a relief now in Berlin (Abubakr, *ibid.*, Pl. 10 and p. 40) is incorrect. The goddess merely stands beside the king while the latter is enthroned. But Abubakr's argument is otherwise similar to that of Junker (*Onurislegende*, p. 64; *Mitteilungen des Deutschen Instituts für Ägyptische Altertumskunde in Kairo*, III, 166); e.g., neither gives any proof for the Lower Egyptian origin of the feather. The two feathers and the ram's horns appear in the hieroglyph for *îty*, "king," and the two feathers are the outstanding attributes of kingship in the Mystery Play of the Succession, where the coronation is effected when they are placed upon the head of the new king. They play a similar part at the Sed festival (see Naville, *Festival Hall of Osorkon II*, Pl. XIV, No. 1: "Horus appears; he has assumed the Two Feathers"). This function of the feathers might well be a direct survival of a custom followed by the House of Menes and perhaps also by other predynastic chieftains, but it certainly makes a Lower Egyptian origin of their use improbable. See also p. 200 above. Sethe would have liked to connect Ta-Tjenen with This, as

we do, but he was prevented from doing so by his belief that Osiris derived from the north (see *Dramatische Texte*, p. 34; *Urgeschichte*, pp. 183–84).

76. After Schäfer, "Die Mysterien des Osiris in Abydos unter König Sesostris III," in Sethe, "Untersuchungen zur Geschichte und Altertumskunde Ägyptens, "Vol. IV (translation revised by Dr. J. A. Wilson).

77. E.g., Schäfer, *op. cit.*, p. 24.

78. Kees, *Totenglauben*, p. 350; Louvre C 15.

79. It would be a coincidence with which we can hardly reckon that there would be another "run" or "procession" of Upwaut in the district of This besides the Great Procession.

80. After Pieper, "Die grosse Inschrift des Königs Neferhotep in Abydos," in *Mitteilungen der Vorderasiatisch-Ägyptischen Gesellschaft*, Vol. XXXII (1929).

81. *Ibid.*, pp. 14–16; see also Schäfer, *op. cit.*, pp. 15–16.

82. This feature was also found in other Osiris sanctuaries. Herodotus, describing Sais, mentions a round pond. "On this lake they enact by night the story of the god's vicissitudes, a rite which the Egyptians call the mysteries" (ii. 171).

83. Wilson, "Funeral Services of the Egyptian Old Kingdom," *JNES*, III (1944), esp. 206 ff.

84. Schäfer in *ZÄS*, XLI (1904), 107–11; C. Robichon and A. Varille, *Description sommaire du temple primitif de Médamoud* (Cairo, 1940), pp. 15–20.

85. Frankfort, *The Cenotaph of Seti I at Abydos*, p. 11.

86. Schäfer, *op. cit.*, p. 25.

87. Pyr. 2108*a*. See p. 95 above. This is yet another argument against a Busirite origin of Osiris.

88. Breasted, *Development of Religion and Thought in Ancient Egypt*. In *The Dawn of Conscience*, he centers his argument on this point.

89. Louvre Stela C 218 after Kees, *Lesebuch*, p. 17, No. 22.

90. Kees, *Totenglauben*, p. 262, referring to Petrie, *Dendereh*, Pl. III; Capart, *Chambre funéraire de la VIme Dynastie*, Pls. 1 ff.

91. On the contrary, when Osiris, because he was king of the dead, was also credited with judging the dead, one finds the absurdity of the dead man, calling himself Osiris So-and-so, facing his judge and reciting a long list of sins which he has not committed. An appropriate spell was carried to silence the heart which might bear witness against its owner and thus destroy the effect of the recitation. See H. Junker, "Die Osirisreligion und der Erlösungsgedanke bei den Ägyptern," in *Internationale Woche für Religionsethnologie* (Milan), IV (1925), 276–90.

92. Published by Jéquier, *Les frises d'objets des sarcophages du Moyen Empire* ("Mémoires de l'Institut Français d'Archéologie Orientale du Caire," Vol. XLVII [Cairo, 1921]).

93. Even in the Middle Kingdom: Gardiner and Davies, *The Tomb of Antefoker;* Blackman, *The Rock Tombs of Meir*, Vol. III, Pl. 23. And they sing royal hymns, such as "The God Comes" in Gardiner-Davies, *The Tomb of Amenemhēt*, Pl. 11. (New Kingdom: Kees, *Totenglauben*, pp. 360–64.) Another Middle Kingdom instance is mentioned by Kees, *Totenglauben*, p. 248; and the fact that the texts written on the Middle Kingdom coffins include many pyramid texts (which means texts originally meant for the king) is in itself a case in point. But we should not conclude as Kees does (*ibid.*, pp. 161 ff.) that the absence from the Old Kingdom graves of texts concerned with the fate of the dead in the Hereafter proves that the thoughts of commoners in the Old Kingdom did not reach beyond the actual interment. Such texts may well have been part of the ritual spoken at the tombs. It is generally admitted that the pyramid texts themselves must have been used in the ritual long before they were engraved for the first time in the pyramid of King Unas of the Fifth Dynasty.

94. Kees, *Totenglauben*, pp. 91 ff., faces needless complications by ignoring this affinity of night sky and death. Sethe, *Kommentar*, I, 47–52, attempts to locate *dat* but meets with the same difficulties that arise in the case of the Field of Rushes. For *dat* is the world of the dead, and the dead move in the cosmic circuit. See above, pp. 119–22, and chap. 10, n. 14.

95. Cf. Erman-Blackman, *Literature*, p. 142.

96. Kees, *Lesebuch*, p. 5.

97. Erman-Blackman, *Literature*, p. 143.

98. Paul Smither, in *JEA*, XXIV (1941), 131–32; cf. Gardiner, *The Attitude of the Ancient Egyptians to Death and the Dead* (Cambridge, 1935), p. 39, n. 17.

99. Book of the Dead, chap. 175; Kees, *Lesebuch*, p. 27, No. 40.

100. Kees, in *ZÄS*, LXV, 73 ff.

101. Kees, *Lesebuch*, p. 17. The curious designation of Osiris as "father" of Re (Lange and Neugebauer, *Papyrus Carlsberg No. 1*, pp. 22, 23) is the result of Osiris' identification with the Nile flood and hence with Nun. Since Nun surrounds the earth and since, consequently, the sun rises every dawn from Nun as he did on the day of creation (*ibid.*, p. 16, l. 8, and many texts), the waters—and hence Osiris—may be said to be a parent of Re. The fact that this combination remained entirely without consequences gives it the character of a metaphor. It may be compared with the picture of Osiris "encircling the Netherworld," in Bonomi-Sharpe, *The Alabaster Sarcophagus of Oimeneptah I*, Pl. 15, and M. A. Murray, *The Osireion*, Pl. 13.

102. An early reference to the lawsuit between Horus and Seth is Pyr. 956–61. A New Kingdom instance is the great hymn to Osiris on the stela Louvre C 286. A late instance, recast to serve as a folk tale, is Gardiner, *Papyrus Chester Beatty No. 1: The Contendings of Horus and Seth* (London, 1931). On the popular character of this story see A. de Buck in *Orientalia*, VIII (1939), 378 ff.

NOTES TO CHAPTER 16

1. Thorkild Jacobsen, "Primitive Democracy in Ancient Mesopotamia," *JNES*, II (1943), 159–72.

2. *Ibid.*, p. 168.

3. The archeological remains of the first settlers in southern Mesopotamia and their descendants belong to the Al Ubaid period. This was followed by the Warka and then the Proto-literate periods, which latter includes the main portion of what was called the Uruk period in older publications. See a forthcoming publication by Ann Louise Perkins, *The Comparative Stratigraphy of Early Mesopotamia*, and P. Delougaz and S. Lloyd, *Pre-Sargonid Temples in the Diyala Region* ("OIP," Vol. LVIII [Chicago, 1942]), p. 8, n. 10. The Proto-literate period corresponds in character (though not exactly in time) with the end of the predynastic period and the First Dynasty in Egypt (see *AJSL*, LVIII [1941], 354–58). These periods in Egypt and Mesopotamia, respectively, represent the transition from prehistory to history with the introduction of writing and of monumental architecture and sculpture and the founding of cities as their outstanding achievements.

4. So I am informed by Dr. Jacobsen.

5. S. N. Kramer, *Sumerian Mythology*, frontispiece; *idem.*, "Man's Golden Age: A Sumerian Parallel to Genesis 11:1," *JAOS*, LXIII (1943), 191–94. The translation has been revised by Dr. Jacobsen.

6. Jacobsen, in *JNES*, V (1946), 134–38.

7. Jacobsen in *JAOS*, LIX (1939), 487, n. 11.

8. With the monarchy abolished, the Greeks attempted to achieve by federation what forceful leaders did in Mesopotamia when they made themselves rulers of the whole country. See J. A. O. Larsen, "Federation for Peace in Ancient Greece," *Classical Philology*, XXXIX (1944), 145–62. For the role of Delphi see *ibid.*, pp. 148–50.

9. See H. Frankfort, *Archeology and the Sumerian Problem* ("SAOC," No. 4 [Chicago, 1932]), p. 49 and Table I, and *Progress of the Work of the Oriental Institute in Iraq, 1934/35* ("OIC," No. 20 [Chicago, 1936]), Pl. VI. Analyses of the sand samples (which will be published in a forthcoming volume of "Oriental Institute Publications") show that they are made of wind-blown, not water-laid, sand.

10. A. Poebel, "Der Konflikt zwischen Lagaš und Umma zur Zeit Enannatums I und Entemenas," in *Paul Haupt Anniversary Volume* (Baltimore, 1926), pp. 226–67.

11. *JNES*, II, 165.

12. *Ibid.*, p. 170, n. 66.

13. Johannes Pedersen, *Israel*, I, 36–37.

14. Job 29:7–14, 21–23; translation of J. M. Powis Smith, *The Complete Bible: An American Translation* (Chicago, 1939).

15. Jacobsen, in *JNES*, II, 166, n. 44.

16. Tablet II, ll. 123–29, after *Speculative Thought*, p. 177.

17. Our knowledge of the temple community is based mainly on documents from Lagash: A. Deimel, "Die sumerische Tempelwirtschaft zur Zeit Urukaginas und seiner Vorgänger," "Analecta Orientalia," II (1931) 71–113, and Anna Schneider, *Die sumerische Tempelstadt* ("Plenge Staatswissenschaftliche Beiträge," Vol. IV [Essen, 1920]).

18. See references in chap. 17, n. 44, below.

19. P. Delougaz, *The Temple Oval at Khafajah* ("OIP," Vol. LIII [Chicago, 1940]).

20. Schneider, *op. cit.*, p. 19. I am told that this number may be too large; under the Third Dynasty of Ur, Lagash contained fifty-four large and small shrines.

21. Delougaz and Lloyd, *op. cit.*

22. Schneider, *op. cit.*, pp. 21, 22. Again I am cautioned that these figures may be too high.

23. Population figures in ancient sources are so divergent as not to make sense: for Lagash, Entemena gives 3,600 people; Urukagina 36,000; Gudea 216,000 (see Poebel, *op. cit.*, p. 234, n. 4). We have computed the populations on the basis of extant ruins, a very rough approximation at most, but perhaps not quite valueless. We started with residential quarters at three sites which we know well: Ur, Eshnunna (Tell Asmar), and Khafajah. The latter is eight centuries older than the other two, which can be dated to about 1900 b.c.; but our figures show no significant differences in the densities of their populations. We found about twenty houses per acre with an average area of 200 square meters per house. These are moderately sized houses, and we reckoned that there would be six to ten occupants per house, including children and servants. Considering the number of activities in the East that take place in the streets or public squares and how easily older and distant members of the family become dependents in the house of a well-to-do relative, these figures do not seem excessive. They amount to a density of from 120 to 200 people per acre. We then compared the area and population of two modern Near Eastern cities, Aleppo and Damascus. In both cases we find a density of 160 people per acre—which is precisely the average of our figure. On this basis, the cities of Ur and Assur, each covering 150 acres, would have had 24,000 people in the Assyrian period. For earlier periods the figures are smaller. We have: Lagash, with a calculated 19,000 people; Umma with 16,000; Eshnunna with 9,000; and Khafajah with 12,000.

24. Deimel, *op. cit.*, p. 80.

25. F. Thureau-Dangin, *ISA*, pp. 74–75 (translated by Thorkild Jacobsen).

26. Ibiq-Adad II, Naram-Sin, and Dadusha. See Frankfort, Lloyd, and Jacobsen, *The Gimilsin Temple and the Palace of the Rulers at Tell Asmar* ("OIP," Vol. XLIII [Chicago, 1940]), pp. 116 ff.

27. R. Labat, *Royauté*, p. 11.

28. A. T. Olmstead, in *AJSL*, XXXV (1919), 75 n.

29. S. H. Langdon, *Sumerian Liturgical Texts* (*PBS*, Vol. X, No. 2), II, 106 ff.

30. See the penetrating study of B. Landsberger, "Die Eigenbegrifflichkeit der babylonischen Welt," *Islamica*, II, 355–72.

31. *JNES*, II (1943), 132–33.

32. Thorkild Jacobsen, "The Assumed Conflict between Sumerians and Semites in Early Mesopotamian History," *JAOS*, LIX (1939), 485–95.

33. Thureau-Dangin, *op. cit.*, p. 53.

34. *Ibid.*, p. 41, Stone A, Column V, 23—VI, 52. Cf. A. Poebel, *Grundzüge der sumerischen Grammatik*, par. 436.

35. Jacobsen, in *JAOS*, LIX (1939), 489.

36. *Cambridge Ancient History*, I, 509.

37. See below, pp. 301–2. The history of Eshnunna (Tell Asmar) gives us an excellent opportunity to follow changes in the status of a local ruler who was first a vassal of Ur, then an independent "governor" under the city-god, then "king," then governor again, and finally a vassal of Hammurabi. The inscriptions reflecting these changes are published and studied in Frankfort, Lloyd, and Jacobsen, *op. cit.*, chap. v.

38. Thureau-Dangin, *op. cit.*, p. 219, I, 36—II, 11, with some changes by Thorkild Jacobsen.

39. The new title did not carry with it any attempt to equate the king and the gods. Kings bearing it were not sacrosanct. Utuhegal, king of Erech, drove out the mountaineers of Gutium who had overrun the land and ended the Dynasty of Akkad. Ur-Nammu of Ur ad-

dressed Utuhegal as "King of the Four Quarters" (*RA*, IX, 114, 1), but later he rose in revolt, overthrew him, and henceforth gave himself that title (George A. Barton, *The Royal Inscriptions of Sumer and Akkad*, p. 274, No. 13, l. 6).

40. A. Parrot and H. Frankfort, "Mari et Opis, essai de chronologie," *RA*, XXXI (1934), 173–89.

41. W. Andrae, *Die archaischen Ischtartempel in Assur* (*WVDOG*, No. 39 [Leipzig, (1922)]).

42. M. E. L. Mallowan, in *Illustrated London News*, October 15, 1938, pp. 697–700; May 20, 1939, pp. 882–84.

43. For a comprehensive treatment see B. Landsberger, *Assyrische Handelskolonien in Kleinasien aus dem dritten Jahrtausend* (*AO*, Vol. XXIV [Leipzig, 1925]). Also Labat, *op. cit.*, pp. 16–17.

44. Labat, *op. cit.*, pp. 17–18.

45. Sidney Smith, *Early History of Assyria*, pp. 198 ff. W. von Soden, *Der Aufstieg des Assyrerreichs* (*AO*, Vol. XXXVII [Leipzig, 1937]), p. 20, n. 1.

46. Knut Tallquist, *Der assyrische Gott*, pp. 13 (n. 2), 16–17.

47. *Ibid.*, p. 22.

48. Gressmann, *Altorientalische Texte und Bilder zum Alten Testament*, I², 264, l. 39; 265, l. 14.

49. Tallquist, *op. cit.*, p. 11.

50. *Ibid.*, p. 54.

NOTES TO CHAPTER 17

1. *Speculative Thought*, pp. 137 ff.

2. *Speculative Thought*, pp. 16 ff.

3. *Paradise Lost*, Book II, ll. 891–94.

4. Thorkild Jacobsen in *Speculative Thought*, p. 160.

5. Rigveda X, discussed by Ernst Cassirer, *Philosophie der symbolischen Formen*, II, 258; cf. pp. 255 ff. for the *creatio ex nihilo*.

6. Other factors contribute to the almost universal acceptance of water as the primary substance. It has long been recognized that myths of creation and myths of the Flood are related. An outstanding contribution to the understanding of these myths is A. W. Nieuwenhuis, "Die Sintflutsagen als kausallogische Naturschöpfungsmythen," in *Festschrift P. W. Schmidt* (Vienna, 1928). Nieuwenhuis emphasizes the inadequacy of current explanations of the myths as memories of catastrophies (J. G. Frazer), reflections of celestial events (G. Gerland), memories of past geological ages (J. Riem), and others. He gives a statistical analysis of several hundred myths of this type from all parts of the world and concludes that the Flood is the device by which the primitive makes *tabula rasa*. Only by doing this can the inexhaustible stream of imaginable past events be dammed up and the existing world allowed to emerge at that point. It is as if he said: "Whatever existed before, it was drowned and done with and then. . . . . " Here follows the creation story. In some countries fire, not water, supplies the required catastrophe.

7. So also R. Campbell Thompson, in *Cambridge Ancient History*, III, 234, and Jacobsen, *Speculative Thought*. Life and conditions in the marshes are strikingly described in Fulanain, *Haji Rikkan, Marsh Arab* (London, 1927); and the photographs in this book allow one to visualize the natural conditions described by the Epic of Creation.

8. Jacobsen, in *Speculative Thought*, p. 171.

9. There are excellent reasons to believe that Enlil was originally the hero of the creation story (see Jacobsen in *Speculative Thought* and F. Nötscher, *Ellil in Sumer und Akkad*, pp. 56, 66). We cannot, however, reconstruct the older version, in which a warlike young god— Enlil's son, Ninurta—played an important part. What matters to us here is the fact that the Marduk story was accepted, at least from the middle of the second millennium B.C., as an account of the origin of kingship among the gods.

10. Jacobsen discusses some Sumerian accounts of Creation in *JNES*, V (1946), 138–43, 151–52.

11. In his treatment of Sumerian myths in *Speculative Thought*, Jacobsen has emphasized how admirably the description of character has been infused with the grandeur appropriate to personifications of natural forces.

12. I, 132 ff., after *Speculative Thought*, pp. 175–76.

13. II, 81 85, after Alexander Heidel, *The Babylonian Genesis* (Chicago, 1942), who uses "frame of mind" for our "mood."

14. IV, 49–64, after Heidel, *ibid.*

15. IV, 13–17, Jacobsen, in *Speculative Thought*, p. 178.

16. H. Zimmern, "Ischtar und Saltu," in *Berichte über die Verhandlungen der Königlichen Sächsischen Gesellschaft der Wissenschaften*, *Phil.-hist. Klasse*, LXVIII (1916), 1 ff.

17. *Speculative Thought*.

18. A. T. Clay, *Babylonian Records in the Library of J. Pierpont Morgan*, Vol. IV, No. 2, Col. I, 6–14 (translated by Thorkild Jacobsen). Cf. S. H. Langdon, "The Old Babylonian Version of the Myth of Etana," *Babyloniaca*, XII, 10–11. See also Jacobsen, *The Sumerian King List* ("AS," No. 11 [Chicago, 1939]), p. 58: "When the crown of kingship was lowered from heaven/When the scepter and the throne of kingship were lowered from heaven."

19. Langdon, *op. cit.*, p. 9. The text is badly damaged, but the sense is clear.

20. So. R. Labat, *Royauté*, pp. 45 ff. Labat suggests that the ruler was first "favorably regarded by the god"; that next "his name was pronounced"; and that, finally, "his great destiny was determined." But these expressions are equivalent rather than complementary. We never hear that all of them have reference to one god; and, as our quotations show, they are only a few of the various set phrases by which divine election is described. Labat's material has been of the greatest help to us, though we disagree with him on several points of interpretation. For the "pronouncing of the name" see p. 246 below.

21. Thureau-Dangin, *ISA*, p. 47, Brick A (translated by Thorkild Jacobsen).

22. *Ibid.*, p. 49, Brick B (translated by Jacobsen).

23. *Ibid.*, p. 107 (Statue B, II, 8 ff.) (translated by Jacobsen).

24. E. Dhorme, *La religion assyro-babylonienne* (Paris, 1910), pp. 150 ff.; Labat, *op. cit.*, pp. 44 ff.

25. *OECT*, I, 23, after Jacobsen.

26. Dhorme, *op. cit.*, p. 150 (Monolith I, 12).

27. Labat, *op. cit.*, p. 45 (K 2801, 14–18).

28. *Ibid.*, p. 46.

29. *Ibid.*, p. 43 (Annals I, 3–5).

30. Dhorme, *op. cit.*, p. 153 (Sippar cylinder I, 4 ff.).

31. *Ibid.*, p. 155; L. W. King, *Chronicles concerning Early Babylonian Kings*, II, 87 ff.

32. Dhorme, *op. cit.*, p. 156; Brünnow, in *ZA*, V, 79, 22 ff.

33. Code, Obverse I, 27 ff. See R. F. Harper, *The Code of Hammurabi* (Chicago, 1904).

34. Dhorme, *op. cit.*, p. 157.

35. A. Poebel, *Historical Texts* (*PBS*, Vol. IV [Philadelphia, 1914]), pp. 17–18.

36. E.g., Urukagina's cone inscription, Thureau-Dangin, *op. cit.*, p. 81, Cols. VII, 29—VIII, 6. In the texts of Gudea Statue B VIII, 11 ff., and Statue I, III, 11—IV, 1, as translated by Poebel, *Grundzüge der sumerischen Grammatik*, par. 659), Ningirsu calls up the personal god of him who is to become ruler.

37. Gudea Cylinder A, I, 1 ff., in Thureau-Dangin, *ibid.*, p. 134 (translated by Jacobsen).

38. Cone of Entemena (*ibid.*, pp. 63 ff. [translated by Jacobsen]).

39. Eannatum's Stela of the Vultures (*ibid.*, p. 27 [Col. VI, 10]).

40. *Ibid.*, p. 93 (translated by Jacobsen).

41. Jacobsen, *The Sumerian King List* ("AS," No. 11 [Chicago, 1939]).

42. *Ibid.*, p. 95.

43. H. G. Güterbock ("Die historische Tradition und ihre literarische Gestaltung," *ZA*, XLII [1934], 1–91) has not proved, to my mind, that the Mesopotamians at any time regarded their history as an alternation of times of blessedness with times of misfortune. Individual cities suffered decline; individual kings were sometimes punished with defeat for their transgressions—that is all that we may conclude from the material.

44. This very important passage from Chiera (*Sumerian Texts of Varied Contents*, p. 25, obv. 14–rev. 23, has been translated and commented upon by Thorkild Jacobsen in *JNES*, II (1943), 171. See also S. N. Kramer, *Lamentations over the Destruction of Ur* ("AS," No. 12 [Chicago, 1940]), and Jacobsen in *AJSL*, LVIII (1941), 219–24.

45. Labat, *op. cit.*, pp. 40–42, adduces evidence which he believes proves the existence of a "race royale," which would imply that the principle of heredity was acknowledged to be valid in theory. The evidence, however, shows only that rulers tended to claim that they and their families were favored by the gods (see also below, p. 310, and chap. 21, n. 21). Thorkild Jacobsen will argue in a forthcoming article that the Assyrian king list stresses descent in a peculiar fashion which can be explained with reference to the conditions under which it was composed.

46. This translation of *bit riduti* I owe to Dr. Jacobsen. See Labat, *op. cit.*, p. 73, for the crown prince's duties.

47. Langdon, *OECT*, VI, 68, l. 11.

48. After Theo Bauer, *ZA*, XLII (1934), 170 ff.

49. Von Soden, *ZA*, XLIII, 255, n. 2, would give "the place of its cover"; and this "place" can only have an "opening" if it is a groove. The sentence becomes clear when we look at the royal sarcophagus actually found at Assur (W. Andrae, *Das wiedererstandene Assur*, Pl. 66*b*), on which the joint of coffin and lid (this, according to our text, was sealed with molten metal) shows clearly.

50. Labat, *op. cit.*, p. 119; after E. Ebeling, *Tod und Leben nach den Vorstellungen der Babylonier* (1931), p. 57, No. 12, and Von Soden in *ZA*, XLIII, 254 ff.

51. See R. Campbell Thompson's new interpretation of Harper, "Assyro-Babylonian Letters," No. 473, in *Iraq*, IV (1937), 35–43.

52. See *Speculative Thought*, p. 13, and pp. 124–25 above.

53. *Speculative Thought*, pp. 4–6.

54. A. Poebel, *Historical and Grammatical Texts*, p. 76. This text was brought to my attention and translated for me by Dr. Jacobsen.

55. Karl F. Müller, "Das assyrische Ritual," *Mitteilungen der Vorderasiatisch-Ägyptischen Gesellschaft*, Vol. XLI, Heft 3 (1937).

56. The exclamation of the priest is commonly interpreted as an identification of the king with Assur, and hence as a proof of the king's deification (Ivan Engnell, *Studies in Divine Kingship in the Ancient Near East* [Uppsala, 1943], p. 17 with notes). This theory ignores not only the fact that the Assyrian king is never identified with a god but also that the king was not yet crowned when he was carried to the temple. The assumption that the priest's phrase refers to the Assyrian king who is to be crowned robs the coronation ceremony of all significance.

57. Müller (*op. cit.*). He suggests, too, that the act of coronation was preceded by an anointment and also points out that the "straight scepter" is a symbol often used to express successful rulership.

58. H. F. Lutz, *Selected Sumerian and Babylonian Texts* (PBS, Vol. I, No. 2), p. 23.

NOTES TO CHAPTER 18

1. L. W. King, *A History of Babylon*, p. 160.

2. Ed. Meyer, *Geschichte des Altertums*, I, 2⁵ (1926), 636–37.

3. F. Thureau-Dangin, *Une relation de la huitième campagne de Sargon* (Paris, 1912).

4. With various qualifications (see R. Labat, *Royauté*, pp. 131–32).

5. Such an appointment was important enough to have a year named after it (see Thureau-Dangin, *ISA*, p. 335).

6. A. T. Clay, *Miscellaneous Inscriptions in the Yale Babylonian Collection* (New Haven, 1915), No. 45, pp. 66–75. The text is studied afresh by F. M. Th. Böhl, "Die Tochter des Königs Nabonid," in *Symbolae ad iura orientis antiqui pertinentes Paulo Koschaker dedicatae* (Leiden, 1939), pp. 151–78.

7. R. Pfeiffer, *State Letters of Assyria*, No. 315, p. 213 (Harper 687).

8. *Ibid.*, No. 276, p. 193 (Harper 895).

9. *Ibid.*, No. 325, p. 220 (Harper 407).

10. *Ibid.*, No. 328, p. 223 (Harper 356).

11. *Ibid.*, No. 265, p. 187 (Harper 78).

12. *Ibid.*, No. 337, p. 230 (Harper 363).

13. *Ibid.*, No. 339, p. 231 (Harper 1278).

14. Von Soden, "Die Unterweltsvision eines assyrischen Kronprinzen," *ZA*, XLIII (1936), 1–31. The dream (*Die neubabylonischen Königsinschriften* ["Vorderasiatische Bibliothek," Vol. IV], pp. 218 ff., No. 1, Col. I, 16 ff.) in which Marduk and Sin ordered Nabonidus to rebuild the moon temple in Harran lacks every trace of numinous feeling and seems therefore a mere literary form, a make-believe; but it confirms that communication through dreams was understood to take place.

15. Gudea Cylinder A (translation by Jacobsen).

16. *RA*, IX (1912), 111 ff. (translation by Jacobsen).

17. Gudea Cylinder B, IV, 13.

18. *OECT*, VI, 73 rev., 5–7.

19. Thureau-Dangin, *Rituels accadiens*, p. 37.

20. Labat, *op. cit.*, pp. 344 and 323–25. Cf. A. van Selms, *De babylonische termini voor zonde en hun beteekenis voor onze kennis van het babylonische zondebesef* (Wageningen, 1933), and E. Dhorme, *La religion assyro-babylonienne* (Paris, 1910), pp. 231–41.

21. Pfeiffer, *op. cit.*, No. 273, p. 191 (Harper 355).

22. Thureau-Dangin, *Rituels accadiens*, p. 35.

23. Pfeiffer, *op. cit.*, No. 270 (Harper 370). See also Labat, *op. cit.*, 345–52.

24. Labat, *op. cit.*, pp. 309–10.

25. *Ibid.*, p. 312.

26. Van Selms, *op. cit.*, 17, n. 6; also K. M. Streck, *Assurbanipal und die letzten assyrischen Könige bis zum Untergange Ninivehs* ("Vorderasiatische Bibliothek," Vol. VII [Leipzig, 1916]), II, 385, n. 8.

NOTES TO CHAPTER 19

1. R. Labat, *Royauté*, p. 353. Labat has carefully studied the substitution for the king (pp. 352–60), and we have used his material extensively.

2. F. Thureau-Dangin, *Rituels accadiens*, p. 37. Cf. below, Epilogue, n. 1.

3. *Speculative Thought*, pp. 10–26.

4. Labat, *op. cit.*, pp. 258–59, after H. Zimmern, *Beiträge zur Kenntnis der babylonischen Religion*, No. 57, p. 172.

5. Labat (*op. cit.*, p. 354, n. 139) shows that this expression of loyalty, common in Kassite times, occurs as early as Hammurabi and persists in the El Amarna letters.

6. *Ibid.*, pp. 355–56.

7. R. Pfeiffer, *State Letters of Assyria*, No. 323 (Harper 629), corrected after Labat, *op. cit.*, 358–59.

8. After L. W. King, *Chronicles concerning Early Babylonian Kings*, II, 12–14, ll. 8–13, and pp. 15–16, ll. 1–7. See Labat, *op. cit.*, p. 103.

9. The profession of Enlil-bani possibly suggests that. The motif is also present in the legend of Sargon of Akkad, who was found and educated by a gardener. On the other hand, a historical event might equally well have become clothed with folkloristic details, and there is not even proof that we have those here.

10. Labat, *op. cit.*, p. 359, after Harper 437.

11. Hence it is quite impossible to connect this rare rite with the annual festival of the Sacaea as Frazer (see Index of *The Golden Bough*, "Sacaea") and many after him did. See Labat, *op. cit.*, 98–110, and Von Soden in *ZA*, XLIII (1936), 255 ff. Also see below, chap. 22, n. 14.

12. There is nothing in the nature of Mesopotamian kingship or in the texts referring to it that would explain the wholesale slaughter of retainers exemplified by the "death pits" at Ur (C. L. Woolley, *Ur Excavations II: The Royal Cemetery* [London and Philadelphia, 1934]). Moreover, the discoveries at Ur possess specific features which have from the beginning thrown doubt on the interpretation represented by the title just quoted. Most important among these is the recurrence of the name "Meskalamdug." Both men bearing this name were interred in the shaft of a "death pit," while in the one case where the burial in the tomb chamber was preserved it contained the body of a woman. One might suppose that the name indicated a role played in a ritual performance rather than a personal name. Sidney Smith has suggested that the bodies represent the participants in a "fertility rite," more specifically the sacred marriage (*JRAS*, 1928, pp. 849 ff.; esp. pp. 860–68); and a similar view is held by

F. M. Th. Böhl, in *Symbolae ad iura orientis antiqui pertinentes Paulo Koschaker dedicatae* (Leiden, 1939), pp. 156 ff. We also tended toward that view formerly and have not properly distinguished the sacred marriage from the killing of the substitute king (*Iraq*, I, 12, n. 3; *JRAS*, 1937, pp. 341 ff.). But in the sacred marriage the king was not, as far as we know, replaced by a substitute or killed. The only ceremonial killing of which the Mesopotamian sources speak is that of the substitute king who functioned in times of emergency. We admit that it is possible that in Early Dynastic times the sacred marriage was followed by the death of its participants, perhaps because they could not be reintegrated in human society after representing deities. But in the absence of all evidence on this matter, we prefer to see in the "death pits" of Ur burials of substitute kings together with their "ladies of the court" and their suites, as described in the texts dealing with Damqi.

13. See *Speculative Thought*, pp. 11 ff.

14. B. Landsberger, *Der kultische Kalender der Babylonier und Assyrer*, I (Leipzig, 1915), 94; Labat, *op. cit.*, p. 149.

15. Thureau-Dangin, *op. cit.*, pp. 118–25.

16. Labat, *op. cit.*, p. 159.

17. *Ibid.*

18. D. D. Luckenbill, *Ancient Records of Assyria* (Chicago, 1927), Vol. II, par. 94.

19. *Ibid.*, par. 699.

20. After Alexander Heidel, *The Babylonian Genesis* (Chicago, 1942), p. 37 (VI, 49–51).

21. Luckenbill, *op. cit.*, par. 702.

22. De Buck, in "Analecta Orientalia," XVII (1938), 52.

23. Breasted, *Ancient Records*, Vol. I, par. 484. This formula is very common at all times.

24. *Ibid.*, Vol. II, par. 303.

25. S. H. Langdon, *Die neubabylonischen Königsinschriften* ("Vorderasiatische Bibliothek," Vol. IV), p. 239, revised by Jacobsen.

26. Luckenbill, *op. cit.*, par. 670.

27. *Ibid.*, par. 649.

28. *Ibid.*, par. 643.

29. Langdon, *op. cit.*, p. 239, ll. 41–42.

30. Labat, *op. cit.*, p. 182.

31. Ernst Cassirer, *Philosophie der symbolischen Formen*, II, 134 ff.

32. Langdon, *op. cit.*, p. 237, ll. 10–14.

33. Breasted, *op. cit.*, Vol. II, par. 339. For the apparent paradox in such a statement see above, p. 149.

34. Langdon, *op. cit.*, p. 244, ll. 56–58. It is observed in actual excavations that temples are often rebuilt through many years, sometimes through centuries, on the same plan. See, e.g., P. Delougaz and S. Lloyd, *Pre-Sargonid Temples in the Diyala Region* ("OIP," Vol. LVIII [Chicago, 1942]). The new walls are founded on the leveled stumps of the old ones. This practice resulted in exceptionally deep and firm foundations, so that experience and belief agreed that the existing layout should be respected. When innovations were made, they were ascribed to inspiration by the gods, as we shall see presently in discussing Gudea's Cylinder A.

35. A complete foundation deposit, in both Egypt and Mesopotamia, contained samples of the materials used in the temple plus an inscription and sometimes remains of the animal sacrificed at the ceremony. At Erech, for instance, an untouched deposit of Ur-Nammu was found. It contained a box of inscribed baked bricks set in bitumen and containing, wrapped in matting, a piece of gold foil; a bronze or copper figure of the king, legless, and ending in a point below, and carrying upon its head the basket with the clay for molding the first brick; one stone tablet (steatite) with the foundation inscription; one piece of wood; and eleven round faïence beads (A. Nöldeke, *Zehnter vorläufiger Bericht* . . . . [*Abhandlungen der Preussischen Akademie, Phil.-hist. Klasse*, No. 2 (1939)], p. 18 and Pl. 22). For Egyptian foundation deposits see, e.g., *Bulletin of the Metropolitan Museum of Art*, 1921, Part II, pp. 10–11, 16, and Figs. 9–11 (Twelfth Dynasty); *ibid.*, 1922, Part II, p. 29; and *ibid.*, 1924, Part II, p. 16, and Figs. 11–14 (Eighteenth Dynasty); Uvo Hölscher, *The Mortuary Temple of Ramses III* ("OIP," Vol. LIV [Chicago, 1941]), pp. 45, 51, 67, 75–76 (Twentieth Dynasty).

36. *RA*, XVI, 121 ff.

37. Labat, *op. cit.*, pp. 182–83.

38. Luckenbill, *op. cit.*, par. 982.
39. Langdon, *op. cit.*, p. 63, II, 40 42.
40. Gudea, Cylinder A, XII, 21–XVII (translated by Jacobsen).
41. K. M. Streck, *Assurbanipal und die letzten assyrischen Könige bis zum Untergange Ninivehs* ("Vorderasiatische Bibliothek," Vol. VII [Leipzig, 1916]), p. xliv.
42. E. G. Heuzey, *Catalogue des antiquités chaldéennes*, Nos. 158, 161, 163, and 164; *A Guide to the Babylonian and Assyrian Antiquities in the British Museum*, p. 146; A. T. Clay, *Babylonian Records in the Library of J. Pierpont Morgan*, Vol. IV, No. 43, Plate 44 and Pl. I.
43. Langdon, *op. cit.*, p. 63, ll. 61–67.
44. Thureau-Dangin, *ISA*, p. 159. Cylinder A, XVIII (translated by Jacobsen).
45. *Ibid.*, ll. 25–26 (translated by Jacobsen).
46. *Ibid.*, XIX, 8 (translated by Jacobsen).
47. The sun-god.
48. The moon-god.
49. Cylinder A, XIX, 20–28.
50. The evidence for the date is not entirely decisive. Gudea's Statue E, Col. V, 1–3 (Thureau-Dangin, *ISA*, p. 123), states that Baba received wedding presents on New Year's Day. Her wedding (Cylinder B, Col. III; *ISA*, pp. 177–81) took place on Ningirsu's return from Eridu on the third day of the month and not on the first (*ibid.*, ll. 8–9). The delay—if there was one—was perhaps due to the extraordinary circumstances of this particular divine union. Ningirsu had left the town while the temple was being built or completed; it may be that the journey could not auspiciously be undertaken during the last days of the departing year. If he started on the first day of the month, his arrival in Lagash and his wedding might be two days later than usual. In any case, it would still be part of the New Year's celebrations.
51. Thureau-Dangin, *ISA*, p. 195, Cylinder B, XVII, 18; XVIII, 13 (translated by Jacobsen).

NOTES TO CHAPTER 20

1. See above, pp. 51 and 157. It may well be that the so-called "pessimistic" prophecies and complaints of Egyptian literature are misnamed. The one which we know in its entirety, that of Neferrohu (*Journal of Egyptian Archaeology*, I, 100–106), ends with the prediction that a king shall rule and "the people of his time shall rejoice." Other texts, describing the same period of disintegration which followed the downfall of the Old Kingdom, may have ended on a similar note. The tendency of the Egyptian texts would seem to be to stress the temporary character of the disturbances of an established order. On Egyptian "pessimistic" texts see Miriam Lichtheim, "The Songs of the Harpers," *JNES*, IV (1945), 178–212, esp. 210 ff.
2. *Speculative Thought*, p. 215.
3. Charles Maystre, *Les déclarations d'innocence* (Cairo: 1937). I do not understand how E. Drioton, "Les confessions négatives," in *Recueil d'études égyptologiques dédiées à la mémoire de Jean-François Champollion* (Paris, 1922), pp. 545 ff., can claim that chap. 125 of the Book of the Dead betrays a high moral standard. See also above, p. 209, and chap. 4 of my forthcoming *Ancient Egyptian Religion: An Interpretation*.
4. E. Ebeling, *Tod und Leben nach den Vorstellungen der Babylonier* (1931), pp. 9–19.
5. Ebeling, *Keilinschriften aus Assur religiösen Inhalts*, p. 23, obv. 22, 23, after A. van Selms, *De babylonische termini voor zonde* (Wageningen, 1933), p. 50; see also our quotation on p. 248 above. Van Selms's disquisitions on guilt and sin are illuminating, since he is familiar with the philological as well as with the theological aspects of the problem.
6. Van Selms (*op. cit.*, p. 89) expresses this by saying that the gods appear as guarantors of the rules of taboo. Note that at this point alone we meet the "law of retribution" which Hans Kelsen, *Society and Nature* (Chicago, 1944), offers as a clue to early man's view of the world. The material presented in our pages demonstrates the inadequacy of that theory.
7. Van Selms, *op. cit.*, p. 51.
8. See *ibid.*, pp. 92 ff., for an interpretation of *Shurpu II* (H. Zimmern, *Die Beschwörungstafeln Šurpu* [Leipzig, 1901]; Gressmann, *Altorientalische Texte und Bilder*, I², 324–25), not as a catalogue of sins, but as a means of discovering (by looking for some portent during the

recitation of the text) what transgression has actually been committed and thus must be expiated.

9. Thorkild Jacobsen, in *Speculative Thought*, pp. 139–40.

10. *Ibid.*, p. 146.

11. *Ibid.*, pp. 150–68.

12. The significance of these lists for an understanding of the mentality of the Mesopotamians has been discussed by Von Soden, "Leistung und Grenze der sumerischen und babylonischen Wissenschaft," *Welt als Geschichte*, II (1936), 412–64, 509–57. The oldest texts are published by A. Falkenstein, *Archaische Texte aus Uruk* (Berlin, 1936).

13. Thorkild Jacobsen, *The Sumerian King List* (Chicago, 1939).

14. While astronomical portents always concerned the state, not the individual (A. Schott, *Zeitschrift der Deutschen Morgenländischen Gesellschaft*, XIII [1934], 313), the questioning of the gods and the purifications and penances by means of which the private individual expiated his guilt are quite similar to those which the king performed on behalf of the community. Van Selms (*op. cit.*, p. 74) notes that the nature of the deity to whom prayers and psalms are addressed makes no difference at all. We found the same to be true in the case of the king's prayers. The distance between man and god is so great that any differences between the gods dwindle to insignificance in so far as the supplicant is concerned. Only the personal god (see pp. 303–4) is felt to be nearer to man.

15. This is Thorkild Jacobsen's interpretation of Imdugud.

16. *Iraq*, I (1934), 2–29; "Analecta Orientalia," XII (1935), 105–21; "Oriental Institute Communications," Nos. 16, 17, and 19 (Chicago, 1933, 1934, and 1935); and, for the same phenomenon considered in the history of religions in general, A. Bertholet, *Götterspaltung und Göttervereinigung* (Tübingen, 1933).

17. So also Bruno Meissner (*Babylonien und Assyrien*, II, 47–48), who lists Urash, Ninurta, Zababa, Nabu, Nergal, Ditar, and Pasagga as identified by the ancients with one another; to this number he adds: Pabilsag, Abu, Shulmanu, and Shushinak. Sometimes the device of claiming a family relationship is used as a means of expressing affinity and distinctness simultaneously. Tammuz (Dumuzi) appears, for instance, as the son of Ningiszida in one text (Zimmern, "Sumerisch-babylonische Tamūzlieder" [*Berichte über die Verhandlungen der Kgl. Sächs. Gesellschaft der Wissenschaften, Phil.-hist. Klasse*, Vol. LIX (1907)], No. 1B, l. 14) and as the son of Ea in the An-Anum list. But Ningiszida was the son of Ninazu, the "Lord of Water"; and water was Ea's element. Such combinations have an interest for the detailed study of Mesopotamian cults, but their secondary nature is clear.

18. See below, pp. 313–17. For Enlil see Zimmern, "Sumerisch-babylonische Tamūzlieder," p. 248; Ebeling, *Tod und Leben*, pp. 31–32. Dor Anu see *ibid.*, pp. 32–33. Other captive gods are Sumuqan (*ibid.*, pp. 26–27) and Enmesharra (*RA*, XVI, 148–49).

19. F. Thureau-Dangin, in *RA*, XIX, 175 ff.; A. Poebel, *Historical Texts* (*PBS*, Vol. IV [Philadelphia, 1914]), pp. 24 ff.; Jacobsen, in *JNES*, V (1946), 150.

20. Scheil, in *RA*, VIII (1911), 61 ff., ll. 8–9, 20–21.

21. Kramer, *Sumerian Mythology*, p. 39.

22. W. W. Baudissin, *Adonis und Esmun* (Leipzig, 1911), pp. 56, 480 ff., shows how the uses of certain Semitic verb roots reveal distinctions corresponding with those existing between the Great Mother, source of life but not necessarily intensively alive, and the young god, so vital as to overcome periodic death but not necessarily a source of life.

23. We do not find in Mesopotamia the contrast so acutely recognized by Baudissin in Syrian religion (*op. cit.*, pp. 15–56, esp. 54, also 181). The Syrian Ba'alim are heads of tribes and towns, not necessarily connected with natural phenomena at all, while Adonis has no social function. In Mesopotamia the gods who are cosmic powers in the first place also appear as city-gods. This contrast between Mesopotamian and Syrian religion, and the fact that our fragmentary information when it bears on this problem at all (e.g., Gudea's account of the sacred marriage where the goddess and not Ningirsu is dominant, chap. 21, n. 7) supports our view, incline us to generalize and to maintain that as symbols of natural life a predominant mother-goddess and a "son" dependent upon her were universally acknowledged in Mesopotamia.

24. I once viewed this combination as "the interpretation of Sumerian mythology in terms of Semitic belief" (*Iraq*, I, 6; *Cylinder Seals*, p. 96), but now consider it a mistake to treat Mesopotamian civilization as a compound (see above, pp. 225–26). In any case, the

argument of our text shows that the combination of hero-god (*quradu*) and the suffering god can be accepted without recourse to the theory that two distinct traditions were combined.

25. Ebeling, in *Pauly-Wissowa*, Vol. XIV, Part II, cols. 1669–70.

26. Zimmern, in *ZA*, XXXV (1923), 239.

27. Baudissin, *op. cit.*, p. 107.

28. Quoted from Meyer Schapiro, "The Religious Meaning of the Ruthwell Cross," *Art Bulletin*, XXVI (1944), 238.

29. The subject is discussed with an extraordinary combination of careful scholarship and a profound understanding of ancient religion by Baudissin, *op. cit.*, in which almost all the conclusions concerning our subject remain valid notwithstanding the enormous increase of our material since its publication.

30. Sir James G. Frazer, *The Golden Bough*, Part I, Vol. I, p. 10.

31. Baudissin, *op. cit.*, p. 177.

32. The predominance of male deities is altogether characteristic for Egyptian religion. Even when the sun is viewed as the child of heaven (chap. 14), the god is dominant and the goddess a mere vehicle of rebirth, worshiping her son:

> "Thy mother Nut hastens towards thee, O Lord of Eternity,
> And speaks to thee words of praise which come from her heart."

(Scharff, *Ägyptische Sonnenlieder*, p. 81). In a similar way the goddess is but the receptacle of an immortal substance when a god renews himself in the mystery of the Kamutef. See above, pp. 169, 180, 188–90. The view even survives in Plutarch *De Iside et Osiride* 53.

33. See below, p. 324. The comparison of Nabu and Ninurta with Horus, who avenged (better, supported) his father, has been made repeatedly (Ivan Engnell, *Studies in Divine Kingship in the Ancient Near East* [Uppsala, 1943], pp. 36–37; Paulus, in *Orientalia*, XXIX [1928], 55 ff.).

34. Ebeling, *Tod und Leben*, p. 47, l. 5.

35. Baudissin, *op. cit.*, pp. 111 ff.

36. Dussaud, in *Les religions des Hittites et des Hourrites, des Phéniciens et des Syriens* (Paris, 1945), p. 375. We have not otherwise brought the very complex mythology of Ras Shamra into the discussion, since the decipherment of the texts is still incomplete and many translations are problematical.

37. De Genouillac, *Textes religieux sumériens*, No. 8, ll. 118–29 (translated by Jacobsen).

38. Zimmern, "Sumerisch-babylonische Tamūzlieder," p. 208.

39. Frazer, *The Golden Bough*, Part IV, Vol. I, pp. 236 ff.; Baudissin, *op. cit.*, pp. 138 ff.

40. Junker, "Die Mysterien des Osiris," *Internationale Woche für Religionsethnologie*, III (1922), 419 ff.

41. G. Glotz, "Les fêtes d'Adonis sous Ptolémée II," in *Revue des études grecques*, XXXIII (1920), 169–222.

42. L. R. Farrell, *Greek Hero Cult and Ideas of Immortality* (Oxford, 1921), p. 27; *ibid.*, pp. 19–52, for parallels with the Tammuz cult. See also Machteld J. Mellink, *Hyakinthos* (Utrecht, 1943) (in English), chap. 3.

43. Plutarch *De Iside et Osiride* 15.

44. Lucian *De dea Syria* 7.

45. The Egyptian documents seem to mention a tree-god in connection with Byblos; but this is not Osiris, for they do not connect him with that city. On a cylinder seal belonging to the third millennium B.C. the goddess of Byblos is depicted with the horns and sun disk of Hathor. This monument and Egyptian texts referring to "the lady of Byblos" are discussed by P. Montet, *Byblos et l'Égypte* (Paris, 1928), pp. 61–68, 275 ff., 287 ff. See also Erman, *Religion*, p. 349.

46. Walter F. Otto, *Dionysos* (Frankfurt, 1933), pp. 81–85.

47. This point is the basis of Alan H. Gardiner's excellent criticism of Frazer, who used classical sources in the first place (*JEA*, II, 121–26).

48. Jacobsen, *The Sumerian King List*, pp. 169 ff.

49. Baudissin, *op. cit.*, pp. 142–60. Baudissin (p. 152) doubts, however, that this feature of the Adonis myth was ancient.

50. Book of the Dead, chap. 112. See Sethe, *Die Sprüche für das Kennen der Seelen der heiligen Orte*, pp. 51 ff.

51. In Pyr. 1268 Horus is called "blinded by a boar." The text is discussed by E. Drioton in *Mélanges Dussaud* (Paris), II (1939), 495–506.

52. Percy E. Newberry, in *JEA*, XIV, 211–25.

53. Sidney Smith, "The Relation of Marduk, Ashur and Osiris," *JEA*, VIII (1922), 41–44. In the Epic of Creation (VII, 1–2) Marduk is called "Asaru, bestower of verdure, who has established the granaries; creator of grain and plants, causing the grass to spring up." The name "Asaru" occurs already in the third millennium B.C., on Gudea's Cylinder B, IV, 2.

54. Baudissin, *op. cit.*, pp. 161–66, esp. p. 165.

55. *JNES*, III, 198–200.

NOTES TO CHAPTER 21

1. The deification of Mesopotamian kings is generally treated as if the use of the divine determinative before the names of some of them were quite unequivocal; the conflict of this usage with the prevalent trends in Mesopotamian thought is ignored, and the divine character of Pharaoh is quoted as an illuminating parallel. Yet we must realize that when cultural phenomena are compared "the whole determines its parts—not only their relation but their very nature. Between two wholes there is a discontinuity in kind and any understanding must take account of their different natures, over and above a recognition of the similar elements that have entered into the two" (Ruth Benedict, *Patterns of Culture*, p. 52). An extreme case of the neglect of the individual nature of distinct civilizations is presented by Ivan Engnell, *Studies in Divine Kingship in the Ancient Near East* (Uppsala, 1943), criticized at length by Theodor H. Gaster, *Review of Religion*, IX (1945), 267–91. Engnell forces one single pattern upon the extensive material which he has collected, thus destroying the rich variety of pre-Greek thought in the name of "comparative religion." The same criticism applies to S. Hooke's *Myth and Ritual* and his *The Labyrinth;* E. O. James's *Christian Myth and Ritual* (London, 1933); and A. M. Hocart's *Kingship*. In different degrees these overshoot the mark of comparative research, which should counteract the narrowness of viewpoint entailed in devotion to a particular field but should not in any way infringe upon the individuality, the uniqueness, of each historical actuality.

2. An enumeration of the gods whose weddings are mentioned in the texts (E. Douglas van Buren, "The Sacred Marriage in Early Times in Mesopotamia," *Orientalia*, XIII [1944], 2–3) includes all the major gods of Mesopotamia.

3. Translation of Chiera, *Sumerian Religious Texts*, No. 1, Col. V, ll. 18 ff., by Thorkild Jacobsen. See also Langdon, *JRAS* (1926), 15–42.

4. So at the birth of Hatshepsut (p. 44).

5. *OECT*, Vol. I, No. 15, Col. V, ll. 17–21 (translated by Jacobsen).

6. S. H. Langdon, *Sumerian Liturgical Texts* (PBS, Vol. X, No. 2), p. 148, ll. 4–5.

7. Gudea Cylinder B, V (Thureau-Dangin, *ISA*, pp. 179–80). The structure of the text brings out in a curious way the passing of the initiative from Ningirsu to Baba. The passage starts by describing the god's tempestuous entrance into his shrine with striking metaphors (see below, p. 330). When the consummation of the union is described, the verses continue to pivot on their similes, but this continuity of structure emphasizes the fact that the subject of these sentences is no longer Ningirsu but Baba.

8. VI, 6 ff.; Leonard, *Gilgamesh, Epic of Old Babylonia* (New York, 1934), pp. 26–27.

9. H. Zimmern, "König Lipit-Ishtars Vergöttlichung" (*Berichte über die Verhandlungen der Kgl. Sächsischen Gesellschaft der Wissenschaften, Phil.-hist. Klasse*, Band 68 [1916]).

10. After Thorkild Jacobsen.

11. R. Labat, *Royauté*, p. 280, where references are given.

12. *OECT*, Vol. I, No. 43, l. 15. See Labat, *op. cit.*, p. 248, with n. 67.

13. Cylinder A, III, 6–7 (Thureau-Dangin, *ISA*, p. 139).

14. Labat, *op. cit.*, p. 55, with n. 19.

15. *OECT*, VI, 68, l. 13.

16. Labat (*op. cit.*, pp. 55–56) quotes other rulers who claim a variety of divine mothers. He wavers curiously in the interpretation of the phenomena, sometimes stressing the humanity, sometimes the divinity, of the king. Cf. his pp. 111–12 and 284–85. with pp. 8–9.

17. Labat, *op. cit.*, pp. 63–69 (as do Witzel and Paffrath).

18. *OECT*, VI, 73, ll. 15 ff.

19. D. D. Luckenbill, *Ancient Records of Assyria* (Chicago, 1927), Vol. II, par. 765.

20. Labat (*op. cit.*, p. 58) quotes numerous examples.

21. Labat, like us, considers that the claim of divine parentage differs from physical parentage. Hence it is difficult to understand why he assumes a Mesopotamian belief in a "race royale," a true dynasty (*op. cit.*, pp. 40–42), which has meaning only when the king is of divine descent and differs in his very substance from ordinary man. The absence of a "race royale" in Mesopotamia becomes evident when we recall medieval views which were based on a truly dynastic conception: "The whole dynasty, not merely the individual, was called to the throne. . . . . This claim of the family, this 'kin-right' or 'blood-right,' . . . . conferred upon the individual ruler an independent, subjective *ius ad rem*" (Fritz Kern, *Kingship and Law in the Middle Ages* [Oxford, 1939], p. 13). The contrast with Mesopotamia is also pronounced in the following respect: "Germanic kin-right . . . . contained no idea of office at all, but only a claim for the family, and the original foundations of this right were not so much a duty enjoined upon the family, as an unusual power, a fortunate virtue, a special divine vocation" (*ibid.*, p. 21). We can only admit that the passages quoted by Labat show that the gods, when well pleased with the ruler, granted the succession to his son, or rather chose the son for the succession and suitably influenced the formation of his personality on both the physical and the spiritual planes (see also above, p. 243).

22. After Jacobsen, "The Concept of Divine Parentage of the Ruler in the Stele of the Vultures," *JNES*, II (1943), 119–21.

23. Thureau-Dangin, *ISA*, p. 41 (galet A, Col. VIII).

24. Thureau-Dangin, *ISA*, p. 27 (Stela of the Vultures, Reverse, VI, 8–9). Neither Eannatum nor any of his contemporaries used the divine determinative; his marriage with Inanna could not have formed part of the cults of Lagash but might have taken place in some of the cities he conquered, perhaps even in Erech.

25. Frankfort, Lloyd, and Jacobsen, *The Gimilsin Temple and the Palace of the Rulers at Tell Asmar* ("OIP," Vol. XLIII), pp. 134–35. *Gimil-Sin* is now read *Shu-Sin*.

26. *Ibid.*, p. 196.

27. T. Fish, "The Cult of King Dungi during the Third Dynasty of Ur," *Bulletin of the John Rylands Library*, XI (Manchester, 1927), 322–28.

28. Code II, 55.

29. C. J. Gadd, *The Assyrian Sculptures* (British Museum, 1934), p. 16.

30. A. Schott, in *Festschrift P. Kahle* (Leiden, 1935), p. 6.

31. C. Jeremias, *Die Vergöttlichung der babylonisch-assyrischen Könige* (*AO*, Vol. XIX [1919]), p. 13, n. 5, collects some references. A statue of Ur-Nanshe was still "worshiped" under Lugalanda, one of Gudea under the Third Dynasty of Ur, one of Shulgi in Assyrian times. The evidence consists of lists of offerings presented to these statues at the same time as offerings were made to gods. Jeremias suscribes to the view we hold incorrect—namely, that offerings to statues implies divinity for the kings who erected them.

32. Thureau-Dangin, *ISA*, p. 105, Gudea, Statue B, I, 13–20. The inscriptions of Statues C and K end with even fiercer curses against all those who would remove or damage them.

33. *Ibid.*, p. 113, Gudea, Statue B, VII, 21 ff. (translated by Jacobsen).

34. *Speculative Thought*, p. 194.

35. Disregard of the juristic implications of the term "shadow" has saddled the literature of our subject with a proverb which seems of fundamental importance and is nothing of the sort. It was first used in this connection by Gressmann, *Der Messias*, p. 28, and modified by F. M. T. Böhl, *Der babylonische Fürstenspiegel* (*MAOG*, Vol. XI [1937]), p. 48. It is also used by Labat, *op. cit.*, p. 222; Jeremias, *op. cit.*, p. 9; and Engnell, who places it as a motto at the head of his book. It reads:

> "The shadow of God is Man
> and men are the shadow of Man.
> Man, that is the king
> (who is) like the image of God."

Dr. F. W. Geers and Dr. Jacobsen have pointed out to me that these phrases occur in a letter from an astrologer to an Assyrian king which deals with the question of when it is propitious to give audience (Harper, *Assyrian and Babylonian Letters*, II, K. 652, ll. 9–13). It is therefore not permissible to translate "shadow" with all the implications that word possesses for us. One must remember that in Akkadian it means the protective "overshadowing" of a client by the power of his patron in a lawsuit (see also Engnell, *op. cit.*, pp. 193–94, for a list of epithets of kings and gods in which they are described as "protectors" or "protecting shadows"). Geers and Jacobsen would view the last two lines as a gloss on the first two. This gloss explains that the king (Man) represents the protection which God provides—the king is the executor of the God's protection. The nobles ("men"—*amelu*), in their turn, represent the protection which the king extends over his subjects. This function of the nobles is expressed in the second half of the statement—the second line in our quotation.

36. Thureau-Dangin, *ISA*, p. 67: Cone of Entemena, V, 19—VI, 8 (translated by Jacobsen).

37. *Speculative Thought*, p. 12.

38. For Mesopotamia see Pohl in *Orientalia*, VIII (1939), 265–66; a basin for sacred water, a drum, and other objects are mentioned as receiving offerings, together with statues. As regards Egypt, a very explicit statement is contained in a decree of King Pepi II (Neferkare), who provided that a statue of his, made of Asiatic bronze with gold inlays and called "Neferkare is justified (viz., in death)" was to be brought daily to the temple of Min in Koptos to share in the offerings presented to the god. Certain fields were laid aside to produce these offerings for the god and the statue of the king. See Sethe, in *Göttingische gelehrte Anzeigen*, CLXXIV (1912), 715, after R. Weill, *Décrets royaux de l'Ancien Empire égyptien*, Pl. IV, 2.

39. "OIC," No. 18, p. 54.

40. Labat, *op. cit.*, p. 144; Engnell, *op. cit.*, p. 32, who refers to the literature. For Egypt see E. Schiaparelli, *Il libro dei funerali* (Turin, 1882–90); E. Wallis Budge, *The Book of the Opening of the Mouth* (London, 1909).

41. In the Early Dynastic temples of Mesopotamia many statues of nonroyal persons were erected; those inscribed are mostly of priests. Their purpose was no doubt the same as that of the royal statues—to recall the donor perpetually to the god. Private people were sometimes allowed to set up statues in temples during the New Kingdom in Egypt. There can be no question of divinity in these cases.

42. Jacobsen, in *JNES*, II, 118.

43. See above, pp. 245–46. We are reminded here of the *dii certi*, the "Sondergötter" of Usener's "Götternamen"; but the Mesopotamian gods are vividly conceived and easily personified, in contrast with the gods of the *Indigitamenta*, though some remained "functional half-impersonal 'numina' " (see L. R. Farrell, *Greek Hero Cult and Ideas of Immortality* [Oxford, 1921], pp. 78 ff., for a penetrating criticism of Usener).

44. So also J. J. Stamm, *Die akkadische Namengebung* (*MVAG*, No. 44 [Leipzig, 1939]), p. 118.

45. Before the First Dynasty of Babylon the oath formula was *mu lugal*, "by the name of the king"; then the custom changed and the king was named alongside certain deities. We find, for instance, the formula: "by Shamash, Aya and (king) Sin-muballit"; or, "by Nanna, Shamash and (king) Hammurabi" (Labat, *op. cit.*, p. 226). The custom remained in force in Assyrian times, clear proof that it did not imply that the king named alongside gods was himself thought to be a deity.

46. Berend Gemser, *De beteekenis der persoonsnamen voor onze kennis van het leven en denken der oude Babyloniers en Assyriers* (Wageningen, 1924), pp. 28–29 (Sumerian names); 178–82 (Akkadian names).

47. *Ibid.*

48. *Ibid.*, p. 37.

49. *Ibid.*, p. 179.

50. *Ibid.*, p. 182.

51. The phraseology of letters is misunderstood as much as the personal names are. A letter of Adad-shum-usur to Esarhaddon (Pfeiffer, *State Letters of Assyria*, No. 160, p. 118 [Harper 2, K. 183]) is quoted often (e.g., by Dhorme, Labat, Engnell) as evidence that the king disposed of the forces in nature. Yet this is not so. Though the terminology is exuberant, the statement remains within the bounds of orthodoxy. The gods are said to favor the king by granting him "a favorable rule, righteous days, years of justice, heavy rains, full streams,

good prices." No wonder that "old men dance, young men play music, women and maidens gladly perform the task of womanhood, procreation is common." If the letter does not claim substantially more than Assurbanipal claims himself (p. 310), the fulsome phraseology is easily explained, since Adad-shum-usur is attempting to get his son admitted to the royal presence, although "at the court there is no real friend of (his) who would accept a present that (he) might give him and intercede for (him)." The letter must, all by itself, obtain the king's favor; hence, it goes as far as it well can go in acclaiming his power. It is therefore disqualified as an illustration of common beliefs; though it does not conflict with them, it shows an excess of adulation which is due to the peculiar circumstances under which it was written.

52. We quote after Gressmann, *Altorientalische Texte und Bilder*, I², 273-75, where the bibliography of the text is given.

53. Thureau-Dangin, *ISA*, pp. 282-83, Brick E, ll. 10-11 (translated by Jacobsen).

54. H. Grapow, *Die bildlichen Ausdrücke des Ägyptischen*, p. 31.

55. Tukulti-Ninurta I, Adad-nirari II, Assurnasirpal, Shalmaneser II, Esarhaddon. See Engnell, *op. cit.*, p. 23.

56. Labat, *op. cit.*, p. 232.

57. After Langdon in *JRAS*, 1925, p. 490, l. 26. Cf. Labat, *op. cit.* The long text in which this phrase occurs is a prayer for Ur-Ninurta in which the king appears like anything but a god.

58. James, *op. cit.*, p. 52.

59. These phrases are collected in a large and revealing excursus by Engnell, *op. cit.*, pp. 178-95. He interprets the terms in the manner we reject.

60. B. Landsberger, "Die babylonische Theodizee," *ZA*, XLIII (1936), 32-76, ll. 295-97.

61. Labat, *op. cit.*, p. 278; *OECT*, III, 11, ll. 23-24.

62. Labat, *op. cit.*, pp. 280-81; but the term does not suggest, as Labat maintains, that the king "fertilizes the land with his magic powers."

63. Luckenbill, *op. cit.*, Vol. II, par. 769.

64. Labat (*op. cit.*, pp. 281-82) quotes several kings who used this expression.

65. Luckenbill, *op. cit.*, Vol. II, par. 127. Cf. Gordon Loud, *Khorsabad*, Vol. I ("OIP," Vol. XXXVIII [Chicago, 1936]), pp. 132.

66. After Engnell, *op. cit.*, p. 28. Dr. Jacobsen tells me that the line is damaged and its meaning really uncertain; he considers Witzel's restoration entirely unconvincing.

67. Engnell, *op. cit.*, p. 28, after Witzel, *Keilinschriftliche Studien*, V, No. II, 30, 56. Engnell, following Hooke, simplified the problem beyond recognition by squarely identifying the king with the tree of life (pp. 25-29). Personal names, like "Shulgi is the Plant of Life" (Gemser, *op. cit.*, pp. 28, 32), prove no more in this context than those which we quoted above (p. 306); nor is it relevant to refer to such obviously metaphorical phrases as "The Kingship like the plant of life may profit the welfare of the people" (*Beiträge zur Assyriologie*, III, 254, 10 ff.).

68. Erman-Blackman, *Literature*, p. 306; Erman, *Religion*, p. 141.

69. Another hymn to Shulgi which Engnell quotes after Witzel, *op. cit.*, V, 53 ff., contains the phrase "endowed with divinity"; but Dr. Jacobsen tells me that the line is damaged and that there is question of necklaces or other tokens of divinity, not a direct pronouncement that the king is divine.

NOTES TO CHAPTER 22

1. Our wording represents, of course, the relationship between the New Year and Creation as the ancients saw it. If we consider this relationship historically, we must say that the annual rites, the participation of the community in the critical change in the seasons, probably existed before there was any well-defined creation story, or at least before the myth had been given the form we know. For "the New Year rites and conceptions go back to the direct dependence of primitive man upon nature, and from this dependence spring the popular representations; they have their roots in the ancient, purely religious conception of nature, which finds a new creation in each new season. The creation that they witness is projected back into primeval times. *Thus have arisen cosmogony and cosmology*" (A. J. Wensinck, "The Semitic New Year and the Origin of Eschatology," *Acta Orientalia*, I, 169-70).

2. *Ibid.*, p. 168. "The Mishna calls the first of Nisan the New Year of Kings. That means that the whole of the New Year symbolism of the first of Tishri is attached to the kingship on the first of Nisan" (*ibid.*, p. 179).

3. The temple of the mother-goddess in Erech.

4. "Cuneiform Texts in the British Museum," XV, Pl. 26, 1–21 (translated by Jacobsen). See S. Langdon, *Tammuz and Ishtar* (Oxford, 1914), pp. 10–11.

5. Note that VAT 9555 (Langdon, *The Babylonian Epic of Creation*, pp. 34 ff.) treats the death of the god throughout as an event which has taken place already (ll. 13, 14, 29, 68). Pallis, *The Babylonian Akitu Festival*, acknowledges on p. 239 that no proof of the enactment of the death of the god exists; yet on p. 249 he treats its enactment as a certainty. Zimmern, "Das babylonische Neujahrsfest," *AO*, XXV (1926), 14–15, illustrates the danger of preconceived ideas or the application of abstract labels (in this case "Jahresgott"). He places the death of Marduk at "the beginning of the dark winterly half of the year," and then, remarking rightly that the Mesopotamian climate does not fit this view, he wonders whether the ritual did not reach Mesopotamia from some northerly region, so that European parallels would be valid!

6. Scheil, in *RA*, VIII (1911), 161 ff., ll. 103–7.

7. *Ibid.*, pp. 170–71.

8. We do not deny that the New Year's festival showed historical accretions, such as, for instance, the introduction of the god Assur in the Babylonian ceremonies, which can be explained only as a result of the Assyrian domination over Babylon. The evil power Zu, who counted as Assur's opponent in the north (E. Ebeling, *Tod und Leben nach den Vorstellungen der Babylonier* [1931], p. 33, ll. 24–26), may have been introduced with Assur. On the other hand, he may have been introduced in very early times, since he was the opponent, also, of Ninurta, Enlil's son, and we have seen that Enlil was originally the hero of the Epic of Creation. However, the acknowledgment that certain features of the celebrations show the influence of historical incident does not amount to dubbing the festival a conglomerate of features of widely different origin, as a number of scholars (e.g., R. Labat, *Royauté*, p. 167) maintain. We cannot describe the Assyrian celebrations in detail. They differed in some respects from those at Babylon, especially in the part played in the north by the sacred tree —an artifact consisting of a trunk with metal bands and other embellishments. See Sidney Smith, *Early History of Assyria*, pp. 123 ff.; *Bulletin of the School of Oriental Studies*, IV (1926), 72 ff.; Gordon Loud, *Khorsabad*, Vol. I ("OIP," Vol. XXXVIII [Chicago, 1936]), pp. 97, 104 ff.; and, for the iconography, Frankfort, *Cylinder Seals*, pp. 204–15.

9. The gods of heaven.

10. Thureau-Dangin, *Rituels accadiens*, pp. 129–30; Zimmern, *AO*, XXV (1926), 4.

11. Langdon, *Babylonian Epic of Creation*, p. 41, l. 34.

12. Thureau-Dangin, *op. cit.*, p. 138.

13. Zimmern, *AO*, XXV (1926), 12.

14. The close connection between the New Year's festival and the Epic of Creation favors the hypothesis of Wensinck (*op. cit.*, p. 184) that the humiliation of the king means also that chaos swamps society for a moment to such an extent that even its very summit is submerged. The commotion in the city which we are about to discuss expresses the same thing on another level. This may have a bearing on the origin of the festival of the Sacaea, which, as we have seen, may have come from Persia (see above, chap. 19, n. 11). It may include Babylonian features, although it cannot be connected with the substitute king and is also essentially different from the complete equality which reigned during the sacred peace (p. 274). But we know that one criminal was released at the New Year's festival, while another was beheaded (below, n. 41). If this one had been allowed to play the part of the king for a short while (we do not know that he was), there would be a parallel with the Sacaea; for at that feast, as reported by postclassical authors (Langdon, "The Babylonian and Persian Sacaea," *JRAS* [1924], 65–72), a criminal was released and possibly paraded as king, while in each house a slave was said to give orders instead of the master. Some such usages might have formed part of the Babylonian symbolization of the temporary ascendancy of chaos.

15. See H. Zimmern, "Zum babylonischen Neujahrsfest, Zweiter Beitrag" (*Berichte über die Verhandlungen der Kgl. Sächsischen Gesellschaft der Wissenschaften, Phil.-hist. Klasse*, Vol. LXX [1918]), 2–20; Langdon, *The Babylonian Epic of Creation*, pp. 34–49. The text may date from the tenth century B.C.

16. Knut Tallquist, *Sumerisch-akkadische Namen der Totenwelt* [Helsingfors, 1934], 23–32, 37–38).

17. For the Sumerian myth see S. N. Kramer, *Sumerian Mythology*, pp. 83–96, and "Sumerian Literature," *Proceedings of the American Philosophical Society*, LXXXV (1942), 293–323. For the Akkadian version see Gressmann, *Altorientalische Texte und Bilder*, Vol. I,[2] pp. 206–10, where further references are given.

18. Langdon, *The Babylonian Epic of Creation*, p. 37, l. 14.

19. *Ibid.*, l. 13.

20. Thureau-Dangin, "La passion du dieu Lillu," *RA*, XIX, 175 ff.

21. Wensinck, *op. cit.*, p. 172.

22. *Ibid.*, p. 173.

23. Langdon, *The Babylonian Epic of Creation*, p. 35, l. 7.

24. Zimmern, "Zum babylonischen Neujahrsfest, Zweiter Beitrag," p. 3.

25. Langdon, *The Babylonian Epic of Creation*, p. 35, l. 6.

26. *Ibid.*, p. 35, l. 11.

27. *Ibid.*, p. 35, with n. 5. Lehmann-Haupt, in *Orientalische Studien;* also Pallis, *op. cit.*, pp. 241–43. We do not believe that the significance of the ziggurat is fully explained by stating that it served as the god's tomb. However, during the New Year's festival it counted as the "mountain" which was also the "Beyond" and hence the place where the god was held captive.

28. The names of ziggurats are conveniently listed by Th. Dombart, *Der Sakralturm* (München, 1920), pp. 34–35.

29. Ebeling, *op. cit.*, p. 26, l. 5.

30. Langdon, *The Babylonian Epic of Creation*, pp. 34 ff., l. 9.

31. *Ibid.*, ll. 28–29.

32. *Ibid.*, l. 11.

33. *Ibid.*, ll. 42–43.

34. *Ibid.*, l. 16.

35. *Ibid.*, l. 66.

36. *Ibid.*, l. 67.

37. *Ibid.*, l. 23.

38. Pinches, in *PSBA*, XXX, 62; Zimmern, "Zum babylonischen Neujahrsfest, Zweiter Beitrag," p. 49.

39. Langdon, *The Babylonian Epic of Creation*, p. 35, l. 8.

40. Ebeling, *op. cit.*, p. 33, No. 7, ll. 24–25.

41. On his way to Esagila, Nabu was led to some reed pigsties to inspect the boars they contained. These seem to have represented criminals incarcerated with Marduk. The boars were killed (Frankfort, *op. cit.*, Pl. XXIII, *h* and *i*, and p. 132) and so, apparently, was the criminal; the head of the criminal was tied to the door of the temple of the goddess. Moreover, two jeweled statues, which had been prepared on the third of Nisan, were beheaded on the arrival of Nabu at Esagila (Langdon, *The Babylonian Epic of Creation*, p. 39, ll. 20–21, 24–25).

42. Langdon, *The Babylonian Epic of Creation*, ll. 68–69.

43. Frankfort, *op. cit.*, p. 117, Pl. XXI*a;* other references *ibid.*, p. 118, n. 2.

44. For this reason, among others, we do not consider the Epic of Creation to be the ritual text or original "cult myth" of the Akitu festival in the strict sense advocated by Pallis, *op. cit.*, p. 254. We regard *Enuma elish* as one version (which happens to have been preserved) of the same myth which underlies the New Year's festival. The seal designs depicting mythological scenes not represented at the festival also prove the one-sidedness of the prevalent modern tendency to see all our material as reflections of cult and ritual. Cf. L. R. Farrell, *Greek Hero Cult and Ideas of Immortality* (Oxford, 1921), p. 51 *et passim*. "We also gather the useful conviction that our mythologic science is never likely to explain more than a fraction of the whole and that no great results are likely to be reached by the application of a single idea or a single method" (*ibid.*, p. 52).

45. Both dates are given in an inscription of Nebuchadnezzar (Langdon, *Die neubabylonischen Königsinschriften*, p. 127, Col. II, ll. 54–65).

46. Thureau-Dangin, *Rituels accadiens*, pp. 103 ff.

47. Here, as elsewhere, Anu counts as the most influential god, a "king." But see above, p. 231.

48. *Speculative Thought.*

49. *Speculative Thought.*

50. Labat, *Royauté*, p. 315.

51. D. D. Luckenbill, *Ancient Records of Assyria* (Chicago, 1927), Vol. II, par. 70.

52. *PSBA*, XXX, 62.

53. Thureau-Dangin, *Rituels accadiens*, p. 146, n. 3.

54. Zimmern, "Zum babylonischen Neujahrsfest," (*Berichte über die Verhandlungen der Kgl. Sächsischen Gesellschaft der Wissenschaften, Phil.-hist. Klasse*, Vol. LVIII [1906]), pp. 146–48.

55. *PSBA*, XXX, 62.

56. Zimmern, "Das babylonische Neujahrsfest," *AO*, XXV (1926), 18.

57. Labat, *op. cit.*, pp. 173–74.

58. Zimmern, "Zum babylonischen Neujahrsfest," pp. 127–36.

59. *Ibid.*, p. 131. Kingu was the leader of Tiamat's host after the death of Apsu.

60. Heidel, *The Babylonian Genesis* (Chicago, 1942), p. 32.

61. Ebeling, *op. cit.*, p. 36, l. 19; Zimmern, "Zum babylonischen Neujahrsfest, Zweiter Beitrag," p. 49.

62. Langdon, *Die neubabylonischen Königsinschriften*, pp. 128–29, Col. IV, ll. 7–10.

63. Delitzsch, in *Mitteilungen der Deutschen Orient Gesellschaft*, No. 33, p. 34.

64. Frankfort, *Sculpture of the Third Millennium B.C. from Tell Asmar and Khafajah* ("OIP," Vol. XLIV [Chicago, 1939]), pp. 43–48. This banquet is the one postulated by Pallis, *op. cit.*, p. 173.

65. Langdon, *Die neubabylonischen Königsinschriften*, p. 283, Col. IX, ll. 3–10.

66. The Akitu festival is known to have been celebrated at Assur, Babylon, Ur, Erech, Harran, Dilbat, Nineveh, Arbela. See Thureau-Dangin, *Rituels accadiens*, pp. 86–88; Pallis, *op. cit.*, pp. 19–24.

67. L. W. King, *Letters and Inscriptions of Hammurabi*, III, 163 ff.

68. W. Andrae, *Das wiedererstandene Assur* (Leipzig, 1938), pp. 151–54; *MDOG*, No. 33 (1907).

69. Thureau-Dangin, *ISA*, p. 179 (translated by Jacobsen).

70. This aspect of Ningirsu's character has been well described by Professor Thorkild Jacobsen in lectures at the University of Chicago.

71. R. Pfeiffer, *State Letters of Assyria*, No. 215, p. 156. For another description of Nabu's sacred marriage, see E. Behrens, *Assyrisch-babylonische Briefe religiösen Inhalts aus der Sargonidenzeit* (Leipzig, 1905), p. 38, n. 1.

72. Zimmern, "Zum babylonischen Neujahrsfest," p. 152.

73. As against Pallis, *op. cit.*, p. 198.

74. The ancient city must not be conceived as a contrast to the open country. The city was but a settlement of people who were largely agriculturalists themselves (see above, chap. 16, n. 23).

75. Koldewey, in *MDOG*, No. 59 (1918), pp. 2–7; Weissbach, in *ZA*, XLI (1933), 269–87, esp. 280–81.

76. Herod. i. 181–82, translated by A. S. Godley ("Loeb Classical Library").

77. F. Nötscher, *Ellil in Sumer und Akkad* (Hanover, 1927), pp. 19–20.

78. Sidney Smith, "A Babylonian Fertility Cult," *JRAS* (1928), 850, translating the Ishtar Hymn, *RA*, XXII, 169–77. It is difficult to combine this view (namely, that the *gigunu* belongs to the temple tower) with the existence of a *gigunu* underground (also discussed by Smith) unless the word indicates a type of structure or room that could be placed in both situations. Pallis (*op. cit.*, p. 109) tentatively suggests that one structure in the ziggurat served as both tomb and bridal chamber. But the ziggurats were solid—a fact which, although it did not prevent them from counting ideally as the god's mountain grave during the New Year's festival (see p. 322), excludes the possibility that "a chapel which is the seat of joy" would be located in (instead of upon) them. Moreover, it would seem senseless to have the god celebrate his renewed vitality in the tomb which had served as his prison, had symbolized his death, and from which he had been forcibly liberated. Recent discoveries near Susa

indicate, as Professor George G. Cameron points out to me, that the *gigunu* may well be a structure on the second stage of the ziggurat—be it the gatehouse where the ramp or stairway ended, or a chapel. See R. de Mecquenem *et al.*, "Mémoires de la Mission Archéologique en Iran," XXIX (Paris, 1943), 142–43. Tallquist (*op. cit.*, p. 26 with n. 4) gives a survey of the interpretations of *gigunu*. See also E. Douglas van Buren in *Orientalia*, VIII (1944), 17 ff., 30–31.

79. If the sacred marriage took place on the night of the tenth of Nisan, it would be understandable that at Babylon (as at Borsippa) the eleventh was named after the divine bride. See E. Dhorme, *Les religions de Babylonie et d'Assyrie* (Paris, 1945), p. 244.

80. Wensinck, *op. cit.*, p. 172.

81. *Ibid.*, p. 182.

82. *Speculative Thought*, p. 182.

83. Usually it is not understood that the two sessions of the assembly at which "destiny is determined" differ entirely from one another in character. Pallis, for instance, considers the rite of the eleventh "simply a repetition" of the act of creation in the Bit Akitu (*op. cit.*, p. 247; cf. pp. 192, 196). As we have seen, the Epic of Creation (which Pallis considers the "cult myth" of the festival) gives us a clear indication of the difference. When he states that originally the completion of the rites themselves constituted a determination of destiny for the ensuing year, Pallis oversimplifies the complex festival and the conceptions which went into its organization. It is true that the consummation of the marriage of god and goddess set off the flow of generative force which sustained nature in the year to come—that the completion of this particular event insured a prosperous "destiny" for the year (p. 330 below). But other elements entered into the rites, for instance, the very important one of judgment, of the explicit determination of the destiny of man. The whole of the Sumerian king list, and such texts as the Lamentation over the Destruction of Ur (p. 242), to name but a few, indicate the great age of such beliefs. Pallis' simplification cannot be justified by characterizing the festival as we know it as "urban" and somewhat mechanical and contrasting it with an earlier truly agricultural form; for the contrast "urban-rural" does not apply to pre-Hellenistic times in view of the size of the cities (see above, chap. 16, n. 23) and because the life and interest of the citizens were no less bound up with the farmer's pursuits than is the case nowadays in a fairly large village in an agricultural district or than was the case in Europe up to the industrial revolution. See, e.g., G. M. Trevelyan, *English Social History* (2d ed.), p. 28.

NOTES TO EPILOGUE

1. This view may be too simple and too rationalistic, being based on Greek sources. See F. W. Buckler, "The Oriental Despot," *Anglican Theological Review*, X (1928), 238–49. The fact that in Assyria the king's mantle, and not an official dressed in it, served as a substitute for the king (see above, p. 263) suggests that the conception of kingship "resting on the incorporation of the agents of the king within the king's person and body" (Buckler) did not exist in Assyria and may have originated, as Buckler supposes, with the Medes.

2. "Achaemenian Sculpture," *American Journal of Archaeology*, L (1946), 6–14.

3. *Speculative Thought*, pp. 367–73.

INDEX

INDEX

overthrow of Osiris' enemies in, 193, 204

Neferhotep, 192, 205; chap. 10, n. 7; see also Osiris Neferhotep

Neferkare; see Pepi II

Neferrohu, chap. 20, n. 1

Nefertari, 40

Negroes: appearance in history of, chap. 14, n. 22

in New Kingdom art, 165; chap. 14, n. 21

Nehebkau, 103–4

Neith, 22; chap. 9, n. 6; chap. 13, n. 49

Nekhbet, 81

as combination of cow and vulture, 173–75; chap. 14, n. 69

and Dual Shrines, 96, 107

as moon, 145

as mother of king, 173–74

nursing Hatshepsut, chap. 5, n. 61

as symbol of Upper Egypt, 20–21, 46, 97, 107; chap. 5, n. 61

in titulary, 46

Nekheb, 96, 174; see also El Kab

Nekhen, chap. 15, n. 62

as center of Horus worship, 17, 20, 39, 93, 95

location of, chap. 7, n. 29; chap. 15, n. 69

Onuris as god of, 203

Nekhen, Guardians of; see Nekhen, Souls of

Nekhen, Herdsman of, 81, 83, 91, 93

Nekhen, Souls of, chap. 6, n. 5; chap. 7, n. 14

as ancestors of Pharaoh, 94–95, 115, 159; chap. 7, nn. 21, 42; chap. 15, n. 12

caring for king, 96–98; chap. 7, n. 35

dead king as one of, 91, 93, 95, 117

as Followers of Horus, 91, 93

on monuments, 94; chap. 7, nn. 35, 42; chap. 15, n. 12

Osiris as one of, 117, 207

Servant of, 85, 87, 95

Seth as leader of, chap. 15, n. 12

Nephthys, 138; chap. 13, n. 39

adoring sun, 159

in art, 40, 45; chap. 3, n. 16

in Ennead, 182–83, 284; chap. 15, n. 13

meaning of name of, 183

and Osiris, 30, 31, 112–16, 121, 183, 187, 192, 201; chap. 10, n. 14

Nepri, and Osiris, chap. 15, n. 16,

Nergal, 270, 310; chap. 20, n. 17

Nergal-sharrani, 330

Neshemet boat, 203–6; chap. 10, n. 7

Neterkau, 75

Netherworld (Egypt), 195; chap. 14, n. 76; chap. 15, nn. 94, 101

anti-sky over, 155

dangers of, 119, 156–57

dead in, 120

dead king in, 121–22, 173, 210–12; chap. 10, n. 14

entrance to, 115, 117, 119, 206, 210; chap. 10, n. 13

entrance of sun into, 156–57, 168–69

hieroglyph for, 210

King Teti in, 159–60

Nile emerging from, 190; chap. 10, n. 13

as underground part of cosmic circuit, 118–22, 155–57, 169, 184, 196, 210; chap. 10, n. 14

Netherworld (Mesopotamia), 329

entrance of suffering god into, 286–87, 322–23

Ishtar's descent into, 321–23

mountain of, 315, 318, 321–26

"Netherworld, Book of Who Is in the," 156; chap. 14, n. 46

Netjeri shema, 96

Neuserre, 91

obelisk of, 153; chap. 6, n. 4

reliefs of, 71, 87–88, 166; chap. 6, nn. 5, 15, 22, 30; chap. 12, n. 3; chap. 15, n. 75

New Light, House of the, 265

New moon feast, 265–66; chap. 7, n. 14

New Year: atonement and judgment at, 322–33

death vanquished at, 322

of kings, chap. 22, n. 2

New Year's Day: and accession, 103–4

and coronation, 106

and creation, 150; chap. 13, n. 12; chap. 22, n. 14

dedication of temples on, 274; chap. 22, n. 14

and Nile, 103–4, 192, 194, 314

for primitives, 103

and Sed festival, 101

New Year's festival, 4, 313–33; chap. 22, nn. 8, 27, 78

boar in, 293; chap. 22, n. 41

and creation, 314, 319, 325–26, 328–29; chap. 22, nn. 1, 44

date of, 313–14; chap. 22, n. 2

determination of destinies during, 236, 270, 277, 318, 325–26, 331–33

as expression of religiosity, 313

interplay of nature and society in, 315–16, 318, 327–28; chap. 22, n. 1

locale of, chap. 22, n. 66

mock battles in, 317, 324, 328

mood of, 315–17, 323–24

popular celebrations during 314–17, 321–25

rites of atonement during, 277, 317–20, 332